American Mobbing, 1828–1861

Toward Civil War

DAVID GRIMSTED

New York   Oxford
Oxford University Press
1998

Oxford University Press

Oxford   New York
Athens   Auckland   Bangkok   Bombay   Buenos Aires
Calcutta   Cape Town   Dar es Salaam Delhi   Florence   Hong Kong
Istanbul   Karachi   Kuala Lumpur   Madras   Madrid   Melbourne
Mexico City   Nairobi   Paris   Singapore   Taipei   Tokyo   Toronto   Warsaw

and associated companies in
Berlin   Ibadan

Copyright © 1998 by Oxford University Press, Inc.

Published by Oxford University Press, Inc.
198 Madison Avenue, New York, New York 10016

Oxford is a registered trademark of Oxford University Press

Library of Congress Cataloging-in-Publication Data
Grimsted, David.
American Mobbing, 1828–1861 : toward Civil War / David Grimsted.
   p.   cm.
Includes bibliographical references and index.
ISBN 0-19-511707-7
1. Riots—United States—History—19th century.   2. United States—
History—Civil War, 1861–1865—Causes.   3. Violence—United States—
History—19th century.   4. United States—Race relations.
5. United States—Social conditions—To 1865.   6. Antislavery
movements—United States—History—19th century.   I. Title.
E415.7.G75   1998
303.6'23'097309034—dc21   97-33073

9 8 7 6 5 4 3 2 1

Printed in the United Sates of America
on acid-free paper

FOR JENNIFER, ROLF, AND ALMON

who, growing with this manuscript,
taught me steady lessons about love
and riot control, two things always joined
in any decent home or society

An Introductory "Because"

What apparent cause of any riots may be, the real one is want of happiness.
— Thomas Paine, quoted in Thomas Brothers, *The United States As They Are*

There is the traditional "leveling" instinct, common to all such occasions, which prompts the poor to seek a degree of elementary social justice at the expense of the rich, *les grands*, and those in authority, regardless of whether they are government officials, feudal lords, capitalists, or middle-class revolutionary leaders. It is the common ground.
— George Rude, *The Crowd in History*

Violence is an impulse we all share. The love of violence is, to me, the ancient and symbolic gesture of man against the constraints of society. . . . It is a disaster to treat the impulse as vicious. For no society is strong which does not acknowledge the protesting man; and no man is human who does not draw strength from the natural animal. Violence is the sphinx by the fireside, and she has a human face.
— Jacob Bronowski, *The Face of Violence*

Do not imagine that the spirit which has been invoked to plunder and destroy the hateful and the pestiferous will rest, and nicely discriminate before it proceeds to havock again. Never was the devil conjured and tolerated, without drenching his friends in the red-ink of slaughter before he left them. . . . Your citizens must have winked at all the diabolerie set forth in your newspapers . . . and King Mob will make them wink . . . , for this old King Mob has in all times been remarkable for his most stern impartiality. He will not even recognize the bookish distinction between the good and the bad, the right and the wrong. . . .

A hiss for those by law protected,
Liberty's a glorious feast.
Courts for cowards were erected,
Churches built to please the priest.

With such a lullaby I shall sleep sound. Good night, again, and may God bless you with long life and a cold, tough heart.
— Thomas Corwin (quoting Robert Burns) to William Greene
January 15, 1842, William Greene Papers, CinHS

The moral and intellectual difficulties in handling social violence develop because all four writers—Paine, Rudé, Bronowski, and Corwin—are correct. We want happiness, and in all societies some people benefit more than others, and those comparatively deprived often feel anger that may manifest itself in violence. Yet society deprives not only those who are most clearly excluded from an equitable share of its goods and privileges, but everyone; it is at once humans' home and their prison, and its restraints are resented, often quietly but for all that passionately, precisely because social bonds are inseparable from the very selfhood that senses threat from them. Because all share anger at social restraints, those who react with violence may or may not be those with the best reason to resent them. The probability of violent response commonly depends as much on confidence that society can't or won't retaliate harshly to legal breaches as it does on extent of social injury. And King Mob, even more than those authorized to mete out social punishment, is prone to "stern impartiality" between the good and the bad in choosing his victims and measures. The sphinx of violence has a human face but an animal's body, which often distinguishes poorly whether saints or sinners, the oppressing or the oppressed, come within its arena and its maw.

Social violence, in short, is always human and understandable response to social inequity or restraint, just as it is always dangerous and ambiguous in its total results. From the view of those mobbing and, more quietly, that of the tolerating community, the work is always beneviolence, holy or at least helpful: a technical escape from the law to a realm of unambiguous justice and equity to right a truly good order. However, even in the best of causes, riots provide social "red ink" as well, sometimes writ only in rotting tomatoes but more often in flame and blood. Few people are so dead to moral and social commitments that they would not applaud the social anger or results of some Jacksonian mobs *and* be appalled at those in others. Because of their diverse motivation, method, and result, the 1,218 riots involved amply demonstrate the profound, and profoundly contradictory, truisms of Paine, Rudé, Bronowski, and that sharp-penned governor and senator from Ohio, Thomas Corwin, whose 1842 comment came in the wake of Cincinnati mobs against both blacks and banks.

Because all three writers express chunks of truth, the study of riot is often hurt by treating mobs as a discrete aberrational category. In fact, riots were neither rare nor commonplace in antebellum society but a piece of the ongoing process of demo–cratic accommodation, compromise, and uncompromisable tension between groups with different interests. They were social exclamation points that can't be rightly read without sifting through the complicated immediate sentences that led to them, as well as the many quieter chapters on the same subject that preceded and followed. Rioters always yell, "Intolerable!" "Injustice!" "Villainy!" One has to listen to these cries of fear and hatred sympathetically and skeptically, as well as to the explanatory coda in the words, deeds, and situation of those who send up the self-righteous shouts. One also has to hear them in the jumble of other voices speaking simultaneously, never forgetting those that are often historically faintest of all, those of the victims. And one has to try to catch how this mob conversation contributed to the social dialogue on the issue most obviously at stake, and on others.

This volume is an attempt to reconstruct about half the riotous conversations between 1828 and 1861, those related to the tragic dialogue leading toward the Civil War. The differing definitions of acceptable mobbing in the North and South contributed substantially to the tensions in the nation's antebellum political system, itself a product of dialogue in which riots at times spoke influentially. Political parties and majority populations in both sections saw the wisdom of avoiding discussion of slavery and were racist enough so that turning African Americans into property seemed small cost, or a nice bonus, for union. Yet the antebellum North was never easy with slavery when it somehow became its business as well as that of the South, nor was it happy to give up traditional rights to support Southern rights to enslave more comfortably.

Clear in the riot conversation of 1835 was the idea that the only national answer regarding slavery was not to think, or at least to talk, about it. Such salutary willed neglect, never very successful, broke down in 1848 when new territories prodded new national debate, and this process accelerated in 1854, when the two sectional systems of violence met in Kansas. At this point the Democratic Party, the nation's most significant remaining trans-sectional organization, showed that it would sacrifice even majoritarianism to proslavery, the North elected Republicans and the South elected to secede.

A second book will tell another tale, using the age's incidents of economic, racial, ethnic, religious, and youth tensions to explore how the angers of various groups, often as sharp as those between North and South and with leaders on both sides much less anxious to resolve or dissolve their differences, ended in accommodation and/or continuation in a less costly fashion. Perhaps "Toward Civility" will prove too upbeat a subtitle for it, despite the small prose pleasures of such verbal symmetry. Or perhaps not. The evils of that day will have to wait their turn.

The evils herein are tied to slavery, the nation's deepest and most divisive anomaly, mocking though never mastering the nation's special commitments to rough equality of human liberty, respect, and opportunity. Part I deals with the North's troubled response to the surfacing of the slavery issue and of the South's new insistence that slavery was an eternal good of which any questioning was intolerable. Chapter 1 introduces the drama by discussing the nation's long, cool summer, stretching from late June through October 21, 1835, of maximum mob mayhem, in numbers and variety of riot never before or since surpassed in the United States. The riotous interlude of 1835 offered an introduction not only to the variety of mobs that were to follow but also to the peculiarly explosive potential of those centered on slavery, in contrast to all other issues where disruptions were sharp and sometimes deadly but quickly handled and absorbed. The riotous slavery arguments of these months, aided by the abolitionist mail campaign of religious suasion, changed the South's soothing "someday" about slavery's end to a firm "Never!" It also led to strident demands that either laws or mobs silence those who publicly questioned the institution. Since laws weren't feasible, mobs became the preferred tactic, in the North against abolitionist speakers and associations and in the South against anyone someone chose to call "Abolitionist!" A few Northern mobs of October 21, carefully organized for maximum effect and minimal damage, propitiated Southern wrath, but the stage was set for future troubles.

In this way, the abolitionists less developed than were handed the issues that assured progress for their movement. The South was so slave-committed that it demanded the cessation of white freedom where it touched that issue: petition, speech, press, assemblage, religion, and—in the 1850s—democratic majoritarianism. Every mob against abolitionists offered added "proof" that the peculiar institution demanded that slavery of a sort be integrated and made a national commitment, while, in every future bout of sectional irritation, Southern words advanced abolitionists' argument more effectively than could their own. The South developed its own style of social violence, semisanctioned and rarely opposed, against any questioning of slavery. This effectively silenced its own doubts; when nettled, it demanded that the North do the same. And the Democrats, generally the nation's most popular, ideologic, and racist party, showed in 1835, as later in Rhode Island and Kansas, that they were willing to trim any principle to proslavery demands at crucial moments, despite costs to their support northward.

Chapter 2 handles Northern mobs against abolitionists and those in aid of fugitive slaves, where that section's riots and rights related to slavery came most to the fore. Anti-abolition mobs were the most numerous, though the least deadly, category of Northern riot, clustered in the years 1834–38. Listening to what abolitionists and their opponents said in these common and uncommonly mild mob conversations involves hearing something of their and their nation's dilemma. The abolitionists stressed, comparatively politely but insistently, the age's political and religious truisms that few of their Northern audience (or indeed of their Southern, had there been one) wished to question. Yet the mob reply was grounded in an equally reasonable question, the profundity of which time fully attested: given Southern commitments, where could discussing slavery lead but to disunion or civil war? Thus, slavery repeatedly began the North's discussion, but other topics involving white liberties quickly came to the fore in ways that assured abolitionist victory in ending slavery by precisely those means the anti-abolitionists had long prophesied, bloody civil war. In this painful, mob-filled dialogue, leading in directions neither side wanted, one hears the debates among abolitionists, their steadily increasing numbers of fellow travelers, and their opponents: those Northerners, only a handful proslavery, who preferred any alternative to irritating the South.

Fugitive slave riots shifted the focus of debate, but not its contours or the direction it took the North. These mobs long predated the Fugitive Slave Law of 1850, which established federal authority to cow and control state laws, officials, courts, and peoples to abet slavery. These mobs, sometimes all-black but commonly well integrated, were far fewer than anti-abolition ones but deadlier, though both types shared some inclination to keep violence minimal. Here white Northerners had to confront their direct complicity with slavery in one of its nastier aspects, the forced reenslavement of men, women, and children who had risked more for freedom than had white Americans for generations. The mild sentences given to blacks convicted in these riots suggested how closely the general public followed antislavery people of all stripes in respecting black action to keep their fellow African Americans from being again debased to chattel. These mobs freed only a modest number of slaves— forty-some—but had a chilling effect on slave-hunting in the North. Yet it was the failed attempts that drew broadest sympathy for the black victims, causing growing numbers to modulate their racism and to accept effective resistance, including violence, against enslavement as just.

Part II deals with distinctive qualities and kinds of Southern riots. While almost all varieties of mob existed on both sides of the Mason-Dixon line, Southern social violence took some distinctive forms. Southern riots, unlike those in the North, commonly went ahead unchallenged. While the number of mob deaths between the sections were roughly equal, most who died in the North were rioters killed when authorities acted to control mobs, while the great bulk of Southern deaths came at rioters' hands because authorities rarely cared or dared to repress the mob.

Chapter 3 explores the Southern system of personal violence and its relation to that of collective violence, represented here by mobs against alleged criminals. The South accepted extralegal structures parallel to its flourishing legal system in part because a slave society glorified mastery as its central honorific. Its extralegal systems, personal and collective, allowed Southerners to escape from situations of moral ambiguity and embarrassment into ones of melodramatically simple and dead certain answers. Chapters 4 and 5 explore how especially useful was this pattern of tolerated extralegality in simplifying the moral ambiguities about slavery's ties to both Southern whites and blacks. Chapter 4 explores how the most effective of antebellum riots, the Southern mobbing of "abolitionists," silenced white questioning of the institution, and Chapter 5 considers the insurrection scare riots through which the South periodically purged its own dark fears, even as it more insistently sang its refrain about happy darkies.

A product of the tensions between the nature of Southern slavery and developing proslavery ideology, these riots provided a major means through which this society held together the slavery it practiced and that which it praised. Bourgeois, evangelical, and genteel commitments created some humane ties and much pragmatic accommodation between the races, but the wish to maximize both profits and mastery offered slaves precious little protection against the casual cruelties of the market or the brutish ones that individuals or groups sometimes imposed in twisted proof of power. Attacks against alleged abolitionists were the commonest category of Southern riot, but the much less frequent insurrection scare panics were the deadliest form of Southern mob. There is no convincing evidence that most of the victims in these two kinds of mobs had spoken or planned to attack slavery, but the very random arbitrariness of this violence made these riots (like postbellum lynchings) especially effective modes of social terror.

The unease and at times fury between the North and South over both slavery and systems of violence had to be contained within the national political system, which had its own riotous strains. These are the subject of Part III. Chapter 6 sketches in the nation's everyday hard business of politics and masculine sport of ballot-casting, including the regular use of toughs, intimidation, and brawls. Established parties, recognizing costs if their violence became too visible, played as teams accepting the rough rules of the game. Drinking, betting, intimidating, illegal voting, cheating, chicanery, handing out bribes and jobs, and legal tampering were regular parts of the system, but the reasonable equality of corruption between the parties contributed to some faith in the system's fairness. Serious riots came during shifts in party structure, first as the second American party system fully jelled in 1834–35, the concern of Chapter 7, which also considers some incidents where Democrats advertised their majoritarianism by arguing for "revolution" to secure true democracy, most seriously in Rhode Island in 1842. In the 1850s Nativists and Know-Nothings brought new issues and people to the political arena, the topic of Chapter 8. It was not that the newer parties were more violent than their predecessors but that the established parties, faced with new challenges, tried to stretch their advantages from intimidat-

ing violence, while the new ones, less familiar with the general rules, were less tol-
erant of common abuses. The major mobs of 1834–35 and 1845 were in New York
and Philadelphia, but the worst riots of the Know-Nothing era were in slave cities.
In St. Louis, Louisville, Washington, Baltimore, and New Orleans, class and especially slave interests detonated the explosive issues and expansive hopes for a "new
politics," freed from slavery's concerns, that the American Party brought to politics.

Majoritarianism was also the chief issue in Kansas, where three bursts of riotous
violence established de facto popular sovereignty, despite the determination of federal forces to help mob the majority will. And here everyone knew that slavery's expansion was one issue, and the Democratic Party's belief in anything besides
proslavery appeasement the other. In Kansas, 1856–58, the sections' two systems of
social violence, the South's long-established and the North's developing in dangerous directions, met head-on, and the major victim was the nation's only remaining
major trans-sectional organization. The broad story of Chapter 9 involves the failure
in Kansas of the Democratic Party to juggle its proslavery commitment with its
Northern appeal, which had been its—and the nation's—defining dilemma since
1835.

The Epilogue summarizes this long mob dialogue, so abruptly ended or changed
at Fort Sumter. It explores the Senate's most honest debate on slavery, one triggered
in 1848 when the nation's first antislavery senator caught everyone off guard by introducing an innocuous antiriot bill, and concludes by looking at the extralegal acts
of John Brown and John Wilkes Booth, which bracketed the much more efficient
legally sanctioned slaughter of the Civil War.

In the beginning of a study of rioting is the word, oddly neglected in the theoretical literature. The common legal definition of riot differs greatly from the sense of
the term in both common and intellectual usage, while recent sociological works
emphasize riots' "spontaneity," a concept of little applicability. Most historical
works deal sensibly enough with events already labeled riots, but this procedure
doesn't work for any attempt to catalogue all riots or to define the broad function of
riot in a particular place and period. The one I devised is: "Incidents where six or
more people band together to enforce their will publicly by threatening or perpetrating physical injury to persons or property extralegally, ostensibly to correct problems or injustices within their society without challenging its basic structures." The
defense of this definition is usability, although it is complicated without eliminating
several gray areas between riot and some other kinds of actions. It covers all of the
age's incidents thought of as riots then or since; it also includes many things given
other names, sometimes or commonly: lynchings, popular uprisings, wars, raids,
massacres, frolics, slave insurrection panics, and acts of lynch clubs, Regulators,
and vigilantes when what happened fits my definition. It doesn't include Native
American–white conflicts, actual slave uprisings, or immediate and legal attempts to
quell them.

Back when the world was young and I began this project, I was finishing a study
of American theater, 1800–1850, where I was intrigued by the number of theatrical
riots, always enacted on the grounds that the "people"—rioters judging themselves
the only people that count—had the right to impose their just will on the playhouse
as world. This rhetoric and these acts posed, in telling and sometimes amusing and

tragic ways, the dilemma of minority rights in a vitally, even belligerently, majoritarian society. At the same time, in 1964–68, rioting returned to the United States, and no historian could miss the shoddiness of most of the history attached to the instant analyses the situation demanded. I hope the most recent Los Angeles riot will fail of a host of successors and this study will retain its merely antiquarian relevance. Certainly this book, like other riot studies, offers no clue to why riot ended so suddenly after the violent Martin Luther King wake, and no certainty that it would break out virulently after the Rodney King acquittals, though the latter was a reasonable guess. What people see as gross injustice, made visible by video camera or other process, always may, though often doesn't, abet mob formation. History's role in the dialogue of disciplines is to answer others' generalizations with a quiet, "Yes, but. . . ." History is the record of quirky rather than dependable cause and effect, full of likelihoods but also of quite improbable people, acts, events, and results.

As this work began, I knew of fifty or sixty riots, the ones that appear in standard secondary sources, about the right number for a historian whose statistical skills range, shakily, through long division. As the numbers quickly grew—and kept growing—I counted a lot where that seemed to have point. About midpoint in this work someone dedicated to faith in a better world through numerology said, with that touch of condescension endemic to true believers, that surely I was going to computerize my data. "No," said I, true to my own Church of the Word, "I thought I would considerize it instead." This answer, I soon decided, was wittier than it was wise, the pleasures of counting mobs, bodies, and maimings being finite. So I sacrificed my machine-breaking instincts to create a database of riots organized by type, area, and period, counting on a life of comparative ease. This will also let others fiddle with the data for their own worthy purposes, including helping find where I have erred.

A supplementary work will consider theories of riot related to this data and will outline the categories in which I counted and the rough standards by which numbers were determined in dubious cases, which most of them were. It amply documents the problematics of the figures, but such is the aura of false certitude haloing numbers. I want to repeat one sentence: most of these numbers are not only uncertain but most certainly wrong. That said, I trust they are reasonably useful, like meaty quotations, proving nothing but capable of being chewed by minds with strong teeth toward some sustenance. They were invented with historical conscientiousness, though the sources were inadequate, woefully and ludicrously, and the inventor's desperate leaps of faith much like Eliza's across the ice floes in the nineteenth century's favorite play. I feel confident that, on this topic, the numbers are the best data available, though precious little brag that is.

Some of the weaknesses of this data and book are endemic to the topic, and some to the author. Some of what happened is doubtless beyond the possibility of historical recall, but there are tens and hundreds of events whose literary remains lurk in the court and police records, newspapers, manuscript collections, articles, local histories—the list just begins—unnoticed, unexplored, unread. In modern history at least, the researcher never exhausts the sources, only him/herself. If those who happen to know or care about these things care to send me additions and corrections, I'll see that the database grows slightly less bad every half decade or so, but all that will do this book no good. Its weaknesses should cause no surprise to professional historians, whose situation Henry Adams accurately described in the first issue of the *American Historical Review*: "The historian can hardly expect that four out of five of his statements will be exact . . . , [and] can only wait in silent hope no one will read him—at least with too much attention. He knows the worst."

In addition to the pleasures that come from confidence in not being read widely, the long years of work on this have provided many other rewards. Some of these relate to the excitement of being drawn into questions different from ones I would otherwise have chosen, especially those related to social, economic, and political issues. I've also benefited from learning how every casual letter or mob handbill asks for a reading as complicated and caring as does the richest sonnet, the wisest scholarship, or the rankest melodrama. The very randomness with which the subject had to be researched, with no newspaper or periodical indices of any use and very scant subject indexing in archives and manuscript repositories, insured much time "wasted" in fascinating stuff. I've also met a host of people, to whom I would have otherwise failed of introduction, whom I'll remember as intensely as I do close acquaintances and favorite fictional persons: English-born Philadelphia businessman and diarist Joseph Sill, philanthropist and abolitionist, who lived to grieve his sons' Americanization to gross racism; lively Sallie Holley, whose devotion to abolition whetted her awareness of every quirk and quibble of her comrades in the cause; St. Louis laborer Henry Miller, whose diary catches so well the zest of a young man's entry into the world of work and politics; Virginian Mary Blackburn, who did as much as she—or any Southerner—dared to aid, educate, and comfort slaves within her communal ken; popular politician Robert Potter, who in North Carolina castrated a couple of men, thinking honor would then allow him to wed wealthier, and who continued his successful career in politics and inventive mayhem in Texas, until a man who understood honor equally well mob-ambushed him to gain his land claims; white carpenter Samuel McCorkle of South Carolina, whose dying wish that his black wife and children be freed was supported by the local community but scorned by the state's patriarchs, who lectured the dead man on his paternalist sin of caring for his children.

One meets interesting people, too, in the midst of mobs: canny and quirky Cassius Clay, who alone well enough understood, enjoyed, and despised the Southern system of violence to break its fundamental rule of silence on slavery's wrongs; Georgian Virgil Stewart, who became a Southern hero by writing a mob-justifying "exposé" of a great criminal clan, which the South insisted was factual, although it pictured its life and slavery as grossly grasping and hate-full beyond an abolitionist's dream; rioters Thomas Wentworth Higginson, cheerfully honest about the mixed motives in his long mob career, and North Carolina farmer John Fountain, who led a mob that killed two runaway slaves who killed his son but who then insisted that the law take its course and even refused to "break jail" when the local community tried to free him; and mob victims like an unnamed black Baptist preacher in Enfield, North Carolina, who refused to confess to a nonexistent slave insurrection plot though whipped nearly to death and then crushed in a vice, and Northern Methodist minister Anthony Bewley, whose letter just prior to his Texas lynch hanging was a model of shrewd mob observation and quiet resignation about leaving this vale whose vileness he had good reason to know.

I hope these people and hundreds of others will live briefly in these pages because they lived or wrote incredibly well, or just incredibly. Good history is their stories and comments tugged toward some general meaning.

I've worried at times about excessive involvement with these people and especially with these riots, so rich in drama and emotional red ink. I often found myself yelling with, or at, the mob, "Injustice!" "Barbarous villainy!"—and repeating Thomas Corwin's prayer for "a tough, cold heart" (not to mention "a long life") as I worked on them. Having literally "shed a tear" and then some over the fate of Rosina Meadows, the village maiden, while reading a play about her, I half-expected other suddenly lachrymose research pleasures on this topic. Still, it was, put most mildly, odd to find uncontrollable tears blurring sight and dribbling through my beard as I read in the Newberry Library A. R. Arrington's melodramatic account of the Cane Hill, Arkansas, mob hangings, or as, in the South Carolina State Department of History and Archives, I poured over petitions of hundreds of evangelicals pleading their religious duty to teach their slaves to read the Bible, all sure to be labeled "inexpedient" by the state's elite patriarchs. And as these rains came, I was fully conscious of my folly and half-afraid of being chucked out, quite properly, for excessive sniffling or dripping on documents. I did get a warning in the Cincinnati Historical Society for insufficiently swallowing chuckles as I read a letter of young lawyer William Hauser, who went south to make his fortune and wrote back the next week that Southern violence was much exaggerated—merely thirty rather than the rumored seventy-five having been killed in a recent incident.

The problem is, of course, keeping clear-headed and honest, not forgetting the moral and emotive drama at the heart of every riot but neither forgetting the human and social complexity in those mobs one at heart cheers on, *and* in those most redolent of sickening sadism. I've never had much respect either for those self-oblivious historical claims to being "objective" or "disinterested" or for those self-serving ones that point out "it's all politics" or "ideology" to justify glibly pasting on one's own. People write good history who care most about their topics and bring to them every bit of experience, passion, insight, and commitment they can muster—and who care about and are committed, in a primary way, to honesty, fairness, and deepening, and thus changing, their own understanding. Such ideals—like all others—are considerably easier to state than to live, and I've no doubt failed of fairness almost as often as I've failed of accuracy. Still, I take comfort in knowing that the answers I've carried from the documents were often quite different from those I expected—and better.

One's intellectual debts in a project like this are broad beyond telling. Of the many theorists and historians with whom I've tried to think about riots, none have I found more contributive or sounder than George Rudé. However, as anyone who has read thus far knows, I dissent strongly from his insistence that no mob should be brought into history without being tidied into a respectable crowd. "Crowd" refers to groups doing all sorts of things, like shopping, and the argument for it as term of choice smacks of the verbal fastidiousness of mob-defenders who called, for example, those who burnt abolitionist Pennsylvania Hall "an assemblage of respectable citizenry." Of course, mobs were crowds and assemblages of citizens whose respectability I don't wish to question, but very few crowds/assemblages rioted. Both "riot" and "mob" meant, in 1835 as now, what I'm discussing, and I think their complicated moral overtones, used interchangeably, are appropriate: "mob" a little salty and harsh, "riot" a little antiseptic and neat.

My notes acknowledge my clearest debts to published sources, including those to many recent works on Jacksonian riot and social violence, none of which I've read with total agreement and none without substantial intellectual nurture. Two works I read in the last four years are exemplary of the help I've often gotten, and of the correction doubtless still needed: Jed Dannenbaum's study of women-led temperance mobs quadrupled the two I'd come across elsewhere, and James Black's account of lynching in Iowa, which was published in 1912 and which I read eight decades later, swelled my six riots for that state sevenfold, propelling it from nothing on my violence map to Free State lynch-heaven, along with California, 1848–60. Perhaps my greatest obligation is to a host of antiquarian chroniclers of cities, towns, and counties, whose simple devotion to telling everything, as far as they could, unmuzzled by what professional historians decreed important, preserved rafts of information that would otherwise have been lost. I am particularly in debt to David Matteson, who published nothing but researched much on riots. He gave his extensive notes to the Library of Congress, where I learned of them about halfway through this project. Had I known of them at the beginning, I reckon I'd be about five years younger now, and, without them, five years older.

My personal research debts are greatest to the many curators and archivists who always graciously helped me find materials. If my search was rarely efficient, it was possible only because of their timely aid and striking oddiments of knowledge. Hardly typical but a worthy exemplar was Lloyd Bender, who kept the Noble County (Indiana) Historical Collection in his kitchen, dug out in a twinkling twenty documents from twenty different piles, and gave me my only—and priceless—piece of oral history. My research has proved, as much as anything, that people who love old documents and their fresh use are more dependably good than those who take the easy way out and like dogs or children.

Unfortunately, few people have ever wanted to read any of this, so it's hard to blame others for its faults. James Penick kindly corrected a couple of errors in the Mississippi slave insurrection story, Joe Mannard gave many useful suggestions on the Know-Nothing section, and Terry Alford helped me with some materials and advice on the Epilogue. My son Almon also read the epilogue and opined that it was OK but needed sharpening. Always more kindly, George Callcott read the Southern chapter as all authors wish to be read: shrewdly and overgenerously. Whit Ridgway shared some of his Maryland materials with me, and friend Ron Hoffman offered to read not a word but handed out some advice anyway. Probably, as with his horse race tips, I heeded where I shouldn't have and neglected what would have proved mildly valuable. My thanks to all, even Almon. It did need sharpening.

I also wish to thank a thief in Indianapolis, Indiana, who broke into my car while I worked at the state library and stole my note-card boxes but thoughtfully dumped out the cards. That this was done less in kindness than in calculation of value lessens my gratitude not a jot.

The University of Maryland has offered a good home base for this work, in ways much deeper than the periodic dollops of direct support they—along with the Social

Science Research Council, the American Council of Learned Societies, and the American Philosophic Society—generously provided. The department has had its collective quidities; I once posted a single thesis on my door—"Power corrupts, and petty power corrupts pettishly"—and would have put it up often again did not such home truths quickly sour. But there's been much personal geniality and support, with perhaps a minimum of that corrosive egoism that's the bane of academics, and maybe everyone else. I've liked and respected the minds and commitments of the bulk of my colleagues and have appreciated the total freedom to teach what I thought had most chance to amuse and involve profitably, as well as I could. My students I've always enjoyed: most worked and cared reasonably, and many proved genial companions in the intellectual quest. For a while I kept a list of those who'd done research from which I gained data, always fretting a bit about those who gave as much in less topical ways. When the list of direct contributors topped thirty, I decided, "This is silly. They were good students who know very well they gave me, as I hope they got, some facts, some ideas, and some enthusiasm for finding more." I trust that's true.

My deepest single debt is to Darlene King, who transferred all the longhand-filled yellow legal pads that comprise this book into electronic files, those gifts from the gods that allow one to fiddle endlessly with prose and idea without guilt toward a typist. Darlene is perhaps the only person I know deserving of canonization—undentably cheerful, efficient, and nurturing—who can type eighty words a minute from illegible scrawl. She is the center of a remarkable group of women and one man in the office who provide the department's intellectual heartland, in chats while munching the candy, cakes, cookies, and breads they bring in. It's been amazing over the years what extraordinarily good and able people have worked in the office. I expect the local rise of neoconservative ideas owes most to the fact that, if people begin to take the equal pay for equal work idea seriously, the salaries of the secretaries and of my colleagues and me would be reversed.

One owes debts to places, too. Chaplin, Connecticut; Çekmeköy, Turkey; and Cappamore, Ireland, are not known for their literary traditions, but the rural environs of each provided inspiration enough for this poor prose. In each place there were wonderful people. In Connecticut, friends Wayne and Bill Harbaugh introduced me to the place and provided its human and intellectual heart; Sidney Chrysler provided raspberries and an annual magical puppet theater opera; the Hanneys, Mike and Peggy, Heather and Holly, visited cheerfully for blueberry harvesting and home-made harvest festivals; and Hal and Teresa Ridgeway made applejack and mussel-fests and lovely rugs, in return for which I almost drowned their three children sailing. In Ireland, Niall and Helen Flynn provided our old farmhouse—and warm hospitality, as did our rural neighbors: the Kennedys, who made music; the O'Malleys, who provided agricultural advice and medicinal poteen; and the Ryans, who shared their sheep-shearing with us. In Turkey, my merry sister Mary and her warm family, Tayfun, Perim, and Cem Akgüner, provided arrangements, amusements, and translating services; the Turcans, wonderful all from Grandmother to young Bilge, with that inexplicable generosity most Turks showed us, simply gave us the house we lived in and provided Sunday picnics, rain or shine, on the deck by the pool and tennis courts where the big house was to be built; and Remzi-bey and Nevri-hanam, who shared our peasant duplex and who were refugees from Bulgaria driven out in an early bout of ethnic cleansing because they wouldn't give up their Turkish names and tongue. We spoke little but laughed and liked a lot. At each story of Eastern Europe's recent ethnic horrors, I see Remzi-bey, grumblingly coping by laughter, his blue eyes sparkling in his ruddy peasant face, and his few silver teeth glinting in the sun, and Nevri-hanam fondling her chicks, tears always quick to come to her gentle eyes at thoughts of family and friends left behind. Those smiles and tears haunt with human face those exiles my Jacksonian mobs created.

Cherishing nineteenth-century yeoman farmer superstitions, I have a hunch that what is good in here grew from the soil, cultivated along with my Washington roses, Connecticut kale, Irish potatoes, and Turkish cherries. As to what is bad—well, weeds and blackspot and potato blight are always with us.

The three dedicatees of this volume also grew with this project, if a bit quicker to mature. All things considered, we all had a pretty good time of it, and we're all relieved that we turned out no worse than we did. Patricia Froelicher has long been a good friend and helpmeet, cheerful about devoting half our luggage to my note cards and, like most of the rest of the world, remarkably patient about this being finished.

Not everyone was so kindly, and I often took solace in Wallace Steven's sensible reply to why it took him so long to publish: "A book of poetry is a serious thing." A work of history is at least as deadly serious, and it needs footnotes, too. The thick seriousness of this volume, when unfinished anyway, provided amusement to a wide circle of family and friends for whom age could not stale the finite variety of variations on a theme. "With this global warming, do you think you'll be done before the floods?" "Are you calling it *Molasses in January*?" "Is it required that historians take as long writing as the history took happening?" "Have I finished vacuuming? Have you finished the book?" Such poor humor has done much to create human ties, binding the generations, my parents to my children; the extended family, unnumberable siblings and offspring and Pat's children and friends; and a section of the local community sizable enough. No greater gift can be made to family and community than soldering such bonds of amusement and comfortable sense of superiority. I'm glad to have contributed to them so generously.

In fact, odd as it seems given my awareness of the waste and the weaknesses, I doubt that I could have better spent this quarter century of life's genial Indian summer than in this way and with this book. I often wonder about my on-gliding life's contrasts with those of so many I write—and read—about, ended in sudden brutal or random viciousness. I keep in mind, of course, the first and most genial of historians' themes: only fools label themselves happy before death, because no one knows the twists of fortune ahead. I try to keep worried or huffy enough to pacify Herodotus's gods, perhaps like ours, jealous of excessive joy or even peace. Still, that true justice, personal and social, that rioters and I crave seems almost wholly a chimera—something that I and mobs and judges and other exemplars of often simple-minded self-righteousness would be better for bearing in mind, even as we seek. I suppose Allah in some form decides, and sensible children, before they are four or so, learn to remember to forget to ask persistently out loud, "But why . . . ?"

Washington, D.C.   D. G.
April 1997

Contents

PART I

The North

Fleeing Slavery, Trying Violence

Once some potent event evokes before your eyes the invisible thing, there is no way to make yourself blind again.

—Joseph Conrad, *Collected Letters*

Those who deny freedom to others do not deserve it themselves, and, under a just God, cannot long retain it.

—Abraham Lincoln, to H. L. Pierce, April 6, 1859,
in *Collected Works of Abraham Lincoln*

Jefferson's belief that error was to be tolerated so long as truth can combat it is re-placed by the idea that a stone or a brick-bat thrown from the hand of a mob is a short and improved method of introducing truth within the human skull.

—Petition of citizens of Monroe,
Monroe, Oneida, and Onandago Counties,
New York, 1835, in *Niles' Register*, October 3, 1835

I thank you for the Squash seed, none of which have come up.

—Mary Grimké to her daughters
Sarah and Angelina, April 14, 1838,
in *Weld-Grimké Letters*

CHAPTER ONE

1835

Year of Violent Indecision

> The law
> Protects us not. Then why should we be tender
> To let an arrogant piece of flesh threat us!
> Play judge and executioner.
> —Shakespeare, *Cymbeline*

> The South wants justice, has waited for it long. She will wait no longer. You have not aided her or even heeded her cries. . . . You will find now that your interests are as much South as North. What destroys her institution and happiness will destroy your own. . . . She cannot live while the Republican principles still exist.
> —John Wilkes Booth, speech, 1860,
> in Hampden-Booth Theatre Collection,
> New York City

Angry differences between the people of the North and South had never been so much in the fore as they were by August 1835, but on one thing observers on both sides of the Mason-Dixon line agreed: since early July the nation had demonstrated a penchant for riotous violence that raised doubts about its future stability. "Our whole community seems to be under an unnatural excitement," wrote the Columbia, South Carolina, *Southern Times*. "Mobs, strikes, riots, abolition movements, insurrections, Lynch clubs seem to be the engrossing topics of the day. . . . The whole country . . . seems ready to take fire on the most trivial occasion." The *Richmond Whig* lamented "the present supremacy of the Mobocracy," and northward the Philadelphia *National Gazette* claimed, "The horrible fact is staring us in the face, that, whenever the fury or the cupidity of the mob is excited, they can gratify their lawless appetites almost with impunity." Hezekiah Niles, the most thorough compiler of these events, could only answer, in fumbling explanation of riot rather like subsequent theories, "Many of the people of the United States are 'out of joint.'"[1]

This change, which seemed to turn editing into "the mere chronicling of atrocities," was sudden. The United States had known only few and scattered riots in the nineteenth century prior to Andrew Jackson's presidency, and the most recent and destructive mobs had been Irish immigrant faction fights along the railroads and canals, which roused little fear of indigenous lawless tendency.[2] When a mildly unruly celebration followed Andrew Jackson's inauguration, Supreme Court Justice

Joseph Story could write home amusedly, "The reign of 'King mob' seemed triumphant." Story's casual tone grew from the fact that the term "mob" retained something of the double meaning it had had in eighteenth-century England. It could refer to rioters or destructive crowds, or to Story's usage, "the lower orders in general."[3] By the time Jackson left office, two things had happened that would make Story's choice of word impossible. Mobs were now tied only to violence, and the honorific "the people" had replaced "the mob" as the designation for poorer folk, or even for rioters in mobs which supporters wished to sanctify. In such rhetorical transformations lay much of the meaning of the Jacksonian era.

Numbers confirm editors' impressions. In 1835 there were 147 riots, 109 of them between July and October. In terms of variety as well as numbers, 1835 represented the crest of rioting in the United States. All types of mobs had riotous representation in this year, but over two-fifths of the riots in these busy summer and Indian summer months related to issues at the core of sectional tension: there were 46 proslavery riots (35 against abolitionists and 11 in response to insurrection scares) and 15 racial riots, 11 of these against blacks, 3 in aid of fugitive slaves, and 1 by blacks.

Yet so varied were the triggering grievances that most people saw a need for some explanation that went beyond the issues of the specific mobs. "Such a state of things could not exist," suggested the *Baltimore Republican*, "without a powerful cause, and one that was general in its operation." This Democratic paper was sure what the general cause was—the Whigs—while the Whig papers were equally confident that the fault lay with "the ruling dynasty and its demagogic adherents." Less partisanly, "contagion" was sometimes evoked as cause, but in general, puzzlement rather than explanation prevailed.[4]

Why riot broke out at this time defies easy answer. Certainly the economic and political storms that had agitated the middle years of Jackson's administration were over. Nullification had been nullified, the hopes for immediate recharter of the United States Bank had died even among its most ardent supporters, and federal funds were at work for the politically chosen pet banks to protect the country from the politically corrupting uses to which at least Jackson believed Nicholas Biddle had put them. That controversy had boiled and then simmered down again with no discernible disruption of the economic system. If ending the national bank had discouraged speculation and stock-jobbing as Jackson had promised, American speculators of all stripes seemed unaware of it. Nor had the demise of a national bank led to the financial collapse that Whigs, partly in fear and partly in hopes of changing Jackson's mind, loudly predicted in the spring of 1834. But in 1835 the wolf of depression was at no one's door, and those who had cried wolf loudest were discredited by quiet. The bubble of inflation and good times floated bobbingly but generally tranquilly upward. Jackson's apparent political and economic vindication ensured both a relatively quiet valedictory to Old Hickory's years of public service and Martin Van Buren's probable success in his pursuit of the presidency.

The partisan explanations for the riots of 1835 have notably ridiculous features but were of some influence in a society where ideas were much shaped by a press for whom the party line was sacred truth. The Whig "explanation" of the riots of 1835, if not better than the Democratic, tended more broadly to unify many of the arguments that had led people to anti-Jacksonianism as the two-party system slowly reasserted itself. John William Ward has argued that the American public saw Andrew Jackson's campaign that began in 1824 as one between the "professor" Adams (read "arid intellectual") and the "plowman" Jackson (read those always united terms "honest yeoman"); certainly they did if they read only and believed wholly Jacksonian propagandists. But if they read and took seriously the pro-Adams press, they knew the fight was between that ubiquitous honest yeoman, now in the form of "the simple farmer of Braintree," and his imperious, slave-driving, aristocratic opponent.[5] In democratic politics, broad images regarding candidates matter much. And since Adams and Jackson shared positive images, the yeoman farmer that had been Americans' favorite cliché for goodness for half a century, the negative image—what was voted against—was most telling.

That most people preferred an imperious, slave-driving aristocrat for president over a professor should surprise no academic. Yet behind the nonsensical caricature of both negative images lay elements of real concern to reasonable people. Perhaps Jackson's deepest initial appeal lay in his lack of political background and clear political positions. Andrew Jackson had taken a stand only in New Orleans and Florida, positions guaranteed to offend few voters.

Yet these actions worried a substantial minority of citizens. Jackson was in public life a general, a man trained to act in terms of friends and foes, victories and defeats, rather than in terms of political and diplomatic courtesy and compromise. Moreover, no American general had ever showed such contempt for niceties of procedure as Jackson had in his foray into Spanish Florida. Americans, John Quincy Adams in the lead, were happy to use Jackson's vigor to unclasp the shaky Spanish grip on the Floridas, but for many this was disturbing behavior in a prospective president. Jackson's private life reinforced such fears. The several notorious duels and brawls he'd been involved in seemed supportive footnotes to his public intransigence: a bravely determined man certainly, but one who paid little heed to process or legality if they stood in the way of what he thought desirable.[6]

Such fears centered in foreign policy, which gave importance to the diplomatic triumph of Jackson's first years in office, the reopening of trade with the British West Indies. What Adams's overreaching concern for abstract principle had bungled, Jackson's pragmatic good sense brought about. Yet the domestic policies of Indian removal and the "bank war" confirmed his opponents' worries. In fact, the central charge of the Whigs by 1835 was that the course of "King Andrew," very like that of "King Mob," was "marked by violence, obstinacy, and daring disregard" for any legal restraints on "his violent impulses."[7]

The *New York Journal of Commerce* deemed this charge proved most clearly in his efforts "to rob a defenseless tribe of Indians of their land." Jackson had followed the established process of making clear to the southern tribes that they had no choice and then locating tribal "leaders" who would sign the desired treaties to make the best of a bad situation or the most of a personal opportunity. Northern opposition focused on one group of Native Americans, the Cherokee, who had most successfully integrated aspects of white and Indian culture and who had strong missionary-reform supporters. The harsh process of removal hardened the sense of Jackson's imperiousness, as had Democratic cant about how removal was required for the good of its victims, without mention of the policy's clearest beneficiaries, politically friendly land speculators.[8] If the Supreme Court questioned the policy, it could be ignored. Jackson's alleged remark "John Marshall has made his decision, now let him enforce it," though probably apocryphal, nonetheless represented what both his friends and his opponents felt characterized the man and his ways.

The bank war sharpened Whig charges of Jackson's lack of respect for law, honed much less on Jackson's initial veto than on his pet bank solution of 1833. Most accepted that Jackson's veto, if not wise, was at least a vigorous response to Henry Clay's and Nicholas Biddle's political ploy of pushing for early recharter. Furious was the reaction to the special deposits system, which involved removing first a cabinet officer and then federal funds from the legally designated bank of the United States to politically friendly pet banks.

Jackson's intense personalization of this issue—"The bank is trying to kill me, but I will kill it"—paralleled his response to individual opponents.[9] At one point, Washington rang with rumors of President Jackson assaulting Robert B. Randolph on a steamboat. A black diarist wrote, "The general said the scoundrel let me cane him and they were after Mr. Randolph." When Sam Houston beat Representative Tobias Stansbury senseless on the capital's streets for exposing the president's attempt to bail his old friend out with a very lucrative Indian removal contract, Jackson opined that Stansbury got "what he deserved." Davy Crockett, in part a Whig creation to counteract Jackson's appeal, offered the slogan representative of Jackson's moralistic politics: "Know you're right, than go ahead."[10] No mention was made here of worrying about the process of determining "right" or the road taken to go ahead. Jackson never had any doubt of his rightness nor hesitancy to go ahead as directly as possible. Nor did mobs.

By 1835 Whigs attacked Jacksonian ideology as an adjunct of a personality and policies that took legalism lightly in ways that paralleled "the demoniac leveling spirit of the mob." They criticized especially the party's glorification of unconstrained majoritarianism, which promised more immediate power to the people and idealized the popular will over procedural niceties, clearly related to the ideological positions that rioters assumed. While encouraging a sense of simple answers that could be simply achieved, Jacksonians created a political structure—urban machines, a convention system, a dependably bought political press, a principle of spoils—which caught the mystic "will of the people" in a web of controlling influences and institutions. Mobs thus represented that instance where some citizens held briefly the power "the Democracy," as Van Buren liked to call his party, both promised and frustrated.[11]

The bent of Jackson's intelligence and the pragmatism of American politics somewhat confused other aspects of Jacksonian ideology in 1835. Jackson, caring little for theory, often depended heavily on his advisers to write the arguments in support of the actions he wanted to take. The president's determination to squelch nullification motivated his proclamation, but the broad interpretation of federal powers attached to it was the work of Secretary of State Edward Livingston. Less than a month later, in a major message to Congress on the bank, Jackson's position was encased in an expansive states' rights argument, probably at Van Buren's behest and in Amos Kendall's words. Still, by the end of Jackson's presidency the Democrats had developed as clear a position as American parties manage. A verbal commitment to hard money, seldom turned into policy and never successfully, gave a rhetorical economic adjunct to political majoritarianism and kept alive some of the class thrust of the producers-versus-speculators argument of the bank veto message. And a stress on strict interpretation, states' rights, and Adam Smith's perfect justice if laissez faire replaced governmental interference all contributed both to their "world is too much governed" theme and to the sense, which they carefully cultivated, that they were the safer guardians of slavery.[12]

The desire of both Whigs and Democrats to do something, almost anything, to silence abolition blunted two other aspects of ideological emphasis until later in the decade. By then Jacksonian majoritarianism and glorification of the "popular will" was allied with a tendency to justify selected mobs, whereas the Whigs' procedural legalism became welded commonly to a condemnation of riot. Young Whig Abraham Lincoln used mob examples from 1835 to argue his party's position by 1838 about the social dangers if Americans continued to wink at riots. By decade's end, Jacksonians had also learned that their best defense when accused of proslavery truckling was a virulent racism that charged that their opponents cared more for "bestial blacks," mere "human brutes," than for the noble white race. If one accepts John Ashworth's notion that it's good to label party ideology by opponents' extremest stereotypes, Whig-Democrat struggles after 1840 pitted "negrophobes" and "nigger-lovers" more than "agrarians" and "aristocrats."[13]

Whatever the broad influences of the president's personality, policies, and developing party ideology, Jackson never expressed direct sympathy with mob actions, something fairly common with politicians in 1835, although twenty years earlier he had permitted the mob-shooting of two thieves and had belonged to a vigilante group that whipped about twenty alleged criminals. In fact, he acted to repress mobs more than any other president before Lincoln. In three cases, Jackson sent troops to quell riots, once against blacks who freed two fugitive slaves in Detroit, once against Irish workers in Maryland, and once against Baltimore bank rioters.[14] Secretary of War Lewis Cass, from Michigan, authorized the troops in the first case, while Jackson's actions in the latter two instances protected legal and economic cronies of adviser Roger B. Taney.

The charge that President Jackson supported vigilantism misinterprets the evidence in the case of a murderer lynch-tried and executed before Iowa territory was organized. Asked to pardon the "convicted" killer, Jackson wrote back urging the vigilantes to turn the man over to the legal authorities in Illinois but saying he had no legal right to pardon the man. This letter was clearly intended to sidestep sanctioning vigilantism. Had Jackson pardoned the mob victim, it would have implied that he had been in some sense legally convicted, something Jackson's carefully worded reply, probably drafted by Amos Kendall, strove to avoid.[15]

Jackson's reaction to the abolition riots of 1835, which few newspapers and fewer politicans condemned, revealed something of his general attitude. Even the most "respectable" of these riotous groups, those gentlemen who burned abolitionist mail in Charleston, South Carolina, received Jackson's condemnation. "This spirit of mob-law is becoming too common and must be checked, or ere long, it will become as great an evil as servile war, and the innocent will be as much exposed." Jackson's solution to the problem of abolition literature enthroned public opinion but not violence as an extralegal authority. Until Congress acted to prevent the circulation of this literature, as Jackson believed they had the right to do, postmasters should deliver abolition publications only at the request of the recipient and then publish the names of those who made such request, so that the community could "put them in coventry."[16] "Coventry" was obviously a village neighbor of "Lynchville" but a significant legal-intellectual distance apart.

Democratic charges against Whigs as instigators of riot tended to be narrower, often a counter to the blame directed toward their party. Specific riots were labeled "Whig," especially the 1834 burning of a convent school in Charlestown, Massachusetts, which was offered as proof of the aristocratic hostility and religious prejudice of the Whigs toward Irish and Catholics, although the school was elite, the rioters were workingmen, and Boston's Whig leadership was hostile to the mob. Democrats stressed more the "panic-making" in the spring of 1834. Both real economic fears and the strong desire of Whig and commercial leaders to pressure Jackson toward rechartering a national bank worsened this brief recession and heightened its emotive fervor. Jacksonians suggested that the huge probank public meetings and protests at the time began mob activity. Their favorite particular incident was a meeting in Baltimore where Daniel Webster and Horace Binney allegedly urged revolution, something made more shocking by their doing it on the Sabbath. Critics argued whether the terror or the timing was worse in these "treasonable and blasphemous appeals to Sunday mobs."[17]

Large public meetings have nothing necessarily to do with mobs, nor were Webster and Binney, among the more conservative of the Whig lawyer leadership, very convincing even as Sunday revolutionaries. But the extremity of political rhetoric in these years certainly aimed at unleashing popular passion. Webster said, "There is no Sunday in Revolutionary times," and Binney argued that administration measures must be put down, in common pro-mob verbiage, "peaceably if we can, forcibly if we must." Nor were such comments atypical in these months. The Washington correspondent of a Richmond paper predicted that soon "pistols will be flashed and dirks drawn in the streets" in "a bloody Revolution."[18]

Such comments, while not advocating violence, predicted its coming in a sanctifying way, much like that favored formula of mob supporters, "We deplore all violence, but. . . ." There was an extremity and abusiveness in denouncing Jackson, as the *Richmond Whig* did, as "a ferocious and unlettered bully, with his hellish crew, the kitchen cabinet," that undercut civility of discourse. It was ridiculous for Democratic papers to say riots were to be expected if Whigs called them Tories— and in the same issue to label their opponents "pie-balds" and "coons"—but they got the political coloring right, though it was a pot-and-kettle dialogue.[19] The bruising political hatred between Jackson and his opponents reappeared in a multitude of public guises, from the sleazy diatribes and special pleading of the partisan press to the steady stream of personal brawls and duels of members of the nation's Congress and press.

Beyond the furious rhetoric of early 1834 lurked the question of why this anger did not turn to riot. Politicians demagogically blamed their opponents' measures for economic collapse, in front of huge mass meetings, reputedly the largest in the nation's history, while, in the words of a Quaker woman, "the obstinate old man in the presidential chair remains unmoved."[20] Yet no social violence resulted but only an avalanche of speeches, meetings, resolutions, petitions, and delegations. It was almost as though the clarity of the protestor's goal—recharter in some form—channeled anger along a nonviolent course.

Prior to this mock-Armeggedon bank war in early 1834, the largest and most destructive of recent riots had been fights along transportation systems, especially in Maryland, where Irish laborers were building both the Chesapeake and Ohio Canal and the Baltimore and Ohio Railroad. Some anti-Catholic spokesmen saw in these disputes the seeds of subsequent American riots. Samuel F. B. Morse, painter, inventor, and believer in Catholic conspiracy, put the case for American contagion from an imported disease most forcefully: "If there is nothing intrinsic in our society which is likely to produce so sudden and mysterious effect [as rioting], the enquiry is natural, are there not extrinsic causes at work . . . ? How is it possible that foreign turbulence, imported by the shipload, . . . should not produce here turbulence and excess?"[21]

There was a mote of reality in this beam of assumption, although 1834–35 amply proved that Americans needed no lessons from the Irish in mobbing. For example, the first major riot of 1834, the New York City spring election riot, was in part an adaptation of Irish traditions to their new political situation. After this prelude to the coming of mobs, seven additional riots between April and November took place in New York City, including serious anti-abolition and antiblack disturbances in July. Philadelphia also had a major antiblack mob, followed in October by an election riot that paralleled the earlier one in New York. Irish Catholic nuns were victims of a major mob in Charlestown, Massachusetts, in this same period. But between November 1834 and July of the next year, no major riots took place.

The historian has little explanatory clue to this pattern. While the bank war was the center of both political fury and mass protest just before wide-scale riot erupted, only one riot over bank issues occurred in 1834–35. The Baltimore mob of 1835 was a response to the age's clearest example of wealthy speculators fraudulently stealing a huge amount from the small savings of thousands of relatively poor working people. Leading Baltimoreans—Whigs and Democrats closely tied to acting Secretary of the Treasury Roger B. Taney—first expected to make money from investing in a bank that could count on indirect infusions of funds under the pet bank system. Later these speculators decided they could do better by borrowing heavily from this bank, closing it, spreading false information about its lack of assets, and using Maryland's legal system to prevent both any audit or settlement. Four years later all debts were settled above par, long after most poor and middling depositors had sold their credits at a fraction of their value, money that the bank's wealthy debtors and elite fellow speculators pocketed. No antebellum riot aroused more worry than this one, which tried most clearly to redress a legally fostered fraud. Whigs quaked at its suggestion of "class" warfare, President Jackson promptly sent troops against the rioters, and Taney and the U.S. Treasury worked to further the fraud and the fortunes of his fellow speculators.[22]

The evidence of this riot, like the superstructure of almost all other socioeconomic data, raises doubts about the recent argument that Jacksonians were dedicated opponents of capitalism's "market revolution." Yet the data fits Marvin Meyers's more cautious earlier contention that much Jacksonian rhetoric suggested hostile response to the more aggrandizing and shoddy aspects of the burgeoning capitalism from which they, like other Americans, intended to benefit. For many Whigs the bank war represented a similar response, especially strong when Jackson pressed his pet bank answer, which so overtly put federal money to patronage work and which neglected the mechanisms of currency control in the original idea of Baltimore banker Thomas Ellicott. The pet banks for Whigs, like the U.S. bank for Jacksonians, came to stand as symbol for the nastiness and cheap chicanery that twisted itself onto the financial "progress," personal, communal, and national, that almost everyone wanted.[23]

The relation of such generalized worries to riot are unclear. Certainly strains exist in any society undergoing major changes toward greater democracy, industrialization, urbanization, modernization, market economy—choose your favorite term—to which collective violence is a possible response. It would be reasonable to picture the 1830s as marking a major intensification, perhaps even a "takeoff stage," for all these trends. Political theorist Barrington Moore has suggested that all societies create a certain quotient of violence as broad social change occurs. If a revolution does not accompany the change, the violence is somehow stored within the culture to burst out later, often in fascistic forms.[24] It is conceivable that people, whose storage facilities for hate are as obvious as society's, may feel tendencies toward violence that are diverted toward questions where lack of clear legal alternatives sanction mob response. In this sense, the broad fears and intense passions of the bank war may have flowed toward violence regarding the less politically channeled issues of 1835.

Yet in the peaceful spring of that year, any proponent of this vague quotient of violence idea would have assumed that the anger built in the bank war had dissipated in 1834's mob events. Social harmony prevailed, although between February and April there were three small anti-abolition riots in Ohio which attracted only local attention. In politics the Whigs offered neither clear-cut issue nor candidate, while Van Buren was determined that Jackson cherish old victories rather than launch new attacks in which his enemies might find fresh foothold. In diplomacy the French spoilation claims, which briefly roused old fears about the general's militant belligerence, were successfully and peaceably settled. Jackson's shrewd political sense about when to bark and when to bite had served him well in diplomatic as in partisan warfare.[25] Jacksonian papers hailed their hero as having led the nation into an era of just peace and plenty; the Whigs could only grumble that it wouldn't last.

It, didn't, of course. But it would have taken a remarkably prescient observer to know in the spring of 1835 what things were to promote the worst rioting in the nation's history a few months later. Most obviously, the Whigs were trying to develop a sectional political strategy, and the man making their appeal to the South was Tennessean Hugh Lawson White, a man Jackson judged "debased . . . in an attitude of sacrificing his principles and party for office."[26] In every national election, the South had voted heavily for slave-state over free-state candidates, and Van Buren saw his years of hard labor in conciliating the South threatened. When slavery questions agitated the South in the summer, this electoral reality drove both parties toward readier support of proslave mobs.

Developments within abolition also defined part of the coming controversy. Following Garrison's lead, William Jay and Lydia Maria Child wrote books that increased the difficulty of honestly seeing colonization as even a faint answer to the problem of slavery. Rooted both in antislavery and racist sentiment, the American Colonization Society's plan of sending blacks back to civilize Africa had always drawn much of its support from the illusion it gave of doing something about slavery without "agitating" the issue. But by 1835, Garrison, Jay, and Child undercut its comfort for Americans who really disliked slavery: the number of slaves sent to Africa was but a fraction of slavery's natural increase; more free blacks had been sent than freed slaves; and racist antipathy was certainly stronger than antislavery in many leading colonizationists.[27] Supporters of the Colonization Society were furious not because the attack was unfair but because it was unanswerable.

At the same time, Arthur and Lewis Tappan were prepared to invest money in trying to stir a moral awakening of the South. And what better way to create that than saturating the South with literature expressive of the suffering and evil entwined with the institution? What political realities made desirable, the new speedier printing technology made possible: cheap mass circulation of pamphlets, newspapers, and periodicals.[28] Yet there is no evidence of public knowledge about this until the papers and journals began to circulate in August, after renewed mob activity was well under way.

Two obscure individuals early in 1835 began journeys that were to be tied to several riotous incidents in the summer. George Thompson, English abolitionist, arrived from London and began quietly and effectively speaking on the slavery dilemma. Jacksonian philanthropist Roberts Vaux, who went to hear him in Philadelphia, was impressed with the man's message and his moral tone. Yet he sensed the danger in any foreigner's handling such explosive domestic issues, even if he "said nothing beyond the merits of the case": "The idea of *foreign* interference is very exciting, and the enemies of emancipation will not fail to turn it to the best account."[29] The trail of riot and near-riot that followed Thompson during his New England tour between late July and his return to England in October proved Vaux's perspicacity.

A much stranger figure destined to influence 1835's midsummer madness was Virgil Stewart, a young Georgian who went to Tennessee and learned of petty thief John Murrell. In the spring of 1835 Stewart returned to testify startlingly that Murrell was no mere slave thief, the only crime he'd previously mentioned. Now he claimed that Murrell headed a broad criminal and slave-stealing conspiracy, which news, a local paper said, was "received with the deepest expressions of interest." Murrell was convicted of stealing slaves, and Stewart went south to Mississippi, where, taking ill, he was taken in by a planter near Livingston. Here he put into pamphlet form his alleged adventures with Murrell and the latter's "confession" to him, now expanded into an account of an organized criminal clan blanketing the South.[30]

Once the summer's rioting began, first Stewart's "clan" and then Thompson's "agitation" were frequently invoked as cause of the events. In fact, Stewart may have had some direct tie to one of the first two major riots of 1835, both incidents occurring within a radius of fifteen miles in Mississippi's black belt. The one, in the area where Stewart recuperated and wrote his influential fiction, was an insurrection panic, in which probably ten whites and about thirty slaves were mob-killed. The second was an attack on gamblers in Vicksburg, in which four men were hanged and four beaten senseless and set adrift on the Mississippi; three of them probably died from their beatings. Antigambling mobs spread from Vicksburg to other cities throughout the South, each mob claiming they were removing from their towns gamblers driven there from elsewhere.

The riot chronology here, like much of it for these busy mob months, is puzzling. It's hard to believe there was not some tie between these two first major events, occurring within the same days only fifteen miles apart. Yet initially no connection was made by either local or distant press. The only clear relationship is a process of reverberation: fears, rumors, and actions from one place reaching out to influence behavior in the other nearby locale. Contemporary observers seldom related the two riots chronologically, much less causally. On the other hand, causal connections were quickly made between the Livingston events and the abolitionist mail campaign and subsequent anti-abolitionist violence. Some historical accounts have repeated what contemporary observers came to believe by August: abolitionist activity triggered violent Southern response.[31] Yet this causal pattern is untenable because the insurrection panic took place *before* there was any general Southern knowledge of abolitionist plans for a mail campaign or much talk of a new wide-scale abolitionist threat. The Livingston vigilantes made no mention of abolition until events late in July made such explanation of their imaginary insurrection a comforting supplementary fiction to the Murrell tale.

These Mississippi mobs inaugurated 1835's intense mob season from July through October. In Maine there were two riots against the Irish, in New York City two riots occurred among Irish groups, and in upstate New York an Irish gang attacked some native-born citizens. In Massachusetts, sailors rioted in one case and temperance opponents in another; in Colerain, Massachusetts, citizens tar-and-feathered one man, certainly a Perfectionist and maybe a seducer. Prostitutes were victims in York, Pennsylvania; New Bedford, Massachusetts; and Vergennes, Vermont, profiteering lawyers-businessmen in Baltimore, and passengers on a competing steamship in Catskill, New York. There was an election riot in Arkansas, as well as killings of alleged criminals. A labor riot occurred in New York City, and others with strong ethnic overtones near an Indiana canal and a Florida harbor. A Protestant camp meeting was mobbed in Massachusetts, the Protestant Association by Catholics in New York City, and a family of Mormon converts in Tennessee. In Maryland a brawl after some horse races worsened when ten or so white furnace workers rescued two slave coworkers from the authorities, a mob here labeled, since necessity is the mother of categorization, "Entertainment-sport." The curtain came down on the year's riots with a theater mob in Mobile, Alabama.

Yet two-fifths of the riots between July and the end of October related to the issue that most mocked and threatened the nation's aspirations to liberty and union: the status of blacks, slave and free. Historians have given the 1835 controversy about slavery much less attention than those when the debate was focused in Congress, such as the Missouri argument of 1820 and that over the Wilmot Proviso in 1846. In histories of these debates there has been a hot pursuit of the petty or aggrandizing motive as "cause" of the controversy. James Talmadge was politically ambitious; David Wilmot was in a swing political district. Northern Federalists in 1820 and Whigs in the late 1840s craved an issue to restore their party fortunes.[32]

Such interpretations have been aided by the chief rival explanation, antislavery moral altruism. It has been easy to show that politicians often came very suddenly to antislavery politics, that this interest was never detached from other concerns, and that often racism, opportunism or personal unpleasantness made antislavery politicians dubious moral heroes. Politicians' motives and tactics rarely can be simple, and it's hardly surprising that American historians, like their fellow citizens, often tend to think the more selfish, the more likely. Yet if Talmadge and Wilmot were calculating rather than committed, they must have believed that the stance they took touched a deep popular chord. And it did.

The nonmoral argument against politicians can also be applied to most of their constituents, who showed little desire to destroy slavery, much hate of unambiguous abolition and strong racism. Yet these truths do not prove the corollary historians have often drawn from them: that the concern about slavery was an ersatz issue demogogically agitated by calculating politicians. In fact, whenever the issue came to the fore, slavery touched Northern popular feeings that ran much deeper than most politicians, concerned about both party and union, cared or dared to follow, in 1820, 1835, or 1846.

The sectional crisis of 1835 was telling because it did not center in a congressional debate, and no politician showed the slightest inclination to do anything but quiet it as quickly as possible. Yet the emotion that went into the controversy was intense, exemplified and heightened by the social violence that accompanied it. In fact, because it was not caged in politics, it touched the general populace more generally than the other controversies. Politicians primarily responded to what Thomas Jefferson called "the firebell in the night" in 1820; few citizens were beyond the reverberations of its tolling in 1835, as both sections took highly passionate positions that the other could not accept. Finally the conflict was not resolved but only postponed by being transferred to the political realm, where leaders debated what should be done about abolitionist mail and petitions. But by that time, the animosities, myths, compromises, and areas where compromise was to prove impossible had all been sketched in.

No change was more significant in 1835 than the solidification of riot patterns. By year's end, two sectional systems of, and attitudes toward, social violence were in place that would mark and deepen all future North-South confrontations. The sectional differences in 1835 riots related only in a marginal way to numbers of mobs, the slave states leading, but scantily, seventy-nine to sixty-eight. More significant were several things: the distinction between property and person as focus of attack, the number of deaths, the situation of those who died in riot, the actions of officials, and the differing quotients of sadism. Property was the object of attack in well over half of the Northern mobs, but persons were what Southern riots aimed at in all but ten or so of the incidents there. Southern mobs also aimed well, usually at point-blank range against people wholly in the power of the mob. Eight died in Northern mobs, but Southern riot killed almost eight times as many (sixty-three). The situation of those killed differed between the sections equally tellingly. Half of the Northern victims were rioters: a white actor shot when cooperating with blacks in a fugitive slave riot, two men killed in separate incidents while attacking houses of prostitution, and a "Corkonian" killed by a "Kerryman" in an inter-Irish fight. One death was accidental, that of a New Hampshire woman just delivered of a baby, who went into fatal convulsions when a mob pushed into a jailor's home when disappointed of a legal hanging. Two, or possibly three, were direct mob victims, but there is no evidence that any Northerner was intentionally mob-murdered in 1835.

In the slave-state mobs, only eight known rioters died, about one-eighth of the total victims, five of these killed by authorities in the Baltimore bank mob. Intended mob victims killed one rioter apiece in the Mississippi insurrection, the Vicksburg antigambling riot, and a Louisville instance where a boat officer somehow "offended" what became a mob. About a half-dozen deaths occurred in mob fights where it's impossible to tell who was rioting and who, if anyone, defending. About forty of the Southern deaths were mob executions and another seven or eight such prolonged and brutal tortures that death resulted. One white victim, returned to jail after an inventively sadistic ordeal, hanged himself, and one slave, who refused to confess, bit his tongue off from the pain of his prolonged whipping and died shortly thereafter, reportedly of lockjaw.

In over three-quarters of the Northern cases, rioters faced some serious opposition either from intended victims or from authorities. In about a third of the cases, evidence exists of arrests, and in about a fifth, of trials or sentences. In the South, mobs acted generally in situations where they were completely in control, and with little fear that legal authorities would question their action. In only four Southern mobs was there any hint of officials opposing the mob, and in one of these a man jailed supposedly for his protection was then murdered by a mob member in his cell. The killer's argument of "self-defence" in shooting the unarmed prisoner went unquestioned. There is record of only one mob member being criminally tried, the Mississippian who led the mob-beating of the slave who died of lockjaw, acquitted despite a wide reputation for sadism toward slaves. Outside Baltimore the only Southern rioters to suffer judicially were five of the mob who whipped and branded Alonson Moody; Moody instituted a civil suit against them, and a Tennessee court levied a $2,000 fine for their tattooing of his flesh.[33]

These details suggest in a broad way how the two sections developed different systems of social violence, if one uses "system" to imply a network of customary rather than codified social expectations and possibilities. In both sections riot occurred with some expectation of communal support or toleration, but in the North the boundaries on what might be done were more tightly drawn, and there was more encouragement to fight back. Northern authorities were often supine before mobs, but they also faced some pressure to act if the riot was prolonged or became brutal or deadly. And there were always people to denounce both the mob and the officials who failed to prevent the illegalities after the incidents ended. Northern courts also sometimes acted effectively against rioters even in such popular mobs as those attacking abolitionists. In 1835, members of at least three Northern proslavery mobs were tried, convicted, and charged small fines for their fun.[34] Northern rioters had to worry some about what the intended victims might do, about officials who might come, and about the changing mood in the tolerating community.

Being a Southern rioter meant seldom having to say you were sorry. The only major exception to this came when an intended victim could and did fight back. A rioter's worst-case scenario followed the pattern of an incident at Deer Creek, Mississippi, on July 6, just after the heaviest killing times in Livingston and Vicksburg. As often in small Southern mobs, the story gave no clue about why the clash occurred, but the small mob that a man named Hasburger led to chastize a man named Chancy unluckily found Chancy with friends, too. The gun battle ended with four men dead, two on each side, one a slave.[35]

Unlike the two Northern rioters shot by the owners of the brothels they wished to sack, Hasburger had no fear that the authorities might intervene. Commonly, the more mob violence accelerated in deadliness in the South, the less likely authorities were to interfere. Nor would Hasburger or his friends ever have to explain much to courts or community, had they killed Chancy. A dead Chancy wouldn't sue, nor would officials or community judge it wise to raise any open questions about any corpse a sensible mob labeled scum, gambler, liar, criminal, swindler, abolitionist, or insurrectionist. The evidence against Chancy was as strong as that offered against the four "abolitionists" mob-killed in South Carolina and Louisiana and the over 40 "insurrectionists" dead in Mississippi and Louisiana—indeed, better, for anyone who prefers the possibilities of total silence to self-evident fantasy and fabrication.

The men who killed rioters in the Livingston and Vicksburg incidents suggested the dangers of opposing Southern mobs. When Vicksburg's just formed—or probably still-to-be-invented—Anti-Gambling Association attacked a group, the intended victims returned fire and killed one man. This resistance caused authorities to intervene not to keep the peace but to aid the mob in the day's carnival of death. In Livingston, the mob decided that a justice of the peace proved he was a member of the criminal-insurrectionist clan when he refused to subordinate his legal duties to extralegal convictions. He released some slaves and two whites whom rioters demanded, and when the mob came after him, he held them off, killing one man and one horse and shooting through the coat of the nephew of Mississippi's governor. At this, the mob retired for refreshment and reinforcement. This lone legalist was saved by a relative, the chief justice of Mississippi's supreme court, who protected his kinsman, not by uselessly invoking Southern legal authority. Instead he located a less heated vigilance committee, on which he had friends and to which he could trust the "examination" of his cousin until mob fervor faded.[36]

Southern mobs always offered "proof" of guilt which no one could doubt: victims were "whipped until they confessed"—and implicated others, as the mob suggested. In Southern legal cases, such confessions were regularly chucked out of court because everyone in fact knew that it was indeed a rare individual who wouldn't say anything at some point to save what was left of his hide and life.[37] One great advantage of the Southern extralegal system was that it silenced all public doubting of such whipped-out confessional confirmations that the mob had saved virtue and slain vice. When rioters were in action, cautious good sense dictated the silencing of all doubts. The only convincing evidence against two white victims in the Mississippi insurrection scare was that they showed sympathy for slaves being whipped until they told. Honest Henry Foote was wiser: he conducted the mock defense according to the vigilante script; told a white woman anxious to save her slave, whom they both knew to be wholly innocent, that nothing could be done; and looked the other way as the mob beat and drove from his home a young white he knew and admired. The two whites who protested were hanged, and Foote became a United States senator.[38]

Southern proof, of course, really lay in the convictions of the rioters and of the tolerating community. To doubt out loud in the South any fatal mob scenario was to question that brave and benevolent white power was able to master the always terribly threatening human black passions and passions of blacks. Such self-deception was soothing, but of course had it costs as well. Southerners complained much of the level of general violence, personal and social, in their society. They were quiet only about the specific instances of it, where sharp questioning would puncture the myth of perfect mastery. This was the gift of the South's extralegal system, and the reason the South protected it as a parallel structure. It was the reason, too, that, after every wave of especially murderous mobs within it, Southern politicians and press and preachers would point with horror to the mob-ridden, anarchic North in contrast with their section's wholesome harmoniousness. As with the confessions of victims, who could doubt what no one dared to question?

Because Southern mob actions seldom were questioned, rioters there were free to indulge in sadistic trimming. Northern mobs could be brutal; Philadelphia's antiblack mob, in which the arrested were Irish, included a castration and a rape. And three Northern incidents centered in a festive tar-and-feathering: against an accused seducer in Massachusetts, an alleged "scab" worker in New York City, and a woman said to cheat on her husband in upstate New York.[39] Yet Southern killings, whippings, and humiliations featured more spectacular brutality, in addition to the commonplace whipping atrocities. Slaves were burned alive in Alabama; the flesh was ripped from the back of a white by the claws of a tomcat the mob swung over him; and a Mississippi mob beheaded a victim, played kickball with his head, and threw his body to hungry pigs. Sadism, ordinary or extraordinary, was an element in about a quarter of Southern mobs.[40]

The politics of 1835 both soothed and sharpened the sectional conflicts over the use of mob violence to quiet criticism of slavery. That neither party in 1835 dared to do enough to satisfy the South marked the dilemma of Northern politicians. In 1835 the South made increasing demands on a compliant North until they drove many Northerners to some grudging sympathy for the abolitionists and most to bounds which no Northern politician could exceed. Both sections broadly accepted the other's right to follow its own course on slavery, but the tensions over the precise structure and significance of this compromise were enough to foster much civil violence in 1835, as surely as they led to civil war in 1861.

One of the traits of riot as political tactic is that it inevitably directs at least as much attention to its violent means as it does to the underlying social issues. In the 1835 riots this was, in part, a blessing. By August 1835 people saw the American experiment at risk from mob violence, and this overreaction acted as counterpoise to the sectional animosities that, almost everyone sensed, posed the real challenge to the continuance of the union.

The question of the causes of the Civil War involves the reasons for sectional discord and the failure of the United States' political mechanisms to handle them. That historians have commonly blamed Northern politicians or Northern moralists in many ways makes sense: the South's commitment to slavery was a historical constant, while the disruptive issues or events—the Missouri controversy, abolitionism in the 1830s, the Wilmot Proviso, the Liberty, Free Soil, and Republican Parties—originated in the North. Yet this causal view overlooks a certain constancy in the North as well: most there felt that slavery was a dated and undesirable institution and that the North should not be forced into active complicity with its extension or protection. The North's position accepted the status quo, as did that of the South, but the status quo itself was often an unstable guide in a society rapidly expanding its population, territory, economy, and cultures of violence.

Slavery had effectively ended in the North, and those few who intensely disliked slavery began pondering the question that their opponents were to chide them with for three decades: What practically and politically could they do to touch slavery in the South? In 1835, the Tappan-financed abolitionists responded with an effort to touch the moral conscience of the South.

About three weeks after early July's insurrection panic in Mississippi, three things converged to create the turmoil over slavery that was to torment the United States for several months. The annual report of the American Anti-Slavery Society was released which revealed that there now existed 215 affiliates in thirteen states. The stories of the Vicksburg and Livingston vigilante murders, and the accompanying Murrell legend, appeared for the first time in the Eastern press. And the first batches of antislavery propaganda arrived in large quantities in the South. The conjunction of these things was largely coincidental, but they all came to general public awareness at the same time, so it's hardly surprising that people wove the three threads into a single ominous design. The growth of antislavery in the North made it less easy to pooh-pooh the significance of the movement, as most Northerners had been striving to do. The Mississippi incident suggested an insurrectionary threat to the South, as well as a way of "handling undesirables" that had obvious possibilities in relation to those "hypocritical madmen" whom the North allegedly despised. And the mail campaign provided the smoking gun between the strength of abolition and the reality of insurrectionary threat: the abolitionists were preaching servile war to the slaves. Taken together—and people took them together—these events posed dramatically and scarily the questions of what the United States was going to do about both slavery and slavery's handful of determined opponents.

Much of the subsequent debate centered around a mirage: that the abolitionists were plotting servile war and that their literature was intended to stir slaves to revolt. There was nothing in the literature itself that suggested such intent, nor in the distribution process the abolitionists used: mailings to prominent Southerners. To read any considerable part of it is to see that the abolitionists aimed shrewdly at their announced goal: touching the moral conscience of the slaveholder. Even had slaves read the works, they would have been encouraged not to revolt but to work and hope for a religious-moral transformation of the white South. In *Human Rights* and the *Emancipator* and the *Anti-Slavery Record*, despite some melodramatic and maudlin elements, there was remarkable reasonableness and restraint. Especially the first batch of literature sought not to condemn white Southerners but to picture them as highly sensitive persons who, too, were victims of a system they inherited rather than created.

Of course, very few slaves could read anything, which reduced the likelihood of printed literature being intended for them. Historian Leonard Richards, like Andrew Jackson and some Southern newspapers at the time, questioned this conclusion because of the pictures in some pamphlets. This implies that seeing pictures of events—the most emotional showed whippings or family separations—would create rebellion in a group of people presumably untouched by seeing or experiencing such things personally. These illustrations no more put a stamp of approval on servile war than temperance pamphlets endorsed proletarian revolt with engravings showing landlords driving hapless wives and children of alcoholics from their homes. In fact, the early abolition woodcuts were careful adjuncts of the verbal message. The slave subjects were treated with human dignity but were shown only as passive or pleading victims.[41]

Richards's larger analysis of anti-abolition rhetoric raises other questions. He accurately points out several of its themes—racism, a fear of the new forms of public appeal made possible by quicker and cheaper printing, the resentment at women and children "agitating" political questions, the fury at George Thompson's "foreign intervention." Thus he concludes that anti-abolition was the position of social conservatives who sensed danger in the broad new forces being created in the United States. Richards's accurate intellectual résumé still neglects the pivot of most anti-abolitionist rhetoric around 1835: that the activity of abolitionists, if unchecked, would destroy the Union. It was not the techniques of the antislavery campaign that centrally bothered people; the kind and quantity of the literature was modeled on work being done in the temperance crusade and the Sunday school union, as was the prominent emphasis on involvement of women and children. But now the new "democratic" techniques were being applied to the one issue that might "blow the union into atoms"; abolition was "the only rock on which the Union may probably split." John Tyler, whose speech Richards emphasizes, mentioned the various subthemes, but his argument centered in union, with 1835 reviving the Missouri question "in a new and more terrifying form." While they fumed at all sorts of subordinate things that gave some comforting sense that slavery was not the real issue, populace and political leaders alike were driven by highly rational worries about where abolition might lead.[42]

It was not only chronological coincidences that tied abolition to insurrection fears in 1835. Most Southerners and Northerners had strong incentive not to question that the plundering-insurrectionary plot of John Murrell related to the plans of George Thompson and Arthur Tappan. If abolitionists were in fact bloodthirsty monsters, the South could justifiably demand their suppression and the North comfortably agree. The sectional dialogue on slavery went forth under the camouflage of insurrection between August and the winter of 1835 because the positions of both sections, undisguised, left no room for the accommodation that the great majority desperately wished. Southerners wanted all determined opponents of slavery to cease agitating the question; most Northerners wanted to wash their hands of the issue. The abolitionists were equally annoying to both groups, but only if they were "vile incendiaries" dedicated to stirring "up deeds of blood and violence" could the two sides agree on how to handle them.[43]

In the last week of July and early August there developed a remarkable unanimity in the Southern press on basic demands: the abolitionists must be "put down" by the North if the Union were to survive. While William Jay was right that the mobs of 1835 were encouraged by the parties' competition "to exhibit the greatest obsequiousness" to slavery, politicians were also central in controlling the controversy.[44] Because Van Buren's candidacy was most threatened by sectional schism, Southern Jacksonian papers were more conciliatory in their approach and quicker to accept Northern gestures of support. The *Richmond Whig* and the *Richmond Enquirer* reflect this difference in tone, but the "moderate" *Enquirer* made similar demands: If the North wished to preserve the Union, it must somehow stop the mouths and clog the pens of the abolitionists.

The question of how abolitionists were to be silenced was the sticking point in the sectional dialogue. In the *Richmond Enquirer*'s terminology one can trace the South's rising temperature: in mid-July the abolitionists were to be "put down," in early August "scouted down," by mid-August "beat down." Each phrase had its rough policy equivalents. The articles that urged "putting" abolitionists down neglected all suggestion about how this was to be done. "Scouting" them down was to be accomplished by public opinion pressures, by concerted and clear expressions of public "scorn and disdain." And "beating" down was to be accomplished by making them outlaws, either legally or extralegally, by jailing or mobbing them to silence. Stressing the "higher law" of self-preservation, editor Thomas Ritchie made clear what "beat down" meant. "When a nondescript incendiary is applying the torch to your roof, you do not leave him to perpetrate his crime and your ruin, while you seek a magistrate."[45]

The North was happy to "put down" the abolitionists if verbal put-downs would do the trick. By mid-August urban elites, especially the business community, organized large pro-Southern meetings. Portland, Maine, held the first major one on August 17, Boston the next on August 20, and within the week Philadelphia, New York City, and other cities followed. These meetings unequivocally damned the abolitionists as "fanatics," "firebrands," "false philanthropists," "hypocrites," and "madmen." They also stressed strong disapproval of any attempts by outsiders to agitate the issue. Some contained racist slurs, and all pledged racial unity against any attempt at insurrection. The Philadelphia resolves struck an emotive chord in the South when these urbanites promised to ride to aid their white brethren should racial war break out.[46]

Yet even in these speeches and resolutions, specifically honed to placate the South, slaveholders found disturbing elements. For one thing, most of the resolves, as John Quincy Adams noted, talked about the "evil of slavery." Under normal circumstances, this would not be exceptionable; most Southern newspapers had continued to refer to the institution in such terms. The *Enquirer* itself, two months earlier, had denounced abolitionists because slavery was a problem for Southerners, "who are best acquainted with the evil." And a meeting of 300 Southerners in New York City, intended to warn Northerners about rising Southern feeling in late July, had claimed that "no one will deny that slavery is an evil" and that Southerners contemplated the slaves' "condition with regret." Even in mid-August Southerners could mouth the heart of the antislavery creed. Arthur Tappan could not have been pleased by what the citizens of Petersburg, Virginia, wanted done to him—mobbing

or murder was strongly suggested—but he could only have said amen to their pro-
logue: "The abstract question of Slavery is one on which no candid difference of
opinion can exist among an enlightened and Christian people. But we appeal to the
history of our country for our acquittal from its stain."[47] Yet by the time these Petersburg slaveholders spoke, the South had become less willing to talk about or to
accept other people's talking about slavery's "stain." What comfort was there when
anti-abolition meetings in the North insisted on their moral superiority to slavery?
"The condition of slavery finds no advocates among our citizens," 1,500 leading
Bostonians assured the South in their appeasement meeting. "Our principles revolt
against it."[48]

A second cause of Southern uneasiness about these declarations involved the
camouflage of insurrection. The Southern press itself was full of extraordinary pictures of the imminence of bloody slave revolt in these months. Vigilance Committees were urged to stay "the strong arm of the plunderer . . . , or the dagger of the
cruel and bloody assassin"; "fiend-like fanatics" were about to "stir up the infuriated
slave to fire his master's dwelling, and glory in the ruin of families perishing in
flames"; sable-veiled monsters were "sharpening the knife for the throats of its
women and children." Meeting after meeting suggested that the South felt it was, as
the *Alexandria Gazette* suggested, living "on a volcano at the edge of a crater." It
was "not so much a question of property, as of life," said the *Enquirer*, and again
"the evil may seriously reach our own families, . . . the powder keg may be set on
fire."[49]

Such rhetoric provided a picture of the relation of slave to master more grotesque
than any abolitionist account. If a talk by George Thompson in New York City or a
stray copy of the *Emancipator* in Washington, D.C., might unleash slave rebellion in
which "merciless fiends" with "bloody knives" and "burning torches" laid waste the
white South, the abolitionists were right when they said they were the true friends of
the white South as well as of the slave. After quoting some Southern recitations of
the dangers of "pillage and murder," the *Kennebec* (Me.) *Journal* concluded, "What
a sad condition of things where the free circulation of information or argument of
any sort . . . is attended with such terrible consequences."[50]

Southerners noted the implications of this rhetoric of danger much more clearly
when Northerners mouthed their words. When would-be allies repeated the extreme
picture of slave threat that had become a Southern rhetorical commonplace, the
Southern press was infuriated rather than pleased. Satisfaction at Philadelphia's
promise of armed aid to quell slave insurrection quickly changed to angry denials
that the South needed any help in controlling their suddenly once again "contented
and ignorant" slaves, the one quality obviously judged dependent on the other.[51]

Insurrection also allowed Northerners to promise to put down criminal conspiracy
while neglecting the peaceable agitation about slavery that abolitionists actually
practiced. The South took no comfort when Northern assurances of action focused
on promises to deal with insurrectionists rather than with Tappan or Garrison. In
fact, hint of any real action against the abolitionists, other than public chiding, was
hazy in the North. A Georgian in New York suggested the general reaction to the
Northern meetings by mid-October. All Southern gratitude and euphoria had faded
toward anger at having been fooled: "I strongly suspect that it was intended to de-

ceive us and the whole South! . . . 'Words, words, words' are all we're to have, and they will not at all restrain Tappan and his associates. . . . Action speaks louder than words."[52] Northern meetings in fact aimed less at ending abolition than at pacifying the South. Few could have thought that people who had weathered mob action already would abandon deep beliefs for shelter from the verbal drizzle these meetings produced.

The Columbia, South Carolina, *Southern Times* early stated the view that was soon to prevail about the Northern assurances: "The magnates of the North may complaisantly sing to us the *lullaby* of 'No Dangers.' . . . Nevertheless, until they manifest the sincerity of their declarations by something more substantial than mere 'set phrases' and 'taffety xpressions,' we shall in no wise believe them." Even papers most anxious to soothe sectional anger mingled their praise of Northern words with warnings that now fanaticism must be "intimidated and silenced." The reaction of the *Richmond Enquirer*, as the administration's most prominent Southern journal, attracted most attention. After warm praise of the meetings of "our brethren at the North," Ritchie added a codicil: "But while the North is rising in her strength, it is hoped she will do the business effectively. Teach the Fanatics a lesson they can never forget. Not only beat them down, but *keep them beat down* . . . , preventing the bold incendiary from repeating the effort for half a century."[53] The dialogue in a month's time had moved from a quiet "put down" to an italicized "keep them beat down."

The New York City reaction to the *Enquirer*'s "Calm Appeal"—so Ritchie labeled his demand for a fifty-year cessation of all questions about slavery—prefigured the growing truculence of the North to Southern demands. The *Journal of Commerce* disabused Ritchie about Tappan's motives: though sadly wrong, Tappan did not crave "notoriety" but acted out of honest conviction and with much regret at the turmoil engendered. The *American* snapped that Ritchie's article was "menacing" and "vicious," while—unkindest cut of all—New York City's most respected Jacksonian organ, the *Evening Post*, condemned Ritchie's position roundly. The *Post* decried the tone of the article because "should the North retaliate in the same braggart style, ill-blood might be stirred." Acting editor William Leggett disliked even more the implied principles. "We shall not permit our right to discuss the question of slavery, or any other question under heaven, to be denied."[54] And this was precisely what was at issue.

The Philadelphia resolves had suggested a willingness to develop and pass laws dealing with "incendiaries." All states, of course, had such laws, but they hardly applied to abolitionists, who had lit no fires except those of social conscience and, much more broadly, social worry. The South had trouble suggesting what "effectual and constitutional laws" could end abolition: "treason to the social fabric," "libellers of the South," "trespass" through the public mails, "public nuisances." Governor George McDuffie of South Carolina, happy to presume the South a separate nation, suggested that the North might repress abolitionists "under the principles of international law." The Northern answers were equally fanciful, such as a Boston suggestion that abolitionists could be jailed for instigating riot because their meetings were often signals for mob action.[55] In fact, the one legal channel open was to make it a crime to speak, write, petition, and organize on the question of slavery. The South seldom dared to suggest this total sacrifice of basic liberties, and no Northern press, even those making a career out of pro-Southern sympathies, proposed it.

Mobbing was a much more attractive answer: it was quick, it necessitated neither a permanent legal principle nor, politicians hoped, any prolonged wrestling with the issues at stake, and it gave the illusion of directly handling a problem for which there was no legal answer. Boston's *Mercantile Journal* didn't seriously pursue its suggestion of jailing Garrison for instigating the riot against him, but it gave its blessing, like the rival *Commercial Gazette*, to the October anti-abolition mob. "If there is no law that will reach it, it must be reached in some other way," the *Gazette* concluded, assuring its mercantile readers that such mobbing would not be déclassé: "the resistance will not come from rabble, but from men of property and standing." Administration journals did not stress such riotous snobbery. The *Cincinnati Evening Post* welcomed all to help lynch abolitionists, and the Jacksonian *Boston Chronicle* insisted that mobbing was not an elitist prerogative, even in Boston, but the "property" of the people. The wealth of some abolitionists made them difficult to prosecute legally, but "if the entrance to our courts of law be blocked up with bars of gold, let the people assume 'the balance and the rod'; it belongs to them; it is their property and rarely abused." Boston's intellectual tradition, of course, mattered, even to the *Chronicle*. It was impossible to get "a *mob* in this intelligent community, without there first exists some crying evil to be remedied, which no other means can reach."

The two well-known mobbings of October 21, 1835—that of Garrison in Boston and of the New York Anti-Slavery Society in Utica—along with two less famous ones on the same day were offered and accepted as final proof that the North really sided with the South against the abolitionists in deed as well as word. The chief sponsors of three of these riots at least—businessmen in Boston and prominent local Jacksonians in Utica and Montpelier, Vermont—were the groups most threatened by Southern reluctance to accept purely verbal assurances of support in these troubled months. Such mild mobbings were all that the South was to get, although a far cry from what Southerners did and demanded. James Henry Hammond wrote to a pro-Southern New York editor in mid-August that the Union would be saved only by effectually stilling abolitionists who "can be silenced in but one way. *Terror and Death*." The editor wisely refrained from publishing this letter, and no Northerner dared to suggest responsiveness to such commonplace murderous demands.[56]

The position of Jackson's administration in all this was delicate, because the explosiveness of the situation strained the election strategy that Van Buren and Kendall had carefully, if not always in unison, been weaving. Administration politicians faced two immediate problems. One concerned abolitionist use of the United States mails, an issue directly depending on the national government. The second involved making sure that Southern loyalty to the administration was not transferred to politicians with more sectional appeal than Van Buren.

Early it was hoped that Amos Kendall, postmaster general and the administration's shrewdest strategist, might kill both birds with a single letter. When the postmaster in Charleston, South Carolina, wrote Kendall saying the safety of his post office was endangered if he delivered abolitionist literature, Kendall took several days to answer, during which time a mob of leading citizens broke into the post office and burned the mail. Probably Kendall and his allies planned this to happen to undercut

Northern resistance to the alternative he was to offer. Certainly the administration carefully considered and sanctioned the Kendall plan. Jackson, when apprised of Kendall's idea "to pacify the South," replied ambiguously enough that the law had to be upheld, but he personally wished the abolitionists could be made to atone with their lives.[57]

Kendall's letter to Charleston's postmaster explained the legal situation with his usual precision. He had no right to bar anything from the mails, but he promised his tacit blessing to action against abolition literature by invoking a higher law of social preservation: "We owe an obligation to the laws, but a higher one to the community in which we live and, if the former be perverted to destroy the latter, it is patriotism to disregard them." This doctrine was presented as alternative to riot, but everyone was quick to see that Kendall genially bestowed on each postmaster what mobs demanded: if the situation were deemed serious, pay no heed to the law. And this official sanction for the principle of extralegality drew more anger and protest than the riots themselves, despite some hesitancy to damn Kendall's argument immediately. Yet there was accelerating public acceptance of Philip Hone's private opinion that the view of "the notorious Amos Kendall . . . embodies all the essense of the abominable doctrine on which the Vicksburgh and Baltimore riots were founded; viz, that the people are to be governed by the law just so long as it pleases them."[58]

The South responded well to the Kendall letter, but Van Buren continued to be pressed by his Southern supporters to take an even stronger stance. Jacksonian speculator and political strategist Samuel Gwin wrote from Mississippi that Van Buren's strength depended on how vigorously he condemned the fanatics: "The knife has been raised over us and there is a desperate frenzy prevailing." On August 20 Kendall went further; now he urged that such censoring "responsibilities be voluntarily assumed by postmasters." Two days later, in the final letter in this series, Kendall wrote New York postmaster Samuel Gouvernor to lament that he personally was kept from acting "only by a want of legal power" and urged Gouvernor to keep abolitionist literature out of the post office. Because abolition literature featured "revolting pictures and fervid appeals addressed to the senses and passions of the blacks," it should be destroyed "in palpable self-defense." If that reasoning were right, Kendall had at least equal duty with Gouvernor to defy mere law, but he, and Jackson's administration, preferred to evade personal responsibility, while making each postmaster extralegal moral guardian of the community.[59]

The *Globe* trumpeted these letters, somewhat belatedly, as new proof that the administration was doing something about abolition, but by the time the last appeared, Kendall's position was proving embarrassing. The *New York Times* initially predicted that Kendall's decision "would be approved by all, whatever they may think about the reasoning by which he arrives at it." The doubts suggested in this last clause proved much more accurate than the beginning forecast of unanimity. Papers were quick to point out that Kendall sanctioned a form of personal "mob law" and to argue that his plan was a good deal "worse than the disease." The *New York American* described Kendall's second letter as "wrong and dishonest" in its description of abolitionists and reached a conclusion that the North was to ponder for the next quarter century: "If Kendall is right, slavery in the South and liberty in the North show an utter incompatibility."[60]

The dependably pro-Southern *New York Commercial Advertiser* damned "the doctrines recently avowed by Amos Kendall, speaking, doubtless, the voice of the Executive, in regard to popular violation of the law." Even in the South, Whig and nullifier papers began to raise their voices. In Kentucky the *Lexington Observer* warned of the "disorganizing pretensions" and "revolutionary positions" implied in Kendall's "Post Office Lynch Law." Duff Green's *Telegraph*, noting that a postmaster had refused to deliver the Indiana *American*, suggested that any opposition paper might be withheld, "the sympathies of honest Amos being in his favor." Increasingly, there was acceptance that Kendall's position "strikes at the very root of our civil liberties."[61]

The more liberal Jacksonian press, led by the *New York Evening Post*, was from the outset critical of Kendall's "web of sophistry," which "truckled to the domineering pretensions of slave-holders." The *Post* printed approvingly a letter to the editor which argued that "Northerners have prejudices in favor of free discussion" and would see that Kendall, that "miniature Machievel," offered "a text fit for any homily on the blessings of anarchy, and the good consequences of riot" which only "increased the Southern excitement by acceding to their illegal demands." The *Post* kept track of several other Jacksonian papers that attacked the Kendall position.[62]

The *Post* also reprinted, as did many Northern papers, some comic letters, first appearing in the *Boston Transcript*, from "Postmaster William Lynch of Lynchburg" to Kendall explaining problems he had with his censorship duties. He'd destroyed as incendiary a paper with a story about laying in fuel for next year and an evangelical periodical that admitted to hoping "to kindle a flame," but he wasn't sure if "*all* opposition papers" were to be burned or how much "burning passion" had to be found in love letters to justify destroying them. The second letter came from jail, where Lynch had been thrust for taking money from letters. He was sure Amos would "spring him" because, since money was "the root of all evil," it must be the root of incendiarism, too, and besides, he'd needed it to pay the censors he'd had to hire to protect society. The embarrassing cul-de-sac of Kendall's attempted solution became transparent when Southern papers demanded that the *Evening Post* be denied the use of the mails as an incendiary journal.

By this time, Kendall had wisely abandoned his public advice-to-postmasters column, but, in an official document little circulated outside the South, he continued to use his office to appease slave interests. In the postmaster's report of 1836, Kendall accepted one of the South's most extreme claims: international law permitted mail intercession because the states were in fact separate nations. He argued the need for such power on the grounds that otherwise even British radicals might use the mails to spread their nasty ideas among Northern laborers. Yet even the milder and better-known Kendall censoring letters of the late summer aroused enough opposition to contribute to the passage of a postal bill in 1836 that stressed nonrestriction.[63]

In late September and October, Van Buren resorted to safer proofs of his adherence to slavery. If formal administration pronouncements boomeranged, both resolutions and mobs, formed by Van Burenites in his home territory, might be offered to soothe Southern fears. Resolutions, less dangerous, were first wafted southward as Van Buren's proof of virtue. Those of Albany, in early October, were crafted as a platform which would protect the vice president's position in the South, while doing him as little harm as possible in the North. These resolves bear the stamp of Van Buren's famous political tact. Probably the best written of the batch, they suggested both vigor and moderation, while carefully gliding over those things most likely to irritate either side. The *New York Evening Post* found them largely acceptable, much better than the *Post* had expected given "the servile spirit and sinister motives" that the *Albany Argus* had in calling the meeting. And the *Richmond Enquirer*, tugging on the administration in the opposite direction, enthused that "they were free from all qualification and equivocation—no idle denunciation of the *evils of slavery*—no pompous assertion of the *right of discussion*." Little wonder that Van Buren, pushed to make a public statement, pointed to the Albany Resolves as embodying his credo.[64]

Yet other truths impressed editors less committed to Van Buren's candidacy. The *Richmond Whig*, for example, found them the epitome of Northern deception, meaningless because they intentionally neglected the basic need to act to "suppress the fanatics." *Niles' Register*, noting the Southern pressure on Van Buren to add legislative proposals, accurately concluded that their omission from the Albany Resolves meant that nothing would be pushed legally to silence abolition.[65]

In September and most of October rioting lessened, while slavery debate intensified. Southern rhetoric became more strident, and there developed, Niles reported, "somewhat of a reaction in the North," with anger increasingly directed toward Southern demands. At the same time, the Jacksonian press moved further southward in its sympathies, even though that meant sacrificing immediately the support of liberal Northern Democrats and nonpartisan moderates. The *New York Evening Post* was a particular embarrassment to Van Buren. It early damned Southern demands that all discussion of slavery must cease, then it mocked the Kendall letters, with their doctrine of every postmaster his own nullifier. The administration and the *Globe* adopted a policy of benign neglect toward the *Post* for a while, but because there was no lack of enemies attacking it, the *Post*'s position only hardened.

By mid-September the administration, goaded by Southerners who presented *Post* editorials as indicative of Van Buren's real feelings, cut off patronage to the *Post*, and in September—in the *Post*'s words—"excommunicated" the New York paper from the Democratic brotherhood. The feisty *Post* printed the *Globe*'s excommunication bull on its masthead for several days, inserted a brief notice of how Luther when excommunicated solemnly excommunicated the pope, and proceeded to lump the *Globe* with the *Argus* and plodding *New York Times* as part of the truckling unprincipled party press.[66] New York City's Democratic General Committee, under pressure from Washington, pushed through a resolution denying that the *Post* was a Jacksonian organ, but party liberals ran a big dinner during which people toasted the *Post* and "a free press"; Van Buren and everyone else in the administration regretted this invitation. A stormy meeting on October 29—the famous one where the radicals got the name "loco foco," from the matches they used to light candles when administration forces turned off the lights—ejected conservatives, while the supporters of *Post* editor William Leggett passed resolves for equal rights, free discussion, and liberal principles under the banner, "The 'Times' must change ere we give up our 'Post.'"[67]

At the heart of the Jacksonians' determination to distance the *Post* was the paper's scorn for its strategy of Southern conciliation and Leggett's increasingly honest presentation of abolitionists' views. That the *Post* published the declarations of the American and Massachusetts Anti-Slavery Societies was not surprising; the paper prided itself on publishing reasonable arguments even for positions it opposed. Yet its declaration of support for everything in these abolition position papers, except for what should be done about slavery in the District of Columbia, was remarkable. And after its excommunication, the *Post* concluded that the issues not only of free speech but also of free men should be discussed fully, and it printed long excerpts from the *Anti-Slavery Quarterly*, as well as letters and articles that would not have seemed out of place in any abolition journal. The charge of the *Charleston Courier* in early September that the *Post* was an "incendiary" journal which the post office must not let "pass South" was true by early October, if one deemed any pro-abolitionist literature "incendiary."[68] That the *Post* could take such a stance without undercutting its liberal Jacksonian and popular support suggests how much the furor over abolition related to the stereotype of unreasonable troublemaker.

Besides excommunicating the *Post*, the administration worked in other ways to appease the South. New Haven's anti-abolition resolves, the most extreme in proslavery rhetoric and promises of legal action, were widely reprinted by Southern Jacksonian journals, with assurances from the *Richmond Enquirer* that they were made "directly under the eyes of the Albany regency." Resolutions and grand juries from Van Buren's home area of upstate New York urged extreme policies, again republished mostly in Southern papers.[69]

On October 21 Van Buren played his last and most successful pro-Southern card, in response to demands, waxing since mid-August, that, if legislation against abolitionists was not possible, mobs might do as well. Two things that month directed the South's and Van Buren's attention to Utica. Southern Whigs had learned of a small paper there that was both pro–Van Buren and antislavery and began to quote from it to counter the stream of proslavery resolves from the area that the Jacksonians claimed proved Van Buren's determination to quell abolition. Even more embarrassing was the coming organizational meeting in Utica of the Tappan-sponsored New York Anti-Slavery Society. Both situations sharply contradicted Jacksonian claims that few abolitionists lived in the area and that those were being rhetorically repressed. To these irritants, a well-modulated mob seemed the best answer.

To make clear the mob's political credentials, United States congressman Samuel Beardsley, known as Van Buren's closest associate in the House, headed it as it disrupted the society's organizational meeting and did minor damage to the offending *Oneida Standard and Democrat*. Van Buren's correspondence and autobiography are a blank about this major event in his home district and his presidential campaign, but his political friends in New York rewarded Beardsley with ever higher judicial posts.

The *Globe* assured the world that Beardsley's ties to the vice president proved "the great injustice that has been done to Mr. Van Buren and his friends" in any suggestion of softness on abolition. At the same time, the Utica mob did so little damage that most Northerners, anxious to blame the abolitionists for "causing" all the trouble anyway, accepted it as "rough justice." On the same day in Boston, a mob with broad popular and especially mercantile support pretended to attack the anti-abolitionist's archenemy, George Thompson (when he was out of town); broke up a woman's antislavery session; chased Garrison into protective custody in jail for an evening; and splintered the *Liberator*'s sign. On the same day mobs attacked Henry B. Stanton in Newport, Rhode Island, and Samuel May in Montpelier, with prominent Jacksonians again leading at least the Vermont riot. The day's riotous work was the North's final offering of works to prove the sincerity of its stream of words against abolition.[70]

Southern response indicated that this Northern mob sacrifice propitiated much of their wrath. There was hope that the North was importing its system of sanctified mob violence to end discussion of slavery, and few in the South noted how little damage to property and none to people these careful mobs perpetrated. At least it was clear that this was as much action as the South was going to get. Southern grand juries continued to indict Northern abolitionists, and governors went on demanding "extradition" to the South of men who had never been there, while meetings put prices "on the head" of abolitionists and demanded that the North ban any statement either "incendiary or tending to create discontent in our slaves" in order to stop all attacks on slavery.[71]

Northern legislators and governors, despite a widespread desire to placate the South, were hardly about to ban those paeans to freedom that were the staple of Fourth of July orations. After the mob outburst at the end of October, the *Globe*'s position against Southern agitators hardened; it gingerly inserted some passages attacking mobs in general and finally condemned all demands for legislative action as "unnecessary." New York Jacksonian William Marcy, in his gubernatorial address, wrote windily about his and his constituents' scorn of abolition, the better to mask the murkiness of his proposed controlling legislation in a prodigality of prose. Hearings in the legislature of Massachusetts gave the abolitionists ample chance to prove the vacuity of insurrection charges against them, forcing the legislative committee to resolve lamely that they sympathized with the South and disliked abolitionists but didn't like mobs either. Abolitionists rightly saw this as "conclusive proof of the *progress of things*."[72]

In Congress Jackson proposed a law banning abolitionist "incendiary" literature from the mails. The meaning of "incendiary" was hardly self-evident, but this would not have prevented the Jacksonians' pushing through this de facto press censorship had not Calhoun and much of the South balked. Calhoun's opposition to this law expressed perfectly his analytic intelligence. His pragmatic point was simple and obvious: what the federal government could grant, it could also take away. Hence, to entrust the nation with power to ban abolitionist literature was to empower it equally to facilitate its passage through the mails. It was, in effect, to make this aspect of slavery not a local, but a national issue, with the dangers to the South and to the Union that that entailed. Calhoun's intellectual argument was equally vital, and more fascinating. A handful of Northern senators—all Whig—defended freedom of press and communication from the dangerous implications of the administration bill, but John C. Calhoun made the most eloquent defense of freedom of the press as he moved to his conclusion that the states could end it at will.

There was no logical flaw in Calhoun's argument, which flowed unswervingly from his premises: liberty is society's most valuable blessing, but, because society must precede it in chronology and in importance, no liberty can or should be absolute. The South, because of slavery, was a distinct society, and the union depended on its having absolute control over actions that might endanger it. The South had no right to use the national government to gag the North, but they had an absolute right to prevent entry of whatever threatened their basic structure and safety.[73]

A historical commonplace is that fanatic extremists on both sides of the slavery issue poisoned accommodation between sensible moderates who otherwise would have arranged a peaceful eventual end to slavery. Yet the 1835 controversy revealed an opposite truth. The "extremist" positions—those of abolitionists and of nullifiers—showed a degree of moderation in language and honest reasonableness in assessment lacking in those who saw themselves as conservative or neutral or middle-of-the-road on the issue. Duff Green was among the noisiest of nullifiers, but he accepted that abolitionists honestly grounded their argument in Christian and democratic doctrines, while the South's moderates, both Whigs and Jacksonians, insisted that all antislavery leaders were "black-hearted plunderers" or "bloodhounds" lusting to "revel in blood and carnage."[74] Certainly the abolitionists were not unreasonable in their argument that the American Colonization Society offered no solution to slavery; it was their opponents who insisted it was the one answer, all evidence to the contrary. The abolitionist view of a "slave-power conspiracy" that emerged from these controversies suggested greater unity than existed in the South, but it was a reasonably accurate cartoon of the Southern determination to foster slavery and to silence all questioning of it. Total fantasy were the reiterated moderate claims that George Thompson represented a British conspiracy to subvert American democracy, or that Arthur Tappan and John C. Calhoun were secret co-conspirators to destroy the union.[75] How extreme was a call for immediate emancipation, even without the explanations attached to this term, compared to demands and pledges of perpetual silence about slavery? So threatening was the issue of slavery to the social organism that moderates could deal with it only by inventing impossible villains and imaginary melodramatic plots to quiet the sleeping dogs that abolitionists had awakened.

The extremists were not only less prone to gross fantasy, distortion, and name-calling, but their basic request was that slavery be considered and discussed thoughtfully (abolition), or that it be legally cordoned off from national politics (nullification). It was easy to mock these positions negatively: Where could such intellectual consideration possibly lead? How could one have a free nation without a central controversial institution being a subject of discussion? But it was even easier to point to the emptiness of the moderate argument that slavery would somehow disappear if the issue were never agitated. There were major dilemmas in abolitionist arguments, but there was a strand of comparative realism in its insistence that slavery was entwined with American democracy and would continue to be so until ended. So "reasonable" people yelled "fanatic" and "madman" at those who insisted that slavery's realities should be discussed without subterfuge, and "factious" and "demonic" at those who insisted that the problem be placed wholly beyond the possibility of national action.

Rhetorical abuse, already a flourishing political art, gained broader sanction in these months, but it was not the abolitionists but their opponents who enshrined brutal name-calling as acceptable taste. In the South this art form reached new levels of development in regard not only to abolitionists but often to the North as a whole.

Southerners showed little desire to break the union, but they developed grotesque caricatures of any who questioned slavery's desirability. George Thompson, Daniel O'Connell, and Arthur Tappan couldn't simply be men who believed that one race's commanding the perpetual forced labor of another for profit little accorded with Christian or democratic ideals. They had to be plotting against democracy, demonic hypocrites whose motives were brutal or aggrandizing. That the North refused to silence such "fiends" proved that that section was little better than its abolitionists. And if mob violence effectively silenced all discussion of slavery in the South, the unprincipled North should certainly do as much. In late August the *Richmond Whig*, perhaps the South's most respected opposition paper, announced that the North must start hanging abolitionists to keep Southern trade: "They know too well which side their bread is buttered on *ever* to give up these advantages. Depend upon it—the Northern people will never sacrifice their present lucrative trade with the South, *so long as the hanging of a few thousands* will prevent it."[76]

The "humor" of the South in these months centered in such verbal violence. If abolitionists dared to come South, they would be sure to reach "a more exalted station," if they were not "burned at the stake most tenderly." It was good Garrison was not hanged because "a decent grass rope would have been disgraced by the miscreant's neck. They ought to have drowned him in a horse pond." A North Carolina congressman sent a piece of rope to Arthur Tappan, and the South hugely enjoyed the joke.[77]

Despite hearty agreement that slavery was none of its business, the North did not accept the South's bullying wholly passively. The sympathy that had existed for the South in mid-August was stretched thin by mid-September. Niles began to caution the South that a reaction was setting in and to complain himself that Southern fanaticism was as bad and as dangerous as abolitionist extremism. Even administration papers chided the South for its "almost insulting tone" and "rudeness."[78] There were other signs of revulsion as well. Opponents took over a pro-Southern meeting in Lowell and offered resolves opposing insurrection but equally condemning slavery and Southern demands. The South stormed that Lowell would "crumble to dust" in the face of its economic anger. By the time Democratic governor Peter Vroom of New Jersey, in his annual message, said his state would never pass a law impinging on basic freedoms, it was warmly welcomed except by those mercantile or Jacksonian papers most scared by Southern threats.[79] The contrast between what Governors Vroom and Marcy said was obvious: one a straightforward statement of honest conviction, the other a circumlocutious game played to placate other men's demands. Most Northerners obviously wished to smooth things over, but by October few could help preferring Vroom's principled truthfulness to Marcy's tortuously concocted treacle.

In Niles's words, 1835 saw "the Missouri question . . . revived in another shape and in a highly excited manner." In the South, moderates, even more than nullifiers, proclaimed that no serious questioning of slavery was permissible; terror would be used against it in the South and political and economic threat in the North. The North would say pretty much what the South wanted about slavery, short of praising it, but would take little action against those who damned it. Abolitionists lost hope of instilling serious thought about slavery in the South but less contrived than were pushed toward new tactics: to win Northern fellow travelers by publicizing how the South demanded that free states curb speech, press, petition, organization, and judicial protection so that slave states might rest easier with their peculiar institution and others' commitment to it. The *Boston Courier* disliked abolitionists intensely but, like much of North by the time rioting ebbed in 1835, came to center anger on the excess of Southern demands and rhetoric:

> Is't not enough that this is borne?
> And asks our haughty neighbor more?
> Must fetters which his slaves have worn
>   Clank round the Yankee farmer's door?
> Must he be told, beside his plow,
> What he must speak, and when, and how?[80]

This 1835 controversy was less solved or dissolved than blurred because the controversy was never translated into a clear political issue, nor were the two systems of social violence directly juxtaposed. But the positions taken North and South less died than became quieted among the populace until the territorial accessions of the Mexican war upset the accepted status quo on slavery by creating issues unavoidably national once again, climaxing in Kansas, where the two sectional systems of riot finally and fatally met.

The most telling riots of these months were against "insurrectionists" in the South and abolitionists in the North. Various racial riots, however, suggested other dimensions of the sectional animosities. Some demonstrated that Northerners shared the Southern sense that blacks were a race apart. At the height of sectional furor, citizens in Canaan, New Hampshire, destroyed a racially integrated academy there, a mob that the Jacksonian *New Hampshire Patriot* reported with praise and a story that the *Globe* passed South, removing only the "RIOT" headline.[81] In Philadelphia, Burlington, and Pittsburgh, Pennsylvania, whites used incidents of alleged violence by individual blacks as excuse for mob attacks on the black community. Despite prevalent press condemnation of these riots, they indicated the strength of racism in the North.

Yet in Philadelphia, less than a month before its race riot, a mob of blacks and whites attacked some people trying to remand a woman falsely alleged to be a runaway. In the same month in Buffalo, New York, an integrated mob freed a slave family being returned south. Most dramatically, in Albany, New York, a mob spontaneously attacked officials leading a chained slave through the streets and freed the prisoner. "There is a hard struggle," a letter explained, "between the desire to obey the laws of the land and the laws of God and nature."[82] What these racial and fugitive slave riots suggested was that the sectional excitements of these months were working on a Northern populace both racist and, when forced to sense their involvement with slavery, hostile to the peculiar institution.

The crisis of 1835 passed because of the North's and South's mutual recognition that the only national solution was to forget the question. Yet to forget slavery "now and forever" was not easy for a nation that prated so much about freedom and mission, especially when both foreign sympathizers and opponents were quick to point out how the exploitation and semibestial legal status of men, women, and children within its borders mocked its glowing claims. Those people who lived most directly off the labor of their human possessions could not but fear and fight their growing moral isolation. That section that benefited indirectly from slavery and shared racist presuppositions was irritated by every request that its support of the institution be made manifest. At each juncture that witnessed a clash between the South's desire for less ambiguous support and the North's wish to wash its hands of direct responsibility, the ability and the will to repress passions parallel to those of 1835 faded. The North grew more steadily irritated at every nudge or slur from the South, and the South more readily infuriated that the North could not quite be cuffed nor mastered to impose silence, when Southerners, so much more masterful and loving of their freedom, sacrificed so much on that altar.

The year 1835, then, was a preview of the longer and more politically centered sectional conflict that developed toward civil war after 1845. A minority in the North said, loudly enough so it made it hard to duck the issue, that slavery was a human wrong that should be ended, a position most Northerners thought dangerous, disturbing, and true. Faced with this challenge, Southerners found themselves pushed to shift from the inevitable evil interpretation of slavery to a positive good theory, and to demand that the rest of the nation be also protective toward slavery. The Jacksonians in power—Van Buren, Kendall, Blair, and Jackson himself—showed little more capacity for adhering to principled neutrality than would the weaker Pierce and Buchanan two decades later. And their gestures to the South in an impossible search for total silence and forgetfulness about the issue pushed segments of the North to angrier sectional stances. There was simply no tolerable way of prohibiting Northerners from discussing slavery, even if one accepted the *Globe*'s dictum that such discussion "involves moral treason against the union; the immediate consequence of servile insurrection; and more remotely, but certainly, Civil War among the states."[83]

A letter to the *New York Evening Post* responding to Amos Kendall's instructions to postmasters summarizes the depth of 1835's anger and its similarity to the emotions later to be vented not in riots but in war. Judging from his nom de plume, "Veto," the writer was a good Jacksonian. After chiding Kendall for lecturing "on the advantages of disobeying the laws, and the evils of free intercommunication," 'Veto' sketched in the Northern view that slowly and only partially emerged through the initial tirades against abolitionists:

> You have increased the Southern excitement by acceding to their illegal demands. . . . The rights of the non-slave-holding states are taken away by a federal officer to appease the phrenzy of the planting community. This, sir, disguise it as you may, is not a reflection flattering to our pride. . . . If we have "doughfaces," I for one prefer that they should be kneaded by our own hands, rather than that the work be left to stranger knuckles. It is not we who draw the odious line between the North and South. That is done by yourself, sir, and those who with you think that the North will allow their rights to be sacrificed to soothe the South.

The South, in 1835 as it would in the 1850s, demanded that federal authority abet its trampling on the most basic "rights of the non-slave-holding states," always sneering that all pretended Northern principles would knuckle under to their "dough."

"Veto" then catalogued the Southern demands that freedom be curbed, that men

be mobbed, that all admit slavery was eternal in the District of Columbia and the territories. "Is this dictation to be submitted to? And if it were, what is to be the next
demand? It were as well to know the terms of our surrender." No sooner was a
Northerner a leading candidate for the presidency, "Veto" charged, than the South
increased slavery's demands.

> These matters, sir, are working upon Northern minds, and we are compelled to ask our-
> selves what is the character of that institution which so maddens whole communities, so
> brutifies entire sections of our population, generates such monstrous falsehoods, and so
> distorts the intellect of cabinet officers?[84]

Whenever changing political realities caused the South to demand clearer support
for slavery or forced the North to recognize its shared responsibility for the institution, the hostile sectional stereotypes developed in these months were to become
prominent. From midsummer on, the South invented a North without integrity or
courage, a people who would do anything so long as it wasn't dangerous or expensive. And by October much of the North had reacted with an image of the South as
blustering bully, quick to threaten, call names, or mob the wholly unprotected but
not likely to act if their bluff were called. And there was enough truth in both caricatures to give them bite. That such images alternated with paeans to brotherhood and
union in the writings of moderate editors who wished to end all discussion of slavery suggests how deeply needed the hostile cartoon of the "other" became at times
of sectional crisis. In the 1850s such images reappeared, spread, and hardened, as
once again the North slowly decided the South asked too much of it.

In the meantime, such matters were indeed "working upon Northern minds," and
Southern, even though most wished to forget this 1835 prelude of passion, which
seemed like "what might be expected to flow from an attempt to seal up the crater of
a volcano."[85]

CHAPTER TWO

Riots Hatching Resistance

Against Abolitionists and in Aid of Fugitive Slaves

> Yet the first bringer of unwelcome news
> Hath but a losing office.
> —Shakespeare, *Henry IV*, Part II

> If Garrison could have been answered, he had never been mobbed.
> —Wendell Phillips, *Speeches, Letters, and Lectures*

In early 1836 Kentucky-born James A. Thome, agent of the American Anti-Slavery Society, was invited to a debate by the Akron Lyceum, its members confident of their oratorical skill and the wrong-headedness of the "fanatics." Pleased with this forum, Thome extemporized his initial remarks around the falsity of much of what was said about abolitionism. A young lawyer made the first reply:

> He expressed astonishment at the *disclaimers* which I had made. Said he didn't know but he was ready to go *all lengths* with *me*, but he protested I was a NEW abolitionist and had disowned every distinguishing feature of modern abolitionism. He proceeded then to give his view of abolition, and after he had dressed it up in a bearskin, he fell upon it like a whole kennel of hell-hounds, and he tore it to pieces most adroitly. I complimented him for his skill and voraciousness and hoped that he would have a *happy digestion* of his *bearskin and straw.*

Thome answered by saying what abolition was: "I blazed and threw sky-rockets, talked of human rights, touched upon the American revolution and threw heaven and earth together." His successive opponents, equally disinclined to deny human rights, "emulated the first dog, in barking at the man of straw and trading bear skins." After three hours of debate, the audience of sixty or seventy people decided to continue the next evening, Tuesday. By Wednesday evening the straw man had lost much of his stuffing, and the members of the Akron Lyceum called for the question. They repudiated their own champions and voted 12 to 9 in favor of abolition; the audience voted 40 to 22 in its support. And James Thome reported the formation of an Anti-Slavery Society of fifteen members.[1]

Yet the nation did not go as the Akron Lyceum. The abolitionist straw man of irresponsible fanatic was to remain a comforting fiction until the Civil War, providing some excuse or camouflage for the eighteen riots in Ohio alone in the mid-1830s against abolitionists. Yet other riots suggested how Northerners sometimes responded when they encountered slavery in involvingly personal terms. A judge in 1839 freed a fugitive slave, Black Bill, on a technicality, and when the Virginia slave-catchers tried physically to retain him, Judge Thomas Anderson and towns-people mobbed them mildly, until Bill escaped.[2] These two types of mobs suggest the dilemma of the North, where most wished to flee all concern with slavery. Yet this was hard to do when a few determinedly pointed out the tie, and even harder in situations where citizens had either to help reenslave or free someone risking every-thing to escape slavery. In both cases, most Northerners could protect themselves only by clinging to caricatured abolitionists and racial straw men to avoid encoun-tering the real arguments and real people.

The mobs against abolitionism in the mid-1830s influenced antislavery develop-ment and its relation to changing Northern attitudes and national tensions. Partly be-cause the Civil War has remained almost as troubling in retrospect as it was in prospect, scholarship has largely remained locked in the contemporary debate: abo-litionists' own sense of issuing moral jeremiads to a nation anxious to forget its gravest flaw, or their opponents' sense of them as deluded troublemakers making a difficult situation a good deal worse by self-righteous fanaticism. The abolitionists and their progeny who wrote histories after the Civil War, of course, felt no doubt about the heroically moral interpretation, and this stance has included a number of twentieth-century academic historians, particularly biographers.[3]

Yet the "Progressive" historians largely dismissed abolitionist "moralism" in def-erence to their favored solid economic or geographic truisms. And when World War II and civil rights struggles restored concern with moral-racial realities, the preva-lent scholarship, influenced by where fanaticism might lead in the Cold War as well as in the troubled domestic scene, tended to treat abolitionists as psychological mis-fits, displaced elites, purveyors of paranoid thought, or unreasonable romantics.[4] Historians who wished to both praise and blame abolition retained a dichotomy Gilbert Barnes developed between reasonable Weldites and fanatical Garrisonians, while New Left historians attacked frontally the leading sociopsychological put-downs and sometimes reversed the dichotomous morality by pitting radical Garri-sonians against less principled moderates.[5] Since the mid-1970s a more subtly judg-mental scholarship has focused on the ties of abolition to concerns other than slavery: "the internal dimension of their crusade," their capitalism, their social fears, their theological-intellectual peculiarities, their psychology, or "their private, social, and emotional relationships."[6]

Abolitionists often showed the traits historians have stressed: evangelical faith, middle-class sexual and economic norms, a few oddly stressed ideas, considerable self-righteousness, some concern about their and their country's status, and a desire to be part of a supportive community. Yet abolitionists were never more than a tiny part of the American populace with such commonplace commitments, and no one has shown that such were notably stronger strands among abolitionists than in their fellow Americans.[7]

Much has been lost, too, by the internal thrust of this analysis, because abolition-ists were important not for what stirred them up but for the social reactions they stirred up. Indeed, the movement's attitudes, tactics, and divisions had much less to do with personal traits than with the structural and practical realities the group faced, centrally including the riots against them. They initiated a major debate within the North and between North and South, a raucously complicated conversation that took directions that no one anticipated or wanted. The conversations between the abolitionists and the clamorous Northern meetings, exclamatory mobs, and self-proclaimed moderates contain some essential clues about the nature of the movement, the Northern society that attacked them, and how both changed as the argument wore on toward one that shook the union.

The riotous events that abolitionists triggered composed an important part of the nation's social violence. There were seventy-three attacks on the abolitionists in free states, about 6.6 percent of the nation's total and 18 percent of the mobs in all the free states east of the Mississippi. To this might be added some nineteen riots in the South—fifteen of them in Kentucky—against people or presses really engaged in antislavery argument, which would make riots against abolitionists just under 8.5 percent of the nation's total antebellum mobbings. Half of these, forty-six, occurred between 1834 and 1838, making them the most numerous type of disturbance in these years.

Given their number, the destructiveness of these riots was slight. Only two lives were lost, both in Alton, Illinois, in 1837: Elijah Lovejoy, thirty-four, was killed defending his press after carpenter Lyman Bishop, twenty-three, was killed attacking it. Seven others suffered injuries in this worst of abolitionist riots, three defenders and four rioters.[8] In other riots even injuries were slight and infrequent. One of Weld's band, Marius Robinson, was brutally beaten and tar-and-feathered near Berlin, Ohio, in 1837, while an 1842 Portland, Maine, mob beat John Spear Murray for supporting Garrisonian Stephen Foster. Frederick Douglass was mob-beaten in Indiana in 1843, and William C. Gildersleeve was inked in 1839 in Wilkes-Barre, Pennsylvania. Gildersleeve's temperance enthusiasm may have been equally provocative; part of his mob humiliation consisted of being made to take a drink at the local dram shop. A handful of other injuries were minor: things like Weld's being hit by a rock in the head while speaking in Circleville, Ohio (1835), or black abolitionist William Wells Brown's being pushed from a platform in Harwick, Massachusetts (1848).

Property damage was more extensive, with presses, churches, and meeting halls the favorite targets. Thirteen times mobs destroyed antislavery presses or newspaper offices. Lovejoy's death came trying to save a press after he'd lost four earlier ones—one in St. Louis and three in Alton—to mobs. The Cincinnati *Philanthropist* was sacked three times, twice in 1836 and again five years later. In Kentucky, mobs destroyed Cassius Clay's *True American* and the mildly antislavery Methodist *Christian Intelligencer* of Georgetown in 1845. William Sheve Bailey's *Free South* in Newport, Kentucky, was badly damaged by mobs in 1851 and 1859. The only antislavery paper to suffer mob damage distant from the South was the *Oneida Standard and Democrat*, gently sacked after the New York State Anti-Slavery convention was driven away in 1835, because it favored both Van Buren and abolition. In other instances—Milford, Delaware (1859), and Washington, D.C. (1848)—officials protected antislavery papers from mobs, while Philadelphia's largest newspaper, the *Public Ledger*, armed its friends and employees against a mob angry over its defense of abolitionist civil liberties and its denunciation of the mob that burned Pennsylvania Hall. A Cincinnati mob in 1841 was the last against an abolitionist press in the North.

Pennsylvania Hall was the most expensive structure to fall victim to an anti-abolitionist mob; almost a decade later its owners received just under $48,000 compensation from the Philadelphia County Commissioners for its loss. In other cases, property damage was greater, though more dispersed and less total. In New York in 1834 considerable damage was done to five churches, seven homes, and a business associated with abolition, and to one theater, while in the black community five homes, five houses of prostitution, one church, and a business were largely destroyed. Some abolitionist business property was damaged in Cincinnati in 1836 and 1841, although the mob was much more destructive to black property, as had been true in New York.[9] In Philadelphia and New York "anti-amalgamation" was the rallying bête noire of the mob: one observer claimed that the rioters outside Pennsylvania Hall were quiet "until they saw a huge negro darken the door arm-in-arm with a fair Quaker girl."[10] In 1834, a Presbyterian church in Newark, New Jersey, was gutted after an abolition meeting was driven out, while two years later a mob burned a church in Fowlerville, New York. Minor damage was commonplace, with windows, doors, and sashes the usual casualties.

The chronology of these events showed some fairly clear patterns. The first and worst of these disturbances occurred in 1834 in New York City, center of both Southern trade and Van Buren's machine politics. On July 4, 1834, an abolition meeting was disrupted, though without use of violence, and three days later a scuffle broke out at the Chatham Street Chapel between blacks holding a meeting there and a few members of the New York Sacred Music Society, who had not been told of a scheduling change. Newspapers printed inflammatory stories, and two evenings later the mob began operations, moving from a mock meeting at Chatham Chapel to an attack on English actor George Farren, and then to sacking wealthy abolitionist Lewis Tappan's home. The next evening rioting expanded, but so did official resistance. Limited damage was done to several churches and homes of leading antislavery ministers, and much more serious destruction was perpetrated on black targets. By the next night officials were strong enough to quell the large groups that congregated to continue the riot. Throughout this riot, suggestions of the "uppity-ness" of blacks and the dangers of amalgamation were central, with much rabble-rousing over Reverend Samuel Cox's sermon suggesting that Christ was a "colored man."[11]

The other four anti-abolition riots of 1834 occurred within two months of the New York City mobbings. Possibly citizens of Newark, New Jersey; New Britain and Norwich, Connecticut; and Concord, New Hampshire, followed the lead of the big city, adapted to local events. Two of these outbreaks related to the "foreign interference," excuse for several of next year's riots. Englishman Charles Stuart was attacked in Norwich, and his countryman, George Thompson, faced his first American mob in Concord.[12]

Thompson was the victim of five New England mobs in 1835, two more than Unitarian minister Samuel J. May faced, and the same number Theodore Dwight Weld met in Ohio.[13] Of the other six mobs, three were in New England, one in Ohio, and two in upstate New York. All of these mobs occurred in the areas where abolition was, and would continue to be, strongest; they were responses to organizational efforts serious and successful, in none of which was serious damage done.[14] Weld, the lone injury, was hit in the head with a rock and suffered brief periods of dizziness. Other damage was mostly to windows or doors or symbolic objects, such as Methodist minister Orange Scott's lecture notes or the *Liberator*'s signboard.[15] The most famous of this year's riots, the mob of "gentlemen of property and standing" in Boston, allegedly intended to tar-and-feather William Lloyd Garrison. Given the size of the crowd, however, and communal, press, and official sympathy for it, one wonders how real this intention was.[16] Both sides had a vested interest in exaggeration. The merchants of Boston, like the Van Burenites in Utica, were proving their virtue to the South; the abolitionists were establishing for their movement a heritage of heroism. The year 1835 featured more mobs than ever before, but abolitionists, damned by majorities, elites, and press alike, suffered little harm and very few setbacks other than the need to move meetings from one building to another or to postpone them for an evening.

The anti-abolition riots of 1836 were two fewer in number but followed the 1835 pattern except that New England riots stopped, save for two in Connecticut, where the process of abolitionist organization was slowest. Nine of this year's crop of riots were in Ohio, where antislavery's lecturers were most active, and three in the other center of pressure, upstate New York. Like the four simultaneous mobs of October 21, 1835, at least three of the riots of 1836 had clear political roots and were again presented in the Jacksonian press as proof of Van Buren's and his friends' soundness on the abolition issue. Most prolonged was the social violence in Van Buren's home area of upstate New York. Here the presidential candidate was embarrassed by Theodore Weld's successful campaign, especially in Utica, whose previous year's riot Jacksonians had trumpeted as the end of abolition. After his substantial gains were publicized, Weld faced increasing mob hostility, openly backed by Democratic officials, first in Lockport and then, very dramatically, in Troy. After several mob stonings of Weld and his audience, the Democratic mayor of Troy, who in the previous year had announced that "the South should withdraw from the Union" if the North failed to criminalize abolition, ordered Weld to leave the city or to face forced "transportation" out of it. Weld gave up.[17]

Despite fewer riots in 1836, there was sporadic increase in destructiveness. A church was destroyed in Fowlerville, New York, while citizens of Cincinnati twice sacked Birney's press. In between these mobs came the first sacking of Elijah Lovejoy's *Observer* in Alton, Illinois. By the next year, mobbing abolitionists was obviously a waning pastime—three more riots in Connecticut, two in Ohio, and three in Illinois—before the death of Lovejoy created the first abolition "martyr."[18]

The next twenty-four years were to know fewer Northern anti-abolition riots than occurred in 1835–37. Only four were major: the burning of Pennsylvania Hall in 1838, the inking of an abolitionist in Wilkes-Barre, Pennsylvania, in 1839 and mobs against abolitionists in Cincinnati in 1841 and 1843, the two latter ancillary to antiblack and fugitive slave situations.[19]

Of the eleven mobs between 1842 and 1848 that attacked abolitionists, four were directed at Stephen Symonds Foster, a specialist in denunciation of all who disagreed with him, especially non-Garrisonian abolitionists.[20] The mobs of the 1850s were similar to those of the mid-1830s, although now they drew much less total community support: attempts to soothe Southern irritation by gestures against abolitionist extremists. Four riots took place in 1850 and 1851, three of them in the leading commercial centers of Boston, New York City, and Philadelphia and a final riot in Springfield, Massachusetts. Both New England mobs were aimed at George Thompson, who had returned to the United States for another lecture tour and was still deemed the foreign originator of domestic discord. The 1850–51 riots came as Northern anger over the nation's new Fugitive Slave Law cooled, and conservatives hoped once more that this legislative compromise on slavery might be its final solution. A last group of eleven minor anti-abolition mobs acted between 1859 and Fort Sumter's fall, ten of them after Lincoln's election, the last pathetic Democratic mob offerings to appease the gods of sectional discord and war.[21]

The central question lurking in the anti-abolition mobs is why so many riots so loudly justified led to so little destruction. The answer lies in the fact that these mobs were primarily exclamation points inserted to prove Northern fury to a Southern audience. Most in the North wanted to silence abolitionists and dressed them in bearskins well deserving of flailing, but they quickly saw that any action, even the mildest mobbing with rotten tomatoes or eggs, hatched abolitionists. Both sides had an appealing message, the one suggesting that slavery was un-American and the other that caring more for blacks than the union was unpatriotic. This made it important that neither side do anything to gain the public ear for their opponent's argument. Hence, abolitionists spoke carefully and their opponents acted carefully. It was hard to threaten without a little action following, but anti-abolitionists quickly sensed that their only sound strategy lay in talking and acting as little as possible.

Abolitionists' insistence on talking started the Northern squabble. The problem was that few of their opponents cared to deny what they said. Their reasoning rested on a few simple ideas. The basic proposition was that no human could justly own another, and hence slavery, which made property of human beings, was a moral evil. "God has committed to every moral agent the privilege, the right, and the responsibility of personal ownership," Weld argued typically. "This is God's plan. Slavery annihilates it."[22] Their second proposition was that slavery existed because humans willed it to exist and could be ended if they willed to end it. For Cassius Clay, hearing William Lloyd Garrison for the first time, this was the revelation: that slavery was a product of human choices and not to be regarded "as I did the other evils of humanity, as the fixed law of Nature or of God."[23] For no abolitionist was slavery the only thing wrong with the United States, but for all of them it was the grossest institutional assault on human rights. Third, abolitionists insisted that there was both a personal and national imperative to ponder and discuss slavery at once and to take some action leading to its demise. Fourth, abolitionists insisted that the Colonization Society, as a means of ending slavery, was at best a vapid gesture and at worst a racist prop to the bondage of slaves and the persecution of free blacks. Fifth, the group accepted African Americans as fully human and, as such, entitled to human and American rights.

The form into which such self-evident truths were put was that of the wholly conventional political-religious sermon. Most antislavery lecturers closely followed James Thome's formula: they "talked of human rights, touched on the American Revolution, and threw heaven and earth together." No politician was so quick as

John Quincy Adams to recognize that abolitionists, despite the furor against them, were sure to win the argument because the eighteenth-century "theory of the rights of man" had "deep root in the soil of civil society" and was now "linked itself with religious doctrine and religious fervor." Few Jacksonians, patriots, or Christians cared to dispute Adams's corollary, made in a speech shortly before his death, that "the soul of man cannot by human law be made the property of another," although many denied his conclusion that these truths made the great problem of the age "the extinction of slavery from the face of the earth." A few honest anti-abolitionists like Thomas Gallaudet admitted that the real problem was that the fanatics were so "un-extravagantly reasonable"; that's how they "gild the pill," he complained.[24]

The abolitionist arguments' rootedness in the day's political and religious clichés has led critics to concentrate on three intellectual points: self-righteousness, immediatism, and sin. The latter concern rarely bothered anti-abolitionists at the time, who worked in the same broad religious framework as their opponents. It was later historians who discovered that abolition's stress on the sin of slavery removed the topic from the realm of rational discourse to that of moral tirade and abstraction. For nineteenth-century religious folk the argument was central to any consideration of slavery.

Between the revolution and about 1835, most public thought on slavery, North and South, agreed that the institution was an "evil." Evil was a comforting concept that both admitted the destructiveness of slavery and suggested that no guilt lay in its practice. Evils were acts of God not of human choice, like floods or tuberculosis. By insisting that slavery was a sin, abolitionists were simply saying that the institution's continuation was not an inevitability but the product of human choice. The Roman Catholic Church and large, though decreasing, segments of Northern Protestantism continued to insist that slavery was an evil, a God-sanctioned one, and hence not a sin, so that guilt accrued only in relation to the way it was practiced. Southern Protestantism, however, found it increasingly difficult to argue that slavery, which they wished to expand, was not an institution that existed because of human will. Hence, biblical apologists for slavery accepted the positive good view not because abolitionist attacks on the "evil" theory were faulty but because these divines recognized that they were unanswerably true in regard to man's ability to choose.

Historians have often connected sin with an emphasis on a sectional self-righteousness that destroyed mutual respect, that encouraged diatribe rather than dialogue, and that scotched reasonable solutions. Actually, abolitionists stressed that the North bore equal guilt for slavery with the South. Elizur Wright was understandably amused by opponents' offering as clincher that it was money-grubbing, self-righteous Northerners who'd shipped slaves to this continent in the first place.[25] Broadly, this was precisely the point abolitionists struggled to make the North consider in the 1830s. Surely it was nonsense—though wholly understandable nonsense—for the South to say simultaneously, "Slavery's none of your business" and "You're as guilty as we, because your ancestors started it." If Boston's gentlemanly mob against Garrison were angered at all by what Garrison actually said, one imagines it was less by his calling slaveholders "man-stealers" than by his making clear that conspiracy to man-steal did not end at the Mason-Dixon line. "We have all committed the act of oppression directly or indirectly. There is innocent blood upon our garments, there is stolen property in our houses; and everyone of us has an account to settle with the present generation of blacks," was Garrison's most irritating message to his Boston.[26]

Even as rhetoric became harsher toward the South and emphasized a slave power conspiracy, abolitionists continued to insist on equal Northern responsibility. The resolves of the abolitionists of Syracuse in 1861, prepared for a meeting that never came off because of a mobbing, illustrate the continuation of this principle. Four of the five resolves were to be expected, but the final point makes the document interesting, coming as it did when the last anti-abolition mobs were acting and much grimmer warfare was soon to begin. The North, said these Syracuse abolitionists, were equal "partakers in the iniquity of slavery," a point tied to no moral self-flagellation but to a suggestion that much personal and national wealth should be used:

> to relieve those who may impoverish themselves by setting their captives free; to furnish the freedmen with such comforts, conveniences and implements of labor as they may need; and to establish such educational and religious institutions as will be indispensable everywhere, to enable them, and, yet more, their children and children's children to become what free people, the citizens of self-governing states, ought to be.[27]

Unrealistic, perhaps; certainly the South was not about to give up its slave labor, nor the North to bestow its wealth alike on needy former master and slave. Yet was a better plan possible, outside the perpetuation-expansion of slavery or the answer of war? Toward this latter "solution" the nation moved rapidly because moderates could not bring themselves to consider the principled, fair, and infinitely less costly and deadly solution of the Syracuse "fanatics."

The Syracuse resolves also expose the emptiness of a second charge against the abolitionists: that they never made any positive proposals and that their emphasis on immediatism undercut all sorts of solutions that would otherwise have gradually ended slavery. "Immediate abolition" was a term that bothered or confused some Americans, although one senses that the critics of the abolitionists who harped on the term took comfort in it as the sole proof of their opponents' unreasonableness. The problem with the term was that its obvious opposite, gradualism, was not what abolitionists were attacking, as was clear in the New York group's revision of the phrase to "immediate emancipation gradually accomplished" or, in William T. Allan's more precise formulation, "gradual emancipation, immediately begun."[28] What abolitionists implied by immediate was "now" in contrast to "someday," that favorite rubric of those who didn't want to defend slavery or do anything about it either. Probably most who pushed "someday" believed that it would come, though as early as the mid-1780s the tone of liberal Southerners from Jefferson on down suggested increasingly "someday . . . , maybe," with only "imperceptible" changes desired. Certainly if all would be taken care of someday, somehow, it was always "premature" to discuss or do anything now, and any noticed questioning of slavery violated the imperceptible requirement. Part of the trauma of 1835 was that the abolitionists' "now" smoked from the South that their soothing "someday" had become a loud "never."

The "plans" abolitionists suggested were varied and generalized, but this grew less from having nothing in mind than from willingness to accept many possible alternatives. Almost every major abolitionist journal or thinker at times made reasonable suggestions. Lydia Maria Child's plea that slaves be paid for increasing segments of their labor to ready them for wage-earning freedom or the Syracuse proposal of public money compensating both masters and slaves and providing long-term education were typical. Weld warned his band of abolition evangelists against pressing any particular solution to the exclusion of others but suggested that, when asked, they might suggest that a special code of laws govern freed slaves as they did minors, apprentices, or immigrants as a transition to full citizenship.[29] Abolitionists did reject the "right" of planters to compensation because this right could grow only from a right to "own" humans, but only the Garrisonians after 1840 actively opposed the idea. Abolition proposals were hardly "practical" given Southern refusal to consider any alternative, but they certainly drove out no better ideas, for the compelling reason that "moderates" offered none at all.

Stanley Elkins chides the abolitionists for not pushing improvements in slavery like legal protection of slave families or guarantees of religious instruction.[30] The suggestion here is that people who find an institution at heart unjust should devote their efforts to making it more broadly acceptable by removing its most obviously objectionable features. There seems little doubt that abolitionists would have favored such reforms, both as aiding blacks and as weakening slavery, had the South ever considered them. Certainly they worked hard for all sorts of piecemeal and pragmatic things, such as the repeal of Northern racist laws, establishing schools or communities for free blacks, legal or mob protection for fugitive slaves, and ending slavery in territories and the District of Columbia.

There was honest concern about the union in anti-abolitionist attacks but almost no willingness to deal with what abolitionists actually said. The few pamphlets offering some "moderate" answers to the fanatics best show the difficulty of establishing any clear position between abolition and proslavery. Among the most telling of these efforts were those of William Ellery Channing, Catharine Beecher, and Leonard Bacon, all anti-abolition writers who didn't accept slavery or overt racism either.

Channing's anti-abolition was ambiguous. The mob persecutions of 1835 caused the author to rush into press his *Slavery*, which could be called the most gracefully written of both the anti-abolition and abolition books of this period. Save for its attack on abolition, it eloquently repeated the abolitionist creed at every point, beginning with the contention that holding human beings as property was a sin. Most abolitionists were quick to accept the book, with obvious reservations about its discussion of them.[31]

Channing rejected some of the bearskinning of the abolitionists, who had shown themselves "full of active goodness," free of sectarianism, and pecularily open in their tactics. Yet Channing insisted that abolitionists had "done wrong." They used a motto, "immediate emancipation," that upset people; they set up organizations into which "excitable" and "impetuous" groups like women and colored people were welcomed instead of only "men of strong principles, judiciousness, sobriety"; they acted through groups rather than stressing "individual action." But these things were mere embroidery on Channing's central charge that abolitionists exaggerated slavery's evil and painted the master as monster. This was asserted, Channing admitted, without reading abolitionist works or attending their meetings or lectures, but he was sure "the strong and next to universal impression" must be "essentially true." He went on to talk about the invective of George Thompson and repeated a fabricated tale that the *Journal of Commerce* had circulated about Thompson's urging slaves to "cruel vengeance." In short, Channing condemned the abolitionists for their extremity on the basis of a publicly discredited lie and without reading their readily available writings. Channing in fact could distinguish his position from that of abolitionists only by eschewing their writings in favor of the "next to universal impression" of them, the straw man.[32]

Regarding slavery, Channing also insisted on a distinction abolitionists rejected: holding people in slavery was a sin, but the people doing it were not necessarily sinful. Channing's ideas converged with abolitionists' when he stressed that owners were not alone guilty, but he diverged in insisting that no sin was involved if circumstances or partial and mistaken ideas of wrong justified the action. If slaves were held for gain, Channing decreed guilt; if they were held from mistaken notions of right, no guilt adhered. If Channing truly believed this, his shock at the South's developing "positive good" theory was indeed strange, for only people who genuinely saw slavery as helpful to both its victims and society would be innocent in practicing it. It's an odd theology that says doing wrong to others is all right, so long as you believe it's right. John Thomas has argued that Channing's views were too cosmopolitan for the abolitionists, but the only disagreements lay in a sophistic quibble over sin that Channing himself neglected except when chiding abolitionists, and a misinterpretation of their position because Channing chose to rely on rumor rather than reading.[33] Strange cosmopolitanism, that.

Channing may have attacked abolition partly in hopes of winning antislavery a broader audience. Obviously there was potential advantage to the cause in repeating the standard arguments under the cloak of moderation. There is no doubt, on the other hand, that Catharine Beecher and Leonard Bacon were more anxious to put down abolitionists than slavery in the mid-1830s. John Quincy Adams was right in his conclusion, if not his choice of terms, when he detected something "jesuitical" in Channing's anti-abolition chapter, but Beecher and Bacon attacked more frontally those who had usurped the antislavery position that more conservative Northern moral leaders were hesitant either to accept or to abandon.[34]

Bacon and Catharine Beecher's father, Lyman, represented the predominant strand of reform-oriented Congregationalism in the early 1830s. Bacon's father had been a dreamer whose social visions had accomplished only his family's impoverishment, and his son was not about to make that mistake. After his education, he became pastor of the First Church in New Haven, a position he held for the next forty-one years, becoming close to Congregationalism's replacement for "pope" Timothy Dwight.[35] Lyman Beecher was a much heartier and less cautious man than Bacon but was equally conscious of his role as moral-religious leader. Both men, especially Bacon, had taken some antislavery and problack positions in the 1820s, but both drew back when others made abolition an immediate rather than a someday thing.

Beecher's dilemma developed when many of his Lane Seminary students became abolitionists. For a long while he tried to cajole them into tactical silence, but the issue was one that not even Beecher's immense geniality could paper over; and he saw his best students leave and his high hopes for his college and role in the West leave with them. He'd also seen his antislavery derided and his "hypocrisy" exposed in damning detail by Theodore Weld, the best of his students.[36] His daughter Catharine sat down to prove to the world the baseness of the men who'd shaken her father's equanimity and the pedestal she placed him on. Obviously, much personal experience invigorated her observation that "nothing could be more irritating" to the righteous than to be told they equivocated with evil. Given her desire to vindicate her father, the book's emphasis on respect for traditional ways, theology, gender roles, and authority becomes moving.[37]

Unlike Catharine Beecher or Channing, Leonard Bacon dealt with what the abolitionists said. Bacon, while still a college student, had worked with a black improvement group, but as controversy grew around slavery, Bacon retreated. When citizens of New Haven voted to fight a proposal to establish a black college in the town, the one opponent was not Bacon, although he may have been, as his biographer insisted, out of town. At any rate, he threw himself into the anti-Garrison movement with more enthusiasm than he'd ever shown for antislavery. His magazine attacked Garrison, while trying to work out some middle ground, and he supported both the American Colonization Society and the newly formed American Union for the Relief and Improvement of the Colored Race, the old and new groups in New England dedicated to moderation. Both begged Bacon to head them, but Bacon was far too shrewd to tie his star to groups dying or stillborn.[38] In the later 1830s Bacon spearheaded the effort to ban abolition speakers from the state's Congregational churches and personally strove to prevent any converts among the clergy to immediatism. When Hartford minister Joel Hawes decided to be an avowed rather than closet abolitionist, Bacon was quick to make clear to him that he could expect little religious fellowship if he persisted in acting upon such convictions.[39]

Bacon alone of early anti-abolitionists paid any close attention to his opponents' writings, particularly one of their most influential and logically vulnerable efforts, Garrison's pamphlet attacking colonization. Bacon ably exposed some of Garrison's specious reasoning and sloppy tactics, arguing that Garrison took personal statements by people associated with colonization and represented them as the society's position.[40] Garrison moved carelessly between personal opinions and official stance, but this kind of "simplification" or generalization is a commonplace of politics and scholarship, to be condemned only if it clearly misrepresents. To read the Colonizationist Society journal or the talks of its officers is to learn that Garrison presented his material crudely but accurately, while Bacon indulged in sophistical as well as sophisticated debate.

Bacon's nastiness is clearest in his speeches attacking women's role in abolition. Bacon referred in several speeches to a colonial incident: "During the prevalence of fanaticism in New England, a quaker-woman was known publicly to walk through the streets of Salem—*naked as she was born*—but Miss Grimké had not yet made such an exhibition of herself." When James G. Birney met Bacon on a steamboat, the latter opened civilities, but Birney refused them until he'd asked about the report. Had Bacon said of Sarah Grimké what had been reported? Birney asked. "I did," replied Bacon, and added, "And should I have said she *did*?" Birney left him with a quiet "I wish no further intercourse with you," but, as they left the boat, Bacon told Birney, "You will be ashamed of yourself."[41]

Some suggestion of who was ashamed can be found in Bacon's attempt to answer a letter Elizur Wright penned to his "old Playmate." Wright's obvious affection for Bacon whetted his harsh words about Bacon's "everlasting hair-splitting and equivocation" and his pleas to "make a common cause with humanity against brute force." "I put it to your inmost soul, Bacon. You know that you were wrong in that whole miserable humbug of colonization." Bacon began several replies but could get little beyond saying he "would not make strictures (deserved)" about Wright's style.[42] For anyone whose "inmost soul" condemned slavery, there was little honestly to say against most abolitionists.

Bacon's hostility ebbed after Lovejoy's murder, and by 1840 he had rejoined the antislavery crusade. In 1846 he published a book strongly attacking slavery that a young Illinois lawyer, Abraham Lincoln, found—quite correctly—powerfully argued.[43] There is symbolic rightness in Bacon's carefully timed eloquence influencing the man who was eloquently to lead modulated antislavery to its first presidential victories.

After the mob years, Channing, Bacon, and various Beechers all drifted toward abolition quite simply because there was nowhere else to go unless one were willing to say of slavery, "Forget it entirely, let it live eternally if the slaveholders so wish." Determined moral indifference was an embarrassing position for Northerners who aspired to religious and reform leadership, and they early struck at the abolitionists to argue that the issue was one of tone and temper, rather than the Scylla and Charybdis of opposition to slavery or indifference to it.

No society appreciates messengers who first announce that social choice is between two potential catastrophes, especially if the messengers refuse when requested or ordered to shut up—and have compelling evidence on their side. When abolitionist Samuel May read William Ellery Channing some of his own words about society's needing to be called to its moral senses by passionate frankness, Channing could only smile at May's cleverness and accuracy in applying his own truth to abolition. But Channing was among the mildest of Americans, and one of the few who could accept without ire the presumption of abolitionists who in effect followed Ralph Ellison's wise old black's later injunction: "Live with your head in the lion's mouth. I want you to overcome'em with yeses, undermine'em with grins, agree'em to death and destruction, let'em swaller you till they vomit or bust wide open." Abolitionists triggered such anger because they affirmed to Americans "the principles they themselves had dreamed out of the chaos and darkness of the feudal past, and which they had violated and compromised to the point of absurdity even in their own corrupt minds."[44]

Because historians generally feel as much embarrassment about arguing with the basic ideas of the abolitionists as did moderates in the 1830s, the attack on them has usually centered on tone or peculiar natures. In a sense the abolition straw man Thome had to fight in Akron has continued his imaginary existence to assist the American belief that there had to be an easier or better answer to the troubling issue of slavery than that toward which, with some push from the abolitionists, the nation stumbled. Now as then, yelling "fanatic" or whispering "odd" is easier than spelling out any cogent moderate position.

Complaints about tone or extremity of language have almost always centered on William Lloyd Garrison and his terrible verbal denunciations. Garrison himself enjoyed the image. When supporter Samuel J. May chided him for excessive warmth, Garrison answered quietly, but with the grandiloquence he liked, that he had a "world of ice to melt." His often turgid prose was sprinkled with some epithets; "man-stealer" was his favorite shorthand for the slave's master, borrowed from the Bible via eighteenth-century Quaker Anthony Benezet, a play partly on the frontier's moral outrage over "horse theft." And he had confidence in the vile motives of those who continued to disagree with him, though often most caustically about abolitionist opponents. John Thomas structured his biography of Garrison around the compromise, give-and-take rationality of the ordinary political process and the absolutistic moralism of perfectionist reform, a conclusion possible only if one reads none in the day's partisan press, where name-calling was the most hallowed aesthetic form.[45]

In Garrison's *Liberator* there is less rabid denunciation and much less dishonest distortion than one finds in any example of the political press, Whig or Democrat. Garrison sometimes disturbed his reform-minded friends because their standards were a good deal more attuned to reasonableness and gentle moral suasion than was the world of political journalism in which Garrison honed his style. Such external sources of inspiration were also clear in the one abolition editor who vituperated with the era's best, Cassius Clay. The Kentuckian, for example, described all proslavery clergy as "the robbers of the poor, would be seducers of women, betrayers of friends," Christian ministers in name who were kept "from highway robbery and secret murder" only by their "abject and craven fear." Northern abolitionists never knew quite how to respond to Clay, but anyone familiar with Southern journalism in the era would know the sources of such bloody-bones twaddle. Clay understood Southern ways and wielded his pen, like his bowie knife and pistol, effectively within the tradition.[46]

Garrison was a poorer writer than abolitionist editors David and Maria Child, James Birney, Elizur Wright, William Goodell, and that extraordinary journalist Gamaliel Bailey, who turned the *Philanthropist* in Cincinnati and then the *National Era* in Washington into papers of broad general interest.[47] The one clearly distinguishing feature of Garrison's journalistic prose was his emphasis on "I." When he wrote best, he dramatized himself. Commonly Garrison's introduction to the *Liberator* is judged his most effective piece; here he used first-person pronouns ten times in the first paragraph. His most famous lines "I will be heard" and "I will prevail" are the hallmark of the role: not "the cause will be heard" nor even "we will prevail."

Garrison's central position in abolition is in ways hard to understand. A mediocre writer surrounded by better stylists, a clumsy and careless lecturer competing with highly effective speakers, and a poor organizer often encircled by able tacticians, he was and has remained the chief symbol of abolition.[48] Partly, he got there first with what became most of abolition's standard positions. Partly, Garrison's own liking and need for people, combined with his unshakable serenity that he and his cause were one, made others accept that judgment, although almost none of his followers marched wholly in step with him on his complicated intellectual-reform journey after 1836. Perhaps most important, "Garrison" became the common name for Akron and the nation's abolition straw man, who was the central figure in the intense dispute. People, including Garrison, confused the two.

The testimony of anti-abolitionist mobs, meetings, and moderates strongly second the internal evidence that abolitionists broadly argued only in terms "unextravagantly reasonable." Opposing groups often called names, hurled charges, and repeated fabrications—while carefully avoiding use of anything the abolitionists had actually said or written. Clearly, abolitionist awfulness lay in addressing such a dangerous issue through ideals and terms that their most committed opponents largely accepted.

Since historian David Donald decided abolitionist oddity grew in people being displaced by a status revolution, there has been some interest in trying to understand the movement and its opponents on the basis of their sociological situation. Donald claimed that his sampling showed that abolitionists were of old families who were being left behind in a developing industrial age, but his pattern is the opposite of what one finds in sixty-four abolition biographies in the *Dictionary of American Biography*, where at least 90 percent of that sample achieved more education and success than had their parents, even at the beginning of their abolitionist work. Those who slipped in wealth, like Lydia Maria Child, the Grimké sisters, or Elizur Wright, did so because of rather than before their abolition. Leonard Richards amusingly inverted Donald's argument to stress that the anti-abolitionists were the old elite who felt insecure in the new world order.[49]

Richards is right about the high status of anti-abolitionists if one defines that group by the prominent participants in the 1835 meetings condemning abolitionists. The mob evidence is much more complicated. Those arrested in the New York City anti-abolition mob of 1834 were almost all poor—ex-criminals, sailors, laborers, and a few young craftsmen. In smaller mobs where there were arrests, the evidence of social background is inconclusive.

Abolitionist Isaac Stearns described a "noise" riot in Mansfield, Massachusetts, in 1836 where a kettle drum, bass drum, horn, and church bell quartet wholly blotted out the words whenever Charles Burleigh or his supporters tried to speak. Two teenage musicians, day laborer Charles Williams and clerk James M. Wilber, were convicted of and fined for riot, specifically for pushing Constable S. C. Cobb when he tried to ascend the stairs to quell the racket in the belfry. But Stearns argued that these were simply riotous frontmen for the plotters, wealthy County Commissioner Major Elkanah Bates; his son, Town Clerk William B. Bates; tavern-keeper O. S. Kingsberry; coal merchant Foster Bryant; and well-off Colonel Josiah Bird from a neighboring town, who contributed to the anti-abolitionist argument an insistence that African Americans were not humans. Such prominent behind-the-scenes mob men were abetted by First Selectman Solomon Pratt, who, when called to duty by Cobb, ordered the abolitionists rather than the rioters home. Stearns admitted that none of these leading men acted in the mob except the younger Bates, who probably tolled the church bell over abolitionist speech, but the chronicler clearly judged that the real issue was "whether men of aristocratic feelings shall cease to dictate to . . . us poor fellows." Carpenter Stearns's "poor fellow" abolitionist friends included doctors, lawyers, merchants, and ministers, but his assertion of some class superiority in the mob years of abolition's Northern opponents is probably true, at least for planners.[50]

Of eight anti-abolition riots where arrests are known, two best allow some occupational typing. In Meriden, Connecticut, in 1837, some of the members of Reverend Arthur Granger's Congregational church invited Henry Ludlow to lecture on abolition. Granger accepted their request, announced the lecture from the pulpit without sponsoring it, and invited Ludlow to stay at the parsonage. In the meantime opposition formed, led by Ira Twiss and a church member, James S. Brooks. When Ludlow and Granger walked toward the church, a crowd had formed outside; when he began to talk, a mob began to throw rocks and rotten eggs. Two Thompson brothers got a battering ram and caved in the door, and the mob forced the audience from the cellar meeting hall to the sanctuary by pelting them with rotten eggs. When the audience tried to leave, more eggs flew so that, one observer noted, the abolitionists "looked like a lot of pumpkin pies." Some women reportedly fainted, and three victims suffered minor injuries. Eight men were arrested: two farmers, a laborer, a carpenter, a smith, Brooks, Twiss, and a man who had no occupation listed, seemingly a town drunk. Only the farmers, two Thompsons who broke the door, were convicted; they received a two-month sentence and a $50 fine, while Twiss was assessed over $1,000 in court costs.

The abolitionists active in bringing Ludlow to town included Elisha Cowles, a dry goods merchant, banker, factory owner, and civic leader; Levi Yale, a farmer, bank director, and the town's Jacksonian postmaster; Julius Pratt, owner of the town's largest industry, who had opened the church in Prattsville, a small industrial village near his factory, to Prudence Crandall's black students a few years earlier; Fenner Bush, of old but impoverished family, who worked himself up to become a foreman and then part owner of Pratt's comb factory; Bush's younger half-brother, Zina K. Murdock, who worked at the comb factory for awhile, became a partner in a successful insurance business, and finally bought a large farm; and Homer Curtiss and Harlow Isbell, joint owners of a lock company. Curtiss had been a teacher earlier and became one again after the lock factory, where for several years two fugitive slaves were employed and protected, burned to the ground. Isbell later established a hardware store in New York City after a foray to Kansas to try farming in aid of the Free-State cause.

In this case the abolitionists were obviously the social superiors of the anti-abolitionists on average. All abolitionists were or became businessmen, although at the time of the attempted meeting Murdock was a hand in a factory where his half-brother Bush was a foreman. Four abolitionists were noted as coming from old families, although two of these had been destitute in the preceding generation. Cowles and Pratt, in whose veins "flowed the best blood of the Puritans," were from the area's old elite, while doing conspicuously well in the new industrial order. Curtiss and Isbell were less successful but landed on their feet after some economic reverses, influenced, local historians suggest, by their intense devotion to antislavery.[51]

If this social profile of Meriden abolitionists directly contradicts Donald's general picture of that group, the town's anti-abolition mob at least equally diverges from a traditionalist elite. Six of the eight were small farmers or laborers who appear nowhere else in the extensive local annals—in sharp contrast to every abolitionist.

The two anti-abolitionists who gained some local prominence were both newcomers to town. James S. Brooks, a traveling salesman for twenty years for abolitionist Cowles, had only recently returned to Meriden. He was soon to become a state representative and, again with Cowles, a leading supporter of the local railroad, of which he served as acting director for several years. Did his anti-abolition have something to do with his having worked for Cowles mainly in South Carolina? or with his political ambitions? The Democrats were the majority party in town, and they voted Brooks their representative to the state legislature in the election following his role as mob organizer. Ira Twiss first came to Meriden in 1836, having previously been a clock-maker in Canada. By 1839 Twiss owned a thriving Meriden tavern, and later he was a successful small entrepreneur in lumber and bag-making. Abolitionists Cowles, Pratt, and Bush were Whigs, while Murdock, Curtiss, and Isbell (along with nine other townsmen) managed to vote abolitionist even in 1837. Anti-abolitionist Brooks was a Jacksonian, as was abolitionist Levi Yale, postmaster under both Jackson and Van Buren. While Yale signed the request that Ludlow speak, there is no record that he, unlike all his cosigners, supported additional anti-slavery activities. Yale's signing may have been the result of curiosity or a commitment to free speech; or perhaps his later silence was a matter of party loyalty or desire to protect his public job.

An even smaller sample from a Montpelier, Vermont, mob repeats the Meriden pattern, somewhat modified by the notable Jacksonian party affiliations of leading rioters. When Unitarian minister Samuel May lectured on slavery in the Hall of Representatives in October, a few things were thrown at him. Scheduled to speak again in a Congregational church, May in the morning saw a placard, signed by seven men, ordering him not to speak to "save us the trouble of using any other means to that effect." May consulted with his friends, determined to go ahead, and his enemies decided on "other" means. As May began speaking, half a dozen men shouted out threats. "Down with him!" and "Choke him!" were among the yells. Supporters of May protected him, but only after May's audience sought safety in retreat.

Five of the seven signers of the placard, all of them involved in the church disruption, were tried, convicted, and fined $5 plus costs. These included bank president Timothy Hubbard, editor of Vermont's Democratic paper J. T. Marston, Jacksonian postmaster and tavern-keeper George P. Hill, and Dr. D. P. Russell. These anti-abolitionists were generally better established than the Meriden group, largely because of their party prominence. Marston, for example, was a community newcomer sent up to Vermont by the Jacksonians. Only Timothy Hubbard was a member of the town's elite, and he had recently achieved his financial status by supporting Jackson's banking measures and was soon to lose his bank position. None of May's persecutors held the status of the two men who prominently defended him, Whig leader and editor of Vermont's leading paper Chauncey L. Knapp and merchant and civic leader Colonel J. P. Miller, both of old New England family. The Congregationalist minister also supported May. Miller, who'd gone with Samuel Gridley Howe to aid Greek freedom in 1824, was quite ready to do battle for American liberty a decade later: "Mr. Hubbard, if you do not stop this outrage now, I'll knock you down." Hubbard stopped, and May left untouched.[52]

Here the pro-abolitionists were all very prominent, and the anti-abolitionists less so, though hardly "riffraff," as Knapp called them. To Knapp, Jacksonians were riffraff whatever their class status, and the four Montpelier mob members convicted were Jacksonians. May's three prominent protectors in Vermont were all Whig. In the half-dozen mobs where one learns the party affiliation of some rioters and opponents, Democrats invariably predominated in the mob and Whigs in the opposition, a few in that party either sympathetic to antislavery or protective of the legal rights of the beleaguered abolitionist minority.[53]

The implications of the Meriden and Montpelier samples (like that for Alton, Illinois) is that leading abolitionists and their defenders were in no sense failures or misfits but generally substantial citizens. They suggest that the testimonies of Weld's holy band who evangelized for abolition were broadly accurate in their claims that those who responded to their message in the small towns where most abolition riots occurred were a cross section of the respectable lawyers, businesspeople, doctors, ministers, workers, farmers, and women of the community. A number of recent studies of those who joined abolition societies or signed antislavery petitions have helped to show that rank-and-file abolitionists were drawn from all socioprofessional categories in remarkably close parallel to the percentage of those groups in the general community.[54]

If the Meriden and Montpelier evidence has significance, it is hardly statistical. In fact, close consideration of the personal realities of participants makes doubtful any class typing. The problems are clear if one tries to apply Leonard Richards's dichotomy between traditional commercial-professional sorts and upcoming manufacturers-tradesmen to the Meriden sample. Is Pratt, with inherited wealth from a prominent family, traditional because he carried on the family business, or part of the new order because he expanded and further mechanized it? Was Cowles commercial because the core of his business seems to have been selling, or industrial because he owned and leased factories and invested in railroads? And at what point does one stop these varied antebellum careers to put them in a category? Should Murdock be listed as the factory worker he was in 1837, the insurance magnate he became in the 1840s, or the gentleman farmer he became later? Was his agriculture at all classifiable with that of the mob members, the Thompsons, seemingly lifetime hardscrabble farmers? Was Twiss the craftsman he had been in Canada, the tavern owner he became by 1843, or the lumber merchant he later became? Obviously, all classification by profession makes something of a hash of the complexities it's intended to sort out.

Abolitionists were as varied as the population from which they were drawn. Certainly no people could be more different in appearance than the debonairly aristocratic Edmund Quincy and that slob on principle Charles Burleigh; in personality than the motherly Quaker Lucretia Mott and the imperious Boston Brahmin Maria Weston Chapman; in public manner that the gentle Samuel May and the vitriolic Wendell Phillips; in intellectual training than the truly transcendental intelligence of Sojourner Truth and the extraordinary breadth of knowledge of German-born and trained Harvard professor Charles T. Follen; in social-economic background than the aristocratic Southern upbringing of James G. Birney or Cassius M. Clay and the penny-desperate New England boyhood of William Lloyd Garrison or the Maryland bondage of Frederick Douglass.

A few unremarkable things can be said about the social background of well-known abolitionists. Most were New Englanders, or of New England family, with the next most sizable group being Southern-born and another group, especially blacks and Quakers, coming from the Middle Atlantic states. Most prominent abolitionists were strongly religious: evangelical Presbyterian, Quaker, Unitarian, Methodist, Baptist, and Episcopal, in about that order of proportionate numbers.[55] Only a handful—Cassuis M. Clay, Frederick Douglass, Edmund Quincy, Wendell Phillips—were not profoundly concerned with religion at the point in their lives when they became abolitionists. And most of them were successful in careers other than their abolition work.

A few, like Garrison and his followers Charles C. Burleigh and Wendell Phillips, made full early careers out of abolition to which they joined other reform causes as time passed. This was even more generally true of women and black abolitionists, for whom appealing alternative professions or public roles were scarce. Sallie Holley, for example, moved from her abolitionist home to Oberlin College and on to work as a Garrisonian lecturer; after the Civil War she devoted the last thirty years of her life to teaching and aiding freedpeople in Virginia.[56] Most white male abolitionists had fruitful simultaneous or second careers. Samuel Fessenden of Maine, Ellis Loring Gray of Boston, Nathaniel Peabody Rogers of Massachusetts and later New Hampshire, James G. Birney in the Northwest, Salmon Chase in Ohio, Alvan Stewart in upstate New York, and William Jay in New York City were successful lawyers. Samuel J. May in Connecticut and later Syracuse, William Furness in Philadelphia, Orange Scott and Asa Bronson in Massachusetts, Edward Beecher and William T. Allan (from Alabama) in Illinois, and Edward Weed, John Rankin (from Kentucky), and William Brisbane (from South Carolina) in Ohio were well-liked clergymen in their areas and denominations.

Business leaders included the Tappans in New York City, the Donaldson brothers in Cincinnati, Samuel Porter in Rochester, William Ashby in Newburyport, Francis Jackson in Boston, Julius Pratt in Connecticut, William Birney on Nantucket, Marius Robinson in Ohio, and Joseph Sill and James Forten in Philadelphia. Edmund Quincy, Maria Weston Chapman, and Wendell Phillips in Boston, Gerrit Smith in upstate New York, Cassius M. Clay, and James A. Thome in Kentucky were among the monied-landed elite in their communities. Lydia Maria Child was a popular writer and children's editor before joining the cause, and John Greenleaf Whittier and Rev. John Pierpont popular poets. Elizur Wright was a professor of mathematics before he became an abolitionist; afterward he alternated between establishing the first successful regulation of the American insurance industry and working for insurance companies to bring their rates within lines of the actuary tables he pioneered in developing.

Such data prove only a negative: abolitionists diverged far from the stereotype, popular at the time and since, of incompetent misfits directing ire drawn from personal frustration toward distant evils. Positively, little is self-evident from such data, other than that perhaps relative confidence about one's ability and position were helpful in venturing far into this dangerous topic.

With such broad influences went the host of individual experiences that create or encourage special commitments. Southern-born abolitionists—the Grimké sisters,

Thome, William Gildersleeve, William Brisbane, Levi Coffin, William T. Allan—attributed an accumulating sense of the personal tragedies of slavery to their later fight against it. James Birney's worry about the influence of slavery on his children pushed him out of the role of wealthy planter into that of much-mobbed abolition editor and presidential candidate. Theodore Weld remembered the anger he felt, as a boy of seven, that caused him to join a new black student on a suddenly created "Negro bench" in the back of a Massachusetts schoolroom. John Brown remembered that he became a "determined abolitionist" at about age twelve when a frontier Ohio landlord lavished praise on the white boy but abused and beat "before his eyes with iron shovels" his slave, a "very active, intelligent" black boy of twelve whom Brown liked and recognized "as fully if not more than his equal." Samuel J. May, trying to puzzle out what made him sensitive to abolition, remembered the charm and vitality of a black youth with whom he'd gone to school, and the kindness of an unknown black woman who found him on the street when he'd been injured, helped him home, saw him cared for, and then slipped out before May's worried mother could thank her.[57]

Every mob made some new abolitionists, while some riots gave the cause its wealthiest supporters. Arthur Tappan became an abolitionist when Connecticut spurned his efforts to aid black education, solidified by the laws, mobs, and mayhem that closed Prudence Crandall's school for black girls. Gerrit Smith became a full-fledged abolitionist in response to the Utica mob, though he earlier argued himself toward that position when he tried to defend colonization, much as William Brisbane did when working on a scriptural defense of slavery. Wendell Phillips became active upon hearing Massachusetts attorney general William Austin's racist diatribe against abolitionists at a meeting called to honor the slain Elijah Lovejoy.

Anti-abolitionists noted nothing odd in their opponents' backgrounds but insisted that they must be psychologically twisted, the charge against them that has remained most prominent. Some were odd, though again the group seems well within the ordinary American range of peculiarity. The abolitionists themselves sometimes took pride in their tolerance of the demented. Henry Stanton provided what became a famous description of the front row of an abolition convention: William Lloyd Garrison, all bourgeois fastidiousness, wedged between the patricians Quincy and Phillips, who sat next to white-haired and flowing bearded Father Lampson, "a crazy loon"; unkempt Abby Folsom, "another lunatic"; and George W. Mellon, dressed in Revolutionary War costume in accord with his belief that he was the man he'd been named for. Stanton discussed Lampson, Folsom, and Mellon as victims of the strains put on abolitionists in these years, although there's no record of abolition activity on their part before dementia set in.[58] Certainly, they were not significant figures despite their mythic front-row seats.

Some abolitionists had mental problems. Phileo Calvin, for example, who married Prudence Crandall and caused her more unhappiness than had even Connecticut mobs, was unstable. Gerrit Smith had a severe mental collapse in 1859, in this case quite possibly related to fears generated by the collapse of John Brown's raid, which he'd supported.[59] The public gaucherie of Stephen S. Foster made him a figure of general ridicule (as of affectionate laughter among abolitionists), though his letters suggest a private humor, modesty, and warmth, especially toward his wife, child, and farm. Recognizing his limitations, he thought it better that his wife concentrate on abolitionist work while he tended house and farm, though evidence suggests that Abby Kelley managed these things best, too.[60] The spate of recent psychological studies of abolitionists suggest little beyond the bouts with disappointment and depression that dot human life.[61]

Among effective abolitionists, the one who appeared most eccentric was Charles Burleigh, who refused to cut his hair or beard and dressed so shabbily that Henry Stanton resorted at times to force and subterfuge to get rid of his old clothes and get him into more respectable ones. Yet Burleigh's messy hair covered a mind of quiet vigor and precision, unemotionally crystalline in its mode. An Ohio anti-abolitionist found his looks outrageous, so hairy he "could see little more than his nose and eyes above the top vest button." Yet Burleigh's "language was beautifully chaste, his imagery superb, and the whole manner of his oratory fascinating to a very high degree." His argument, this listener regretfully concluded, would seem "absolutely conclusive and unanswerable" to most people.[62] Burleigh was an excellent organizer as well as orator, and his coworkers gladly tolerated his appearance because of his capabilities and tidied him up when they could get their hands on him.

Theodore Dwight Weld was almost as indifferent to dress as Burleigh, though in a less ostentatious way. Certainly he was a bit strange, if one can believe his self-description to Angelina Grimké, the woman he was soon to marry. He claimed to be oblivious of social niceties; forgetful of times, dates, and even seasons; selfish; proud of his avoidance of vanities; irritable; severe—the latter reflected in a countenance so stern that Stanton claimed he looked like an Inquisitor and frightened young children to tears. Weld continued his catalogue of foibles: he "cut all sorts of boyish capers," and every day, when possible, he liked "to jump and hop and scream like a loon and run on all fours and wrestle and throw stones and play 'tag' and 'hide and seek' and all those childish rompings." He also felt "keen relish" for other more dangerous amusements. Climbing young trees at night, swinging from their tops, and then falling ten or fifteen feet to the ground was "a favorite sport," as were "leaping fences and chasms, standing on my head, jumping or hanging from the limbs of over-hanging trees or from rocks high above the tide."

And, he went on to the woman he wished to marry, he was a mess. He didn't shave until his beard scratched so that he had to act "in self-defense—or until some of my friends beg me to do it." His hair he didn't "comb once a year" but instead dunked it half a dozen times each morning in cold water, "then frictionize it with a stiff hair brush after wiping it dry and then letting it straggle in all directions like the quills on a porcupine." Little wonder that his mother called his hair her oven broom, and less that Angelina Grimké begged him to say something good about himself. He admitted he was not dirty and bathed "all over in water" each day.

Such were the traits of the man historians have labeled the leading representative of moderate abolition. And none of these habits interfered with his role as abolition's best speaker and organizer in the 1830s, the leader of the Lane "rebellion," and the man who did most to create the beachhead for abolition in the West, in the Presbyterian Church, and in Congress. He was the cause's intellectual and tactical genius, who awed all who met him by his extraordinary powers of mind and manner, although he reported that his formal education amounted to "an inventory about equal to that of a learned pig."[63]

After the mob years, some abolitionists took up causes often associated with crankishness, which led to some popular and historical disparagement, though in general these causes had more to do with social intelligence than incapacity. Was an even excessive emphasis on cold water less flavorsome than an avoidance of it altogether, or more dangerous than a commitment to hot toddies? Can the few women who donned pants be judged unbalanced, and the many who wore ever bigger hoops and bustles be seen as exemplars of social sanity? In all societies, some things deemed madness are divinest, or simply common, sense. It's hardly surprising that some members of a group who insisted on raising a nation-shaking issue also questioned some less consequential customs.

Abolitionists' response to mobs, threatened and realized, offers the clearest refutation to the clearest of historians' charges, that of Hazel Wolf, who claimed they possessed a "martyr complex." Surely had "lust for martyrdom permeated the abolitionist ranks," they would have had little trouble satisfying it in 1835.[64] Of that year's many ludicrous charges against the abolitionists—that they were sex-starved, money-hungry, insurrectionary plunderers—none was pushed harder than that they were cowards. If antislavery people really wanted to dedicate their lives to the cause, Southern papers and politicians sneered, they would travel south, where tar and cotton and hemp were plentiful.[65]

No abolitionist accepted these repeated offers of Southern murderous hospitality, but members showed flexible caution and courage in facing Northern violence. Substantial discretion underlay their willingness to cancel or postpone meetings if danger seemed great, to shift meetings from night to day, to disband in the midst of sessions, to change meeting places or times to avoid confrontations. Thompson skipped meetings in Salem and Portland because of threats; Weld changed to afternoon sessions in Troy, then gave up entirely when mobs continued active and authorities made clear their commitment to the rioters. Arthur Tappan's New York City abolitionists avoided a threatened mobbing in 1833 by first changing their place of meeting, then by convening and adjourning earlier than expected; the state society avoided dangerous conflict in Utica in 1835 by meeting early and, when the mob came, adjourning to another town. James Birney and Elijah Lovejoy agreed to remove their presses from slave states to avoid possible riots; Birney published the *Philanthropist* in rural Ohio until its well-deserved reputation for reasonableness gave the illusion of safety to its transfer to Cincinnati. Lovejoy quietly bought a new press three times after mob destruction in Alton before attempting physically to protect the fourth. Prudence Crandall offered to move her school for black girls outside Canterbury to satisfy her persecutors, and she disbanded it when arson and mob terror threatened the students' safety. Weld accepted the recommendation of Ohio blacks that the state antislavery convention should be all-white to lessen the likelihood of mob attacks on it and black communities.[66] Abolitionists built a national meeting hall only when they felt mistaken confidence that the killing of Lovejoy had ended mob danger in the North.

In most cases, the only provocation abolitionists offered was to maintain their right to speak, meet, publish, or teach, while the tone and content of what they said, so far as the evidence goes, mattered not at all as cause of riot. The most frequent mob victims were not the abrasive Stephen Foster or even straw man William Lloyd Garrison but the powerfully rational Weld, the gently tactful Samuel May, and the mild-mannered—if British—George Thompson. Riots often were a surprise to abolitionists, coming when and where they thought trouble unlikely. Prudence Crandall had weathered a long year of petty vandalism and legal prosecution, but she was shocked that her enemies would set fire to her house while she and her students slept. The trustees of the integrated Noyes Academy in Canaan, New Hampshire, thought they'd outlasted communal hostility when the mob attacked. Birney had not expected his press to be attacked, and Weld's account of the Troy riot suggests wonder at his prolonged inability to cajole the mob into listening. George Thompson, after being mobbed out of a meeting in Abington, Massachusetts, a town considered safe because of the strength of abolition there, wondered sadly to Samuel May if people could really believe that he was "an enemy of your country."[67]

Abolitionists did not incite mobs or invite martyrdom but quickly learned of persecution's advantages to them. Samuel May refused to give bail for Crandall so that officials would have to follow through on her arrest, though he saw that the jail was made comfortable for her, something not mentioned when abolitionists described how the young Quakeress was thrown into a murderer's cell for the awful crime of teaching African American girls. The Garrisonians regularly celebrated the mobbing of their hero, as well they should have, given its aid to their cause. Without seeking martyrdom, abolitionists, like Mormons and Catholics, would have had to be blind indeed not to see the value of such events in binding their own adherents to the faith and in creating sympathy among the unaffiliated. Just as Catholics left the ruins of the Charlestown Convent as public testimony to their unjust sufferings, Lewis Tappan left his mobbed New York City home unrepaired for a season or so "as a silent Anti-Slavery preacher to the crowds who will flock to see it."[68]

Their convictions caused some abolitionists to accept personal as well as riotous setbacks. For people in business and the professions, these proved of little long-range harm; presumably these persons provided valuable services to a limited clientele who privately thought no worse of people for being antislavery. Those who gave up most were people whose public status—particularly as editor, preacher, or teacher—made them vulnerable. Lydia Maria Child knowingly sacrificed her profitable editorial labors when she published her plea for African Americans. Elizur Wright traded in his comfortable professorship at Lane Seminary for an antislavery career that at times reduced his huge family to real poverty. Charles Follen, driven from Germany by repression, gained a job tutoring in German at Harvard and finally was given a chair there in German literature—only to be tossed out by Harvard because he wouldn't repudiate abolition.[69] None of these people chased martyrdom, but they chose some hardship when there was no alternative but silence about their convictions.

The pressures on ministers toward silence were particularly intense. Edward Cheever and John Pierpont, both highly able and respected, lost pulpits for their abolition sentiments. Joel Hawes and Arthur Granger in Connecticut also faced intense denominational pressure to leave shortly after their antislavery positions were made public.[70] Little wonder that most clergy were cautious, and the more carefully ambitious unwilling to speak out. Nehemiah Adams gave an antislavery sermon but, when asked to publish it, refused; he soon became an anti-abolitionist and later still a proslavery apologist. His ministerial career was uninterrupted, although in the 1850s he lost his position on the board of the American Tract Society because of his slavery enthusiasm. Weld convinced theologian John W. Nevin to speak out against slavery, but Nevin retracted his promise because, he explained, it might not be helpful to Mercersburg, where he taught.[71]

Those who became abolitionists, despite some immediate difficulties, never regretted their actions and quickly worked out alternatives. There is much more evidence of psychological unease in those who long deferred honest public avowal of their antislavery convictions, such as Rev. William Furness. Furness came to Philadelphia in 1826 at a time when Unitarianism had scarcely a foothold there and built his congregation into one of the city's most flourishing. The detailed diary of his congregant and supporter, abolitionist-businessman Joseph Sill, offers accurate record of Furness's struggle with his convictions.[72] A convinced abolitionist by 1835, Furness first spoke from his pulpit on slavery at the beginning of 1841, calling it "an unmixed evil" in an argument attacking proslavery theology. A note protested his "obnoxious doctrines," but Furness decided, five months later, to touch on slavery again. This time, while specifically rejecting immediate emancipation, Furness stressed "that the people generally should have the independence to think and speak about it fearlessly, and to prepare their minds to its final accomplishment." This plea drew much wrath. Several families absented themselves from church, and Sill feared that a church meeting, should one occur, would lead to censure of Furness. Sill was puzzled by the opposition, which seemed "wild to a degree," coming from people who said they hated "slavery in the abstract" but who were ready to turn out an able and popular minister over such gentle comments.

Furness said nothing more about slavery for over a year, but the Sunday before Independence Day in 1842 he suggested that there was some inconsistency between American professions of freedom and the practice of slavery. At this, half a dozen members rose and stalked out—because "they could not bear to hear the truth," Sill presumed. Furness continued, stressing the way slavery was enslaving opinion in the North and that "the Northern people should plainly wash their hands from its contamination." During this section, many others left the church. Sill strolled from church with a slaveholder, W. H. Robinson, who had not stalked out but was furious. Robinson had recently talked with Sill about a slave sold away from his wife and children, a case so sad "it almost made him an abolitionist." Yet Robinson's predominant feeling was now outrage that Furness should dare to speak of slavery. Several resignations followed, and wealthy Joshua Tevis began a campaign to censure Furness, who this time did not retreat to silence.[73] He spoke the next week on the moral effects of fear of public opinion and, a month later, on the church's obligation to speak out on riots, perhaps in recompense for his silence in the wake of Philadelphia's earlier racial and anti-abolition mobs. Thirty-nine congregants signed a protest, but, in a single day, Sill collected fifty signatures in support, and he soon doubled this number.

At this point a compromise was set up. Furness would satisfy his conscience by speaking on slavery on the Sunday preceding Independence Day, at which time the congregation would include only those willing to hear it discussed; Sill called it "the annual one upon the subject of abolition." The minister was also permitted to mention the topic on special occasions, such as the twentieth anniversary of his pastorate. By late 1845, however, his uneasy conscience drove Furness to speaking out more regularly. A full decade after he'd concluded that abolitionism was right, and almost five years after his own hesitant pastoral broaching of the subject, Furness spoke his convictions openly: the North had a responsibility "to create such a sympathy and compassion for the slaves as should induce their shackles to fall" and to stop treating its own blacks "as if they did not belong to the same family of humanity." With this full revelation of Furness's abolition, congregant resignations poured in, and pressures on Furness, even from his own wife, again induced silence. When the Fugitive Slave Law spurred Furness to renewed attack on Southern slavery and Northern indifference, large numbers again left, undercutting the solvency of the church. But Furness now refused to consider silence; even Sill was bothered by his avowal that antislavery was "the great duty of his existence," a duty so passionately felt doubtless because it had been so long deferred. By this time, however, commitment was safe. Furness's church once again grew, and by 1854, when Furness described Anthony Burns's rendition or denounced the Kansas-Nebraska bill, his hearers seethed with passion, but now in sympathy rather than opposition to their minister's words about that "monstrous and inhuman code" of slavery.

Furness's relief at speaking out paralleled that of most abolitionists, whose letters and periodicals reveal a zest and confidence in their course. Their vision was one of slavery's sure demise, with even today's setbacks a part of tomorrow's progress. Things like the Mexican War and Texas annexation were discouraging, as the Fugitive Slave Law was infuriating, but all were likely, in the long run, to contribute to the cause. The same was true of every riot against them: typical was Charles Burleigh's conclusion that the Garrison mob was "the best Anti-Slavery meeting we have yet had in Boston." James Thome in Hanover, Ohio, expressed the same theme sharply: "Egged the first night. Hatched abolitionists fast."[74] Specific difficulties were often vexing and sometimes insurmountable: newspapers failed, organizations foundered, and meetings couldn't be arranged. But progress was steady in terms of the numbers who were abolitionist, who were willing to talk about slavery, and who found Southern demands intolerable. Abolitionists seldom aroused an attack by their opponents—vide the various congressional maneuvers of John Quincy Adams—without forcing substantially more Northerners to recognize their own basic hostility to slavery. In a twenty-year period the views of a tiny, persecuted minority had become the watered-down stance of the majority in the North. It was not the abolitionists who were frustrated, but their opposition.

The tone of their lives and letters accorded with their conviction that they were both right and bound to win. There is a common warmth and camaraderie in their writings and a frequent humor that attests to their sense of life well lived. A joint letter from James Thome and John Alvord to Weld both described a typical riot and response and suggested the geniality that joined the religious and moral passion of abolition. Thome, after describing his triumph in Akron with which this chapter begins, noted, "Am staying about Middlebury a day or two to take care of John Alvord. He has such a mob-raising tendency that he needs some guardians." At that point Alvord described events in Middlebury: "Last evening Middlebury puked. . . . Spasmodic heavings and wretchings during the whole day. Toward night symptoms were alarming." Evening rumors of an impending mob led the committee of arrangements to ask that the meeting be canceled. "We told them it was their concern—we had no personal fears—and if the house were unlocked and lighted we should be there." Given this choice, one member pocketed the church key and went home, but Thome and Alvord with a sizable audience gathered at the appointed time of six. "Abolition dander got a little started. Two of the trustees of the Church with a growl put out and soon we heard the bell ringing like fire. One of them came and invited us over. Found the door burst in."

Undismayed by this proof of abolitionist violence, Thome lectured till 8 P.M.

When in came a broadside of Eggs. Glass, Egg shells, whites, and yolks, flew on every side. Brother Thome's fact book received an egg just in its bowels and I doubt whether one in the House escaped a spattering. I have been trying to clean off this morning, but can't get off the stink. Thome dodged like a stoned gander. He brought up at length against the side of the desk, cocked his eye and stood gazing upward at the flying missles as they streamed in ropy masses through the house. I fear he'll never stand the "Goose Egg" without winking. He apologizes to me this morning by saying he thought the *stove was crackin*!!!!

After this interruption, Thome lectured for another twenty minutes till "another Egg plaster" arrived. A merchant, Mr. Kent, went out to try to calm the mob of about forty "when a volley was discharged at him and one of them hit him plump in the right eye. He came back groaning most piteously. I understand that he says this morning he is an abolitionist."

At nine the group, still under occasional egg barrage, decided to meet again Friday and set up a committee to bring the rioters to justice. Mob threats were noisy, but Alvord guessed that people wouldn't let them be "mobbed out." Thome added a short reply to Alvord's comic description: "What I have to say is that this story of John's about me 'is just as mean as purssly.' I was brave as a warrior, but I did really think the stove was exploding with a tremendous force. So soon as I was undeceived, I was bold as a Lion. It was ludicrous scene though, after all. Don't you believe me?"[75]

The humor of the description is obviously grounded in the confidence of the two, as their teasing is in affection for Weld and each other. This kind of robust, slangy humor runs through the writings of abolitionists like Alvan Stewart, William Elder, and Elizur Wright. The earthy humor of James Russell Lowell's *Biglow Papers* had roots in the traditions of the group he joined, just as Wendell Phillips's scathing sarcasm followed from William Jay's bruising wit. Angelina Grimké's letters to Weld are full of warmly amusing complaint, as when she had sister Sarah write Weld that Angelina would not answer his letters until he stopped scrawling in pencil because of her belief in fair treatment for women. Even William Lloyd Garrison joked. John White Chadwick remembered an evening on the abolitionist circuit in which a group sat around a fire laughing as Garrison described the oddities of Stephen S. Foster and related an anecdote about Charles Burleigh, dirty, ragged, and hairy as always, coming into a village, at which sight some children ran away screaming in fright to their parents. "A clear case of hair 'em, scare 'em," said William Lloyd Garrison. Chadwick's generalization seems broadly right: abolitionists tended to be genial folk of kindly disposition, serenely confident that they were "engaged in a good work and that the good time was coming right along."[76]

Sallie Holley's witty letters offer good evidence of the pleasant quality of life among even those Garrisonians most known for unbending censoriousness. The daughter of one of New York's most effective political abolitionists, Holley had just graduated from Oberlin in 1851 when Abby Kelley Foster, recognizing her talent, urged her to become a Garrisonian lecturer. That career she pursued into the Civil War. It was a hard life in most ways—constant travel and living in strangers' homes for pathetically little reward in contributions or subscriptions—and yet the editor of her letters is right in saying they describe an "anti-slavery idyll." Holley expressed her warm feelings toward Abby Foster for her intelligence and public skills and for the quiet warmth she brought to her home, her child-rearing, and her friendships. Holley also took some delight in teasing about Abby's husband, Stephen. She reported asking Stephen's mother if she'd ever heard her son lecture and being told that Stephen lectured enough around the house so that she had no desire to go outside to hear him. Holley also mentioned Pennsylvania farm families' pointing out the room where Abby and Stephen met and a parlor where they courted; it must have been for everyone a memorable romance.

Holley depicted genial long visits with the Motts in Philadelphia, with Thomas Garrett in Delaware (who, on each visit, multiplied the number of slaves he'd helped escape) and with Gerrit Smith in New York, who laughingly introduced his bloomer-clad daughter as "the best dressed lady in America." When Holley visited the Welds, she was appalled by the looks of the Grimkés, especially Sarah, who was "shockety in personal appearance. . . . Seeing her is an event in your life. It's like seeing Stonehenge! . . . But then their talk. Oh, it's angel food!" Abolition perhaps required some zest for conflict, which Holley showed much like Thome or Alvord, but it was grounded less in frustrated bitterness than in secure conviction. Despite major disputes and almost constant quibbles, being with one another was "angel's food."[77]

Why and how abolitionists and their opponents spoke and acted in these mob years mattered less than the way the riots changed the political culture in which both groups operated. Cincinnati's anti-abolition riots are a telling example of what happened because they were both extensive and extended over a considerable period, 1836–43. When they began in 1836, both sides were already aware of riot's contribution to abolitionist growth, but fears about the city's dependence on Southern commerce led to accelerating threat, supported especially by the mayor, the party press, and Jacksonian officials, that forced them toward riot when James G. Birney would not pack up his press and leave, as he had done under similar pressures in Danville, Kentucky, just before moving his paper to Ohio.[78]

In an attempt to avoid trouble, Birney decided initially to publish the *Philanthropist* in a village about twenty miles from town. The Jacksonian paper suggested mobbing Birney to protect the city's "merchants, her capitalists, and her tradesmen" from Southern economic retaliation. A few days later, January 22, 1836, Cincinnati's political and economic elite joined in a huge mass meeting to make clear their determination "to exert every lawful effort" to get Birney to leave. What these "lawful" means were went unsuggested other than some hope that the Ohio legislature might pass laws similar to those vaguely suggested by Van Buren's friend William Marcy, governor of New York. The meeting was genteel, Birney was allowed to speak, and the central economic concern about the city's Southern trade and travelers was clear. Only Jacksonian ex-congressman and soon-to-be–U.S. Surveyor General Robert Lytle added to his economic theme a racist diatribe, one urging sterilization of blacks.[79] Unity was possible because the resolves simply repeated the toothless ritual gestures to the South of last summer's Northern mass meetings.

A leading Cincinnati abolitionist, Christian Donaldson, was angry that a friend of his supported this meeting "to suppress entirely that class of philanthropists called abolitionists," but Birney, more politically savvy, lightly mocked the meeting's alleged commitment to a free press and free discussion "except in this instance," their professed concern for the welfare of the slave, and their expectation that gentlemanly social snubbing would cause abolitionists to give up their beliefs. Three months later, having clearly established the "moderation" of his position, Birney moved the *Philanthropist* into Cincinnati. He wrote Lewis Tappan that he thought a mob now unlikely, despite the opposition of "poor creature" Mayor Samuel Davies. He also was sure that if a mob developed it would quintuple Ohio's abolitionists.[80]

His enemies realized this, too: Birney was left alone, even when an April mob burned some African American homes and brutally beat some occupants. Abolitionists feared for their school for blacks, but no threat was made to white abolitionists or their property.[81] Only in July, when the city had its largest number of Southern visitors, did tension resume. It began with Cincinnati blacks' annual July 3 Independence Day parade, which the Mayor permitted only when the marchers agreed to cancel Birney's address to them. Anger developed, too, over a black's getting the better of a street argument with a white anti-abolitionist. On July 12 a mob led by Joseph Graham and comprising three Kentuckians, several resident Southerners, and a few young commercial men did mild damage to the *Philanthropist*'s printing house and threw its type in the river. Birney was able to publish the very next day, and all of Cincinnati's major papers except the Democratic organ gingerly deprecated the mob.[82]

The next day, Graham and a Mr. Wood had a handbill printed making clear that this first mild mobbing was to be "taken as a warning." If Birney reestablished his press, "longer patience would be criminal" because "the business of this place is receiving a virtual stab" from people "engaged in the unholy cause of annoying our Southern neighbors." Threats also poured in from Kentucky, one of them offering a $100 reward "for the delivery of the body" of Birney, who "in all his associations and feelings is black." The anti-abolitionists once again hoped that threat might work, and the *Whig* and commercial *Post* joined the Democratic *Republican* in suggesting that Birney's conduct was arousing riotous response. Only Charles Hammond's independently Whig *Gazette* remained antimob, claiming that petty "pecuniary interest" alone motivated the mob to action. Cincinnati's Presbyterian journal also angrily attacked the threatened riot as both unjust and sure to strengthen abolition.[83] Another meeting was called, now at the Lower Market, where the poorer people active in the antiblack riots would give some bite to elite words. The formal resolves of this July 22 meeting repeated the "all lawful means" rubric but also stated that "only discontinuance can prevent violence" and set up a committee to try to convince Birney to leave. A "volunteer" resolve was passed also, but far from unanimously. Wilson Brown, son of a mercantile family, added that Cincinnatians should follow the "noble and fearless example" of "true-hearted Americans" at Boston's tea party in taking illegal action "to rid our fair land" of a "withering influence."[84]

Charles Stowe claimed that some at this meeting accepted violence; he named Democratic appointees William Burke and Morgan Neville, along with Joseph Graham and Nicholas Longworth, who (with Neville) was the leading investor in a projected Charleston-Cincinnati Railroad. Others such as Whig ex-judge and senator Jacob Burnet, William Greene, Nicholas Wright, and "uncle John" Foote thought threat might work. A third group went to try to soften the resolves. By the meeting's end, however, everyone saw that Cincinnati's anti-abolitionists now had either to scare Birney away or accept/encourage his mobbing. In this situation some who had supported the meeting publicly dissociated themselves from it: lawyer Timothy Walker denounced any resort to violence and said his anti-abolition had nothing to do with money but with fear for the union. Businessmen William Greene spoke out against any violence, and Joseph Vaughn and Stephen Burrows refused to serve on the meeting committee.[85] All were Whigs.

Attempting to frighten Birney, the anti-abolition presses all proclaimed anew their commitment to mobbing. The *Republican* said that abolitionists, all "reckless and unprincipled fanatics," would deserve what they got, and the *Post* decided that it was the abolitionists who were rioters because they defied "popular sentiment." The *Whig* was both more conflicted and more virulent. It printed some antimob letters, one of which pointed out how riots grew abolition, and often protested its hatred of mobs, but. . . . The "buts" revived all the most ridiculous charges of 1835: abolitionists fomented insurrection, were amalgamationists, were "hirelings of the despots of Europe," with Garrison a "hired stipendiary" of the English crown. The editor trotted out the principle of self-defense in English and Latin (*ex necessitate re*), that sanctioned action against "the assassin . . . with a knife at our throat," and rejoiced that the founding fathers "did not deem themselves the slaves of law." All action was justified against these monsters who "menaced the union, tottering on the verge of a dissolution."[86]

The committee went to see Birney, expressing friendliness toward him and their desire to prevent his being mobbed. The committee, who had said they disliked slavery, clearly disliked even more Birney's suggestion that then they should publicly debate how best to end it eventually. Judge Burnet admitted that the tone and content of Birney's writings were not at issue but stressed that a mob of "2/3 of the property holders of the city" would attack if Birney didn't leave. He also complained that blacks were growing "impudent." Robert Buchanan bewailed the profits that Birney's principles were costing the business community as well as the dangers of Southern boycott. Not one to slight an old joke, wealthy Methodist minister Oliver Spencer suggested that Birney might go south to achieve his "glorious martyrdom." Birney politely preferred taking his chances of martyrdom in Cincinnati but promised to refer their information to his paper's owner, the Ohio Anti-Slavery Society.

The committee reported their failure to convince Birney in a public card that also cautiously proclaimed that they were not advocates of violence. The Ohio Anti-Slavery Society elaborated on the position they'd taken just after the Lower Market meeting: to comply with these demands was to abandon freedom of the press, speech, and opinion, at "virtually the demand of slaveholders, who have broken down all the safeguards of liberty in their own states . . . and are now . . . making the demand of us to follow their example." The society stressed basic rights and how "unmanly" it would be to submit to threat simply because the South "had sold its own liberty, and now wanted the North to do the same."[87] Abolitionists had quickly learned that the most effective response to mob pressure in the North was to neglect black liberty to stress Southern hostility to Northern white freedom.

On July 30 another meeting inaugurated the mob. The *Philanthropist* claimed that Jacksonian postmaster William Burke and land receiver Morgan Neville led the meeting, but younger men led the riot, including Neville's son Julien, J. A. D. Burrows, and, again most prominently, Joseph Graham. The mob destroyed Birney's presses this time, but Graham dissuaded rioters from burning the building. They also were frustrated in finding the abolitionists they wanted to tar-and-feather, and they decided not to injure most abolitionist property, though Dr. Isaac Colby's office was sacked. More damage was done against blacks; at least half a dozen brothels, grog shops, and homes were sacked, after initially resisting blacks fled. One rioter was seriously wounded; perhaps other injuries were avoided when the mob decided not to attack the *Gazette* office and Lane Seminary when it was learned they had armed defenders. Mayor Davies went off to a meeting when the mob attacked the *Philanthropist* but returned to watch the sacking of black property. Finally he asked the mob to stop, so they'd disturb no one's rest. He assured them abolitionists would no longer "disregard public sentiments": "We have done enough for one night."[88]

The "we" of the mob and Cincinnati's elite continued to praise their riot. When Charles Hammond, Edward Mansfield, and Salmon Chase called a meeting to condemn the mob on August 2, mob supporters, led by the Jacksonian officeholders, took it over to say once again that abolition caused the riot and to praise the mayor and other officials for their inaction. Still, the results were the usual: Birney resumed publishing within a month, with subscriptions trebled, and moved the paper back to Cincinnati within the year. The mob found themselves portrayed as knaves and fools by the noncity press, and abolitionists found new recruits. Even before the riot a few prominent anti-abolition committee men, like Timothy Walker and William Greene, denounced any violence; afterward they took a moderate antislavery stance. A meeting of some forty craftsmen and small store owners condemned the mob and said they thought abolitionists had every right to speak and publish. Private letters ceased complaint about abolitionists and described the riot with disgust. Young Clarissa Gest wrote that everyone, including "pa," who had supported the committees, was now disgusted with the violence. As a result of the riot, Salmon Chase became the abolitionists' best lawyer and soon Ohio's most effective antislavery politician. And Harriet Beecher Stowe mocked the men "disposed to wink at the outrage" and claimed that antimob feeling was now dominant, though most feared to speak out. She hoped Birney would hold out, with guns if need be; were she a man, she "would take good care of at least one window."[89] Stowe held her fire until 1852.

For five years Cincinnati's abolitionists went unmobbed though their acts in aid of runaways and in helping to free slaves voluntarily brought into the state drew threats. In 1839 a mob drove out a black doctor on rumors of his maltreating two women patients. Beginning in 1840 Cincinnati had a new Democratic paper, the *Enquirer*, that was stridently antiblack, urging the city to expel this 6 percent of its population. Perhaps this was to appeal to the city's burgeoning Irish and German immigrants; certainly it was in line with more overt grounding of Jacksonian argument in racial hatred. Several black-Irish fights climaxed on August 31, 1841, when an Irish crowd chased a black and guns were fired. When the city refused the protection blacks asked, they armed themselves, and when whites attacked their homes, they fired, injuring several rioters. When whites started to bring up a cannon, blacks wrested it from them. "The Negroes were the best soldiers," Nicholas Longworth, leading anti-abolitionist in 1836, wrote appreciatively.[90]

A law-and-order meeting was divided between those who wanted to keep the peace and those who wanted to condemn the blacks. Both sides put pressure on the African Americans to disarm. They did so reluctantly, and as soon as they were taken into "protective" custody, the mob grew brave, yelled for their blood, and attacked the now defenseless black community—after they sacked the *Philanthropist* one more time, and the bakery of abolitionist Cornelius Burnett. Several blacks were beaten and probably two African American women raped, and the crowd stole much black property. At least one white, a Kentuckian, was killed in the first attack, and at least one black later. Officer J. W. Pratt, Sheriff John Avery, and Mayor Samuel Davies, as in 1836, tacitly supported the mob, as did the militia they called out to watch. Violence ended when Whig governor Thomas Corwin happened into town as the rioting was going on and immediately organized volunteers who ended the violence.

Once again the *Philanthropist* almost immediately resumed publishing and subscribers and financial support shot up. Now defense of the mob was left to a single source, the *Enquirer*. It first published letters from Kentucky, one from a Covington militia commander who said his men had come to Cincinnati at the request of authorities but had then just gone home, and another from R. Wallace saying no Kentuckians were involved and it just happened that Birney's presses were sent there. Wallace added that, anyway, the mob bore no guilt but only the abolitionists, "who throw firebrands," and that more riot was needed to ensure Cincinnati's keeping the South's trade. Endorsing these letters, editors John and Charles Brough defended the riot as the natural result of the harm abolitionists did to the Southern trade but also on racist principles. The town "was overrun with Negroes," most of them "characterless vagabonds" who were "crowding out white labor, when they worked at all." No one should believe stories of rape and plunder when they came from what everyone knew were "lying niggers." All whites should join to protect "our rights and our interests" and our market economy. Whigs clearly had "African affinities" and even allowed Brown County to exist "where niggers and whites are classed together." The *Enquirer* called a meeting on September 21 to condemn the abolitionists for "assisting the blacks to mob and shoot the whites." This meeting set up an Anti-Abolition Society and resolved that the black community got what they deserved and, while "inhumanity" to the African American was not good, all should "endeavor to fix him to his proper place."[91]

The rest of Cincinnati's press expressed shock at the mob, its brutalities, and the city's compliant authorities, although the official Whig paper faintly echoed some of the *Enquirer*'s racism for a few days before deciding that condemning the mob rather than blacks was the best politics. Edward Mansfield's independent Whig *Chronicle* was the most honest problack, antimob general paper, and his position was seconded by all the religious press. The *Western Episcopal Observer* gave its support to the "strong reacting feeling of sympathy and kindness to the blacks," and John Purcell's *Catholic Telegraph* strongly condemned the attack and urged, if any Irish were involved, that they be punished. Perhaps the repeated brutality of these mobs led Bishop Purcell to be the only American Catholic leader in the antebellum years clearly sympathetic to antislavery. Of the forty arrested, twenty (eight with Irish names) were convicted of riot and sentenced by Democratic judge D. K. Este to one day in jail and a one-dollar fine.[92]

Probably sympathy for the blacks was widespread. Birney found few who cared "to palliate the ferocious—the bloody—the brutal—the lustful outrage," where the police arrested male blacks so that a drunken mob "led on by a corps of Kentucky negro-whippers" could burn, beat, rob, and rape in safety.[93] Yet the *Enquirer* was probably right in concluding on offensive racism as the best defense. The Democrats won the local elections, and the *Enquirer* quickly became the central Jacksonian journal in Ohio. Yet in the long run there were costs, too. Rather than driving out abolitionists, the mob expanded their supporters, even among old enemies like Nicholas Longworth. Rather than driving out African Americans, the mob strengthened their support. And the Democrats created the issues that would slowly drain their Northern support when sectional issues reemerged after the Mexican War.

The *Philanthropist* in 1841, now edited by Gamaliel Bailey, defined the issues that would undergird the political shifts toward civil war. It described and deplored the extraordinary viciousness of the attack on blacks and mocked the mayor and his militia, especially that led by *Enquirer* editor Charles Brough, as "mobocrats in uniform." But it especially stressed that Kentuckian mob prominence showed that the mob's supporters were happy to make the city "a conquered province of the slaveholders." In the following issues Bailey more clearly developed what became antislavery's and then the Republican's theme: the Democrats obviously held no principles so sacred as "consolidating their alliance with slaveholders and slave-holding prejudice." Their presses like the *Enquirer* were increasingly "unscrupulous, violent, vulgar, and incendiary," with the party taking "mobocracy as well as slavery under its wing." The Democrats, working so that in the North as in the South "no law reigns but Lynch-law," were bringing Kentucky "justice" to Cincinnati: "The Queen City! It is the Mob City—the Queen of Mobs."[94]

After this mob, the *Enquirer* and the *Philanthropist* jointly made extreme denigration of blacks and extreme cooperation/truckling with the South partisan issues. Given the nation's racism, the first issue was a winning one for Democrats—though not one that in the North could survive many such brutish manifestations as this mob. The second issue in the 1850s would prove the Democrat's losing one, though Northern Whigs' concern for the union and for its Southern base would keep them from defining it vigorously. Abolitionists like Bailey sensed where victory lay and made their saddest compromise in subduing their antiracism to stress Democratic–slave power conspiracy, a process launched by earlier anti-abolition mobs. Bailey, like abolitionists in 1835, said supporters were not insurrectionists nor "Negro stealers" nor antiwhite, nor did they entice blacks to Ohio or encourage "amalgamation." Abolitionists continued to support black schools and communities, and most accepted the fully equal qualities and rights of humans, in Thome's words, "bleached and unbleached."[95] Yet the mobs they faced, and the opportunities they saw, led them to attack racism less often and Southerners more.

In 1843 occurred the last mob threat to Cincinnati abolitionists. A Louisiana planter brought with him a slave girl of nine to Cincinnati—whose mother had told her she could be free in Ohio if she ran off and gained protection. She did so, and her master tried to raise an anti-abolition mob over the issue, first believing she'd been stolen and then even angrier when he learned the truth. He printed placards about the slave-stealing and visited grog shops to collect a mob of a hundred or so. He couldn't get them to attack, however, except at Cornelius Burnett's, and there rioters ran off when defenders showered them with bricks, felling two, one with his skull fractured, before William Birney, James's son, could have his fourteen armed men fire at the group he believed to be mostly Kentuckians. All the press condemned this clearly Southerner-initiated riot, though the *Enquirer* ritually opined that the abolitionists caused the disturbance and expressed shock at their violence.[96] So ended Cincinnati's antiblack and anti-abolitionist mobs, but not before the sectional issues that would soon lead to bloodier conflict had been well defined, intellectually and partisanly.

Two books illustrate the influence of mobs on abolitionist thought and strategy that the Cincinnati case history makes clear. Both were highly influential and, like most abolition literature, careful about fact and cautious about personal condemnation. Lydia Maria Child's *An Appeal in Favor of Americans Called Africans* of 1833 and Theodore Weld's *American Slavery as It Is* of 1839 show how the riotous virulence against the group between 1835 and 1838 dictated some positional change.

Using the accounts of both Southerners and travelers, Child argued the economic disadvantages of slavery and its psychological costs to whites, both slaveless and slave-owning, and to blacks. But her central case rested on the laws of slavery themselves, which systematically denied human dignity and potential: laws that refused protection to the black family or black women; that freely permitted harsh punishments to blacks and set up great obstacles to legal prosecution of even the extremest cruelty or sadism; that enforced black ignorance and circumscribed slave religious development; that demanded that one race work, for life and for generations, for the others' benefit, without chance of possessing or protecting property, family, or their own capacities and lives; that made it hard or impossible for slaves to gain or be given freedom; that made slaves legally things to be bought, sold, and appropriated like cattle. Such legal realities demanded, Child insisted, that all who cared about human rights work to end slavery with thoughtfulness about the future needs of slaveholders as well as slaves. Some method, perhaps a system of gradual wage work so slaves might "redeem themselves progressively," would allow blacks to gain a sense of personal responsibility as they gained freedom.

Finally Child, recognizing that the only moral justification of slavery was racial inferiority, presented data demonstrating an environmental explanation for those "facts" commonly used to denigrate blacks. Here her target was as much Northern as Southern practice; she claimed that the former's racial injustices were even less justifiable than the latter's slavery. Child recommended the abolitionist program at this point: people should think about and treat blacks as fellow beings with fully human capacities and aspirations. Were this done, Child concluded, indifference to slavery would disappear, as would the nasty caricaturing of blacks, "our cold-hearted ignoble prejudice," that created thoughtless condescension in even well-meaning people that "often cut deeper than the lash" in the North.[97]

Weld's *American Slavery* came six years after Child's *Appeal*, during which time old abolitionist hopes and tactics had been shattered and new ones developed. The South had made clear that it would not listen to any appeal on slavery, nor tolerate anyone else's listening if they could help it, and now insisted that slavery was no evil but a peculiarly blessed and benevolent institution necessary for a superior society. Second, the North's attempt to silence abolition at the South's behest had created a dichotomy between oppression and liberty—of speech, of press, of assembly, of petition—that gave weight to the abolitionist attack on the South among people willing enough to ignore pleas centered on black freedom. Although there was no name-calling in Weld's pamphlet, its tone was uncompromisingly harsh. It systematically destroyed those arguments Southerners used to portray slavery as the higher kindness with words drawn from Southerners, most of them writers and advertisers in Southern newspapers who unconsciously revealed the realities of Southern society that its apologists ignored or noted only as rare evils.

Gone was Child's determined gentleness of tone, and most of her stress on antiracism. Present was a catalogue of specific human tragedies and acts of personal viciousness or indifference that Weld used to destroy favorite proslavery arguments that touched immediate treatment of slaves. Hardly could whipping, branding, mutilation, slave-catching, slave-selling, breaking up families, and extreme violence be rare if these documents were true; hardly could respectable Southerners scorn such actions, when Southerners, many eminent indeed, could publicly show such acts and attitudes quite obviously without second thought or worry that anyone might be bothered by them. And the quotations were accurate. The newspapers were cited exactly, and the testimonies bore many marks of Weld's injunction that no one exaggerate or offer as evidence what they knew only as rumor. The book was strong in the way Engels's account of the British working class was strong: one-sided obviously, but informed by a conviction so firm that cold fact, carefully unexaggerated, served its ends—and often in opponents' words that proved Weld's points more effectively than could any friendly argument.

What Weld wished his readers to recognize was that slavery's injustice was inextricable from its existence and that personal or national acquiescence in it endangered all human dignity and freedom. Now not national racism but sectional slavery was the enemy. The book chronicled violence and brutality to whites as well as to blacks in the South, victims in subtler ways of the tyranny bred of slavery. It was not that Weld was any less concerned about racism than Child, nor any more inclined to absolve Northerners of their responsibility for the continued degradation of blacks.[98] It was that the task of abolition was now to hasten an inevitable political realignment in the North between pro- and antislavery parties.

The changes in emphasis in Weld's compilation and in the *Philanthropist* as it was mobbed underlay the divisions in the abolition movement that are often seen as proof of personal quirkishness that made "organizing them . . . like binding crooked sticks in a bundle." In part, abolition developed in a legal-political context bound partly to blunt and complicate specific goals. The nation was formed in a document accepted because it carefully avoided mentioning the dirty word, yet sanctioned slavery's continuance. Hence, unless abolitionists were willing to burn the Constitution (as Garrison finally did) and with it their bridges to a larger public, they had to attack corollaries of slavery rather than the evil itself. Things like the debate over whether the Constitution was a proslavery or antislavery document, with both sides indulging in desperate special pleading, were products of the abolitionists' unavoidable practical-legal dilemma.[99]

The mobs between 1835 and 1837, as the virulently anti-abolition *Democratic Review* pointed out, had nurtured "the infancy of abolitionism into the hardy energy of youth."[100] Yet in these years one door closed sharply where abolition wanted to enter; the South would not listen nor permit anyone to speak. The strategy of 1835 to mount a publicity campaign to touch the conscience of the South bore strange, and mob-embittered, fruit. By 1837 it was clear the abolitionists had a growing coterie of followers and fellow travelers in the North but no chance of serious communication with those citizens on whom alone legally depended the continuation of slavery.

In this situation, abolitionists understandably diverged, partly because they now tacitly accepted the charge that their opponents had long made: serious agitation of slavery could lead only toward disunion or civil war. No one early posed the question more starkly than revivalist Charles Grandison Finney to Weld in the summer of 1836. Finney was upset particularly by the revival's loss of many of its leading young ministers to abolition, but his central concern went far deeper:

> But Weld is it not true, at least do you not fear it is, that we are in our present course going fast into civil war? Will not our present movements in abolition result in that? . . . Nothing is more manifest to me . . . unless your mode of abolitionizing the country be greatly modified.

Finney said that Weld, who certainly could "not but discern the signs of the times," should understand his motives. And he had an alternative: push the revival in the South so that change in men's hearts would eventually ensure abolition's triumph. Without it, Finney warned, abolition "will roll a wave of blood over the land." Unable to convince Weld, Finney turned his attention to four Lane rebels who had been laboring for abolition. They all resisted Finney's plea that the "unholy excitement" being raised by the abolitionists could end only in civil war and "that the only hope of the country, the church, the oppressor, and the slave was in wide spread revivals."[101]

The fissures in the movement became open in 1840, when Garrison imported a boatload of supporters to New York City to take over the American Anti-Slavery Society. The specific issue here was women's role in the movement; when the Garrisonians closely won on the vote to make Abby Kelley an officer, the Tappanites withdrew. This enabled Garrison to carry back the name to Boston but gave him control of little else.[102] And behind this specific fight lay Garrison's increasingly encumbering abolition with his new causes: nonresistance, women's rights, perfectionism, and anticlericalism. Non-Garrisonians saw the disputes primarily in pragmatic terms: why tie abolition to other unpopular causes, many of them vague and all of them sure to drive off some potential antislavery converts, when the goal was to win adherents?[103]

Yet behind the disputes lay profounder realities for antislavery after the mob years of the mid-1830s. The South and its political allies suggested that no freedom was so precious as the right to enslave without question, a position that the North could not swallow. The abolition movement splintered in the late 1830s into not just three movements—Garrisonian, Tappanites, and Liberty Party people—but into many individuals and factions responding variously to their desire to remain active when all paths led meanderingly and always dangerously toward the approaching goal.

At the time and since, the Garrisonians have been seen as the most "extreme" faction. Though everyone's favorite straw man, Garrison was most extreme in but one sense: his castigation of abolitionists who disagreed with him. Yet this grew neither from Garrison's fanaticism nor his radicalism but from stress on the maintenance of purity among abolitionists. A common practice in pietistic groups faced with a world entrenched in evil is to emphasize their distance from it. The Garrisonian odyssey was more complex than this because it was grounded in concern with ending a particular social practice in this world, but it stressed steadily the preeminent need for ideological and personal purity.

There were radically anarchic implications in Garrisonian political theory, as in much other Jacksonian political and social thought.[104] And there was a strain of nastiness in Garrisonian treatment of opponents: Garrison's smug dismissal of Orange Scott, who did much to make Northern Methodism antislavery, as "morally defunct"; Abby and Stephen Foster's cheaply self-righteous insistence that a resolution in praise of Joshua Giddings, who'd led the abolition fight in Congress for years, contain a codicil that he was "as faithful as his false position will permit him to be to his duty"; in Edmund Quincy's glib brutality to Elizur Wright, reduced after years of service to abolition to selling his translation of LaFontaine door-to-door to support his large family. Yet such personal asperity was rare among abolitionists, rare in all but a handful of Garrisonians. Purist Abby Kelley, invited to stay at the home of an Ohio Liberty Party leader, felt obliged to tell her host that she had "come to kill the Liberty Party" before entering. The host's reply was more typical of abolitionists' response. "Come in, Abby," said Quaker Jacob Heaton, smiling, "and we will kill thee with kindness."[105]

While Garrison's group was small enough so that most of his stances became official policy, the leader was both too genial and too canny to demand more than pro forma adherence to his many positions so long as there was acceptance of his leadership. Maria and David Child, as editors of the most successful Garrisonian paper, printed the society's formal positions without ever taking many of them up seriously, and while giving respectful attention to all antislavery tactics and shades of opinion. Samuel May, who considered himself a Garrisonian, advocated only a few of the Garrison causes and never lessened his warm and supportive relations with other abolitionists of all stripes. The movement's leading feminists—the Grimkés, Lucretia Mott, Elizabeth Cady Stanton, and Susan B. Anthony—were never Garrisonian exclusivists. Even among the handful dedicated to Garrisonian pietism, the willingness to disown coworkers, churches, country, and Constitution was enmeshed in a socially mild stand that tried to deny the main threat associated with abolition.

The stress on nonresistance in the late 1830s was quite simply an assertion of nonviolence in a situation where vast violence was increasingly likely, an argument that truly good ends were best served by peaceful means. Neither Garrison nor Henry C. Wright, the main architects of the nonresistance doctrine, excelled at systematic thought, but a belief that in their truth lay gentle answer illumined their political writings, such as the original declaration of sentiments of 1838:

> The history of mankind is crowded with evidences proving that physical coercion is not adopted to moral regeneration: that the sinful dispositions of men can be subdued only by love; that evil can be exterminated from the earth only by goodness . . . that there is great security in being gentle, harmless, long-suffering, and abundant in mercy.

Such hope that in pacifism lay "omnipotent power" was a notable response to the predicted threat of civil war.[106]

The relationship of this stance to the end of slavery was obscure, but essentially it was a more abstract version of Finney's proposal: change men's hearts, and from this, other changes will painlessly flow; from personal purity will come social reformation. The "no government" implications of this doctrine solidified Garrison's position as *the* radical abolitionist, although Nathaniel Peabody Rogers was soon to carry it to an extreme that led to a conflict with Garrison, certainly not about to apply such disintegrating principles to the organization he'd so neatly stolen from the Tappans.[107] Yet as with much pietistic radicalism, its extremity in damning existing power offered little real threat to any order except one that demanded total uniformity. Of all abolitionist tacks after 1837, that of nonresistance offered the least threat to the union or even to slavery.

Perhaps because of nonresistance's mildness, vagueness, or practical emptiness, Garrison took up disunionism with relish in 1842, with his society accepting the doctrine in 1844. Certainly it was a position radically unpopular with both general citizens and other abolitionists, but it was much less a condemnation of society than a position that for the first time suggested that abolitionists put all the blame for slavery on the South in a self-righteous way.[108] Behind the radical theater of Constitution burning lay a theory that the North's failings grew largely from contamination with the South, that the Mason-Dixon line separated good from evil. Nonresistance had suggested purity through separation from the nation's political structure; disunionism promised purity through casting off the South. This idea of slave-power contamination was the Garrisonians' pietistic version of the Liberty Party's simultaneously promulgated social theory of slave-power conspiracy. Abby Foster clarified the central idea and emotion of disunionism when she wrote to Garrison in 1843 that she would have to withdraw from his organizations unless they condemned the union as well as the churches: "I must clean my hands from the blood of the slave that is spilt by support of slavery in church and state."[109]

To most abolitionists, the most troubling aspect of disunionism was that the Garrisonians, in washing their hands of guilt, seemed also to wash them from responsibility to the slave. Garrison at times offered explanations—slavery only existed because the North upheld it, and once separated, slaves would end the institution "by their heels"—but such answers were not very convincing, nor was Garrison himself much enamored of them. A minister in early 1861 filled his diary with a long statement of the kind abolitionists had long made against Garrison's disunionism, still being urged by some antislavery spokesmen, in this case Henry Ward Beecher, as an alternative to war. "Beecher said, 'I don't believe the South will secede, and I don't care if it does.' One must forget the slaves to say that heartily."[110]

The Garrisonians never forgot the slaves; they simply forgot their other propositions when conflict developed. Yet had Garrison exerted controlling influence after 1840, slavery would not have been tied to politics, the North would have allowed (if not initiated) secession, and slaves would have had to take care of their own freedom as best they could. Of course, the leader followed events. When in 1861 the *Journal of Commerce* taunted the Garrisonians with opposing what they'd been urging for some seventeen years, Garrison pungently answered that, when he'd said the Constitution was a covenant with death and a pact with hell, he had not known that death and hell would try to secede. Reasoning was never Garrison's forte; to spend well over half a million lives to keep hell in the union must rank as the oddest justification of the Civil War. Yet the answer worked on the level of rhetoric where Garrison was most comfortable, not losing his pungent aggressiveness even when saying he was wrong.[111] Garrison's post-1861 claim that he'd never meant nonresistance or disunion absolutely but only used them to draw attention to abolition was disingenuous. Yet there was a bit of truth, too; Garrison's political theories were ad hoc structures to house his abolition, while long denying the violent answer that all changing circumstances drew closer.

Political activity, the most obvious and popular alternative to Garrisonianism, took full shape in the Liberty Party by 1840. Reform movements tend to go from moral suasion to political-legal enforcement as people prove reluctant to act in response to the best-laid arguments for their improvement.[112] The Liberty Party had another attraction. It allowed abolitionists to do something, at a time that they felt acutely their critics' taunt that talk was all they did. Weld's marginal approval of Liberty organization, because many would "work in that *harness* who will work in no other," suggests the appeal of the movement. Yet the early Liberty Party shared many Garrisonian emphases. It was purist politics with little chance of gaining power.[113] A few Liberty people, especially those like Myron Holley or Alvan Stewart, who really enjoyed politics and who believed the "Old Anti-Slavery horse" would thrive if fed "ballot box oats," were willing to add some attractive issues to abolition. Yet the party's emphasis on moral integrity was what set it apart, an emphasis insured by candidate James G. Birney, who insisted that the platform attack not only the abuse of slavery but injustices toward Indians, Mormons, and free blacks as well. He also expressed his doubts about that Jacksonian holy of holies, the absolute perfection of the American democratic system. His positions tended to be both true and truly democratic but were well calculated to drive away all but faithful abolition enthusiasts.[114] Through the Liberty Party, abolitionists could do something and yet refrain from most of the compromises that promise of power brings to democratic politics. Only with the Free Soil Party did pragmatism wage a winning battle with purity in the antislavery political movement. And most old abolitionists had some trouble swallowing the new political realities that Free Soil involved, especially when accompanied by Martin Van Buren, who had been running for the presidency for a decade on declarations of support for slavery and gestures of repression toward abolition.

Other abolitionists either took different paths or gave support to them all. The Tappans, despite their financial setbacks in 1837, remained willing and able to contribute to a variety of efforts they or their friends devised and organized. When Garrison took over the American Anti-Slavery Society, the Tappans organized the American and Foreign Anti-Slavery Society, modeled on its British counterpart. This organization never attracted large numbers, but for a few years it provided a group that abolitionists could join who weren't inclined to damn all churches, burn Constitutions, or throw a vote away on a third party. Indeed, it was a group that "moderate" but real abolitionists could join while denying they were "fanatics" like Garrison. It also kept the South morally isolated by its close ties to the reform-religious community in Britain and sponsored a good deal of well-researched abolition literature, such as a series of reports on the success of West Indies emancipation. The Tappans also continued to supply funds for social and educational aid to free and escaped blacks, such as Augustus and Susan Wattles' work in Ohio or Hiram Walker's in Canada. And they financially aided attempts to settle anti- or nonslave communities in the South, such as John G. Fee's community in Kentucky, as wedges against the system.[115]

Abolition's other leading contributor, Gerrit Smith, followed an independent course similar to that of the Tappans. He used a sizable part of his New York estate to found farming communities for poor whites and blacks, a good many of them too inexperienced to benefit much from his bounty. Often supportive of the Liberty Party, in the 1850s he was elected to Congress on a uniquely egalitarian platform, both racially and economically, and a bit later contributed to the Free Soil struggle in Kansas and John Brown's stab at guerilla warfare.[116] In fact, there were few aspects of antislavery work which did not draw from Smith's deep pockets at one time or another.

Theodore Dwight Weld's course and convictions demonstrated the profoundest, most accurate, and bleakest vision of abolition's role after the mob years. Weld's power of thought, oratory, and organization made him the central figure in the spread of abolition in upstate New York and the Middle West between the mob summer of 1835 and late 1837. Both the South's rhetoric of 1835 and the mobs that half-heartedly opposed Weld and his "holy band" created the issues that allowed them to leave a coterie of abolitionists in most communities, people who hated riotous bullies as anxious to limit white freedom as they were to support black slavery. Weld, with other abolitionists, sensed that the groundwork had been laid for eventual victory, but, unlike most, he also understood the process. As future sectional conflict arose, there would be a group of respected people in every Northern community who would not allow politicians to toady so spinelessly to Southern demands as they had in 1835 without driving increasing numbers to an unambiguously anti-Southern, if not antislavery, position. And as Northern resistance hardened, so would Southern demands increase, cutting the ground from under those willing to accept any compromise to save the union.

Weld's personal speaking ended on a note of failure. In Troy, New York, in 1836 Weld was unable to repeat his usual success in quieting the mob and using it for his own ends. Unusually well organized and acting under the direction of the town's Democratic officials, this mob continued until Weld gave up. The failure was disturbing to him. He "lost" his public speaking voice for five years and never again took on the role of public speaker. Yet this defeat corresponded with a victory that gave broader impetus to Weld's style of promoting antislavery. The American Anti-Slavery Society accepted Weld's plan of fielding a group of "seventy" lecturers to canvass the nation the same month Troy's Democracy ejected him. He turned to the new project with zest and set it up with his usual success.

Weld's next project was going to Washington to aid, educate, and organize a small group of congressmen who would provide the political core for Northern resistance to Southern demands. Joshua Giddings, Seth Gates, William Slade, John Mattocks, Sherlock Andrews, and especially John Quincy Adams were the first legion in this political adjunct of the popular groups already formed. Any new crisis would find legislative resistance channeling a popular anger against Southern demands which would doom slavery. In a letter to James G. Birney in which he said he thought the Liberty Party beside the point, Weld expressed his vision of antislavery's future:

Whoever has not seen, ever since so long ago as Jackson's veto of the U.S. Bank, that from every quarter, the elements of conflict, the last conflict between liberty and slavery, were rushing headlong into the central focus—has been asleep. . . . They must drive against each other until one of them goes to the bottom. *Events*, the master of men, have for years been silently, but without a moment's pause, setting the basis of two great parties, the nucleus of one slavery, of the other freedom. . . . Where half of a government live by their own work and pay as they go and the other half by other's work and by the longest possible credit, and where these halves are made by *Climate*—a mighty pecuniary convulsion *must*, if of long continuance, hurl these two systems of labor and of living into mortal conflict. *The end must come.*[117]

Weld's vision of sectional hostility, economically as well morally based, to be embodied in two parties and ended only by "mortal conflict," was grimly accurate. Weld's historical usage as moderate and reasonable counterpoint to Garrison's "extremism" has tended to mask the harshness of his central vision. The uncompromisingly grim honesty of *American Slavery as It Is* was repeated in Weld's private letters. Southerners who refused to repent of the sin of slavery were damned—including, he wrote Sarah and Angelina Grimké, their beloved mother, and their brother who had recently died.[118] To Finney's prediction of coming civil war, Weld in effect replied, "So be it." It was just punishment for a nation which, while it prated of liberty, practiced or let others profit from slavery. Some of the excesses and some of the charm of the Garrisonians grew from their conviction that the fate of antislavery depended upon their efforts and purity. Other abolitionists tended more reasonably to assess their importance after 1837, though none so clearly as Weld, who ceased all antislavery activity in 1843 because he believed that no longer men but *events* controlled abolition's eventual and probably bloody triumph.

When Weld went to Washington, a Mrs. Sprigg hesitated to take him as a boarder because she judged that an abolitionist would keep her house empty. Weld convinced her, as he did most people, and by 1843 hers was the Abolition House and the only one in the city that was filled. Its only empty beds were those belonging to two slaves who had run off, under the influence and with the aid of Mrs. Sprigg's boarders. It was a moving abolition lecture to the landlady, who decided henceforth to employ free black help.[119]

The incident illustrates one area in which abolitionists could and did act. Elijah Lovejoy and John Brown were abolition's famous martyrs, but in between the greatest sufferers were those who worked to free not all slaves but particular slaves. Much of the stature of John Brown before 1859 grew from his identification with a slave raid in Missouri that freed eleven blacks. For a long time abolitionists had praised people who gave their lives to aid slaves—Charles Torrey, who died in prison in Baltimore, or Seth Concklin, killed when being sent back to Alabama for slave-stealing; Alanson Week, Aaron Burr, and George Thompson, imprisoned in Missouri; Calvin Fairbanks and Delia Webster, jailed in Kentucky, Asa Mahan, in Ohio, and Daniel Drayton, in Washington; and Jonathan Walker, branded in Florida. John Greenleaf Whittier, a weathervane of abolitionist sentiment, wrote poems about most of these people and their sacrifices.[120]

Abolitionists insisted, quite correctly, until well into the 1840s that their movement was nonviolent and noncriminal, and historians have argued about why they "changed" in the 1850s.[121] Yet from the beginning they accepted certain kinds of violent or illegal action. While Southern charges of insurrection support in 1831 and 1835 were fantasy, abolitionists always condoned the efforts of slaves to escape, or of whites to aid them, as self-defense, even if violent. If violence was never the highest morality nor usually the best policy, neither was it wrong when related to ending anyone's slavery. Gerrit Smith voiced the accepted position when he argued, "If a fugitive slave may not fight for his liberty, and stand for his life, who may? If blood is shed in pursuit of him, the whole sin of it is on the pursuer."[122]

No evidence exists of any abolitionist supporting insurrection prior to 1856, but Alvan Stewart stated the prevalent view when he argued the need to end slavery by political action

> or else it will be accomplished by slaves *rising*. As to their rising and by one mighty effort overthrowing their bloody masters, God grant that way if no other mode can be found out. The South would not be entitled to the commiseration of the civilized world, if before tomorrow's sun went down one universal deluge of fire and blood were to flow over the South.

Stewart's comment, in a private letter to a fellow abolitionist, was more apocalyptic than that of public statements but in fact said no more than Jefferson had half a century earlier: should the situation come to insurrection, a just God could never side with the white South. John Quincy Adams publicly voiced general abolitionist convictions when he said in Pittsburgh, "May the slave in the South be free, even if it should be through blood."[123]

For abolitionists, if violent slave insurrection was an abstraction, escaping slaves were the living embodiment of their ideas. Every abolitionist was, along with William Elder, "disposed to steal, and aid in receiving and concealing the stolen goods and chattels that think fit to steal away" from slavery. Strategically located abolitionists, like those Reverend John Rankin led in Ripley, Ohio, centered efforts on helping and encouraging slave escapes. Black entrepreneur John F. Parker, himself a self-purchased ex-slave, offered one of the best descriptions of these activities, full of moving, amusing, and tragic detail and sometimes punctuated with accounts of a little fighting or even the exchange of shots. Parker claimed he kept a record of 315 slaves he helped escape until his growing wealth, and fears aroused by the Fugitive Slave Act, led him to burn the potentially dangerous document. He gave 440 as the reasonable number for his total "assists." His account testifies not only to the intelligently daring dedication of his Ripley group but also to his own visceral response to "an excitement about the game."

Such escapes were vicarious excitement for abolitionists less strategically situated as well. In fact, intense enthusiasm for instances (though not a policy) of slave-theft, or property-stealing to end man-stealing, provided the clearest common ground for abolitionists of all stripes after 1838. The Garrisonians had no greater bête blanc than Charles Torrey, before he was convicted of helping slaves escape. When he died in a Baltimore jail, Torrey became a noble martyr for them, as for other antislavery people. Nor was private irritation allowed to dim public praise for even the most dubious of such saints. Abolitionists lost $25,000 when William Chaplin, accused of aiding slaves to run off, jumped bail. As usual, Gerrit Smith paid over half of this cost, which must have sharpened his response to letters revealing that Chaplin, back safe in New York, preferred keeping company with a brothel madam to lecturing for the cause to help defray the cost of his freedom. Yet Smith bit his tongue and contributed another mite to publish a pamphlet proving Chaplin a hero, neither criminal nor cowardly—much less debauched.[124]

Fugitive slave incidents, long predating the Fugitive Slave Act of 1850, raised for North and South alike troubling issues. For Southerners, escaping slaves both provided active satire on their idealized claims about slavery and suggested most directly their frightening dependence on others without commitment to their system. For the North, these escapees most movingly put the peculiar institution in human terms, while mocking the favorite conservative pretense that the North had nothing to do with slavery. And when that pretense was punctured, Northern indifference to slavery deflated.

For abolitionists, fugitives had additional meaning. Taunted that all they did was talk, abolitionists found in fugitives a chance to act in ways that showed they cared enough to endanger self in aid of slaves. Here was the spice of both personal danger and meaningful action, while for everyone, fugitives offered proof that slaves were fully human, men and women willing to take greater risk for freedom than had white Americans for generations. When Northerners saw blacks who risked all to be free, sometimes blacks who long had proved, despite racist constrictions, their ability to care well for themselves and their families, arrested on Northern soil by Northern officers, it became impossible to pretend that slavery was only the South's business, and difficult for most to avoid feeling a stab of respect or kinship for someone being chained for life while a liberty-loving, or at least -talking, people looked on. Abolitionists noticed how many of those normally hostile to them shared their sentiments on such occasions.

The best-known of the fugitive slave riots—those in Boston, Syracuse, and Milwaukee in the early 1850s—have obscured some important aspects of these events. In the first place, hostility to the Fugitive Slave Law of 1850 was not the source of this type of riot, although many mobs occurred between this date and the Kansas-Nebraska Act. Yet the number of incidents in these years was no larger than for the period of intense anti-abolitionist activity, 1833–37. And in most early fugitive slave riots, blacks took the leading role, in contrast to the 1850–54 riots, where prominent white abolitionists generally organized the well-integrated mobs.

No category of mob was clearer in specific objectives than fugitive slave mobs, and none so generally successful in achieving them. Of the 34 riots that took place, 26 resulted in freedom for slaves. Of the 8 riots that failed, 5 of them occurred in the 1833–37 period (failure rate of 50%), and 5 of them were in the cities of Philadelphia, New York, and Boston, where police control was strong (failure rate of 71%). At the same time, the numbers rescued through riot was small: in the 26 successful Northern riots, only 45 slaves were freed. In Marshall, Michigan, 6 were protected in 1845, 4 in Buffalo in 1835, and 3 in South Bend, Indiana, and Harrisburg (both 1850). Seven others helped 2 slaves to remain free.[125] At the same time, the numbers of fugitives and free blacks aided by these mobs obviously much exceeded the numbers rescued. Every such mob was a warning to owners and slave-catchers that their work would not be easy. Much more frequent than riot was intimidation that discouraged arrests and, perhaps even more, a general sense that risks might not be worth the benefits.

Fugitive slave riots occurred commonly where antislavery was strongest: Boston, upstate New York, rural Ohio and Michigan, and especially Quaker-influenced rural Pennsylvania, where ex-slaves were active in their own protection; over a third of both riots and rescues occurred in Pennsylvania. All these were areas through which escaping slaves often traveled on their way to Canada. In addition, all these areas had by the 1840s organized groups, black and white, that regularly aided fugitives. Rioting was usually a last-ditch response by groups who commonly gained their illegal ends more peaceably. Only a few of the early mobs were largely spontaneous, such as those of 1835 in Albany, New York, and in Burlington, New Jersey, the next year. Here the capture of hard-working and respected Severn Martin, who'd lived there the seventeen years since he'd escaped slavery, unleashed a mob of townsfolk who drove off two boats and a ferry carrying arresting officials before the mayor coaxed them into acquiescing in the law.[126]

Since police and marshals were often those attacked, it is also unsurprising that arrests occurred in about half the incidents. Jail terms resulted in five cases: Philadelphia in 1835; the 1842 Latimer mob in Boston; the 1847 Carlisle mob, where slaveholder Kennedy was killed; the Wellington, Ohio, rescue of 1858; and Sherman Booth, in Milwaukee in 1854.[127] Sentences were short; no one served more than eight months. In most cases where blacks were found guilty—in Detroit in 1833, Buffalo in 1835, and Palmyra in 1850—they were simply fined, despite death or serious injury in each case. In Carlisle, Pennsylvania, eleven blacks were sentenced to three years, partly to appease Southern anger at the acquittal of the white man incorrectly alleged to be the mob leader. The Pennsylvania Supreme Court overturned their sentences after they had served eight months. Perhaps Syracuse officials miscalculated when they avoided trying Gerrit Smith, Charles

Wheaton, and Samuel May, all of whom proclaimed their involvement in a slave rescue there, to try a poor black, Enoch Reed, who was acquitted.[128] Juries commonly showed substantial sympathy or sense of extenuation when blacks rioted over such issues.

In two cases, civil suits required rioters to pay for the slaves they rescued: Brookville, Pennsylvania, in 1835 and South Bend, Indiana, in 1850. Even lost trials usually provided valuable publicity for abolitionists and blacks. The unselfishness of their motives and their courage won respect from even those angered by their actions, much as John Brown was to do by his death. In several cases slaveholders and slave-catchers also suffered jailings, for legal failings (alleged or real) in their procedures. Associate Judge Elijah Heath and Justice of the Peace J. M. Steed of Brookville, Pennsylvania, assured freedom to two fugitives by actively assisting an intimidating mob and by having the two Virginia slave-catchers briefly jailed for violation of Sunday travel laws.[129]

During the 1850s, legal maneuvering by fugitive slave rioters became more complex. In Boston old Judge Loring was almost impeached by the legislature for his use of the military to return Anthony Burns to slavery, and in Michigan a slaveholder was jailed for two years for his attempt to regain a slave. Perhaps most spectacular and ironic was the prolonged legal fight over the Sherman Booth case in Milwaukee, in which the Wisconsin Supreme Court briefly enunciated a doctrine of nullification to uniform abolitionist applause, and the South, with equal unanimity, lauded the subordination of state to federal judicial power. By this time, however, the great surprise was that a jury convicted Booth, despite indiscrete galloping through the streets to organize the mob that rescued Joshua Glover.[130]

The often perplexing interplay between courts, community, and various groups willing to indulge in violence was well illustrated in what occurred in Harrisburg in August 1850, when twelve men from Winchester, Virginia, ran down three slaves and had them taken to court for remanding. A group of whites and blacks convinced the court to release the slaves on a writ, with the judge rejecting the Virginians' plea that the escapees be kept in jail because they'd stolen horses as well as themselves. The judge explained to the Virginians that the horses were not stolen but appropriated for an escape, which was no crime in Pennsylvania. The Virginians tried to handcuff the slaves on leaving the court, which led to a mob attack. One slave escaped in the melee, but the Virginians held onto the other two, in part because a group of Irish laborers were attracted to the scuffle on the proslavery side. At least two blacks and one Virginian were injured before the judge had arrested the Virginians, the slaves, and a few of the slave protectors and had a posse disperse the Irish. When a second release led to a second scuffle, the judge repeated the arrests, this time letting the slaves leave first and keeping the Virginians, on grounds that they had used other than legal means to procure their slaves, until all danger of further fighting or of the reclamation of chattel was ended.[131]

A few Northern free blacks were also remanded or stolen into slavery. A threatened mob in Philadelphia foiled one such attempt, and the near-miracle of the return of New York black Solomon Northup to freedom after he was taken, drugged, sold, and kept a Louisiana slave for twelve years offers the best-documented case. Gangs of crooks specialized in this crime and never lacked safe market if they got their human loot south.[132] Legal protections for Northern free blacks, until the Fugitive Slave Law of 1850 largely erased them, entailed some delay between arrest and rendition which gave slave rescue mobs time to plan, organize, or at least congregate. In most cases, the mob's beneficiaries were certainly slaves, since riot was usually unnecessary to defend free blacks once public attention was directed to their plight.

After the promulgation of laws or legal opinions in Northern states freeing slaves brought voluntarily there, abolitionists could sometimes assist this process. Railroad officials blocked an attempt by Buffalo blacks to offer freedom to a slave traveling with her master in 1847, but other attempts were more successful. Some Garrisonian abolitionists in Salem, Ohio, were holding a convention when they received word that a couple from Tennessee was traveling with their twelve-year-old slave girl on a train to pass through Salem in about an hour. The abolitionists, thrilled by the chance to substitute action for abstraction, went to the depot with much of the town in sympathetic attendance. When the train stopped, Charles Burleigh and Henry Blackstone boarded, explained the law to the slaveholding couple, and asked the girl if she wished to be free. She did and was whisked off the train and to a meeting where speeches were made as prelude to the presentation of the black, surrounded by white girls her own age. Amid "thunderous applause" she was rechristened Abby Kelley Salem, in honor of the woman who had converted the town to abolition and the town which had handed her her freedom.[133]

The fugitive slave riots differed in that they used violence to effect their ends. Sometimes the degree of violence was slight—a quick thrust to get the slave out of the hands of the captors and then enough intimidation to let him or her escape. Yet the situation was always dangerous if authorities took seriously the guarding of their human goods. In the Jerry rescue in Syracuse, nonresistant Samuel May, along with Martin Stowell, took a leading role in devising the plot, which called for so many abolitionists to push into the room that the authorities would be made inactive. The idea worked, but one policeman got off one shot that wounded a rescuer, and another leaped out a window, breaking his leg. Meanwhile, Jerry made his escape through the massed bodies and into a waiting carriage. Knowing the roads from the city would be closely watched, plotters May and Gerrit Smith had the slave hidden in a home for several days until he could be smuggled out in comparative safety. A similar tactic in 1850 had freed Shadrach in Boston; lawyer Charles W. Davis, Elizur Wright, and many blacks cooperated in the effort.

The same tactics proved useless, however, for arrested slave Thomas Sims in Boston, so in 1854, when Anthony Burns was arrested, a more elaborate plan was developed. Martin Stowell, who'd been active in the Jerry affair, was imported to concoct the scheme. Thomas Wentworth Higginson was to lead five whites and Lewis Hayden ten blacks into the courthouse, while John L. Swift was to yell out in a Wendell Phillips meeting that blacks were rescuing Burns so that all could rush there and aid the escape by their presence without being legally responsible. The plan almost worked, but guards managed to get Burns into a room which could be barricaded—after Stowell had fatally shot guard William Batchelder. The abolitionists, so shocked at the similarly unintended murder of Lovejoy, showed little concern at the death of this man who had acted to uphold the legal system. He was simply a "hireling" of slavery.[134] The passionate quality of fugitive slave riots is clear in the death tolls. There were but two victims in all the Northern anti-abolition riots, but nine were killed in fugitive slave affairs—two officials, two rioters, two slave-holders, and three slaves.

In almost three-fourths of the slave rescue riots, blacks played a leading role; in a few they acted without, or with minimal, white support. For example, in the first of these rescue riots, those active were entirely Detroit blacks. Ruth and Thornton Blackburn, although they'd been Kentucky slaves two years earlier, were among the most respected of Detroit's black community. Their arrest caused a great stir, and their quick and superficial trial the next day deepened black anger. The Southerners who'd come to get the Blackburns asked the sheriff to turn them over on Saturday after the trial, but he refused. Sunday Mrs. Blackburn escaped by contrivance when Mrs. George French visited her and stayed behind in Mrs. Blackburn's clothes, while the slave walked away dressed as her friend.

The next day blacks, led by a one-armed barber named Cook, rioted when Black-burn was to be sent South, and after a struggle, in which one black was seriously hurt and Sheriff John Wilson badly mauled, Thornton made his way to Canada, where he became a successful businessman in Toronto. Several blacks were ar-rested, and in early July efforts were perhaps made to free them. At least this was the way whites interpreted an attempted firing of the jail on July 11 and the burning of a stable attached to it on July 15. A week and a half later Detroit mayor Marshall Chapin asked that United States troops be sent to protect the town, and Jacksonian Lewis Cass quickly dispatched them. The trials resulted in convictions for the blacks, but remarkably light sentences, given that Sheriff Wilson was so badly hurt that he never fully recovered and died within the year. A woman, Mrs. Lightfoot, was fined $25 as a leader, and the other six convicted were assessed $5 or less.[135] The mild chastisement for blacks who so openly attacked white authority suggests a degree of respect for the justice of these riotous acts that transcended the era's racism. The prominence of Mrs. French and Mrs. Lightfoot in the Detroit mob also suggest the generally greater role women played in black riots, as both leaders and participants.

Most of the post-1850 riots were more associated with prominent whites than blacks, largely because the whites—Thomas Higginson, Theodore Parker, Austin Bearce, Wendell Phillips, Samuel Gridley Howe, Samuel May, Gerrit Smith, Elizur Wright, Henry Stanton—were more socially, rather the riotously, prominent. There were always black leaders involved as well. William Nell and William Brown were active in the Buffalo rescue of 1835, Henry Tracy led the attempt to rescue Latimer in Boston in 1842, and Baptist minister J. W. Liquen in Syracuse and William Nell and Robert Smith in Boston were equals in the later planning there. The cooperation between whites and blacks was well illustrated in the Burns case, where the resisting guard was first stabbed by black leader Lewis Hayden and then shot dead by white leader Martin Stowell and where nine were arrested—five blacks and four whites— all to be released by legal technicalities, or "by the side door," as Higginson put it, to avoid the communal embarrassment of a trial. When action could be aided by a crowd, large numbers of now anonymous blacks always appeared, a tribute to African American moral commitment to their fellows less free than they.[136]

The best-known of black leaders of fugitive slave mobs was escaped slave

William Parker of Lancaster County, Pennsylvania. Because Parker published his version of his activities in the *Atlantic Monthly* in 1866 and because a major trial followed the incident, most is known about the black fugitive rescue mob of 1851 at Christiana in southern Pennsylvania, for which twenty-seven blacks and three whites were tried for treason. The rural area around Christiana, of easy access to Maryland runaways, offered fugitives work and some protection because of the large numbers of friendly blacks and whites, mostly Quakers and Presbyterians. Though most whites were "neutral" about slavery, most tolerated the escaped slaves, who worked hard and cheap. The Fugitive Slave Law, however, revived efforts of slaveholders to regain their chattel and strengthened both black and white resistance. Parker, who'd lived in the area since his escape from Maryland slavery in 1839, claimed to have set up a protective league among blacks in the early 1840s and reported an unsuccessful riot to rescue a captured fugitive about 1841.

It was only in the 1850s, however, that Parker's activities received enough attention to draw corroborating evidence. Slave-catchers took a woman named Elizabeth from the home of Quaker Moses Whitson, probably in 1850. The catchers' stop at a tavern gave Parker and a half-dozen confederates, informed by Benjamin Whipper of the abduction, a chance to catch up. Whipper followed the wagon on a highly visible white horse so that Parker and company knew what to attack when the wagon passed Gap-Hill. The woman escaped north, and the blacks beat the slave-catchers so brutally that, Parker reported, two and possibly three of them eventually died of their wounds. Parker also staged a barn-burning against a tavern-keeper who'd said he'd welcome slave-catchers, and attacked two blacks believed to be informers. One of the latter was badly beaten in "an appeal to the Lynch Code," and another had his house burnt down around him, although he escaped to a neighbor's rather than being shot to death when he ran out, as Parker had planned.[137]

Parker's final pièce de résistance attracted nationwide attention. Four slaves of Marylander Edward Gorsuch escaped in late 1849 and went to the Christiana area. An informer told Gorsuch where they were in August 1851, and the Methodist deacon, known as a kind master, decided to retrieve his property. With his son, cousin, nephew, and two neighbors, Gorsuch went to Philadelphia for the proper papers and there, joined by U.S. Marshal Henry Kline and two officers, took the train to Christiana. On the train was a black Philadelphian, Samuel Williams, going to inform blacks that the posse was on its way. Williams let the posse see him; quiet intimidation was more effective and less dangerous than violence as protective strategy. Kline's two men were frightened back to Philadelphia, leaving the Gorsuch party of six and a reluctant Kline to push on toward the warned fugitives. Kline's lack of enthusiasm kept the party from acting as originally planned on Wednesday, September 10, and during that day Williams's warning circulated among the black community. William Parker's narrative suggests that Wednesday night two of the fugitives came to his house, where a decision was made to hide or fight rather than to leave.

What's known suggests a more probable interpretation: the blacks thought the posse had already been intimidated and had left. At dawn on September 11, at any rate, one of the fugitives, Joshua Kite, went from Parker's house off toward work, singing. When he saw the posse turn into the lane, he ran back to the house to give the warning to the other blacks, still sleeping upstairs. Kline and Gorsuch entered the house, and the slaveholder told his fugitives that they wouldn't be punished if they returned with him peaceably. From the second floor the blacks replied by throwing things at the men in the yard, staggering both nephew Dr. Thomas Pierce and cousin Joshua Gorsuch. Kline then announced his official position and threatened to come upstairs; Edward Gorsuch started to go up but retreated when the blacks threw an ax and a pronged fish spear at him. Gorsuch moved out of range, and Kline read the warrant, before both retreated to the yard. A shot was fired, each side claiming the other fired first. Parker described elaborate conversations in which he and Gorsuch debated scripture and the blacks sang a hymn to embarrass the good Methodist deacon:

Leader, what do you say
About the judgement day?
I will die on the field of battle.
  Die on the field of battle,
With glory in my soul.

At any rate, a couple of hours passed, probably in less symbolic intellectual combat than Parker reported. The odds were fairly even, seven whites against seven blacks, two of the latter women. The blacks were in a stone house, as good as a fort against bullets, and the whites had no way of effectively acting against them. Kline, seeing no profit in battle, wanted to leave, but Gorsuch probably thought time was on his side. If Parker's account of what happened on the second floor is true, Gorsuch was right: Parker was already having trouble controlling some of his small band, including his brother and sister-in-law, who wished to give up.

At that juncture help came, not for the posse but for the blacks. Black Isaiah Clarkson had seen the posse when it first arrived. He'd quickly gone to warn white Quakers Elijah Lewis and Joseph Scarlett, who then began to call together others, including Castner Hanway, a white miller. Hanway went to Parker's place, doubtless to spy out the situation and to proclaim the nearby aid. His appearance with a large number of armed blacks changed the attitude of Parker's group from wavering to spirited defiance. Kline requested aid from Hanway, who warned him that he'd better leave quickly or blood would be shed. Kline thought leaving was a very good idea, but Gorsuch went toward the house. The blacks attacked and Gorsuch was killed, possibly "finished off by the women," as Parker said, although the coroner's report recorded no signs of the multiple wounds Parker's account implied. Gorsuch's son tried to help, but was badly wounded himself; the cousin and nephew, slow to run off, suffered some minor buckshot wounds. Hanway reportedly protected the two relatives from being killed when they fled; the Quakers saw that Gorsuch's son was well cared for until he recovered.

Those blacks most obviously involved in the attack—Parker, the males in his house, the other Gorsuch fugitives, and two blacks who were wounded—left for Canada that night. Parker was hidden in upstate New York by fellow Maryland fugitive Frederick Douglass, whom he'd once heard speak, until Douglass could put him on a boat for Canada.

There seems little question that whites and blacks worked together in the Christiana escape, but it's also probable that there was a difference in strategy between the blacks inside and the whites and blacks out. What Hanway and the "outsiders" tried to do was what Samuel Williams attempted earlier: to intimidate the party into leaving. Lewis pretended that he acted only until he found out it was not an illegal kidnapping, and Hanway pretended to be just observing. Yet what they did was calculated to drive the slave party away and would have worked had Gorsuch not been so determined. It probably also would have worked had not Parker, seeing the numbers and arms suddenly turn in his favor, determined to attack Gorsuch's group as Kline and others were leaving. Parker reported dramatically turning down Kline's offer of peaceful withdrawal: "I told him it was too late. You would not withdraw when you had the chance,—you shall not now." The dialogue seems improbable given Kline's quite successful retreat, which hardly required Parker's permission, but it suggests Parker's attitudes.

The violence was probably a mistake. Because of it, blacks were rounded up wholesale in the area, and possibly as many as six of them were remanded to slavery, including the mother of Parker's wife. Parker's wife and sister-in-law were left behind to be arrested and were released only because the prosecution decided it would injure their case to include women among their "traitors." Two others escaped only because Marshal Anthony Roberts let them disappear when they were identified as slaves. Some thirty-two blacks—twenty-seven defendants and five witnesses—and three white defendants spent several winter months in the Philadelphia jail. Potentially even more harmful to his friends, Parker in his haste left behind a large packet of letters from other fugitives and resisters that might have done much damage had not Quaker Levi Pownell found and burnt it.[138]

Just as Parker's violence was both understandable and probably unwise, so was the reaction in the South. Blacks had murdered a white Southerner acting wholly legally, with the white North figuratively looking on. The South saw treason, and to pacify the region, Hanway and the rest were tried for this crime; Maryland attorney general William Brent was imported to direct the case. And gradually, as black leader William Still made clear, the hostility against black violence was shifted toward anger at Southern interference, while respect grew for the dignity and courage of those on trial, very ably defended by old abolitionists David Paul Brown and political leader Thaddeus Stevens. Increasingly, Northerners agreed with the explanation Hanway gave his wife from jail: "I do not regret my course; I simply did my duty." Certainly it was hard for Americans to deny the conclusion of the Boston *Christian Register* that Parker did simply "what any white man would be applauded for doing."[139] It was another in the long series of events in which North and South defined duty oppositely and showed progressively weakening regret at the violence their "duty" entailed.

These spectacular cases featuring mobs, violence, and death or injury were atypical. The few fugitives mob-saved were a fragment of the at least 191 blacks, over 82 percent of the cases that arose under the Fugitive Slave Law, who were returned to a life of slavery. They were even a smaller fraction of some thousands who remained free because large numbers of people acted illegally or intimidatingly to aid blacks fleeing. Yet when federal officials and magistrates got their hands on blacks, they served their slave-masters faithfully. Such was the nation's racism and legalistic unionism that in most cases that came to federal courts, nothing was done to protect blacks, and the North by and large did its duty to the South by watching the return of men, women, and children to their proper legal status as chattel.[140] Yet for Northerners to see slaves so humanly, and to see their section's role in mocking such moving aspirations to liberty, was to glimpse their own abolition.

Margaret Garner provided human dimension to these black people who had risked everything to be free only to have that dream crushed. When she, her husband, his parents, and her four children were captured in Ohio after putting up substantial resistance in which an arresting officer was seriously wounded, Garner managed to free one of the party. She fatally slashed the throat of her daughter but failed in her attempt to kill two sons and herself, for whom she preferred death to slavery. A sympathetic crowd let state officials act, and state officials, also sympathetic, accepted federal orders to take them back to their old Kentucky slave home. And their owner sold them down the river to avoid Ohio antislavery Governor Salmon P. Chase's one legal means of offering help: issuing a murder warrant for Margaret Garner. "Such things may be expected," Ohioan Joseph Osborne noted in his diary, "while this horrible system of Wrong is continued in our country."[141]

Despite common Northern acquiescence in the fugitive slave law, it was the uncommon dramatic incidents of resistance that drew people's attention and that created growing sense of disgust with the South's demands that the North sacrifice its principles and use its resources for active support of federal imposition of the planter's right to profit. Hence, there was political accuracy, as well as factual falsity, in the perception, North and South, that the Fugitive Slave Act failed miserably.

There was no major revolution in abolitionist or Northern thought on violence in the 1850s, but there was intensification of extenuation, toleration, and even pride in its use. As early as 1833 a black Detroit mob received little punishment when they badly beat up a sheriff to rescue a slave; in Burlington, New Jersey, and Albany in 1835–36, white mobs quite spontaneously turned to violent action, in one case when an old black resident was threatened, and in the other when a crowd saw a strange black dragged in chains through Albany streets. In all cases the communities were certainly racist and agreed that slavery was the South's business. Yet even in these virulently pro-Southern months, Northerners were sometimes willing to use violence rather than acquiesce in the acts of slave-catchers. By the 1850s the South had dwindling reservoirs of patience and goodwill to draw on in the North; Joseph Sill's Philadelphia diary reports the strong public joy—and anger—felt over the results of quieter fugitive cases there.[142] During the 1850s events forced more Northerners to think about their relation to slavery and pushed them toward conclusions that duplicated—if often palely—the positions of abolitionists for decades: slavery was contradictory to the nation's basic political and moral truisms, and at the very least, Northerners should avoid positive aid to the extension of "the horrible system of Wrong" over territories or individuals.

Harpers Ferry shocked the nation, partly because it marked a new phase of violence and partly because it was obviously a continuation of the line of argument abolitionists and more reluctantly their section had been slowly accepting. Abolitionists had long praised the slave rescue attempts of Harriet Tubman and Jonathan Walker and Charles Torrey and Daniel Drayton and Seth Concklin, had stimulated and plotted fugitive slave mobs, and had shown no qualms about the master John

Brown's men killed in Missouri or the guard Boston's vigilance committee had slaughtered there. Suddenly these people found these principles dramatized in a way which gave them pause but which they couldn't repudiate. And the majority in the North, as they often had when abolition was put in movingly personal terms, were moved toward support rather than alienation. In a real sense Harpers Ferry was dramatic counterpart to the Fugitive Slave Law and the *Dred Scott* decision. Riot, statute, and legal ruling all argued in effect that slavery was a concern of Northerners too, and all underlined how untenable was the moderate hope that the North need neither support nor reject slavery but could simply stand clear of it.

The "abolitionists hatched" by a few speakers' numerous eggings of a quarter century before were moving toward their goal, as "events," in accord with Weld's prediction, convinced millions of the position that James Thome and John Alvord had worked so hard to induce a handful to accept in Ohio in 1835. And this time the stove really was cracking.

PART II

The South

Asserting Mastery, Terrorizing Doubt

Memory believes before knowing remembers. Believes longer than recollects, longer than knowing even wonders.

—William Faulkner, *Light in August*

The [slaveholder's] creed . . . is reiterated all the oftener and more loudly from a lurking doubt of its perfect truth. The slave owner defends his position ostensibly against the Abolitionist, but in reality against his inner self.

—James Stirling, *Letters from the Slave States*

When truth and justice are more than hollow words, the idea of honor is such as to exclude all fear, except of wrong-doing. Where the honor is to be derived from present human opinion, there must be fear, ever present, and perpetually exciting to or withholding from action. . . . I doubt whether they can even conceive of a state of society, of its ease and comfort, where no man fears his neighbor, and it is no evil to be responsible for one's opinions.

—Harriet Martineau, *Society in America*

      And plunged them down
Straight into his own eyeballs, crying, "No more,
No more shall you look on the misery about me,
The horrors of my own doing. . . .
From this hour, go in darkness!" And as he spoke,
He struck at his eyes—not once, but many times;
And the blood spattered his beard,
Bursting from his ruined sockets like red hail.

      —Sophocles, *Oedipus Rex*

CHAPTER THREE

The Peculiar Institution of Southern Violence

The whole commerce between master and slave is a perpetual exercise of the most boisterous passions, the most unremitting despotism on the one part, and degrading submissions on the other. Our children see this and learn to imitate it. . . . The parent storms, the child looks on, catches the lineaments of wrath, puts on the same airs in the circle of smaller slaves, gives a loose to his worst of passions, and thus nursed, educated and daily exercised in tyranny, cannot but be stamped by it with odious peculiarities.

—Thomas Jefferson, *Notes on Virginia*

His insulting language and manner came not from the heart, but from the head. They were part of his system, a method of controlling society as he controlled his Negroes.
—Henry Adams, *John Randolph*

"I don't like that shooting from behind a bush. Why didn't you step into the road, my boy?"
"The Shepherdsons don't, Father. They always take advantage."
—Mark Twain, *The Adventures of Huckleberry Finn*

A young lawyer from Cincinnati, William Hauser, wrote his cousin, Julia Conrad, as soon as he arrived in Helena, Arkansas, in 1841. He had high hopes that he could establish his legal career quickly in the South, and he didn't want Conrad to worry about him just because she'd probably read that a mob had recently drowned fifty to seventy-five "gamblers" in the area. He lectured that it was "such exaggerated accounts" that gave the South "a more abominable complexion" than it deserved: "In this instance I have been assured from the best authority there were not more than thirty men shot or otherwise killed." Hauser didn't mail the letter immediately, hoping to provide more precise details about where he was settling. Eight days later he added a postscript from Mills Point, Kentucky, having concluded, "I would have to sacrifice everything and endanger life to live" in Arkansas.[1] He was on his way home to Ohio.

The Southern violence that drove the young man so quickly northward relates to the central dilemma of antebellum history, bounded as it is by the vastly heavier bloodshed that ended it. To what degree and in what ways did the South differ from the North? And why was the American political structure unable to reconcile, finesse, or forget these differences, as it has all others, without civil war or political fragmentation? The many answers that have been given—distinct economic, constitutional, political, social, moral, or ideological stances—all take shape in the shadow of slavery, the central variation obvious to everyone then and now.

Patterns of social violence, too, varied between North and South, although in a broad context of regional sharing. The numbers of incidents and deaths in social violence were roughly equal in the two sections in proportion to their population. And, with the exception of insurrection scares, there was no kind of violence of which there were not incidents in both regions. The most telling difference came in the situation of those who died in riots. In the North, most of those killed were rioting when authorities acted against them. The South's body count consisted very predominantly of mob victims, killed in situations where authorities rarely acted. In broad outline, Northern officials moved against mobs, often tentatively and usually reluctantly, but with enough frequency and vigor to create substantial costs for rioting. In the South, social violence of most kinds was only rarely repressed or punished, so it became a tolerated, even a sanctioned mode of social control. In addition, Northern criminals and mobs tended to endanger property rather than injure people, while prototypical Southern rioters, like their counterparts in crime, attacked persons more than property. Southern mobs were much likelier to be murderous in intent and/or sadistic in mode than were their Northern counterparts. In these crucial ways, the communal boundaries, or definitions, of what was tolerable mobbing diverged greatly between the North and South.

Southern mob violence was related to distinctive patterns of personal antagonism. The duel, although probably the least common and destructive mode of extralegal injury in the Old South, has drawn most attention because it fits most comfortably the favored image of the antebellum Southerner as a bit irascible but bravely dedicated to the highest standards of honor.[2] Clement Eaton and John Hope Franklin did most to rescue the subject of Southern violence from what amounted to this gentlemanly glorification.[3] Recent studies have, in a sense, circled back to folkish justification: southern violence was the product of a distinct code of honor, now capable of considerable nastiness, but in the service of communal and familial protection. In essence, the recent kettle of Southern violence features a dash of bloodily Celtic or Sicilian spice in the older Sir Walter Scott romantic stew.[4] This study tries to weave the complicated strands of Southern personal/social extralegal violence together into a fuller tapestry of meaning for both this slave society and the nation's sectional fraying.

All varieties of sources for the antebellum South are redolent with violence. Random newspapers revealed eighteen violent deaths in a single week in 1835 in Arkansas, fifteen deaths by violence in a two-month period in a sparsely settled area around Grand Gulf, Mississippi, and a tally of twelve murders in a week in 1837 New Orleans. Twenty years later a Louisiana attorney general's report argued that only a small part of the same city's violent crime was handled judicially, although the present pending cases in the city of about 116,000 entailed twelve for murder, three for manslaughter, sixteen for attempted murder, and fifty-two for assault with a deadly weapon or with intent to kill.[5]

Personal writings even more sharply attest the everyday quality of Southern violence. The Rev. William Winans, a Methodist leader returning to Mississippi after a two-month stay in the North, wrote in 1836, "Many violent deaths and some by disease occurred in the circle of my acquaintance during my absence from the country." Only in the antebellum South could a clergyman return after a visit to find his acquaintances decimated a bit by disease but substantially by violence. Winans understood that the mayhem was grounded in social refusal to punish such crimes which "licences the vicious and the violent to act upon the suggestion of their passions." Less analytical was the lament of a Kentucky slave owner in 1847: "What does not die naturaly or is not kild in Mexico is kild here at home."[6]

Other Southerners reported public violence without such sense of distress. A Mississippi doctor described two such events in his neighborhood in late 1859. Two colleagues, Dr. Fullerton and Dr. Reynolds, drew weapons in the street after trading epithets of "liar" in a quarrel originating when Reynolds opined that Fullerton had bungled a case. Reynolds, getting his knife first, stabbed his enemy three times before turning him loose when Fullerton begged for mercy. Fullerton went about ten steps, turned, and "very deliberately pulled out a colt and commenced firing at R approaching R all the time until he fired the last and fifth time the pistol was almost in contact with R, who was just then sinking to the ground from the severe wounds in his body. R, who stood unarmed and unresisting, eyeing his adversary, made one remark which was—'You d—d coward, you are shooting me after I have spared you.'" The letter's next paragraph presented an almost equally grotesque, if less tragic, incident that occurred "the same day" in the tiny hamlet of Raymond. Joe Gray, an ex-mayor, put two bullets into Tom Ford at a distance of three feet. "One ball took effect just below F's eye and the other struck him on the forehead and glanced off." Both Ford and the letter writer took all this calmly: "Ford says Gray was too stingy to put enough powder in his pistol or he (F) would have been a goner. This I think closes the fights and exhausts my stock of news."[7] For that day, anyway.

Southern casualness about violence gives a macabrely humorous edge to many of these accounts. Amelia A. Boswell wrote from Eldorado, Arkansas, to her "Cousin Lizzy" in Pike County, Alabama, urging her family to join them: "The land is better and then the society is as good as is to be found in almost iny part of Georgia, being composed mostly of Georgians." She went on to local events: "Rogers that killed that man in your country is here at uncle Elisha's." Boswell inquired if there was a reward on Rogers because Dave might capture him—if there was a reward. "Tell all the children howdye," Amelia closed. A young South Carolina girl, Mary Hart, in 1847 noted that a crazed schoolteacher named Backus stabbed a Mr. DuBose (who had assumed his position at Darlington Academy) while the latter strolled down a road. Hart concluded the diary entry cheerily, "It was a splendid spring day." And in 1842, forty-seven voters of Orange County, North Carolina, asked the governor to pardon James Hicks, convicted of "biting off the ear of Samuel Hudson." After all, Hicks's family needed his support, and besides, the petitioners argued, "his case was not an aggravated one." R. R. Rose in Texas wrote his brother "about the fus between Wiley Ingram and Carivele," which "commenced about a peas of land." "They were both killed on the ground they fell in five feet of each other they have not forgot how to fight in harrison County yet," Rose concluded, proudly noting that Marshall had some deadly conflict "every week or two."[8]

The comments of perpetrators or supporters of violence were even more uniformly filled with prideful enjoyment. Virginian James L. Stirling wrote his brother about their friend John McDermott's having killed old James M. Bradford. "He sent the poor old fellow to the other country," Stirling wittily reported, "both drunk and with a pain in his belly, that being the place where John's knife made acquaintance." Stirling was also delighted that everyone pretended the murder was "an unhappy accidental circumstance." New Orleans editor J. C. de St. Romes illustrated well the crowing braggadocio style of most winners in his account of his "rencontre" with fellow editor John Gibson. De St. Romes claimed that Gibson struck him from behind when he was peacefully watching a backgammon game in a tavern. He soon got Gibson down on a gambling table and began strangling him, "but seeing the rascal would not give up his soul, I let my right hand loose to take up my pen knife and open his guts, but I had left my pen knife at home." Taking his opponent's dagger, de St. Romes "made some effort to nail the coward to the table where I had carried him, but, as I was going to execute this meritorious act, I was torn from a prey that could no longer escape, by a crowd of friends and enemies." Proud of his near "nailing," de St. Romes worried only that the public remember his many other "affairs of honor" and not misinterpret his promise to seek only legal satisfaction from Gibson.[9]

Like riots, most Southern personal violence was done openly in a situation of assumed moral clarity and with expectation of communal and legal tolerance. The commonest explanations of this pattern of public murder have referred to traditions of the frontier, or of chivalry and honor. Yet there are difficulties with such answers. Most of the violence occurred not on the frontier but in long-established areas. Incidents happened about as often in Virginia and Charleston and New Orleans as in Arkansas or Texas. James Norman Smith's amusing autobiography covers the ups and downs of his troubled role as "peacemaker" in Texas in the 1840s, but he records no more violent incidents than did Andrew Schirmer in his journal of life in Charleston, South Carolina, where apparently no one played peacemaker, or black barber William Johnson's account of Mississippi's urban center, Natchez. A frontier environment may have accentuated public killings, but they remained a regular part of slave-state life long after the frontier passed.

Johnson's careful diary of his adult years in Natchez, 1835–51, offers a good résumé of the patterns of Southern violence in one locale. Johnson chronicled 2 small riots in which no one died; 4 duels in which two deaths and two minor injuries occurred; and 128 brawls, affrays, and public murders that took at least eleven lives and left nineteen men permanently or badly injured. The causes mentioned were almost always political or economic, and the latter by far predominated. The three duels where cause is clear involved "a barrel of oysters," "cattle," and a financial judgment in a legal case where the losing disputant challenged and then killed the judge who ruled against him. Typical of the fatal brawls was one where "something about a 20 ct. hat was the origin of the fuss." Johnson knew how little a code of honor had to do with it, and that the system worked to prove "Whatever is, is right"—or whoever won. Johnson didn't live to record the public murder that ended his account. Baylor Winn, a fellow free black, in partnership with a white banker, had been stealing logs from Johnson's land. When court action threatened such profitable theft, Winn turned to the South's extralegal system and killed Johnson from ambush. Winn, like almost all these killers, suffered no legal punishment for this public murder that rounded out Johnson's catalogue of Southern honor.[10]

Though Johnson's proportion of affrays to duels reflected general realities, the duel was the most discussed form of public murder and the one Southerners most vigorously tied to honor.[11] One can see both the trappings of honor and the personal motives in duels such as the famous one between Richmond editors John H. Pleasants, fifty-five, and much younger Thomas Ritchie Jr. The rhetoric followed the expected name-calling formula: Ritchie called Pleasants an "abolitionist" and "a rank coward," and Pleasants replied, "Liar."

This duel was not, like several Washington ones, a pro forma affair staged to impress constituents but one of personal fury. When three shots led only to a minor wound for Pleasants, the duelists turned to swords. Ritchie plunged his into the abdomen of the much older Pleasants, who fell senseless and died two days later.[12] No one thought that this result proved Pleasants an abolitionist, much less a coward, or made Ritchie any less gross a liar, about these issues anyway. Yet it clearly was "vindication" of Ritchie's right to label anyone abolitionist, something young Southern Democrats were increasingly prone to do against old Whigs they judged insufficiently enthusiastic about slavery's virtues and expansion. Both men, watching the disintegration of the two parties they had seen as offering true protection to both Southern and national interests, accepted escape from the irritated sparring and half-deceptions of partisan editing to the comforting mythic moral simplicities of violence's realm.

This affair suggests the problem with seeing duels and other public violence as the mark of a society with higher standards than those of "trading" regions, or as a means by which the virtuously strong protected the weak, or which insured, in Benjamin Perry's words, "a greater courtesy in society and a higher refinement."[13] Honor was usually invoked, but there is little evidence of its ties to any code of behavior beyond formulaic invocation of certain terms when violence was deemed the best way to win a dubious argument. The system in fact sanctioned the "rights" of those who wished to be abusive, while intimidating more decent people who might want to be honest or fair. Southerners like Perry and Robert E. Lee never resorted to the extralegal system because they were secure, civil, nonirritable, self-controlled.

Perhaps sometimes the epithets that usually decorated duels were causative. Nathan Warren had a case when he asked a Mississippi governor to remit a $50 fine "for fitting a sertain man by the name of Jas. Ramsey after caling me a dam liar three times repeatedly which is two much for any man to take that stands fare in his Contry." Yet "liar," "cheat," and "coward" were less charges than code words anyone could invoke who determined to escape the uncertainties of the everyday world for the dangerous excitement of extralegal absolutes. A Texan shrewdly described the common situation in his report on an upcoming duel between two editors. "Some reflections of Marshall's on the private character of Norton is the cause immediate of the trouble, and politics the cause remote." The challenge occurred at a time when "politics run pretty high with us"—and when Marshall began to fear that the votes would not vindicate his position. In hard situations, Southern men knew they could resort to personal violence, as one glorifier of the duel put it, to "reap whatever eclat is derivable."[14]

Harriet Martineau was dead right that Southern honor depended centrally on "present human opinion," so that violence served less any communal code than a system of individual winning by intimidation. The South's semisanctioned public murders provided a court of appeal usually for petty or mean self-assertion based largely on "fear, ever present, and perpetually exciting to or withholding from action." William Lowndes Yancey admitted as much in a letter to Alabama Baptists bothered by his bouts of violence. "Laws which public opinion had formed," he said, forced men to set at naught all obligations to God, state, and family.

Certainly Yancey had some expertise in the field. In his best known "rencontre," a seventeen-year-old boy at militia drill reprimanded Yancey—possibly called him "a damned liar"—for Yancey's calling General Whitner a "blackguard." Yancey slapped the boy but later heard that the lad and his father, Dr. Robert Earl, were in town "with clubs." Yancey claimed that when he met the doctor on a Charleston street, Earl called him liar, refused a duel, and came at him with a cudgel. Others saw the two men arguing, then saw Yancey draw a gun against the unarmed Earl, shoot him through the chest, and hit the fallen man on the head with a pistol until that broke before ramming him through with a sword cane. Yancey was arrested but was let go, probably because, as he said, of the support of "the public," which in the South was almost always sympathetic to winners. In jail, Yancey gloated to a relative: "He who grossly insulted me lies now with the clod upon his bosom. . . . If not so passionate, I might have used a cane only and been beaten. As it is the blood of the only man who ever called me a 'd—d liar' is now, unwashed, upon your stick. And there let it remain, a legacy to my son, and a warning to others who feel like browbeating a Yancey."[15] This relic did act as a warning, letting others know that Yancey had earned some license to blackguard whom he pleased and that others needed to be cautious in doing the same to him, or in being the fathers of lads who may have. In Southern politics no license was more valuable.

Yancey's most famous duel occurred in 1845 with fellow U.S. congressman Thomas Clingman over a debate that revolved around who was the truest Southerner. It was one of the de rigueur affairs, fought almost exclusively by politicians, in which many notes circulated before the two men helped to insure each others' political prominence by missing. The duel commonly served such practical ends as gaining political clout, avoiding paying bills, winning property, eliminating rivals, settling court cases one was losing, silencing opinions one couldn't refute. Despite the feudal gloss put on dueling by its enamored chroniclers, it was in the Anglo-American world an institution that gained popularity in the eighteenth century, one perfectly suited to an embarrassedly bourgeois world, where the comforting rhetoric of heroic disinterestedness was well integrated with the reality of calculated advantage. The various "guides" to duelling amusingly paralleled the raft of etiquette books bourgeois society required: minute behavioral instructions to assure the insecure that their action would be, in one of their favorite words, "high-toned." One dueler's manual was remarkably similar, in its detailed correspondence guide, to those helpful handbooks published to teach the aspiring acceptable modes of composing business or personal letters. It thoughtfully included a survey of properly impressive gestures for the dueling ground as other books catalogued them for the parlor or lectern.[16]

While duels at least had rules, a striking feature of most affrays was the unconcern for much semblance of fairness. Yancey explained, with perfect self-righteousness, that he could have fought Earl with a weapon equivalent to the doctor's, but then he might have "been beaten," so why take risks when you could safely shoot the man and beat and stab him to death after he'd fallen? Yancey's well-calculated passion, de St. Romes's disappointment at being prevented from nailing his helpless opponent, Dr. Fullerton's cold-blooded killing of his professional rival who had just spared his life were, in general mood, typical. Numerous instances were even more savage. A Dr. Emory first seduced the daughter of a patient, James De Baun Sr., and, when the latter publicly threatened to kill him, murdered from ambush both the father and brother of the girl, leaving without support the widow and five daughters, the one pregnant with his child. In Georgia, a man named King, furious when he learned his daughter had eloped with a Casey boy, went with his sons and killed old Mr. and Mrs. Casey, at the same time managing to kill one passerby and to wound two others.[17]

In cases like the latter two, the murderers were commonly expected to leave the area or submit to arrest, but they were seldom pursued by the law. Dr. Emory had been publicly threatened; King, in his own eyes, had been publicly injured; and such paltry excuses usually palsied Southern justice. Even communal exile was unnecessary if the murderer was very prominent, if there was a semblance of a fair fight, if the victor was clearly not the party who started the public affray, or if liquor was labeled "cause" of the trouble. Then the murderer could turn himself over to the authorities and await legal acquittal or minimal fine as gesture to legality.

When Col. John Milton was acquitted of shooting Joseph T. Camp dead without warning—pumping a second shot into him as he lay bleeding from the first—there was some dissent, because there was no evidence for Milton's excuse that Camp had threatened him. The *Milledgeville Federal Union* complained that such verdicts meant "assassination is legalized." Perhaps as significant was the editor's assumption that the killing was all right if any prior threat had occurred. When Louisianan Tom Chaney "killed old Mr. Coursey's son"—"he slipped up behind him when he was eating his supper and struck him dead"—Chaney had to take his negroes and leave the area since there wasn't "any cause for killing him, only that of Tom's being drunk." When public official William Tripsett stabbed to death constable Robert Frail, the local *Little Rock Gazette* quaintly reported that, since there had been no provocation, "it was hoped and presumed" that the killer "was laboring under an aberration of the mind at the time."[18] Such hopes and presumption sprang eternal in the South.

Acts of Southern public violence which drew little or no official response provide a stomach-churning catalog of butchery. In Georgia, a gambler first bit off the nose of a policeman and then attacked the editor of the *Augusta Chronicle* for his failure to appreciate the earlier deed. An Alabaman shot dead a poor man moving west with his wife, children, and a small flock of sheep, when the traveler mildly complained of the man's repeatedly riding through his flock. In Vicksburg, Mississippi, one assailant, after a fist fight was broken up, fruitlessly tried to catch his opponent and then out of frustration beat and stabbed, possibly fatally, an "inoffensive German." In nearby Jackson, one Captain Flack, claiming Hugh Roark had threatened him, attacked Roark in bed, stabbing him twice, first in the back and then in the abdomen, "letting out his bowels." In Louisiana, Dr. Joseph P. Hawkins pretended to make up his quarrel with an actor, drank a toast with him to reconciliation, and then literally stabbed him in the back. The editor of the *Hagerstown* (Md.) *Courier and Inquirer* reported the "gouging out of my right eye" by one Charles Macquill, who took exception to his political views. In Tennessee, four Jones brothers—Lafayette, Chamberlayne, Caesar, and Achilles—went to the house of relative Col. A. G. Ward in a familial-financial dispute and threw him a gun to make it a "fair fight" before shooting and stabbing him, then trampling his body.[19]

Such incidents suggest how sneak attack, attack from ambush, attack on the unarmed or even the sleeping, attack on one by several did little to detract from the honor of these public maulings or murders. When James M. Smith decided to chastise a Virginia editor, he took along Marcellus Bell to hold a gun on everyone else who might interfere with his beating Thomas Terry insensible with a cane. Bell used the gun to wound George White, who responded to a constable's request that something be done to save Terry's life. Philadelphia-born Dr. James Hagan fought a number of brawls and duels as editor of the *Vicksburg Sentinel* before, sickened or maybe just tired by the battles and blood, he announced that he would no longer fight or go armed. Encouraged by this announcement, a young Southern gentleman gunned him down on the street and submitted to the favorite Southern legal action in such cases, a quick acquittal.[20]

Nor did third-party victims in these affairs arouse much criticism, either the few George Whites who tried to interfere out of a sense of fairness or feistiness or humane concern or civic responsibility, or those who merely watched. In a duel between Louisville editors George D. Prentice and Reuben T. Durrett, the men not only hit each other several times but also hit bystander George D. Hinkle. In an affray at Chuckatuck, Virginia, the two parties were both killed, but so was a free black observer. Vicksburg celebrated Christmas (five months after vigilantes announced they'd purified the community with an impressive mass murder) with at least two tragedies. A traveler recorded, "Last night, at a drinking house, two men fought with knives. A third attempted to part them and got stabbed. One of them is dead, and another is in danger." The next morning, the traveler saw "a horrible spectacle. A man had been shot in the street last night and was still lying exposed at breakfast time. There was a bullet in the center of his breast and three buckshot near the heart. He was shot by his cousin, Tom Thatcher, because he would not give up a dirk that he wore with which he wished to attack another man."[21] Southern peacekeeping took strange and tragic forms.

Even the presence of women didn't prevent violence. One letter writer, describing a prebreakfast affray with gunshots and bludgeoning, was amused that the ladies were somewhat upset, although there was "no serious damage." In Mississippi two men fought with knives and buckshot at a hotel dinner table, fatally for a nonparticipant. This inspired the Massachusetts *New Bedford Gazette* to create a Southern dinner conversation:

> Mr. Snooks, I'll trouble you for a slice of that beef.
>
> No trouble at all, sir, but excuse me until I shoot the doctor who is sitting at the head of the table. (Fires and blows a stranger's brains out.) Oh, bless my soul; pardon me, my good friend, I beg you won't mind my awkwardness—that bullet was intended for the doctor not you; but *n' importe*. Boy, a glass of brandy.

Yet heavy satire is hardly so amusing as the etiquette lesson drawn from the incident by the editor who reported it: "Street fights meet with due disapprobation, but a fight

at dinner table with pistols charged with buckshot and split bullets is unpardonable."[22] It seemed, however, a matter of manners, not murder.

Cases about which most is known best illustrate the function of this public violence
and cast the most doubt on the common justificatory explanations of it in terms of the
frontier, of the lower-class origins of its brutal aspects, or of a code protective of the
South's communal and family values.[23] Robert Potter and Thomas B. Chaplin were
both Carolinians who lived in areas long settled, and both were slave owners of
substantial wealth or prominence in their communities. And both moved into the
realm of extralegal violence out of pique, frustration, or calculation grounded wholly
in service of self.

Potter was a North Carolina congressman when he began his spectacular career in
public mayhem by castrating two Methodists, Lewis K. Willie and Rev. William
Lewis Taylor, alleging adulterous relations with his wife. In fact, he had determined
to marry a wealthy woman, and he acted to discredit his wife so he could divorce
her. His plot failed when his ulterior motive was revealed and when his victims and
wife convincingly denied the charges. Potter went to jail very briefly. Yet so little did
this gross brutality, intended to dishonor a wife so he could marry more money,
bother his constituents that Potter was elected to the state legislature immediately on
release. Ejected for the more serious crime of reneging on a gambling debt to a fellow lawmaker, Potter went to Texas, where he successfully resumed his career of
politics and violence until violence ended it.[24]

South Carolinian Thomas Chaplin revealed a more ordinary case of public violence in his diary account of his hassles with planter neighbor J. R. Toomer. "Rode
up to demand apology for some scandalous talk he had taken the liberty to make use
of towards me. The fellow hesitated rather long for my patience to endure so I
merely gave him a genteel flogging with a small cane. Made him beg like a negro,
swearing he would not prosecute or do anything else if I would let him go." As
Chaplin drove off, Toomer shot at him, "but did no more harm than putting one shot
in the horse and shooting off the hat of my boy John." Three days later, Chaplin
noted: "Saw my friend J. R. Toomer who looks as though he had been pretty severely handled by someone—I wonder who it was? . . . I suspected he intended to
indite me for assault and battery, and sure enough it was so. But the affidavit was not
properly drawn so he could not compel me to keep the peace, as he wished to do, *the
infernal coward.*"[25]

Worth noting in Chaplin's account is the integration of the systems of legality and
of violence. Chaplin forced Toomer to promise not to sue him and took great pleasure
in the procedural mistake that prevented his being ordered to keep the peace.
Toomer's resort to law occurred only after his shots missed their target, merely injuring a horse and nearly killing a slave. Second, Toomer's crime was that of telling the
truth. He'd simply said that Chaplin had lived very high on borrowed money, a charge
Chaplin often repeated himself in his diary during the preceding months. Toomer's
"scandalous talk," his "lies," were in fact what the whole community knew to be truth.
Chaplin wanted not to hear an explanation from Toomer but to chastise him quickly to
transform sordid truth into violent vindication. What people dared say somehow was
what was true, while the public testimony of Toomer's bruises somehow showed
Chaplin's mastery, as did Toomer's begging "like a negro." A week earlier Chaplin

mentioned the pleas of his slaves whom he was selling for debt; the images and structure of his account suggests how his discomfort over this transaction contributed to
his illusion of just mastery over Toomer. Before moving on to his central concern,
self-pity, Chaplin noted the sadness of slaves separated from families "all to pay for
your own extravagances: People will laugh at your distress and say it serves you right,
you lived beyond your means, though some of the same never refused to partake of
that hospitality and generosity which caused me to live beyond my means. Those beings I shall find out and will know how to treat them."[26]

Chaplin's concluding threat here, to be acted out against Toomer a week later,
suggested precisely how Southerners often found an enemy to escape dueling with
self. That Chaplin's only interlude of violence occurred at the lowest point in his
prewar fortunes underlines how the Southern fracas allowed escape from the burden
of personal depression or of wholly justified self-blame. Fellow South Carolinian
John Lyde Wilson's book on dueling suggested the same psychological and social
landscape as Chaplin's diary entries, against which the Southern gentleman sometimes had to take up arms. Wilson mocked the Christian's ethic of forgiveness as
wholly unnatural in a world where human, animal, and vegetable life all waged "a
continual warfare for supremacy," happily destroying "the more weak and delicate."
Chaplin's sense of his social peers as people who would gleefully bite the hand that
had well fed and wined them, once it was palsied by misfortune, was very like Wilson's brutally competitive pre–Social Darwinian generalities. In such a world,
Chaplin's actions and Wilson's words proclaimed, no one of "manly independence"
would fail to find and punish someone who "had sapped and undermined his reputation," upon whom could be blamed "all his misfortune and misery" when he saw
slipping away his wealth, friends, and social standing.[27] Toomer had nothing to do
with Chaplin's debts, but making him a blood, or at least bloodied, sacrifice for them
was atonement of sorts in the viciously competitive struggle for position that the
duel glorified and the rencontre glossed.

While justifications of Southern violence have abstracted the topic from specifics,
antebellum planters who wrote humorous sketches were much more forthright about
its nature and its appeal: it provided excitement, clarity of result of the kind that is
the charm of all sports, and a system of intimidation highly useful to those willing to
brazen its dangers. The sporting excitement involved in these controversies was
generally given most literary emphasis from Augustus Longstreet's 1835 *Georgia
Scenes* on. In the tale "Georgia Theatrics," for example, a would-be assailant is
overheard playacting a brutal victory over an opponent, and in "The Fight" cowardly and bloodthirsty townsfolk egg on a vicious brawl.[28] Later Southern humorists
less changed Longstreet's picture than presented it less moralistically. Of these humorists, none wrote better than Alabama planter Thomas Kirkman, two of whose
stories, widely reprinted in humorous collections, cut to the core of Southern violence. "Colonel Jones' Fight" is a fairly conventional account of a brawl described
by one of its participants. When Colonel Jones sees from the courthouse window a
rival in the street, he goes out to fight him. The cause of the quarrel is vague, Jones a
bit unsure of it himself, but Kirkman suggests nicely the desertion of formal court
justice for the parallel system of street justice. Everybody follows the colonel out,
including the judge, who declares for the record, "I can't do anything about it," re-

ferring to the breach of peace he is rushing out to enjoy. The judge can, however, prevent the parson from doing anything about it so the fight can go on while the community watches with the enthusiasm and sharply evaluative eye of all sports experts. The colonel proudly reports that several in the crowd told him that his eye-gouging was a "beautiful specimen of the art" until he unfortunately sprained his wrist. Then he had to bring new tactics to this field of Southern honor:

> So, being like the fellow who, when it rained mush, had no spoon, I . . . went in for eating. . . . While he was chewing my finger, my head was between his legs; his woolen jean britches did not taste well, but I found a place, where the seat had worn out, and meat in abundance, so I chewed hold of a good mouth, but the bite came out; and finding his appetite still good for my finger, I adopted . . . the patent method of removing teeth without the aid of instruments, and I extracted two of his incisors; and then I could put my finger in and out at pleasure. However, I shall have, for sometime, an excuse for wearing gloves without being thought proud.

The long description of varied mayhem ends with the colonel assuring us it was only because he, his opponent, and his communal audience were all growing a bit bored with the show that "at laaast, I hollered."

Kirkman's "Quarter Race in Kentucky" dealt with another popular form of Southern sport, in which the author's central joke involved the handiness of Southern honor in defending cases that were morally and legally hopeless. The narrator in this case is a gentleman—much like Kirkman, one supposes—betting on a race, cautiously putting money on both sides so he won't lose much. The race ends literally in a fog of uncertainty. When the narrator goes to get back the money he wagered, one person has absconded, and the second has spent the narrator's funds on drink and cards. When the narrator suggests that he considers such stealing ungentlemanly, Southern honor is offended. The Kentuckian draws a dirk, demands "civility," and proclaims that he's "as honest as any man in Harris Co., Kentucky," and says he "always pays those who wait, but won't be pushed." Both men know the rules of the Southern extralegal game, and the narrator, deciding that the $20 stolen is better sacrificed than his life, chooses to be amused rather than infuriated by this honorific representative of chivalric chicanery.

Kirkman, like most of these Southern humorists, less condemned than enjoyed the world of conflict and conning he described. Their society was one rife with democratic demagoguery, economic conniving, and aggressive enthusiasm where the most violent, the most viciously calculating, the loudest and least honest often floated toward the top. The greatest of literary bourgeois con men, Johnson Jones Hooper's Captain Simon Suggs, was Southern-born, bred, and primitively baptized, and his scheming progeny blanketed the South, the rhetoric of honor simply one of the many tools useful for folks so vigilantly on the make and take. Suggs was a disciple of the least common denominator of bourgeois morality—"It's good to be shifty in a new country"—and the bottom line of laissez-faire economics: when he or his family were hungry or thirsty, he knew somebody had to pay for it—and he went out and found somebody.[29] These stories, of course, are no transcript of Southern truth. Like other humor of the period, they represent an exaggerated version of the underside of everyday reality, the side that serious writers neglected, in order to uphold a moral ideal they wanted—or wanted others—to believe. Partly because the Southern ideal tended to be so sentimentally bloated, Southern humor was an especially active emetic. There is no question that Southern humor skirts closer to the reality of antebellum public violence (though it divests it of its tragedy) than do serious treatises about a Southern code of honor in service of communal morality, the protection of the weak, or the hegemony of the plain folk.

The issues involved in cases of public violence and murder underline the truth of Kirkman and Hooper's comic insights. The "causes" in Southern public mayhem and murder suggest that the rhetoric of honor was less tied to gentlemanly rectitude or folk communalism than to competitive angers, ambitions and frustrations grown of a bourgeois-democratic society. Familial protection or revenge was ostensibly involved in from about a fifth to a quarter of these cases, though often in perverted ways such as Potter's castrations. Familial aid in mayhem was frequent, understandably, because reputation in a bourgeois society is always partly a relative matter. At the same time, about a fifth of these public murderings and maimings involved interfamily quarrels; killing cousins, like the Jones brothers who murdered Ward, were not uncommon, and records show public murderers who chose for victims brothers, fathers, wives, husbands, even a grandson.[30]

Woman's honor occasionally entered these quarrels. A Memphis woman accused a prostitute of slave-stealing, and that woman avenged her honor by horse-whipping her accuser while a street crowd watched. When amused bystander William Gholson commented that the women seemed two of a kind, a relative of the nonprostitute, Albert Jackson, demanded retraction and, not getting that, a duel, in which Gholson died and Jackson was badly hurt.[31] Such was an unusual case, and not only because it involved a woman's resort to public violence. Duels and affrays were more commonly used by husbands to proclaim their wives' dishonor than to uphold their honor.

Common cases centered around money and politics. In Montgomery, Alabama, a long series of public killings that stretched over five years seemingly began in a dispute over the cost of a saddle. In Louisville, Kentucky, in 1838 the purchase of a coat that either did or did not fit Mississippian Dr. B. R. Wilkinson became the cause of two men's deaths and the severe beating of another. In New Orleans in 1843 prominent Whig Alcee La Branche challenged Walter Heuston, editor of the *Baton Rouge Gazette*, over political differences. The men fired four times before Heuston was killed. Two Georgia planters, young John A. Wylly and Dr. Thomas F. Hazzard, published elaborate and personally vicious cards in the local press in an argument over a bit of land, publicly working out a duel where the winner was both to grab the territory and to decorate it with the poled head of his rival. The duel was averted when the older planter met and shot dead in a hotel his young antagonist, whose widowed mother was lucky enough to bury his whole body.[32]

Women, family, or clear wrong-doing much less often inspired mayhem among Southern males than did things like a horse, a "peas of land," a bungled case, occupation of "a chair," the cost of a coat, "a slight difficulty about some hogs," or, especially, the claims of Whigs or Democrats.[33] Most of the cases where cause is stated or implied—from 75 percent to 80 percent—involved quarrels of the bourgeois public sphere: over profits, property, professional position, or politics.

The charm of public violence was that it gave the illusion of stepping outside the realm of such mottled issues even while offering hope of gain within them. Robert Potter could announce after his viciously calculated castrations, with who knows what emotive truth, "I felt I had undergone purgation and purified myself of defilement"; Potter's mood precisely paralleled Chaplin's savoring the public visual evidence of his "genteel flogging" of Toomer. "Genteel," odd as it may seem coupled with bullying brutality, was an apt term. The genteel tradition of the nineteenth century was in large part a determined effort to cling to moral absolutes in a world where sense of immediate divine sanction for most conduct seemed insecure. In a sense duels and affrays, even in their most cunningly brutal forms, were "genteel murder," the most extreme and perhaps the most satisfying of the many attempts to impose moral simplicity on the necessary compromises and ambiguities of bourgeois democratic life.[34]

Alcohol was often an important ingredient in public murders. It was not a matter of chance, everyone knew, that so many affrays occurred in or just outside taverns. Missourian Mary Gregg wrote to relatives in Texas about their brother, Ellis: "with heavy hart I must inform you that the third time he went to Fayetteville he drank too much and him and Mr. Clift had som difference. The cause I scarcely know but a fight insued, he finding himself too weak he drew his knife and stabbed him in the neck and he fell a lifeless corpse." Probably Mrs. Gregg's hope was justified that Ellis would be let go or acquitted, since drink and name-calling was involved. It is also possible that brother Ellis had little better idea than his sister why he'd killed Clift. Certainly old Thomas Maddox couldn't remember the reason for his duel with Samuel L. Wells, though he remembered drinking wine with him before and after.[35]

Most Southerners, of course, neither practiced violence nor wholly approved it. Private distress about it was common, though more so in the writings of women than of men. And public pleas and efforts to curb violence were frequent. In South Carolina, where lower- and middle-class political power was most limited, hundreds signed at least thirty-seven legislative petitions asking restrictions on the carrying of deadly weapons in order to curb a system of social bullying and intimidation. Typical was one from Abbeville District in 1838 asking for a ban on the carrying of private arms such as the "murderous Bowie knife, Dirks, Pistols, Sword-Canes, etc. Your petitioners look upon this practice as a violation of civilization, barbarous in its origin, derogatory to our free institutions, shackling the liberty of opinion, and at war with the laws of God and civilized man." In several Southern states less dominated by slave owners, laws were passed against dueling and for knife and gun control. Southern leaders steadily bragged of their section's commitment to legality, and often, more honestly, they deplored its acceptance of illegality. Governor Hugh McVay raised common fears in his address of 1836 to the Alabama legislature: "We hear of homicides, in different parts of the state continually, and yet how few convictions for murder, and still fewer executions. How is this to be accounted for? In regard to assault and battery with intent to commit murder, why is it that this offense is so common?—why do we hear of stabbings and shootings almost daily in some part or other of the state?"[36]

As the most debated form of public murder, duels offer a window on the contradictory reactions Southerners showed toward violence. Southerners repeatedly mocked the duel, as one can see in Andrew Shirmer's terse description of one in Charleston: "the former shot in the foot to keep him from running and the latter in the mouth to keep him from jawing." And one could go too far. When a young man named Barnwell came to Charleston in 1857 carrying "a revolver, pistols, rifles, and a half-dozen challenges," his designated opponents had him arrested for lunacy. Too, the line between the duel as tragedy and as farce was often close. A North Carolina girl described one of her father's opponents: "Capt. Daniel rages about like a madman, abusing the old man wherever he goes. He is a laughing stock for all the town." The girl believed no one feared him much, although he had been practicing for some weeks, "shooting at saplins in the woods."[37]

Editorials frequently damned dueling, perhaps because editors were often its victims. In 1836, for example, the *New Orleans Courier* labeled the duel "a barbarous relic of a barbarous age" and quoted a New York paper: "Men who render themselves notorious and ridiculous by their acts of bravado, and swaggering, bullying, over-bearing carriage should always receive the special attention of a free press. . . . A common duellist is either a fool or a blood thirsty, malicious assassin." The editor's opinion went unchallenged, perhaps because he wisely quoted someone else.[38]

Legal answers were hardly difficult; simple enforcement of existing laws would have ended most public murder. While legislators sometimes raised penalties for dueling to discourage the practice or lowered them to encourage convictions, there was a fairly easy legal answer to dueling, one similar to the *Washington Globe*'s 1836 suggestion that would have made victorious duelists responsible for the debts or family obligations of killed or badly wounded opponents. Creditors and families of victims would simply have access to civil suit so that there would be some price for the deaths and injuries inflicted. The *New Orleans Courier* made brutally explicit why it was generally recognized that this kind of law would be effective: "It will be found that tenderness of the pocket excels that of the heart in preventing sanguinary appeals. *Mercenary* selfishness will prove more than a match for the *honorable* selfishness of duellists."[39] Such laws were rejected not because there was much doubt of their effectiveness but because there was so little—and because they would have showed how thin was the chivalric veneer on the calculated realities.

This steady criticism never translated into effective action. Criminal conviction proved nearly impossible, and public opinion usually swung behind the duelists and other murderers who won. Southerners never argued that victory proved virtue, but violence silenced any public questioning of one's chosen vision of self in a society where "honor" in fact depended less on character or adherence to a code than on what people dared to say publicly. Had Captain Daniel killed someone, people would have stopped laughing. It was an effective way of silencing criticism and of transcending any need to ponder the complicated motives of self and community.

Public murder and intimidation took on added vigor from a society where status and character were tied to mastery, to the numbers of people over whom one wielded unquestioned domination. Little wonder that Southerners thought better of themselves and their leaders if they reenacted rituals asserting a mythic right to rule, even when the details of particular transactions were considerably less than glorious. All Southerners agreed that no competent planter could rely on law or argument to

control slaves but had to depend on mastery, gentle or gross. Public interwhite violence allowed occasional resort to the simplicity of this system. To question these events too closely was to raise to scrutiny the relation of power to right—worrisome in all societies, but peculiarly so in a slave society within a world skeptical of the justice of total ownership of other humans. The continuance of dueling and affrays in the South owed much, as the *Democratic Review* asserted, to the "peculiar causes" of the region.[40]

Of course a system of tolerated public intimidation helped silence not only private uneasinesses but some public ones as well. The liveliest of Southern journalists, George D. Prentice, retained his free-wheeling independence largely because he was as quick with his gun and his fists as he was with his pen. The South's only antislavery politician, Cassius M. Clay, survived because he was tough and lucky and enjoyed a fight at least as much as his opponents. Texan A. B. Burleson expressed what broadly was at stake in the South's system of extralegal violence: "Me and old Rip [Ford] had like to got to fighting the other night and dam him I will whip him if he does attempt to stop me from speaking my sentiments at any place or time in these states, God dam him." On the issue of slavery, practically all Southerners opted for silence, most of them for the deeper silence of even refusing to think about the issue, except in the socially sanctioned terms, rather than fighting with the desperate hope that the gods of violence might claim their enemies rather than them. Joel R. Poinsett described the politics of terroristic intimidation on slave-connected issues well: many people, including himself, were "adverse to violent men and violent measures, but they are frightened into submission—afraid even to exchange opinions with others who think like them lest they should be betrayed."[41]

The most famous act of Southern antebellum public violence makes clear how sectional misunderstandings on this issue contributed to impending civil war. Largely because they had swallowed the South's chivalric picture of its extralegal code, Northerners were puzzled and appalled by Preston Brooks's caning of Charles Sumner in the Senate. Later Southerners decided Brooks's act was one of family honor for some allusions in Sumner's speech to Brooks's senator relative, allusions that were neither false, salacious, nor especially personal but true and, in terms of Senate rhetoric, commonplace.[42] More generally, of course, Sumner had raised major questions of the morality of slavery more explicitly than was common in the Senate. He had also centered the speech on "the crime against Kansas" just as federal authorities, their territorial appointees, and various bands of Southern emissaries were about to launch their final solution of violent intimidation against the Free-Staters of Lawrence.

Brooks and his myriad of Southern admirers insisted that his act was an attack on political abolition. Brooks's mode of action—coming up behind Sumner and beating senseless a man who would not physically fight back—shocked the North but not the South, which had slowly evolved a different view of the proper standards for silencing ideas one disliked. Certainly Brooks had no doubts of the glorious rightness of his deed, which he described as heroic politics:

> I struck him with my cane and give him about thirty first-rate stripes with a gutta percha cane which had been given me a few months before. . . . Every lick went where I intended. For about the first five or six licks he offered to make a fight, but I plied him so

rapidly that he did not touch me. Towards the last he bellowed like a calf. I wore my
cane out completely but saved the head which is gold. The fragments of the cane are
begged for as sacred relics. Every Southern man is delighted and the abolitionists are
like a hive of disturbed bees. They are making all sorts of threats. It would not take much
to have the throats of every Abolitionist cut.[43]

Brooks's crowing was part of the cock-a-doodle-do ritual of Southern public violence. The sneak attack against an unarmed man proved honor and skill, while
Brooks hymned his speed and accuracy of blow in terms that suggest a remarkable
feat of arms in a holy cause. Shattering gutta percha on a prone man, then pocketing
the gold, proved that the victim and his friends were animals or insects and that the
chastiser was the gentleman that gold made and violence sustained. And the glory
could be easily extended to wide-scale assassination by throat-cutting, certainly an
effective way of silencing opposition.

Perhaps "every Southern man" did not exult in Brooks's heroics, but few voiced
reservations. Public exultation prevailed, in most cases clearly tied to a briefly renewed Southern hope that public violence now could be extended to the North and
be used to silence any serious questioning of slavery there, as it had long done in
slave areas. The *Richmond Whig* hoped "that the ball may be kept in motion. Seward
and others should catch it next." William Seward was the Southern press's almost
unanimous choice for next victim, as the South proclaimed that indeed "it would not
take much" to silence all Northern public reservations about slavery. The leading
Democratic paper in the South, the *Richmond Enquirer*, stressed the expectation that
the Southern system of public violence would function well in the North if only a
few "mealy mouthed Pharisees of the Press" would shut up about petty reservations
over the honor, bravery, and justice of Brooks's caning:

> We consider the act good in conception, better in execution, and best of all in conse-
> quences. These vulgar abolitionists in the Senate are getting above themselves. They
> have become saucy, and dare to be impudent to gentlemen. . . . They are a low, mean,
> scurvy set . . . as utterly devoid of spirit and honor as a pack of curs. The truth is that
> they have been suffered to run too long without collars. They must be lashed into sub-
> mission. . . . Let them once understand, that for every vile word spoken against the
> South, they will suffer so many stripes, and they will soon learn to behave themselves
> like *decent dogs*—they never can be gentlemen.[44]

In abolitionists, as in slaves, saucy impudence to authority was the ultimate
crime. And slaves, like dogs, if they failed to yap steadily in praise of the master,
could and should be whipped to submission, caned to compliance. The Southern
system of public violence could be used to silence all kinds of questions, most of
them personal, but the greatest of these issues involved mastery. Occasionally violence was needed to abet general geniality and steady quiet intimidation to keep
curs, slaves, abolitionists, the North, and, with by far the greatest effectiveness, the
white South itself from questioning the slave system in which the fundamentals of
honor were quite simple: wielding rather than feeling bullet, knife, cane, the whip.

When Southerners talked about their section's reverence for law compared to the
North, or about abolitionist fantasies of cutting their throats, they inverted reality.

When they self-righteously claimed that the South was free of the mob threat one found in the North, they were less wrong. In the South some forms of collective violence were much less common. On the other hand, the South had its own kind of riots, many of them directed toward stilling social uneasiness over slavery.

The riot patterns in larger Southern cities show no great differences from those in the free states, with the exception of much greater 1850s Democratic–Know-Nothing political violence in the border or river cities of the South—Baltimore, Washington, St. Louis, Louisville, and New Orleans. Since rioting in three slave jurisdictions—Delaware, Maryland, and the District of Columbia—showed much greater affinity with Northern patterns, these areas are excluded from the consideration of distinctively Southern mobs.

Of the 403 Southern riots, about 66 percent fall into three distinctively Southern categories: mob punishment of alleged criminals (68); insurrection scare mobs (35); and mobs against those labeled abolitionist, although usually there was no evidence of abolition activity (162). Thus, only about a third of Southern riots parallel the kinds that occurred in the North, and this percentage would shrink to about one-fourth if one excluded the cities of Louisville, St. Louis, and New Orleans.

Deadliness from the three categories of riot varied inversely from their frequency. The riots against people labeled abolitionists were most heavy in the two years before the Civil War, when 115 incidents occurred. In these two years, twelve people were killed, while only seven had died in the previous thirty years. Despite frequent sadistic elements, mob attacks on people who allegedly questioned slavery were the least destructive of distinctively Southern riots. In over half the cases, the only punishment was the mild humiliation of being ordered away, often out of slave territory entirely. Such mob punishment was harsh for permanent residents, some of whom had considerable property that fell to the mob or its tolerators. For travelers, such punishment was more annoying and frightening than deeply harmful. Similarly, the most common fate of alleged criminals was ordering out, though in this case usually after whipping. Yet 188 died at the hands of anticriminal mobs; 104 of these deaths occurred in Texas and Arkansas. About a quarter of the victims of these mobs were blacks, mostly slaves. The less frequent insurrection scare mobs were much deadlier; the body count in such mobs reached a roughly estimated 382, and well over four-fifths of these victims were slaves. This figure excludes the deaths in the real uprisings of Nat Turner and John Brown, as well as in the immediate legal repression of these actions.

While mobs killed a few alleged criminals in the North and quite a few in California and Iowa, Southern riots were distinctive in several ways in addition to their greater deadliness. One feature involved the use of the whip to extract confession, literally to beat out the "truth" the mob had determined. For example, in 1835 a Mississippi mob took Mary DuBose, the fifty-some-year-old widow of a man recently murdered, "partly naked" from her bed to the woods and whipped her till she passed out. Revived, she confessed as the mob directed to avoid another beating. This confession was then used in a legal conviction that resulted in a sentence of thirty-nine more lashes "on the naked back of a decrepid old woman."[45] Such a case shows the commonly cooperative interplay of the South's judicial and extralegal systems, as well as the nature of the "truth" that often satisfied in the South. Commonly Southern courts threw out convictions involving whipped-out confessions that clearly were made to avoid the continuation of excruciating pain, but no one appealed the mob's extorted "truth." If rioters could coerce a victim to say what they wanted to hear, the community usually closed its mind, or at least its mouth, to all doubt.

Such whipped-up truth contributes to the deep vagueness and uncertainty that often clouds the "cause" of Southern mobs. In the majority of non-Southern criminal riots, the crime being punished is clear, even when the charge seems doubtful or even deceptive, as in many vigilante descriptions. In Southern mobs, general social acceptance of violence negated the need for explanatory detail. One has no sense of the evidence against DuBose or who mobbed her and why at that time. A story in an 1837 issue of the *Vicksburg Sentinel* about recent mob actions in that vicinity offers a good example of the problem. The more "minor" incident was most fully described: when a jury acquitted an "aged wretch" of giving passes to slaves, he was taken up by a mob at noon, stripped, and badly flogged while his wife and children looked on; the whole town heard his screams. Here the basic situation was clear, though the newspaper didn't offer any clues about why the jury acquitted or who composed and what justified the mob. The editor only said this outrage seemed less serious than two other recent ones: in one, a lawyer named Scott was dragged from his house and hanged, and the second was against "a respectable planter" named Saunders whom a mob castrated "besides cutting off his nose and ears and scarifying his body to the very ribs!" The editor gave no explanation for the mob punishments of these two men.[46]

It's possible the editor didn't know more than he wrote about the work of these small mobs. Yet probably the editor's ignorance was feigned, or at least half-willed. To raise questions about what mayhem groups of citizens accomplished might, in the South, justify deadly assault. Courage, perhaps foolhardiness, would be needed to discuss very closely groups that were hanging and "scarifying." Suggesting that Saunders was "respectable" might even be dangerous; it was safest to offer only negative judgments of victims like the "wretch" a jury acquitted but a mob condemned. Regional as well as local sensibilities encouraged silence. By this time, the South well knew how things casually printed in ad or article might be effectively used to mock the South's favored image of idyllic communalism. So one guesses that the lawyer hanged was probably accused of a criminal act and that the planter creatively carved was guilty of a "moral" infraction, perhaps openly consorting with blacks or, more probably, clearly accepting a black mate and children as family. The severed nose and ears suggest someone who smelled and listened too closely to his slaves.

In addition to whipped-out truth and neglected detail, Southern mobs, as Saunders's body testified, featured distinctive gore. Other American mobs destroyed homes and churches and occasionally beat, humiliated, or killed people, but seldom, until the draft riots of 1863, did they feature the calculated mob sadism of the Saunders or even the DuBose sort. Whether sadistic elements appear in the majority or minority of Southern criminal riots depends on the evaluation of whipping, both a common punishment and a decreasingly used legal, educational, and military mode. As administered by Southern mobs, whipping was often a gory brutality. Saunders might have been "scarified to the ribs" by knives, but a whip, too, could have been the instrument. Whips could turn flesh to pulp, and numbed relief could be restored to sensation by the favored disinfectant of Southern mobs and planters, salt and vinegar. The whip's use in interrogation encouraged furious viciousness against anyone who refused to confirm what the mob wished to hear. Sadism seems clearly involved in the actions of a Mississippi mob led by a man named Hardwick, which took up a slave rumored to have made an "offensive remark," stripped him, tied him over a barrel, and gave him over 1,000 lashes, during which torture the slave bit his tongue in two; he reportedly died of lockjaw.[47]

There are records of about a dozen incidents, half against alleged criminals, of whippings so prolonged that their sadism is clear; at least six victims, including Hardwick's, died. In several cases, whether death resulted is not surely known, especially if victims of beatings were then set adrift, a tactic frequent in mobs along the Mississippi River. It's known that a Vicksburg mob of 1835 gave four victims 1,000 lashes and then set them adrift in an oarless boat as a way of involving divine providence in mob judgment. The later story of a jailed criminal that he was the sole survivor of this trip is probable: he said that one man was dead before the group was launched and that his two other companions died of their wounds under a broiling sun before the craft drifted ashore. There's no evidence of the fate of three men, a father and his sons, caught stealing, so it was said, by "Regulators" from Randolph, Tennessee, under the leadership of planter Orville Shelby. There's no doubt about the pride with which Regulator Joseph Williams later described the "mercy" shown these men. They were not killed but were stripped and lashed with a three-and-a-half-foot cowhide "all night," the rioters working in shifts as their arms tired. Near dawn, the three presumably senseless victims were fastened down, naked and face-upward, and gagged—and set adrift without oars. Williams remembered in pleased tranquility how, as they drifted, "their upturned faces greeted the first rays of the morning sun."[48]

Such whippings represent the least inventive form of Southern mob sadism. More imaginative cruelty is recorded in about one-fifth of these incidents. One form was reserved for black criminals, slave or free—burning alive; in two instances a "slow fire" was recorded as the murder weapon. Twenty-six black criminals were mob-hanged or shot, seventeen of them were burned to death, two were whipped to death, two were drowned, and two accused of poisoning were poisoned; about four-fifths of these were slaves. Most black victims were accused of murder, but some were charged with theft and rape. One free black cook on a steamboat was bound, gagged, and thrown into the river by some passengers merely for being found alone in a storeroom with a deaf-and-dumb German girl. One victim of a slow fire also suffered decapitation after he'd died; his head was put on a pole, a ritual otherwise used only in slave insurrection scares. This Mississippi victim was punished for a rare instance of Southern personal violence directed toward avenging a wife's honor: the slave killed his wealthy master, a native of New York, for sleeping with his wife. One slave woman was hanged in Arkansas for killing her mistress during a brutal beating.[49] In at least six of these cases, the mob executions occurred in front of large numbers of slaves rounded up to learn wisdom from the salutary bonfires.

The best described of these deaths by fire was the only one that occurred in an urban area and the only one about which there was any protest. In April 1836, a free black from Pittsburgh, Francis McIntosh, injured a St. Louis constable and killed a deputy sheriff in a scuffle following the officials' attempt to arrest two of McIntosh's friends. A mob took McIntosh from jail in the evening, chained him to a locust tree, and lit in. The sheriff briefly resisted the mob, perhaps only symbolically; reportedly his daughter lit the blaze. At any rate, that was the last protective gesture by the authorities. Twenty-some men fed the flames, about 2,000 looked on, and a St. Louis alderman swore he'd shoot anyone "who would dare to loose the chain." What this mob watched was fully described not in the St. Louis press, which agreed that "the veil of oblivion" should be drawn over the event, but by an Illinois reporter:

> All was silent as death while the executioners were piling the wood around the victim. He said not a word till he felt that the flames had seized him. He then uttered an awful howl, attempting to sing and pray, then hung his head and suffered in silence. After the flames had surrounded their prey, his eyes burned out of his head, and his mouth apparently parched to a cinder, someone in the crowd more compassionate than the rest proposed to end his misery by shooting him. But it was replied that he was already out of his pain. "No, no," cried the wretch, "I am not. I am suffering as much as ever. Shoot me! Shoot me!" "No," exclaimed one of the fiends standing by the roasting sacrifice, "No, he shall not be shot. I would sooner slack the fire if that would increase his misery."

None in the immense crowd cared or dared to end McIntosh's ordeal, which flamed fifteen or twenty more minutes before he died. A correspondent for a New York paper reported the piercing shrieks and groans of the victim and concluded, "To observe one limb after another drop into the fire was awful indeed." A diarist wrote that when McIntosh assured his watchers he still felt pain, "The lower part of his legs were burnt partly off. . . . The flames had burnt him so as to let out his bowels." Finally, when he "was burnt to a crumb," with "only a part of his head and body left," some in the mob poked those remains into the flames, while "some boys present threw on more fuel." A Mormon in the crowd noted the frequent "civilized yells" of the rioters as limbs dropped off: "The negro had been tried by fire, and the honor of 'Seventy Six' melted, while the cinders of a human being said: man without the spirit of God is worse than the wild beast of the forest."[50]

Those who penned revulsion were all Northerners, though none acted on that revulsion. In the records found, Southerners were silent or supportive of these actions; Judge Luke Lawless, friend and protégé of Thomas Hart Benton, discharged the McIntosh murderers, on the ground that no crime could be committed by a large group of people who represented the popular will. When Elijah Lovejoy denounced the Lawless opinion, he and his press were mobbed from the city. In the accounts of rural mob burnings, there is never any sense of dissent. When two runaways who had killed and raped were burned alive in Louisiana in June 1842 with a "great many to witness it and several hundred negroes," wealthy planter Bennet Barrow felt only that "burning was even too good for them."[51]

No other type of mob punishments were so racially segregated. A black was castrated before being killed in Louisiana, while a white in the same state was castrated without being killed. White women in Barton County, Missouri, were raped when they tried to interfere with rioters whipping their husbands, allegedly counterfeiters.[52] Both comparatively mild mob humiliations like tar-and-cottoning (or -feathering), riding on a rail, or squirting with sewer water and bloodier acts like scalping, "skin-ning," "scarifying," branding, and chopping up were, so far as the records go, re-served for white victims only. It was a white citizen of Louisiana whom a Texas mob captured, imported, and started to bury alive. When he managed to run off, they shot him, cut him up while still alive, and hung various parts of his flesh from various trees. The victim thus became strange fruit for the crime of suggesting that these vigilantes were contributing little to social betterment.[53]

The best recorded of such sadistic mob actions against a white criminal was the lynching of James Foster, of a leading Mississippi planter family, who probably killed his wife. Upon his release from a Natchez jail, a mob of 200 to 300 greeted him at the courthouse door, took him to the edge of town, stripped him, and gave him 150 lashes "until his back was cut to pieces." Then Foster was "partially scalped," tar-and-feathered, and paraded through town to musical accompaniment while a crowd of perhaps 1,000 watched. A suggestion of mercy at this point was quelled by a leading lawyer's yelling that Foster had shown no mercy to his wife, but propositions to brand, hang, or set adrift were also rejected. He was finally tossed back into a jail cell, from which he quickly escaped. The participation of Fos-ter's lawyer in the mob, the ease of Foster's escape, and the communal unconcern about the "monster's" getting away suggests how mob equity could be used by the wealthy and powerful in the South and reveals the interplay of its two systems of justice. In all probability the mobbing and escape were part of a plea bargain whereby communal anger was sated, festively, while Foster's life and freedom were assured.

This "rational" structuring of the event was not opposed to, but was predicated on, the ritual sadism of the mobbing. "Yesterday was a great day here," crowed one mob member, "none but gentlemen of *good standing* flogged him." The *Natchez Courier* reported the incident with a greater sense of sympathy and symbolism. It was a "horrible sight" to see the young, handsome Foster

> pale and trembling, the blood trickling down his neck, tar and feathers making his ap-pearance that of a monster. So far from recognizing *Foster* we could scarcely realize he was a *Man*. The mob believed that he *was a monster* AT HEART, and were determined that his external appearance should correspond with the inner man.

Such ritual correspondence was clear in all these humiliating and sadistic mobs. The attempt was to turn people into mock birds and beasts, to dehumanize them, even to annihilate the flesh so that the visual reality justified the cessation of human sympathy. All such actions unleashed the gleeful "shouts of the multitude" that ac-companied similar mob action against a man acquitted of murder a couple of weeks later in a nearby Mississippi town. The *Rodney Telegraph* proudly captioned its ac-count: "The way they do things in Jefferson County."[54]

Southern humorists again provide literary and explanatory corollary to mob sadism. North shared with South most aspects of antebellum humor: con stories, hunting and sporting yarns, tall tales, puns, conversational ramblings, and sexual suggestiveness. Only violence distinguished Southern humor with its zest for humil-iation and its often uneasy boundaries between humor and horror. The writings of Louisiana doctor Henry Clay Lewis offer an intense example of this. A typical

Lewis story tells of the lynching of someone who brought on board a steamboat a rattler, which got loose and bit a man. The speaker explains that the passengers didn't kill the owner, "sich as cuttin' his throat . . . for that would have been takin' the law inter or own hands." Instead, they behaved in a civilized way and

> guv him five hundred lashes, treated him to a coat of tar and feathers, made a clean crop of one ear and a swallow-forked-slit-under-bit-and-a-half crop of the other, an' put him on a little island up to his mouth in water, an' the river risin' a plum foot an hour.

The humor of this creative sadism fades somewhat in the light of its closeness to reality.

In other Lewis stories, the pathological gouges the comic into submission, as in one in which he narrates his necrophilic fascination for a dead black baby that leads to his stealing it from the medical school's dead room, or in a tale about how he and some fellow medical students punished their kindly, if very curious, landlady. Knowing she would open anything, they elaborately packaged a face they scalpeled from a terribly deformed albino slave cadaver. Leaving the bundle in their room, the students secretly watched as the widow carefully removed the wrapping. When it was open at last, the landlady neither screamed nor threw the macabre object down but, after a pause, began to laugh wildly. The students feared the woman had gone mad, a misconception cleared up when the widow apologized to the townsfolk, attracted by her screaming laughter, for worrying them. "I was just *smiling aloud* to think what fools these students made of themselves," she explains, "when they tried to scare me with a dead nigger face, when I had slept with a drunken husband for twenty years."[55] In this story stalks the horror lurking in much Southern humor: the intensity of hatred within families, friendships, and communities; the defaced white Negro as externalized mask of blacker white passions; an existential nihilism no less powerful for being encased not in portentous Kafkaesque allegory but cheerfully Americanized into grisly practical joke.

All these tendencies are clearest in the early nineteenth century's most powerfully original Southern writer, Tennessean George Washington Harris. His Sut Lovingood yarns are cut from a general pattern: Sut, the outsider and "nat'ral born durn'd fool," spends his life plotting ways to introduce mayhem into a world he can't join or leave alone. So he is always letting loose lizards or gnats or bulls or horses or hornets or steers or stenches to break up social occasions, to drive people out of their clothes and their senses and their lives, to create the comic chaos in which alone he's successful and comfortable. Constables and circuit riders and his father and greedy innkeeps, those representatives of state, church, family, and business, are enemies by definition, as is anyone who crosses or irritates him. Yankees and Negroes, of course, need do nothing to become deserving victims of his often deadly, always brutal humiliations. He is a one-man Southern mob made scarily attractive by the honesty with which he admits his cowardice and understands that he, rather than the designated enemy, is the moral outlaw beyond the human pale. And why not? Sut asks in his anarchic creed:

> Whar thar ain't enuf feed, big childen roots littil childen outen the troff, an' gobbils up thar part. Jis' so the yerth over: bishops eats elders, elders eats common peopil, they eats sich cattil as me, I eats possums, possums eats chickins, chickins swallers wums, an'

wums am content tu eat dus, an' the dust am the aind ove hit all. . . . An' I speck hit am right, ur hit wudn't be'lowed.[56]

Sut's world is without end, demonic providence incarnate, unsullied by the self-righteous pietism with which societies and mobs cloak their grossest brutalities.

As in these stories, so in the accounts of sadistic mobs rings laughter, human enough partly because it was directed at thing rather than being: outlaw turned to sightless, flightless tarbaby bird or sexless, featureless blood-smeared stalk, flesh into flowers or dying embers. Elias Canetti's macabre observation hovers over all such scenes: the only other laughing animal, the hyena, does so when he cannot eat his prey, while man laughs not only at seeing his enemy fallen and powerless but because in that situation he refrains from eating him.[57] Some Southerners roasted enemies, but they didn't, as other peoples have, eat them, even blackened and feathered "chickins," black chattel, or "cattil" like Sut.

Slightly more common in these mobs than sadistic embroidery was simple killing, especially of white victims. In all forty-nine mobs against alleged black criminals, the punishment resulted in death, and only about half of those cases involved straightforward methods of shooting and hanging. The 100 percent black death rate, of course, doesn't mean that white groups did not mete out many other punishments to blacks but simply that Southern laws gave so much power to white masters, patrols, and even the general populace over blacks that little unfatal action was considered extralegal. Less than half the white incidents ended murderously, but still the numbers of whites killed, 128, was far greater than the number sadistically handled.

In only twelve of the sixty-one fatal instances were more than two victims killed. Three of the larger killings involved blacks. Near Jackson, Louisiana, in 1829, planters shot eight runaway blacks to death, rounded up in response to the slave group's cutting off the legs of a slave boy they believed had informed on them and leaving him to bleed to death. In Madison County, Texas, in 1856, planters killed five free blacks and drove out thirty families with some "black blood," to put their property into the hands of these pure white upholders of law and order. The ploy's success was limited when the victims, some 150 strong, along with "a few whites and Spanish," set up a counter-vigilante group that made it possible for many of the dispossessed to return. And in Louisville, Kentucky, in 1857, a mob killed three slaves, despite serious protective efforts by the mayor; a fourth slave committed suicide to avoid falling into their hands. The slaves had been acquitted of murdering the Joyces, their white owners, so a Joyce son, infuriated (he said) by the legal decision, led a mob. When they trained a cannon on the jail, the authorities allowed them their prey.[58]

Some of the larger-scale incidents involved broad local struggles. A feud might be the proper name for the 1849 Gerard County, Kentucky, killings where two groups, centered on family animosities of obscure origin, ran up a total of nine deaths, some inflicted by assassination and others on captured people. And in Shelby County, Texas, from 1840 until 1844, with a final slaughter in 1847, two factions fought each other, always in the name of law and order and in fact in the service of personal and property aggrandizement. The circumstantial annals of this Regulator war identify twenty-eight victims killed, most assassinated but some murdered in mob hangings and butcheries as well as pitched battles. This total includes those killings done by the two Moderator groups and other people who opposed the Regulators but not those killed in the affair's 1847 epilogue, in which a Moderator named Wilkerson invited many Regulators to a wedding, where he poisoned a dozen or so old ene-mies—or members of their families. For this act of Southern hospitality, the groom was shot, and Wilkerson, the guardian of the bride, was caught in Arkansas and mob-hanged.[59]

The other two large Texas criminal mobs were lesser in their destructiveness. One was the only case of an extralegal group that punished the socially more protected race for crimes against the more helpless, crimes for which the criminals might well not have been legally convicted. In South Sulpher, Texas, citizens set up "court" to judge five men—L. Rhea, Andy Jones, Mitchell, White, Read—when the drunk Rhea confessed they'd killed three Indians—two men and a boy—in conjunction with robbing them. The "jury" convicted the four accused men unanimously and, by a majority vote, decided to hang Rhea too, despite his "state's evidence."[60] The other group followed the Shelby County pattern more closely, though happily in miniature. In Panola County, a group formed around William Pinckney Rose osten-sibly to "regulate" horse thieves and, in fact, to kill or drive off rivals for political office and land rights. A descendant of Rose defended his ancestor by arguing, quite correctly, that many came west "to find a safe retreat from the terrors of the law where they might not be molested or made afraid in the widest exercise of personal liberty." Such libertarian principles in making free with others' lives and property often prevailed. North Carolinan Robert Potter, who, like so much moral scum "could only float in troubled waters," also drifted to Texas. Potter and Rose quickly became rivals for political power and land, and President Lamar put a price on Rose's head for his killings, perhaps at Potter's request. Potter went to arrest Rose, who hid under the house while his son lied about his whereabouts. The next day Rose and many cohorts swept down on Potter and a friend, ordered them to run, and shot them dead; Potter was shot after he'd leaped into Lake Caddo and was trying to swim away. Rose and the other murderers were indicted but used both legal friends and Regulating intimidation to stay out of court. Rose's group killed at least six and suffered two casualties, while driving out a dozen families.[61]

In 1859, in the Attakappas area of Louisiana, Democratic ex-governor Alexander Mouton formed groups of vigilantes who killed perhaps eight people, some of whom were charged with vague crimes and others with being ethnic-moral unde-sirables. A moderating reaction brought the group to an end after a long career, but not before the Know-Nothing and Unionist opposition to Mouton had been much weakened. Two of the deadlier mobs in Arkansas were the only criminal ones to have integrated victims. In Chicot County in 1857, a mob caught a gang of reported murder-rapists; they hanged the white "leader" and burned four or five blacks. In Cane Hill in 1840, a mob of "leading citizens," many of them ministers, quickly hanged a mulatto slave girl who had axed her mistress to death while being brutally beaten. A week later, a white man and three children were murdered, and the extrale-gal group reconvened to exact punishment. Unable to find any clues, they turned on five whites, two local wastrels and three who had criticized the vigilante group. All had alibis, but the probably bought testimony of a prostitute and the whipped-out confession of one man (who had to be corrected as to who his "accomplices" were) led to the hanging of all five.[62]

The final Arkansas mob killed twenty-three people—more than any other at one sitting, though there were more lives taken in the Shelby County, Texas, murder-battles. A Mississippi sheriff in 1841 crossed the Mississippi River to lead a mob against alleged "horse thieves," a strange occupation, it would seem, for island dwellers, a literary problem vigilante fabricators recognized by making them counterfeiters in later accounts. The first vigilante account gave the usual lament "that it was a fearful thing for men to take law in their own hands," followed by the usual excuse that "an outraged and insulted community cries loudly for justice" and topped by the constant happy conclusion "that virtue had finally triumphed over vice." This account had it that the mob first dared the crooks to fight but that, crooks being cowards, the mob had to trick them into coming onto a flatboat. In fact, brave Sheriff Poindexter and the mob lured the men onto a "trading" boat and there captured the unsuspecting "crooks," who apparently expected to find only cheap booze. They were to drink more than they counted on. Poindexter, Barney Bedford, Harrod, and Burgess collected at least twenty-two victims and, on deserted Island 70, bound and drowned them in the Mississippi. They shot at least one man to death on the way. Eleven bodies washed up near Napoleon, Arkansas, the next day, while the vigilantes returned to drive off women and children—the other men had fled—and burn their homes. At least some of the virtuous mob took over some of the "vacated" property.[63] It was word of this mob that greeted William Hauser, whose brief adventures in Arkansas began this chapter and who cautioned against exaggerating its significance because "not more than thirty" had been killed.

Mississippi Sheriff Poindexter's involvement in this mass murder of Arkansas citizens symbolizes a final peculiarity of these Southern anticriminal mobs. Southern officials much more commonly cooperated than interfered with mobs, even mobs engaged in killing and maiming. Fairly typical was a sheriff in Tully, Missouri, who arrested four Mormons accused of theft after a mob brutally whipped three of them. The official defended himself to the public by saying he'd not beaten the men but just watched and taken them off the mob's hands when it finished with them. Neither he nor his community considered arresting the perpetrators rather than the victims of the mob beating. A few Northern officials led or participated in mobs, especially in cases of abolition or economic-territorial rivalry; often mobs occurred because it was known that officials sympathized or would not act.[64] Yet no Northern mobs with any support from authorities acted so openly, so prolongedly, and with such brutality as did distinctively Southern ones.

In the South the legal and extralegal systems usually comfortably cooperated. Southern mobs took people they wanted to punish directly from courts and jails with no opposition. In at least six cases, victims moved immediately from courts where they'd been acquitted or released into the hands of the mob for punishment. In the Foster riot, the mob took their victim from the court and later threw his bloodied body back into jail. In Columbia, Missouri, a trial of a black whom a Miss Hubbard had accused of attempted rape was ended by a mob when the man's lawyer began to question seriously Hubbard's testimony. When they tried to hang the black, the rope snapped, and they "started to burn" him. At this enough people balked so that the accused was returned to jail. But the next morning, to prevent any continuation of the trial, the black was again taken from jail. This time the rope held and the rape was "proved."[65]

In the larger anticriminal activities, sheriffs, justices of the peace, and judges were mob participants and victims, sometimes both. In Panola County, Texas, the Rose group killed the sheriff so their leader could assume his office to sanction marauding thefts, and in Shelby County, a man soon to be elected sheriff, Alfred George, arranged the first murder there and made it his first official duty to obtain the acquittal of the assassin he'd hired. At this trial, Charles W. Jackson's men surrounded the court, Judge John M. Hansford fled, and the prosecuting attorney refused to present evidence. The defense told the jury these small circumstances shouldn't prevent a verdict, and they acquitted on the grounds of self-defense. Four years later, rioters killed Judge Hansford when he refused to give up slaves they claimed he'd used his legal office to steal, but Probate Court Judge Samuel McHenry of neighboring Harrison County was an immediate victim of the acquitted Jackson. Jackson captured McHenry and had him sent to Louisiana, where there was a $200 reward on him as a slave thief. One of Jackson's men collected this money because Louisiana also had a price on Jackson's head. Much later, the election of Amos Llewellan as sheriff created difficulties for the Regulators in manipulating the legal system, and attempts to drive out him, his deputies, and about twenty others in 1844 as "obnoxious disturbers of the peace" brought state action.[66]

As the Texas example shows, mob activity, like personal violence, was less an attack on legality than an alternative system to which Southerners could resort when it offered securer promise of gaining "justice," revenge, power, or property. It was often justified in terms of weaknesses in the formal legal system in ways that were dubious but telling about its alternative status. Later accounts sometimes claimed lack of established courts, which never was the case. They also stressed, in ritual litany, the weaknesses of jails, but most (though not all) of the frequent jailbreaks were a part of the established extralegal system, concurred in by officials and communities. More honest was the argument that mobs avoided the law's delays and circumvented the obvious monetary influences within it. The mobs who squirted sewer water on a judge who gave bail to a man expected to vamoose, the attack on the wealthy father of Matt Ward in Louisville when the young man was acquitted of killing a schoolmaster, and the mob defilement of Foster all were in part protests against the American reality that there was far less equal justice under the law than justice for sale, usually to those who could bid highest. In such instances riots had aspects of reasonable social protest; however, they tended not to challenge the system but to support it by directing and dispelling anger. Despite the egalitarian potential of both guns and riotous gangs, money and social position were generally at least as advantageous in the extralegal as in the legal system.[67]

In well over 90 percent of these Southern criminal mobs, there was no legal protection of victims nor legal action against perpetrators. In the one case of a jail sentence for mobbing whites, sixty-seven Mississippians signed a petition arguing that William McMurty acted only like other "most respectable citizens" in "lynching" a man, Sam Hoague, "against whom a well-grounded suspicion" existed of theft and miscegenation. So commonplace were such activities that, his fellow citizens claimed, McMurty "acted under mistaken notions of the law." Given Southern practice, McMurty indeed whipped in accord with the unwritten law, though in this rare case what was writ led to a year sentence. Sheriff R. L. Hamilton endorsed this petition, and perhaps he helped the "hale, hearty, industrious and skilful mechanic" McMurty, along with an accused murderer, break jail. The suspicion was that the sheriff was bribed to allow the escape of the wealthy killer, although he claimed he was framed and indicted by his fellow Claiborne County citizens who actually perpetrated the freeing.[68]

Civil suit more commonly offered redress to victims. In at least half a dozen cases white Southerners received some compensation from people who had mobbed them, although in several cases the minimal awards were close to a gesture of support for the mob. Such tended to be the fines that were meted out to the Alabama Slickers in the early 1830s for the beatings of seventy-year-old Woody Martin, William Hall, and Alonson Huff, the latter represented by lawyer James G. Birney, shortly to become an abolitionist spokesman.[69] In 1854, South Carolinian James Petigru did better for a Yankee client, treated "worse than a dog" by a mob who pretended he'd been trading with slaves. The $2,500 collected in that case was slightly larger than the $2,000 Alonson Moody was awarded in Brownsville, Tennessee, 1835, from five men who beat and branded him after he was legally acquitted of slave-stealing. Such attempts at redress through civil suit, however, could prove costly, as the Pepper family learned in 1840 in Union, Missouri. When they came to court in a suit against lynchers who had whipped them, the court officials recessed for a drink with Regulator supporters, leaving a mob free to chase the Peppers out of court and town. "Old Pepper" was both shot and "lacerated with stones" in this second mobbing, and another member of his family was badly hurt. The case was held over indefinitely.[70]

Legal action against Southern criminal mobs, surprisingly enough, occurred most often when the victims were slaves or free blacks. One of the more serious efforts by Southern authorities to quell a mob occurred in Louisville in the murder case after the Joyce slaves were legally acquitted. The rioters who roasted McIntosh in St. Louis were at least arraigned, and Mississippian Hardwick was tried, though acquitted, for the fatal mob-whipping of a slave. A case in Texas where two blacks, suspected of the murder of a notoriously vicious overseer, were whipped so brutally that one died and the other could not walk for months led to a civil suit by their owner.[71]

The most interesting case occurred in North Carolina and provided the single instance of a criminal jail sentence being imposed on mob members for killing alleged black criminals. A group of runaway slaves hid out near Kenansville for some time, living partly off stolen cattle. Several groups had tried to hunt them down, but none of these failures proved as tragic as the success of a party led by seventy-five-year-old farmer John Fountain. When they stumbled on the slaves, gunfire caused them to retreat, but not before Fountain's only son was killed. Three of these slaves later surrendered. They were jailed and would perhaps have been left to the law had one not escaped. That night a mob of twenty-five or so took the other two, Balsam and Howard, from jail and shot both dead. The Whig *Fayetteville Observer* not only condemned this "high-handed outbreak against the supremacy of the law" but, in an unprecedented way, hoped "that justice will be dealt out in a rigorous manner" against those whose discovery could not "be a very difficult matter." It was not; indictments were issued for twenty-three men, all "poor farmers."

The incident might have ended there, remarkable for even this much legal action. In a year and a half, no law officer got around to arresting the men, but in April 1842, all the indicted men surrendered to the law. Perhaps they thought conviction was improbable; perhaps old John Fountain, "a most exemplary character as both a citizen and a christian," thought they should. Twelve prisoners were dismissed for lack of evidence, but eleven were tried for murder and acquitted because, Judge William Battle explained, "the current of public sentiment was so strong in their favor." Technically, the jury's excuse was perfect certainty of identification, but everyone knew that public sympathy made the murder conviction "impossible." But for some reason, perhaps Judge Battle's determined legalism, conviction for riot proved possible. The men were all given six-month sentences.

Of course, petitions for pardon immediately flooded Governor John M. Morehead, stressing the extenuating circumstances and asserting that "they done only what every spirited man would do though it was a violation of the law." Morehead, however, was a legalistic Whig, one of the earliest antebellum governors in the South to refuse to use his pardoning power for political leverage. If the jail were insecure, it should have been repaired, he tartly told the petitioners; weighing the law's dignity against old Fountain's suffering was not easy:

> My sympathy for the poor old father, who lost his only son, scarcely allows me to do my duty, as I deem it. But the law must be enforced—or we are not safe, and it is by disregarding its violation in extraordinary cases that makes us familiar with its violation in ordinary ones.

The law failing them, the community arranged a jailbreak, and all escaped except old John Fountain, who refused to leave though "entirely at liberty" to do so. At this rare proof of commitment to law, Judge Battle urged and Governor Morehead signed a pardon for the old farmer, whose principles they shared.[72]

The legal integrity of the *Fayetteville Observer*, the *Wilmington Chronicle*, Judge Battle, Governor Morehead, and John Fountain in a case involving black runaways guilty of serious crimes, including the killing of a white, was remarkable, anomalous, and telling. The results, despite untypicality, suggest in a way the strength of legalistic commitments in the South. Extralegal mob actions in the South, despite frequency, frequent sadism, and semi-official support or toleration, remained untypical, too: an alternative system available for use but, compared to legal processes, not commonly used. This creates ambiguity about the general social function of these anticriminal riots. A handful were obvious attempts to correct what were deemed errors in the legal process, but the great bulk of these cases fell into two categories. About half were actions against people like McIntosh, many of the slaves, and at least seven white victims whose guilt was clear enough and social position weak enough that legal conviction was almost inevitable. The other riots attacked people, often for reasons of personal aggrandizement, charged with crimes too vague or too poorly supported to have allowed legal conviction or even prosecution. In short, these mobs neither gave much aid to justice nor contributed to changing the Southern system of law but were a parallel adjunct to it, related to Southern idealization of personal mastery.

This adjunct extralegality became much more important to the South when used to intimidate the two types of potential opponents of the slave system, white and black, through "anti-abolitionist" and insurrection scare mobs. It was a system grown of commitments to total mastery, and it was accepted because it terrorized to silence almost all public doubts about the peculiar institution that fathered it.

CHAPTER FOUR

White Fears

Silencing Questions

> The white people of the South are essentially a fine kindly breed. . . . Perhaps their early and fatal mistake was that they refused long before the Civil War to allow the South differences of opinion. . . . Men act as they do in the South, they murder, they lynch, they insult, because they listen to but one side of a question.
>
> —W. E. B. Du Bois, *Black Reconstruction*

> We are both heartily sick of this atmosphere redolent of insane violence. . . . There is a strong party adverse to violent men and violent measures, but they are frightened into submission—afraid even to exchange opinions with others who think like them, lest they should be betrayed.
>
> —Joel Poinsett to Benjamin F. Perry,
> December 16, 1850, Perry Papers, Ala DHA

After 1835 Southern ideology put one category of person, abolitionists, farther beyond the human pale than even their ambiguous chattel. No one, at least publicly, demurred from the bloody-bones rhetoric that passed for description, as in this typical enough letter in the *New Orleans Bee*: "The murderous designs of these fiendlike fanatics would not only place the firebrand in our dwellings, but prepare their knives for the cutting of our throats." The self-contradictory elements that followed in this description of the "hydra monster" suggested how abolition became a pastiche of villainy that blotted out any need to think about the real motives of any person questioning slavery and that even obviated rational structuring of the stereotype. They were "sickly sentimentalists" *and* "wretches, who delight in confusion and disorder, merely with a view to plunder." Their bloodthirstiness led to "untiring exertions to accomplish the extermination of the white population of the South," *but* expectation of making money was "the true secret of the humbug." They were "bloodless hypocrits" *but* were driven by uncontrolled lust for blacks and "unnatural tastes" that were "peculiarly disgusting" in women.[1] The abolitionist became not only Evil and the Enemy, but a mirror deflecting northward the darker aspects of Southern realities, precisely when the South first came to insist, with at least outward unanimity, that slavery was no evil at all.

Such abolition stereotypes were less surprising than was the vacuum of any attack on them, of any more reasoned analysis. The Jacksonian *Globe* steadily pretended that abolition was a British plot to destroy republicanism, a view also propounded by the *Democratic Review* for two decades. The most respected Whig paper, the *Na-*

tional Intelligencer, alternated appeals for Southern calm with descriptions of abolition as "a crime of so deep a dye, in comparison with which murder and midnight
incendiarism are acts of white-robed innocence." A handful of Nullifier editors, especially Duff Green, provided some more reasonable evaluation, but by the late
1830s their rational counterpoint was silenced by the usefulness of the image that
South Carolina governor McDuffie, in cooperation with Southern moderates,
worked to enshrine in 1835: motivated only by "envy and ambition," the abolitionists were "wicked and deluded fanatics," cloaked in "hypocritical benevolence, muf-
fled up in the saintly mantle of Christian meekness, to fulfill their fiend-like errand
of mingling the blood of the master and the slave, to whose fate they are equally indifferent, with the smoldering ruins of our peaceful dwellings." Given abolition's
devotion to this "saturnial carnival of blood," McDuffie straight-facedly urged all
states to enact for anyone opposing slavery the penalty of "death without benefit of
clergy."[2]

The mythic quality of this "abolitionist" perhaps explains the tendency of Southern anti-abolition mobs to be especially arbitrary in their choice of victim. At the
same time, the vileness of this apparition and the extremity of the remedies rhetorically urged makes strange the comparative mildness of punishment in cases where
abolition was charged. With relative infrequency did Southern mobs inflict on those
labeled abolitionist the "death without benefit of clergy" that McDuffie urged as legal remedy in the North and that Southerners, riotously and privately, comparatively
lavished on other "enemies."

Only a small portion of the "abolition" victims of Southern mobs had any claim to
inclusion in that group, even if one uses the vaguest possible membership requirement. About 5 percent of these mobs were directed at people who were in some
sense antislavery, all but one of them in border areas and the majority in Kentucky.
The attack on Cassius Clay's *True American* in 1845 was an unambiguously anti-
abolition riot of the kind found in the North. The attacks on people involved with
Marion College in Missouri were against committed abolitionists, and William
Shreve Bailey's paper, mobbed twice in Newport, Kentucky (1851, 1859), and
Adolf Douais's German-language *San Antonio Zeitung* (1856) mildly questioned
slavery. Another Kentucky paper, the Methodist *Christian Intelligencer*, mobbed in
1845, and Elijah Lovejoy's *St. Louis Observer*, driven out in 1836, disliked slavery,
though the Methodist journal refrained from urging action against the institution.
The mobbing of the *Observer* was a direct response not to Lovejoy's then mild uneasiness with slavery but to his vigorous questioning of the exoneration of the mob
who roasted McIntosh.

In several cases, mob targets were people of antislavery persuasion who had not
publicly advocated that idea in the South. Three in 1835 were young men in the
South on other business. Dr. Reuben Crandall was briefly the target of a largely antiblack mob in Washington, D.C., when it became known he was brother to Prudence Crandall, already famous for being mobbed out of Connecticut for the crime
of teaching black girls. Amos Dresser was whipped in Nashville after a hostler
found some abolitionist papers he'd carelessly left in a carriage he sent to be repaired. Georgian John Lamb was sadistically handled in 1831 for subscribing to *The
Liberator*; at that time the South was starting to accept the comforting fiction that

William Lloyd Garrison's abolition rather than Nat Turner's Christianity was the inspiration for the Southampton insurrection.³

The longest series of these riots, nine between 1855 and 1861, attacked settlers around Berea, Kentucky, under the leadership of antislavery ministers and laypeople. These partly integrated communities were set up, with some Tappan brother financing, to create a beachhead for free labor in slave territory. Under John G. Fee's general guidance, these farmers and rural mechanics were dedicated not to speaking against slavery but to demonstrating its inferiority. Given their pacifist inclinations, these groups would have been forced out earlier had not Cassius Clay made clear to the mob that he could organize to attack as well as they. Only when Clay withdrew his threat of protective violence did effective mobbing start.⁴

Southern mobs might label anyone suggesting questions about the sociopolitical status quo an abolitionist: Republicans, Northern Methodists, Quakers, and, in the years just before the Civil War, Unionists or people who happened to be from the North. Seven incidents involved the mobbing of Southerners affiliated with the Republican Party—three in western Virginia, two in Kentucky, and one each in Missouri and North Carolina.⁵ Seven mobs, most of them in Virginia and Texas, attacked Methodist pastors or congregations who tried to associate with the Northern branch of the church after the sectional split in 1844. Yet over 60 percent of all Southern anti-abolition mobs attacked people against whom there was no evidence of even such ambiguous abolition. Beyond vague charges like meddling or tampering, rioters didn't commonly feel a need to detail any charges against its "abolitionist" victims. This tendency to mob those who were innocent of all ties to the movement paralleled a willingness in the South to let the legal system handle those few incidents where antislavery people in fact broke Southern law, most dramatically at Harpers Ferry. The southern legal system handled actual abolitionism and even insurrection; Southern mobs attacked primarily representatives of phantom abolitionism and delusionary slave uprising.

The problems of two Englishmen, one named Robinson and one Robertson, in Virginia suggest the evidential basis on which Southern mobs condemned abolitionists. Robinson mentioned in a private conversation that he believed blacks were entitled to freedom like other people. This opinion, aired less than a month after Nat Turner had spoken forcefully against slavery, became excuse for Robinson's being taken outside Petersburg, stripped, and "scourged almost to death" for his indiscretion. In the wake of Southampton, Southerners found it comforting to act against a stranger who certainly said no more than many leading Virginians had said earlier but whose punishment was a comforting explanation of the Turner killings.

In 1835, following another insurrection scare and the furor over abolition literature, an Englishman named Robertson happened to be traveling in Virginia. David Robertson's crime was to have a name similar to Robinson's and also to be an Englishman. Rumor spread that he was Nat Turner's "helper" who'd been lynched previously; a mob formed, and Robertson narrowly escaped and was hidden by a planter until the truth could be told with safety. In the meantime, reports circulated that Robertson had been hanged, which the *Norfolk Beacon* judged a helpful "warning to the fanatic of the prompt punishment which inevitably awaits him South of the Potomac." A week later, the *Richmond Compiler* offered some practical advice to mobs-to-be, urging "the public to be cautious in venting its indignation not to get hold of an innocent individual, who may be so unfortunate as to have the name of the offender against its peace." Or a name somewhat similar.[6]

But in these situations, rumor, even refuted rumor, often ran stronger than fact. Two weeks later, Robert Gage wrote a relative about the "storm" abolition had raised:

> Several have been tried by Judge Lynch, condemned and hung without a world [sic]— among them a most notorious son of John Bull Robinson who was the grand cause of exciting the Southampton Insurrection some years since—he was caught in the same neighborhood and at the same business and hung.

This farce had one more act. In Georgia in 1836, an Englishman was arrested for "insurrectionary activity"; four months later, the man was acquitted when all the "evidence" proved fatuous, but his prolonged illness in jail made observers conclude that he'd soon die. This man, whose name was Edwin Roberts, was another victim of name-nationality confusion with John Robinson, the Englishman who had privately suggested, half a decade earlier, his belief that liberty was a basic human right.[7]

The structure of this comedy of errors—though hardly funny to Mssrs. Robinson, Robertson, and Roberts—was common to these cases: an innocuous statement latched on, an innocent person suspected, action taken or avoided, and whatever happened turned to a warning to all outsiders and to comforting assurance that the South could quickly handle all threats. In a real way, the crazy arbitrariness that often marked these riots was a central aspect of their social utility. They were intended to quiet all questioning of slavery, and nothing did this more effectively than knowledge that at almost any time, for almost any reason, almost any punishment might come. Terror as political system works best when rules are vague, and Southern mobs acted often and arbitrarily enough to make terror visible and felt.[8]

Southerners seldom admitted this arbitrariness, of course, any more than they did with more famous postwar black lynchings that utilitarianly did so much to keep the black race cautiously in its "proper" place. Had Robertson been hanged or brutalized, it's unlikely that the *Richmond Whig* would have proclaimed him an "honorable and innocent man": that would have made the "prompt energy" of the section appear to be irrational hysteria. Only rarely would the *Whig* and a handful of other conscientious Southern journals admit mistake when punishment actually was applied. For example, when it published Robertson's innocence, the *Whig* also regretted the severe mob-whipping of an old man near Farmville, Virginia. Though charged with slave tampering, the man was "a harmless, inoffensive and pious" person who had been preaching to slaves at the request of their master. The *Enquirer*'s response was more typical. It approvingly reported the chastisement and was silent after its injustice became known.[9]

The details of over half these Southern anti-abolition riots are so scant that there is almost no clue about what was done to earn punishment. For example, papers all over the country in 1835 repeated a story that two men had been mob-hanged in St. Helena Parish, Louisiana, for "stirring up the blacks." The report evidently had a single source, and its only variation was in the designation of the victims, sometimes called "abolitionists," sometimes "ministers," and sometimes "abolition preachers."[10] No follow-up stories or letters appeared to enrich or complicate a sense of what happened. Presumably the specifics of the case so poorly bore out the initial explanation for the mob that no one from the area cared to report further. Certainly it is improbable that anyone would have preached abolition in that area and time or that Southerners would not have delighted in any evidence of an abolition threat. Probably such was also the case in the three anti-abolitionist incidents in South Carolina in 1835. For two, including the one where "Judge Hang" presided, no data exists to explain the mob action. For the third, the *Aiken Telegraph* slangily reported that "Judge Lynch pinned into a chap a few days ago," then added a couple of unconvincing details: the victim had "feigned partial insanity" after being "caught with the blacks," but this hadn't fooled the lynchers. What the man had been doing, or why the mob concluded his dementia assumed, the account didn't suggest.[11]

Most is known about the incidents where victims, generally persons of relatively established social position in the North, lived to tell their story. James Otis escaped in 1835, although he was or had been a bona fide abolitionist, and in spite of the best efforts of his political enemies. Otis was visiting White Sulphur Springs in Virginia when the furor of 1835 broke and an official Jacksonian organ, the *Portland Argus*, decided it would be fitting or funny to embarrass an old political enemy. The *Argus* published a story that Virginia was now hosting an "abolitionist emissary" from Maine, James Otis. Not knowing he was a marked man, Otis, while traveling on a stage, let a Captain W. draw out his views. Either out of caution or a sense of the Southern definition, Otis deprecated abolition but also criticized lynch law as something full of empty "bravado," aimed at political intimidation. When these views were reported, a mob went to lynch him, but Otis escaped by smooth assurances that he was an enemy of immediatism and that his condemnation of lynchers had nothing to do with the present respectable assembly. Once safely in the North, Otis wrote letters attacking the *Argus* as "a vile receptacle of falsehood and filth" and withdrew from the Anti-Slavery Society, perhaps to deflect the jeers of the *Argus*, which claimed he'd lied to save his skin.[12]

Rev. Aaron Kitchell, traveling in Georgia the next year, was less abolitionist, less lucky, and perhaps less glib than Otis. The wealthy grandson of a former New Jersey senator, Kitchell was judged an abolitionist for "talking with the slaves." Kitchell, who'd damned abolition the previous year, claimed he'd merely casually chatted with two slaves he met fishing. But he was Northern, educated, and a minister, so the Hillsborough mob acted. They stripped him, shaved part of his head, tar-and-feathered him, and rode him on a rail while fife and drum played the Rogue's March. He was let go after about an hour's harassment on the promise, readily given, that he'd leave the area within ten days.[13]

The concentration of incidents in 1835–36, when the South first worried deeply about Northern abolition paled before the commonplace actions during 1859–61, as the Civil War approached. The details of these riots are often fuller, in part because the Republican press gave large play to them as proof of Southern brutality. Garrison's American Anti-Slavery Society also published two pamphlets, sloppy compilations of clippings, often without specific date or attribution, from the contempo-

rary press, a kaleidoscopic summary of the culmination of a quarter century of tolerated mobbing. While none of these mobbings electrified the North as had Kansas's
simmering and Sumner's caning, they steadily reinforced the feeling patterned by
those earlier events: that the Southern commitment to mastery exacted the right to
cow not only all opposition to slavery but also all legal and procedural restraints.

A few of those incidents involved actual statements against slavery. In 1859, one
John Fletcher said that, while many fellow Virginians were afraid to say they hated
slavery, he was "free, white and twenty-one" and wouldn't be intimidated; a mobbing changed his mind. In a tavern in Columbia, South Carolina, twenty-three-year-
old Irish stonecutter James Power, having drunk too much, voiced his view that
slavery caused white workers to be looked down on. When a vigilance committee
formed a few weeks later, Power's comment was reported. He was arrested and
jailed for nine days, during which time the mayor interviewed him and then turned
him over to a mob that included both the mayor and the jailor. Led by a troop of
horse, Power was literally dragged through muddy streets, hooted by thousands, including the speaker of the South Carolina house and other legislators. Amid yells of
"Brand him," "Burn him," and "Spike him to death," Power was stripped naked,
given thirty-nine lashes by slaves, rubbed with tar, and covered with feathers. They
let him put on a pair of pantaloons before throwing him on the Negro car of a train to
Charleston and deportation. At each stop a new mob greeted Power, one of which re-
furbished his tar-and-feather dress, while a Charleston man who gave him biscuit
and coffee was threatened with lynching. Jailed in Charleston, he was put on a train
north a few days later. Power, like most Irish-Americans a lifelong Democrat, became a Republican on his return North.[14]

Most alleged antislavery statements that justified Southern mobs came from people who were young, Irish, and/or drunk. All three of the adjectives described a man
named Tait who allegedly, of a Saturday evening, told a group in front of the Salisbury, North Carolina, post office "that he was an Abolitionist, and that he hoped before long every slaveholder's throat would be cut." If this vigilante account contained any truth, it was certainly mistaken in its picture of Tait as "very cowardly,
and, covertly very malicious, spiteful and revengeful." Again, action is clearer than
cause. The mob first shaved off Tait's "luxuriant crop of dirty red hair," then stripped
him, "humanely replaced" his clothes with "a very neat fitting garment of North
Carolina manufacture—tar is the name," dunked him several times, and threw him
unconscious in jail. The mob decided not to hang Tait, something the reporter regretted because "the necessities of the times imperatively demand terrible examples."[15]

Terrible examples were not lacking in cases even where the cause was silly. A Virginian was almost lynched in Alabama when he passed a banknote from Massachusetts, and vigilantes drove out a peddler from South Carolina for his "impertinence"
in having, with his other goods, framed copies of the Constitution of the United
States. A young daguerreotypist in New Orleans, advertising his wares by pictures
of presidential candidates, was beaten because these included one of Lincoln. And a
Northerner selling Fleetwood's *Life of Christ* at a Methodist conference was driven
out, his tormentors stated, simply because a Northerner selling a Northern book
was "presumptive" evidence of abolition. He was paraded out of the county marching to music and led by a militia group. One Alabaman from the North, who'd lived

in the area nine years and married a Southerner, refused to play in this band, so the mob drove him and his family from their home. What better proof of abolition than failure to make music for any mob claiming to be defending slavery against a peddler of *The Life of Christ*? In Mississippi a man was hanged for wearing a large red sash, the insignia, his killers asserted, of a not-so-secret "secret abolitionist society," the Mystic Red.[16]

Unsurprisingly, John Brown's raid justified mob actions in parts of the South far from Harpers Ferry. In Alabama, a book-selling reverend named Albertson was legally imprisoned when vigilantes found in his trunk one letter from his employer making him "chief agent" and another letter he drafted to his subordinates urging them "to be faithful." He was let go north when his employer paid $60 in jail costs. In Clio, South Carolina, a father and son named Hitchings, naturalized citizens of English origin, were taken up when an invoice for arms, belonging to another son who was a guide on the Santa Fe Trail, was discovered; there was also a letter of introduction praising Hitchings as a railroad contractor, interpreted as a code word for underground railroad worker. For the mob, this was "ample evidence" of their guilt, but it voted fifty to eleven to order them out rather than hang them. Less lucky was James C. Bungings, who'd been, we are told, "prowling around several days" near Chappell's Depot, South Carolina, when a search "revealed" his ties to Brown; 150 people helped with his hanging. As Bungings began to ask God to forgive the mob for their mistake, the mob knocked out the ladder on which he stood, breaking his neck. The body was left swaying for three days and then given to the medical school for dissection.

An Alabama case best suggests the odd combination of malice and mirth in these mobs. Two Italian organ-grinders asked directions at a tavern to the next town. Wiseacres gave not only directions but also a "letter of introduction" to a tavern-keeper there—which in fact said they were John Brown agents seeking their fellow insurrectionists in the area. The crowd where they showed the letter whipped them before sending them off.[17] Here, as in several cases, fun is more apparent than any real fear.

Calculation of personal profits also entered into some of these mobbings, tellingly illustrated in cases where victims wrote about their experiences when they went north. On December 29, 1859, the *Augusta* (Ga.) *Evening Dispatch* reported that James Cranagle had been jailed for talking abolition when drunk; the *Charleston Mercury* two days later said he'd been tar-and-feathered for his abolitionism. Once back in New York, Cranagle told his story. A lawyer of Irish background, he had gone south to work for Gray and Turley, a dry goods firm of Savannah and Augusta. Gray and Turley soon let him go, but Cranagle became deputy court clerk of Chatham County, Georgia, and successfully sued Gray and Turley for lost wages resulting from breach of contract. The Georgia Supreme Court upheld Cranagle, but no one in Savannah would issue the warrant; when Crangle went to Augusta to try to get the money, John Neilly of the vigilance committee ordered him out as an abolitionist. Cranagle denied the charge but found it repeated when he went into court to press his claim; there he also learned that the source of the charge was Andrew Gray, brother of the senior partner in the firm that owed him money. That night at 2:00 A.M., two constables and twenty vigilantes dragged Cranagle from bed to jail, then threatened to hang him if he didn't give up the keys to his trunk. When no abolition literature was found, Mayor Foster Blodget Jr. signed an affidavit alleging abolition against him, and the vigilance committee set up a trial. Perhaps what saved Cranagle was that a prominent Augustan, Colonel Cumming, defended Cranagle, threatened to publicize how Southerners used abolition to take Northerners' property, and paid the "court costs" after the vigilantes stole Cranagle's money.[18]

Maine seamen reported more typical mobbings in Christmas activities near Jeffersontown, Georgia. In 1859, a captain, his wife, and a mate went to have Christmas dinner with an old planter friend while most of the sailors visited a tavern. David Brown, leading a small mob composed mostly of relatives, caught four sailors, giving three of them 50 lashes and one, more recalcitrant, 100. A bit later, this mob intercepted the other party returning to the ship, gave the captain and mate 54 lashes each, and threatened the wife with the same if she didn't stop her "damned crying." Brown's only charge was that they were Northerners. By the next year, the Jeffersontown mob was better organized, now a formal group of vigilantes under Duncan L. Clinch, chairman. Their committee, having resolved to hang the first abolitionist they found, were hard-pressed to discover one. But they picked up Captain E. W. Ryder and Mate Joseph E. Ryder of Maine. The problem was that committee members had said "abolitionist" rather than "Northerner," and the Ryders were questioned for two days while their captors scratched their heads trying to think up a charge. Happily, rumor came to their help; they "proved" that some mulatto had been telling the slaves they could rise if Lincoln were elected. This stray fact somehow showed that the Ryders "held improper and dangerous conversation and intimacy with negroes." Since the evidence was not "conclusive," the vigilantes reluctantly concluded to flog rather than hang. Few mob publicists were quite so naively honest as scribe William L. Bird of the Jeffersontown vigilantes, who expressed gratitude to Mr. Naylor of the Savannah, Augusta, and Georgia Railroad for kindly providing the rumor.[19]

The commutation of the preordained sentence of the Jeffersontown vigilantes from hanging to whipping helps explain a peculiar trait of many of these riots. Given the horrendous image of what abolition was and the willingness to "prove" guilt with empty evidence, why was the usual treatment of victims so mild? Seemingly, rioters' tendency to let the punishment fit the crime and evidence braked the harshness with which the mob would have joyfully handled a real abolitionist. Of the slightly more than 300 personal victims of Southern abolition mobs, 198, or just over 64 percent, were ordered away without the infliction of other harm, usually out of the section but sometimes only out of the county or state. This was costly punishment for some who had to abandon homes, farms, businesses, or credits, but not to transients who escaped uninjured. Perhaps this wave of mobs was most costly to whatever small hopes of avoiding war existed. Each instance gave Southerners a sense of power over a cringing joke of an enemy and sharpened the Northern sense that blacks were not the only people that the South was determined to treat with barbaric brutality should they fail "to pay lick spittle to their prejudices" at all times.[20]

Of the remaining victims, fifty-two (17%) were whipped, and thirty-nine (13%) were humiliated—tar-and-feathered, dunked, shaved, branded, and so on—in addition, in most cases, to being whipped. Whippings were often brutal; James Cranagle's body from ankles to neck was still a "mass of scars" some weeks after his ordeal. Yet most abolition victims were given only thirty-nine lashes, generally used as the cutoff point between punishment and injury. Tar-and-feathering was the commonest humiliation, but there was much variety, as the first victim of these mobs, John Lamb, who lived in rural Georgia, came to know. Lamb reportedly subscribed to the *Liberator*; in November 1831, this was possible. When the South discovered Garrison after Southampton, a mob took Lamb from his house and tar-and-feathered him. Then the mob struck on an unusual gambit: they poured oil on his hair and set fire to it. Then Lamb was put on a rail, carried to a river, and dunked several times. After this fun came the punishment: he was tied to a post, whipped, and ordered out.[21]

Southern abolition mobs killed seventeen men and one woman, about 6 percent of the people they victimized. In addition, one mob member died: Dr. Shepherd, once head of the Texas Navy, who criticized fellow vigilante James Blair for reading love letters found in a trunk of a suspect named Brown. Blair proclaimed such questioning of vigilante thoroughness proof that Shepherd was an "emissary," and Shepherd caned him for the insult, but not thoroughly enough to prevent Blair's firing a fatal shot. Perhaps the total of abolitionists mobbed to death should be increased to nineteen, as the evidence for Shepherd's being an "emissary" was not notably scantier than in most other cases.

All except one of the abolition executions were intentional murders. In the case of John Byler, a native of New York who'd been a grocer in Savannah for many years, death was unintended. The charge against Byler was that he'd dined with blacks. Denying this misdeed and refusing to leave, Byler was taken to City Park through a mob entertaining itself by such things as spitting tobacco juice in his eyes. On arrival, he was hit by pistol butts, his clothes were torn off, and he was forced to kneel and lie prone while he was whipped and occasionally kicked. This changed Byler's mind about leaving; he was ordered to run off while the mob swung things at him. He had almost run this gauntlet when a policeman's pistol butt felled him. (The Savannah police, we are told, kept order "in the Park while the mob worked.") Sometime during the next several days, Byler died.[22]

The most sportive of the fatal mobs of this kind occurred at Friar's Point, Mississippi. From this hamlet on the Mississippi River, W. J. Weiss wrote his mother on January 6, 1861, of the tragedy he'd watched:

> *Mob Law* reigns supreme. Let me recount some of the deeds of horror I have witnessed. Last week I was at the steamboat landing on the Mississippi River. A Gentlemen there who was a native of Ohio was waiting for a boat to go up the river. While there he remarked that he would soon be in a free state. He was closely questioned, and found to entertain principles not compatible with the Southern institution. He was seized, crowded into an empty pork barrel, and headed up tight and was then rolled into the river. Three men, natives of some Northern state, were hung two weeks ago.

For lack of time, Weiss refrained from reporting "hundreds of atrocities."

The *Memphis Argus* provided earlier information on Friar's Point activity. When fire destroyed two gins and part of a slave quarters, the vigilantes hanged three carpenters from the North. The evidence: a slave was whipped until he said that one of the hanged men told him all slaves would be free after Lincoln became president. After hanging the three, the mob burnt their bodies, and the next day they ordered out all Northerners, after branding some of them "GB" for "Gin Burner." Later they thought up their barreling tactic that Weiss and others observed; at least three victims slowly bobbed until they drowned.[23]

Unlike some mobs against criminals, those against abolitionists drew no Southern public criticism. A very few Southerners quietly offered protection to mob victims, probable indication of an undercurrent of dissent or disgust, but one that surfaced only in rare cases, as in that of a Georgia marshal who took one victim out of the mob's hands at gunpoint, or Augusta's Colonel Cumming, who probably saved Cranagle's life and endangered his own by speaking the sober truth that it was morally disgusting when mobs used abolition as a pretext for avoiding legal debts.[24]

These anti-abolitionist mobs' cavalier indifference to giving even a veneer of convincingness to their claims makes clear how fully they could depend on public support no matter what they did. Their accounts stressed not explanation, but the easy exertion of power over those expelled, disgraced, or killed, monstrous symbols of a general threat. The chronicler of the North Carolina mob that tormented Tait crowed, "Now to a man of mind, principle, and honor, such a degradation would be worse than death, but of such men Abolitionists are not composed." That victims asked legal protection proved them cowardly tricksters; that they denied the principles attributed to them showed they were unprincipled weaklings; that they allowed themselves to be stripped, shaved, turned to animals, and annihilated demonstrated their lack of dignity and honor. In short, each of these local rituals asserted the power, moral and actual, of the South; its enemies, not it, were isolated, vicious cowards. The ritual was too appealing, and too twisted, to question.

Mobs against "abolitionists" also were too pragmatically effective to allow doubting. These riots encouraged silence, caution, and fear about broaching anything but unqualified praise of slavery. On the simplest level, the experience of John Lamb and others prevented not only them but society in general from reading what real abolitionists argued, so that the fiction of the bloodthirsty, plundering insurrectionist-abolitionist could go unquestioned. And if abolition were human vileness, this was little different from disliking any aspect of slavery, and Republicanism no different from that, and being for the "dumpy, stumpy Douglas" little different from that, and supporting Bell and Everett or Unionism still no better.[25] These mobs showed what awaited not only abolitionists but those who sold or read the wrong books, made careless statements, adhered to the wrong church or party, questioned the wrong riots, and thought dangerous things—and all who might lack vibrant enthusiasm for proslavery thought or action.

A Missouri case of 1842 offers a clear example. A young Northern woman who came to Warsaw to teach attracted a large school by her abilities but offended the area's slaveholders: although she did not speak against slavery, she sometimes showed sympathy to slaves. This "abolition" activity led the pro-Whig and planter-dominated "Slicker" leader, "Black Jack" Wilson, to warn her out and led planter wives and their slave women to "charivari" out of town the young woman and her father, a Methodist minister from Illinois, who had come to take her home. The woman's closest friend in town, a young druggist from New Jersey, Charles Pancoast, who disliked slavery too, urged her to leave when she got the warning-out note and said and did nothing, despite his deep disgust, as the planter wives humiliated her. Later he carelessly told a friend he thought the women should be indicted. Southern friends tended to talk, especially if it promised interesting trouble, and a large planter and steady drunk, Robert Everett, called at Pancoast's drugstore to demand an apology to his wife. This refused, Everett moved to cane the Northerner but changed his mind when the latter drew a gun. Pancoast had been in the South long enough to know the rules of the game, which involved "the necessity of carrying deadly Weapons" and sometimes using or threatening to use them, preferably against people like Everett, "very unpopular, even among his own kind." Yet Pancoast also knew his limits. Here, no matter how unjust and cowardly and communally destructive was the action against a wholly innocent, contributive, and unprotected girl, he "carefully held my tongue: not altogether through cowardice, but from the fact that I was powerless and knew that anything I could say or do would only aggravate her troubles and bring destruction on my own head."[26] Such sadly self-evident truths bespoke the fearful foundations of the South's mob and personal proofs of mastery.

Because many Southerners dissented from extreme proslavery and saw or knew of things that happened daily that mocked positive good pieties, the threat of riot was especially effective against the region's own moderates. The total silence of Southern communities about even the flimsiest pretext or most vicious mobs spoke loudly the effectiveness of these riots. They created caution in outsiders like Pancoast, but even more, they bred home habits of holding one's tongue, killing one's doubts, burying one's reservations. In the early 1830s, a dozen or so Southern planters became abolitionists, most prominently, of course, Alabaman James G. Birney. After the South's sanctification of the mythic abolitionist and the anti-abolition mob, almost no Southerner dared consider the option of open opposition.

No one represented this total obeisance to the mob while mouthing legal pieties more strikingly than Charles Colcock Jones Jr., alderman and then mayor of Savannah at a time when it, along with neighboring Augusta, was the most active mob city in the South and the nation. This wealthy, well-educated, unbellicose Southerner presided over Savannah during a year when mobs drove out scores of people, natives, long time residents, and transients; brutally beat and humiliated over a half-dozen people; and killed two. His courts, his police, and his friends fully cooperated with these mobs, and he did nothing to discourage them, though one victim said that Jones promised him protection that was not forthcoming. When first elected to office in late 1859, Jones claimed his only commitment was to "law and order," and he became mayor as alternative to the extreme Southern candidate. On taking office, Jones mentioned the need for legal vigilance against "scoundrels . . . and suspicious persons . . . tampering with our Negroes," but he never noted the many mobbings he tolerated. His letters mention no riot until May 1861, after the outbreak of the war and the ebbing of the mob, when he reported the help he'd given two young Northern West Point graduates, who'd been in Florida trying to defeat consumption and who were mob-threatened in Savannah while going home, obviously, Jones reported, soon to die of the disease.

Jones's verbal protection of these "poor fellows" was decent, but his reflections on the incident were peculiar, coming at the end of the South's and Savannah's peak mob years, when the North had had few riots, and none bloodily sadistic, like commonplace local events. Of all things, Jones wrote his father, he most hated "mob law," while he rejoiced, "It is a proud and enviable peculiarity of our Southern cities that while riots and lawless mobs are perpetrating all kinds of excesses at the North, reminding of the darkest hours of the French Revolution, we have up to this time been law-abiding citizens, preserving the peace, the good order and the dignity of the community in which we live." His minister father, the epitome of antebellum planter Presbyterian piety, wrote quickly of his complete agreement with his son about both "mob law . . . , the beginning of the overthrow of justice, mercy, truth and order," and his conclusion that "the law-abiding mass of the American people lies South of Mason and Dixon's line."[27]

Since both Joneses had to be familiar with the repeated and brutal local mobs in the last year, gleefully detailed in the area press, one is tempted to conclude that indeed the "mass of the American people lies south of Mason and Dixon's line." Yet not only the personal decency of these two exemplars of evangelical-bourgeois propriety but also the regularity of this genteel legal pietism in the South after each conspicuous bloody wave of riot creates a sense of how deep and deeply needed was the gross self-deception that Southern abolition myths and mobs sanctified and threatened.

The patterns of anti-abolition riots in two states, Virginia and Kentucky, one reasonably typical and the other richly anomalous, offer summary of how and why these Southern mobs functioned and to what ends. The Virginia riots differ in no major ways from those in the other slave states south of Washington and west through Texas. They sharpen the pattern's outlines, however, because the sectional divisions in the state, partly involving differing enthusiasm over slavery, raised regionally the question of the permissibility of mild doubt and dissent. In Kentucky, the whole state's handling of slavery was transformed because one man, Cassius Clay, disrupted the quietus imposed by anti-abolition mobs by his willingness and ability to threaten and return riotous violence in spades.

The first Virginia riot occurred shortly after Nat Turner's revolt, seemingly an attempt to soften that event's terror by connecting outside instigators with the home-grown reality. Nat Turner did what the political principles of Virginia's founding fathers and the brief evangelical thrust against slavery had failed to do: caused the commonwealth to give serious consideration to ending slavery. The effort failed, and never again was Virginia to consider seriously the slave issue. This stance hardened in 1835 in Virginia, as in the rest of the South, as a half-dozen mobs attacked "abolitionists": a Northerner at a health spa whose abolition was proved by his dislike of Southern mobs and "bravado"; a man whose name bore similarity to that of the earlier Nat Turner "instigator"; an old man preaching to the blacks. Two riots were especially telling. Vigilantes in Louisa County, Virginia, heard that two citizens had dangerous literature, which the mob read, judged inflammatory, and burned. The threatening work was elderly Virginia preacher "Father" John Hersey's *Appeal to Christians on the Subject of Slavery*, which urged decent treatment of slaves and hoped that gradual emancipation tied to colonization might somehow occur.[28]

The final abolition riot in this batch occurred in the far western section of the state, the area where ambiguous antislavery was strong enough to create the state of West Virginia in 1861, when final decision about commitment to state or nation was made. And it was here where most subsequent Virginia riots against those who allegedly threatened slavery took place. For the 1835 riot, the only account is the product of the mob. Accused of trying to entice away blacks, four Ohio "abolitionists" were taken up, two of them whipped, and all ordered to leave in twenty-four hours. Two went unwhipped, we are told, for "lack of evidence," though this didn't prevent their expulsion. Given that the report presents none of the "evidence," one suspects that victims Joe Gill and Old Drake were hardly carrying membership cards in the American Anti-Slavery Society. But the myth the lynchers accepted and propagated was clear. "Here we have strikingly illustrated the beneficial effects of the publications issued at the north by those damned philanthropists, Garrison, Tappan, and Co." In effect, Garrison and Tappan lashed the Ohioans. Certainly such activity was not the choice of this swearing mob of "gentlemen of the first respectability who are not only willing but anxious to be governed by the law, when it is adequate for the protection of their firesides and property." Southern mobs commonly spoke of slaves in relation to their fundamental function: property.

Had Gill, the Drakes, and Ross been stealing slaves for their profit or that of the blacks, the law, of course, could handle the issue, but the mob was creating a section of "the cordon sanitaire" the *Richmond Enquirer* said the South would need if the North did not permanently silence all questioning of slavery. Many others were suspected and probably would be leaving the area, the rioters concluded ominously, in an attempt to warn everyone to raise no questions about slavery in a sphere much broader than was reached by Old Drake's "yells."[29] The hapless Ohioan barreled into the Mississippi at Friar's Point in 1861 was not unwarned when he carelessly said he looked forward to being in his free-state home again.

Virginia's abolition riots of 1838 and 1839 were again ostensible warnings to outsiders as well as proofs of the South's ability to protect itself. Of the first riot, all that's known is that citizens near Richmond scourged a New Jersey man. In the second, Virginians carried the war to free territory: a mob from Guyadotte crossed into Ohio, grabbed a man believed to aid fugitives, took him to Virginia, and tar-and-feathered him. Slavery's reaching across borders understandably displeased Ohio and was to give weight, in its many manifestations in the 1850s, to a sense of the aggressiveness of slavery, the instability of a house divided, and the sorry joke of the South's proclaimed dedication to states' rights. But the Southern argument here was the same as in the Drake-Gill mob: danger to property justified any action. Here Virginia law was indeed powerless in face of the offense, more probable in this instance. Certainly by 1838, to get at open abolitionists one had to cross into free states. Ohio had its share, and its citizens had ceased doing their "duty to the South" by mobbing the monsters.[30] Virginia mobs made other raids into Ohio to arrest/kidnap residents of that state in 1845 and again to beat abolitionists in Quaker Bottom in 1854.

The next three Virginia anti-abolition riots occurred in 1845–46, all in western Virginia, all involved with both a new national threat to slavery and the deepest source of local reservations about the institution, religious belief. The evangelical faith that spread in the South in the antebellum years justified slavery but also gave most support to limited slave "rights": decent treatment, religious experience, Bible-reading, family protection, soul equality.[31] When the Methodist Church split sectionally over slavery in the wake of the sharpening division the Mexican War honed, Virginia mobs acted to make sure that no groups took advantage of the rift to stiffen their religious commitment to slaves as opposed to slavery.

While most Virginians gravitated without much debate to proslavery Methodism, this choice was not automatic in the western part of the state until mobs used fear to foreclose other options. In Parkersburg, a survey of Methodist Church members revealed that 102 favored the Northern branch and 82 the Southern. In the face of this threat to "our property," proslavery people called a mass meeting to form a vigilance committee, which drove out Rev. John Dillon when he came to set up the new church. When Northern Methodist minister Valentine Gray tried to speak in Salem, Virginia, a proslavery mob literally dragged him from the pulpit, and authorities and courts, of course, refused him any legal protection or redress. Freedom of religion meant no more than freedom of speech or press, mobs made clear and society acknowledged, if they were in any way construable as questioning the right to enslave. At about the same time in Guilford, a mob's shouts, stones, and shots ended an alleged "abolition" sermon by Reverend James Hargis, who presumably spoke in favor of Northern Methodism.[32]

In 1851, a mob drove John Cornutt from Virginia in another religious quarrel. Cornutt was accused of backing a Northern minister who had been quietly pushed out of the area for his alleged antislavery views. A mob of 200, "mostly yeoman farmers," visited Cornutt to demand that he renounce his "abolition" views. Cornutt, stubborn and principled, was unwilling to abandon his views at the mob's bidding or perhaps to renounce views he'd never held. So the mob, after stripping him, brutally beat Cornutt until he finally agreed to sell his home and farm and leave the state. Before going, Cornutt braved the mob again by seeking legal protection, but in such cases, Judge Lynch's court remained the highest tribunal, from which Southern legal authorities rarely accepted appeal. In instances of stubbornly defective conscience, like that of Cornutt, the neighboring *Salem (N.C.) Free Press* moralized, "a summary process is the only effective remedy."[33]

By 1856, a political threat to slavery was waxing in the North: a party dedicated to geographic constriction of the institution. Since Republicanism appealed to some western Virginians, mobs hastened to squelch it. A mob broke up a meeting near Wheeling where Dr. G. P. Smith was to discuss the new party, and Smith was jailed for his protection. When Dr. John C. Underwood, whose wife was a cousin of "Stonewall" Jackson, had the temerity to attend the Republican National Convention, mobs forced him and his family to leave Clarke County.[34]

The next mob action occurred at Harpers Ferry. John Brown was the personification of the South's mythic abolitionist-insurrectionist, but because the threat was real rather than imaginary, the problem was left largely to the law. And during the months just before and just after the Republican triumph of 1860, which made official the section's minority status, Virginia, like the rest of the South, experienced a spasm of anti-abolition mobs to prove that the old methods were still in control. In Pulaskie County, some "philanthropic pilgrim" was hanged five times, and each time he was cut down just before expiring. A Hansonville, Virginia, mob caught Fred Smith talking to blacks, and several "best citizens" tarred, feathered, and railed him. In Haineytown, Albertis Patterson was almost choked to death when he said he'd vote Republican. In Clarke County, a proslavery mob unable to get at John Underwood instead sacked his house and bayoneted the protesting wife of his tenant, a Methodist mother of fourteen children. They also drove out a number of peddlers, but they didn't sack a newspaper, as the *Richmond Enquirer* wished, that reprinted some articles from the Northern press. At Sandy Creek, Virginia, a mob ordered out a sixty-year-old Baptist minister guilty of having a copy of the *Albany Evening Journal* in his home, forcing him to sell his farm at great loss. A Martinsburg mob found another dangerous emissary, a young blind girl from Indiana visiting relatives. Suspected of insufficient love of slavery, she was mobbed out of town. In another section of the state, Fairfax County, a mob amused themselves by stripping a suspected Lincoln voter and covering him with printer's ink to create the archetypal "Black Republican."[35] Only the Civil War, which prompted Virginia to leave the union and Virginia's western section to leave the state, ended mob intimidation of those in the area with less-than-perfect enthusiasm for slavery.

In Kentucky, in contrast to the rest of the slave South, some open discussion of slavery lasted through most of the antebellum years. There was one reason that antislavery papers were published, antislavery communities existed, and periodic debates over continuing slavery occurred in Kentucky: Cassius Clay. His success was the product of his being a stellar product of the Southern system of violence. He survived, as for long periods did papers, groups, and political causes he supported, quite simply because he used his bowie knife and pistols and fists more competently and courageously than those determined to silence him and what he supported. No one could quarrel with Clay's conclusion when he first decided that slavery was not an inevitable evil but a correctable wrong: "Prudence would have said to me, be wise—be silent!" Clay attributed his decision to speak not only to "faith in the omnipotence of truth, and in the gradual improvement and perfectability of the human race" but also to "constitutional organization."[36] Clay liked a good fight, and a few very good fights permitted Kentucky what no other Southern state allowed: some serious public discussion of slavery. He refused to become what he said most Southerners were: slaves of slavery who gave up their liberties as surely as they stole freedom from blacks.

In 1841, when Clay opposed the removal of Kentucky's restriction on slave importation, the charge of "abolitionist" was hurled at him, but the threat attached to the term—"bowie knives and belted pistols and the imprecations of maddened mobs"—did not silence him. In fact, he used a careless remark by opponent Robert Wickliffe to demand a duel. Forced to fight or give up the campaign, Wickliffe fought but refused the second shot Clay requested after both missed. Aided by this evidence of his mastery, Clay won the election in fact, though a dishonest election board accomplished what the mob couldn't.[37] In the election of 1843, Wickliffe plotted Clay's murder in a carefully orchestrated act of public violence. In a campaign meeting at Russell's Cave, Samuel M. Brown, a "political bully," attacked Clay. As expected, Clay drew a knife and was pinioned by several Wickliffe associates, while Brown drew a pistol, told the crowd to stand back, and readied his shot.

Let loose for the "honorable" kill, Clay saw that his only hope lay in rushing toward the gun. Brown shot Clay at close range just before Clay struck him with his knife, cutting out one eye and laying "his skull open about three inches to the brain, denting it." Clay lived because Brown's bullet lodged in the scabbard for his bowie knife. Indicted for mayhem, Clay was defended by Henry Clay, and his acquittal was assured when Brown, irked when his allies threw him over a fence after the brawl, confessed the plot between Wickliffe, Prof. J. C. Cross, Jacob Ashton, and Ben Wood, a "police bully" hired from New York City by South Carolinians to plan Clay's killing.[38]

Clay claimed that Brown and Ashton were leaders of a vigilante group, the "Black Indians," who called themselves "police assistants," intended ostensibly to control black law-breaking but actually to terrorize and drive out free African Americans. Clay's attack on this organization was the only public condemnation of an active Southern mob against blacks. The question, Clay asserted, involved whether "our towns and cities" were "to be yet more infested by lawless bands of robbers and ruffians, who, under the specious garb of police assistants . . . spare from violence neither age nor sex, bond or free, so that they be guilty of a partially coloured skin . . . , under the infamous pretense that the laws are not sufficient protection." Clay concluded sarcastically: "If slavery be 'the foundation of liberty,' then most surely is the corollary, that Lynch Law is the foundation of good order and pure morality." A society capable of such reasoning might find even "'Black Indians' most honorable men." Admitting a degree of personal racial aversion, Clay always insisted that blacks deserved equal legal and political rights, and he was willing to take risks to protect the Black Indians' intended victims. Clay's fight against this mob made him deserving of the praise Philadelphia blacks gave him: "He was a white man with a black heart."[39]

Northern abolitionists had defeated, and benefited from, mob opposition by peaceful firmness, but sectional differences in riot realities doomed such response in the South. Though he was commonly cautious, Clay correctly knew that his willingness to use force was his chief protection. These qualities of calculating realism and brave belligerence were clear in the brief history of his paper, the *True American*. When Salmon P. Chase and others urged him to set up an antislavery journal, Clay resisted, explaining in 1843 that "a moderate paper would do much good if insinuated into the South" but that a paper avowedly antislavery "at present cannot live" because of Southern mob realities. In January 1844, he argued more fully that "a free press could not stand against *violence* here" because slaveholder power insured protection and "impunity" to slavery-dedicated mobs. Yet the next year, he changed his mind, influenced partly by covert favorable response in Kentucky to his antislavery talks in the North, partly by Northern praise, and partly by his impatience at restraint. Possibly proslavery taunts that Clay said in the North what he wouldn't dare argue in the South may have been crucial to his beginning to publish the *True American* in May 1845.[40]

There was never any question of its being a "moderate" paper. Clay began by replying in kind to those who had threatened to mob the proposed paper. He'd challenged "Junius" to a duel, but the man had refused because "*mob-leaders* are inevitably *cowards*." "A Whig" on the other hand was a mere "tame and harmless

villain." Clay saved his chief fire for Judge Robert Wickliffe, the father of an old political opponent, who was lucky that those whom he

> has robbed by the dishonest *jugglery* of the law—men who have seen the beds stripped
> from the sick and helpless women—bread from the mouths of crying infancy—the
> plowshare run sacrilegiously over the buried ashes of their fathers, mothers, brothers,
> sisters, and children, by this inexorable fiend of the law—have not come up in mass, in
> their great and remediless woe, and thrown his torn limbs to the dogs. And yet he stands,
> at the age of seventy, advocating violence. Let the old man beware! . . . Remember
> Russell's Cave; and if you have still thirst for bloodshed and violence, the same blade
> that repelled the assault of assassin sons, once more in self-defense, is ready to drink the
> blood of the hireling horde of sycophants and outlaws of the assassin-sire of assassins.

The diatribe ended with a request that his enemies take care not to "turn us from our
purpose of avoiding, if possible, all personal controversies."[41]

Passages like this made abolitionists (and some subsequent historians) question
Clay's sanity or stress his bullyism. Certainly no other abolitionist wrote like this,
but Clay's prose fitted the pattern of searing abusiveness of the Southern press in its
constant bouts of irritation. And pragmatism underlay this diatribe against those
who'd publicly threatened Clay. He quickly proclaimed two things: that violence
against him would have its cost and that those who refused such obvious bait for
duel or affray were afraid of him. Clay hoped for peace not by the impossible tactic,
given his message, of avoiding trouble but by quickly calling the bluff of those who
would silence him in this strange but well-established and almost universally accepted game of Southern chicken. Clay and every Kentuckian knew the *True American* existed not because of the truth, the falsity, the extremity, or the moderateness of
anything Clay said or might say but simply because he'd braved and survived the attempted murder plot, sicklied over of course with honor, of proslavery people at
Russell's Cave.[42]

Clay's tactic worked for two months, during which time the subscription list of
the *True American* increased dramatically, from 300 to 700 in Kentucky and from
1,700 to 2,700 outside the state. Clay believed, probably rightly, that it was his serious illness in August, with its promise of safe mobbing, that destroyed his press. At
least the excuse for the mob was found after Clay became bedridden, an editorial in
fact no more extreme and less personal than several of its predecessors. In arguing
the cowardice of Southern mobs and in condemning slaveholders' luxuries in contrast to the impoverishment of their society, Clay delivered one of his threats: "But,
remember, you who dwell in marble palaces, that there are strong arms and fiery
hearts and iron pikes in the streets, and panes of glass only between them and the sil-
verplate on the board, and smooth-skinned woman on the ottoman. . . . The day of
retribution is at hand, and the masses will be avenged." A group of citizens chose to
interpret this as encouraging slave insurrection, although the "masses" in "the
streets" obviously referred, Clay pointed out, to the free rather than the slave population. Yet the passage suggested insurrectionary possibility or intent far more
clearly than in any other abolition case, giving a modicum of truth to the rioters'
contention that they had to act "to protect the safety of our homes and families."[43]

Clay's first reaction to the letter warning him to desist was in character: "Go tell your secret conclave of cowardly assassins that C. M. Clay knows his rights and how to defend them." He did. Two cannon were mounted on desks aimed at the *True American*'s doors "at breast level," and an escape door to the roof accompanied "a keg of powder ready to set off to blow up any intruders." Yet both Clay and his opponents knew he was too ill to handle gun or knife, cannon or keg effectively at the moment. Thus, on August 15, Clay went to a suppression meeting of some twenty people, mostly Democrats and his political enemies, where he took what for him was a conciliatory stance, assuring Thomas Marshall, a former Whig congressman recently converted to the Democracy, that he referred to white rebellion, not black, and that talk of insurrection, especially among Kentucky's wholly outnumbered blacks, was "only used by slaveholders as a bugaboo, to maintain" their ascendancy.[44]

Clay's illness, apparent at this meeting, was so great that he couldn't attend the public meeting of August 16. Instead, he dictated to his wife a respectful appeal disclaiming knowledge prior to publication of the offensive passage and promising to be more careful in the future and even "very materially to restrict the latitude of discussion." Clay had friends at the meeting; he so considered James C. Clay, Henry Clay's son, and William Kincaid, who had helped him set up the arsenal inside the *True American* office. But all that they felt they could do was join the committee to sack the paper in order to keep destruction at a minimum. The speeches by Robert Metcalfe and Thomas Marshall carried the day. Marshall stated the usual argument for the Southern abolition mob. When anyone questioned slavery in the South, they brought "into the bosom of a slave state . . . fire to a magazine." Citizens had made "a wonderfully mild request" that Clay extinguish his editorial fire, which "the haughty and infatuated fanatic" had rejected. So "self-defense" demanded action that the law would be too slow to supply. If Clay should resist such reasonable mob suppression, "the consequence be upon his own head."[45]

Even unable to rise, Clay could frighten a mob. When Clay had himself carried on a cot to his office by a few friends, the mob neglected their deadline. But on August 19, they had Judge George Trotter issue an order that Clay give up the keys to the office and leave. That night, they entered the empty building and carefully boxed up the press and type and shipped them to Cincinnati. Within a month, John Vaughan published the *True American* from Ohio, and later he returned the antislavery paper to Kentucky. The mob "Committee of Sixty" gave themselves up to their co-adjudicator, Judge Trotter, who assured their acquittal by telling the jury that no mob existed if people were simply abating "a public nuisance," the favorite ploy for those wishing to make promiscuous rioting legally chaste. Clay, however, brought civil suit against mob members and in 1848 was awarded $2,500 damages. The criminal trial and the civil suit were the only Southern legal action taken against a mob that yelled insurrection or abolition, although the charges were much less fatuous than in other cases and the mob action milder.[46]

Several things about this riot are suggestive. The riot did not end open abolition but only transferred it to other hands; if Vaughan touched Kentuckians less deeply, most Northern abolitionists felt more comfortable with his gentler religious stance. And while Kentucky Democratic papers praised the mob, the Whig press gingerly condemned it. "We are compelled to disapprove," the *Louisville Journal* concluded.

"Ours is a country of laws. Freedom of speech and action are to be restrained only by law." Clay's defeat was, all in all, a remarkable victory—the most impressive one in a slave state—for free discussion. Horace Greeley, like much of the North, thought that by showing the cowardice or at least great caution of the rioters, the case removed "all panoply for mob violence either in courts or public opinion."[47] Yet the situation showed most deeply how someone could and had to appeal to the Southern system of violence if he were to be given any hearing. The restraining influence was the dues Clay had paid to the Southern violence system, as well as his clear willingness to up anyone else's ante, almost beyond the limits of the physically possible.

Clay appalled abolitionists with his next action, just as he had earlier by going North to campaign for his old lawyer friend, Henry Clay, against the Liberty Party: he went to fight the Mexicans in a war that no one more strongly condemned as a proslavery injustice than Clay himself. Clay offered explanations. Henry Clay's defeat, he said, would assure annexation and war dictated by slavery. When war came, Clay argued that all citizens had an obligation to support the decisions of their nation, legally made. On the first point, Clay's prediction was accurate, and it is possible that, had a few more Liberty people in New York accepted it, the United States' most obviously imperialistic and profitable war might not have occurred. The second point involved not result but principle, the legalistic abstraction of which fits with Clay's general Enlightenment form of thought. Clay also hoped to triumph politically on the antislavery issue in part by consolidating some support from the Whigs of Kentucky by returning to his native state a military hero.[48] He did, and in 1850 he made the Kentucky Constitutional Convention a referendum on slavery— the first real consideration of the issue in the South since the months after Nat Turner frightened Virginians.

His opponents again tried assassination. As he argued with Cyrus Turner during the election campaign, a fight broke out, and about twenty people attacked after someone grabbed Clay's only weapon, his bowie knife. Clay was beaten, kicked, and stabbed several times and survived a gun's being fired against his brow only because it thrice misfired. Covered in his own blood, Clay broke loose somehow, grabbed back his bowie knife, cutting his fingers to the bone, and ran at and felled Turner. All observers thought Clay would die, but he recovered and Turner expired. But with Clay quieted, the electorate quieted Clay's hopes effectually. It was a sound defeat, but Clay's forces gained about 40 percent of the vote, despite proslavery chicanery and intimidation, as good a clue as exists as to the depth of antislavery feeling in the South when not mobbed to silence.[49]

Clay's continuing to speak owed something to his friendliness as well as to his lucky ferocity. A Northern observer recorded an 1855 stagecoach conversation between a slave-owning farmer and a storekeeper who agreed that their Kentucky had no braver, better, or more benevolent man than "Cash Clay." The farmer said:

> "I like a man that, when he's an abolitionist, frees his own niggers first, and then ain't afraid to talk to other folks."
> "He's a whole man, if there ever was one. I don't like an abolitionist, but by God I do like a man that ain't afraid to say what he believes."

"I hate an abolitionist, but I do admire a Kentuckian that dares to stay in Kentucky and say he's an abolitionist if he is one."

Here the driver interrupted to opine, "There ain't many men I reckon, that has more friends than Cash Clay," to which the storekeeper replied,

"They are good friends, too."
"He's got a good many enemies, too."
"So he has; but, I tell you, even his enemies like him."
"There's some of his enemies that don't like him much."
"I reckon they'll let him alone, after this, won't they?"
"Well, I should guess they'd got about enough of trying to fight him."[50]

The recent "after this" the Kentuckians referred to was Clay's protective efforts against a mob threatening the antislavery evangelicals situated around Berea. In 1855, as Missourians organized to drive Free-Staters from Kansas, the Democratic *Louisville Courier* encouraged an attack on John Fee's community, long established as a free-labor bastion in the state. A mob of Lincoln County men formed to drive away the passive resistants, but Clay determined that "they shall not do it without fighting at all events—although they have cannon from Frankfort to meet us with!" Clay armed a band of seventy-five men and went to Lincoln County; the mob chose to talk rather than fight and soon "agreed to disarm and to allow Fee to preach on the same ground peaceably! God defend the right!"[51]

Despite much tension between the passionate rationalist and the intense evangelical, Clay continued to defend Fee until the latter defended John Brown. Clay believed the Republican Party might take hold in Kentucky, but not if antislavery in fact became insurrection; he also believed riot was wrong on both sides of the slavery issue. And if one claimed John Brown's attempt to be right or even all right, Clay asked, on what grounds could one damn the acts of Sam Brown or Thomas Marshall? Clay's legalism, both intellectually consistent and tragic for Fee's community, was sharpened on his political ambitions and instincts. The rise in the North of a political party that was antislavery, despite immense compromise and evasion, made the position of political moderates in the South difficult and had a similar influence on the region's only "whole man" who had denounced slavery. The rise of the Republican Party made Clay's home state more belligerently proslavery and also opened to Clay possibilities of national political influence that depended partly on quieting Northerners' uneasiness about what they saw as his erratic excess. Faced with broader violence at home and probable political slippage northward even should he once again intimidate it, Clay decided to distance himself from his evangelical ally, an honestly simple man for whom slavery was simply a moral wrong.[52]

When Clay washed his hands of protective responsibilities, mob and state cooperated in driving off and humiliating citizens they knew wouldn't fight back. In the end, Kentucky's distinction was that it was very late in accepting the unquestioned sway of the proslavery mob.

The strangely lucky career of Cassius Clay in Kentucky makes clear how broadly effective the South's policy of terror against invented abolitionists was. In one sense, the South's anti-abolitionist riots were, as Joel Poinsett suggested, "insane violence," attacking randomly and sometimes barbarously the usually wholly innocent on the basis of fabricated or whipped-out evidence. Yet the social sanity of the practice from the proslavery perspective was evident. For a mere eighteen bodies and a few hundred whippings, maimings, and exiles, all Southern states except Kentucky for a quarter century kept their citizens from raising any questions about the sanctity of slavery. The riots against pretended abolitionists in the South worked precisely the way Southerners and many Northerners had hoped that those of 1835–38 would work in the North. For anyone who might have questioned slavery, these mobs in the South effectively "not only beat them down, but *kept them beat down*."[53]

CHAPTER FIVE

Black Fears

Mastering Dark Realities

> Thou hast also given me the necks of mine enemies, that I might destroy them that hate me.
>
> They cried, but there was none to save them; even unto the Lord but he answered them not.
>
> Then did I beat them small as the dust before the wind; I did cast them out as the dirt in the street.
>
> —Psalms 18:40–42

> We are a band of brothers and native to the soil,
> Fighting for the property we gained by honest toil.
> . . . .
> Hurrah! Hurrah!
> For Southern rights, hurrah!
> —Harry McCarthy, "Bonnie Blue Flag"

If the impulse behind the South's mobbing of alleged abolitionists was to make any white questioning of slavery unthinkable, the fear driving insurrection scares was black: slaves, working each day near whites in fields, gardens, kitchens, nurseries. Insurrection scares both expressed the darkest fears of a slave society and allowed a sense of mastery over both the realities and nightmares that could never be fully controlled.[1]

Just as Harriet Tubman, John Brown, and others proved that the Southern vision of abolitionist slave-theft was not wholly hallucinatory, so Nat Turner underlined insurrectionary possibility in the antebellum South. In Rapides Parish, Louisiana, slave tradition bears out the basis, if not the details, of the white version of an insurrection plot in 1837.[2] Doubtless slaves plotted other uprisings, but the records about other "insurrections" testify to white fears rather than black action. The number of victims killed in these scares proclaims the depth of Southern fears about their slave population. Although there were only thirty-five instances of extralegal action against alleged insurrectionary plots, 448 persons were killed, 447 of them mob victims. Of these only 26 were whites and but 8 stately free blacks. The Southern press and letter writers gave scant detail about slave victims, including numbers, because of their marginally human social status. Yet there's no question that mobs of this sort destroyed property to the amount of hundreds of thousands of dollars, a cost that went largely uncounted because these killings gave illusion of white power. Antebellum Southern mobs were willing to pay—or have their neighbors pay—heavily for the terror periodically craved to slack the thirst for total mastery.[3]

Most of the killings centered around four major panics. The first group, concentrated in Virginia and North Carolina, but with minor incidents in South Carolina, Georgia, and Tennessee, as well as "rumors" throughout much of the South, followed Nat Turner's rebellion. Excluding both the actual suppression of Turner's band and the legal actions that followed in its wake, this panic involved the random mobbing of blacks in situations where no slaves were in rebellion. Connected with these mobbings were three riots that shortly preceded the 1831 uprising, especially a wide-scale scare in North Carolina around Christmas 1830, concentrated in the area just south of Southampton.

The second group of panics, less than five years later in the summer of 1835, centered in Mississippi, with important spillover in Louisiana, Georgia, and Tennessee. Most often the panic has been tied to fears aroused by the abolition mailings of this summer, but this scare preceded not only the mailing itself but also any general concern about new abolition activity. As the Denmark Vesey plot marked South Carolina's development of the idea that slavery was a positive good, so this panic, along with the year's subsequent abolition campaign and spectrum of varied riot, solidified a new Southern ideology. Slavery was no longer an evil, Southerners came to argue, but the best of social systems for profits, stability, and humane treatment of the black race.[4]

The rise of the Republican Party related to the two final outbursts of insurrection hysteria. In 1856 a broad insurrection panic took place in Tennessee, another in Alabama, and a number of lesser incidents in Texas. Texas became the center of the 1860 panics, although stray information suggests that major scares occurred in all but the seaboard slave states at this time. By these years the South was very anxious that outsiders have no sense of internal uneasiness over slavery, so aside from the reasonably well publicized Tennessee and Texas ferment and killings, the historian finds information about what happened only in private letters or diaries. One presumes that much more occurred than is known, or even can be known.

The extralegal attacks on blacks after Nat Turner's uprising are easiest to understand. Blacks had perpetrated wide-scale indiscriminate slaughter of a kind to touch the deepest fears of a slave society. That whites reacted with passionate violence was less surprising than the oddities of the pattern of response. Those slaves active in the insurrection were either killed (one) during the immediate repression of the incident or legally tried, resulting in nineteen executions, eleven transportations, and several acquittals. The Southern justice system acted reasonably in response to real insurrection of an awful sort, but in the alternative system of Southern mobs, brutal violence prevailed where there was no evidence of any wrongdoing at all. Puzzled by this anomaly in 1831, planter E. P. Guion explained that at first blacks were jailed because the extent of the slaughter was not known, but when the details came out, "not one black was spared that fell in their hands." Yet the first reports of the insurrection exaggerated the numbers killed and spread the notion that hundreds of blacks were in arms, led, some rumors claimed, by "500 Yankees."[5]

The mass killing and sadistic maiming of blacks began after the militia units arrived in the area to find most of the guilty jailed or dispersed, though Turner was still at large. Those killed and hurt after the rebellion's suppression were innocent victims of white citizens who exorcised their horror through atrocities on stray blacks. John Pleasants, editor of the *Richmond Whig*, offered the most public acknowledgment of these random killings, suggesting that "possibly more than forty" blacks had been mob-executed in the immediate Southampton region. An acquaintance of Pleasants bragged of personal involvement with the killing of "ten or fifteen" blacks and admitted letting a slave woman be killed he thought innocent. Pleasants tried to soften his report of atrocities, which other editors refrained from mentioning, by suggesting that they were committed mostly by maddened relatives of white victims. In fact, the primary murderers were, as a local clergyman and eyewitness wrote, "thousands of troops, searching in every direction," who arrived in the area after the threat was quelled. "Many negroes are killed every day," he reported. "Men were tortured to death, burned, maimed, and subjected to nameless atrocities." Some of these troops made their murdering profitable, pocketing their victims' possessions on the grounds "that they had might as well be paid for their troubles as not."[6]

The clergyman's observation that "the exact numbers [of these victims] will never be ascertained" is right. The estimates of from 100 to 120 murdered or seriously maimed slaves are reasonable in light of the scattered evidence of atrocity locally and throughout the state. A letter from Emma Mordecai, living near Southampton, gives vivid sense of the means of interrogation used on blacks and the ritual brutality exercised on those who refused to confess to end their torture. "They burnt off the foot of a negro whom they had taken upon suspicion, and found at last that he was innocent. They had one of the ears cut off of another . . . , and after rubbing the wound with sand, they tied him to a horse, had the horse mounted and rode, and then turned loose into the woods. . . . This Indian-like treatment casts a great reflection on the troops by whom it was authorized." A postscript in another hand added that these incidents of roasting and dragging to death, "so far from being the common mode of treatment," were "exceptions to a course of conduct both just and clement." The postscript illustrates the general historical problem: a minister or a woman might write the truth, but most Southern men realized that silence or lies about their race and sex's sadism was essential proslavery policy.[7]

Concentrated around Southampton, the panic spread in milder forms to other parts of the state. Eight legal executions occurred in Sussex County, one in Nansemond County, and one in Prince George's County, but scattered evidence again suggests that much more was done extralegally than legally. Mary E. D. Manning, for example, reported that two slaves "who were offended by the patrols" which nightly checked on Negro houses had made threats and were "taken up and transported." One of these victims was a "daughter of Stephen belonging to this estate."[8] In these days, any slave attitude other than abject servility toward the community's guardians was proof of insurrectionary intent.

In Charlottesville, V. I. Trist reported a "panic" with patrols searching for insurrectionists in his house "twice within the week." His sister, Jane, was distraught and begged their brother, Jeff, "to sell all his property here and go to live in Cincinnati." He'd suggested he might for awhile, but he was now determined to stay, in part, the writer suggested, because "the merciless manner in which all who were suspected have been shot down or hung" should quell "any thought of further black rebellion."[9] Trist's letter makes clear the social realism underlying the frequent senseless sadism of the killings and actions. They taught all blacks to fear and convinced whites that they indeed controlled the dark peril.

Southampton triggered white mobs not only in Virginia. The reaction of neighboring North Carolina, less horrible and extensive, is better documented. In the North Carolina scare, there were also clearer indications of the rampant rumors that fed fear and of occasional intentional propagation of panic. In North Carolina, Nat Turner's uprising did not begin the panic but merely directed its second movement. Less than a year earlier, around Christmas of 1830, occurred a scare which was harder to reconstruct but whose results were legally greater: the enactment of much harsher laws against blacks, slave and free, in accord with those in other Southern states. Centered in the part of the state near Southampton, the panic may have given ideas to a sensitive slave there who derived the promise of apocalypse and millenium from the Bible's captivity narratives.[10]

The 1830 panic was tied to rumors about Boston free black David Walker's pamphlet justifying slave violence. Possibly some copy fell into slave hands; probably some whites decided to use the pamphlet's inflammatory rhetoric to arouse white fears to promote a more stringent black code. At any rate, in 1829 James F. McRae told Governor John Owen about the dangerous book, "an open appeal to their natural love of liberty," and the next year state representative Tryam McFarland, whose campaign for reelection he reported had "again proved suckcessful," wanted to be sent Walker's pamphlet so he could demonstrate to some angry constituents that concern over the slaves' Christian right to read the Bible was based on "false philanthropy." In September 1830, L. D. Henry in Fayetteville reported to the governor that he was using "secret agents to pervade the black community" so that any pamphlets around "will and must come to light." In mid-November W. Burgwyn and John L. Paskur reported that a condemned slave, Moses, had said some things that led "to an impression on their minds that a conspiracy among the black people of this and neighboring counties exists for the purpose of exciting an insurrection." The men asked a stay of execution for Moses, perhaps as the latter had wished, so that fuller details could be learned.[11]

Lack of evidence led to no lessening of fears but to increasingly specific rumors of impending insurrection, now scheduled for Christmas Day. By mid-December, the governor was getting and satisfying requests for arms to fend off the danger, though he was anxious to avoid "creating unnecessary expense or alarm." New Bern was said to be the center of the infestation. Rumor at one time located sixty armed slaves there and also had them all conveniently killed by vigilant North Carolinians. On Christmas night, nothing happened except for a few groundless arrests in Chatham and a "few fires . . . upon a parcel of trees, blindly taken by these Don Quixotes for negroes." Those who'd been seriously frightened became the butt of jokes; one young man was said to have walked to and from school backward to prevent the blacks from sneaking up behind him. Even the slaves spent the post-Christmas holidays "in incessant gigling up their sleeves at our fear." At the end of the month, Thomas Ruffin wrote his wife that all fears were "without one tittle of foundation." The whole business was "a mere *bugbear*" spread by beings "who have no pretensions to be called men except that they shave and wear breeches."[12]

Blacks may have secretly laughed at the whites' groundless panic, but the joke was to turn on them, as white fear came to justify black repression. However unsubstantial the stories about Walker's pamphlet and the insurrection were, they led next spring's legislature to stiffen the state's black code, with fifteen of thirty-six laws devoted to this end. Punishments were upped and black gatherings and manumissions prohibited. Most controversially, a new law prohibited the teaching of reading or writing and the giving of books to slaves. Evangelical Protestant concern about the importance of Bible-reading to Christian nurture gained a sizable minority vote against this last law.

The 1830 panic made a few things clear. No shred of reasonable evidence was required for insurrection fears and rumors to reach huge proportions. It also showed the danger of whites' doing nothing to prove fantasy true. Had whites killed some blacks, this would have become de facto proof that the plot was real and would surely have squelched public mockery of the panic. If all was fantasy, those loudly vigilant were not heroic bulwark but cowardly victims scared by the mere shadow of slavery. It was comforting to pass laws that suggested the fear had been well grounded; in fact, a few probably encouraged the Walker scare to spur North Carolina's catching up with the legal harshness developed in other slave states. These laws attacked free blacks even more harshly than slaves, despite lack of even rumored free black involvement, in a common displacement. The fear centered on slaves, but if the wisdom of slavery itself were not to be questioned, blame had to be directed against the small group that proved that blacks need not be slaves. If free blacks—or abolitionist agitators—were really to blame, the problem wasn't slavery but these people's baleful influence.

Southampton justified fear enough, and North Carolina's truncated trauma of 1830 probably assured that panic would cross state lines, first in the areas near Southampton, but later in those of greatest black concentration. By November, when the hysteria ended, fourteen North Carolina slaves had been legally convicted of insurrection, and twelve of these executed. There are records of about fifteen blacks—only one of them a freeman—being killed extralegally. Probably many more were killed; certainly hundreds of slaves suffered vicious beatings and torture. And all this occurred without a tad of serious evidence of any slave violence or plot.

The first killings occurred in Murfreesboro, near the Virginia line, where Turner had slaughtered. Robert S. Parker described the two certain killings. When an unfamiliar slave from Ahoskie Ridge was passing through Murfreesboro, someone decided he was on his way to Southampton and "there were about 8 or 10 guns fired at him by the guard. They then cut off his head, stuck it on a pole, and planted the pole at the cross streets." The same day, a carriage driver, perhaps on seeing the head and the exposed body of the murdered slave, "behaved imprudently"; at least so said his frightened mistress. He, too, was killed and his head poled in proof of white power.[13]

Having begun killing, citizens of the area set out to prove a plot. Blacks, especially preachers or slaves of ministers, were rounded up, whipped, and tortured. General Samuel Whitaker wrote the governor on August 26 from Enfield: "I have this moment learned in their great zeal to put down insurrection the good people about town have taken a free negro to the *Vice* and screwed him up to extort confessions and failing in their object threaten to shoot him forthwith." Perhaps the courage of this black, a Baptist preacher, in refusing the desired confession despite such barbarous vices, prevented further harm. At any rate, the populace arrested five blacks—the free preacher; Primus, slave of a white Baptist minister; and three other slaves. By the time of their trial a month later, citizens were willing to admit the total lack of evidence for a plot, and all were acquitted. It was a rare case in these situations of reward for deep integrity under horrendous pressure, presumably aided by some interracial religious bonds.[14]

The worst of the North Carolina scare began in early September in those parts of the state of heaviest black concentration. Panic started when a free mulatto revealed an extensive plot to Mr. Usher. Probably made under torture, this revelation certainly led to the brutal beating of the slaves implicated by it. Sheriff Morrisey's Dave and James Wright's Jim were the first suspects, whose whip-extracted confessions made them the ringleaders and implicated many others. Jeremiah Pearsall described well the process of proving a conspiracy: "Dave was committed and after *very* severe punishment criminated several others, the whole of which was taken up and whipped without mercy (some will probably yet die of the wounds) and those who were the most guilty bore the most punishment, yea some almost died before they would make a disclosure." Such was the central reality in all these cases: interrogators wanted not truth but confession, so failure to say what the mob wanted became proof of greatest guilt. Of the many blacks taken up, those who complyingly lied were "severely whipped and set at liberty." The most tragic irony of the Salem witchcraft trials of 140 years earlier was repeated in these scares: those who confessed and named names were often freed, while those with enough integrity to deny what wasn't true were killed, in the Southern cases usually after vicious beating and torture.[15]

With some sixty-five "ringleaders" in custody, danger would seem slight, but the most hysterical rumors came a week later, on September 12. Stories suddenly spread that hundreds of slaves were in arms, that seventeen white families had been murdered in Sampson County and the courthouse burned there and that the slaves were marching to rescue Dave and Jim, and then on to Wilmington to burn it. Indeed, other reports had Wilmington already in flames. The oddest thing about these rumors is that leading citizens described them as accomplished facts in letters to the governor and to the press. Supposedly the slaves were marching toward the farm of Pearsall, who testified to his own bravery; "As for myself, I cared not much about it, but the cries of my wife and children distressed me greatly." For their sake alone, Pearsall hightailed it to town, as did about 600 other rural people. Once in town, Pearsall and his fellow Duplin County citizens acted. Jim and Dave were "brought out, shot down, their heads severed from their bodies, and elevated in the air." These gory talismans of white power worked; the black threat vanished, striking comfort into the hearts of those who killed the "savage miscreants."[16]

Pearsall was sure there were a lot of conspirators in Wilmington, too, and that "if they could receive such treatment as some got here they would disclose—from one hundred to three hundred cracks of the paddle." Wilmington, already once burned by rumor, set out to prove its danger. Rounding up its batch of suspects and whipping them into confessed insurrectionists, the Wilmington mob had its executions eight days after the Great Rumor led to the murder of Dave and Jim. The local *Recorder* enthused over these "public examples" the next day:

> Summary justice was executed yesterday morning by the *PEOPLE* on four of the ringleaders. . . . The guilt of these monsters in human shape is established beyond a doubt. A deep conviction settled in every bosom that the measure was indispensible to the safety of the community.

No evidence was mentioned, save the "deep conviction settled in every bosom." Five blacks were to be hanged, but one escaped in the confusion of the event. Some plans were afoot to kill four more the next day—the one who'd escaped earlier was to be burned—but cooler heads prevailed by then. At Wilmington, as elsewhere, the heads of the executed were lopped off and set on poles at the corners of the town. No one could enter except under such signs of white mastery over the Cape Fear area.

Before Wilmington citizens raised this pole tax on "these monsters in human shape," the court in Duplin County, during the week following its mob executions, tried six alleged insurrectionists legally. Three of these were convicted on the basis of earlier confessions. There followed legal convictions of slaves in Richmond (one), Sampson (two), and Wilmington (seven). All these were hanged, save one at Wilmington, who was ordered transported, and one in Duplin, who was reprieved.[17]

The latter case was revealing. Two of the three slaves convicted in Duplin, as well as one mob-executed, were owned by James Wright. Immediately after the trial, Judge John R. Donnell asked and gained a respite of sentence for Jerry on the grounds that bedridden, seventy-six-year-old James Wright Sr. had urged all his slaves to confess to avoid being "tortured to extract confessions, with unusual severity." On sober second thought, many citizens supported the petition for pardon, including five members of the jury, but it aroused counterpetitions from 163 citizens who argued that not only Jerry's confession but those of ringleaders Jim and Dave proved the former's guilt. Obviously, if Jerry's confession were discounted, those of Jim and Pizgah were equally untrustworthy, and the state took a significant step toward branding the whole business hysteria.

Donnell, aware of this problem in his initial petition, tactfully assured the governor "that the execution of the other two will for the present answer all the purposes of justice." James Wright's position accepted the same pragmatic standard of "justice." Pointing out that his father had already sustained loss "in behalf of public example," the younger Wright asked only Jerry's release. Jerry was twenty, with a lifetime of slaving for Wright before him; the sacrifice of Wright's "old Pizgah" for the sake of justice or rather legal sanctification of communal action was much less costly. Whig governor Montfort Stokes pardoned Jerry but allowed the rest of the convicted to be hanged, including Pizgah.[18]

Here, as in the other Southern insurrection panics, communities insisted on the reality of the threat long after people knew how tainted the "evidence" was and how fabricated the "facts." Certainly others must have felt the amazement William Gaston expressed that "men of high respectability" presented as fact wholly false information: "We had it in written orders to the Colonels of the different counties for summoning the militia that seventeen white families had been extirpated and the servile war was yet unchecked. It turned out that no white individual had been in-

jured or threatened, and not an armed slave had been discovered." Surely it was hard
to have "confidence in the capacity, calmness or judgment to ascertain a hidden Plot
of those who could *fancy facts*—startling, numerous, and impressive facts—which
had no existence." Gaston's explanation had some truth: "When fear arises in *multi-
tudes* . . . , it deprives them of judgment and humanity. Like a herd of cattle terrified by the screams or supposed scream of a panther, they rush forward, unconscious
of the ends toward which they are hastening." And then followed a determination,
equally blinding to truth, to present the action as heroic, not hysterical.

During the fear mobs happily swallowed the self-evidently ridiculous, such as
Isaiah Spencer's request to the governor that "your majesty" send arms to Hyde
County because an insurrectionist "went to one Mr. Gibbs and asked if he would
join them for they were about to rise." Slaves who so politely inquired about white
support were odd threat indeed. All panics reflected a profound mistrust of all
blacks, and no Southerner denied that slaves were "our internal enemies." In Sampson County at the height of activity, leading citizens claimed that they possessed
"testimony that will implicate most of the Negroes in the county." Even more remarkable was the statement signed by over 100 citizens two months later that the
plot was so cleverly contrived "that not one out of fifty of the guilty can or will be
detected."[19] The emotive release of insurrection panics suggested how richly
blended within Southerners were black shadows with the technicolor rosiness of the
official doctrines about happy darkies.

Panics also suggest how religion complicated the Southern response to slavery. In
1830, Representative McFarland wanted to use Walker's pamphlet to swing his constituents to a position their evangelicalism contested: that slaves should be denied
the great human right and obligation of searching the Scriptures. Religion principally tied whites and blacks in an emotive network that alone raised questions about
the slave codes' strictures against reading, and that sometimes gave teeth to the
much vaunted (but of course never legalized) Southern concern for the sanctity of
slave marriage and family.

In panics, there was implicit recognition of how evangelical faith, their own and
their slaves', threatened the peculiar institution. "Their leaders, who you know are
preachers," wrote a citizen of Murfreesboro, "have convinced many of them that to
die in the cause in which they are engaged affords them a passport to heaven." First
suspicion fell on preachers or slaves of preachers. The first slaves arrested in
Murfreesboro were the "educated preacher David," whom a Sampson County mob
killed; the one slave executed in Richmond County and at least three of the ten
legally killed in the central scare area were ministers or owned by ministers.[20] The
timing of the plot was to be during a revival meeting, while the previous year's one
was to be at Christmas. Revivals and Christmas holidays offered unusual chances
for slaves to congregate, but only because the shared religion here disrupted slavery's routine.

A letter from Charlotte Hooper in Wilmington catches some of the Southern response. There had been "no instance of violence or unnecessary severity in the
mob," she assured her son just a paragraph after she had talked, in carefully evasive
passive voice, about the execution's occurring "in a manner which would gladly
have been avoided." But "four viler, more degraded wretches never suffered the

penalty of their crimes"; their guilt could not be questioned, and their ingratitude was staggering when one considered that they were "in every respect better situated than poor white people." Nor could any idealism be connected with these monsters. The insurrectionists had no intention "to release their oppressed brethren," but wanted to rob the banks and sail away to Santa Domingo. The slaves, pampered ingrates in one sentence, become "oppressed brethren" in the next when Mrs. Hooper let her intellectual guard down. Just outside Wilmington, Moses Curtis filled his diary with similarly confused reflections, along with the common thought that either abuse or indulgence might drive slaves to revolt, but the greatest of these was indulgence: "No class of beings . . . take such vile advantage of favors as blacks." The Wilmington murders caused Curtis to conclude that he must be strict in insisting that his slaves brush his boots well. Mrs. Hooper's conclusions seem more to the point. She wished to go north: "I think I could not leave this world in peace if I thought my children would inhabit a slave state twenty years hence."

Hooper's solution was a womanly answer. Men reached more toughly twisted conclusions. If Moses Curtis's commitment to the better blackened boot was idiosyncratic, that of Lewis Williams was typical. Williams recognized that the plot showed that "something ought to be done on the subject of slavery," but he suggested doing something only about free blacks, whom he wanted removed "beyond our limits."[21] Such a conclusion flew bravely above the facts that of the dozens implicated only two were freemen (and only one of those convicted—Dan, a Wilmington drayman); and that the only two blacks said to volunteer information about the plot, one in Duplin and one in Wilmington, were not fondly faithful chattel but freemen. The fear was of slaves, but after the fact, men like Williams took comfort in scapegoating free blacks.

The hysteria of these events didn't undercut their pragmatic contribution. Heads staring from poles created black fear and white sense of control. A phrase runs through the accounts of these murders: "killed as examples." Such examples explain the strange indifference that those looking at the executions from a distance often expressed, or carefully avoided expressing. Governor Stokes himself wrote to his South Carolina counterpart, "There has been no insurrection of slaves in North Carolina," and he admitted that "some, who were innocent" had been killed. Yet he took no action to protect the innocent, other than to reprieve Jerry so that his owner wouldn't have to contribute unreasonably to the price of the public example. Stokes, like the Wrights, was happy to pay the innocent life of old Pizgah as small contribution to his state's exemplary justice.

Proslavery people used the gory acts and examples to repress all doubts about slavery. Three of the four trials that resulted in convictions were presided over by Judge Strange, a man "before whom a slave never found favor." In Richmond County, where one conviction took place, the legal record book contains an enigmatic extra comment: after sentencing Reverend Crawford's Avery to hang, "Judge Strange left the court house and without returning left the County." The petition that accused Strange of judicial prejudice against slaves begged reprieve for a convicted slave rapist on the grounds that the alleged victim, Lavinia Swink, had accused another of Mrs. Kelly's slaves first and changed her mind only after it was shown that the original accused was not in the area at the time of the claimed crime.

W. L. Menouson assured the governor that leading citizens would favor pardon except "for prudential motives" caused by the insurrection scare. The counterpetition urging execution admitted as much by stressing "the present excited state of the country as regards the Black population, and the evil example that would be set to said population." Guilt mattered less than the need to prevent an "evil example" of blacks questioning white versions of truth, no matter how patently false. Sometimes property had to be sacrificed to protect it, insurrection scares and the Southern legal system regularly recognized.

In North Carolina, the 1831 scare was bounded by some legalism and skepticism about the reality of any plot, but the results were typical. The North Carolina governor, who believed no plot had existed, nonetheless blamed it on "fanatics of their own complexion, and other incendiaries" and urged stricter supervision.[22] The North Carolina legislature agreeably passed a new parcel of laws, over half of them aimed at free blacks.

Governor Stokes's "other incendiaries" may have included William Lloyd Garrison, whose *Liberator* the Southern press discovered about a month after Southampton and immediately installed as cause ex post facto.[23] At any rate, the North Carolina panic remained a local affair, wholly overshadowed by the Virginia tragedies, insurrectionary and conventional, that preceded and followed it. But no matter how softened or distorted, Turner's rebellion stained proslavery ideology. By 1835, the South was eager to replace his terrifying memory with an insurrection scenario infinitely more fanciful and, hence, comforting. This panic took place in Mississippi, centered in the black belt around the village of Livingston.

The documentation for the Mississippi scare is rich. The area's vigilance committee published a brief official account in the *Clinton Gazette*, while general interest in the event led to the publication of many letters describing or discussing what happened. Although none of these letters essentially attacked the mob actions, Thomas Shackleford, the vigilantes' designated historian, nettled by some of the data disclosed and questions raised, dubbed them the products of "officious letter writers." Shackleford wrote the official justification of the mob in a pamphlet rich equally in detail, invention, and omissions. Two leading Mississippi politicians, Henry Foote and John Claiborne, much later provided some information about the events in which Foote, especially, was closely involved. In addition, the Mississippi panic quickly became integrated into the myth of John Murrell's criminal clan, one of the most honored and telling of popular Southern visions of their society.

The 1835 panic was less deadly than the preceding ones in Virginia and those that came over two decades later in Tennessee and Texas. One vigilante lost his life, while the mob killed seven whites and at least a dozen, probably over two dozen, blacks in early July, while later in 1835 at least eight whites and one black were killed in related insurrection–Murrell clan outbursts in Mississippi and neighboring states.

The affected area was one adjacent to the Mississippi River that featured rich soil, sprawling plantations, and men on the make on a large scale, many both very wealthy and much in debt. Settled a quarter of a century earlier, it had boomed in the "flush times" of the early 1830s. There were complaints that "the state of society" suffered because a few wealthy planters, many of them absentee, aggrandized the land. The ratio of blacks to whites was high and had grown in a decade from just over one-third to over two-thirds. The banking panic of 1834 shook the prosperity of the region because most planters were heavily dependent on credit. The early summer of 1835 had been very rainy, without a fully clear day between mid-May and mid-July, the kind of weather a witty Louisiana editor called "Southern days with Northern principles." The rain had kept the slaves idle much of the time and created fear that the crop would be small, perhaps even ruined.[24]

Shackleford's account claimed that in mid-June whites first got whiff of a plot when a Madam Latham, living on a rural plantation at Beattie's Bluff, some nine miles from Livingston, heard a female slave disputing the necessity of killing a particular white child. The black woman then confessed to her mistress the insurrection plot, but Latham gave out only "hints" of the plot for almost two weeks. On June 26 she first told her story to some gentlemen from Livingston. Instead of investigating, these gentlemen rode back to Livingston to call a meeting, chaired by the nephew of Mississippi's governor, to see if there was any evidence of insurrection there. There can be no explanation of such delay, and of the slave woman's never being further quizzed, other than that the tale was either generally unsubstantiated and disbelieved or invented later.

The mob at Livingston soon resorted to lash evidence, though without quick success. A black driver finally told owner William Johnson that an old slave had told him that Ruel Blake's Peter had mentioned to him an insurrection plot. The old slave denied Peter had ever said anything of the kind until the committee "ordered him to be whipped until he would tell what the conversation was." "A biting thong wielded by a strong and practiced hand," went one account of the confession of Johnson's slave, "is the most irresistible of human arguments with those whose minds have not been refined to that pitch of intelligence which is capable of martyrdom." "After a most severe chastisement," the old man confirmed "in every particular" the driver's story and implicated Thomas Hudnold's Ned along with Ruel Blake's Peter. Ned escaped, and Peter refused to confess despite a brutal whipping, given over some protest from his master, a ginwright with whom the elderly mechanic worked closely. Shackleford later claimed that Peter repeatedly said that he'd never tell what his master had told him not to reveal. Shackleford also claimed that none of the vigilantes noted this unusual way of denying knowledge of a plot.[25]

Back at Beattie's Bluff, the mob more efficiently proved insurrection. Jesse Mabry learned of Madam Latham's story on June 28, but he and the other citizens of the bluff merely held "a small meeting" three days later, the day after the first whipped confession occurred at Livingston. They quickly made up for lost time. On July 1, they selected two slaves, one of whom, old Weaver, "a preacher," refused to confess "under the torture of the lash when even his executioner was nigh to fainting with his task." Such clear proof of stubborn courage and, hence, guilt led to Weaver's immediate hanging, which banished all doubt about the plot from white minds or tongues. The second slave, Jim, was wiser and, after "being cruelly lacerated with the whip, at length gave in, and promised to tell all if the flagellator would hold his hand." Jim told all he was told to tell so well that his life was spared, living proof of the hope confession offered to those accused. The next morning, after "scrutinizing and patient examination," the mob hanged five more slaves, including another "preacher" whom Jim had fingered at their behest. Jim was then taken to Livingston to continue his work.[26]

The day before Weaver's death and Jim's confession proved the plot, the mob at Livingston took action that assured that some white co-conspirators would replace in Mississippi the wholly hypothetical ones earlier posited in Virginia and North Carolina. Ruel Blake had to flee town because of anger about his lack of enthusiasm for the beating of his slave. And "steam doctor" William Saunders, perhaps frightened, perhaps vengeful, perhaps shrewdly competitive, told the committee that his former partner, Joshua Cotton, had traded with blacks who brought him stolen property. Saunders left town but, going to Vicksburg, unwisely repeated his charges to another mob segment whom he met on the road and who decided that such knowledge implicated Saunders. No sooner did report come of the strange fruit hanging from trees nine miles away than the mob at Livingston strung up the three slaves they had in custody: Peter, William Johnson's old slave, and one other. Shackleford admitted that this may have been done "precipitously." The next day 160 citizens appointed a formal Vigilance Committee of Thirteen to guide future local extralegal activities. They immediately turned their attention to Saunders and to Cotton, who'd been found hiding in a swamp. Both men were whipped, and a cringing Saunders quickly agreed that Cotton had told him about the plot. Cotton, stronger-minded than his former colleague, confessed only when it became clear he was to be hanged; then he promised further revelations about his white confederates if he were spared for awhile. His ploy for delay didn't work. The committee wanted action more than "evidence," and they celebrated on July 4 by hanging both white steam doctors from the bars of the jailhouse window.

More slaves were hanged in the following days at Livingston and in the general area, but no one provided numbers. One or two dozen seems a reasonable guess; the larger estimate would put the total number of blacks killed, all but one of them slaves, at about thirty, the estimate most often given. The additional white victims drew more attention. The mob ordered out at least seven whites after three of them, including a seventy-two-year-old man, were given severe beatings with a "coleman"; members took turns striking the naked victims, who were pegged to the ground. One of these, steam doctor Lee Smith, was only ordered out but was beat by less formally organized rioters as he left. Henry Foote watched but did not dare to offer protective word for the young man he liked and respected. On July 8 the vigilantes hanged Albe Dean, whose crime was association with Cotton and Saunders, and Angus Donovan, a corn trader from Kentucky, who was guilty of evincing disgust at the bloody brutality of the slave whippings at Beattie's Bluff.[27]

Another victim who had proved his abolition by objecting to whipping slaves "almost to death" was Ruel Blake, hanged at Livingston on July 10. The final white deaths in Livingston occurred on July 16. A committee from neighboring Warren County "arrested" John and William Earle and handed them over to the Livingston committee. That night a mob took William Earle from jail and tortured him. Shackleford claimed that Earle confessed "without any fear or compulsion." In fact, he was whipped senseless and then revived when the crowd decided it would be fun to lacerate his back with the claws of a tomcat swung over him by its tail. After pouring melted sealing wax over his wounds, rioters threw Earle back in jail, where he managed to hang himself, vigilantes said; they hanged his brother John in the morning. The only Earle crime hinted at was his being related to Andrew Boyd, "convicted" by the mob but never caught.[28]

Courage and connections saved one other intended victim, Patrick Sharkey. He and James Kilborn, local justices of the peace, angered Livingston vigilantes when they let some slave "suspects" go and refused to turn over some poor whites who came to them for legal protection. The mob peppered Sharkey's house with bullets, shattering Sharkey's right hand. He still could shoot with the other, and the mob rode off when Sharkey killed Hiram Perkins and a horse and badly wounded Robert Hodge Jr. and one other. Sharkey also came within inches of killing the governor's rioting nephew, who left with a bullet hole through the collar of his coat. The vigilantes expected to capture and kill Sharkey the next day. Instead Patrick's cousin William Sharkey, chief justice of the Mississippi Supreme Court, knowing the protective weakness of Southern law, had Patrick give himself up to the neighboring Clinton Vigilantes, where he was held in protective custody until passions abated. The Clinton committee contented themselves with hanging but one black, a free mulatto who had a hidden gun, which he used to hunt squirrels.

The last known mob murder occurred two months later. A slave of Thomas Hudnold, Ned, was, along with Blake's Peter, the first accused. He escaped and remained out of sight, probably with his master's connivance. Hudnold, the wealthiest member of the Committee of Thirteen, probably thought danger had ended, but threats from a less organized mob caused the committee to hang Ned under their genteel auspices.[29]

These Mississippi events gain suggestiveness from three things that were used to explain them. From the time of the first white hangings, the insurrection plot became connected with a mythic criminal clan that Southerners insisted was at the center of the contemplated black rebellion. And shortly after the Mississippi outbreak, Southerners began to revise this story to blame abolitionists for the trouble or, more commonly, to insist that abolitionism and the criminal clan were a unified conspiracy. Finally, the comparatively formal organization of the group at the center of the scare led to a written glorification of its activities; this account gave shape to the argument usually left implicit in insurrection panics.

Shackleford's committee-sponsored history is similar to many vigilante accounts, differing significantly only in that it deals with a black rather than a white threat, so terrible that citizens heroically and necessarily rose up to save the community. For Southern mobs, a little Latin lent a lot of respectability, and Shackleford's motto for the committee was "salus populi est summa lex," which he translated: self-defense was "the first law of Nature derived from our Creator as essential to the preservation of our lives itself," the argument used by thinkers from Thomas Jefferson to Sidney Hook who wanted to sanction actions deemed illegal or unconstitutional. Indeed, an 1835 Mississippi newspaper reprinted Thomas Jefferson's argument as theoretical justification of the mob activities.[30]

The argument for self-defense depended on showing why legal officials could not handle the situation, and Shackleford recited the usual litany. The jail was small and unsafe, while a guard would have "left many families defenseless"; of course, the committee kept all its victims there, safely guarded. His other assertion was that "immediate example, and its consequent terror, without hope from the law's delay or evasion, seem as in truth, it was indispensible to safety." Shackleford's stumbling grammar and punctuation reflect the awkwardness of the argument that the full discovery of the plot, and the jailing of the leading conspirators, black and white, would not have prevented the insurrection. Even "the execution of a few negroes, unknown and obscure," Shackleford claimed, would not "have kept whites from perpetrating their horrid design." Supposedly a plot, by all accounts dependent for success on absolute secrecy and general slave support, would have been carried forward after full public revelation by the dozen or so whites who had planned it, even though half of them were in custody already.

Shackleford insisted that the committee acted only with "the most patient exercise and calm deliberation of their judgments." He claimed that the accused had "all the privileges allowed to criminals in courts of justice" and then some: all were treated with respect and were convicted only on "evidence convincing to *all*." To support this vision of perfect rectitude, Shackleford failed to mention the whipped-out confessions, black and white, and embarrassing incidents like the attempted killing of Patrick Sharkey. He also neglected to explain why the investigators hanged Cotton before he revealed his co-conspirators, unless the committee didn't care to learn the truth. Henry Foote, who was allowed to represent Angus Donovan before the committee, wrote much later that "the examination was conducted in a very rapid and informal manner, and without the least regard to the established principles of law and evidence." Foote didn't dare even to cross-examine the witnesses against Donovan, whom Foote was sure was guilty of nothing except some sympathy with blacks being beaten.[31]

Because of its formality, this committee offers evidence about the social position of mob members. Historian Edwin Miles found that twelve of the thirteen members were middling to large slave-owning planters from the region. The person who first proposed the committee was Dr. Joseph Pugh, and its chair was Dr. M. D. Mitchell; perhaps it was wholly coincidental that three of the whites hanged and one exiled were their medical competitors and that a blacksmith named Mitchell was the only initial arrestee released unpunished. While the committee's pretense of calm judiciality was a joke, there probably was some desire to curb as well as sanctify "the wild sallies of passion, and not infrequently private revenge" of mobs. The wealthiest member, Thomas Hudnold, furnished the horse on which Ruel Blake initially left town and clearly tried to protect his slave Ned. Such realities suggest that he may have joined to check as much as channel communal fear and desire to act.[32]

The victims were certainly less well-off than their formal tormentors. Six of the eight whites killed had never lived in Madison County, allegedly the center of the plot, and two of them, Dean of Kentucky and Hunter of Tennessee, were merely traveling through; nine of twelve others accused by the committee lived elsewhere. Cotton had lived near Livingston for only a few months, and Ruel Blake for only a few years, though in that time Blake had bought slaves and land. The one longtime resident was seemingly a marginal drunk whom Cotton thought safe to name without fear of effective contradiction. Cotton, Blake, and Albe Dean were native New Englanders. Shackleford presented a lot of melodramatic rhetoric: all of the white victims were "highway robbers, murderers and abolitionists," labels forgotten when the author penned his equally bloody-bones description of each villian. Blake, for example, now was "noted for cold-blooded revenge, insatiable avarice, and unnatural cruelty" and had gone to sea as a boy, probably to become a pirate. The unspecific and improbable character of such charges append disbelief. It is clear that action was easier against relative strangers, perhaps especially Yankees, even though this choice undercut the credibility of a local plot.[33]

The argument became that the insurrection plot was not local but sectional when the mob began to jail and whip whites. By the time Cotton and Saunders were hanged, the affair was firmly affixed to the criminal clan that Tennessean John Murrell allegedly headed. Those whites killed and driven off, the story said, were white criminals who plotted insurrection as a distractive ploy to allow them to plunder comfortably. Despite the ridiculousness of this plan, there was no public Southern questioning of it in the antebellum years. It remained, in the later words of Mississippian John H. F. Claiborne, "one of the most extraordinary and lamentable hallucinations of our time," even after its literary creator was discredited.[34]

The story of Virgil Stewart, on which the whole case for a criminal clan rests, needs only be read to be disbelieved. Even for people content to consider thousands of white Southerners happy to plan a massacre of their race allegedly to abet robbery, Stewart's account should have seemed wholly implausible. One had to be willing to believe that the head of this clan, John Murrell, continued petty thefts against his neighbors as he laid plans for the great conspiracy; that he, who first reduced crime "to an organized system," began telling his various adventures to Virgil Stewart within hours after meeting him as a stranger on the road; that in two days Murrell accepted Stewart into the clan and revealed the great conspiracy to him; that Murrell never noticed Stewart jotting down notes on Murrell's revelations with a needle "on his boot legs, finger nails, saddle skirts, and portmanteau" as the two rode along; that upon meeting the leaders of the clan Stewart gave a speech on the social justification of crime; that Murrell insisted on giving Stewart a list of 300 clansmen's names on parting, a list that was only partial and contained initials instead of first names because of a paper shortage; that after having Murrell arrested for stealing a neighbor's slaves, Stewart was not hurt by the powerful clan, although he was known to have a list of its members and was living surrounded by clansmen; that for six months after Murrell's arrest, Stewart never mentioned the awful conspiracy in order to protect the clan leader's right to a fair trial, and only partly told the tale at the trial itself; that with the plot exposed, 450 of their number named, and their leader in jail, the conspirators did not drop their great insurrection idea but moved forward its commencement. Suffice it to say that the names on Stewart's list of Mississippi conspirators matched none of the victims at Livingston but did jibe with two of the vigilantes.[35]

Stewart's character no better supported the truth of his tale. Stewart was born in Georgia and reared there by his widowed mother. At one time of substantial means, the family's finances sank, so that Stewart at fourteen was deprived of the education he desperately wanted. He worked in the printing and cotton gin businesses near his home until 1830, when he removed to Madison County, Tennessee. In June 1833 he moved again, now to the newly opened Choctaw purchase, where he tended the store of Matthew Clanton for several months. Stewart returned to Tennessee in

January 1834, just after three slaves belonging to Parson John Henning disappeared. Henning probably hired Stewart to track his slaves, although Stewart insisted that the adventure began only because "the noble young man" voluntarily endangered life in the pursuit of justice. When Murrell and Stewart returned to Tennessee, Murrell was arrested. Stewart continued his futile pursuit of Henning's slaves, then returned to the Choctaw purchase. Now threatened by his former employer, Matthew Clanton, with prosecution for theft, Stewart organized a vigilance committee for "his own and the community's protection." When the group refused to drive away Stewart's enemies, including Clanton, the young man retreated to Tennessee.[36]

At Murrell's trial in July he told about Murrell's theft and hinted at a much broader plot in a way that attracted some notice in the press. One paper suggested that Stewart's testimony, "if well arranged, and embellished, would form the subject of a story, or novel, unsurpassed by anything produced in fiction." Some months later, while convalescing from an illness in the area of Mississippi where the panic was to center, Stewart arranged, embellished, and published his legend of Murrell's mystic clan. That the panic arose in the area where Stewart wrote may not have been coincidental. The committee member who first whipped out the desired "truth" and began the hangings was Jesse Mabry, who wrote a letter, incorporated in Shackleford's book, describing the first Beattie's Bluff whippings. This letter is much in Stewart's melodramatic style, as is a later one, more circumstantial in its account, describing the first Beattie's Bluff beatings, attached to a *Police Gazette* reprinting of Stewart's Murrell story. The case is far from certain, but it's possible that Jesse Mabry's actions and only known writings were the work of that man of many pseudonyms, Virgil Stewart, and the Livingston bloodshed an unusual, and unusually successful, book promotion campaign.[37]

It's not surprising that Stewart's book achieved substantial popularity. It has the coarse vigor and imagination, the melodramatic incident, and the personalized explanation of problems that characterized a fairly large body of plebian literature on both sides of the Atlantic. These tales of crime usually provided a happy ending, with much moralizing and little suggestion of structural change, but their format permitted expression of some of the harshest appraisals of the unpleasant underside of social realities. Stewart offered much of what Eric Hobsbawm rightly sees in the European exemplars: strong popular protest lurking beneath melodrama and moralistic whitewash.[38]

Stewart's account is fascinating as a myth that much of Southern society insisted was unquestioned fact, even though it depicted a wholly ruthless society where no man could trust his slave or his neighbor. The Mississippi legislature welcomed Stewart as hero; the New Orleans City Council republished the tale, "the truth of which cannot now be doubted," to awaken citizens to the dangers surrounding them; the legislature of South Carolina voted a reward to Stewart for his services, and newspapers throughout the South praised the tale with no questioning of its validity. Such was the currency and endurance of this myth that the South's leading novelist, William Gilmore Simms, based two popular works on it and, when one of these was reissued in 1854, added a preface asserting that Stewart's facts about this "wild and savage confederation" were "beyond question." Robert Coates, in the guise of history, and Eudora Welty, in decently fictitious format, have continued Stewart's legend.[39]

Beyond question was the fact that this pamphlet argued that Southern society's vicious class competition and favoritism justified the robber chief, whose talents were

> as creditably employed as are the talents of many who are accounted pillars of society. In this world every man must take care of himself; some do it by siding with the majority, and by helping to enforce set laws, while they violate higher moral obligations themselves, without scruple; a smaller portion despise hypocrisy, and set themselves in open opposition to the rest. It is a mere difference of opinion which makes one party lock the other up when they get them in their power, and which makes the other power retaliate by plundering or killing the first whenever they get a chance. It's a game. . . . I believe, sir, in respect for the law, when the law takes care of all classes alike, but when war is open between classes of society, I say let the hardest fend off.

In the United States, having money, no matter how procured, was the only escape from the sneers of "opulent wealth" and the sole basis of "character, popularity, and power." Murrell showed that the "terrible power" of the clan was no greater or more vicious than that of the law over its victims; at least the clan avoided "hypocritical pretense of affection for the object of its vengeance." Murrell went on to discuss lynch law. "A respectable lynch mob" had set out to hang him, but when they found him prepared to defend himself, they "showed their respect for the law by dispersing and going home." Murrell's analysis of vigilante heroism, if harsh, was fairly accurate, as was his comment on the broader principle behind it: "Ah, sir, society will seldom venture to trifle with the powerful but it will trample on a beggar and disdain to calculate the wrong."

In his alleged address to the Mystic Clan, Stewart argued that divine as well as social realities justified criminality in a dark premature variant of social Darwinism, parallel to that in John Lyde Wilson's dueling guidebook. Animals lived by killing other animals, and man preyed on his fellow man so that "if there be a God he has evidently given his sanction to this system of violence, and impressed it upon nature with the force of law." Stewart, poor, badly educated because he was poor, ambitious, frustrated in his various success schemes, in trouble with the law himself, gave himself, not Murrell, the harshest lines against the brutalities of class and cash in American society, including the basic moral; "If I live in hell, I will fight for the devil."[40]

Yet in Stewart's account, class and competitive hatreds were linked to slavery. On this issue, too, the melodramatic format allowed expression of fears too deeply held to be handled in more proper tracts. Stewart made clear that Murrell's success as a "Negro thief" grew out of the basic discontent of slaves. At one point Murrell demonstrated his skill to Stewart on a slave they met by chance on the road:

"Well, old man, you must have a d—d hard master, or he would not send you to mill this cold day."

"Yes, maser, all ov 'em hard in dis country."

In a few minutes, the black had agreed to run off with Murrell, to be sold and restolen a couple of times before being given his freedom, and to bring along several of his fellow slaves. "You shall not be with your d—d old task master much longer to be cuffed about like a dog," Murrell promised the old man on parting. Then the bandit informed Stewart, "Fifteen minutes are all I want to decoy the best of ne-

groes, from the best of masters." Such was the vision of slave treatment and loyalty
in this pamphlet which Southerners insisted was factual.

The way Murrell won blacks to his insurrection plot also provided a comment on
white uneasiness about slavery. Murrell's appeal to them was not put in terms of
plunder or revenge. Rather, social justice and the moral isolation of the South were
stressed in a formula more tough-minded than that of any Northern abolitionist. The
clan told slaves, Murrell said, that

> they are entitled to their freedom as much as their masters, and that all the wealth of the
> country is the proceeds of black people's labor. . . . We remind them of the pomp and
> splendour of their masters and then refer them to their own degraded situation; and tell
> them that it is power and tyranny that rivets their chains of bondage, and not because
> they are an inferior race of people. We tell them that the West Indies are all free, and that
> they got their freedom by rebelling a few times and slaughtering the whites, and con-
> vince them that if they will follow the example of the West India negroes, that they will
> obtain their liberty and become as much respected as if they were white; and that they
> can marry white women when they are all put on a level. In addition to this, I get them to
> believe, that the most of people are in favor of their being free, and that the free states in
> the United States, would not interfere with the negroes, if they were to butcher every
> white man in the slave holding states.

When vengeance was invoked, it was done in terms of the brutalities suffered by
slaves: "We have long been subject to the whips of our tyrants, and many of our
backs wear the scars."[41] It was not the brutal black but the informed and perceptive
slave, the black who sensed what Southern whites sensed, that haunted Stewart's
nightmare scenario, when strangers talking justice could readily turn all slaves into
executioners.

The Madison County hangings, like Stewart's tale, were premised on the idea that
outsiders could securely induce large numbers of slaves to join a plot to murder all
whites without one faithful soul ever mentioning it to a master, although the
Nashville Banner, much after the fact, invented a prototypical faithful slave infor-
mant. In the Livingston incident, as in Stewart's tale, suspicion focused on especially competent blacks. In the early "official" report of the killings in the *Clinton
Gazette*, the blacks involved were described as "*the bold, the sagacious, the desperate*," particularly "Negro preachers, always the greatest rascals." At least two of
those executed at Beattie's Bluff were preachers. When the hysteria quieted and
people made light of further danger, citizens commonly referred to slaves as "ignorant but contented," the two traits essentially joined in the Southern mind.[42]

There was almost no public questioning of the reality of the Livingston plot,
though on July 8 George Wyche urged the governor to rescue the government from
"the hands of the mob" because all danger ended when the conspiracy was discovered. Perhaps the best indication of private response came in a long letter from Dr.
William H. Thomson to his sister Hannah. After expressing some worry about professional competition from "the steamers," he talked about the "alarm and stir" and
said rampant rumor made it "impossible at present to arrive at the truth." He'd heard
that the plot had been discovered by a planter in disguise at a black meeting, and
now "every negro they meet who does not give a good account of himself they take
up or shoot down." He claimed that twenty blacks and five or six whites had been

executed, some of them steam doctors "whose remedies were found to avail them nothing against hemp." He recounted the near-murder of a black woman passing through his town, and how Sharkey's opposition to lynchers' methods brought "upon himself their exterminating vengeance." How far "the phrenzy" would go he didn't know, but already "the innocent with the guilty" were attacked. Clearly, he concluded, "the regulators need regulating."[43]

The public wrestling with the issue was highly telling. A single issue of the Jackson *Mississippian* offers good résumé of the complicated response to the panic and the tensions within slavery that underlay it. The editor, anxious to assure continued immigration and investment to the area, complained that too much had been written about the "contemplated insurrection." All the guilty had "been hung—as all such wretches should be—without judge and jury." Mississippi had almost known a similar scene to the Southampton affair, but after all, it had only been "a neighborhood affair" and "the negroes generally had nothing to do with it." In a separate article the editor defended the governor for not sending the militia to Livingston because "many families would have been unprotected while their dwellings were surrounded by the enemy." Such contradictions mirrored deep uncertainties about how real the danger was or could be admitted to be: blacks generally had little to do with it, but it was almost another Southampton; it was a neighborhood matter, but taking militia from other parts of the state would have left men's families surrounded by enemy slaves. The editor's final assurances to the world were tellingly equivocal: "property and life are as safe here as in the other states where slavery exists," because slaves were "raw and untutored."

There also was a communication from B***, who frequently wrote chatty articles on Mississippi's past and future. Rather than playing down the threat, B*** argued that without prompt action "our towns and villages would have been reduced to ashes, all honest men and their wives and children butchered up by the white villains and negroes." The fright was nothing new, said the old Mississippian: "From my youth I have at times heard of plots and insurrections, and much alarm has frequently been given, and a Capt. Nat has done considerable murder in Virginia, and many have their fears that at some period, our slave population will do us much mischief." B*** went on to explore the moral problem of slavery. The Bible did not condemn holding slaves but

abundantly condemn[s] unkind treatment to them, there lies the sin of slavery. And who more likely to risk the consequences of an insurrection than those who have hard masters. . . . It is God that sits in the heavens who controls the affairs of nations. . . . Though conspiracy after conspiracy has been attempted, yet no weapon that has been found against us has prospered. . . . By treating servants well they can perform better service, will last the longer, we can well afford it, we will have a place in their affections, they will betray the white villains and their plots will never succeed. . . . The name of the Lord is a strong tower, and have their plots not always been disclosed by negroes who had kind masters?

As response to the alleged plot and the real mass murder, B***'s perplexed simplicity of mind and kindness of wish showed the South's tangled response to its slavery. If there was reason to doubt that Madam Latham overheard positive evidence of the plot, the rest of her story—probably all she originally told—was convincing, even typical. She had noticed that many of her slaves recently showed "a disposition to be insolent and disobedient" and had overheard them use "contemptuous language" about her. She also heard a favorite slave remark that "she wished to God it was all over and done with, that she was tired of waiting on *white folks*, and wanted to be her own mistress the balance of her days, and clean up her own house." And what could B***'s kindness be in a system where such normal human desires were in truth insurrectionary?

On the last page of the paper where B*** reflected on God's approval of kindly slavery were the usual runaway notices. Adjacent to B***'s letter was one from Brandon, Mississippi, which told of a captured runaway, John James, belonging to a Mr. Ward below Natchez. Rather than be returned to his master, James had put "a period to *his slavery*" by hanging himself from a three-and-one-half foot ladder in his cell. The Brandon writer told the story of James "for the benefit of such as treat their slaves with barbarous severity and such wanton cruelty to make them prefer death itself to their condition."[44] The letter writer's moral anger spoke well for Southern decency, but such open talk about cruelty to slaves was itself in the process of being mob-hushed as fear of outside hostility to slavery mounted. Positive good insistence after 1835 increasingly demanded an essential commitment to not noticing anything that happened that was positively vicious.

One element that became entwined with this panic was wholly missing from the early accounts of it and from the first Stewart pamphlet: abolition. In mid-August, a month after the panic, the state learned of the abolition mail campaign. On August 14 the *Mississippian* responded virulently, charging that such writings were intended to promote insurrection. Yet the connection to recent local events was tentative: "Who knows but that their doctrines were the chief cause of the South Hampton massacre and the recent attempted insurrection in Mississippi?" In the same issue, "A Voter" from Clinton claimed that if the plot's discovery "had not been made by negroes," destruction would have been terrible and some slaves would "have made their escapes to their abolitionist friends at the north." Yet those in the affected area awaited cues from the North before they discovered that Blake and Donovan were abolitionists and the great criminal Clan an adjunct of Arthur Tappan's philanthropy. The welcome news came from the *New York Commercial Advertiser* and the *National Intelligencer*, passed on by *Niles' Register* under the *Intelligencer* caption: "The fruits of fanaticism. Behold, ye 'liberators,' 'emancipators,' 'abolitionists,' the fruits of your extravagance and folly, your recklessness, and your criminal plots against the lives of your fellow men."[45]

Local revision of the plot then began. A letter in the *Woodville Republican*, for instance, decided that the distinction in Murrell's clan between the "grand council members" and the "strikers" offered the key to the role of "those abolitionist fanatic murderers": "Now the only difference between Murrell's clan and the abolitionists is this—Murrell is a man of strong mind and intelligence," but his "strikers" were "nothing more than weak-headed Abolitionists who through a false religious zeal would think they were doing God service to murder all the white inhabitants of the United States who do not believe just as they do." The South was creating its cherished "abolitionist": a religious fanatic who was also a retarded bandit-murderer.

By December leading citizens of Wilkinson County gathered "in reference to the dangerous machinations of the clan of Murrell and the abolitionists." This meeting concluded "that the hour of danger has not passed off and that the most energetic measures" were needed to handle the many Murrellites-abolitionists "not only living on our borders but prowling amongst us." They set up a committee of vigilance to hunt down such persons; if "clearly ascertained" to belong to either group, "he, she or they should suffer death."[46]

This blending of John Murrell with Arthur Tappan also occurred in soberer private thoughts, such as a letter from Methodist leader William Winans to his brother. Winans wrote that he'd welcome "the day when the footstep of no slave should press the soil of our country," but the tragic results of abolition were clear: "*They* have shut out thousands of slaves from the gospel and its means of grace. They have rendered the police, in thousands of instances, more rigorous than it was before— they have caused the deaths of many slaves, and will probably occasion the death of thousands more." The deaths he referred to were those near Livingston; although 120 miles from "the chief scene of these massacres . . . I was near enough to the volcano to hear the rumblings and feel the agitation of the crater." Winans said the trouble was "owing to the incendiary publications of the abolitionists, and the discovery of an association of villains, one of whose projects was to incite the slaves to rebellion." He deplored the vigilante violence, "lawless and blind as it was," but found much excuse for it "in the foreign and flagitious meddling of abolitionists and in the formidable designs of the almost equally wicked Murrellites." Winans concluded, as he wished to believe, that the tragedy grew from the joined efforts of Murrell and the worse Tappans rather than from slavery itself, which he sincerely disliked but which he always publicly defended.[47]

The entwining of abolition with the Murrell plot also occurred in Shackleford's report and Stewart's tale. Shackleford made Donovan an "emissary of those deluded fanatics at the North," even though the one thing Donovan's "defense attorney," Henry Foote, had been allowed to establish was his client's racial loyalty. For the 1836 edition of his history, Stewart suddenly remembered that Murrell was an accomplice of the abolitionists, with the destruction to be led by "a poisonous swarm from the 'great northern hive' of fanatic incendiaries." A long "note," awkwardly stuffed in, asserted that Murrell expected financial support from "an English lecturer on slavery." Yet even in this quick historical revisionism Stewart's Murrell spoke with a tough-minded honesty about abolition in the South that one finds nowhere else. Religious or rational appeals might convince the North and West of the evil of slavery, but the powerful Southerner would count "the cost of his slaves and his annual income" and harden his heart. Only if blacks revolted "and let loose the arm of destruction . . . so that the judgments of God might be visibly seen and felt" would they touch "the flinty heart of the tyrant."[48]

For all its hard truths, Stewart's myth proffered Southern comfort." The . . . brutal affair at Southampton is still fresh in our memory," wrote a North Carolina minister in 1835. The attraction to the South of Mississippi's myth joining Murrell's "clan" and the "abolitionist" came from its providing an insurrectionary model less harrowing than that of Southampton. Southampton had illustrated what Stewart's pamphlet asserted: that large numbers of slaves not peculiarly mistreated were yet willing to slay all whites they could lay their hands on. Stewart's legend played on this terror but also softened it. Blacks were still a threat, but now they were also dupes manipulated by whites, so the power of darkness became partly illusion. And the source of danger was less the people Southerners deprived of freedom, dignity, and familial stability so that some whites might rest and profit than a society of bandits, men of leisure equally imbued with the profit motive. The main threat, too, was distanced and cut off from "the disagreeable state of living to be ever suspicious of those with whom we live" and from the uneasy "suspicion that Nat Turner might be in every family." Instead, it was the stranger whose distance made him a much more comfortable object of fearful hate.

The Mississippi addenda to the legend promised that prompt action could forestall all insurrectionary slaughter. The bodies decorating the trees, jail windows, and gallows in Madison County in early July, like the piked heads earlier in North Carolina, were human sacrifices promising protection against demonic terrors. The bloody Livingston Fourth of July "truth to say . . . was scarcely less a holiday than if the proceedings had been peaceful."[49] Stewart, as myth-maker, deserved the accolades the South gave him; he created a mythic Murrell much less fearsome than the real Nat Turner.

This angry insurrection-abolition summer marked changing Southern emphases about slavery. What the Denmark Vesey scare abetted in South Carolina earlier, the Mississippi panic of 1835 marked throughout the slave South: the move from justifying slavery as an evil for which all cures were worse than the disease to a position that said it was good, the basis of a profitably stable society and the kindest form of child care for a race of such deep inferiority that its freedom could only mean its destruction. It was, as Eugene Genovese has said, one of the South's "major turning points."

The clearest motif in this new tangle of ideas was that all the unhappinesses of slavery were wholly the result of abolition. On this issue Mississippi governor John Quitman's message was typical of what the South's political leaders, editors, and people agreed on. Cryptically referring to what had happened in his own state, Quitman quickly turned his eyes to the North, where abolition was sure to produce "partial scenes of violence and bloodshed" in the South, despite what he called "the interesting relations" between the master and his "faithful slave." Not what happened in Livingston but what went on in Boston and Utica became the key to the ties, beatific or bestial, between planter and slave. Northern agitation had "already, in some measure, disturbed the domestic tranquility, subjected the master to the care and anxiety of stricter vigilance, and induced curtailment of the innocent enjoyment of the slave." In spite of the recent insurrection panic—or more probably because of it—Quitman constructed an idyllic world of innocently happy slaves and gently carefree masters before the Satan of abolition disturbed Mississippi's tranquility. Immediately after the panic, Mississippians claimed that "white men" alone were responsible for the "ignorant and generally contented African's" sudden resolve on "indiscriminate butchery." By early 1836 Quitman had distanced white men to "abolitionists," softened the "butchery" to mere lull in "domestic repose," and turned hysterical executions into quiet "stricter vigilance."[50]

A second theme about which Southerners came to agree when put on the offensive was that slaves were better off than free laborers, black or white. Almost every Southern governor referred to the greater degradation of European labor, if they were moderate, or of Northern workers, if they were more radical or angry, and newspapers and public meetings followed suit. The cautious *New Orleans Bee* was pleased that city's anti-abolition resolves dropped the most virulent attacks on the North, but the paper insisted that slaves were much better off than all free blacks or white workers, particularly those in Europe. "Slavery exists here but in name," the paper concluded, while in England "pauperism is slavery."

A third theme in the argument was given sharper emphasis by the sense of threat: the inherent inferiority of blacks, beings so hapless they'd disappear were it not for the kindly discipline of the wiser race's total control. In the decades after Thomas Jefferson carefully planted his "mere doubt" that blacks were a lesser species of human, "scientific" racism had become in the South, and much of the North, a comforting certitude. Black freedom, Quitman and others assured abolitionists, the world, and themselves, would insure their "extermination" through violence or decadence. This was no new doctrine for Quitman, who a decade earlier had privately laid out his belief that blacks were "a happy, careless, unreflecting, good-natured race who, left to themselves, would degenerate into drones and brutes" but who became the "most contented of laborers" by the "wholesome restraint and stimulus" of slavery. A proslavery Northerner, Joseph Ingraham, visiting in Mississippi at the time of the panic, expressed the planter ideas he heard. There never really was any fear of blacks because the race was "wholly destitute of courage," with "fear, awe, and obedience" of whites "interwoven" into their very nature, as well as a deep contempt for their own race. Under slavery they were well treated and happy, though "there is no animal so averse to labour . . . as the African." Thus, they had to be forced to be happy—against their nature—by constant labor, since "there is no vice in which many of them will not become adepts, if allowed even temporary freedom from restraint, one day in seven." Ingraham's "theories" were perfectly congenial with the mishmash of self-contradictory but socially useful clichés of proslavery racism.

A fourth theme involved property. Southerners on guard offered idyllic pictures of kind masters and contented darkies, but after 1835 when angry and honest they warned the North about any interference with "our property." No other Americans at this time stressed so unanimously the absolute sanctity of private property over all other moral and communal considerations. The moderate *New Orleans Bee* was as insistent about "the integrity of our property" as were the rabid resolves from Norfolk, Virginia, which proclaimed that Southerners would not allow anyone even to discuss "the validity of their title to their slaves." Every Southerner would rather die, these Norfolk citizens went on, "than voluntarily surrender five hundred millions of their wealth." Just as Thomas Jefferson was the first American to acclaim the ideas of Adam Smith, his planter descendants throughout the South were the first to proclaim unambiguously the absolute sanctity of property as its primary commitment.[51]

Two arguments that followed in the immediate wake of the insurrection offer summary of these tendencies, one a series of letters by a North Carolina minister widely published in Southern papers and the other the resolves of a citizen group in

Clinton, Mississippi, near-neighbor of Livingston. Methodist Rev. E. Battle addressed his public letters to R. G. Williams, abolitionist editor of *Human Rights*.
Since that publication began, Battle told Williams, Southerners had suddenly noted
"a restless and disaffected spirit among our deluded servants." The minister was
willing to admit that "much evil" was tied to slavery, but given the nature of blacks
there was no alternative: a kind Virginian had recently freed a family of blacks but
soon had to hire an overseer to make them work for their own good. Battle claimed
that in his life he'd seen a slave whipped only once, though he'd also heard of one
other case in Burke County, Georgia, where an overseer whipped someone urging
insurrection. Surely Williams couldn't want to steal "our property," Battle concluded, or believe that Southern Christians would hold slaves "with a guilty conscience." How could any Christian believe that the South "would be so abundantly
blessed of the Lord, spiritually and temporally," if God were not an enthusiast of
slavery? For Battle the "Protestant ethic" of profits that proved divine favor was not
to be questioned. Battle's sympathy lay with the poor blacks in the North who had
"no kind master to protect them" and were hence degraded and often beaten by
mobs. Battle simply forgot Livingston's dead slaves of the month before or those
whose heads had decorated poles in his native Murfreesboro four years earlier, courtesy of their masters' protective efforts.

The Clinton resolves put the same argument in more secular terms. The nation
faced a grave crisis, these Mississippians argued, because abolitionists had perpetrated "the most grave encroachments on the rights of property in the south" and had
shown themselves willing to pursue this "nefarious object by blood and carnage."
These planters admitted some "cruel and tyrannical masters" existed, but it was
somehow those states who permitted abolitionists to speak who were directly responsible "for all the discontent, oppression, cruelty, stripes and carnage" that occurred. Slavery largely protected blacks, for "in truth the condition of our negroes is
infinitely more comfortable than that of the poor working class in the North. . . .
They are more contented, . . . an ignorant race." Besides, the Bible sanctioned
slavery, while Danish boors, Russian serfs, and French and English vassals still
lived in a state "not . . . less subversive of the equal rights of mankind." Northern
philanthropy could be better directed to the "enslaved inmates of their factories, and
the lack-land tenantry of a bloated aristocracy." The union was doomed if the North
did not end all abolition interference with "our rights, our property, and perhaps our
lives." And any discussion of the right to enslave, any consideration of "whether
slavery . . . be abstractly right or wrong" was intolerable interference with the
property of this otherwise "peaceful society."[52]

Such arguments did not attack bourgeois or evangelical or democratic values—
not even "the equal rights of mankind"—but simply used them in a way that made
not slavery but its questioning the evil. It was abolition that promoted violence,
threatened property, neglected real enslavement, encouraged "bloated aristocracy,"
caused all the ills of Southern bondage, and failed to see that the profits of slavery
proved God's endorsement. In all these writings there is no hint of the hierarchical
organicism that William Harper of South Carolina at times sentimentalized and
George Fitzhugh turned gingerly toward a science a decade later, when lasting sectional tensions created formal proslavery apologias of all stripes. Then antidemocra-

tic and hierarchical arguments waxed, though they never prevailed in the theoretical literature and barely dented the popular formulation of 1835. What organicism existed in the general argument related not to prebourgeois hierarchy but to a Burkean conservatism that damned insistence on rights—except those of property—when abstracted from social reality and historical roots.

The public statements in the wake of the Mississippi scare glossed the classic defense of slavery Virginian Thomas Dew wrote shortly after Nat Turner led Virginians briefly to debate the institution. Dew stressed the gross racial incompetence and inferiority of blacks, talked of how superior slaves' condition was to white labor in Europe, and defined the chief intellectual enemy in Burkean terms: sentimental emphasis on abstract rights that endangered the functional decencies of society that had been honed over time. One right, however, Dew insisted, was part of Southern functional reality: the absolute right to property that was the copartner of slavery in establishing modern progress away from feudal stagnation. It was "monstrous absurdity" to argue, Dew concluded, that Virginia should sacrifice the economic basis of its greatness, its wealth in slaves, or its huge profits as "a *negro* raising state for the other states." Since "the exclusive owners of property ever have been, ever will, and perhaps ever ought to be, the virtual rulers of mankind," no informed Virginia planter would give up his absolute control of all profits derivable from slavery.[53]

Such bourgeois ideology of slavery was in harmony with Southern reality, which participated in the essential facts of American life, often with special intensity: a market economy based on private ownership and international trade; competitive mobility related largely to money and conspicuous consumption; status based on individual/family economic effort, cleverness, or luck, with little communal or governmental interference; a definition of self dependent on family success and communal opinion integrated with wealth and position; much litigious self-assertion, and political power that was lawyer-dominated; deep involvement in democratic politics; rhetorical concentration on individual "liberty" and "rights"; steady agitation for economic growth and advantage, personal and communal; a deep and deeply evangelical Protestantism. If such a society was not bourgeois, one wonders what had to be added or subtracted.[54]

Certainly slavery interacted with every aspect of Southern society, from its system of violence on up. But such interaction didn't create different basic values and institutions from those of the North. Unquestioning commitment to slavery weakened the more questing and questioning social and intellectual trends of the North, but this to a degree sharpened the intensity of embrace of a bourgeois bottom line: position dependent on highly competitive individual and familial effort in gaining or retaining social status essentially tied to wealth. With slavery's help, the South maintained a more patriarchal family, an intense evangelicalism less related to communal activism, and a slightly louder democracy. It also featured slightly more volatile personal fortunes tied more wholly to an international market economy. And it tolerated assertive violence as a sometimes useful, although not commonly used, machete in John Lyde Wilson's competitive jungle.

Few Southerners would have disputed Karl Marx's claim that Southern slavery was "a calculated and calculating system." It was what they said themselves. Looking back, Ezekiel Powell remembered entering the 1830s as a teenage lad without a cent and using "unlimited credit" to become a Mississippi planter; looking on, a Virginia traveler noted the state's "incredible frenzy in speculating in land and negroes." The region's planters had no more dependable eulogist than Joseph Ingraham, who praised the "enterprise" of Southerners' steady pursuit of profit and expansion: "To sell cotton in order to buy negroes—to make more cotton to buy more negroes 'ad infinitum'" was the goal of every "thorough-going cotton planter," while to have a large plantation "well-stocked with hands" was "the *ne plus ultra* of everyman's ambition." The *Mississippian* described neighboring Warren County with glowing admiration as "one of exceeding interest, especially to the individual devoted to pecuniary profits." That its citizens were "shrewd, calculating, industrious, and enterprising" ensured their "extraordinary success in accumulating wealth," where it was "almost impossible to interest the people in any subject, except it is connected with making *Dollars* and *Cents*." Madison County was working to catch up to Warren; an editor in an ad for a paper there praised the county's exemplary "rapidity of growth" and its "vast resources," both "present and prospective."[55] The language of the region was that of bourgeois capitalism: flush, credit, speculation, enterprise, investment, industry, growth, profit, rapidity, resources, dollars, *more*.

The South's central economic commitment was as clear in writers labeled paternalist as in the laissez-faire capitalism of Thomas Dew. George Fitzhugh's essential motive in *Sociology* was no different from that of every Southern commercial convention: to devise a way by which slavery's immense personal profits would enrich the South as region rather than the North. South Carolina Chancellor William Harper put economic profits at the heart of his complacent hierarchy in both his proslavery tracts and his judicial opinions: his fundamental proposition was that "Property—the accumulation of Capital, as it is commonly called—is the first element of civilization." Thus, enslaved blacks contributed "to the advance of civilization, (by the results of their valuable labors)," but if freed they became "a dead weight to the progress of improvement," because blacks were such instinctual animals that "they make no provision for the morrow." Enslaved, they provided the money and leisure that let the "best" of the superior race promote human progress. So also said James Hammond: "The question is whether free or slave labor is cheaper to us."

Private records make even clearer the prevalence of the profit motive. "It is a sordid, avaricious, jockeying people, this," wrote Alabaman R. F. Charles of his wealthy neighbors: "a community of men who possess wealth without character and influence without worth." And questions couldn't be asked because "murderers and outlaws stalk abroad at noonday" so that "no one can feel anything like security of person." Most Southerners were less moralistic about slavery as a money-making matter. Kentuckian J. W. Menzies wrote a friend in Ohio about the stupidity of abolitionists "who instead of thanking God and our ancestors for the liberties of white people, and the privilege of *working negroes*, will be grumbling because the negroes are not *free too*." He was amazed that people could be so blind to interest and urged his friend to return to a more sensibly calculating society at least for July 4: "Come out from among them, if it is only to spend the glorious anniversary of *liberty* and *slavery*." But the strongest evidence of commitment to bourgeois enterprise was the steady discussion in letters and diaries of investment, credit, costs, calculations, and profits. It was a literature full of wholly casual bourgeois business comment, such as that of perhaps the wealthiest Carolinian, Robert F. W. Allston, to his wife; "I have sent to Charleston a bill of 16 of my negroes for sale—intending to hire a gang of 30 odd next year." On another economic and spelling level, but with the bourgeois orientation not a jot different, was the letter of Texan R. R. Rose: "Well, I have now Seven Hundre Doller wurth of the Best of poperty for this Cuntry Concisting Cattle Oxen and Niggers afer wich I make far profits for the amount invisted." In both cases, "far profits" were the goal.[56]

At the same time, evidence is scant for any commonplace personal caring for slaves that went beyond economic good sense and real, if carefully constricted, evangelical ties. There were occasional rituals—"howdy to the folks" in letters or Christmas pageants of planter benevolence and slave gratitude—but one finds little indication of sustained dedication to their care. Mary Chesnut mentioned her mother-in-law's sewing layettes for slave births, but as an oddity tied to her Philadelphian background. The clearest record of systematic concern and effort for slave welfare comes in the diary of planter wife and abolitionist Fanny Kemble. In a few months, she devoted more thought and personal energy to the welfare of her husband's Georgia slaves than did the several neighboring Jones women, pious and kind mistresses though they were, in their several lifetimes, at least so far as the extensive records reveal.[57]

Some confusion comes from the verbal linkage between "paternal" or "patriarchal" and kindness, and, in Marxist vocabulary, between "bourgeois" and exploitation. Slavery, in any form, involved profound exploitation but was not notably brutal in its bourgeois guise. On the contrary. The closest comparative studies—between the slave South and Brazil or Russia—have suggested much less deadliness and horror in United States slavery, something always underlined in its enslaved race's reproductive expansion. Whatever their theories of organic noblesse oblige, modern semifeudal or patriarchal societies' assumption of absolute rank and power commonly incorporated much protective neglect. The South's commitment to pragmatic productivity led to more sensible caringness for slaves than did patriarchal theory, and its bourgeois-evangelical decencies offered more restraint on the brutalities inherent in absolute power than did the sometimes noble pronouncements of patriarchal Catholicism or Orthodoxy.[58]

Southerners, until the war began, stressed how the profit motive encouraged reasonably decent treatment of slaves, pointing out regularly how owner interest created concern with the chattel's basic welfare. As one South Carolina slavery enthusiast put it, good treatment meant a healthier and less recalcitrant workforce, and "increased efficiency meant more money." Mississippian John Claiborne stressed that Southerners saw slaves as "hereditary heirlooms," that is, property treasured because "interest taught" that it was "wise to cherish what was to be the permanent means of production and profit." Slaves understood this as clearly as whites, as is evident in the comment of a Texas black woman about the notably humane treatment of her former owner, Dave Cavens: "The Cavens allus thunk lots of their niggers. Why shouldn't they? It was their money."

It was, and many of the things tied to moral motivation—providing religious training or preserving families—were also well anchored in economic good sense. Some respect for the black family not only encouraged reproductive profitability but was also the best brake on the most costly form of slave protest; running away. Southerners knew this. When a Kentucky couple feared correctly that a slave family planned to escape, they insisted that the slave baby sleep in their bedroom each night. This was a melodramatic illustration of the everyday reality of deep kin commitments constricting slave options. Religious training often not only instilled a sense of responsibility in blacks but gave essential meaning and dignity to life within slavery. Little wonder an Alabama planter considered his support of a "missionary" movement to slaves, "from a money standpoint, the best investment he ever made." This is not to question the sincerity of planter moral motivation but only to state the truism that decency is likely to prevail more generally where it dovetails well with advantage. It was the principle that Thomas Jefferson recognized when he instructed his overseer not to overwork pregnant slave women because a healthy birth provided more money than could any extra labor. "In this, as in all other cases, providence has made our interests and our duties coincide perfectly." Whatever providence's role, general Southern decency to slaves and interest in profit were tightly linked.[59]

How greater tolerance of brutality walked hand in hand with patriarchal pieties in the South is clear in that best of primary sources on antebellum slavery and racism, Helen Catterall's invaluable collection of judicial records. When patriarchal platitudes waxed in the 1850s, the South's always limited willingness to respect some human rights of slaves or to punish clearly inhuman white treatment of them notably diminished. Some Georgia examples are typical response, especially there and in Virginia and South Carolina. In 1854 a slave named Jim killed an overseer after the latter tried to hit his head with a maul. The Georgia court ruled that "those whose interests are involved" could not be asked to abridge in any way *"their right"* to deal with slaves as they saw fit. "The slave must submit" in all cases, for "servile insurrection and bloodshed" would result from any hint that they might "judge . . . as to the reasonableness of the extent . . . of that patriarchal discipline which the master is permitted to exercise," including the right to maul skulls. In this case, the court suggested that a mauled slave might "trust to the law, for his vindication," but it proceeded to make such protection increasingly improbable. The next year the court ruled that a slave who drowned while the dogs of the men who hired him were tearing him up was not maltreated because the Georgia code prohibited only "unnecessarily biting or tearing with dogs." Having dogs chew a runaway slave who was drowning fell under the right to tear necessarily. The court ruled that through defection the South had already lost 60,000 slaves "worth between 25 and 30 millions of dollars," so no court could diminish those punishments needed "for the security and enjoyment of this sort of property."

True enjoyment of such property required not only the inalienable right to tear necessarily with dogs, the court ruled, but the right to beat nearly to death, though in this case the victim, Dinah, had not been guilty of the terrible crime reported of her: she wouldn't send back the dresses she was ironing until they were properly finished and "forty devils and the defendant couldn't make her." The report of such a comment led Dinah's renter Johnson to whip her, sock her, kick her in the stomach, knock her teeth out, partly in the kitchen and partly in the public street where Dinah ran for succor, which she found only in insensibility. Feared to be dying, Dinah recovered enough to be able to get out of bed in two weeks. The court thought that Johnson's treatment was "excessive" but that he was innocent of any crime given the necessary rites of mastery, though the plaintiff was not Dinah but her owner, Lovett, who sued Johnson for losses on his damaged property; this was the kind of case where Southern courts were generally more actively protective.[60]

Had Dinah died, the possibility of some legal action, even in the Georgia court's high patriarchal stage, would have increased, as an overseer, Jordan, learned in 1857. He whipped to death a thirteen-year-old slave girl, Mariah, giving her "400 to 1000 lashes"—one does lose count—with a three-ply leather whip, knocking out the "boy" Spencer, Mariah's father, when he tried to protect his daughter and curtly rejecting a suggestion to stop from another overseer, given quietly so that no one would deem him in support of insubordination. The high court upheld Jordan's fine for the "manslaughter" of Mariah, having, as Justice McDonald delicately put it, "looked in vain for a single mitigating circumstance." Their search was less futile the next year when they found a technicality to clear Green Martin, who with his son Godefroy spent three hours one night beating and choking to death a twelve-year-old slave, alternating the entertainment by sometimes putting a saddle on the boy and riding him as the other Martin continued to beat. Martin was freed because, after a previous acquittal for sadistic whippings, one of his recent jurors had remarked that he must be a bad man. The slave was tortured and killed for the crime of having told Godefroy Martin, a boy about his age, "to kiss my ass." The Martins rode to legal safety largely because the court believed, as it ruled in an earlier case, that all suggestions of seriously limiting paternal mastery threatened slavery, "a condition that is to last, if the Apocalypse be inspired, until the end of time."[61]

If hard cases often make bad law, they make good social history. The Catterall volumes are rife with incidents and individuals illustrating both the decencies and indecencies of the institution. These late Georgia decisions could be replicated in earlier years in almost every slave state, but they were commonly mixed, especially in North Carolina and Western states, with other decisions much more generous of some measure of justice to blacks. They are also mixed with cases testifying to interracial love, sexual and nonsexual, and clear commitment by some slaveholders to religious and political principles never at peace with slavery. Most abundantly, they show the economic chicanery involved with slavery; the determination to cheat slaves, to defy family wishes, to con one's neighbor, to make some money by hook or crook off the institution's possibilities. And they show the South's judicial elite—about equally divided between the generous, the realistic, and the harshly unconcerned—struggling with cases that all hinged on slaves' being both person and property, with thinghood having to be the prevalent part of the equation.[62] There were also the telling unemphasized patterns, such as the number of cases of brutality that centered on hired slaves, where justice concerned itself only with white money and neglected wholly the slave's dead or broken body.[63]

Finally, there are the asides by those involved and those judging that suggest commonplace assumptions. Joseph Lumpkin, for example, author of some of Georgia's expansive legal patriarchal rhetoric, considered one case involving a man's race, which he said was crucial because as soon as the black truth were known, the person "became Sambo." But it wasn't easy to judge: "Which of us has not narrowly escaped petting one of the pretty little mulattoes belonging to our neighbor as one of the family?" Patriarchs understood that real family had to be all white, and they could only hope narrowly to escape instinctive gestures of affection toward those who looked like children but who in fact were things. The court codified its paternalist stance in this case by ruling that "the status of the African in Georgia, whether bond or free, is such that he has no civil, social or political rights."[64] It had made clear he had almost no legal ones as well.

The violence of 1835 inaugurated the South's full-fledged acceptance of slavery as a total good: economically profitable, socially decent and desirable, and divinely favored. At the same time, it inaugurated a cordon sanitaire of violence around most honest observation and dealing with the institution's bleaker realities. Southerners became adept at not noticing what diverged from the ideal. Both slave-labor and free-labor capitalism had deep tensions within them, and North and South handled these within a nationally shared genteel tradition, or moral dualism, which posited two realms, one of absolutes where perfect moral principles reigned, and the other of everyday realities that might diverge from the ideals but was also held in check by them. This gentility, which kept moral principles pure by some segregation from sullying realities, could promote hypocrisy, or attempts to draw reality closer to the sacred ideal, or both. In the South, violence, social and personal, made what Mary Chesnut called "the ostrich game," the ability to filter out or forget all that contradicted the moral ideal, an essential social virtue.[65] But there were costs in this intellectual system of rigid apartheid, as there were in the racial system, evidenced less in guilt than in irritability, a quickness to anger, a dedication to settling issues not by argument but by violence.[66]

The issue of the separation of slave families offers a good example of the twisted obliviousness with which Southerners came to think about their peculiar institution. Planters had strong moral and pragmatic reasons for commonly respecting slave families, but they had equally strong reasons to wish to break up units whenever personal circumstances and market realities dictated buying, selling, or renting in convenient lots. The commonest notices in newspapers and commonest scenes in the slave markets made clear the system's commitment to maximum economic flexibility, rarely inhibited by any concern for the slave family. Yet almost every proslavery thinker piously announced that no "decent" planter ever sold families apart and that all looked down on slave traders. They knew well, however, that very few planters did not at times break up slave families and that slave traders who did well were not only essential agents of the planting structure but leading citizens. If decent Southerners disliked slave traders, Cassius Clay reported, the decent were a small minority; he offered to name several traders in the Kentucky legislature at the moment and two who had recently represented his county there. Nathaniel Bedford Forrest was only the most professional of the Southerners who turned slave-trading to profit and hence much-respected prominence. Andrew Jackson was simply the most famous of many planters for whom a brief career in the chattel trade brought no ostracism but bought—or rather helped to buy—eventual social and political leadership.[67]

Occasionally, proslavery proponents hinted that some laws protecting slave families might be nice, but no one seriously urged this. A representative discourse was Thomas Cooper's 1835 argument that such laws were unneeded because selling families apart was "so rare"—though he surely knew that the law would not be passed because such sales were so common, and so uncommonly profitable.[68] On a personal level, it is rare to find any white sympathy for slaves sold away from the husbands, wives, or children they loved.

Thomas B. Chaplin felt sorry for himself when his debts forced him to market "about ten prime negroes," breaking up several families. "I cannot express my feelings," he wrote, concluding the entry, "I hope they bring a good price." After the Civil War Chaplin appended a note in pencil bitterly claiming that he was the victim here "for in truth the negroes did not care for us as we cared for them." Equally realistically, he concluded that had Southerners foreseen events, "I and everyone else would have gladly put them in their pockets."

Southern whites often stressed the unfeelingness of blacks when they most strongly showed their own. It was three Northerners whom Washington free black Andrew Shiner found to get money and help when "my wife and children were snacht away from me, and sold on the 5 day of June 1833 on Wednesday from near White Alley. . . . i shal never forget them." A Virginian suggested his section's response to these tragedies. "Poor Sarah," a free African American, had come to beg him to buy her slave husband, who otherwise would be sold to Mississippi. Though Sarah pleaded tearfully that she was willing to give all her wages to pay back anyone who would aid her, this kindly man, who either couldn't or wouldn't help, comforted himself with the white platitudes so fully mocked in his very description of this black woman: "Poor thing, she will never see him again! How little the most humane feel for negroes. Yet that little is more than they feel for themselves, I believe."[69]

Perhaps Southerners cultivated no sadder blindness than to the humanity of blacks. Despite steady prating about their depth of understanding, no Southern description, personal or literary, of a slave moved much beyond adjectival cliché: crafty, contented, abused, brutal, simple, sly, happy, irresponsible, faithful, unfeeling, and (most repeated) ungrateful. William Gilmore Simms shrewdly analyzed Southern whites even when he most self-consciously embroidered Southern myths, but his portraits of slaves were always so flat that Harriet Beecher Stowe's effort possessed comparatively Shakespearean depth and variety. A better stylist than either, Mary Boykin Chesnut surpassed Simms only in her admission that she knew nothing of slaves beyond the "masks" they wore, while the sharply perceptive Southern humorists used blacks only as hapless butts of jokes or, more rarely, symbols of viciousness.[70] In this company, even the blacks in Virgil Stewart's melodramatic chapbook were comparatively human.

It was only the handful of Southerners after 1835 with some real antislavery feeling that noted the slaves' depth of hurt in these situations. Virginia housewife Mary Blackford often lamented her usually futile efforts to prevent or repair the separations of heartbroken slave women from husbands or children; one woman had had all of her six children sold away, the youngest when but two years old. Blackford thought such losses should have "a hardening effect" on slaves, but instead she found repeatedly "devoted attachment," with grief barely numbed by long passing years.[71] Whites created Sambo, Nat, Mammy, Dan, or Jim Crow because such images of limited and lesser humanity best protected their sentimental image of themselves.

Miscegenation was another area of Southern family life where the "ostrich principle" and the ability to exclude blacks from human feeling were essential. Even the person who talked about this reality most honestly, Mary Boykin Chesnut, saw it as only the white woman's burden and expressed nothing but scorn and blame for the black women with no choice and the mulatto children whose paternity everyone recognized on plantations other than their own. Yet formal obliviousness was expected. The Jones family of Georgia avoided noticing the slave children of their close friend, but they were apparent to Fanny Kemble Butler after a week's residence. Rachel O'Connor noted with indignation her overseer's intercourse with her slave women when she was angry with him but forgot it when Patrick produced an unusually large crop of cotton for her. In fact, she noticed nothing for five years of fat profits. Only when Patrick left in a wage dispute did O'Connor again note anything, now that her slave Charity had produced a child "just like Patrick," except he would be enslaved.

The sin of miscegenation for Southerners lay not in its practice but in its recognition, especially any acceptance of children as humans to be cared for rather than property to be used. Nothing infuriated planter Bennet Barrow more than a neighbor's mulatto offspring who were "indulged" as children; he exulted in taking his dogs and his gun to scare them when they deigned to use a road that went on his property. And while Northern Whigs smeared Van Buren's vice president, Richard Mentor Johnson, for fathering an illegitimate slave family, Southern Whigs concentrated on his sins of acknowledging his slave mistress and educating and seeing well married their daughters. Southern Democrats waxed most wroth over the terrible charge that Johnson was husband of a black. "*He was never married*," a Mississippi paper assured Jacksonian partisans; each press that reprinted the story had the same problem with space: "We are sorry we have no room to reply more fully . . . on this subject."[72]

When proslavery talk was loudest, judges and legislators regularly rejected the requests of white men who wished to free or protect their slave women and children, the paternalists in power making clear their disgust at the crime not of procreating mulatto offspring but of caring for them. Few legal documents are sadder than those that chronicle the fate of South Carolina carpenter Samuel McCorkle's six children. When the craftsman died in 1839, McCorkle's executor, Elisha Blackman, asked the legislature to free his slave Lydia and her six children, which was McCorkle's deepest dying wish. His will went on: "I do further desire that my black woman Lydia to have, and her children after her death, my bible, my feather-beds, my bed-steads, my four quilts (being homespun cloth), my blankets, sheets, pillows, etc., my big spinning wheel." W. F. DeSaussere's legislative committee immediately quashed this request, but the slaves (except for Lydia, who died shortly after Samuel) lived as free people by community consent. Six years after McCorkle's death, Blackman submitted a second petition, supported by forty-four citizens, asking the freedom of the six children and now making explicit what was clear in the first: the children were McCorkle's by Lydia, who had lived as his wife for over twenty years.

This second petition came because two lawyers, Amos Blackman and Raleigh Hammond, had voided McCorkle's will, with the help of the South Carolina Supreme Court, so that his property would go (against his express wishes) to his nearest legal relative, whose interest in the estate the lawyers had already bought for $1. Legislator J. D. Wilson curtly rejected this second petition on McCorkle's behalf as "not only contrary to express statute, but the true interest of the state." The true interest of the slave states was to reenslave John, Bob, Lund, Isaac, Simpson, and Harriet McCorkle, despite the community's recognition that they were industrious, well-behaved, and contributive, so that Amos Blackman and Raleigh Hammond could make a handsome speculation on a dead couple's beloved children. In the decision enriching the two crafty lawyers, one South Carolina justice derided the "superstitious weakness" of McCorkle's paternal concern and his "astonishing ignorance" of slavery's "solid moral and scriptural foundations," while William Harper, always complacently callous, praised his own kindness to the blacks involved because it would be "harsh to send these slaves to a new and uncongenial residence."[73]

At least the dead McCorkle didn't have to hear such cant, unlike William Primm, who in 1848 apologized to the Texas legislature for his neglect of "the laws of moral restraint" but begged for the freedom of "these his only children" because he loved them "with the full attachment of a parent for his offspring." The official Texas reply sanctimoniously lectured that when someone like Primm violated both law and public sentiment, "he ought to bear his misfortunes with the resignation of a martyr." The sins of white fathers were to be visited only on their half-white offspring, unless weak unwillingness to treat those children as chattel imposed just martyrdom for the paternal sin of noticing that one's children were human.[74]

Blindness to gross brutality must have been, for some, an even harder social rule, and one even more dependent on segregating blacks from ordinary human sympathy. Louisiana planter Bennet Barrow didn't like that one neighbor whipped a slave to death and that another, A. G. Howells, cruelly maltreated his slaves: he'd caught one young victim trying to run away with irons around ankle, thigh, and leg, his body "nearly a solid scab" from beatings. But Barrow confined his horror to his diary, and it didn't interfere with his attending Howells's parties and fish fries. Propriety demanded that one ask no public questions about any owner's style of mastery, neither Howells's love of the whip nor neighbor Wade's practice of half-starving his workforce. After all, some might question Barrow's own frequent mass whippings of his slaves, his use of "ducking" for punishment, his intentional shooting of one runaway in the thigh, his intent to shoot him dead if he saw him again, and his hands-off way of watching dogs rip runaways "to pieces" until they were nearly killed. Barrow was so excited at the sport that he repeated the ripping in front of other blacks back home.[75]

Even when the whole community was aware of conspicuous sadism, generally no one publicly noticed; South Carolina Baptist minister Robert Sandiford bound a crippled slave in a chicken house on a winter's night for the crime of not collecting enough oysters, so that the slave froze and/or choked to death, with no injury to Sandiford's position in church or community. Protest was confined to the diary of a neighbor who judged the murder "despicable," partly because he judged the amount of oysters the victim collected large. Willful obliviousness to even ongoing sadism was the rule. Free black William Johnson reported much talk about the screams of a slave as his master Murcheson, in the heart of Natchez, slowly beat him to death with a picket with a nail in its end. The torture went on for over an hour in early evening and midcity before "Arthur was herd to hallow no more," but no one in Natchez deigned to notice or interfere. And all legal action ceased when a doctor proclaimed death the result of "Congestion of the Brain," much to Johnson's perfect unsurprise: "Thus it was and thus it is, etc."[76]

Of course, it was not always quite thus. Charges, and even convictions, occurred for brutality, especially fatal brutality, to slaves. Yet usually there was only an "investigation," intended to end all talk through legal absolution of the white killers, such as the one called by Langdon Cheves when two of his "difficult" slaves were beaten to death. When Alabaman William Orr and friends killed Orr's Jerry after prolonged torture, Dr. Pendleton was called in to provide the autopsy whites wanted. Jerry was first beaten, then hit over the head with a fence rail, then whipped several more times, and these activities were interspersed with sportive chases of the slave; during one of these chases Jerry rolled down a steep hill (intentionally, claimed his killers) and died. Pendleton concluded that Jerry died from a skull fracture caused by a "rough blunt instrument," but this might have been a stone he hit rolling downhill, or death might have been caused by the water Orr and friends gave Jerry when he could no longer move. Pendleton also inventively concluded that Jerry was angry and that "the passion of anger, if highly aroused in such a person, might, in the absense of any other cause, have produced death." Since death by spontaneous combustion from ire was likely in the case of such "insolent and passionate" slaves, Jerry's bludgeoned and bloody body was immaterial to Dr. Pendleton's medical conclusion.

Some cases came to court. Between 1827 and 1854, thirteen cases of cruelty to slaves reached the Sumter County, South Carolina, Sessions Docket; of these six were dropped, five people were convicted, and two pled guilty, but the only punishment recorded was a $1 fine in a single case. When slaves were killed, white punishment was sometimes greater. Alabamian Henry M. Hall, convicted in 1837 of killing a slave boy, was given two months in jail and fined $500, while two ten-year sentences were given in that state in 1843–44. In North Carolina there were three capital convictions of owners. In 1839 the court sentenced to death a man named Hoover, whose slave Mira, in late pregnancy, was, over a four-month period, beaten with clubs, chains, and whips; denied food, clothes, and shelter; burned; and sexually abused until she died. Hoover justified his conduct on the grounds that Mira had stolen turnips. In 1842, Mary Hinkel received a death sentence for beating a slave girl's head to a pulp with a ladle. One hundred ninety citizens asked for her pardon on the grounds that Hinkel was an "uneducated and weak-willed woman of violent passions" who must have been insane to destroy her own property. When Governor John Moorhead refused to spare Hinkel, the community resorted to the simpler procedure of letting her break jail and flee. In 1855 a man named Robbins was convicted on the testimony of his stepchildren, who watched his grisly torture murder of his sixty-year-old slave Jim in a dispute over whether Jim had fed a horse. Robbins first beat him with an axe helve, then stamped on the man for ten minutes, beat him for about half an hour with the butt end of a whip, then poured scalding water with salt on his wounds, and beat that into him for another hour. He left the mangled man lying in the yard, and some three hours later the children heard the slave breathe his last.[77]

South Carolina executed four slave-murderers, all of them nonowners of their victims. The most famous were Thomas Motley and William Blacklege, two "sports" who took their hunting dogs to the sparsely settled part of Colleton District in 1854 to injure and terrorize stray blacks. Probably two or three blacks were killed by this pack of beasts before their reign of terror ended with another murder at Parker's Ferry "after inflicting the most outrageous and inhuman barbarities hitherto without a parallel in a civilized country." The pair's conviction was followed by widespread petitions for pardon, arguing that the two killers were young and of "good blood" and that the example of whites being executed for harming blacks was dangerous. The governor was unmoved and called out the militia to prevent popular rescue of the two who had killed others' slaves merely for fun. Shock at this case elicited petitions both urging lesser penalties to encourage convictions and harsher ones to discourage such conduct. Over fifty citizens of Charleston wrote in support of the latter change: "The unlawful beating and stabbing, and otherwise maiming of slaves is increasing and becoming a very serious evil, to the injury of our property and what is infinitely worse revolting to human nature." J. Hamilton Read, for the committee, simply pointed out that any real remedy would involve "an entire change in our social system."[78]

Skill at not noticing was bound to grow in regard to an institution where responding to even the grossest viciousness led to such a social cul-de-sac and where notice almost always showed as much concern for slaves as property as for slaves as people. When young Basil Manly wrote home about one of his aunt's slaves, a thirteen-year-old girl who, while rented out, was beaten so severely over the head that she "lost *all sense*," the boy expressed sorrow for his aunt's feelings and losses but none for the child, near his own age, reduced to a zombie "who has been lingering"—the wording just hints at "malingering"—"in aunt's hands for sometime." And few Southerners would have probably noticed anything but the slave's great value when the *New Orleans Courier* fumed at the street murder of a slave believed to be a runaway: "This atrocious act has occasioned the owner of the slave a loss which $3000 cannot compensate."

A young Alabama doctor illustrated how the rule of public silence gagged even those who felt moral outrage at fatal brutalities against slaves. George Wharton described a local killing of slaves in a letter to a friend:

> Yesterday, ten miles off, an overseer stabbed one to the heart for "sarceing" him. Last week, below Pikeville, another driver attempted to flog a boy. Four of the plowmen stopped their mules, and taking out their swingletrees, advanced upon him in battle-array. He retreated to the "house" and informed the owner of the slaves. They armed themselves with double-barreled guns and returned to the field. Again the black swingletree militia presented a phalanx. The white men aimed their guns and slaughtered the four incontinently. While these victims were weltering in their gore like stuck hogs, they tied up the offender, and administered two hundred lashes upon his bare back, well laid-on. Hurrah! God and Liberty!"[79]

Wharton's private anger, disgust, and decency about such casual chattel killings were clear, but no clearer than his acceptance of the Southern rule of public silence. Such reports could go only to close, "safe" friends who also understood the restrictive requirements of the slavery game.

Still, the need for general acquiescence in all aspects of a system that glorified absolute power weighed on good people, in slave times even more intensely than in the post–Civil War era that W. E. B. DuBois described:

> Deeply religious and intensely democratic as are the mass of the whites, they feel acutely the false position in which the Negro problems place them. Such an essentially honest-hearted and generous people cannot cite the caste-levelling precepts of Christianity, or believe in equality of opportunity for all men, without coming to feel . . . a flat contradiction to their beliefs and professions.[80]

Yet little guilt appears in Southern discourse, private or public, on slavery. The myths of incredibly vicious threat to all decency and life from slaves and from white intruders, myths etched in incidents like the Livingston panic, staved off self-doubt and stilled both social observation and questioning.

The older Southern justification of slavery as an evil that couldn't be ended offered at least room for recognition of the suffering and injustice that was a part of any slave system. Less devious defenses demanded a steady downplaying of the irritating and grim realities, everyday as well as occasional, that were its inextricable result. Southerners must have often blanched at what they knew happened in slavery, over which no public action was taken and no private voice could be raised, including their own. Diaries and letters often suggest such feelings, and in riot they were occasionally evidenced as well. One vigilante account labeled one planter-victim a sadist who was known to have tied one slave in a swamp to be bitten to death by mosquitoes and pushed another into an oven and baked him to death. This chronicler explained why these locally notorious acts went unpunished and publicly unmentioned and also why the vigilantes drove out the man not for slave-murder but for the crime of hog theft: "Should a planter kill a negro by slow torture, his honest neighbors would become indignant but would not dare to prosecute for fear of weakening the institution of slavery." A mob rose in fury against a prominent New Orleans woman, but only because a fire, perhaps an act of God and certainly that of her brutalized cook, revealed in her pantry seven chained slaves who were terribly scarred, emaciated, and worm-infested, "a sight so horrible we could scarce look upon it." Officials permitted the riot but perhaps helped the woman escape, and they vigorously intervened when some in the mob suggested looking into the houses of others suspected of similar sadism to slaves.[81]

The importance of violence in enforcing the segregation of silence between ideals and reality is clear in the conclusion Southerners drew after each of their conspicuous surges of mob destructiveness: theirs was a peaceful and unified community free from the riot rampant in the North. In 1835, mobbing was a national pastime, though the most deadly and sadistic riots occurred in slave states. Within the year the *Southern Literary Journal* would praise the section's slavery-based stability while insisting that the North verged on mob chaos, partly because it didn't mob abolitionists severely enough. Just over a month after its big day of mob murders, a Vicksburg paper found room in its columns, crowded with news of varied local mayhem, to print made-up reports of riot from "north of the Potomac" under the heading "Very Likely to Be True in 1860."[82] Southerners steadily kept up with the Joneses of Savannah, so far-sighted in their vision of violence that they noted, with pious horror, the mote of mob in the North while never seeing the beams of whip and hemp close at hand.

Subsequent insurrection scares generally followed the 1835 Mississippi pattern. Most divergent was the next one that occurred, in 1837 around Alexandria in Rapides Parish, Louisiana. In this case the plot was actual, and the slave who betrayed it had organized it. Lewis Chaney thought slaves might be able to take advantage of widespread sickness in the area to kill those whites who remained and to escape by boat to Mexico. When differences developed among the blacks over the question of killing all white women and children (no one doubted the desirability of exterminating all white males), Chaney despaired of the plot's success and hit upon a safer if less heroic way of gaining his freedom. He betrayed the plot and those blacks he'd induced to join it. Some forty African Americans were arrested, and at least twelve were killed legally and extralegally, including three free blacks. The grateful legislature of Louisiana, forgetful of their recent paean to the greater happiness of blacks as slaves, rewarded this model "faithful servant" with what they knew was the best gift they could bestow—his freedom. This is the only plot after Nat Turner's that has any reliable confirmation. Solomon Northup, a New York free black who was kidnapped into slavery and spent a dozen years in this region of Louisiana, after his release described the black version of the events and the intense hatred for Chaney and his treachery that smoldered years later among the area's slaves.[83]

The Louisiana plot of 1840 seems much less probable, though some details ring psychologically true, such as the gallows statement of a slave of Cesar Mouton that his greatest wish had been to whip his master to death. Still, no evidence exists of anything beyond frightened fantasies proved by whipped-out confessions. Wholly false were the original stories of an insurrection, such as that in the *New Orleans Picayune*, reported with the contradictoriness that Southerners so often failed to notice: "Four hundred happy and peaceful slaves broke out in furious revolt on the 25th in the Parish of LaFayette." Probably the rumors grew as part of the emotional carryover from the hanging and beheading, seemingly a legal procedure, of six runaways. The day these blacks were executed was the day the insurrection plot was "discovered."

The plot reportedly existed in half a dozen parishes—good sign of white hysteria—but immediate action was taken only in Vermillionville. Nine were quickly hanged there, including two "leaders"; a free mulatto named Prefere and the slave son of a Mr. Clouet. Later two slave brothers, Henry and Don Louis, were also hanged. "Four white abolitionists" allegedly instigated the plot, but they were let go after a flogging, reports claimed, because blacks could not testify against them—a strange reason given that no legal procedures were followed. Two weeks after these killings, an offshoot scare occurred in St. Martinville. In this case quick legal action led to five guilty verdicts; three of the convicted were hanged, while one committed suicide. Again, two whites were said to be guilty but were mob-flogged rather than tried, probably to prevent any real inspection of the "evidence."

The wife of one of the slaves hanged revealed the St. Martinsville plot, as also happened in 1844 in Wilmington, North Carolina. In this latter case the slave woman's husband "had beaten her severely," suggesting that these women may have used white fears to gain domestic relief or revenge. In the North Carolina case, a white allegedly instigated the trouble but was let go when investigators found "nothing positive," although the letter writer went on to ascribe to the white actions and statements that easily would have convicted him.[84]

Whites in later Louisiana panics showed more restraint. In late 1841 an insurrection scare allegedly led by a Choctaw Indian evaporated when the intended victims were held long enough to make clear there was no real evidence; a year later a scare in several Louisiana parishes similarly turned out to be groundless. In between these scares occurred a wider panic in the most commonly affected areas of Louisiana, Mississippi, and Texas. Here it's perhaps worth quoting the original yarn, so like those in other insurrection scares, although the detail is more convincing than usual:

> The overseer of a plantation of Robert J. Barrow of West Feliciano arose from his bed one hot night and heard two slaves discussing a rising against the whites. This led to an examination the next morning of the two slaves who confessed the facts and gave information that led to the arrest of several others. The alarm was spread, arrest was made on various plantations and it was found by confession that all agreed to the main facts. This was that there was to be a general rise on the 1st of August. A white man, a carpenter, was also arrested on suspicion and examined. He said that he had nothing to do with the plot, but the Negroes had informed him of it.

The report continued that at a nearby town "numerous slaves confessed to the same facts," while in another "several gentlemen recollected occurrences" confirming that slaves planned to revolt. The writer claimed that the plotting slaves were owned by the "most wealthy and respectable" planters.

Here was the usual pattern. Some hint, real or imagined; whipped-out confessions that must be true because they meshed; a white instigator; the spread of the story, with all planters who heard it being able to remember suspicious things in their vicinity; the gradual geographical extension of the plot. This case, however, was handled slowly so that the falsity of all the evidence became clear. The principal witness testified that he lied about the plot to end his whipping, and the white man arrested was mentally retarded, hardly a man plotters would choose to abet their schemes. All the slaves were acquitted of the charges, as was the carpenter, although the latter was "invited to make himself scarce."

Bennet Barrow, the nephew of Robert, kept a diary during the time of the scare. On July 17 he received a note that five of his slaves were implicated, and he went to Robert H. Barrow's to find out about the evidence. He claimed that there was only a hearsay charge against one of his slaves but that "six negroes were found guilty in the first degree," each from a different plantation. Barrow spent the next week investigating and reported finding several Negroes "deeply concerned," but he seemed unconcerned on July 27, when he noted, "Negroes all cleared."[85]

No more panics occurred in Louisiana until the late 1850s, but in 1846 the state had one further insurrection. In February, about ten miles outside New Orleans, the overseer on Hewitt, Horan, and Co. plantation ordered a black driver to beat a slave who had threatened that "no man should whip him and live." When the driver refused, the overseer brought another overseer and planter Sidney Story with twenty slaves to enforce the order. In the interim, however, the driver and several slaves decided to rebel. Led by the driver and using their tools as weapons, the slaves approached the Story group, yelling, "Let us kill them all—Liberty or Death." Story's slaves provided no support to the three whites, who were all wounded with hoes when some hunters on a passing train came to their rescue. The driver and one other slave were killed, eight or nine escaped, and the remaining members of the briefly insurrectionary group were "severely whipped."[86]

Northern politics influenced the last major insurrection scares of the antebellum South; the growth of the Republican Party was the obvious stimulus. Shortly after the 1856 elections, rumors of a Christmas insurrection spread throughout the South. Tennessee became the center of the scare, but in all slave states except Delaware and Maryland there were reverberations of panic. The diary of Alabaman William P. Gould offers one of the more circumstantial accounts, although he intentionally kept details vague. On December 23 he noted that seventeen slaves had been condemned in Livingston, Sumter County, and were to be hanged the next day. On December 24 he noted that in the morning "there seemed to be a foregone determination to put some of the accused negroes to death," but a glance at the evidence showed that "nothing positive could be fastened on any of them." Yet the very extent of the rumors convinced Gould that "where there is so much smoke, I fear there must be some fire." Gould regretted that no executions had occurred because "a few examples would deter them from further efforts of this kind." Sensitive and sensible as Gould seems in his diary, he still would have preferred to see few blacks killed despite the lack of evidence of a plot.[87]

The clearest evidence about the killing of blacks in the 1856 panic exists in Texas and especially Tennessee, in the latter case chiefly industrial slaves, who worked in its many small iron furnaces. The origins of the plot were obscurely tied to the Frémont canvass: "the negroes, hearing so much of Fremont, began to think that if he was elected they would all be free." A young slave in Kentucky supposedly revealed the plot, which involved a long insurrectionary march from central Tennessee through Kentucky to Ohio, plundering banks—another common white projection—along the way.

Rumors piled up. A keg of dynamite was found under a church near Louisa furnace, though no thought was given as to how this keg was to aid the plot. Several "white minister" instigators were invented, and one black suspect, who died halfway through his sentence of 900 lashes, turned out to be, rioters claimed, a white man who had "dyed" himself. In the usual fashion, slaves were rounded up "and under pain of severe punishment or death were made to confess," and confessions proved "identical in every particular," of course. Some fifty-six blacks were hanged, at least nine-tenths of them slaves; two or more, in addition to the "dyed" white man, were beaten to death. After the first hangings in Dover, Tennessee, many victims were beheaded, and, hoisting "the ghastly gory relics" on poles, citizens paraded the streets in triumph. People soon became aware of the hysteria, but, because men had been murdered, no one publicly questioned the plot, though most sources soon denied it was very "widespread" or "organized." Of course, if the plot were not widespread and organized, the confessional evidence was all false.

Private doubts were strong. Whig planter William F. Cooper wrote his father from Nashville on December 29:

> We are trying our best in Davidson County to produce a negro insurrection, without the slightest aid from the negroes themselves. Whether we shall succeed remains to be seen, but it is certain no more effectual means could be adopted than those our wiseacres have adopted. . . . The lash properly administered is quite . . . efficient. It breaks no bones, while it satisfactorily elicits whatever confessions or disclosures the ministers of extralegal justice are anxious to procure.

In "sober seriousness, no shadow of foundation" existed for the hysteria, and Cooper could only hope that he and his friends might prevent "an outbreak—*among the whites.*"

The recollections of a smaller planter who experienced the panic near its center told the same story:

> Some hot-headed whitemen, taking counsel of their fears, imagined that they saw indisputable evidence of insurrection, and the poor negroes upon whom suspicion fell were taken up and unmercifully whipped until they confessed that such a thing as an insurrection had been frequently discussed. In order to be relieved from this severe and unmerited chastisement they would often implicate others without any foundation, and thus the excitement and suspicion grew until whole counties were involved.

Years later this farmer still remembered acutely the "pitiable sight" of humans "tied up day after day and flogged in the most inhuman manner" simply to appease their tormentors' "morbid imagination."[88]

If morbidity and tragedy marked the insurrection scare triggered by Frémont's defeat, the major outbreak accompanying Lincoln's triumph added elements of personal and political calculation as well as a tone of bullying bravado. Texas had an insurrection panic in 1856 second only to that of Tennessee, but that was to prove pale prelude to the terror of 1860. In 1856 a German editor sympathetic to Frémont was driven from San Antonio by a mob, and five free blacks were mob-killed and others were driven out after one of them killed law officer Samuel Deputy in the early summer. In September an insurrection panic in Colorado County led to the hanging of five slaves and the whipping of over a hundred. One white instigator, William Mehrman, was caught and ordered out of the state, and another, Durden, escaped. All the Mexicans in the county, about twenty of them, were driven out as well, on the grounds that they had been in league with the slaves. Obviously ethnic hatred and real estate acquisitiveness were entwined with this insurrection scare. Plots in several other locales elicited less action or less publicity. In Lavaca County five whites and thirty blacks were whipped, but only an "Ohio abolitionist" named Davidson was further punished. He was ordered out rather than hanged because, the mob said, he agreed to confess.[89]

Two incidents of 1859 were, in retrospect at least, tied to the 1860 panic. At Timber Creek, near Bonham, Texas, some Northern Methodist ministers held a convention, which 300 citizen-mobsters dispersed. The *Texas State Gazette* applauded the action because "we would rather see a hundred such dogs bleed than one victim of a slave insurrection." Southern Methodists may have organized the mobbing; certainly they sanctioned it. Leader Rev. Homer Thrall wrote that there was no mob action at Timber Creek and that anyway some mobs were all right. When the furor of 1860 erupted, Texans remembered that their slaves had become discontented at just the time this meeting occurred. Prior to that meeting, the *Dallas Herald* wrote, "masters and servants lived in harmony, but ever since certain of the latter have become sullen and disobedient—evidently under some secret influence so changed is their deportment." "Abolition emissaries," probably "sent out by the disgruntled clergy," were obviously at work.[90]

The more moderate *Houston Republican* blamed this sudden discovery of slave discontent not on abolitionist agents but on "old man McKinney's friends." Texans had reason to hate sixty-year-old Solomon McKinney, a Campbellite minister from Kentucky, and his fellow preacher, William Blount of Wisconsin, not because they had caused slaves to sense they were not fully happy but because they had so fully exposed the calculating greed behind one Southern proslavery mob. Both men were lifelong Democrats, and Blount had attacked Republican "extremism" on slavery. However, McKinney made two mistakes in Texas: he agreed to collect a friend's debt from Mr. Sprowle of Dallas, and he deplored brutality to slaves in a conventional way in a conventional proslavery sermon on the duties of masters. Sprowle, deciding it was cheaper to lynch than pay, got up a mob over the "abolition" sermon. Blount made one mistake; he defended McKinney.

Both men were put in "protective custody" in jail, from which they were given into the hands of a small mob, stripped to their underwear, given seventy or eighty lashes respectively, and, after being relieved of their cash, ordered to leave. Local citizens, of course, gloated over this triumph over "cowardly" abolitionists. But because both ministers lived and enjoyed some prominence in their sect, they told their story widely. Texans were furious, especially when the legislatures of Wisconsin and Iowa petitioned for redress for the two men. They were "liars," fumed the *Dallas Herald*, which proved their dastardly cowardice in the usual way: let them return and "they will be re-dressed, and no mistake."[91]

The McKinney-Blount exposure made these men the favorite target of blame for the hysteria of 1860, almost a full year after their retreat north. A series of major fires—in Dallas, Denton, and Henderson—in July 1860 triggered the panic. In the South, suspicion of arson often fell on blacks, probably sometimes correctly. Well-poisonings were also reported, though these were wholly unsubstantiated rumors. A plot with a leader and a subagent was quickly whipped out of slaves, and wide-scale hanging and burning to death of blacks began. The slaves reported that abolitionists were to join them in August, about a week before the slaughter was to commence, this time scheduled for election day. The number of blacks killed is unusually uncertain in this case but is certainly high. Claims by both pro- and antivigilante sources put the number of victims into the hundreds, but it is reasonable, if conservative, to accept what appears a fairly careful count by one vigilante who claimed that "only" ten whites and sixty-five blacks were murdered.[92]

Several of the white victims were ministers—Dr. Shreves, Rev. Willette, Rev. Bewley—and one white woman killed, Mrs. Foster, was the wife of a minister, confirmation of Texans' belief that the emissaries were "chiefly professional ministers of the gospel" sent out to avenge either the breakup of the Northern Methodist meet-ing or McKinney-Blount. The best-known of these victims was Anthony Bewley, a native Tennessean who had been a minister in that state before the Northern Methodists sent him in 1855 to head their church in Arkansas and Texas. His church in Bonham, Texas, had 53 members, and the rest of Texas had only 179 Northern Methodists. The Northern church was opposed to slavery but pledged to uphold the law rigorously and in the South tacitly accepted the ban against saying anything negative about slavery. Bewley, who'd spent most of his life preaching in the South, knew the rules well and certainly would not have broken them as tensions mounted.

Charges that Bewley knew Blount and McKinney were circulated by the *Dallas Herald*, and reprinted in Bonham, just after a vigilante "found" discarded on the roadside a letter to "William Buley" urging arson as an aid to abolition. Bewley left with his family for Arkansas, but sometime later the Fort Worth–Sherman vigilantes put a $1,000 reward on his head, which was enough to spur the patriotism of A. G. Brayman, Joe Johnson, and several others. They captured him in Missouri and took him back to Ft. Worth, where the vigilantes hanged him on September 13. Before being killed, Bewley wrote a letter saying he expected to die despite the falsity of all charges: "In these times of heated excitement, molehills are raised mountain high, and where there are none it is frequently imagined that they see something." The quiet honesty of his letter was clear, but it didn't matter. The Texas *Advocate* was sure he must have been guilty of something, and even an old friend and admirer of Bewley, D. R. McAnally, concluded in faraway St. Louis about the death of this man kidnapped for hire in Missouri so he might be killed in Texas, "The people very nat-urally arose . . . for their own protection."[93]

Another case suggests how conscious Texans were, after McKinney and Blount, of letting no one tell the truth about vigilante actions. German-born Frederick An-thon escaped from Henderson, Texas, in 1860. A resident of Texas for fourteen years and a naturalized citizen since 1856, Anthon got in trouble with the local vigilantes for denouncing the fatal whipping of a young man named Evans from Illinois for the crime of mildly admitting he preferred the free states and didn't really like slavery. The *Henderson New Era*, which claimed Evans was a proven thief and abolitionist, gloatingly reported that Evans's body was left as food for buzzards and hogs. An-thon spoke out to friends against the mob, and the mob came to kill him at 2 A.M. Warned, Anthon was awake, armed, and ready, so the Texas mob skulked off. An-thon said he'd never uttered a word against slavery and asked for a hearing. Five vigilantes examined him; he came armed, so they found him innocent. Another meeting of the "leading men" or mob of Henderson was called, and Anthon, warned by friends, hid under a porch to hear their plans. None of them thought he was an abolitionist, but there was agreement that he might escape North to "tattle." Fearing Anthon's prowess with a gun, the vigilantes decided to pay $2,500 to a professional killer to dispose of Anthon. Forewarned, Anthon jumped the hired gun but decided that he himself had to leave—and leave behind his extensive property, which he be-lieved was the major mob motive.[94]

There is no doubt the panic was used to discredit political moderation in the state. In an able thesis, Walter Smyrl gathered much evidence in support of his argument that abolition and insurrection were largely convenient bugbears in intimidating all reservations about secession. The scheduling of the insurrection on election day and the panic's enactment in the two weeks immediately before it suggests a social ritual to underline the argument that Constitutional Unionism was like Republicanism was like abolition was like insurrection. This strategy probably insured secessionists their slender victory.

The insurrection scare was an effective social variant of the personal intimidation widely used by secessionists throughout Texas and the rest of the South. A political meeting at Palo Pinto offers a typical incident. When Judge Evans said Brecken-ridge represented a "secession, disunion and dangerous" party, Colonel Terry found it easier to threaten Evans than to answer his charges. He drew a gun and ordered Evans out, saying "he would show the people where Evans properly belonged, for we need no political missionaries in this county to tell us how to vote." The term "missionaries" was obviously intended to tie all Bell supporters to the clergyman-insurrectionists that Texans had recently spent considerable effort hating and hang-ing. The results in this precinct suggested the effectiveness of such intimidation and rhetorical damnation: Breckenridge—100; Bell—4.[95]

The hysterical elements in these events seem authentic, despite the frequent prop-erty or political dividends. "Nearly all negroes" were involved in some counties, people insisted, and their confessing to precisely the same tale "under the lash" left "no earthly doubt" about their and the abolitionists' bloody plans. Stories went well beyond what anyone would invent for mere political effect: fantasies of well-poi-sonings that had killed hundreds and imaginary accounts of women and children fleeing homes and in flight-fright becoming "almost confirmed maniacs." Sexual fantasies, only late and pale additions in the early panics, were given much greater stress in Texas. "Our houses, etc. were not only to be burned and our citizens mur-dered," foamed a Ft. Worth letter writer, "but the young women and little girls were to be saved to become the wives and concubines of these fiends of hell." Possibly the writer and others really believed that the plot was headed by Abraham Lincoln, whose "Abolition Aid Society" he knew had already sent John Brown to Virginia.

Beyond such stuff and the usual assertions that all action grew out of "stern cool justice" lay a tone of brutal bravado, a social equivalent of Preston Brooks's earlier braggadocio. In one letter that argued the commonplace sentiment that "it is better to let ninety-nine innocent men hang than let one guilty one pass," a man from Mar-shall, Texas, blustered:

> Unless the churches send out new recruits of John Brown this summer, I fear the boys will have nothing to do this winter (as they have hung all that can be found). The school boys have become so excited by the sport of hanging Abolitionists, that the schools are completely deserted. . . . [They] will go 75 to 100 miles on horseback to participate in a single execution of the sentence of Judge Lynch's Court.[96]

The insurrection panic had obviously become one of the South's major educa-tional institutions, a school of chosen attendance whenever in session, where the murder of the helpless proved proslavery power and rightness. Those who escaped, like McKinney, Blount, and Anthon, might lie about its truth-proving stature, but the Reverends Bewley and Willette and Mrs. Foster and the tens, possibly hundreds, of hanged and burnt blacks paid silent testimony to God's sanction of the human sacrifices gleefully offered up to it. The myth was too socially functional, but also too fatuous, to permit public doubt in a section long grown accustomed to skirting the world's and its own questions about its peculiar institution with myths of docility and intermittent fantasies of violence.

And yet the public bluster of the Texas letter writer was not the last word in what was surely a complicated tragedy for morally sensitive people. An Alabama woman, Lucilla McCorkle, recorded her response to one of the many insurrection scares of 1860–61 that were given no publicity. On August 26, 1860, she noted, "Much excitement prevailing in reference to politics and insurrection. Black republicanism likely to give us much trouble." McCorkle went on to explore her own thoughts. "I myself should feel a natural repugnance to slavery if I did not find it existing and myself an owner lawfully and scripturally." She comforted herself, too, with the thought that slaves were "comparatively happy" and "when converted, having comparatively few temptations, they are most consistent" religiously. In her next entry— two weeks later—she noted that on August 27 her slave Dave was arrested for insurrection. The evidence finally proved false, but "Payne was hung who it was believed was instigating the Negroes." But the panic didn't pass, and on September 30 she reported that four negroes were to be hanged on Friday, "alas, as the consequences of idleness and dishonesty and sabbath-breaking, fruitful causes of rebellions and insurrections." Not the consequence of slavery, of course, but Mrs. McCorkle prayed for the protection of the innocent as well as the detection of the guilty. "May our country be delivered from civil war and faction!," she concluded. "May she stand forth a monument of the grace of God, notwithstanding the spirit of wickedness in high places—and the fanaticism of the mob which threatens to break up our beloved union."[97] In this housewife's diary shone the decency of the South in difficult times—perplexed, sensitive within the context of conventional wisdom, caring. The Alabama woman represented the private heart of the South, just as the man from Texas presented the braggadocio that had become part of the section's public stance. But neither of them questioned the argument that a quarter century of insurrection-abolition extralegality had come to legitimize. "The fanaticism of the mob" had nothing to do with the mob actions they worked and watched but only referred to Northern disinclination to give full enthusiasm to that institution Southern mobs ostensibly protected and controlled.

PART III

The Nation

Political Affrays and Fraying

While they promise them liberty, they themselves are the servants of corruption: for of whom a man is overcome, of the same is he brought in bondage.

—2 Peter 2:19

How should freemen spend their time, but looking after their government, and watching that them fellows as we gives offices to, does their duty, and gives themselves no airs. . . . I'd rather have my son drunk three times in a week, than not look after the affairs of his country.

—American citizen, quoted in Frances Trollope,
The Domestic Manners of the Americans

A people who have lived in a political bawdy house so long as we have and have become no *more* corrupt than we have, will probably last a while longer.

—E. Peshine Smith to Henry C. Carey, October 17, 1856,
Edward Gardiner Papers, HSPa

Glory be to God for dappled things.

—Gerard Manley Hopkins, "Pied Beauty"

CHAPTER SIX

Times That Tried Men's Bodies

The Manly Sport of American Politics

Lead us ~~not~~ into temptation.

—Mark Twain, "The Man That Corrupted Hadleyburg"

Cursing, drinking, sometimes fighting, getting black eyes, bloody noses, and when the election is over coming home with coat torn off and sometimes minus a hat—verily they appear to be the number of the elect . . . in those times that tried men's what? Souls—it may be; but I should think the body was most exposed.

—Henry B. Miller, "Diary," March 23, 1838, HSM.

Politics is a contact sport.

—"Tip" O'Neill, *Man of the House*

Henry B. Miller was in St. Louis when he participated in his first elections. The initial one, for city officers in the spring of 1838, was a memorable induction for the young man into the sport of American politics, even though "it went off middling quiet, as far as regards fighting." The second, in August of the same year for state and national positions, was a notable brawl which "learnt me," Miller wrote, "that there was as many rowdies amongst the Whigs as amongst the Democrats." Miller's first voting experiences included many common aspects of belligerent antebellum democracy and suggest how much intimidation, bruising, and violence the American system incorporated into its democratic virility.

In the "middling quiet" city election, Miller recounted many "amusing sights":

Each one exerting himself for his respective candidate, talking loud and fast . . . , raising the one above the superior class of mankind and sinking the other below the lowest of mankind to whom the Devil himself would be virtuous . . . , bringing forward the voters telling them who to vote for, and challenging the votes of everyone with who they have the faintest shadow of a chance; handing out tickets, crossing out names, with many arguments pro and con.

Around this genial mayhem swirled the swearing, swilling, and fighting, the black eyes and bloody noses and torn coats that made this a time that tried men's bodies "by smart raps and sound kicks."

If the spring election provided days that tried other men's bodies, Miller's own was to be tested in the three-day August election. The voting process was "Viva Voce, that is everyman's vote is read off at the Polls and the name of the different candidates taken down that he votes for." This was obviously a slow method made much worse by the fact that there was only one place in the city, the courthouse, to vote. This poll was open from 9:00 till 6:00, but the first day proved that no more than 500–600 could vote during those hours. The temperature was 90 degrees, so all voters "had to take a full sweat for it, many were crowding from morning to afternoon . . . and then gave it over for a bad job and went away without voting." Presumably the Democrats had set up but one polling place because they believed that the slow viva voce method would let them essentially "collar" the poll and insure their victory. The plan didn't work because the Whigs proved they were not "too gentlemanly" to use the same tactics; both parties were "resorting to all the plans in their power both Fair and Foul" to win.

By the second election day, both parties had decided that the only way of getting in their votes was to ship their voters to adjoining townships and polls. Each hired a number of carriages to transport the electorate "free of charge," and each chartered a steamboat to take people to vote at Carondelet, seven or eight miles downriver. This latter outing probably had greatest appeal to young men; at least, Miller went to Carondelet for a long day of democratic politics. A band on the boat whipped up enthusiasm by playing songs like "Yankee Doodle," but this was dampened when the Democratic cargo arrived to find Whigs surrounding the polls. Still led by their band, they bravely joined ranks in a procession and marched to vote. As they got close, the Whigs started yelling, and the Democrats joined in what became "the greatest Medley concert I ever heard:"

> Hurra for the Whigs! Pull down the banner. Kick them, drive them away! Keep the polls! Hurra for Darby! Hurra for Sublette! Hurra for Benton and Democracy! Hurra for Jackson! Hurra for Hell, see who'll get there first! . . . Some halloed one thing and some another. Some imitated the Barking of Dogs and some the Roaring of Bulls, all making as much noise as they could.

Though contributing to this hell of happy animalism, the Democrats hesitated to go to the polls because they were outnumbered and "consequently rather shy." They planted their banner at a distance and engaged in "considerable fighting in which fair play was a scarce article and the Democrats generally [were] licked." The Democrats decided the better part of valor was "to crowd up to the polls quietly," and Miller arrived at about the same time as several other Democrats. The Whigs, thinking "they were in a Free country, consequently they had a right to let vote who they pleased," proceeded to throw off the porch and down about five steps all recognized Democrats. When they asked Miller if he were a Jacksonian, he answered honestly: "No sooner said then three or four caught hold of me and the way I was sent down the five steps was rather faster than when I . . . walk leisurely out of church." "Angry" but feeling "like a whipped dog," he gave the exulting Whig toughs—from a distance—"some remarks on the liberty of suffrage, etc. etc."

Miller retreated to the protection of numbers under the Democratic banner, and, after a wait, he and his friends went to the poll and voted, undisturbed, for Thomas Hart Benton and the other Jacksonian candidates. That duty done, Miller found a seat on a fence that gave "a fair opportunity to see the greater part of the fighting," more than he'd seen in all his previous life and "some of the bloodiest, too. Dirks,

Bowie knives, clubs, handkerchiefs with stones in, with all the other kind of tools that the occasion might require." Veins of humor as well as blood were opened, as several fighters were too drunk to hit anyone, and as the Whigs, hoisting a 350-pound man on their shoulders as symbol of how they'd carry the state, suddenly dropped him as "a bad job, or wrong calculation." When the steamboat returned to St. Louis in the evening, the Democrats marched in procession to the courthouse, where they were told that the Whigs "drove the Democrats away entirely" after the steamboat left.

Miller's conclusion about all this was balanced. The election amply proved that the Whigs were not "too much of Gentlemen to do such things" and had "a number of blackguards in their ranks to match the Jacksonians." He also concluded, probably naively, that party leaders had nothing to do with the violence but that the fault lay with a group of men who were dedicated to drinking and brawling—and who preferred brawling for the strongest side. The toughs had supported the Jacksonians when that party was clearly strongest, but now they were more equally divided, like the general electorate. The two-party system had come to St. Louis, and "no party has any right to blame the other" because now there was rough parity of rough intimidation.[1]

Miller's adventures in casting a vote, if not Everyman's story in these years, contained elements common in other elections in other communities. This type of rowdyism happened enough to create a serious lacunae in historical thinking about politics in these years. Interest in what and whom parties represented, or in why particular groups voted as they did, has absorbed historical attention, and almost no consideration has been given to the mechanics of the process. Richard McCormick, in his able study, *The Second American Party System*, argued that historians need to watch the feet more than the mouths of politicians, but he himself largely counted votes rather than paying attention to the complicated realities of casting them that Miller and his fellow citizens often experienced.[2] To consider antebellum political violence is to follow the money and mayhem, the feet and the fists—and, more tragically, the bullets and bowie knives and bludgeons—that citizens used or felt on occasion in the rarely wholly peaceful working of the American democratic process.

Politics was a separate sphere, an arena of culture where the traits deemed peculiarly and even dangerously male had especially free reign, sanctified by their integration to patriotic duty. Elections generally were held at least twice a year, providing holidays for men, in settings legally defined as free from women's influence. The animal sounds, the barking and bulling Miller mentioned, were symbol of the ties of politics to the "lower" instincts—fighting, cheating, conning, drinking, humiliating, lying, making a quick kill—that women and home influences were to check. As arguments about women's incompetence faded, men had a vested interest in keeping convincing the argument that voting would sully female decency.[3] Men, especially young ones, enjoyed regular escape from the heaven and haven of the happy home to the livelier happy hell of politics, sanctified by that most praised of tripartite ideals, white manhood suffrage. "Hurra for hell," yelled the men of St. Louis, all of them fighting to get there first.

To look at the election paintings of George Caleb Bingham is to see the nature and meaning of politics in this era. Men of varied classes exult and despair, fight and drink, bet and calculate, jump in the air and grovel in the dirt, the liquor keg more in evidence than the ballot box. No homes or females are in sight, though young boys crowd the scene learning the pleasures of patriotism that await their maturity—or majority, anyway. Bingham's political towns are public and business buildings, most centrally taverns, over which Old Glory waves through the dust and fumes.[4] Yet there is nothing bitter in Bingham's vision. A gentle autumnal glow pervades and unites the scene, while the individuals are pictorially joined within a block of solid citizenry. These are gentle genre paintings, evoking the good old days despite their bad old ways. About this, too, both Bingham and Miller were right: usually the process worked fairly well, without being grossly destructive. Violence and chicanery were checked because, if uncontrolled, they tended to interfere with the main purpose of this male sport and business: winning convincingly. Things verged toward destructiveness only in the early 1830s and the mid-1850s, when new political alignments brought into the fray groups unfamiliar with the vague rules by which established teams had agreed to play the political game, especially when what was supposed to be safely centered in women's dominion, profound moral issues, intruded into this virile sport.

Brawling and intimidation of the sort Miller noted complicate the definition of riot. A conservative definition is followed here, so what Miller described does not constitute riot because there is no evidence that coherent groups, larger than the three or four who tossed him down the steps, cooperated in perpetrating the violence, or that the threat was truly destructive in intent. Miller claimed the brutality was personal rowdyism, though parties probably sanctioned the fighting covertly, just as they openly collared polls, printed tickets, challenged voters, and provided bands and boats and booze. Still, these political fights became riotous only when the commonplace tactics of irritation, delay, intimidation, and personal brawls heightened to serious group-perpetrated injury or pitched battles between large groups. Using this quite restricted definition of political riot, there were at least seventy-two political mobs in these years, which killed at least 110 people and seriously injured 341. All these figures err conservatively and of course exclude the commonplace "bloody heads and broken noses" of the kind Miller mentioned in private political fisticuffs.

There were two broad categories of political riots: electoral riots that occurred while voting was going on, and partisan mobs directed at political speeches, meetings, festivities, symbols, or headquarters when no election was in progress. In terms of numbers, riots divided roughly equally into these two categories, but those that took place during elections, with their immediate link to results, were commonly far more destructive to both life and property. Election riots took eighty-nine lives and other political sorts only twenty-one, while the ratio of injuries in the two types was even greater, about ten to one. Property damage was minor except in the Nativist conflicts; the most destructive of these was the 1844 affair in Philadelphia where Nativists destroyed Irish and Catholic buildings after Irishmen fired deadly shots into a Nativist political gathering.[5] Widespread property destruction also occurred in some of the Know-Nothing conflicts in the mid-1850s, especially those in Louisville and St. Louis.

Nowhere is the myth of American peaceful progress more misplaced than in regard to the antebellum voting process, where the worst of these incidents are treated as "anomalies" grown of Nativist or Know-Nothing paranoia or xenophobia. Though the worst of the political violence did in fact involve Nativism, this movement became threatening to the system only when linked to the ultimately divisive moral issue, slavery.

The place of violence in the rules of the political game owed much to the electoral structure in the United States. Elections of a winner-take-all kind were frequent; major ones occurred in most localities at least twice a year. Riot statistics followed this pattern: of thirty-five election riots, twenty-four occurred in the fall season from late August to early November, when national offices were at stake, and eleven between March and early June, when the elections commonly centered on local offices.[6] Such frequency of political contest reflected not only democratic ideals but also male commitment to poll-going holidays.

Ostensibly to let everyone vote and certainly to lengthen the excitement, urban polls were open for two or commonly three days for each election. In rural areas where elections often lasted but one day, the day commonly chosen was Monday, so the whole weekend centered on the approaching polling. A rural Alabaman remembered that men would congregate near the polls on Friday and Saturday for political talk, quarreling, and drinking, would keep reasonably quiet on the Sabbath, and, when that ended at midnight, "began campaigns in earnest."[7] The excitements of such lengthy contests, especially if close unofficial results were announced after each day's polling, spurred all sides to tactics as extreme as they thought they could get away with. Toughs, volunteer or subsidized, were also around to promote particular parties' general welfare in less formal and hence more dangerous ways. Different election dates in different locales in turn created an intensified sense of what had to be done locally to ensure triumph or stave off disaster in many state and national contests.

The emotion and violence of these all-male rites were whetted at the whiskey keg, fueling the male indulgence and aggression that kept women off the streets. A Texas housewife recorded her observations of an 1856 election day, all made from her own porch: "There is a great deal of drinking going on tonight. At least one would think so from the hollering, screaming, cursing, and swearing that is constantly saluting the ear. I have seen more intoxicated men today than I ever did see at one time."[8]

The price was right, too; at elections liquor flowed free. Candidates had no greater electioneering expenses than those for alcohol. Anson Buttles noted why a local Wisconsin tavern caucus nominated him as town clerk and justice of the peace: "The caucus cost me $5.64 for treating today." Two months later at the general election, Buttles won the justiceship but lost as town clerk, perhaps because he spent for liquor only "about $15.00." A North Carolina congressman wrote a play in which he depicted the general view of part of the electorate to democratic duty: "No, I ha'nt voted yet. I'm waiting to see who treats me the best—I votes for them that give me the most grog. I have not had but four drinks today. I'm not drunk enough to vote yet!"[9]

David Crockett's account of his political rise gave perhaps the richest survey of the essential tie between generous treating and political success, but no one denied the connection. In one St. Louis election, party taverns gave out beers labeled with the picture of their congressional aspirant. Any rumor of stinginess with the "strong stuff" was proof to many of political incapacity. Henry Foote reported that one respected Mississippi judge failed of reelection when his opponent hit upon the idea of extending freedom by letting voters fill their own glasses rather than having barkeeps measure out the drinks. "I'm no politician, nor ever shall be," sang one happy voter:

The joy of my life is to go on a spree.
Whoever is president is all one to me,
While I can get gloriously corned.[10]

Probably in some areas when temperance was strong such practices were curbed, but general attempts to segregate liquor and electioneering failed. A paper in the nation's capital sadly concluded, because it was impossible to end election-day drunkenness, that those wishing to avoid trouble had better "keep cool, vote early and go home." Voting-day excess was only an accentuation, of course, of the way politics went hand-on-bottle with liquor on an everyday basis. A Texan heard that well over a month before an election for sheriff, "Uncle Buck has supplied himself with a Barrall of good stuff and keeps open house." Three weeks later Buck Williams was still "going it with a whoop," but by that time all the candidates were "beginning to hump themselves" over their own kegs. Taverns were also everyday centers for politics in both urban and rural areas. An Ohio farmer spoke well for his fellow Americans when he told Frances Trollope that it was the duty of all good citizens to go to the tavern often and that any "true born American" would rather have his "son drunk three times in a week, than not look after the affairs of his country."[11]

The intense masculinity of elections owed much also to their participatory pageantry. The "hard cider" campaign of 1840 brought liquor use, mass involvement, and voter participation to a new level in the United States, but most of its specific tactics had been used before.[12] Mass banquets and parades, organizations and uniforms for young men, political rallies, debates, balls, and a humorous popular literature exulting in the sport of politics, all helped assure that voting days became the climax of contests in which large numbers of men felt deep involvement. In the weeks before an election, the two-party system provided an unbroken party system.

Thousands at times attended the banquets and barbecues and feastings of politics. A woman wrote her husband in 1856 that Democrats had "engaged a hundred hams and lambs and pigs and other things in proportion" for a Nashville rally to which a thousand men from Sumter County, Tennessee, were riding down, a grand climax to the "barbecues and mass meetings almost daily" in the immediate area. Men's memories were often fuller of amusing detail. Milwaukee historian James Buck recalled a Wisconsin rally where the Whigs, "an unlucky set," had their roasting ox stolen by the Democrats, who "had one good square meal" anyway. The Whigs kept their liquor, and one Pettibone, who donated the ox, jumped on the table in a fit of pique and kicked off the plates. Fred Wardner and W. A. Webber proved happier drunks, the first sliding down a hill to East Water Street in a champagne basket, and the second rolling the same course in a hardware cask.[13]

More formal clubs for boys and young men preceded presidential elections, each distinguished by elaborate costumes. In 1836 young Edmund Cooper in Tennessee wrote his brother that a Van Buren Company was forming in town to compete with the "White Guards," who supported Hugh Lawson White, and the company to which he belonged, the "White Oak Sprouts," whose man was Harrison. The sixty White supporters donned "plain fur hats with White Feathers," while the thirty-five Harrisonites wore "a red roundabout with three rows of Bell Buttons, White Pantaloons and White straps." The boy concluded proudly, "We have cockades which dangling from our hats show off in fine style."[14] Such groups became the center of the huge preelection parades in large towns and cities and were sometimes part of the "forces" parties kept near polling places to aid their cause. Torchlight parades of these men and boys in full regalia drew thousands to the streets.

These rituals became more respectable when women were included. Women and children watched with men the huge parades that moved through city neighborhoods for hours. Women played a more important role, of course, in the fund-raising party balls that were introduced in the late 1830s. And as women and families become more welcome and more numerous at certain kinds of political gatherings, such as picnics, speeches, or debates, these events became more sanitized and serious. Drinking lessened and fighting and rioting disappeared, while issues and ideas were more responsibly addressed in meetings that women attended. The greatness of the debates between Stephen Douglas and Abraham Lincoln owed most to these candidates' ability and to the depth of the questions and tensions involved but owed something as well to the fact that women and families listened in numbers sufficient to discourage the abusive sportingness of wholly male rituals.

In the Whig campaign of 1840 women for the first time appeared in political pageantry, in one case wearing sashes that proclaimed, "Whig husbands or none." Thereafter, women increased their input to the virtual political representation allotted them in various ways, including rioting in the 1850s in support of temperance. The change was clear, too, on the more private level. Missourian Minerva Blow wrote her daughter Susie in early 1861 about her fears that Susie's grandmother might die of disease and mental excitement fueled "by injudicious neighbors who talked with her about politics."[15] Of course, by this time, men were turning to the playing fields of Bull Run and Antietam in a different sport, one where their gender dominance still went uncontested.

The campaign of 1840 capped the opposition's response to the changes that came to politics with Jackson. The Democrats furiously damned the new paraphernalia, especially when its effectiveness became clear: the *Democratic Review* proclaimed that it was "nothing short of High Treason to the whole spirit of their and our country." Yet the songs and symbols and cartoons and rallies that made up that campaign were neither new nor undemocratic. Since the Peggy O'Neill cabinet blowup in 1830, the Whigs had been developing all these things, partly as political tactic and partly as a way of wryly accepting democracy while puncturing some of its cant. Some things the Whigs simply borrowed from their opponents: their "Liberty poles" were "Hickory poles" turned Whig. And Jacksonians had long employed songs about "Johnny" Quincy Adams "lounging on crimson and down, and stuffing both pockets with pelf" while "Brave Andrew" saved the nation at his own expense, or about Henry Clay living blithely on his "good bank bribes." The major change in the Whig songs was their often considerably more good-humored quality.[16]

Good humor also characterized much of the most original Whig contribution to American party warfare: the cartoons and the newspapers verbal humor, especially the classic Jack Downing letters. All this Whig humor showed a zesty delight in American folkways, sports, slang, and dialect and a solid faith in the common sense of the common man to retain balance amid seas of demagogic cant. Davy Crockett, Jack Downing, and the cartoon and verbal caricatures of Andrew Jackson all presented genuine democratic heroes, sometimes foolish or naive, but with reservoirs of good sense, competence, and basic decency behind folk simplicity; the best were the verbal equivalent of Whig George Caleb Bingham's paintings. Throughout the early Whig humor ran a calculatedly genial faith in the American people and political process along with shrewd recognition of the seamy underside of democratic pieties.[17] To be sure, much of this was quickly embedded in strata of cynical political manipulation; Whigs were seldom "too much of Gentlemen" to let mere good taste daunt their essential commitment to winning, another trait they fully shared with Democrats.

The *Democratic Review* cried treason, as subsequent historians have cried cynicism, out of a belief that the Whigs had drowned "in a wild tumult of popular shouts and hurrahs all that calm and intelligent discussion of the great issues at stake, on which alone should depend" democratic decisions. The problem with this argument was that until 1840 American political campaigns had never offered any serious discussion of issues. Candidates ran on the basis of their character and public service. In the early Republic, it had been considered undignified to appeal for votes by policy promises; in the later Republic it was deemed dangerous to let the public know clearly where you stood. Ambiguity was hard to attack; clarity allowed too many people clearly to decide you were wrong. James Russell Lowell's politician spoke honestly for the American breed:

> I stan' upon the Constitution,
>   Ez pruedunt statesmun say, who've planned
> A way to gewt the most profusion
>   O' chances ez to *ware* they'll stand. . . .
>
> Ez to my principles, I glory
>   In hevin' nothin' o' the sort.
> I ain't a Wig, I ain't a Tory,
>   I'm just a candidate, in short.[18]

The attraction of Jackson as candidate was not only his military popularity but also the fact that no one had any clear idea of where he stood on any major issue in either 1824 or 1828; he and his advisers carefully lost none of this advantage in the campaigns. In 1832 Jackson's veto of the charter for the Bank of the United States provided an issue, but again Jackson carefully avoided offering any hints—much less intelligent discussion—of what he thought should replace it. Van Buren spent most of Jackson's second term cautioning against letting serious issues develop, and he ran as heir apparent rather than as advocate of any specific action, except assurances, mob and verbal, of his commitment to repressing abolition. Candidates of both parties ran on "democratic" and "republican" principles and with praise of "equality" and "the people," to which almost no people objected, and against "privilege" and "corruption," which very few favored, in theory at least.

Though in 1840 both parties avoided any thought about slavery and fudged the sectionally disruptive tariff issue, the Whigs campaigned forthrightly on limiting executive power and renewing, in some form, a national bank. Whigs came to power in 1840 having given voters a clearer sense of intended political program than had any previous party. Unlike Jackson or Van Buren, Harrison made campaign speeches that showed his general political orientation and the two issues Whigs chose to stress. Yet what most aroused voters was less speeches than the songs and gimmicks, things like rolling a ball across the country to illustrate the party's rolling ahead, or the fun whipped up at hard cider and log cabin "festivals." The Whigs chose a candidate associated with military exploits (in obvious imitation of the earlier Jacksonian strategy) around whom vague uneasiness and vaguer desire for change could coalesce, a politics of mass appeal with a nostalgic twist. If some of the tactics were new, the images and songs were not: log cabins with the latchkeys out, nicknames like "Old Granny," new words for "Auld Lang Syne." "Nothing serves so much in party matters as a sign, a symbolic word," Francis Lieber explained to his son, and hard cider awaiting the stranger in a log cabin captured well a longing for yesteryear's always more comfortably kind, less corruptly competitive society and politics.

The Whigs' greatest democratic contribution was to make politics attractive fun for more Americans, the ones left out of the organizational gangs and clubs Jacksonians pioneered. Late in life Ohioan Jesse Strawn retained as his first memory a scene from 1840. The four-year-old was amazed to see thirteen yoke of oxen pulling a wagon carrying a log cabin about ten by fourteen along a road by his parents' farm. The cabin was topped by a huge flag and decorated with a stuffed eagle, coonskins, and a live raccoon. "The coon interested me greatly. . . . He would climb the pole as far as his chain would permit him and then come down." Following the cabin were wagonloads of "cheering men and boys" from neighboring farms, their cheer owing something to the cabin's rear door, from which "girls, who were busy inside, would hand out cups filled with cider to the men to drink."[19]

"The country was perhaps never before so *alive* to an election," noted a Philadelphian in 1840. That sentiment echoed around the country. An Ohioan traveled to Dayton in mid-September to hear Harrison and found 70,000–80,000 others there for the same purpose, "not office holders or office seekers or lawyers, speculators and merchants"—this Whig list of chosen nonpeople identical to that of Jacksonian rhetoric—but "the hard-fisted farmers and mechanics of the valley, men who left their ploughs in the fields and their tools in their shops to confer together on what had best to be done in the present crisis." Harrison spoke for two hours in "one of the most thrilling speeches I ever heard," clearly audible at least eighty yards from the platform. The "people's shouts almost made the heavens ring," this Methodist noted. Jacksonians recognized the same reality, although they were less happy about it. A Missourian feared that "merchants" were turning his state into a "Tipacanoe Club," but he kept "ploughing, hoeing, sowing, and planting—and affraid to go to town. Your party are rather rambunksious for a modest man like me."[20]

Personal advantage abetted mass emotion in keeping elections "rambunksious." Behind the partying and parades lurked the solider loaves and fishes of power and money. Much was at stake in elections in terms of jobs, fees, judicial protection, and personal power. The spoils system attracted most attention, perhaps as much because of Jackson's and his followers' words as their actions. Such a defense Rhode Island's Democratic congressman Dutee J. Pearce put most dramatically when he declared any officeholder who was not an active partisan a "recreant traitor" who sinned against the "cardinal principle" of democratic politics: "Support those who support you." By 1837 both parties regularly lamented the way patronage sickened politics. "Office—office—office," hissed a Connecticut Whig, glad to be out of "the public kitchen," with "the President of the United States down to that of Constables and tithingmen . . . , bartering for them all the sole leading principle." In its first issue in 1837 the *Democratic Review* called patronage already "a weight and a clog" on democracy, and eight years later it advocated electing even postal clerks as the one means of combatting "the chief depraving agency" of American politics.[21]

The extent of patronage replacements when parties won and lost power was often extraordinary. The Know-Nothing victory in New Orleans led to dismissal of the whole police force as well as schoolteachers and street sweepers, all of them Democratic political appointees. The age's political correspondence is full of letters like that from Philadelphia clerk Joseph M. Cord in 1857. Cord begged to be kept on by the new Democratic administration until October so "he could get into some other business as I have a family to support"; he reported that he had "voted and done all I could secretly" for the winning party. Any project or institution that received government funds might be affected. Democrats accused Anti-Masons of forcing canal workers to vote for their governor's reelection in 1838. He lost, and an engineer on the Pennsylvania canal cautioned a coworker that they'd better hide their support of Harrison to ensure keeping their jobs in 1840.[22]

Patronage gave elected officials heavy burdens as well as power. James K. Polk's diary is a plaintive lament on how office-seekers sponged up his time, and even the least significant political collections are dominated by requests for jobs. When Elisha Pease became Democratic nominee for governor of Texas in 1853, he was inundated with patronage plea letters. A sampling of correspondence from would-be secretaries of state suggests the variety of approaches taken. W. D. Moore used the common unctuous style: "Now, Col., if in the dispensation of your judgement," this "humble servant" got the job, his "greatest aim will be to discharge the functions of that post in a manner that will reflect lustre on you as the giver, myself as receiver, and upon the entire state as a third party." P. DeCordova was frankly greedy: "The office is a mere clerkship, but the salary of $1,000 per annum would be a great service to me." Edward Clark explained he had to vote for his wife's uncle, but he considered this no reason Pease shouldn't aid his ambitions: "I am fond of public life . . . and for higher positions than I have heretofore held; I would be pleased to have from you the office of secretary of state." James M. Bell was brusque: "To come at once to the point, I wish you to give me the post of secretary of state," because the job would give him fulltime to devote to his writing. Little wonder that Pease, like Polk, quickly grew "bored to death with office seekers."[23]

The pettiness of the system, however, didn't lessen its political utility. Parties succeeded by practicing it diligently and unabashedly. New York's Thurlow Weed and Pennsylvania's Thaddeus Stevens made the Anti-Masons, Whigs, and Republicans into vital opposition and majority powers by using the patronage tactics Van Buren and the Jacksonians pioneered. Whigs in New York City wailed about Tammany's gross manner of buying men and power, and Democrats howled at Philadelphia mayor John Swift's tactics, such as dismissing half the city watch in 1834 because they voted Jacksonian—fifty-eight men with, according to Democratic count, precisely 275 children to support.[24] Yet Tammany dominated New York City for half a century, and Swift ran Philadelphia for two decades. In politics, sanctimony weighed little against such success.

So clearly were "loaves and fishes" the grail of parties that humor became the wholesome response. J. L. Jenckes wrote William Greene that he shouldn't worry about the Cuban consulship being lucrative enough because "scripture" assured "that 'where the treasure is, there shall the heart be' and 'where the carcass is, there will be the eagles gathered together.'" Jenckes thought it might be good if "the Powers" put off a decision for some weeks: "Only think how many are studying Spanish with a zeal that must tend to their rapid improvement and to the speedy dissimulation of that noble tongue throughout the land." When a janitor at Columbia Law School asked for a recommendation for a consulship, George Templeton Strong complied: "I cheerfully contribute my mite to relieve the Law School of a sweeper and maker of fires who has so little knowledge of his profession." No one had harsher things to say of politicians than that literary figure who knew many intimately, Nathaniel Hawthorne: "They cease to be men in becoming politicians," he wrote his wife; "their consciences are turned to india-rubber—or to some substance as black as that, and which will stretch as much." A classic of a kind is Hawthorne's endorsement for office of one Zack Burchmore, because he was "a poor miserable, broken, drunken, disagreeable loafer, contemptible as an enemy and only troublesome as a friend." If the party denied him office, Hawthorne feared he might feel guilt at Burchmore's grave, "the fumes of rum oozing up through the sod."[25]

Patronage's success created some political fears, partly related to the fact that, between Andrew Jackson and Abraham Lincoln, no president was reelected. However much John C. Calhoun's theories were grounded in a defense of slavery, his plea for a "concurrent majority" was partly a response to a broadly shared grim reading of politics: no matter what the crop of offices harvested after an election, more men would go unfed than would gorge, with the hungry going into the other party. As Baltimore Know-Nothing Henry Winter Davis explained, "The disappointed have ever joined the defeated to eject the victorious parties." A Maine politician pointed out that when politicians worked largely "for the loaves and fishes, they must expect trouble when they are distributed."[26]

Calhoun's argument that the American winner-take-all political system undercut the accommodating civility needed in democratic government was even more clearly true. No publications were more abusively duplicitous in the era than the party press. If Whig and radical Loco-Foco journals at times showed mild independence, it was noticeable only in comparison with the mainstream Democratic press, where the party line varied only in response to sectional calculation. The expansion of the penny press in the 1830s and later owed much to its comparative honesty and

sometimes its breadth of social concern.[27] The frenzied prose of moderate Southerners in 1835 became national in the 1850s as the "Young America" movement encouraged foreign adventurism and domestic abuse as antidote to rising sectional tensions. "Young Americans" steadily berated their general enemy, "incapable and
incurable old fogies," and had vituperation aplenty for any individual they disliked;
in the Senate, for example, Sam Houston labeled Thomas Jefferson Green as someone no decent person would touch "with a fifteen foot pole without wearing gloves
of double thickness—and then he'd better throw away the pole." Centered around
the *Democratic Review*, Stephen Douglas, and Franklin Pierce, this group claimed
that all discussion of slavery was a plot of "anarchists" *and* Whigs and that the issue
should be buried along with all "old personal hacks and public harpies," those "political niggers" trying to make the nation "a huge asylum for the indigent and imbe-
cile . . . and to empty its industry and genius in spoonfeeding them." "Personal vituperation and abuse" became "the staples of stump oratory," noted a St. Louis
Democrat who attributed his own victory to "having become rather famous" for his
"cutting language."[28] And such linguistic bullying bore direct tie to the many political duels and brawls and riots.

"Though I love my country well," wrote one patriot, "I love it because I myself
am in it." This Texan wanted his governor to prove himself *"useful"* as well as orna-
mental by paying him generously. Politicians often served their supporters' welfare
in such ways. The pattern was clear in the administration of Andrew Jackson. Robert
Walker worked through Jackson's closest friend in Mississippi, Samuel Gwin, to get
large chunks of the best Native American lands at minimal rates for his affiliated
speculators, and in the process he assured himself Jackson's backing for the United
States Senate. Roger B. Taney and friends made fortunes, directly taken from poor
people, through their legal manipulations of a bank failure after they failed to make
much money through speculating in the stock of a bank where Taney sent federal
funds. Jackson and Sam Houston were both furious when public attention led to rejection of a Native American removal contract that Jackson intended largely as a
subsidy to his old friend.[29] It was not that this kind of favoritism was notably Democratic or predominantly federal but that the pattern had precedents at the highest
level.

The buying of support went on at all levels of American politics. Shortly after
speculators bought land around Massac, Illinois, they feared that competition from
nearby Metropolis might sink their project "beneath the attention of even Loafers."
They dispatched to Washington General John M. Robinson, who successfully got a
national armory contract for Massac when he was able to "log roll it with Senators
and representatives and Secretarys of War and Navy." Still, Massac had so few occupants that its would-be founders believed state support to be essential to make it
the county seat. William Wilson headed this effort and gave out town lots to key
state legislators to gain their support. Representative Owins especially required considerable priming: "If his attention had not been called to the subject by his interest,
he might not have considered the subject sufficiently to appreciate its importance."
Wilson piously concluded that handouts were "but justice, too, to those, who from
patriotism and a sense of justice, have exerted themselves to promote the prosperity
of this end of our state."[30]

Owins's patriotism fitted perfectly a vision of "politics as a trade to make money by," but the manifest self-interest never threatened the functioning of the political system. In 1853 the *North American Review* praised the responsibility and responsiveness of American democracy, despite much surface corruption and a general complaint that office-seekers were "a hungry, impudent, conscienceless set." Shrewd Republican observer E. Peshine Smith argued that nothing better showed American resiliency than that people had "lived in a political bawdy house so long" while becoming "no *more* corrupt than we have."[31]

Broad economic favoritism contributed less to political violence and intimidation than did the close ties between elections and the legal system. Policemen were often the intimidating party arm, for their jobs were at risk if defeat came. In two cases, one in a Philadelphia suburb and another in Cincinnati, police were convicted of riot, but this represented only a highly unusual conclusion to a fairly common reality.[32] The police conflicts were most apparent when Know-Nothings or Republicans mounted serious challenges to entrenched Democratic city regimes in the mid-1850s, in cities like New Orleans and New York City. A historian of the New Orleans conflict makes clear that the initial Know-Nothing aim was to break the political intimidation and control of the Democratic police force. New York police were often "appointed . . . as a reward for party services performed at the polls," and their personnel contributed to riots in places as far away as Rhode Island, Kentucky, and San Francisco. The mayor of Northern Liberties, a working-class suburb of Philadelphia, perhaps spoke honestly when he refused to call out the police on election day because they often "intimidate the right to suffrage."[33]

Even when police functioned responsibly, aldermen and magistrates might absolve the guilty who had the right political credentials. Members of certain fire companies and gangs, prominent urban brawlers, enjoyed this kind of protection in return for their political loyalty. The arrests of election toughs followed by immediate discharge by party-appointee judges was a common method for recycling political violence. Failure to cooperate with the system sometimes endangered the honest policeman's life as well as his job. At least a dozen policemen died repressing riots, and one was killed by a candidate for New York City alderman who tried "to rescue some rowdy political friend of his from the ministers of the law."[34]

Gubernatorial pardons were a common way to reward or curry political favor. At times such pardons were a part of an equity system that represented the true enough feeling that punishment, especially jailing, only compounded the social costs of crime for everyone. Some Mississippi petitions of the mid-1830s suggest the prevailing pattern. Eighty-nine citizens of Adams County wanted William Alco pardoned because he'd killed his victim in "self-defense" and because he had "an aged mother . . . whose gray hairs will be brought down with snow to the grave." Judge James F. Trotter and fifty-five Kemper County residents thought that convicted horse thieves Charles Van Horn and John Smith should be freed because their families were respectable and they probably took the animals with no "other view than to assist them a little on their journey." In Green County, eighty-two people thought that $50 was too high a fine for James Williams's part in an affray because he "had a weakly, sickly wife and a lot of small children to provide for." William Peebles Sr. had similar problems, twenty-eight supporters testified, as well as "a crop in the

ground." In petitions such as these, there was commonly no or very half-hearted effort to suggest lack of guilt; instead, there was emphasis on the sad realities of im-
prisonment: costs in sorrow and suffering to families and in money to the community, which had to feed and house the prisoners and sometimes their dependents as
well. A Texan asked freedom for one crook who "richly deserved all the punishment
assessed against him, but in punishing him a large and helpless family is punished
with him."[35]

Such considerations made pardons a chief form of communal patronage, in heavy
use in the first three decades of the century. For example, of 3,175 New York State
convicts sentenced to the penitentiary for felony between 1810 and 1823, a full
three-quarters were pardoned. In Ohio between 1815 and 1829, well over half those
convicted of major crime received pardons. Such percentages fell sharply as the century wore on, in the North especially in the 1830s and in the South and West about a
decade later. The sharpest downward shift came under non-Democratic governors in
the late 1830s, partly reflecting anti-Jacksonians' emphasis on legalism and on limiting executive patronage.[36]

When Pennsylvania's Democratic governor, David Porter, 1838–44, reversed this
pattern and pardoned over 900 people, his policy drew increasing public attack. Porter
freed 32 murderers, 10 rapists, 22 counterfeiters, 27 burglars, 14 arsonists, and 25
men convicted of manslaughter. Most controversial were his 55 pardons of political
friends prior to trial, such as 3 Philadelphia vote fraud specialists indicted for election
tampering. Yet even the dependably party-line *Pennsylvanian* attacked, after he left
office, Porter's "special delivery to the worst offenders." By 1850 pardoning had been
reduced toward its modern scope. Salmon Chase explained in 1856 that seldom were
pardons now issued "from mere sympathy, a regard for the respectability of families,
the influence of connections, or other personal considerations."[37]

So important to election success was another group of officials that the election of
ballot judges sometimes began an election's fighting season. The counting, like the
casting, of votes was often party-manipulated. In Maine in 1832 and in Ohio in
1848, the legislatures came to a halt when rival candidates both claimed victory in
certain districts and the two partisanly balanced houses of each legislature were unable to come to a decision for awhile. Such cases were rare only because one party
usually had the majority and decided all such issues in accord with its power. Elections for U.S. congressmen reflected an identical pattern. When Nativist congressman Charles Naylor defeated Jacksonian Charles J. Ingersoll by 775 votes, Democrat judges "lost" one poll's returns and so rejected all votes from working-class
Northern Liberties, where Naylor had a 1,200-vote lead. They declared Ingersoll the
winner, although the Whig state election judges certified Naylor. The Democrats
who controlled the U.S. Congress simply upheld their Philadelphia lawyer at the national level.[38]

"Irregularities" occurred regularly. Votes were for sale and political managers
bought them. Greeley's *New York Tribune* claimed that its reporter watched the
Democrats bring fifty men from the Williamsburg section of Brooklyn to New York
City to vote at $1 a head. A Hartford man claimed that the Republicans used
$100,000 to buy votes in Connecticut, purchasing 20,000 in his city alone. Republi-
can organizer E. Peshine Smith reported that the party had no need to appease influ-

ential American Thompson in upstate New York: "We can buy him for $1,000. Three years ago (this is *private*) we did buy him for $1,200 to betray his party in this county." Cassius Clay blamed his loss to Kentucky democrat Robert Wickliffe on illegal votes but freely admitted his own practices. "It is true we bought votes that offered themselves on the market; unhappy country where such things are." There was truth in the maxim, though maybe not in its attribution to Simon Cameron, that "an honest politician is one who, when he is bought, stays bought."[39]

Since this market was open to both parties, only the largest scandals drew much attention. John Slidell earned a post in Mexico when he carried Louisiana for James K. Polk by shipping 5,000 people from New Orleans to Plaquemines Parish to vote there, and some years later Judah P. Benjamin assured his place in the Democracy by organizing a "cab squad" to vote repeatedly in different parts of the city. The fullest documentation exists for the New York City Whig "pipe-laying campaign" of 1838. The Whigs gave money to John Glentworth to recruit Philadelphians to vote in New York. Philadelphia mayor John Swift and others directed Glentworth to "contractors" who agreed to furnish groups of men at from $20 to $30 a head. The wittiest of these enthusiastic voters was Robert Looney, a Philadelphia city plumbing employee, who wrote assuring Whigs he could supply nineteen workers, some of them "old hands who could lay pipes in any place." Looney thus gave the nation its first plumbers' scandal and its first indigenous term for gross election corruption: pipe-laying.[40]

Democrats learned of the fraud in 1838 but restrained their wrath until shortly before the election of 1840 to give the scandal maximum political impact. One man testified that Glentworth told him the Philadelphians cast at least 1,600 ballots; one man voted seventeen times. Evidence also showed that the Whigs transferred some prisoners from Blackwell's Island to the almshouse so they could vote. Physical action capped the trial when Glentworth, aided by Whig sheriff Acker and some toughs, tried to remove key documents during a session. Recorder Robert Morris held onto the documents and parlayed his role at the trial into the mayor's office. All that minimized damage to the Whigs was general acceptance of much truth to their claim that were trying to create parity of corruption with Democratic practices. When Police Judge Robert Taylor began to investigate Jacksonian poll frauds, Morris decided reform had gone far enough and had Taylor removed. Surely Democratic governor William Marcy knew of what he spoke when he feared that the "Barnburner" faction of his party might "pipelay, etc." more effectively than his faction could.[41]

"Unless the Whigs lay more pipe than I think they can," James McCullough wrote a friend in 1844, he considered Clay "a gone coon" and Polk "the best bet." McCullough used the last phrase literally. He and his correspondent were concerned with election results not as political but as gambling contests. Betting on results was as central to the politics of the 1840s and 1850s as it was to be to other sports over a century later. "Hundreds of thousands of dollars are already staked on the results," wrote the *Philadelphia Public Ledger* early in the 1838 campaign; "the destinies of the State are in the hands of gamblers." While some states passed anti-election-gambling laws, enforcement was rare. The Van Burens, Martin and son John, at times bet heavily on elections, and fairly openly as well. A Pennsylvania court decision reflected the odd public attitude toward this practice. The court ruled that those who bet on elections could not sue to collect their winnings but that guardians of the poor might initiate suits in their stead against recalcitrant losers and use the money for the general welfare.[42]

The extent of political gambling was great. A young man mentioned one Baltimore citizen betting $12,000 in 1844. One gambler reportedly put out $40,000 in a number of bets in a small Massachusetts town in 1840. In 1848 a Louisiana schoolteacher reported "thousands and thousands" staked in his area, while "even my school boys have large bets for boys." A Kentucky American Party organizer wrote in 1856 that that state's central committee was working out a system of quickly telegraphing election returns in elaborate code to party regulars, "by which our mutual friends expect to be benefitted," being helped to bet carefully indeed. Newspapers sometimes printed odds and large offers to bet and regularly reported big stakes.[43] When elections involved a "tight race," a little mayhem often meant immediate money in some men's pockets.

Only one variant of the many forms of electoral fraud and intimidation had a clearly predominant party source. Democrats were certainly the main beneficiary of the quick illegal naturalization of foreigners to swell voting ranks at crucial elections. Constant Whig complaint attested Jacksonian preeminence at this political tactic. Martin Van Buren's political machine pioneered this practice, which tied urban immigrants to long-term loyalty to the Democrats. Immediate naturalization was criminal but almost never led to prosecution, in part because local courts, under party thumb, controlled the process. New Orleans city judge Benjamin Elliot was impeached in 1844 for selling naturalization papers to the Irish, probably because personal greed was in this case so integrated with party duty. Yet no one considered voiding the 1,700 illegal naturalizations for which the Democratic Party paid good cash.

The first wide-scale reports of illegal naturalization for a particular election occurred in 1834 during New York City's troubled spring voting. The *Commercial Advertiser* reported "the melancholy and amusing" sight of hordes appearing at the court and emerging five minutes later to be "sent off to the polls to support the Constitution and break men's heads." In Cincinnati 1,200 were naturalized the day before the election of 1844 and almost as many the day prior to the 1848 voting. In the latter year, about 100 immigrant St. Louisians voted the same day they became citizens. The many unnaturalized immigrants whom New Orleans Democratic policemen herded to the polls were believed to comprise the bulk of the 3,000 rise in the number of voters in 1853.[44] In Maryland, politicians "vied with each other . . . in cramming boarding houses with aliens, whence, scarcely recovered from the dizziness of the sea voyage, they were driven to the polls."[45] The practice was one of the major things that stimulated the periodic waxing of nativism.

Rural elections were often as corrupt as urban ones, though usually less riotous. In by far the least democratic of American states, South Carolina, the evidence of all forms of electoral corruption and intimidation is as strong as anywhere; "Grand Jury Presentments" regularly complained of fraud. Abbeville citizens protested the political uses of the pardoning power and the lack of control over "unprincipled men voting at several different boxes." People from Barnwell in 1850 asked that those who bet on elections be kept away from the polls. Colleton District in 1852 pleaded that treating at the polls, "a species of bribery," be ended. One-day elections were often urged: by Marlborough in 1841, by Lancaster in 1851, by Kershaw in 1848, to curb "the many illegal voters," and by Fairfield in 1851 to lessen "bribery and corruption." Kershaw in 1846 added a plea to aid honest elections by requiring that each voter cast his ballot "in his own beat." Chester district in 1842 suggested that one-day elections would help control "the demoralizing influence of this system on the Community," where "various acts are resorted to by the designing to defraud the unsuspecting voter" and where a great many went "to sell their votes to the highest bidder not for thirty pieces of silver, but for the last drink of Grog." South Carolina politicians rejected most of these ideas as "inexpedient." Obviously, the state's aristocratic features simply made commonplace forms of corruption cheaper and easier.[46]

Parties used electoral poll watchers or vigilance committees to try to prevent illegal voting. As early as 1832, Philadelphia businessman Joseph Sill was surprised to be asked to serve on an anti-Jackson "Committee of Vigilance." In 1860 both parties still had vigilance committees in Philadelphia, and the Democratic one was told to "have an eye on the pipe layers and stop their contemplated travels." They also worked to get out the right voters. For example, those in a small Illinois town were told "to see all Whigs and see that they vote in the election."[47]

The most obvious way to stop fraudulent voting was through registration laws, but these were unpopular with Democrats, probably because Democrats benefited more from the illegal votes. Part of the objection was practical and ideological, however. Initially the practical objection concerned a mobile population's right to vote, but even when the principle of district voting was accepted, Democrats denounced registration as a slur on freemen and a curb on freedom. Why this was true if election frauds were real—as everyone admitted—was hard to say unless the Democracy was aided by political cheating.

The Whigs and then the Republicans led the fight for voter registration. When the Baltimore battle was won in 1838, the vote was a party-line affair. The five wards that voted heavily against registration gave large margins to the Democratic mayoralty candidate; the four heavily Whig wards gave registration strong support; the two wards in which the parties were evenly matched provided the slight plurality in favor of registration. In New York City the same pattern is clear. In 1840 Democrats perpetrated a minor riot to break up a meeting in support of registration, beating a couple of participants in "a severe and cruel manner." A weak law was passed that year, but a New York Whig thought even this law offered his party "a fair prospect of doing well at the general election." Republicans got a strong law through only in 1859, in the wake of the crumbling corruption of Mayor Fernando Wood. Heavy fines for illegal voting were also an important deterrent; Boston, where immigrant voting power remained checked till after the Civil War, used this system effectively.[48]

In a system that worked through mutual party intimidation, a covert threat of violence was helpful. To have large groups of voters vigorously pushing their opinions—and maybe their opponents—was a part of election-day strategies. Though voice-voting faded, the system that replaced it equally encouraged intimidation. Ballots were privately printed, often on colored paper, so that everyone's party preference was clear to those who wanted to know. These private ballots allowed some chicanery: members of one party would print tickets for the other on which names were misspelled or middle initials changed so judges could subsequently toss them out. Anson Buttles almost lost an election when tricksy opponents had ballots printed for "Anson Butler," who came within three votes of beating his near-namesake. But primarily the party ballots allowed judges or bullies to know exactly who should be questioned or intimidated. Democratic distaste for the secret ballot, on the grounds that it promoted "hypocrisy," suggested that they again benefited most from opening every vote to public knowledge.[49]

Cities were the centers of greatest violence and corruption, but in all sections, American antebellum politics was a tough and professional profit-making sport. Illinois governor and historian Thomas Ford claimed that most early elections in Illinois were controlled by "butcher-knife boys, rowdy Davy Crockett types," while a Mississippi short-story writer claimed that elections always drew huge crowds "for the triple purpose of voting, spreeing and lastly for the peculiar pleasure of witnessing the beginning—aye 'The Opening of the Fall Fighting Campaign.'" Andrew Schirmer's diary makes clear that such actions also happened often in that most aristocratic of political settings, Charleston, South Carolina. Schirmer claimed that "never was bribery and corruption more exercised" than in the September 1831 elections, and he reported the burial of Jack Ashe, who was shot to death during the election by "Mr. Weyman, . . . a bully for the Nullifiers." The next month in a special election "the managers after counting the vote several times contrived to give the Nullifiers a majority of eight votes." In September of the next year, war almost broke out between the parties when a man fell to his death from the fourth-floor window of Unionist headquarters; it was avoided when both parties agreed to "set at liberty those persons they had locked up." The election continued full of "disgraceful acts" that were "sufficient to cause the most awful visitations from a just and offended God," and the 1834 election events were "too disgraceful to record."[50]

Much intimidation was personal, like a Mississippi governor's threat to give a rival "hell" once the election ended, or a Texas politician's advice to friends; "Tell Perkins to be alive, I'll lick you and him both if I'm beat." But the personal tended to become general if acted upon. Nimrod Porter claimed that he was abused by one of his opponents, Col. T. G. Hunter, who "got knocked down which he ought to have expected. A general row took place and some right pretty fighting ensued." Some eighteen of Porter's friends were arrested and fined, and Porter promptly paid the fines. It was worth it. "Col. Hunter quit the chase the next day after the battle royal."[51] Intimidating violence was usually less effective only because both sides used it, usually more equitably.

Antebellum elections were commonly, in the words of a New Orleans editor, "a hell's holiday of drunkenness and perjury and bludgeons."[52] Voting days were American male holidays, alcohol-enlivened and likely to feature much fisticuffs and finagling. But the roughly amusing political sport usually avoided real destructiveness—unless new players and passions loosened the always slippery rules.

CHAPTER SEVEN

The Mobs of the Second Party System

> Politics is the gizzard of society, full of grit and gravel, and the two political parties
> are its opposite halves . . . which grind on each other. Not only individuals but
> states have thus a confirmed dyspepsia.
>
> —Henry David Thoreau, *Life without Principle*

> America! America!
> God mend thy every flaw!
> Confirm thy soul in self-control,
> Thy liberty in law!
> —Katherine Lee Bates, "America, the Beautiful"

Niles' Register reported with horror the October 1834 election riots in Philadelphia. Rowdies sometimes formed "such a mass of living matter" that the feeble or aged gave up their vote, and even the strongest could stay only if willing to sacrifice their clothes. Elections were becoming the province "of a villainous mob—sets of wretched creatures, hired at so much for *the day's* work, to do the bidding of their employers!—to block up the passage or 'knock down and drag out.'" A letter from a Philadelphia woman, Julia Grew, corroborated Niles's account. "Such immovable mobs collected around the polls," she wrote, "that the common method for a gentleman to present his vote was by a conveyance across the heads of the multitude. During this delightful transportation, some gentlemen of the opposite party would snip a seam in his coat, and tear it as far as possible. Some had their clothes literally torn off, and many persons were much injured." Some chose other means of access; one man, Niles reported, fixed a knife against his abdomen to clear a path toward the polls.

Niles and Grew agreed that the violence was the product of both parties. And Niles recognized that such practices, though their extremity had "immeasurably increased," had long existed, going at least as far back as 1798, the most intensely partisan year in the development of the first American party system.[1] Niles's historical memory related to the broad pattern that antebellum political violence was to take. What had happened (relatively mildly) in 1798, what was happening in 1834, and what was to occur with greater destructiveness in the mid-1850s suggested a repeated pattern. At times when new party realities were jelling, electoral violence of some seriousness occurred. When two strong parties emerged, major violence faded as rivals learned that the common tactics of corruption, trick, and intimidation were undercut by clear destructiveness. The Whigs were not more violent than the Democrats in 1834, nor were the Know-Nothings more vicious than their opponents in

1855, but the old boys used old weapons more indiscriminately when faced with a new threat, while the new boys were less attuned to the always vague boundaries between electoral roughness and real destruction. In these transitional eras of American party development, the threats common to electoral politics often spilled briefly into social violence in localities where the political stakes were highest and communal restraints least secure.

Eighteen thirty-four was a crisis year of the second American party system, as party alignment became a national reality. Van Buren's ordination as successor allowed administration opponents to coalesce in the South, just when anger over other issues reached the boiling point. Jackson's bank policy became clear only with his adamant refusal to consider recharter in any form and his unveiling of the pet bank system. This solution confirmed the opposition's angriest fears: Jackson was willing to neglect statutes, the financial needs of the country, and monetary restraint to create another rich source of political patronage. Jackson's actions also invigorated the devotion of his supporters, who saw a leader who would never knuckle under to established interests—and who would win. Such were the yeasty emotions raising partisan intensity in 1834.

Growing party ideologic clarity gave bite to such feelings. Jackson's refusal to budge enhanced the Democratic sense that the presidency represented popular interests in a way that the legislature and judiciary did not, while the unwillingness to provide any currency control embodied a commitment to laissez-faire, with its twin promises of quick profits and justice to all through government inactivity. For Whigs these same realities whetted concern about legislative and judicial checks on executive "tyranny." It also clarified commitment to the idea that social justice was partly a product of governmental choices about the general good, in contrast to the Jacksonians' sense that government action alone represented unwholesome favoritism.[2] These hardening party lines boiled into violence during elections in the nation's two largest cities, New York and Philadelphia, where size and rapid growth enfeebled older patterns of communal restraint.

The most injurious election riot of the Jacksonian era erupted during New York City's spring voting, when furor over the pet bank policy was at its apex. The New York election was municipal, with the mayor's office the chief plum, but both Whigs and Democrats saw it as a portent of coming events. "The salvation of the Country depends in great measure upon the defeat of the Jackson Party," Whig Philip Hone noted in his diary. In Washington, Daniel Webster hoped the election would inaugurate "a favorable change in the affairs of the country." For Democrats, the election was a referendum on the administration's position, while the ties of the contest to Van Buren's prestige revved up his political machine.[3] The Workingman's Party had recently muddled traditional Tammany control, and the Whigs knew that current controversies gave them a solid chance of victory.

The riot grew out of Whig determination to prevent the intimidation that Tammany "bullies" had used in earlier elections; their anger had been whetted by wide-scale naturalization of Irish immigrants in the days before the election. The *Commercial Advertiser* was probably right in seeing the 1834 violence, in retrospect, as the result of a ten-year practice of "bullies" who "annoyed people to discourage the 'respectable classes' from voting" and "insulted by noise and threats of violence every decent man who opposed them publicly at the polls."

The *Advertiser*'s comment made clear the limits the "bullies" accepted: noise, annoyances, threats, and even personal fighting were all right, but not serious injury. This explains why, in the presidential election of 1832, New York City papers could report a few injuries and some actions of an "unpardonable character" but also say that the voting went with "more civil deportment at the polls than was anticipated and with apparent good temper." Intimidation wasn't desirable, but it was not too serious, either, if limited to certain areas and if the "numerous fights" resulted in little more "than a black eye" here and there.[4] Bullies commonly acted around polls where their party predominated, and nonbelligerent voters could always go to another to vote.

Democratic bullies were largely unopposed and undestructive in the city until 1832, when the opposition began to take permanent form. In 1834 the Whigs were not about to let such one-sided intimidation continue, nor were the Democrats ready to accept the Whigs' new tactics of innovative mass appeal. That a good deal of the trouble focused on the Sixth Ward was inevitable: this poor, largely immigrant ward was where the party's Irish bullies lived and where they had traditionally been able most readily to control the polls. As their electoral emblem, the Whigs constructed a model frigate labeled *The Constitution* manned by seamen, which was dragged through the streets accompanied by two bands and hundreds of supporters. In Philadelphia in 1832 the first of the second party system riots occurred when Jacksonians attacked a Whig center that showed a huge transparency, a painting on translucent cloth with lights behind it, that illustrated "The Downfall of Tyranny."[5] As party battles heated up in the early 1830s, the Democrats hated the new Whig popularizing measures, while Whigs decided to resist traditional Jacksonian intimidation tactics.

Whig editor James Watson Webb, always fumy for a fight, presented the party position most loudly on the first day of the election; "Let us all go to the polls with a full determination to keep the peace, but also with a firm resolve to deposit our votes in the ballot box and enable our friends to do so—or die in the struggle." The melodramatic quality of Webb's pose and prose encouraged a feistiness that was likely to cause trouble. The advice of the most respected Whig paper, the *American*, probably caught more accurately the prevalent Whig mood; "If we do not protect ourselves, we deserve to be victims of ruffians."[6]

Some of the Jacksonian tricks could be publicized and controlled. The Whigs learned that their opponents had resorted to the ruse of printing ballots with mayoralty candidate Gulian Verplanck's name misspelled. But with the "bullies," the only control was the dangerous tactic of meeting threat with resistance. On the first day of the election, Jacksonian toughs tried to protect their Sixth Ward prerogatives by driving their opponents from Whig headquarters. Former Democratic alderman George D. Strong led about a hundred rioters into the Whig building, tore down their banners, destroyed their ballots, and beat fifteen or twenty Whigs, some of them unconscious. They also beat a constable insensible who tried to stop them. Democrats claimed provocation in the form of Whig comments and inflammatory articles, but this form of Jacksonian defense makes clear that the initial violence was one-sided.[7]

Democratic mayor Gideon Lee refused to protect at the polls; he told Whig leaders that the police were all busy. Lee perhaps thought that the Whigs, faced with a
choice of fighting or fleeing in Ward Six, would give up the game there. He was mistaken. Rumors, including that of a death, circulated, some of them possibly Webb's
creations. At a general meeting Tuesday night, Whigs damned the actions of "a band
of *hirelings, mercenaries,* and *bullies,*" and in a Ninth Ward meeting contingency
plans were made for each ward to provide 100 citizens to make up a mobile peacekeeping force wherever "ruffians may attack peaceable citizens while exercising the
Sacred Right of Suffrage."

Mayor Lee, faced with this reality, decided to return the Whigs to their headquarters. This was accomplished peaceably, and moderate Whigs were mollified. Still,
Webb turned out with 200 men to protect voters' rights in the Old Sixth. The situation was explosive with men spoiling for a fight when the *Constitution* passed
through. A melee broke out, but the parity of partisan strength and the presence of
police brought it quickly under control. Another scuffle later in the morning also
ended quickly, but not, in this case, before a few Whigs were severely beaten. In this
affray, some Jacksonian rioters were arrested, and a Whig "posse" prevented them
from being rescued on their way to jail. Rumors of more deaths resurrected Whig
fears and their determination to turn out a large protective force. The mayor also decided that if he didn't act, others would. He laid plans for having 300 watchmen at
call, something he'd said was impossible a day earlier.[8]

On the final voting day, police kept the peace in the Sixth Ward, and in the neighboring Eleventh they quickly acted when the Jacksonians sealed off the entrance to
the polls to all but their supporters. Subsequent troubles followed the course of the
Constitution, with some Jacksonians hissing and threatening wherever it went. In
one morning scuffle, Mayor Lee, now determinedly leading the police, was struck
on the head with a stick. About ten o'clock near the Whig Masonic Hall, Jacksonian
threats and stones triggered a response. The Whigs rushed from their hall and drove
off the attackers, hurting one or two Jacksonians. The defeated Jacksonians retreated
to the Sixth Ward and returned at about high noon reinforced for vengeance, but
now they faced police rather than Whigs. The rioters routed the badly outnumbered
watchmen and brutally beat about twenty of them, the fury probably heated by rioters' surprise at facing opposition from their party's police. Eight police were hospi-
talized with severe wounds; one lingered unconscious and near death for weeks.
During the day, twenty Whigs, two Jacksonians, fifteen watchmen, and the mayor
were also hurt, but it was the brutal near-fatal beatings of the policemen that
shocked everyone.[9]

This worst encounter triggered the Whigs' long-brewing fears. Thousands filled
the streets, and about 500 of them went to the armory, which, rumor had it, the Jacksonians were determined to take. Refused arms, the Whigs entered anyway and
armed themselves. Before they could leave, the mayor arrived with a militia unit,
again promising legal protection and melodramatically pointing out the dangers:
"Do not cause the streets of our city to be dyed in blood! Do not call down upon
your heads the curses of the widow and the homeless orphan." Probably the posse's
presence more than the widow's curse caused the Whigs quietly to return home. All
violence was over, even though thousands of partisans filled the streets the next two

nights, first to hear that the Democrats had won the mayoralty by 181 votes, then to learn that the Whigs had narrowly triumphed in the city council struggle. Thus quietly ended the contest that some thought put the city "in the midst of a Revolution" two days earlier.[10]

Some thirty men, mostly Irish, were arrested, and at least six, four of whom had previous prison records, were tried and convicted. Possibly the more respectable rioters made use of political connections to be freed, but the criminal records of several of the prominent rioters give ballast to the charge that these men were political "mercenaries." No newspaper questioned the Irish centrality in the rioting, but party affiliation determined one's interpretation. Davy Crockett in his *Tour* called the rioters both "Van Buren's warriors" and "the wild Irish," individuals "worse than savages" who were "too mean to swab hell's kitchen." Niles labeled the New York Irish rioters "fighting machines" but insisted that the real problem lay in "the bad hearts of those who arrayed and *stimulated* them, rather than in their own wrong *heads*." The Irish arrested were "victims of persons 'behind the scenes' less *brave* but more *cunning* than they." Whig papers closer to home were careful to avoid blaming the Irish generally and gave wide currency to the talks of Irishmen Dr. William Macneven and William Sampson, who argued that the Irish generally were not responsible for the actions of the bands of political hirelings. The penny-press *Sun* summed up the general view of Whig and neutral journals: it was "illiberal to condemn the Irish as a body, for the disgraceful conduct of a few of their ignorant countrymen." It was the Jacksonian papers that minimized political explanation by emphasizing an ethnic version. Taunts had caused the Irish, "always easily excited," to attack, argued the hack *New York Standard*, while William Cullen Bryant's Jacksonian *Evening Post* claimed that the troubles grew from "peculiarities of the Irish character. Quick, irritable, and generous, with a clash of nationality, and particular inclination to a row. . . ."[11]

By the fall elections of 1834, both parties in New York settled for peaceful process, or rather circumscribed commonplace voting violence, but Philadelphia experienced a deadly and destructive fall riot marking that city's rites of passage to the new two-party system. In the City of Brotherly Love, the initiation of violence was more bipartisan than in New York, although the Jacksonians perpetrated the greatest destructiveness before it was over. The first fatality was that of a young carpenter, William Perry, who, during the selection of election judges for the coming contest, was stabbed through an artery in the leg as a gang of roughs of both parties ran by. Perry, not active politically, was probably the victim of bad luck in a situation where a lot of people were running around with clubs, knives, and guns. But the Jacksonians, still carrying the burden of blame for the New York election violence, decided to make him a Democratic martyr. Though none of Perry's friends saw what happened, the Jacksonian *American Sentinel* screamed that this was "the diabolical crime of the Bank hirelings" and invented, as the victim's last words, "Success to Jackson and Democracy." With elaborations, this story was spread through the Jacksonian press, particularly in New York, whose fall election was close at hand.

Two days later, its account demolished locally, the *Sentinel* half-apologized for its earlier story, but national Democrats had Philadelphia officeholders stage a huge funeral, for distant consumption, in praise of this "martyr." Public funerals have been held for less deserving souls than this "good, peaceful" boy, probably a Whig, whose mother at least believed "he had no enemies" and was a martyr to party-encouraged violence. To quiet tensions before the election, authorities released a coroner's report that showed the improbability of any partisan motive, although it emphasized how Perry's death suggested the dangers violence posed for American elections "should they become the arena for political and mercenary Gladiators." The coroner's jury recommended banning weapons near the polls, an idea that the Jacksonians rejected at a public meeting under wealthy banker Robert Patterson, which also decried all supervision at the polls by a "secret spy system" of either police or party "committees of vigilance."[12] The Democrats obviously believed they'd benefit most from "toughing out" the election.

The actual election was very rough from the beginning, with many harsh scuffles and both sides doing some poll-barricading in their strongholds. On the night of October 14, the violence verged out of control. The Jacksonians destroyed a Whig transparency and some election ballots but failed in their attempt to cut a Liberty Pole which the Whigs, with mirth aforethought, had made of metal instead of the usual wood. Whigs attacked some Jacksonian liquor tents and felled a Hickory Pole. In the Moyamensing area, the worst trouble developed when Jacksonians attacked Whig headquarters, in a brick building rented from James Robb. Initially driven off after some damage to windows and shutters, the Jacksonians returned with reinforcements. Whigs fired first blanks and then buckshot at the attackers, wounding about fifteen, but were driven out when the Jacksonians set fire to the building. Several of them were beaten, one of them, John Nell, fatally by Democrat John Zane, "wielding a cane over the fallen victim." The Democrats also beat constables and firemen, trashed an engine, and cut fire hoses, so all five substantial buildings in "Robb's Row," worth about $6,000, burned to the ground. Besides Nell, two others were killed, Whig James Lamb and Jacksonian John Bath.[13]

Some of the Democratic claims about these two major riots of the second American party system were true, but hardly exonerating. In New York, Whig poll watchers, some of them clerks or workers given time off to electioneer, irritated Democrats; much verbal abuse, political and ethnic, occurred, as always; "one to four" Democrats were attacked and beaten; Webb's rhetoric was excessive. In Philadelphia the Whigs were as involved in rough intimidation at the polls as Jacksonians. Yet the Jacksonians perpetrated the great bulk of the injurious and destructive violence and were attacking to destroy when they suffered their only real losses. And the violence was far beyond the bounds of what had occurred previously in the nation. In no antebellum riot did so many police suffer such serious injury as in the spring New York political riot; the number of deaths in Philadelphia in the fall was unprecedented in an election riot, and the intentional destruction of property was paralleled in very few mobs.

Quite simply, this degree of violence created communal disgust that threatened the party most tarred with it. Hence, as their justification the Jacksonians resorted to their ethnic interpretation of the excitable Irish, unduly riled by words. Nor was the Perry funeral their only gesture to point out the horrors of Whig violence. In New York, Jacksonian appointee Commissary General Henry Arcularius published a report damning the Whig mob that briefly took over the arsenal, adding an amusing portrait of his and his wife's bravery.[14] A soldier in the Seventh Regiment, to which Whigs turned over the arsenal and its arms, remembered Arcularius's report as "so exuberant and overflowing in grandiloquent bombast, and ridiculous egotism, and unmitigated 'bosh' that it remained a standing theme for jest and merriment."[15] Of course, it was not intended for home consumption but for evidence in less knowing areas that excess violence was a Whig tactic.[16]

Both parties learned these riots' lessons. After 1834, they reestablished rough parity and propriety in use of electoral intimidation, cheating, and brawling. Seldom did an election go by without dirty tricks, nasty threats, and fighting. Yet this brief "reign of terror" ended, and no political violence on the 1834 level recurred until the emotive issues of nativism and slavery disrupted the Whig-Democratic rules of the game, especially in Southern urban centers, where the major political mobs in the 1850s occurred.[17]

After 1834, the chief violent incidents of the second party system were more verbal than realized. At times the Democratic Party cheerfully urged revolution over its favorite issue, democracy: in Maryland in 1836, in Pennsylvania in 1838, and in Rhode Island's less farcical "Dorr War" of 1842. The Jacksonian's favorite rhetorical ploy of wrapping themselves in the robes of "the people" and "the Democracy" had little policy corollary because American suffrage was about as "universal" as they wished it. This created enthusiasm for events showing that opposition to "aristocracy" was a bit more vital than the two parties' steady quibbles over the precise balance of majoritarianism with legalism.

Such an opportunity the party seized in Maryland in 1836. Agitation began when, after losing a close election, Jacksonians discovered the need to embody "the will of the people" and to end "aristocracy" by immediately ending the Maryland state constitution. Yet the Baltimore rhetoric of the local spring election—"Reform or Revolution," and an end to the present system "peaceably if we can, forcibly if we must"—vanished in the statewide fall campaign because at that time Jacksonians weren't anxious to endorse a change that was unpopular in the older rural parts of the state.[18]

The problem was an odd system Maryland established at the time of the Revolution. In county and city jurisdictions people voted for electors, whose job was to choose senators for a five-year term. In turn, with the directly elected assembly, these senators chose the governor. One of the most extreme institutional attempts to balance government by mixing popular and "disinterested" judgments, the system was long questioned, less for its "indirection" than for its regional-numerical injustices. As population grew in Baltimore and the larger western counties, these areas were increasingly underrepresented by the electors. In 1833 and 1836 bipartisan groups in Baltimore and Frederick County urged reform. There was general agreement that the system should change, but complexities about how and at whose expense supported inertia. Neither party talked about reform in the fall campaign of 1836.[19]

The results of this election triggered the trouble. Jacksonians gained a small majority in the popular vote, but the Whigs narrowly won the contest by carrying twenty-one of the forty jurisdictions. The Jacksonians at this point decided to boycott the meeting at which the senate was to be elected, preventing a quorum and hence most governmental activity—unless the Whigs agreed to give them eight of the fifteen slots. The "Van Buren electors," as the nineteen were called, issued a proclamation announcing that acceptance of legalities would be "tame submission" to gross abuse of majoritarian principle. Whig electors promised reforms but rejected the Van Burenites' solution. Jacksonian meetings extolled the charms of revolution, while Whigs lamented "the gigantic strides of a youthful nation in the paths of precocious corruption." In this political gridlock, Maryland voters were given a clear choice between either the nullification of existing institutions for popular sovereignty or promised change within the established constitutional framework.[20]

Faced with this choice, the popular will for legalism in Maryland routed the Jacksonians' "revolutionary" majoritarianism. In successive months, Maryland voters first elected a house of sixty Whigs and nineteen Jacksonians and then supported William Henry Harrison over Van Buren, despite the latter's comfortable win nationally. The only area where Jacksonian support did not fall off precipitously was Allegheny County, where Democrats repudiated the action of the Van Buren nineteen. With the reform issue central, these two elections convinced enough Jacksonians to heed "the will of the people" to allow an elector quorum. The established system went ahead, and Maryland avoided falling into what Whigs breathlessly called "a state of nature" that might "involve us in all the horror and unspeakable calamities of anarchy, intestine commotion and *Civil* War." A month later Whigs followed through on their reform pledges, voting to abolish the electors, directly elect both senators and governor, and apportion house members by population rather than region, the latter an important gesture toward equitable democracy that the Jacksonians had not raised.[21]

Never did the nation's voters have such clear chance to decide, after full debate, on extraconstitutional popular sovereignty, and Marylanders were clearly disinclined to turn their government into "a nursery of *future revolutions*." If Whig fears of "anarchy" and "Red murder" were much overheated, they were matched by Jacksonian pretenses that their postelection attempt at a power grab grew from their willingness "to surrender, upon the holy altar of disinterested patriotism, power and office with all their allurements." By the time the Democratic "revolutionary" convention met, it was an empty gesture in which the party praised its principles but admitted that "circumstances"—not the popular will, of course—made it "expedient" to adjourn "temporarily." Baltimore's *Niles' Register*, which had long argued that the Maryland constitution had "plague spots" needing removal, claimed that "none would have dared to have resisted its purification if it had not been seized by the hand of violence. That act changed the current of public feeling." That the violence here was all rhetorical and theoretical only made stronger the evidence for "our love of constitutional law."[22]

The threat of violence in Pennsylvania, two years later, featured similar Jacksonian rhetoric and strategy in a situation where the party acted successfully to frustrate "the will of the people." Appointees of the Van Buren administration led the sorry affair, though Washington moved quickly to repudiate them once the business was done. Pennsylvania house Democrats later conducted an investigation that concluded the party line: it was a struggle "between the people and a corrupt minority administration," full of "wicked and designing men," that resulted in "the triumph of republicanism over bank aristocracy." These politicians assured a mostly laughing world that without the heroic mob threat, "the right of the majority to govern . . . would have been obliterated . . . and our government ceased to be a republic." The testimony in the report suggested that American democracy was flourishing, though in shoddy form, which needed but a little mobbing to become material for, in the words of *Niles' Register*, "a bitter satire on our institutions and the public intelligence." The riot became known as the "Buckshot War," another of several proofs of how laughter helped expose the nineteenth century's inflated moral rhetoric as slipcover for its more tattered furnishings.[23]

This "war" could have turned tragic but happily provided even better farce than satire. The affair grew out of a hotly contested election in Pennsylvania in 1838 that led to grosser than usual cheating by both sides, with trouble centered in the Northern Liberties precinct of Philadelphia. With the returns from this working-class district, the Whigs/Anti-Masons would have carried a congressional seat as well as the state senate and house, assuring themselves of a U.S. Senatorship. Without the Northern Liberties returns, the Democrats, who won the governorship, would control everything but the Pennsylvania senate. Charges of vote fraud were rampant and justified, but the Democrats managed to lose one polling sheet to justify tossing out all votes from Northern Liberties. To prevent any legal-political action at the state level to readjust this decision, Democrats decided to send to Harrisburg a couple of trainloads of intimidating armed "citizens." It was one of a number of disputed elections that occurred where there was no attempt to do justice, only to base the solution on who had political power at a slightly higher level.

Setbacks in other places made national Democrats especially anxious to make a congressman of Charles Ingersoll. His opponent, Charles Naylor, was one of the few politicians in either party with real ties to working men, while Ingersoll was a wealthy lawyer whose main contribution to "the Democracy" was his virulent anti-abolitionism, including praise for the recent mob-burning of Pennsylvania Hall.[24] While the 1837 depression hurt the Democrats nationally, it also destroyed Anti-Mason governor Joseph Ritner's reelection, because he had invested heavily in internal improvements as well as public education. At the same time, Ritner and his party's strategist, Thaddeus Stevens, were the leading Northern politicians to take a seriously antislavery position, while Naylor had gained most fame for his vigorous reply to South Carolinian George McDuffie's speech claiming that white workers in the North were more degraded than slaves. Local Democrats had another reason for wanting to disrupt any quick action in Harrisburg. When they thought Ritner's reelection likely, they'd pushed a constitutional amendment restricting gubernatorial power and patronage. Now that they were victorious, they wanted to make sure these changes were scotched.[25]

On December 3, Ingersoll urged "popular action" to prevent the organizational sessions in Harrisburg, and the state Jacksonian organ endorsed immediate action: "Civil government is at an end," it proclaimed, and "the day to speak out has come. Silence is treason." Philadelphia's Jacksonian paper announced that it wouldn't mind "hear[ing] of the *spilling of blood* and *the risk of life*" to assure Ingersoll's election: "Democrats! Be determined! Be resolute! Liberty or Death!" Democrats set up "A Committee of Safety" or "provisional Government" and sent trainloads of men to Harrisburg; those from Philadelphia were led by three federal employees, John J. McCahen of the post office, James H. Hutchinson of the custom house, and Charles F. Meusch, a deputy U.S. marshal. A correspondent of the *United States Gazette* reported that on December 3 "every car, stage, or boat comes heavily laden with live freight, men of every cast and character, many of them, doubtless, panting to play some distinguished part in the melee which is expected to come off tomorrow." Possibly some were, as Whig Thomas Williams charged, "patriots at one dollar and a half a day," "heroes of the cockpit and grog shop" purchased "by rewards and rum." The Democrats claimed that large crowds poured in merely out of a concern for law, but party officials didn't deny the purchase of tickets for the patriots and of subsidizing some Harrisburg taverns to assure the continued warmth of their legal action.[26]

The action in this war occurred early. On December 4, the Senate met long enough to seat the two Whig candidates from the disputed district before a mob broke in, many of them with guns. Their demand was that defeated Democrat Charles Brown be allowed to speak, which was agreed to so long as the speech was peaceable. Brown proceeded to announce a popular "revolution" and reportedly asked the crowd if they were willing to "trample the Constitution and shed blood" for justice, to which his audience replied with shouts of "Yes, yes, we will, we will; and accompanied their assent with horrible cries of give us blood if we cannot have our rights." Probably the cry for blood was rhetorical, but Whig senators who were the special objects of mob wrath took no chances and jumped out a window to safety. They were followed outside by most of their colleagues, denying any semblance of legality to the rest of the session. Governor Ritner declared a state of insurrection and requested federal troops, while Thomas Williams wrote his wife, "We are in the midst of a Revolution" where legislative procedure bowed to "an infuriated mob composed mainly of the butchers of the Faubourgs of Philadelphia."[27]

Williams's picture of "the bloodhounds of party . . . baying at our very throats" and his comparisons with the French revolution were overdrawn. Ritner's firmness and his clarity in pointing out the ties of the mob to federal officials led to the Democratic Party's retreat from action. Secretary of War Joel Poinsett denied Ritner's request for the aid of federal troops, but the head of the arsenal in Philadelphia issued weapons, and two contingents of militia turned out to insure the peace, one led by wealthy Philadelphia Democrat Robert Patterson, who came both to quell violence and to insure that no action was taken against the mob. Some mob members tried unsuccessfully to get the troops to desert, after giving up a plan to derail or blow up the troop train when they learned that many Democrats were participating.[28]

The new constitution went into effect, and the Whigs and Democrats compromised on other issues. The Democratic majority later wrote a report on the affair for distant consumption, the conclusions loudly Democratic and the testimony a muddled but rich account of both parties' low toughs and tactics, though the Democrats' most creative chicanery only came to light later. To protect the right of repeated suffrage from a registry law, they inserted forty pages of forged names in the books. Ingersoll partisans beat one potential witness so badly he couldn't testify; this was the only injury in the affair.[29]

Democrats were embarrassed by the Buckshot War's farce and its clear tie to the Van Buren administration. Postmaster General Amos Kendall announced that McCahen had visited Harrisburg between appointments, the U.S. marshal said Deputy Muesch hadn't been connected to the business of the office for months, and customs collector George Wolf said he told his workers not to go and had now fired Hutchinson for his efforts. Such backtracking illustrated once again how unwise political violence (or, in this case, its mere threat) was if it became great enough to attract particular attention. General was private condemnation ("What fools!") and public damnation, none stronger than that of Pennsylvania's largest and best paper, the *Philadelphia Public Ledger*: "What a beautiful commentary upon the assertion so often made in stump speeches, by unprincipled demagogues to unthinking crowds, and so often blazoned in capitals by editorial prostitutes in venal pages, that the Americans are the most enlightened people in the world."[30] Neither political party welcomed any incident that triggered such honest reaction to the self-complacent platitudes that formed the substance of their campaigns and editorials.

In Rhode Island the issues had more substance, as did the man who became the spokesman and the victim of the Democracy. Thomas Dorr was a sensitive and mildly intellectual man who took seriously democratic rhetoric. Yet events were to show how honest naiveté is often more dangerous than cynicism when it follows ideology beyond the established rules of the game.

In 1840 Rhode Island still operated under its colonial charter, which was simply turned into a state constitution at the time of the American Revolution and had changed little from that time on. Given the nature of Rhode Island as a colony, this involved a fairly democratic structure of government, one not nearly so aristocratic or layered by property as those, in 1840, of South Carolina or even Virginia. It had survived so long in part because it gave the state's agrarian interests a decided political advantage. Hence, local and farming interests often favored the constitutional status quo as a measure of protection against the state's substantial but declining commercial interests and its major and growing industrial sector. In relation to what Americans had come to call "universal suffrage," Rhode Island procedures were radically defective—apparently only about two-thirds, though the Dorrites claimed but one-third, of the adult white males were eligible to vote. Yet the injustices favored many less financially advantaged voters and sections. People with "a cabbage patch" were often given more power, complained one Dorr supporter, than men of "great talents" and "property."[31]

Besides a broad-based interest in the politics of inertia, there were other issues that complicated electoral change. Rhode Island was discriminatory against naturalized citizens, and there was some fear of the notoriously quick citizenship procedures of New York City and Philadelphia. Native-born farmers were disinclined to hand over chunks of their power to the increasing number of foreign-born industrial workers. A second complicating issue was the question of black suffrage. Whig suffragists tended to favor black inclusion, on both moral and pragmatic grounds, while Jacksonian suffragists' universal principles were clearly meant for white males only. Whatever stance a suffrage proposal took, opponents could and did use this issue as excuse for general rejection.[32]

These realities kept Rhode Island from making any changes or even showing much concern over the issue until the 1830s, when Jacksonian political success in the state, under wealthy merchant John Brown Francis and banker Thomas Sprague, gave the Whig party some incentive to question the status quo. The first national "agitation" on the issue came in 1833, as Martin Van Buren began efforts to consolidate support as Jackson's successor. Six citizens, their professions written after their names to suggest the range of class support, asked the vice president for his views on suffrage so the candidate might reply that universal suffrage did not endanger property and point out the great success of the "universal" democracy he had given New York. Such carefully pointed inquiries and preordained platitudinous reply were the stuff of which campaigns were made at the time; moreover, Van Buren did not intend to attack the "freehold" system that Rhode Island Democrats largely supported. In 1834, with some Whig encouragement, Thomas Dorr began his political activity to extend Rhode Island's suffrage. A decade later, his battle largely won on terms he refused to accept, Dorr was in jail— suffering in a dungeon where the enemies of popular sovereignty had hounded him, national Democrats insisted, or comfortably situated with a good prison library at hand because of simpleminded stubbornness that kept him from taking an oath of allegiance to a government now constituted as he'd wanted, Whigs claimed. No one disputed Dorr's claim that, during his twenty months in jail, he painted over 8,000 fans, each with from one to twenty-five figures of flowers and fishes.[33]

To his friends in 1830, Dorr's ending up practicing this genteel craft must have seemed more likely than his becoming a political martyr. Dorr's father, a wealthy manufacturer and insurance magnate, sent both sons, Thomas and Henry, to Phillips Exeter, to Harvard, and then to study law under Chancellor Kent. Thomas Dorr didn't practice law but lived the life of a New England gentleman of means, more drawn to his mother's cultural and social activities than to his father's business. For awhile he headed Providence's school board, where he led the fight for more general and better public education. Elected as an anti-Jacksonian to the Rhode Island Assembly in 1833, he actively opposed both a law that would have made banks favored creditors and the gestures of restraint suggested against abolitionists. Dorr's antislavery convictions were deep. In 1837, during his bid as Democratic candidate for Congress, Dorr wrote a letter that favored the abolitionist position on several issues: the right of petition, abolishing slavery in the District of Columbia, and opposing Texas's annexation. When he was defeated, James G. Birney tried to get him to become an antislavery agent, a job he refused while announcing his faith in "the extermination of Republican slavery."[34]

In 1834, Dorr's actions were moderate. He organized and financed the Rhode Island Constitutional Party, dedicated to bringing full suffrage to the native and naturalized, the white and the black male adults of the state. He did what had to be done—buying the allegiance of a newspaper, printing the required ballots, inducing people to run on the ticket—but the small vote in that year and the even smaller one in 1836, always less than 10 percent, spelled doom to the effort. Dorr's early Whig support also turned against him when his candidacy threatened Whig chances in a congressional race. There were ironies in the situation: most of the Whigs who repudiated Dorr, including his future nemesis Samuel Ward King, were on record as in favor of constitutional change, while his new Democratic allies, including popular

John Bacon Francis, had the previous year urged followers to bring into the field "horse, foot and dragoons" in support of "the last fight of the Landed Interest!!!," where a loss would let the Whigs destroy "their freehold system!!!!!!!" With all these exclamation points behind the old system, Francis was never willing to support Dorr, but other Democrats were more flexible when they thought his movement might aid their return to power.[35]

Dorr's early efforts in the usual third-party vein failed both because of lack of popular concern—the readiness of nonfreeholders to be "willing slaves" was amazing, one Dorrite reported—and the difficulties in integrating its principles to either major party.[36] This contributed to Dorr's distrust of politics and his irritation with its mechanisms of compromise later on. Yet Dorr's rapprochement with the Democrats forced his acceptance of one compromise that must have rankled his idealism: his suffrage proposals from then on excluded blacks. For the shy, gentlemanly Dorr, both political failure and the essential racist accommodation he made may have hardened an idealism that neglected even minimal political realism in later situations.

The ablest Democratic leaders in Rhode Island were never Dorr enthusiasts, but the outside ideologues of the party were pleased to locate a political struggle where principles beyond the division of loaves and fishes were at issue. Dorr's second failure in traditional politics came when John Bacon Francis adamantly refused both Van Buren's and Dorr's pleas that he lead a unified Jacksonian-Suffragist ticket in 1840, probably out of loyalty to Rhode Island's "freehold system," with its favoritism of farmers, who had always been his chief support. Jacksonian hopes were in fact so desperate without Francis that they waited too long to accept his refusal to give adequate support to their second choice.

Francis's pragmatism led him to distrust Dorr and to like Van Buren, on the same grounds as one of his South Carolina correspondents. Since democracy must rule the country, "give me, then, for President a man who knows how to 'wield the democracy.'" On the other hand, he thought Dorr "should be put down" both for his "free suffrage heresy" and because no one could do much good "if he stand sternly upon an abstract and impractical notion of duty."[37] At the crossroads, Dorr got many letters from prominent Democrats—Silas Wright, Levi Woodbury, Thomas Hart Benton—but, unschooled in real American politics, he took them as proof of support rather than as gestures announcing that public approval was not to be expected, at least until success was certain. Francis's refusal to run in 1840 and what one Dorrite called "the *bona fide* panic that has at last got hold" led to an overwhelming Whig victory.

The second part of Dorr's strategy in early 1840 fared little better. He arranged for some representatives of the Jacksonian intellectual-oratorical elite—Robert Rantoul, Alexander H. Everett, Orestes Brownson—to speak on democratic political theory. Rantoul ran into opposition at Newport, in the form of catcalls and a tossed potato. William Ennis reported bitterly the passing of politeness along with "the gentlemen of the old school" and told Dorr "it would be almost as easy to raise the dead" as to arouse the area to suffrage enthusiasm. The only memory of Rantoul's talk was "the missile potato which is pinned in one of our grocery stores against the handbill which announced the lecture."[38]

Yet much more had come of Dorr's efforts than the mockery of a rotting potato.

The publicity given the issue locally and nationally, as well as the pressure of shifting economic-demographic realities in Rhode Island, had turned a neglected issue into one about which most of the political leadership in the state agreed that something had to be done. In six years Dorr, like many another American reformer, had lost every battle and won the war. It was at this point that he hit upon his most inventive strategy, one that might have capped rather than clouded his work had he treated it as potent democratic theater rather than tying it to the always shabby world of real power with threats of violence that, luckily, proved largely ludicrous.

Dorr's idea was to deny the existence of Rhode Island's legal structure on the grounds that it was not democratic and to call an election of all the people—that is, the people who alone counted in American Democratic and democratic eyes at this time, adult white males. If the majority of these citizens voted as Dorr wished, the "People's Constitution" and its representatives would become Rhode Island's true government. Alexander H. Everett was right in calling the idea "a curious and interesting experiment in the practical workings of our institutions."

Everett was also right that the peaceful way Dorr and his supporters went ahead with their plans for a vote to end the existing government, while that government did nothing to stop them, was "pretty good proof that the sovereignty of the people is . . . a substantial and practical reality."[39] Yet equally clear on both sides was an at least as substantial commitment to procedural orderliness. The Whigs in power responded largely by speeding up action on their plan for suffrage reform, which retained some mild property qualifications for naturalized citizens and for voting on taxes but also gave black males voting rights.

Dorr calculated that victory required 12,000 votes but that 14,000 would be good, just to be safe. The People's Constitution, it was announced, gained just over 14,000 votes. A large number turned out to support Dorr's constitution, but there's little doubt that the official returns were considerably inflated. With one group controlling, counting, and keeping loose record of the vote, it's hardly surprising that the People's Party achieved just a whisker better result than it felt it needed. The official Democrat-Suffragist paper, the *New Age*, initially reported just under 12,000 in support of the Dorr document, stressing that 4,019 votes by freeholders was more than half of the suspected 8,000 in that group, but it discovered 2,000 more votes a week later. An opponent who later checked the tallies that were kept for Newport claimed that of 1,202 favorable votes reported there, at least a third were fraudulent: 213 were by unnaturalized foreigners, 52 by soldiers temporarily in town, 20 by other nonresidents, and 5 by minors, while 20 people were listed twice as voters, and many of those counted claimed not to have voted.[40]

The vote on the new Whig-sponsored Constitution, where all voters proposed to be enfranchised were allowed to vote, was better regulated but did nothing to clarify the situation. In April 1842, it was rejected 8,689 to 8,013, the triumphant opposition divided fairly equally between old freeholders and new Dorrites. In the meantime, the Rhode Island Supreme Court unsurprisingly ruled that the People's Constitution, which invalidated that court, was not valid. Toward the end of the month, elections for officials were held under both the old charter and the People's Constitution, with 7,000 voters taking part in the former and but 6,000 voting on the People's candidates; again, that figure was probably inflated and certainly reflected slippage in enthusiasm for now "Governor" Dorr's strategy.

Had Dorr had much political sense or experience, he could have assured his own political future by announcing the justice of his cause and his refusal to corrupt it by resort to the brute force that was the last resort of Rhode Island's illegal and now desperate opponents of democracy. Those opponents passed a law with harsh punishment against anyone attempting to take over official duties outside the prescribed legal structure. The Dorrites labeled this the "Algerine law" to evoke earlier failed attempts to enslave Jeffersonian democracy, and the Whig action would have seemed excessive had not Dorr upped the extremism considerably by suggesting military action to enforce the will of the people. Such bravado, with its potential for danger, withered his local support and destroyed what might have been, for better or worse, an impressive precedent for the occasional reassertion of direct democracy over procedural primacy in American society.

Dorr's folly came not for lack of sound advice. Dorr had no closer friend in the Democratic Party than its chief intellectual spokesman, John L. O'Sullivan, editor of the *Democratic Review*. O'Sullivan's majoritarianism led him to support Dorr's "little revolution," though his concern about the South subdued his support for any inherent popular right to chuck over all structure that might interfere with "laws of nature." He urged a "prudential philosophy": "Before putting my head down the fox's throat, like the silly crane, I must feel perfectly safe about being able to draw it back again."[41]

If O'Sullivan's counsel was sensible, that of Dorr's brother, Henry, was more thoughtfully perceptive than anything published either for or against the movement. The younger Dorr had a clear sense of American democracy not as abstraction but as an organism binding popular feeling to a set structure. Hence, as his brother's plans for the people's vote took shape, Henry thought the idea worthy, despite his worry that political hacks could easily distort it. Basically, he judged that the time was ripe and that Dorr was helping to make change not just the work of "a few enlightened persons" but of the people, in a positive way. He worried more as the election drew near and "the inconsiderate threats and revolutionary harangues" of many Dorrites made the freeholders enemies, when in fact to exclude their support was to kill "the popular will."

When the election was over and the Suffragists announced that their document was the constitution of Rhode Island and that any attempt to resist it should be met by force, Henry Dorr wrote a long analysis of the intellectual and practical dangers. The greatest of these, Henry Dorr warned, was that the Suffragists were staking out a position that they might be obliged to maintain by force. And if this came to pass, the movement would both fail and slay the very ideal of the popular will freely expressed. Using arms out of conviction that one represented the majority could only sow "inextricable confusion," and the federal government would have to see announcements about "the right of revolution" as "insurrection," which it had the responsibility to crush.

Even more convincing was the younger Dorr's reading of the pragmatic situation in Rhode Island, with its "quiet—too quiet—people." While the Suffragists had aroused general support of the broad changes they wanted, they'd created almost no commitment to "resistance to the laws." The state showed no sign of "that feverish recklessness" that would encourage people "to take forcible possession of their rights, in cold blood and cold weather," so the more violence the Dorrites talked, the less they represented the popular will. Henry Dorr thought this situation tragic, not only because of the potential bloodshed but also because it undercut the good the Suffragist agitation might do to change the state's citizens:

> Their minds are encrusted over with the prejudices of 200 years. The dust of antiquity has settled thickly down upon the institutions and the feelings of the state. It is full time that it is removed—that the clogged political machinery should be lubricated, and the improvements of modern times be introduced. The people must be awakened, and taught to read and think for themselves, and the subject of suffrage seems to be the proper one to give them the opportunity.[42]

Whatever Rhode Islanders' provincialism, Henry Dorr was right about their response to the possibility of violence and about the way this trampled upon the intellectual contribution Suffragism otherwise might make.

Why, in the spring of 1842, Dorr continued to welcome violence as a solution "if necessary," as local support declined and warnings grew, is murky. There is no doubt that his acceptance of violence in late May and June destroyed his movement; though happily the almost immediate "absquatalation" of him and his "troops" prevented much physical harm. Outside support doubtless had some effect, most notoriously New York City's Loco Focos. Levi Slamm and Mike Walsh announced from New York City that a bit of bloodshed would make Dorr's a second American Revolution, and Alexander Ming Jr. and Abraham Crasto suggested that New York City militia units or police accompany Dorr to Rhode Island. Dorr was to confer about this "honor" with "Quartermaster Slamm."[43] Similar empty promises of help came from similar sources in Philadelphia and Massachusetts.

Nor was Dorr without more respectable encouragement. Seth Luther and Orestes Brownson assured him, in the latter's words, that "there are warm hearts and strong arms enough in the union to support you" Brownson promised that he himself "would shoulder a musket and fight if need be." Brownson, like most New York City theoretical heroes, never noticed Dorr's need when the Rhode Islander followed his advice; Brownson next went to Rhode Island a year later to lecture on the social dangers of democracy if interpreted simplemindedly, à la Dorr. Probably more influential on Dorr were the views of political leaders such as the Democratic governors of Maine, New Hampshire, and Connecticut, the last of whom was kept by "prudential views" alone from sending out the militia to fight United States troops if President Tyler should dispatch any. Prominent national Democrats Levi Woodbury, Silas Wright, and Thomas Hart Benton sent letters of support which Dorr found of a most gratifying character but which in fact suggested that no serious aid, even of a verbal kind, was to be expected. The letters began with notice that they were strictly private, and ringing statements of faith in Dorr's principles were followed with injunctions to avoid "violence" and "excesses." "Caution, caution, caution; forbearance, forbearance, forbearance. Suffer wrong, but do no wrong," wrote Wright, who also asked Dorr to burn his support letter because it might "be misrepresented." Congressmen

Edmund Burke of New Hampshire and William Allen of Ohio, who had less reputation to lose, gave more belligerent encouragement.[44]

Out of some flaw of judgment or character, Dorr listened to the coarsest advice he got. To read his letters is to sense not only Dorr's basic kindness and decency but also the weaknesses of the mild gentleman-intellectual as politician. He had some taste for himself as a man of action, or at least for metaphorical militarism. Even before the Suffragist constitutional election, he talked about his supporters' being "*old soldiers* in the *last war*" for democracy and claimed that their actions had to be "on the Bonapartean order." As the 1842 crisis approached, he found it "time to repeat the memorable words of Waterloo, 'Up guards, and at them." Perhaps he hoped, too, that talking tough might lead to triumph.

There's no doubt that in early April, he still thought it would be only "a paper war," with the vigorous action by the governor and legislature meant "only *to frighten the common sort of folks.*"[45] After that time Dorr paid much more attention to national reaction than to that of Rhode Island's "common sort of folks." While Governor King worked steadily to combine gestures of threat and conciliation with promises of reform that neutralized the bulk of Dorr's Rhode Island following, Dorr apparently thought Rhode Island had already spoken and presumed the voice of the people should be silent, having once announced for Dorr's constitution.

King acted to gain national support by requesting that President John Tyler send troops to quell the Suffragist "insurrection." Tyler refused on the grounds that no insurrection was in progress, but he recognized what Henry Dorr had called the nation's "visitatorial rights" and promised that he would not "shirk from the performance of a duty" in sending troops should insurrection occur. King cleverly used this hazy promise to show national recognition of his government. Northern Democracy was committed to Dorrite principles for home and Rhode Island consumption, but it had no intention of paying the tariff of Southern alienation for them. So the Jacksonian Senate boldly proclaimed that they wouldn't endorse Tyler's position but wouldn't condemn it either. Dorr's Washington lobbyist, brash Dr. John A. Brown—he judged he could "soft soap" the president, "the greatest ass I ever see that had the name of an educated man"—alienated many congressional supporters by making public those endorsements of Dorr they were happy to make loudly in private.[46]

All action and reaction that mattered much was local, and all of it weakened Dorr. His government organized on May 3, following a procession of some 2,000 supporters, about one-third of them conspicuously armed. Dorr immediately formed militia units and requested that the King government share its revenues with him, while his legislature "repealed" the "Algerine law" against it. On May 4, King's legislature met, reaffirmed its position, urged obedience to law, authorized the arrest of the Suffragist officials, and organized a citizen patrol in Providence, the only place where the Dorrites retained strength. Dorr left the state in pursuit of support, while King carefully developed it at home. The crisis came quickly when Dorr returned to Rhode Island at midmonth and King ordered arrests, including Dorr's. Some jailings were made, while crowds prevented others, including that of Dorr. On May 17, Dorr brought out two cannon to threaten the arsenal, and King brought out his carefully organized 600- or 700-strong "law and order" patrols. The next day Dorr's legislators all resigned en masse and asked Dorr to leave, but Dorr again marched on the

arsenal with several cannon. The arsenal was well guarded—the many defenders included Dorr's brother and father—and Dorr's troops disappeared as they moved
within shot of their goal. Dorr fled the state, and the authorities worked out a peaceable surrender of arms from the remnant of Dorr's militia.

Perhaps the laughter at this farce, which seemed more a test of will and public
sentiment than a resort to force, dictated Dorr's second debacle, when he clearly intended to establish the popular will at bayonet point. As he ran from the state on
May 19, Dorr wrote his "general" Henry De Wolfe that he "deemed it expedient to
withdraw" to save lives but that he would return "should your post be defensible."[47]
De Wolfe found his position defensible only when he got back to Massachusetts, but
a few Dorr friends encouraged a return to the field with better preparation. There
was some talk that July 4 would be the right day to renew the war, but Dorr's 200
troops at Chepachet were surprised by a clash with Charterite scouts. The few
rounds of shot in the dark took one Dorrite life and injured at least two others, and
Dorr led the flight to safety in Massachusetts. The dozen men Mike Walsh led from
New York, he immediately led home again. High political theory gave place to a raft
of low political satire:

> His men had sworn not to desert
>   Their gallant leader come what might.
> But, when they saw "he cut dirt,"
>   True to their oath, they joined in flight.[48]

A new constitution was approved, and the broadened electorate overwhelmingly
supported anti-Dorr candidates. Several Dorrites were tried, convicted, and quickly
pardoned, commonly on taking an oath of allegiance to the government of Rhode Island. Only Dorr refused and stayed in jail, until 1845, when the Rhode Island legislature, led by a Whig governor, who had won with some old Dorrite support, pardoned Dorr but denied him his civil liberties until he took the oath of allegiance. In
the end, Dorr was one of the few adult male citizens of Rhode Island both unincar-
cerated and unable to vote.

In many ways, Dorr's political position was as much muddled by his long refusal
to compromise as it was sullied by his acceptance of violence. The most obvious intellectual question was the degree to which democracy was a sovereign concept outside of the structural realities that encased it. Dorr himself never much sharpened his
argument beyond saying "the whole people became tenants in common of the right
of sovereignty." The most formal argument of the Dorrites, that of their "nine
lawyers," claimed that in republican government power resided "in the *People
Themselves*" and that "the mode of proceeding by the people is immaterial."[49] The
Dorrite opponents tended to argue either simply the sanctity of law or, more complexly, the folly of any claim to a popular will divorced from the procedures set up
to express contractually who could do what under which circumstances. John
Quincy Adams, forced into the conflict when his offer to defend his old and hapless
friend Dutee Pearce was interpreted as support for Dorrism, most clearly mocked
"the mirage of universal suffrage," when no one intended to include women, children, or slaves, and stressed the need to keep faith with social contracts or to change
them by established procedures.

In fact, Dorrism caused the Democracy to back away from an unconstrained popular sovereignty. John L. O'Sullivan remained personally loyal to Dorr, but his June 1842 comment about the struggle's proving that "the people" could change the government any way they wanted became, the next month, the claim that while "the whole" had power, the whole had nothing to do with the insane, children, women, or slaves, even though it was mere practice and not reason that excluded the latter two groups.[50] Why such "practices" were sacrosanct when Rhode Island's were sacrilegious, O'Sullivan and his fellow Democrats cared not to consider, but never again did the Democratic Party try to prove its purity by invoking the right of revolution against all limits on the popular will. Daniel Webster, whom Dorr saw as the nation's leading antidemocratic Tory, had the last word: great good had come from the Rhode Island controversy, which had rid "the political atmosphere from some of its noxious mists" and turned "men's minds from unfounded notions and delusions" toward truer ideas about "representative government."[51]

The irony of the victory of Rhode Island's broader practice of democracy with defeat for the principle of popular sovereignty above all procedure was no greater than the personal one. Dorr had made himself not only the state's premier disenfranchised adult male but Rhode Island's preeminent stickler for constitutionalism, clinging to the absolute supremacy of his charter long after the state's people had lost interest in it.

For all the dangers in Rhode Island, actual violence was minimal. The "will of the people" in lynch, Regulator, and vigilante groups often offered an excuse for much deadly violence, but only because these groups made clear that their actions were simply a pro tem strategy to right, rather than rewrite, the constitutional order. When faced with clear choices, the American people refused to uphold "first principles" over procedural propriety or to make extraconstitutionalism a part of the unwritten American political constitution, decisions promoted in part by Jacksonian unwillingness to push their rhetoric where slavery reigned.

Such legalistic choices also solidified willingness to resist what most Northerners viewed as a Southern determination to junk the national compact at the time of the Civil War. This argument of Civil War, however, was preceded by the nation's only successful extraprocedural assertion of popular sovereignty—in Kansas, where another idealistic New Englander, "Governor" Charles Robinson, established a "majority" government and cannily managed to steadily strengthen its local support for several years. And here the Democrat Party was forced, much more openly than in its earlier Northern "revolutions," to make clear that its concern for majoritarianism was as nothing compared to its commitments to slavery.

The Dorr War marked the end of the riotous political violence of the Whig-Jacksonian era, though the tough tactics and personal violence that Henry Miller described in St. Louis remained a vital part of political sport. Few elections passed without accurate charges of cheating or disturbance, but so balanced was the chicanery and so bounded the brawling that power passed back and forth or stayed in one party's hands, largely in accord with accepted popular sentiment. Elections were often very close, and victory sometimes went to those who bent the rules best, but both rules and results were in accord with a popularly developed rough definition of how to measure the American popular will.

CHAPTER EIGHT

Trying to Forget Slavery

Nativism and New Riots

> If you put a chain around the neck of the slave, the other end fastens itself around your own.
> —Ralph Waldo Emerson, "Self-Reliance"

> The field of politics always presents the same struggle. There are the Right and the Left, and in the middle is the Swamp. The Swamp is made up of the know-nothings.
> —August Bebel, *Address to the Social Democratic Congress*, 1903

After the Dorr debacle of 1842, Whig and Democratic rivalries stayed rough but nonriotous. This owed something to the withering away of issues of a deeply divisive sort. After 1840, the major problems of earlier debate, the tariff and the bank, faded. James K. Polk put to sleep the tariff issue after the long quiet ushered in by Henry Clay's compromise of 1833, and the national bank died as surely as the president from William Henry Harrison's sudden postinaugural illness. The last legislative legacy of the 1835 anti-abolition eruption, the gag rule, disappeared as even the most belligerent Southerners tired of giving John Quincy Adams another chance to bait them. The clearest ideological difference between the parties—the Jacksonian stress on government inactivity and the Whig insistence that government had some responsibility for promoting the general welfare—developed no policy correlatives at the national level, nor did the different rhetorical emphases on legalism, racism, and proslavery. Only when relative political outsiders brought into politics volatile issues with profounder social roots did political violence return. Religion and immigration gave the best-known incentive to new parties tied to violence, but such tumult became worst and most dangerous when integrated with the explosive question of slavery.[1]

Only one large political riot occurred between 1834 and the 1850s, that in Philadelphia in May 1844. This has been commonly treated as an ethnic-religious clash, and the brutal attack on Catholic property and Irish homes on the second night of the riot wholly fits this description. Yet the triggering event was political, the shooting from an Irish firehouse into a Nativist Party rally in "Nanny Goat Square," an Irish-dominated section of Philadelphia. Three Nativists were killed in the first skirmish, and ten later on, as well as one Irishman, making it the most deadly of antebellum non-election political mobs. Nativists destroyed much property, though no lives, the following night. Although this riot and the anti-Catholic one that followed in July are best discussed in terms of the nation's ethnic and religious travail, its political origin, involving essentially the 1834 question of protecting political rights in an ethnic district determined to exclude an opponent's activity, deserves notice here.

New York City, although it had its own influential Nativist movement in these years and even richer controversy over public schools, avoided violence at this time. Philadelphia had a less centralized structure than New York City, but of clearest relevance was Archbishop John Hughes's effective announcement that he would protect his New York City churches with armed men. The Philadelphia violence led to the Nativists' decline. By 1845 George Templeton Strong traced their "bad luck" to the Philadelphia riots, which caused "the Sect of Ecclesiocausts" to verge "fast toward dissolution."[2] Yet this political sect revived as the Whigs faded following their presidential defeat in 1852. Whig nominee Winfield Scott had competed with the Democrats in courting votes from the foreign-born. He talked often of his love "of the familiar accents" of German citizens and of "that rich Irish brogue," but such blarney, or what Democrats quickly labeled "honeyfuggling," did him little good and perhaps sharpened some public reaction. The political void left as the Whigs declined, Nativism quickly filled.[3]

Two major interpretations of Nativist politics have predominated. More generalizing accounts have explained the movement in terms of psychopathology: fear, insecurity, and paranoia grown of rapid social change that found a comforting explanation of evil in xenophobic and bigoted responses.[4] Closer local studies have been more appreciative of the party's appeal to groups outside the lawyer-business elite that controlled politics, and of Know-Nothing support of programs like integrated public education or women's property rights.[5] What's certain is that the emotive issues of religion and immigration attracted new people to politics who were willing to consider a range of topics more experienced politicians deemed dangerous to bring up. A third aspect of the American Party's quick though brief success is underlined if one explores the party through the lens of the social mobbing associated with it. Always clear has been the Know-Nothing failure caused by inability finally to forget about or fudge on the issue of slavery, but less recognized has been how deeply the party's appeal rested in offering emotive issues that represented a prounion distraction from the proslavery and racist politics that both Northern and Southern Democrats increasingly stressed.

The Know-Nothing movement waxed in the early 1850s, when fear and talk of disunion was great, and sprang to success in the years just after the Kansas-Nebraska Bill accelerated national political realignment. The party was dedicated to a return to eternal forgetfulness about slavery but arose in a context of irritated worry that the Democratic Party had become determinedly proslavery. The Know-Nothings attracted adherents for a host of reasons, but at a time when no one was oblivious to threatening discord over slavery. A Kentucky Nativist made clear in his diary how disparate issues melded: he primarily resented what he sensed was the illegal manipulation of immigrant voters by the Democratic Party, but he also disliked "politics" in general and those of the Catholic Church particularly and was pleased that Know-Nothings directed "their forming energies" also against "Abolitionism, secession, and drunkenness." This voter, like his party, was anti-antislavery and anti-proslavery, safely coded as the ever popular social villains of "Abolition" and "Disunion," as well as for and against several other things that focused attention away from that issue.[6] The Know-Nothings inherited the Whigs' greater dedication to avoiding all action or discussion of issues touching slavery, which comprised the "moderate" position, but in a context where Weld's—and James K. Polk's—"events" made passionate redirection seem the best alternative to slavery's dangers.[7]

Overt Know-Nothing antagonism centered on Catholic and immigrant influences. The influx of immigrants following Ireland's potato famine and Germany's turbulence of the late 1840s was immense, enough to worry any thoughtful person, even though both good sense and evidence suggested the truth of Henry Ward Beecher's jest against fears of foreign influence: "When I eat chicken, the chicken becomes me, not I a chicken." From the 1830s on there were reports, many authentic, of English and German towns sending their poor, ill, or criminal populations to the United States as the cheaper solution.[8] Statistics steadily proved that in almshouses, charity hospitals, asylums, and prisons, the percentage of foreign-born was much higher than that of native-born people. For instance, New York City figures for 1853 showed that the foreign-born, about a quarter of the population, contributed well over three-quarters of those in the almshouse, in Bellevue, in the insane asylum, and in jail, and an even higher percentage of those getting "out-relief."[9] Everyone knew that such realities were the product of the suffering and strain poor immigrants faced, but few liked paying the necessary taxes any better for that knowledge. The frequent plaints, especially against the Irish, of excessive drinking, brawling, and rioting were easy enough to document with instances in a one-sided way. The political orientation of foreign-born voting blocs on special issues—temperance, slavery, the public schools—also created animus among people with inclinations on the other side of such questions.

The deepest and most reasonable grievance in the Know-Nothing arsenal centered on the tie of immigrants to commonplace practices of political corruption and demagogy. Most Know-Nothing writers accepted that such failings were not unique to immigrants, who anyway were much less to blame than the native power brokers who used them. As most Nativists put it, the point was not the peculiar corruption of immigrants but the corruption of the political system that absorbed them. This disgust at the failings of American democracy ran deep. In 1844 an Ohio businessman, Joseph Osborne, wrote his governor begging that all new citizens be given the federal and state constitutions in their native language on arrival and that Congress act "to prevent the undue and illegal foreign influence on our elections." Osborne wished this action because he abhorred and feared the prospect of parties forming that "will draw a line of demarcation among our citizens that will be marked with blood."[10] Many like Osborne lamented the sorry realities of American politics as much as the immigrant's sometimes conspicuous place in them.

While the Nativist attack on immigrants was far from fair, it was commonly balanced with acceptance of their contribution and with statements of discrimination between valuable and unfit individuals, usually defined in classic Jacksonian terms of "productive" versus "parasitic" members of society.[11] About the most controversial—and impoverished—immigrants, the Irish, a kind of romantic racialism predominated among their attackers, their supporters, and themselves: excitable, sometimes too fond of the battle and the bottle, but honest, generous, and open in character and dealings.[12]

The anti-Catholic argument was harsher and more psychologically twisted. Perhaps the oddest of anti-Catholic arguments, and one of the most central and silly, from the Maria Monk "exposé" to the convent "investigation" by Massachusetts Know-Nothings, concerned nuns. Some of this, like Monk's salty tale, involved sheer fabrication, some of it elaborate embroidery on real incidents, and all of it near-hysteria. Partly these tales represented pornography for the proper, the essential fetid fascination rendered respectably in reform garb. Partly as Joseph Mannard has argued, they represented the fears and fantasies of male patriarchs about groups of contributive working women who managed their own worlds well. That some women like Catharine Beecher used the Catholic example as a model for parallel Protestant "sisterhoods" that professionally extended women's nurturing sphere doubtless made Nativist men no easier.[13] A law of opposites was probably also at work. Non-Catholics praised no Catholics more than the convent teachers of the 1830s or, later on, the courageous and devoted women religious who nursed during epidemics. An anti-Know-Nothing in St. Louis thought that party's anti-Catholicism, "shocking as it is, the most respectable" of its ideas, because Catholic abusiveness could "lead astray a Protestant of heated brain and defective judgement." Yet the work of Sisters of Charity, when "no others can be found for love or money, to perform the perilous service of taking care of the sick" ought to be enough to "make every persecutionist hang his head in shame."[14] Nuns in part were central in the most scurrilous of Nativist writing and attacks because they were also the most respected representatives of their church in the larger community.

A few riots testified to some social depth to the antinun phobia, but more formal attempts to exploit it ended in social joke. Maria Monk's second illegitimate child, this time delivered while under the sponsorship of Protestant divines, wrote a farcical finish to her—or someone's—already discredited fantasy. And the Massachusetts Know-Nothing convent investigators earned for themselves laughing designation as the "Smelling Committee" when the world learned that their chair had taken his mistress along, at public expense, on his search for moral turpitude within convents, while finding no evidence of sexual licentiousness outside his own hotel rooms.[15]

Other aspects of Nativist anti-Catholicism shared some of the paranoia over nuns, but there were also legitimate issues, related to the church's ultimate position on civic freedom and religious toleration. American Catholic leaders were quick to announce, perfectly honestly, their perfect acceptance of the American system of rights and the equal rights of all faiths before the law; those from Ireland indeed had long struggled against the church established in their homeland. Yet these men and their church could hardly proclaim this as one of their "universal" truths: where they held firmest power, they preached and practiced differently. Certainly Pius IX (Pope from 1846 to 1879), whose "infallibility" American Catholics accepted, was unfailingly hostile to, as Charles R. Morris puts it, "the core propositions of the American Bill of Rights, including freedom of speech, press and religion." Nativists asked, didn't this mean that Catholics would work to curb American freedoms should they become, as some of them predicted and as seemed possible, the United States' dominant faith?[16]

This improbability joined an even more theoretical concern that Catholicism's claim to unchanging truth cut it off from the open nature of democratic enquiry.[17] Since every American faith proclaimed its own certitudes about essential things, and since all churches lived by their adaptability to changing circumstances, any Protestant-Catholic distinction was one of emphases, although Catholic apologists insisted that they indeed represented the only rock of certitude. If any distinction existed here, it was simply that the Catholic Church enunciated a bit more loudly the position Protestant groups broadly shared: their creed best encouraged good thought and action and checked bad. Tocqueville was perhaps right that Catholicism's longer uninterrupted history and authoritarian structure made it especially useful and attractive in democratic society, but such modest differences were hardly the stuff of which mobs or parties were made.[18]

Much anti-Catholicism involved theological argument that could quickly become mental mud-wrestling between defenders of particular faiths. Led commonly by the heirs to the United States Protestants who cared most about theological issues, the Presbyterians, its heart was little different from the Catholic Church's anti-Protestantism.[19] Among few Protestant or Catholic leaders did the taste for frontal assault loom large, although some prominent Protestants like Lyman Beecher dabbled in anti-Catholicism, along with almost everything else, while a handful, like brothers John and Robert Breckinridge, formed their pastoral careers around the anti-Catholic movement, or perhaps it around their careers.[20]

John Breckinridge's lengthy printed debate with John Hughes in 1833 established a certain parity of both ability and abusiveness on the part of those who chose to argue loudly over Western Christendom's central schism. Both clerics showed more zest for the controversy than any reader could have had as the attacks and replies went on and on. Major issues existed over the nature of human liberty, religious authority, and the contributions of each faith. There was also a good deal of nastiness in the picture of the other's crimes and leaders and history. Both divines exhausted their tolerance when they announced that they weren't attacking the mere ignorant dupes of erroneous doctrine and calculating clergy. Hughes, who occasionally brought a touch of humor to the intellectual brawl, certainly proved that Catholics could give as well as they got in terms of both argument and demeaning vituperation. Probably both men satisfied their intensest partisans and left those less committed to the debate thinking the two deserved each other.[21] Crowds would turn out to hear a good debate on questions of religion as on anything else, or to listen to the testimony of a renegade priest. Catholics were similarly fond of public recitations by converts to their cause.[22]

As in polemics, Protestant-Catholic mobbing worked intricate influences. The leadership of American Catholicism in these years were men from Ireland who, while sharing the common language and the common touch, were untouched by looser American notions of hierarchy and authority.[23] Products of Ireland's tortured history, they well knew how much the oppressive other could contribute to strong religious adherence. While they found a strand of virulent anti-Catholicism ready-made, they were quick to use it, or even to sharpen it by visits of men like Papal Nuncio Gastano Bedini, whose acts of repression of Italian liberalism insured that his tour would trigger the fury especially of many Germans. Bedini was ready and anxious to return to

Europe when Archbishop Hughes insisted that he travel west, with the Catholic press steadily reporting riots against him, though the only real violence came when Cincinnati police attacked a parade peacefully protesting his presence.[24]

Aside from the few dozen anti-Catholic tracts and sermons and three or four small periodicals, anti-Catholicism in the mainstream Protestant press was minimal, and in private correspondence one finds very little concern divorced from the public issues—politics, slavery, temperance, and schools—that were the subject of legitimate and necessary debate.[25] Of these issues, temperance was least divisive, the area where at least an important strand in the Catholic Church paralleled Protestant concern. In this crusade, immigrant groups, not their favored church, were the enemy, especially the Germans, many of them non-Catholic. Here Catholicism sometimes contrasted its moral restraint to Protestants' determination to influence politics, in amusing reversal of the charges against them, but Father Mathew's temperance themes were at one with those of American Protestants. Abolitionists were aware of Catholicism's general acceptance of slavery in the United States, which led a few of them like Elijah Lovejoy to statements against Romanism, but they commonly threw much greater condemnation at Protestant faiths' failures to damn slavery.[26] The issue of the public schools was the deeply divisive one, directly in the center of the early 1840s Nativist urban thrust and in fact defining the role of Catholicism and of many Catholics in America for the next century.

Catholic leaders were remarkably effective in creating a special position for their church in American society. Policies on intermarriage and refusal of any formal cooperation in religious or benevolent matters contributed to separatism, but it was over school policy that Catholics built their strongest institutional fence to abet the precepts, traditions, and weekend institutions all church groups used to keep their members both a part of and apart from an amorphous democracy.

The school controversy has often been presented as one over "Bible-reading," but this was a peripheral—though often passionately argued—question. By 1840, when the inclusive public school system that Horace Mann had developed in Massachusetts was being initiated in most free states, Archbishop John Hughes in New York City made clear his church's quest for public funding for church-run schools. The openness of his urging Catholics to use politics in demanding that the state fund his church's schools, an old New Yorker remembered, "much increased the general feeling of alarm among our citizens."[27]

Newly elected Whig governor William Seward was anxious to strike a deal with Hughes on the school issue, in hopes of at least denting Irish Democratic loyalties. He was also anxious that public education include all and was sympathetic to Hughes's plaint that Catholics should not have to pay for schools run by Protestants. Seward's plan of allowing "local" control so Catholic schools could be effectually funded failed, and he settled for making public education nonsectarian only to find that this irritated both some Protestants and the Catholic hierarchy. Hughes made clear that an "infidel" school system based on "deism" was as bad as a Protestant one in his eyes and that taxes for education were improper if his church were not allowed to control the classrooms of its adherents. At the same time, when congregations of Jews and Scottish Presbyterians said they'd like funds for their religious schools, Hughes dismissed their requests as "prayers against our rights." He also attacked the morals of all who attended public schools, especially Quaker youth, who, possessing no respect for authority, corrupted Catholics. By 1852 Catholics regularly damned public education as encouraging Protestantism's progeny, including "Socialism, Red Republicanism, Universalism, Infidelity, Deism, Atheism, and Pantheism"—everything "except religionism and patriotism."[28]

Catholicism never got public funding for its schools despite some strong efforts, first in New York, then in Maryland and Ohio in the early 1850s, each push abetting American Party successes. Ohioan James Lakey noted in his diary in 1853 that "the Catholics are making a fierce onslaught upon the Common Schools: they ask to have their share of the public money by itself so that they can have separate *religious* schools." Lakey's sense of the incompatibility of the nation's nonestablishment principle with giving public money to institutions dedicated to strengthening a particular faith prevailed, despite politicians' occasional willingness to serve with public money their Catholic constituency. As Philip Hone predicted when Hughes conducted what New York's former mayor considered his "unblushing attempt to mix religion up with politics," the funding of church schools was to prove "an unpalatable dish in this country."[29] Unable to stop the public school movement, Catholics were finally forced to settle for what Seward had offered in New York: basic sectarian neutralism in the public arena, and funding its own system privately.

Outside New York, where Catholic leaders were more circumspect than Hughes, Bible-reading or prayer issues camouflaged the deeper controversy. In Philadelphia, Catholic objections to reading the King James Bible led to a compromise of permitting students to read the Bible of their and their church's choice so long as the divine word were not encrusted with human commentary, the school commissioners either not knowing or having learned that extensive notations were a part of the Douay Bible. In Philadelphia a sharp controversy arose when a Catholic school commissioner fired, or at least sharply reprimanded, a woman teacher for leading prayer in her classroom. By the 1850s the parallel systems—public and parochial—were well established in the North, the latter providing what the *North American Review* called, with some exaggeration, "an imperium in imperio" over much of the immigrant population.[30]

The Know-Nothings' initial success owed something to legislative moderation. From 1835, when the Nativists first broached political action, they had clearly advocated a single policy: a twenty-one-year (instead of five-year) wait for immigrants to be naturalized and to vote.[31] There were amusing aspects to the notion that if it took true-born Americans twenty-one years to vote, it would take Irish, English, and Germans at least as long to both unlearn old political ways and learn the new, but the policy was hardly proscriptive of Catholics or immigrants. The measure in fact suggested how rooted the party was in American disgust at political corruption. Against the Catholic church, the Know-Nothings suggested—if anything—only investigations of convents. From such inquiries, the Massachusetts example well proved, Catholics had nothing to fear and their opponents much. In addition, Know-Nothings personally pledged not to vote for Catholic or immigrant candidates.[32] This was the party's one lasting success, largely because they asked for what already existed: Protestants, Catholics, and members of ethnic communities very predominantly voted, as did Southerners, for "their own" in cases where a choice existed.

Equally vague, but crucial, were the Know-Nothings' assurances about ending "politics as usual," whatever that might mean. Because voters like to whine about the betrayal of their always virtuous disinterestedness by cunning politicians—and politicians cunningly assure them that such is true—there's often great readiness to welcome leadership by those who announce they are not politicians. Given the fears of drifting toward civil war because of politicians, as well as disgust at the dubious compromises politicians manufactured to avoid it, the idea of popular purity rising to the miraculous rescue in this decade was especially attractive. Even skeptics like Ralph Waldo Emerson, who saw the Know-Nothings as "an immense joke" and recognized the danger of "joking with edged tools," knew that the laughter grew because people rightly saw that the old parties were "plainly bankrupt."[33] While Know-Nothings depended on experienced politicians aplenty, the party did offer political entree to many new men and substantial influence to groups other than the lawyers, planters, and businessman who ran the older parties.[34]

Despite the silliness of the pretense of a nonpolitical politics freed from the compromises democracy demands, the Know-Nothings' criticisms of the electoral game had some substance and profound appeal. Louisianan Charles Gayerre caught well the strand of vigorous and cogent criticism found in many American Party tracts. Once parties had had some meaning, but now all differences had vanished, leaving only "the greediness of demagogues, the kissing and licking of the toe of every popular prejudice." The country was ruled by "the veriest jackasses in the land," while Louisiana Democrats were "those eunuchs of the intellect" whose only aim and skill was to keep power, largely by manipulating foreigners for "fraud, corruption, and intimidation in voting." A Catholic, Gayerre disliked the Know-Nothings' suggestion that members of his faith not be elected to office but thought this overridden by their "hostility to the corrupt means of party," the constant "rewards for political subservience," and "the wild hunt after office." Like all Southern Know-Nothings, Gayerre saw the Louisiana Democrats as foolish in their insistence that the nation serve slavery. If an effort were not made "to form, on an honest basis, a national party," inevitably "geographic parties will be hatched" which would be sure to unleash "an immense field of devastation and ruin."[35]

Gayerre, naive in his projected solution, was bracingly honest in his analysis of the faults of American democracy and of the extreme danger of proslavery's demands on the North. Since the Democrats had long cultivated those voters most proslavery and antiblack, the American Party's appeal to people was as deeply negative as positive, including its appeal to some Catholics and immigrants, for whom union remained the greatest good.

The initial "secret" nature of Know-Nothing organization was part of its nonpolitical credentials.[36] This, like everything else, had to change for the party when its early surprising success made it in fact a viable political alternative to the Democrats. Thus, the Know-Nothings were weakened by every step they took to secure political growth, most notably by their fatal attempt at national politics in 1856, which forced them to say something about slavery. After that campaign, the Know-Nothings lasted only in Baltimore and New Orleans, urban areas most conscious of political corruption and latently resentful of proslavery politics, where strong elements of class steeled the party's other appeals.

Nationally, twenty-two political riots involved Know-Nothings and killed seventy-seven people, injured several hundred, and caused property destruction of over $100,000. About three-fourths of these riots occurred between 1854 and 1856, the years of American Party success. Three of the riots happened in Northern cities—Brooklyn, Cincinnati, and Chicago—and the rest in large urban centers of the slave South: Baltimore, New Orleans, St. Louis, Louisville, and Washington. The latter had but one riot, while St. Louis had two, Louisville three, New Orleans five, and Baltimore eight. Five deaths occurred in the free-state clashes and seventy-two in the slave-area battles, as well as a parallel portion of the injuries; the South was the site of almost all property destruction. St. Louis in 1852 had the earliest riot in this category at a time when the Know-Nothings were not yet the official opposition but an active element supporting the Whig candidates, a situation that the city repeated in 1854. In the other cases Americans and Democrats vied directly for power, though the Know-Nothings early ran within "Reform" coalitions and the Democrats called themselves the "Reform Ticket" in the elections of 1857 and 1859 in Baltimore. An anti-Know-Nothing vigilance committee aided Democratic "reform" in New Orleans in 1858.

In few of these cases was the violence one-sided. In two-thirds of the fifteen riots where there is some agreement about the initial event, Democrats began the violence, and in one-third, the Know-Nothings. At the same time, ethnic groups tied to the Democratic Party suffered greater losses, especially in the deadliest Louisville riot, and bore the brunt of property destruction, which was concentrated in Louisville and St. Louis. While the partisan press whipped up much of the fury and party officials often failed to make real effort to keep order, these riots were less the product of party control than of free-floating popular passions politically channeled.

In this volatile mix, direct anti-Catholicism was perhaps least important. However, one kind of religious mob was indirectly a product of Know-Nothingism, as well as locally a stimulus to the party's growth. In 1853–54 there was repression, legal and mob, of "street preachers," some of them anti-Catholic and all of them irritating to Catholics when they preached in their neighborhoods. Unaffiliated and little educated, some of these men were unbalanced—or at least bizarre—such as one John Orr, who called himself the "Angel Gabriel" and appeared "with a three-cornered hat and a cockade on his head, and an old brass-horn in his bosom" with which he would trumpet his message. He kept Boston crowds amused and police alert during his regular preaching outings in 1854. Other street preachers were less peculiar souls moved to share their religious convictions, partially by the public debate over Know-Nothing issues by this time.[37] Sometimes Protestant mobs grew from the arrests, actual or attempted, of these open-air orators; some Catholic mobs acted to drive them and their audience off.

George Templeton Strong recorded the general dilemma in his 1853 comment on "the prospect of a No-Popery riot" in New York City. There'd been a "bitter indignation meeting" on December 14 "growing out of the arrest of a loafer who undertook to preach native Americanism and anti-priestcraft last Sunday." The arrest was intended to prevent riot, or at least was excused on that basis, but threatened to have an opposite result. The preacher "sets up for a Protestant martyr on the strength of his detention" and was determined to return preaching to the street corner of his crucifixion by cops. So one could expect "a mob originating with the Irish and German Papists if he's not arrested, and with the Order of United Americans and the godly butcher boys of the Hook and First Avenue if he is." The fact that Irish policemen often did the arresting did nothing to lessen the tension.[38]

New York's most serious clashes of this kind came later than Strong predicted, but on May 28 and June 4, 1854, Irish Sunday mobs attacked street congregants, and numerous injuries resulted. A locus of these conflicts was the Williamsburg section of Brooklyn, where a political riot with some street-preacher roots occurred during 1854's fall elections. This ward had Brooklyn's heaviest percentage of both immigrants and Know-Nothings, and Know-Nothing challenges about citizenship papers angered the Irish, who beat to death the election official handling the challenges. Then several hundred Irish attacked and drove off nine deputies sent to protect the polls and all American Party voters; one deputy was killed in the fracas. This was the only political riot where women were reported as among the perpetrators; some threw "stones and flat irons," and one Mrs. Murphy urged the crowd to "kill them bloody Know-Nothings."[39] Mrs. Murphy's mob killed only two men but beat and mangled several deputies and perhaps a dozen would-be voters. Here Democrats injected a strong dose of racism into the situation by insisting that the Nativists wanted to put blacks above immigrant whites, in what the *Brooklyn Eagle* came to call the hellish union of "Know-Nothingism and Niggerology."[40]

The funeral of the killed election official, a popular fireman, understandably attracted a huge native American attendance. When it ended, the crowd decided to "arrest" the rioters. When they found the authorities there and the Irish gone, someone yelled, "Get the Church." Again the authorities prevented all damage at both the Catholic church and the Methodist one where the Irish met to "retaliate" should damage be done by the other mob.[41] In fact, in all these Know-Nothing riots almost no harm was done to property of the Catholic Church. Authorities quelled a threat to a church in Louisville, targeted on the rumor of arms stored there, even though the destruction of homes and commercial property was extensive. In Baltimore occurred the only church damage: a few broken windows that the Nativists claimed the Democrats had stoned to discredit them.[42] Whatever its truth, this claim showed recognition of the counterproductivity of any religious destruction and suggested how the anti-Catholicism involved in the American Party tended to be more theoretical than active. Nativists probably remembered how the violence against church property in Philadelphia in 1844 had burned their movement.

The other two Northern Know-Nothing riots were also in part continuations of other kinds of mobs, reflecting the gnarled wood of ethnic and issue divisions that fueled the party. In Chicago at the spring election of 1857, when Nativists made their last attempt to hold power, one German was killed and one native American badly hurt in brawls little different from those commonplace at polls. It attracted much less communal attention than an earlier riot that came when newly elected American mayor Levi Boone decided to raise saloon license fees from $50 to $300 and to enforce Sunday closing laws. The saloonkeepers, supported by Irish and especially German citizens, protested, and a large parade initially disrupted the court cases. The next day, April 21, 1855, police kept the marchers, headed by drum and fife, from preventing the court session; in a scuffle there were some minor injuries

and four or five arrests. Serious consequences came in the afternoon, when the pro-
testers returned to demand the release of those arrested and someone yelled, "Pick
out the stars. Shoot the police." The crowd and the police exchanged shots that
killed one rioter and left two other citizens and two police badly wounded; one of
the latter had to have an arm amputated. All agreed that Germans had organized and
led the protests; the *New York Tribune* correspondent even wrote that "the Irish covered themselves with glory by keeping out of the affray." Yet the only two convictions and the majority of the fourteen tried for the riot were Irish.[43]

If Chicago's "beer riot" featured Irish-German cooperation against Nativist temperance interests, Cincinnati's communally disruptive riot that acted as prelude to its
one Know-Nothing mob centered on German-Irish religious antagonism. Cincinnati's liberal Germans were infuriated by the visit of Bedini, famous for ordering the
death of a priest who supported Garibaldi. As their large torch-lit parade, carrying a
gallows and a mitred effigy, moved toward Archbishop Purcell's residence, where
Bedini was staying, they marched under banners proclaiming, "Down with the Roman Butcher" and "No Priests! No Kings! No Popery!" Police Chief Thomas
Lukans ordered his men to "pitch in." One German was beat to death and several injured, and one policeman was killed by a shot. The police claimed that they were
fired on first, but communal belief was that the shooting happened well after the
melee was launched against a peaceful protest, whose nondestructive intent was
proved by the presence of large numbers of women.

Anger turned on Democratic mayor David Snelbarker, associated with the
proslavery, pro-Catholic "Miami tribe" wing of the Democrats. Nativists joined
German groups in part because Snelbarker was also blamed for his recent arrest of
an anti-Catholic street preacher, Hugh Kirkland, while the mayor had provided an
elaborate police guard for a Catholic procession. Snelbarker refused to resign but
was forced to fire his police chief and to watch a judge of the police court and several of his policeman, all Irish Catholics, tried for riot, while all of the arrested
marchers, who claimed police abuse and denial of medical attention in jail, were
freed.[44] The unprecedented legal proceedings against the police reflected not only
community anger, but also a desire to make police more accountable to law and less
to politics. Cincinnati lawyer and legal scholar Timothy Walker made an able argument, tied to this event, that police actions constituted riot if officers' violence occurred without clear sign that illegality was intended, with excessive force against
nonresistants, *or* with brutality and baiting after arrests were made.[45]

One of the stimulants to Nativist support in large cities was the general feeling
that there was need, in Walker's words, for careful "inquiry into the true boundaries
of police power," when the often foreign-born police tended to serve party first. In
Cincinnati, for example, about 15 percent of the population was Irish Catholic, but
well over 50 percent of the over 100-man police force belonged to this group. This
patronage question was at issue two years later, when Know-Nothings made a concerted drive to gain power in the city in the spring election of 1855. Trouble erupted
in the Eleventh Ward in the city's "Little Germany," where polls were controlled by
Germans but voting was open to both sides, in part because of German divisions in
the election. One Nativist was beaten on the first day of the election, and much fighting followed. A cannon, which the Germans had set up to protect a polling place,

changed hands several times, and brawls killed one Know-Nothing visiting from Indiana and one brewery foreman, murdered, some reports said, for refusing to "treat" a section of the Know-Nothing crowd. Injuries were substantial—ten or twelve—and Know-Nothings destroyed the Eleventh Ward ballots and some in the Twelfth, claiming polls had been stuffed by either German schoolboys or visiting proslavery Kentuckians.[46]

The diary of Cincinnati shopkeeper William S. Merrell suggests how readily the local public digested its allotment of violence. On April 2 he noted, "Great excitement in some wards. Some riot and bloodshed and the ballot box of the 11th Ward destroyed." The next day he reported, "Great trouble over the canal. 12th Ward ballots destroyed—military called out—great difficulty in preventing a civil war." On April 4 Merrell wrote, "City at last quiet, but much mob feeling. No legal election effected. Rain after a long dry spell." The next day's news notation was that his wife and sister were papering the "small chamber," and April 6 included his last mention of Cincinnati's latest riot: "Fair, but cool. Excitement subsided. Sister Lu and wife paper room. Letter from Mama. Business pressing—store till 11PM."[47]

The rioting in Southern cities would prove less easy to forget locally and would also suggest much greater difficulties in preventing "civil war." Here proslavery forces were more vitally concerned about a party professing indifference to the cause they felt central and attempting to use religious, ethnic, and class cleavages among whites to gain strength. In the urban South especially, the class appeal of the American Party to the native-born poor was great, grown both of resentment at the planters who manipulated the system and at the immigrants they used to do so. One St. Louis observer despised the Know-Nothings in part because he saw that "the most energetic of the rank and file are native American mechanics who are as jealous as possible of foreign labor."[48] Democrats in these cities had much to worry about if white fissures hardened in the South. In St. Louis and Louisville the rioting was concentrated in elections where the Know-Nothings achieved their greatest success before other parties or factions replaced them. In Baltimore and New Orleans, the American Party represented a more lasting effort at urban reform politics, in one case beaten by proslavery interests just before the Civil War and in the other defeating them.

In St. Louis in 1852, the earliest of all these Know-Nothing conflicts proved not especially destructive but dramatic enough. One of the nation's most successful writers and rabble-rousers, E. Z. C. Judson, better known by his pen name of Ned Buntline, came all the way from New York City to participate, riding through the riot scenes on a white horse, no less. Buntline was one of several New York City political-literary men who drew working-class support because they both expressed and blunted class anger in flamboyant form. Buntline, about as serious and as flippantly scurrilous in his class tactics as were Democrats Levi Slamm or Mike Walsh, came, mounted like one of his Western good guys, to lead his native working-class following to the promised excitement.[49]

Others in fact created the situation in which Buntline saw dramatic opportunity. Editor Henry Boerstein of the *Anzeiger des Westens*, believing Germans were cheated of their fair share of local offices, had urged St. Louis's German community to vote uniformly for the Democratic ticket, led locally by Thomas Hart Benton, so that party would clearly recognize, and repay, their support. What Boerstein desired was precisely the "foreign influence" the Know-Nothings said corrupted American politics, and Buntline had long been a spokesman of sorts for native-born working-men against foreign favoritism. Judson may also have come out of ties to an old New York political crony Robert O'Blennis, who now worked for Missouri's proslavery Democrats. O'Blennis did what he was best at during the riot: tending the whiskey keg.

In the German First Ward on the election morning of April 5, Germans prevented all Whigs from voting. A German later reported that the excitement was intense "be-cause they intended none but Democrats to vote. A German told me I was not to live in the 1st Ward if I voted the Whig ticket." A German band blocked the poll's door and, one observer claimed, "would not let anybody but a Dutchman with a Demo-cratic ticket come in."[50] In response, a large group of natives, a few of them Demo-crats, moved to the polling place, and two Whig candidates invited, in both English and German, all voters to vote as they saw fit. The election went forward with no more than the usual scuffling and shenanigans, possibly including Buntline's ripping down a Democratic poster and some stone-throwing. Then shots rang out—Whig supporters thought, from Neumeyer's tavern and house. Joseph Stevens was fatally hit and a few others hurt, either from this first shelling or as Buntline's group moved toward the tavern, which they sacked and burned. The people in the house were res-cued, including a sick Mrs. Neumeyer. Authorities quickly turned out to quell the fighting, contain the fire, and, much later in the evening, check the mob movement against the German newspaper. The riot was all over but for the shouting, which Buntline did by telegraph to New York:

5 o'clock
Ned Buntline had a horse killed under him—he acted like a man—fired several time and each ball took effect—Bob O'Blennis scattered the Dutch blood like dew.

11 o'clock
Great riot—*Anzeiger* office mobbed—military ordered out—member St. Louis Fire Co. killed,—Stevens—Neumeyer's house . . . burned—250 Germans gone to Illinois.[51]

Events more closely approximated the workings of Buntline's imagination in the second St. Louis Know-Nothing riot two years later. And there was an intervening riot in St. Louis, one whose two victims made it more deadly than the election mob of the year before. The oddity of its inception shows how small events, given the belligerence of any large city's variety of young men, could trigger serious vio-lence—and how important this doubtless was in riots related to clearer "issues" as well. Two men on a boat's crew were fighting their dogs, on which their comrades had placed bets. A passing fireman, seeing one dog getting the worst of it, rescued him, for which offense the dog's owner and the crew attacked him. His fellow fire-men came to his rescue and drove the Irish to dockside buildings, which the firemen then lit. Two Irish died in the melee. The pattern of this "sporting" riot was remark-ably similar to that of the two election riots: a personal act served as catalyst for un-leashing group belligerence against the "other."[52]

The inciting event for the 1854 election was similarly personal and idiosyncratic. The *Missouri Republican*, the newspaper supporting the Whig and Know-Nothing coalition candidates, urged the examination of naturalization papers of the foreign-born to make sure their votes were legal, a measure sure to slow voting and irritate those questioned. In the Irish Fifth Ward, tempers sharpened as some would-be voters were rejected, and violence erupted when one rejected voter stabbed a boy. The man ran off to hide in a mechanics' boardinghouse, a large crowd followed, shots came from Irish homes and taverns, and the now-mob began to sack them. The Irish arrived in force, shots were exchanged, two were killed, and the mob expanded its destruction of Irish homes. After most of the trouble had subsided, the police came. They again protected the German paper that had been central in the 1852 riot.

The militia were called out the next day. Some Irish were determined to retaliate but waited until ten that night, when various deadly skirmishes began. Three militia members were badly wounded; two leading citizens, one of them wealthy ironmaker E. R. Violett, trying to keep the peace, were killed; a saloonkeeper was murdered, reportedly for the deadly sin of not wanting to slack riotous thirst. The next morning the mayor organized citizen patrols, in part because it was thought that the mostly Irish police force had abetted Irish rioters. The trouble ended with ten men dead, some thirty seriously wounded, and, according to one account, precisely ninety-three pieces of property injured or destroyed. Twenty was the usual number given for the homes and drinking places destroyed.[53]

In this case, party leaders and press, rather than using the violence for maximum political profit, were shocked by it, so it became a stimulus for reform. The general response was caught in a man's letter to his wife: "The Mobocracy is getting altogether too fashionable in St. Louis. Society seems to have relapsed." More circumstantial was a letter of Henry Hitchcock, who partly blamed "the extremely ill-judged course" of the *Republican*, which "had set people to looking for a riot," as well as the election's significance and the precedent of the 1852 mob: "Doubtless the newly organized strength of the Know-Nothings may have come in here or there to help, but it was at no time either a regular party riot nor even a sectarian (anti-Catholic) mob."[54]

Such response allowed strong reforms to come from the event. The Whig City Council passed regulations for better controlling elections, and the Democratic state legislature passed a strong antiriot bill, giving local authority to close saloons and set curfews and making all rioters financially responsible for all mob damage. Hitchcock wrote that the volunteer patrols were organized because "the regular city police, who are almost all foreigners," were "suspended from duty for the time." When Know-Nothing Washington King became mayor the next year, he reorganized the police force, making it more independent, though King's changes in personnel meant it was much less Irish and Democratic. King's own antimob credentials were established when he demanded and got a normally peaceful and open election in 1856, when there was fear of local mob history repeating itself.[55]

An additional influence helping real reform result from the St. Louis riots was their relation to the state's political divisions over the slave issue. In Missouri this controversy never hardened into bipolarity by party because the deepest hatreds centered within the Democracy. The proslavery wing of the party concluded that long-time leader Thomas Hart Benton had "done more for abolition than all its open, reckless and God-defying advocates." Benton never questioned slavery, but he was unwilling to see its interests as paramount to those of union, a position that put him beyond the pale of the Southern Democracy by this time. The old statesman, who had once physically brawled with Andrew Jackson and then long intellectually brawled for him in the Senate, entered the political ring swinging again. He became the hero in one of George Caleb Bingham's most positive political paintings and divided Missouri into three political parts until the Civil War. He proved to his main enemy, senator and soon-to-be-border-ruffian David Atchison, that he had "enough in him for five Roman tyrants" when he became the candidate for the St. Louis–area congressional seat in the violent elections of 1852 and 1854.

Benton's working-class and especially German support in St. Louis allowed him to win a three-cornered race in 1852. Yet what he called "the clandestine and incessant" intercourse of nullifiers and "Nullities" (as he liked to call the Whigs), who acted "together in dark places, and . . . as man and wife, whether lawfully married or not," when joined by Know-Nothings in a ménage à trois of convenience in 1854, led to his defeat. Essentially the proslavery Democrats gave only a few hundred votes to the party candidate and doubtless helped the Whig win this two-sided race.[56] Such political complexity allowed "law and order" efforts to be real in St. Louis rather than the rhetorical camouflage for political advantage over the slave issue they were in other riot-torn Southern cities.

There was greater destruction in Louisville where the issue of slavery openly heated the party struggles between Democrats and Nativists. The riot there of August 1855, the most deadly and destructive of the lot, followed two earlier ones; the first occurred in 1854 as the Know-Nothings came to power, with the Democrats initiating most of the intimidating violence. By the spring of 1855 the Know-Nothings ruled the city and initiated some violence in the First and Second Wards, where Germans predominated. Here Know-Nothings beat a few German and Democratic voters and, when some young men fought back, chased them into Merkel's brewery, where the rioters demolished a bar and some furniture and roughed up the inhabitants, including Mrs. Merkel. Some of the beatings were harsh, but only one serious injury was reported. A Mr. Grey, who was struck after voting, drew a gun, shot, and was shot twice in the thigh. This led the police to act, protecting Gray and taking him home for medical treatment.[57]

One could judge who perpetrated most of the violence in these two riots by the reports of Louisville's highly partisan press. George Prentice, whose *Louisville Journal* was long the organ of Kentucky Whigs, raged at the electoral violence of 1854 but mildly suggested after the 1855 riot that "if there were any truth to the charges" of Democrats, "legal remedy should be sought, not rumors propagated." The "moderate" Democratic *Louisville Courier* called the violence of 1854 "disgraceful" but claimed parties had nothing to do with it, while for the spring 1855 trouble it denounced the Know-Nothings as "a crowd of jackals, hyenas, and bawdy house bullies." Proslavery Democrats in 1855 set up their own journal, the *Times*, to compete with the *Journal* in bruising wit. It quickly labeled the Know-Nothings a "political Bruiserocracy" and "mere puppets moved by fat-headed editors." It also urged naturalized citizens to arm themselves against their opponents' intimidation.[58]

The *Times* and the *Journal* bellowed the flames that were to flash out in August. Both papers were masters of the great art of gross abusiveness, although Prentice's was leavened—and sharpened—with unusual wit and intelligence. The *Times* was established by proslavery forces to push the theme that the Know-Nothing "issues" were a mere cover to antislavery to justify the "lowest depths of servile toadyism to the North, besmeared with abolitionist slime." Prentice, oft reminded of his Northern birth, supported slavery but only on the old grounds of its being an evil that would eventually disappear. The *Times*'s line of attack caused Prentice to emphasize the new party's religious argument to an unusual degree, especially Roman Catholicism's animus to tolerance where they held authority and the allegiance to Rome and priest that allegedly undercut individual judgment. He also stressed the most common Know-Nothing theme, the need to prevent illegal foreign voting by checking naturalization papers.[59]

The intense political campaign, in which Know-Nothings spread their early local victories statewide, insured that the passions of the press and the public never wavered. In mid-summer, a citizen noted in his "Memorandum Book," "Great excitement such as was never perhaps known here . . . centered in questions of allegiance to the Pope and the extension of the time required for naturalization" and made more volatile because "the Democrats have the foreigners all on their side." He knew that "the bringing of religion into politics will doubtless engender great excitement and bitterness of feeling in the country—People seem to forget that there is a God or a hereafter."[60] Within three weeks, political riot was to help twenty-two citizens of Louisville personally learn whether there was a hereafter.

The Democrats made some proposals to preserve the peace and protect their interests as the election approached: opening new polls to make voting quicker, setting up a two-party poll-watching group, or having two sets of election officers in each ward. A bipartisan peacekeeping group might have prevented much of the trouble, but it would have meant that Know-Nothings sacrificed their duly elected position of power, something Democrats had never suggested when in office. Both sides' press continued to press vituperation and violence. The *Times* labeled Prentice an "impotent old biped" and "press hyena . . . who has outraged humanity from the moment of his birth" and urged all good citizens to check the Know-Nothings' "onward march of treason" against slavery and the nation. It sent its readers to the polls with the assurance that no one would be deprived of voting who was not afraid, because "a bully is always a poltroon." The *Journal* was even worse in its urging voters to "rally to put down an organization of Jesuit Bishops, Priests and other Papists." Prentice argued that, to be sure, all violence should be protective, then concluded: "Let the foreigners keep their elbows to themselves today at the polls. There's no place for them in the ribs of the natives. . . . Americans, are you ready? We think we hear you shout 'Ready!' Well, fire! and may heaven have mercy on the foe."[61]

In the morning, the election went fairly quietly, though there was a knife fight between an Irishman and an American, both of whom eventually died, the Irishman in jail. In midafternoon things grew worse when Germans fired into some American election carriages, killing two men, and Know-Nothings attacked and burned five or six German homes and a coffeehouse from which the shots apparently came. The Know-Nothing mayor dissuaded them from attacking the Catholic church. In the next few hours, random Germans were attacked, at least three fatally, and other homes and a brewery burned down. Irish in Ward Eight attacked three Americans, killing at least one, and Know-Nothings followed their retreat to a house, burned them out, and killed three. Another American death led to an attack on Quinn's Row, a block of Irish homes, and some others, twenty in all, which were burnt. Patrick Quinn was shot and his body partly burned, and rioters beat victims fleeing the fire and, rumor declared, drove some Irish trying to escape back to a fiery death. The Know-Nothing police, inactive and maybe helpless in the shootings and burning of private property, protected the hated *Louisville Times* when a mob later threatened it.

The mayor's strong proclamation and preparation against violence the next day, abetted by the horror of what had happened, ended all mobbing, although the rumor or reality of another Irishman's injuring an American briefly threatened renewed trouble. The Know-Nothings carried the city and state by a landslide, but the extraordinary violence of "Bloody Monday" helped discredit them nationally. The *Journal* and the *Times* quite accurately traded charges of inciting to riot. In 1860 the city of Louisville paid property damage claims, but there was no compensation for the twenty-two lives—six or seven Americans and the rest "foreigners," about equally divided between Germans and Irish—lost in this deadliest of American political riots.[62]

Few failed to be appalled at what happened, but few failed to fit the tragedy to their vision of the political threat of foreign or Know-Nothing influence. American Party apologists used it as another example of the troubles begun by immigrant voters, and the Democratic Party, effectively after the Know-Nothing demise, argued that it proved the essential violence of the supporters of religious fanaticism. Private reaction similarly followed partisan proclivity. A future historian of Louisville, Stoddard Johnston, lamented in his journal "that Kentucky has been the scene of such villainous, cowardly proceedings," but, having voted the straight Democratic ticket, he knew the fault lay with "Know-Nothings instigated by their leaders and lodges." Diarist L. C. Porter also decried "the most painful and disgraceful tragedy that happened in the history of our national existence" and spread his blame more widely: "the pleading politicians . . . , the passions of men . . . incited by . . . partisan editors," and "especially the foreigners who, naturally slavish and bloodthirsty, were easily induced to resort to acts of violence."[63] As always, there were plenty of people deserving some blame.

If Baltimore and New Orleans never quite had a "Bloody Monday," political violence was their steady portion in the years when the Know-Nothings contested and won power and then defended it from proslavery forces as the Civil War approached, when these two cities remained the lone holdouts from Democratic control in the slave states. Baltimore Know-Nothings didn't survive their adoption of measures to control the polls in 1859, measures that went much further than was customary; in New Orleans the party defeated their opponents' attempts to use uncustomary violence against them in the form of a vigilance committee modeled on the San Francisco Vigilantes of 1856.

Baltimore had its "predecessor" riots, in this case a long series of fireboy disputes of an unusually destructive kind that gave much impetus to the change of direction the Know-Nothings offered. From 1846 to 1851 every year had its major fireboy clash, as well as a steady diet of smaller skirmishes. Injuries were common, including some serious harm to authorities who tried to check the "fun," but weapons were used with enough care that there was but one fatality, that in 1847. Part of the tolerance for this violence grew from the political services and influence of these organizations. One old Baltimorean wrote that the fire companies served as the "organized fighting force in the community" and "the natural ally or instrument of the contending political parties. From the firemen's riots, pure and simple, it was but a step to the election riots that disgraced Baltimore."[64] Certainly it was a complicated step, but professionalization of the fire department and the introduction of the steam engine, always the crucial moves in ending the volunteer system's rowdyism, were reforms contributing to the "reform" credentials of Baltimore's Know-Nothing Party, though renewed deadly fireboy clashes in 1855 and 1856 provided the immediate stimulus.

Baltimore, like New Orleans, had a complicated relation to Catholicism, with an "old" elite American Catholic tradition that was not wholly at one with either the new hierarchy or its largely immigrant congregants. Too, Baltimore continued to host national Catholic Councils of Bishops, where the power and the great expectations of the church were major themes. The city also was home at times to both Presbyterian minister Robert Breckinridge and Andrew Cross, among the most respectable of those few ministers for whom anti-Catholicism was a central dedication. One of their congregants, Anna Ella Carroll, became the most active of the American Party pamphleteers, the only woman in the era to write extensively on partisan matters and a good example of the "new" people Know-Nothingism attracted to political activism.[65] Baltimore in 1839 had had its "escaped nun" and anticonvent mob, one that city officials handled in a model manner that avoided all destruction. In 1853, as the Know-Nothings first publicly organized, it also became the only Southern city with a street-preacher controversy. Police arrested the blind orator, and a large enough crowd formed in protest that the law officers decided it would be wise to release him.[66] Giving impetus to the new party was the near-success of the Kerry Bill, which would have funneled Maryland state funds into Catholic schools.

The Know-Nothings inherited some fighting power through the Whigs, when General Watkins in 1852 lost the Democratic nomination for mayor and became a Whig, leading, Jacob Frey tells us, the toughs of west Baltimore with him to the new camp. Shortly thereafter the Know-Nothings held their first city meeting, where Col. H. K. Elliott argued for extending naturalization and also sang "Home, Sweet Home" and "The Old Oaken Bucket"; "the songs," Frey reported, "were most enthusiastically received."[67] In many ways such as this, the Know-Nothings brought a celebratory as well as a condemnatory quality to their patriotism. In spite of their reputation for violence, all the lives lost in Baltimore rioting in these years were far fewer than the twenty-eight killed in a railroad accident when the Know-Nothings overfilled a train taking people to a Fourth of July picnic.

A major Baltimore strike in 1853 gave clarity to the class issue often tied to Southern urban Know-Nothingism. Ironworkers staged strikes for higher wages against several owners, which proved largely successful, despite the vehement opposition of Democratic politicians and industrialists. This fact, along with the Democrats' usual use of pro-immigrant patronage, helped to shepherd native-born workers into the American Party fold. The Know-Nothings cemented their loyalty with public works programs that much improved water, sewer, and transportation facilities in poor urban areas and by their refusal in 1857 to quell strike action, despite the fulminations of city Democrats and the readiness of state Democrats to send the militia to defeat the railroad workers and preserve "law and order." Baltimore's politics in this decade suggests strongly how useful was the Democratic ideology for both Southern planters and industrialists: government had the responsibility to protect absolute rights of property but should otherwise practice laissez-faire, leaving all real power in their private hands. The elite would act paternalistically, for the good of all—unless foolishly upstart slaves or workers infringed on their absolute authority. Such industrial paternalism, an offshoot of slavery ideals, was made explicit in city Democrats' return to power at a time of economic collapse in 1860. They set up soup kitchens, while denying all attempted protection for wages, jobs, or public works.[68]

Baltimore's early Know-Nothing riot history was similar to Louisville's: minor skirmishes between toughs of the two parties as the American Party won control of the city in 1854, and more serious trouble in the fall of 1855, as the Know-Nothings' triumph spread from city to state. Yet Baltimore's 1855 riot remained mild. There was some intimidation at the polls and fighting in the Irish wards led by Democratic toughs, and much random Democratic violence at the Americans' victory parade after the election. Baltimore's equivalent of Louisville's Bloody Monday came a year later, when between September and November 4, fourteen people were killed in political clashes. Yet the violence in Baltimore was of a different kind from the "maddened" quality of the Louisville mob. It was primarily the struggle of the organized toughs both parties had developed, with heavy doses of both sport and calculation.

The first mob action in this long fall political campaign did not pit Democrats against Americans and may have been a cooperative effort, though it was led by one of the Democratic club answers to Know-Nothingism, the Sag Nichts. At any rate, cheers were heard for both Buchanan and Fillmore as the mob broke up, near its end, the first Republican Party attempt to hold a meeting in Baltimore. The damage was minor: Quaker F. S. Cockran offered some passive resistance and was pushed about, lost his hat, and had his coattails cut off, with pieces passed around as souvenirs. The largely German gang also threw some rocks and broke some windows at a liberal, Republican-respecting German newspaper office.[69]

This preliminary round of September 11 sharpened the "boys'" desire to make points against their real opponents. The next day Democrats attacked with guns and clubs a "Fillmore Fishing Party," which, after fishing excursions, paraded in Baltimore with their dead catch labeled "Buchanan," etc. One young man was killed and several badly hurt in this clash. The next day, the two major American clubs, the Rip Raps and the Wampanoags, again marched past Democratic Seventeenth Ward headquarters, were insulted or attacked, attacked and were driven off, returned and fought—until four were badly hurt, one of whom later died. In this second clash, perhaps by preagreement, guns were not used, but only bowie knives and slingshots.

Further trouble awaited the elections in October and November. Riots began in early October—one of them lasted twenty minutes, until police "stopped the fun"— but became fatal three days later, during the election. There was some fighting and injury in Ward Seven and more in Irish Ward Eight, where Democrats collared the polls, drove off a gang of "investigating" Know-Nothings, and wounded a bus driver when one of his passengers yelled "Hurra" for a Know-Nothing candidate. The Know-Nothings fought back, long and fatally, when their opponents tried to collar the Twelfth Ward near Lexington Market House. After Rip Raps drove some Democrats away, the Democrats fired at people going to the polls, shooting from the Democratic New Market Fire House, center of the worst fireboy riots. The Rip Raps won this battle, too, and sacked the firehouse. At least four were killed in the Twelfth Ward rioting; vague reports of deaths in the Eighth Ward also circulated. Over fifty people were hurt in the day's skirmishes.[70]

The violence a month later was similar. It began with the wounding of two Know-Nothings demanding naturalization papers. In the afternoon two deadly battles occurred. In Ward Two, Democrats first drove off Know-Nothings to control—or open—the polls, but the Americans returned and retook the polls after adding guns to the knives of their first charge. In the Irish Ward Eight police were decoyed away, while Democrats held a pitched battle with the Know-Nothings in Belair Market, the Democrats firing guns and a small brass cannon from the meat house at the Americans, who, true to their fishing party image, shot from the fish market. Most of the day's eight deaths occurred at this last locale in a long struggle that again smacked of prearrangement. A few days later a few more injuries were added to the some 150 on election day, when political "clubs" again fought with guns after the Democrats tried to fell the American electoral pole.[71]

When the state returned to Democratic hands, that party's strategy was to blame all violence on the Know-Nothings so that militia could be sent in to aid proslavery Democrats. Governor Francis Ligon issued the first of the "reports" that would come from Democratic sources (and would become the "history" of these riots) in the midst of his campaign to "cooperate" with the mayor in insuring election peace. Not noticing that the Democrats had often taken the lead in fomenting violence, Ligon argued Know-Nothing guilt and "the inability of the police to grapple effectually with the diabolism that has broken loose in the community." He was particularly irritated that the community "affected a morbid ignorance of the true nature and dangers of the lawless element" and remained unenthusiastic about rallying to "vindicate its insulted honor." Ligon's report was timed to coincide with Baltimore's local elections, where someone broke windows at the German Turner Hall and Democrats assaulted a Know-Nothing procession. A policeman was killed in the usual Ward Eight melee, and police confiscated caches of arms in Democratic Jackson Hall and New Market Engine House. Yet the election was deemed "largely" peaceable.

When Ligon moved to put the city's polls under military control, the recent quiet voting and the general feeling that the rioting had never been one-sided frustrated his attempt. The local militia, including the Germans, generally refused to follow his orders: the Buchanan administration sent him arms and Governor Wise of Virginia offered troops to protect the sanctity and proslavery of Baltimore's elections, but Ligon had to give up on his plans. The penny-press *Baltimore Sun*, Democrat-leaning, claimed that "in the view of almost the whole of our citizens," Ligon's partisanship was so transparent that even those most upset by the violence thought his planned intervention worse than doing nothing.

Two days before the election, someone threw bricks through some windows at the

Church of the Immaculate Conception. When this drew quick police protection and claims from Know-Nothings that Democrats did the deed to discredit them, Ligon rescinded his order. The election went quietly under Know-Nothing control.[72] Baltimore's failure to welcome Ligon's offer owed much to the recognition that the violence was largely confined to the young men who enjoyed it. Like intra-Irish faction fights or fireboy brawls or, for that matter, boxing or wrestling matches, some people found them an amusing and others a brutal and repulsive sport, but one that could be tolerated so long as its chief victims were its enthusiasts.

In 1858 several things changed, especially Southern Democrats' insistence that all opposition was abolition. At the same time, the isolation of the Baltimore Party, its uncertainties or arrogance or both, caused its always rowdy clubs to practice extreme intimidation. By 1857 the Rip Raps and Wampanoags and "fishing parties" were joined by the Plug Uglies and Blood Tubs, the new names suggestive of the new aggressiveness. Mayor Swann's bland insistence that the political violence in the city was a product simply of heated debates in grog shops suggested the party's growing willingness to let its clubs do what they roughly pleased.[73]

The election of 1858 went smoothly, with a few scuffles, though the opposition claimed much intimidation. The "Reform" candidate withdrew during the election, his defeat certain, but claiming he sacrificed his candidacy to save the public peace. By 1859 the intimidation was blatant. In this "awl out" campaign, the shoemaker's awl became symbol of the class orientation of the party. There was much to say for the awl as electoral tool compared to the guns Democrats and Know-Nothings had used earlier, and much of the emphasis on it was a joke about the violence attributed to the city party. Slogans like "Come up and vote; there is room for awl" or "The Third Ward is awl Right" were intended to cause humor more than horror.[74] Still, it was a very pointed joke, and its sharpness told on the public. For the first time the moderate press reported wide-scale, one-sided intimidation. The *Baltimore American* claimed the "Reformers" were the victims of "organized ruffianism and fraud," while the *Sun* declared, "The whole city was literally disenfranchised, defied, and laid helpless and prostrate at the feet of violent men." The Democratic state legislature took power over Baltimore's police force away from the mayor (following the pattern Republicans in New York State had used against city Democrats), expelled Baltimore's Know-Nothing members, and passed much proslavery and antiblack legislation. In the fall of 1860, half a year before Civil War, Democrats returned proslavery forces to political control in the city.[75]

In New Orleans the Know-Nothings had their most lasting success because the party intimidated more effectively and less flamboyantly there than in Baltimore and because it struck deeper class roots. At the same time, the city's older Catholic tradition was unchallenged by any anti-Catholic movement, and many of Louisiana's old Catholic families supported Nativism. The movement began with Whig and nonpartisan support for reforming principally the corrupt, almost all-Irish police force under the thumb of state Democrats, who used them with little subterfuge to control elections. It ended only when the Union army captured the city, still in the hands of an able Know-Nothing mayor of labor background. A series of five riots in 1854–56 punctuated the party's rise to power, and a dramatic conflict in 1858 gave it an impressive victory over proslavery Democrats.[76] The

American Party succeeded best in New Orleans because there its positive promise—reform and a new, less elite politics—came closest to fruition, while its negative themes were more readily jettisoned.

The political movement began with a reform meeting in mid-March 1854, endorsed by a spectrum of leading citizens, though "with precious few Democrats." These reformers immediately organized poll watchers to check corruption at the election coming up in two weeks. The movement did in fact represent, as Democrats charged, a coalition of Whig–American Party interests, which aimed, in the words of the Whig *New Orleans Bee*, at "the despotism of faction" in the city. Central were the police, who provided little citizen protection but were "a powerful, well-disciplined, and unscrupulous electioneering machine," whose primary duty was "to influence doubtful contests and compel the ballot box to render a Democratic victory."[77] The election on March 26 featured much fighting as Democratic police and gangs drove off poll watchers and voters in several wards. Two people were killed, one of them a policeman named Mochlin, stabbed to death while leading a gang against Reform Party observers. At one poll some Reformers destroyed a ballot box when poll watchers said it closed with 700 ballots in the evening and opened with 1,100 in the morning. Some in this mob were indicted, as were the poll officials.[78]

The Reformers lost the mayoralty race but won most other contests. Know-Nothings were also helped by rioting that erupted in September. Another dog started the trouble. An Irishman wounded the animal in the "American section" of the city, and the pet's owner asked a policeman to arrest the culprit. The Irish policeman instead tried to arrest the owner, and his neighbors came to his rescue. Shots were fired by both the owner's and policeman's friends. For several days rumors—one held that the Catholic cathedral was to be attacked—and random beatings occurred. Both sides were active. Americans shot into an Irish coffeehouse, but most of the violence and all the many beatings were laid to the Irish. A woman wrote to a relative, "The details of the Irish riots are really fearful, for it seems there is no safety for the most peaceable people, walking the streets. . . . Do not expose yourself to the rough hands of those infuriated rowdies." Citizens set up a private force to suppress the violence, because it was believed the police and the mob were one. There was reason; among those arrested were two Irish policeman and former police chief Stephen O'Leary. Some twenty people were beaten or injured, and two killed. The dog, according to the *New Orleans Bulletin*, also died.[79]

In terms of the "Reform" cause, he died not in vain, for the riot paved the way for Know-Nothing electoral victory. It came, however, with violence; Know-Nothings now took the initiative in aggression. They were angered in November 1855 by a flagrant example of one of the Nativists' chief grievances: three days before the election, a court naturalized eighty-six men whose period of residency was questionable. This led to a determination to check naturalization papers closely, and one German came to the polls with his naturalization papers in one hand and a gun in the other. When he fired, wounding a poll watcher, he was shot dead. One Irishman was also killed, and Know-Nothings destroyed two ballot boxes where they believed aliens had cast ballots.[80]

The Know-Nothings consolidated their control of New Orleans in the June election, again with some poll collaring. The victims in this election belonged to a new Democratic ethnic group, Sicilians. When a Sicilian voter was challenged, District Court Clerk Norbert Trepagnier came to investigate. The would-be voter and a companion shot and stabbed Trepagnier fatally, wounding two other Know-Nothings with French names as well. Some Know-Nothings at the poll trailed the killers to a house on Old Levee Street, where they caught and killed two Sicilians. Democrats were embarrassed when the mayor learned they were storing arms for election "work" in the office of the *Louisiana Courier*, the party organ that most vigorously attacked American violence. Perhaps more significant than the Democrats' loss of weapons was their loss of jobs. Several policeman resigned when the mayor ordered them not to wear weapons to the polls, and the Know-Nothings quickly replaced most Irish policeman, and even street sweepers and teachers.[81]

The clashes in the election in the fall of 1856 were nonfatal, though in places masked men intimidated voters and beat some Irish. The next March the state appointed John B. Cotton election superintendent for New Orleans. Rumors of plans to mob him flew, but his protective readiness and promises of impartiality allowed him to restore elections that were tolerably fair. The most serious violence of 1858 came because the Know-Nothings, now attracting many working-class immigrants, did even better with nonviolent elections. In June Democrats tried to resort to more inventive tactics.[82]

They, like the Know-Nothings earlier, now worked under a reform banner and had "leading citizens" nominate P. G. T. Beauregard as an independent candidate against Gerard Stith, a printer on the *Picayune* and head of the Printers Association and hence of what little labor was organized in New Orleans. These proslavery reformers had another precedent as well, the San Francisco Vigilantes of 1856, who, under the guise of moral purification, purified the city largely of Democrats.[83] The vigilantes of New Orleans used precisely the same rhetoric as the San Franciscans and other Western vigilante groups, but their political objectives were too obvious, while their political opponents proved more competent than they.

The campaign certainly lacked subtlety. Two days after Beauregard's nomination, the Democratic press noted that "rampant party spirit has brought forth its fruits, corruption, riots, bullyism and assassination" and now New Orleans's "well-meaning citizens" had to use all means necessary to "compel obedience to the law." About a week before the election, Captain John Duncan, in town for his trial as a filibusterer in Nicaragua, became "law and order's" champion, took over the arsenal, and quickly signed 700–800 people on as vigilantes. The Democratic *Courier* and *True Delta* published the vigilantes' documents, which were by this time formulaic: New Orleans was the world's center for crime and corruption, so that good citizens had to either acquiesce in their own degradation or rise up to throw off the yoke of evil. Throughout New Orleans, placards proclaimed: "After years of disorder, outrage and unchecked assassination, the people" were rising against the ruffians, "unwilling to abandon the city in which their business, their social sympathies, and their affections cluster." When the Know-Nothing mayor briefly resisted, the vigilantes declared the authority of mayor and police suspended, said they would "provisionally act in their stead," and told the vile generally that they "must leave or perish." "The people" had decided: "Vox Populi, Vox Dei." With this bit of Latin as final proof that they were gentlemen of property and standing, the Democratic papers quickly announced that "all respectable citizens," including the decent Know-Nothings, supported the vigilantes.[84]

The mayor by this time no longer dared to be one of the vile few who were unenthusiastic about vigilantism. On the urging of some business leaders, he authorized Duncan's men as "special police" and took protection with them. The Know-Nothing city council then legally deposed the mayor and appointed in his place one of their members, H. M. Summers. Summers enrolled large numbers of deputies of his own and posted his own bills threatening all who might try to take the law into their own hands. "Inflammatory!," fumed the Democratic press. A visitor described the intense excitement, with "the whole city under arms and expecting a great battle among themselves on account of the Division in the Election for Mayor." Citizens crowded the parks and the roof of the St. Charles Hotel for a good view of the promised mayhem. Meanwhile, the vigilantes arrested one criminal, the editor of the *Picayune*, which opposed them, for "drunkenness."

Summers was lucky. Or perhaps the editor of the *Picayune* was not the only one under the influence in the vigilante camp. Captain Duncan, who had already killed one opponent when his cannon went off "accidentally," fired it more effectively the second time. He now managed to kill four of his vigilantes, three Irishmen and a German, and wound nine others with a single shot. This discouraged Duncan's backers from continuing their purification campaign, Summers supervised what everyone agreed was a fair and peaceful election, and the Know-Nothings won in what was the nation's only real balloting on the constant vigilante claim that they represented all the decent people in the community.[85]

The vigilantes accepted the election and, to prove their anticriminal credentials, promised they would disband if "six thugs" were arrested. They disbanded, with some expressions of regret by Democratic papers and politicians that "something more decisive" hadn't helped "restore the former good character of the city." Perhaps the greatest national contribution of the New Orleans vigilantes was to raise doubts about the extralegal myth San Francisco's 1856 action had come to sanctify: the perfectly virtuous unanimously punishing the perfectly vile to restore perfect order.[86]

Locally, Stith proved a very able mayor, active especially in promoting public health and in modernizing and depoliticizing the police force. In another quiet election, another Know-Nothing workingman, a stevedore, became mayor in 1860 with wide support generally, including among the immigrant community.

Before the final riotous Know-Nothing elections in Baltimore and New Orleans, a far deadlier voting day occurred in Washington, D.C., one in which United States troops were the primary actors. Know-Nothings in the mid-1850s strongly contested elections in the nation's capital, a fact that was embarrassing to the proslavery Buchanan administration. In a hotly contested election in June 1857, Buchanan sent out a troop of 110 marines under Democratic mayor William B. Magruder to protect the polls. In the morning, two people had been wounded at one poll where Know-Nothings from Baltimore intimidated and fought foreign-born voters. This disturbance was long over when fatal events occurred in the afternoon. The marines fired on a crowd of people around one poll, killing at least ten and wounding about

twenty-five. The Democratic press trumpeted this action as a triumph of law and order. "A great principle has been established by the recent tragic occurrences," D.C.'s
Democratic organ *The States* intoned; "the majesty of the law has been maintained."
Local citizens also briefly rejoiced in the action as helping put down "rowdyism,
filibusterism and fanatical abolition." No one presented the original version of
events that circulated more honestly than the town's black diarist, Andrew Shiner:

> June 1, 1857 there was about fifteen or twenty men come on from Baltimore in time the
> election was going on and call themselves pluguglys and they went to the poles and they
> interfered with the election and raised such an excitement that the mayor and the whole
> police force could not stop them and they was forced to call on the . . . aid of the US
> marine forces to preserve the peace. . . . There was about 110 in number. . . . There
> was stones throwed at them and one of the marines was shot in the face and severely
> wounded and it is supposed that the marines fired through a mistake of order and there
> was several people killed.[87]

Within a week or so this story began to unravel. Observers testified that voting
had been going on peacefully for some time when the marines came. A Methodist
minister chaired a meeting of over 500 local citizens, who condemned the mayor
and marines for unjustified homicide. The coroner's jury reached similar conclusions in gentler language. Almost all the killed and wounded were Washington citizens; the two Baltimoreans were both Democrats, the dead man a railroad worker
and the wounded one belonging to Baltimore's leading Democratic gang, the Empire Club. The wounded began to testify that they were peacefully voting or watching when the mayor, obviously drunk, suddenly gave the order to shoot. A doctor
testified that the wounded marine, whom he treated, told him he was shot after the
troops had fired. Democratic officials later made much of trials of some Baltimore
Know-Nothings involved in the morning violence, but nothing suggested their afternoon involvement or refuted the testimony collected in the pamphlet alleging "Military executions." Magruder, elected by a majority of 13 out of about 5,000 votes in
1856, gained only 147 votes of the 7,000 cast in 1861.[88]

This, the strongest action to repress Know-Nothing electoral violence, occurred
where no violence was going on and took the lives of at least two Germans, two
blacks, two teenage boys, and some other local citizens, only one of them a known
American Party supporter. It was a slaughter of Americans peaceably voting by
marines ordered out by a proslavery president under a drunk proslavery mayor. Not
since 1807, when Jefferson decided to achieve international peace by using soldiers
to enforce the embargo on his own citizens, had U.S. troops fired on the country's
citizens, and never with such fatality, although Buchanan's record would soon fall
when Republicans applied his precedent in 1861 in Baltimore and St. Louis.

The years 1854 to 1857 were the most violent politically that the country experienced. There was no special Know-Nothing propensity to violence, nor, except in
the Louisville incident, much passional tie to issues. Rather, most of the violence
suggested the dangers existing in traditional political practices in a situation of party
flux, if both sides at times shared willingness to stretch the vague rules a bit. The Republicans, whose leaders had a long apprenticeship in coalition and Free-Soil politics, avoided violence as a political tool. The exception was vigilante actions in the

West—Montana, Colorado, Idaho—on the 1856 San Francisco pattern, their politics, unlike that of the New Orleans Vigilantes of 1858 or the Attakappas area groups in Louisiana in 1859, successfully camouflaged as disinterested communal purification rites. Once the Know-Nothings lost power, Democratic legislatures diligently turned out reports on the awful violence of those opponents to distract attention from their own use of it sporadically in the North and very systematically in the South, where mobbing and intimidation made impossible any Republican opposition and weakened Douglas Democrats and Constitutional Unionists, the political inheritors of the Know-Nothing desire for nonthinking about slavery. The political rioting in 1834 made clear the counterproductivity of open violence. That had not changed, and for proslavery forces in Kentucky and Maryland and Missouri, the best defense of their violence against the camouflaged "abolitionists" who inherited the Know-Nothings' stance was loud caricature of the mob viciousness of their former opponents.[89]

Yet the Know-Nothing memory in these border areas, although Democrats managed to rewrite the prevalent "history" of the movement, largely served other purposes locally. They provided patterns of resistance to proslavery politics that allowed the solidly Unionist majorities in most of these cities, with federal help, to avoid the kind of intimidation that was effective in other sections of the South. That four of the five slave cities which Know-Nothings had contested were the centers of those states and that district (along with anomalous Delaware) that never left the union was not wholly a product of geography. Federal troops had to quell the last efforts of proslavery forces in Baltimore and St. Louis to use the mob to protect their interests, but they were abetted by the recent patterns of counterviolence developed when the American Party had briefly flourished.[90]

The importance of Know-Nothingism to creating a beachhead for nonslavery politics in the South is clear in the anti-Nativist writings of proslavery politicians in the chief riot years of 1855–57, where the lurking issue was, as one American put it, "'the colored gentlemen in the fuel' or (if I may be permitted to express it in vulgar parlance) 'the nigger in the woodpile.'" Certainly this colored gentleman fueled Southern rhetoric against the Nativists. "An Old Clay Whig" from Kentucky, one who claimed to have voted for but two Democrats in twenty years, warned that the old plot, widely discussed in 1835, between British aristocrats and American abolitionists to destroy the United States had revived. Now those "black banners" neared triumph "with a coarseness of vituperation peculiar to that school of fanatical traitors," as the Republicans used Know-Nothings to divide the white South and to elevate "the negro race to a social and political equality." Such interests would render "that species of property dangerous" to its Southern owners and would cause one to see "delicate ladies . . . hanging upon the arm of a sooty African." The South faced "a more intolerable yoke of bondage than that which is now worn by our own slaves," if it did not coalesce with Northern Democrats, whose party was now fully purified of all those not dedicated to slavery.

This former Whig was sure that most Southern Nativists were sound "upon the great question of southern rights" but were in fact "fomenting division in the South."[91] Such was the theme that abler Southern speeches emphasized. Congressman William Sebastian of Arkansas well represented the "moderate" version; he, like the "Clay Whig," found the only hope in "a national party, whose principles will command allies in the North," as would popular sovereignty. Such had to be the South's proper course because "the balance of power has vanished forever," Sebastian argued, "and we are now in a fixed minority." The "mad fanatics" who would "rend the Union to crush the slave power" on one side and the "misguided efforts" of those who fought "a foreign influence" on the other were both "sporting with the peace." Know-Nothingism was especially dangerous in the South because now issues were argued that left core concerns "undefended through which the Union itself is endangered. Why should *we* fear a race or religion by which our rights have never been endangered?" Certainly no responsible Southerner could support a party that in the North worked "to degrade its alien-born white citizens from the right of suffrage, and extend it to its native Africans."[92]

Sebastian's theme of the folly of Southerners' questioning white solidarity since that might divide them on black subordination ran through these speeches and was strongest in those that glorified slavery. U.S. Representative Lawrence Keitt of South Carolina agreed with Sebastian that Know-Nothingism represented reformism and innovation unsuited to Southern soil, but he also stressed its roots in "the struggles of labor to adjust and protect its relations with society." Social tension came because "the Almighty has planted the love of" not paternalism but "power in every human breast." Hence, sharp class or racial divisions were "essential to the peace of society," and the Know-Nothings attacked immigrants in desperate imitation of the innate principle that Southerners alone satisfactorily handled: "the ambition to be masters, the resolve to have inferiors beside them." Not recognizing that "Heaven has appointed" blacks "to be cringing servants," the American Party "would trample their own race into the status of inferiors. They are too pure, too philanthropic, too holy to deny citizenship to the black man; but they will disenfranchise the white man. The Ethiopian will not be an alien among the snowdrifts of the North."

The South had "the patriarchal relation," born of the "unselfish antagonism of the races" (whatever that might mean), to embody and ennoble this universal lust for mastery. "Slaves of capital" were European and American workers just now beginning to rise up "gnashing in hate and blindness." The South, free of all "strife of classes," had much reason not to "build up castes among the whites." The Know-Nothing movement was simply a misdirection of free workers' fear and anger that, in helpless fury, would soon demand "a remodelling of the industrial machinery" toward socialism, which was the ultimate "social slavery." Protesting his deep friendship for laborers, Keitt explained that he could never aid these friends to "revolutionize government, and remodel the organic forms of society to establish an Utopia." Society had to choose: "Take you now slavery and safety, or free labor with paper rights and starvation."[93] Such a position, of course, could appeal to none of those Northern Democrats whom the "Clay Whig" and Representative Sebastian saw as the core of safety for their section. By 1860 proslavery politics made Douglas Democrats as dangerous to "our property" as all three men deemed the Know-Nothings to be in 1855–56.

Some things were sorted out in this crucible of Nativism, such as the relation between religion and the nation's public and parochial school systems. It also became certain that there would be no formal discrimination against white ethnic and religious newcomers. The already strong bond between the Democratic Party and Roman Catholics hardened and contributed to the developing one between Northern Protestants and the Republicans. Political reforms such as registration laws advanced, as did social ones involving professionalization of urban police and firemen. In the Southern urban centers where violence concentrated, the Know-Nothings developed the groups and the techniques of resistance that checked the proslavery pattern of control that prevailed elsewhere as civil war approached. The Know-Nothing experience also showed how hard it was to maintain a party in the South around the issues of class or alternative prejudices when so many powerful interests, and passions, were dedicated to the politics of keeping blacks, and the wealthiest whites, in their place.

The Know-Nothing episode underlined a final lesson: the sorry joke of the occasional American pretense about instituting a politics of purity in a sport where the rules were always too rough and the stakes too high to discourage whatever chicanery, cheating, and bleating parties judged they could get away with profitably.

CHAPTER NINE

Bleeding Majoritarianism

The Sectional Mob Systems Meet, Mingle, and Mangle

A man cannot be too careful in his choice of enemies.
—Oscar Wilde, *The Picture of Dorian Gray*

When the votaries of freedom sacrifice also at the gloomy altars of slavery, they will at length become apostates from the former.
—William Pinkney, "Address to the Maryland House of Delegates," 1789

I have no objection to the liberty of speech, when the liberty of the cudgel is left free to combat it.
—Alexander H. Stephens to Thomas H. Thomas, May 25, 1856,
Stephens Papers, Emory University

While slavery lurked in Know-Nothingism despite the party's desire to duck the is-sue, it loomed fore and center in "bleeding Kansas," where the two systems of sec-tional violence met and merged under the uneasy supervision of the federal govern-ment. And of all the deaths in this Kansas conflict, by far the most important was that of the principle that Representative Sebastian and most Northerners saw as the union's last best hope, the majoritarianism embedded in popular sovereignty. This principle was lynched when it failed to deliver Kansas to slavery as expected, though the Douglas Democrats quite reasonably clung to its mangled corpse as preferable to the alternative deadly courses being pursued.

The political situation in Kansas bore broad similarity to that in Southern cities where Know-Nothings contested proslavery interests, wishing not to end slavery but to stop being intimidated and manipulated in its support. Yet the differences ensured Kansas's greater importance. Here the federal government was involved, not simply in sending a few arms to Baltimore or in authorizing a fifteen-minute marine opera-tion in Washington, as in 1857, but in prolonged decision making. Here slavery was overtly the focus, uncamouflaged by a host of other issues and interests. And here both sides recognized that the resulting "truth" would derive partly from Scriptures out of the mouths of border ruffians and "Beecher's Bibles." Missouri artist George Caleb Bingham, early in the Kansas conflict, planned as the grim conclusion to his political series a painting titled *The Border Ruffians in Kansas,* a design he never ex-ecuted as the deeper designs on Kansas grew clear.[1]

The gift to the South Stephen Douglas carefully packaged in the Kansas-Nebraska Act, intended to smooth a presidentially ambitious Northerner's troubled courting of that region, was to destroy the suitor's political fortunes. Douglas early recognized that both his hopes and the peaceful union's rested on finding some principle that would placate and quiet the South, while stopping the drift of the North toward anti-Southernism.[2] Territorial popular sovereignty was, as Sebastian saw, the only principle that might hold the North and South together. The Kansas-Nebraska Act offered the South a good chance for new territory and the North a solution based on majoritarianism, praised by all and the special grail of the Democracy. To the union it offered, like the Missouri Compromise, a mode of territorial solution where the national government need not get involved. It was a clever unionist strategy that foundered only on developing fact. When it became clear that slave states would get no addition, that Northern Democrats paid no long attention to any principle questioned by the South, and that the nation had to be steadily involved with the issue of slavery in its most volatile form, the whole idea worked precisely the opposite of the way intended.

Instead Kansas brought into conflict the sectional patterns of violence that had been developing for two decades and focused them on the slave issue. The South believed that geographical proximity to Missouri would make Kansas a slave state, aided by a little proslavery intimidation. Yet, as with the later New Orleans vigilantes of 1858, the political ends and means were too clear to allow optimal implementation. Northerners understood that what many of them considered a long tradition of toadying to slave interests was to climax with the nation's giving the South a prize for their happy use of intimidating violence. Failure to act in a case where the intended extralegalism was proclaimed was to become what the South was fond of saying Northerners were: calculating cowards willing to act on nothing not decorated with dollar signs. This created some organized effort to "save" Kansas in the North. The leaders of the New England Emigrant Aid Society tended to be not old abolitionists but men who had long been less antislavery than anti-abolitionist, like Amos Lawrence and Henry Ward Beecher. Their uneasy consciences appreciated this chance to act.

Northern "aid" groups planned, as their chief benefactor Amos Lawrence wrote David Atchison, that "the fight be a fair one": to send intended bona fide settlers, armed for protection, to win the democratic contest by the announced rules. Henry Ward Beecher explained his plan to a potential supporter: arms were being bought for settlers as a "means of self-defense, each to be accompanied by a Bible with a motto inscribed on its cover: 'Be ye steadfast and immovable.'" The South intended to rely on what "honor" had come to mean: if you couldn't win by any stretch of the regular rules, violence was the effective court of appeal, one especially fun to use against people deemed curs and cowards, as all were who doubted Southern property rights.[3]

The importance of Kansas lay less in the bloodshed than in the political reverberations of the conflict, as the country became divided on a sectional basis between controlling parties dedicated centrally to slavery's constriction and to slavery's expansion. A Kentucky Democrat could point out in early 1856, that, for all the talk about "bleeding Kansas," up to that time Kansas had but a fraction of the deaths that occurred in Louisville's 1855 Know-Nothing riot. After Kansas's bloody summer of 1856 that conflict had passed Louisville's body count. Yet the three years of periodic violence that shook Kansas and the nation between 1855 and 1858 produced only fifty-two corpses, some twenty-five fewer than occurred in Know-Nothing political clashes in about the same period of time. Partly it was the publicity; the Kansas victims were not anonymous, a cypher in the numbers mentioned. Reporters gave them names and families and circumstances and made them victims or villains or heroes. Iowa vigilantes in the 1850s killed more victims than did Free-Staters in Kansas, but the Iowa deaths mattered to no one beyond their families and neighbors; "choking Iowa" was of but local interest.[4] Historians who have debunked "bleeding Kansas" on the grounds of insufficient casualties may be right about the numbers, sufficiency being a matter of taste, but not about their importance as prelude and influence on the coming more efficient bloodshed.

The casualties were predominantly Free-State settlers, 36 to 16—or 18 if one extends the trouble to 1860, when James Montgomery hanged 2 people, an alleged proslavery murderer and a fugitive slave hunter. The circumstances of these Kansas deaths similarly suggested preponderant proslavery violence. Twenty-eight Free-State casualties were murders; only 8 died in battles between the groups. On the other hand, 5 proslavery victims died in battle, and 2 were killed accidentally by their own violence; 8 were murdered, 5 of these killed by John Brown, 2 hanged extralegally for a murder they clearly committed, and 1 shot to death while disrupting a meeting. Because most Free-State deaths were in controlled murderous circumstances, injuries were more equally balanced between the groups and probably ranged under 200 altogether. Expulsions are even harder to measure. Reports of many people turned back and driven out by Missourians in the early years were common, perhaps exaggerated or perhaps underestimated. At the end of the summer of 1856 Missourians burned out some 50 families and expelled 150 more. In late 1858, with the Free-Staters finally in de facto control, James Montgomery drove out perhaps as many as 300 settlers from Linn and Bourbon Counties.

The Kansas violence was immensely complicated. It was the nation's most influential extralegal violence for social ends, though as always the personal was often deeply influential as well. Most of the violence occurred in five concentrated periods of mob action, the first and last distinct bookends around the three central clashes, each of them occurring when federal officials and the military most fully cooperated with, or coopted, proslavery groups from Missouri and elsewhere in the South to gain the results that Democrats desired: Kansas's being made securely a slave society. After two elections so grossly dishonest that they failed of their proslavery intent, Southerners began the initial mobbings from the spring of 1855 to January 1856, hoping terror would work. The final riots, concentrated in December 1858, featured Montgomery's actions against proslavery settlers that marked the now-assured Free-Staters' victory. Much deadlier were the three federal-proslavery attempts to quash Free-State resistance: the violence of May and June 1856, centered in an attack on Lawrence and its much bloodier retaliatory reverberations; the three-week period in August and September of that year when a proslavery killing led to Free-State retaliation that federal officials decided justified deadlier action by them and their local proslavery allies; and conflict in the spring of 1858, when violence was used in a last attempt to gain acquiescence in the Lecompton Constitution, favored by proslavery and federal officials.

Federal officials and troops played an ambiguous role in Kansas because Presidents Pierce and Buchanan wanted them to do two incompatible things: make Kansas a slave territory yet act with some semblance of peacekeeping fairness.[5] When they tilted much toward their proslavery goal, violence erupted that made it impossible to push on without its costing much more in blood and reputation than any of them were willing to pay. The South sent a number of its native sons: David Atchison of Missouri, Jefferson Buford of Alabama, G. D. Fleming of South Carolina, Henry Titus of Florida, and Charles Hamilton of Georgia, with groups of men who were happy enough to do a bit of mayhem for the good cause but did not stay long when they met real resistance. Free-Staters had their champions as well: New England Emigrant Aid leader Dr. Charles Robinson, fresh from involvement with Sacramento's "squatter riots" in California; James Lane, who came to revive his political fortunes; and, intermittently but dramatically, John Brown.

Years afterward Free-State leaders and their historians argued loudly over the glory, and the guilt, due to individuals, but there was much less division at the time.[6] Whatever the various competences of their leaders, the Free-Staters' victory owed most to two things. First, their less violent actions could be seen, in all but two instances, as being reasonably protective or retaliatory. Second, they represented, from early on, the clear majority. If the principle of popular sovereignty were to be anything but a mockery and a subterfuge for slavery *über alles*, they had to win.

The quick turnover of the federally appointed Kansas governors in these years reflected such realities. Each appointee was a Democrat who came initially with sympathies for proslavery groups. Yet the violence and popular sentiment they found in the territory drove the ablest of them—Andrew Reeder, John Geary, and Robert Walker—quickly toward de facto Free-State support, while those governors who were most dependably proslavery had to be recalled when what they tolerated embarrassed the federal administrations whose wishes they worked to support.[7]

For all the political ramifications of the Kansas situation, most settlers came with the usual frontier motive: the desire for new opportunities and better land. Their antislavery was less a moral commitment than what they saw as the policy that best served their just interest and influence. And the threats, bombast, and violence of proslavery groups offered blaring testimony for abolition's most effective theme from 1835 on: slave owners were as determined to master and debase whites who disputed their dominion as they did the blacks they owned.[8]

Proslavery interests tried to secure victory in Kansas quickly. At the end of November 1854, about six months after the Kansas-Nebraska Act became law, the first election was held, though scant settlement had taken place. The number of votes counted in places equaled dozens, even hundreds, of times the number of actual settlers, which cast some reasonable doubt on their legitimacy and caused Governor Reeder to void the grossest returns. Another election was called for March 1855. By this time many more Free-Staters had arrived, which drew crowds of Missouri nonresidents to ensure slavery's triumph. Proslavery won handsomely, buoyed, a congressional committee later suggested, by Missourians' casting well over two-thirds of the votes, as well as by threatening suspect settlers who wished to vote. The proslavery legislature met primarily to pass a host of capital laws against any "interference" with slavery.[9]

These laws were intended to codify the bullyism that had long been apparent. David Atchison and Benjamin Franklin Stringfellow, proslavery Missouri Democrats, were the chief organizers of this movement, which took in money from all over the South. A South Carolinian wrote Atchison that his group was sending four men to him "to instruct them where to settle, how to vote, and, if necessary, when to fight." Because these four were paying their own expenses, this South Carolina emigrant aid group had decided to give Atchison $800 "to be used at your discretion." The Missouri organizers had their own interests as well. Atchison wrote a friend, "You know my abhorrence of labor of any kind," which made him anxious to regain a seat in the U.S. Senate. A letter to Atchison suggested some of the local "interest" in his activities: if Missourians couldn't go to Kansas "with all our property of every kind" it was best left forever to the Indians, "better neighbors than the abolitionists, *by a damn sight.*" In fact, this correspondent concluded, should Kansas "become 'free nigger' territory, Missouri must become so too, as we can hardly keep our negroes here now."[10] The "all slave or all free" choice that Republican orators were to develop had much to do with such commonplace Southern claims that the insecurity of their "property" in slave states bordering free ones was intolerable.

Atchison's early tactic was to see if bluster would do the work of violence. He organized societies—the Blue Lodge, the Sons of the South—that announced their dedication to slavery and to expelling all "foreign invaders." The Missouri town of Westport became a center for public meetings where proslavery leaders announced determination to remove from Kansas all people who had ties to the Emigrant Aid Society and later promised to expel those in Lawrence. Atchison also paid to establish newspapers in Kansas, such as the *Squatter Sovereign*, that announced "public opinion" in accord with the highest standards of intimidating Southern braggadocio: "We are determined to repel this Northern invasion and make Kansas a Slave State; though our rivers should be covered with the blood of their victims, and the carcasses of the abolitionists be so numerous in the territory as to breed disease and sickness."[11]

Such verbal drivel against the public health was the early substitute for action, though there were some unsystematic efforts at turning back settlers from the free states. Atchison's groups early expected to win Kansas for the South by quick fraudulent voting. The first acts of violence grew out of anger at those daring to question the sacrosanctity of the elections proslavery forces stole. When Governor Reeder noticed an occasional oddity in the 1854 election, a Missouri newspaper opined, "The infernal scoundrel will have to be hemped yet," but an editor only roughed him up a bit. Real riot awaited the second election farce, when it became clear that proslavery verbal suasion was not enough. In Missouri a mob put out the light of the *Parkville Luminary* and nearly that of one of its editors for doubting the perfect rectitude of the proslavery vote.[12] Kansas lawyer William Phillips, who swore the election was fraudulent in his district, was punished in ways intended to be exemplary to anyone publicly doubting proslavery truth. A Kansas vigilance committee pledged similar action against all who posed "a danger to their domestic institutions." Taking Phillips to Missouri, the mob half-shaved his head, tar-and-feathered him, took him on a mile-and-a-half rail ride, and had blacks sell him for $1. A few days later proslavery Kansas officials at a public meeting endorsed the appropriateness of this punishment for Phillips, "the moral Perjurer."[13]

The first Free-State death occurred at about this time, when some proslavery men shot a young man for his reluctance to donate his horse to their cause, but the common reliance was on symbolic and mob-amusing violence. Some Atchison men drove out their first Free-State man and, when a minister named Pardee Butler said he disliked "the spirit of violence" of the paper that praised it, conducted a mob frolic on him. They lashed Butler, with his baggage and some bread, to two logs and set him adrift under a flag reading "Cargo insured—unavoidable danger of Missourians and Missouri River excepted." There was also a flag showing a man riding off with a black labeled "Agent of the Underground Railroad," put there, Butler believed, to justify someone's shooting him. The *Squatter Sovereign*, whose editor led the mob, exuberantly described Butler's handling and underlined its moral. Such would be the fate of all challenging "our time-honored institutions"; Northerners should remember that "our hemp crop is sufficient to reward all such scoundrels."[14]

Reverend Butler, twice to be a victim of proslavery mobs, was about as guilty of slave theft as most of those mob-punished in the South for this crime, or the first person driven from the town of Atchison, J. W. B. Kelly. Kelly's trouble began when a slave woman owned by Grafton Thomasson, a hard-drinking tough, drowned herself in order, it was believed, to escape her owner's physical and sexual abuse. Kelly's crime was to mention to someone his moral respect for this woman's preferring death to continual debasement. Thomasson, told of this home truth, badly beat up the slight Kelly, and proslavery interests decided to expel Kelly, as a "warning" and as a "proof" of their claim that all Free-Staters were abolitionist slave-stealers. The *Squatter Sovereign* announced that the slave woman had been

> persuaded by one of this lawless gang to destroy herself rather than remain in slavery. In fact one of this gang was heard to say she did perfectly right in drowning herself. . . . We cannot feel safe while the air of Kansas is polluted with the breath of a single Free-soiler. . . . Self preservation requires the total extermination of this set.

Kelly never returned to Kansas, but Butler disobeyed the mob's orders and came back to his farm, church, and ex-Missouri neighbors outside Atchison. When he went to town as proslavery forces readied their attack on Lawrence, the mob again took him up. They'd promised death if he returned, but Butler was partially protected by his local popularity. The mob settled for a tar-and-cottoning.[15]

By the fall of 1855 the political and mob situations in Kansas were changing. Angered especially by the restrictions on basic freedoms in the proslavery constitution, Free-Staters accepted a strategy of establishing, much on Thomas Dorr's Rhode Island pattern, a "majority" constitution and government theoretically replacing and actually paralleling the proslavery ones deemed "bogus" because of electoral fraud and minority support. Divisions over several issues, especially free blacks, threatened the movement, but the "radical" Dr. Charles Robinson (again like Dorr) reluctantly accepted a document excluding black voters to broaden the appeal of the cause. Unlike Dorr, Robinson took care to strengthen steadily local adherence to his constitution, while avoiding action that would give excuse for federal repression.

Many historians have disparaged the moral seriousness of the Kansas conflict by pointing out that most Free-Staters were more unambiguously racist than they were vigorously antislavery.[16] This is true but is a misleading truth if Kansans' stance is not related to the growing sense that black slavery was the deadly enemy of white freedom and democracy. In Kansas for the first time the nation paid attention not simply to the explanatory rhetoric of the Southern system of violent intimidation: unprecedented vileness and danger demanded drastic action to save society. The revelation of Kansas came because now the nation noticed how and against whom and in what circumstances violence was actually used. While Republican Party journals made the most of the conflict, they created neither it nor the system of mob intimidation made crystalline on the plains of Kansas. Certainly the Kansas "crusade" was rife with the moral limitations grown of the nation's racism, but this was just one more way it was pertinent "prelude to the Civil War."

The shrewdest Free-State leader, Charles Robinson, was strongly antislavery and antiracist. Too much of an ideologue to be successful for long in ordinary politics, Robinson had a clear sense of what needed to be done in Kansas to injure both slavery and racism. He never hid his personal views but presented them in ways that assured other Free-Staters that the emphasis that separated them mattered less than the cause upon which they agreed: Kansas and Kansans should be free. No powerful orator like his frequent rival, James Lane, Robinson made his most important speech on July 4, 1855, when Free-Staters were looking for both a strategy and a morally unifying position to oppose the "bogus" government. Robinson's central idea was to argue that Missourians were trying to do what England had tried to do fourscore years earlier: not simply impose slavery but demand that "we must become slaves ourselves." Replying to proslavery insistence that a free Kansas would endanger slavery in Missouri, Robinson's argument reconciled his position with the feelings of "free white" Kansans and expressed what Republicans in the North would move gingerly toward over the next half decade. The "liberty of governing ourselves" was the fundamental principle:

If Kansas or the whole North must be enslaved or Missouri become free, then let her be made free. Aye, and if to be free ourselves, slavery must be abolished in the whole country, then let us accept that issue. If black slavery in a part of the States is incompatible with white freedom in any State, then let black slavery be banished from all.[17]

Robinson pragmatically accepted accommodation. Lane and his supporters were anxious both to retain power in the Free-State cause and to refute the common proslavery charge that they were "abolitionist nigger lovers." Hence, they pressed Robinson to accept a constitution with "white male suffrage" and with a subsequent popular vote to determine the issue of black exclusion. The votes on both these issues went antiblack by about a 3-to-1 margin, but Robinson judged that fact unimportant because it strengthened the basic cause. He himself was glad both to express his conscience and to allay Lane's fears of him as a political rival by voting against both the "white" and the "male" suffrage restrictions.[18]

The victory of antislavery in Kansas, however, was much less Robinson's than that of common people who were only a bit less racist than most of their opponents. The congregants and neighbors of the Reverend Pardee Butler, who was roughly handled twice by the proslavery mob, were fairly average Free-Staters. Butler described his situation and that of his friends simply, unheroically, and honestly. A farmer and sometime Campbellite minister from the Midwest, Butler went to

Kansas, despite some fear of trouble, because its land was, he judged, cheaper and better than that elsewhere. He'd never thought much about slavery until, traveling toward his new home through Missouri, he was repeatedly asked if he was an abolitionist and warned that it would be wise for him to keep secret any nonenthusiasm for slavery.

Quietly troubled about how a decent man who just wanted to farm and maybe preach should respond to these pressures, Butler quietly staked his claim in the proslavery area around Atchison because he found there a large number of fellow Disciples of Christ, most of them from Missouri. He liked them and they liked him, in part because they were troubled by the same issues. The Missourians had come to Kansas believing that the issue of slavery would "be determined not by the nation, not by Congress, but by themselves" and had just seen the spring election of 1855 mocked by invaders from their home state. Butler's neighbors told him "with pain, and shame, and bitter resentment" of being pushed aside at the polls, which made them feel "held down under a reign of terror" and "sick at heart. It was a deep, unspoken, bitter and shame-faced feeling" that troubled the whole community.

Butler understood that most of his neighbors wanted "a free white state" and resented blacks as they resented the Southern aristocracy, both of which were associated with the limitations of thought and opportunity under which they had earlier lived. By the summer they were ready to support the Topeka Constitution as "the feeling of dissatisfaction, that had all along been festering in the hearts of the people, began to come to the surface." And this commitment was hardened as the legislature passed its "savage and bloody laws" that put into statutory form what Southern mobs had long legislated: no freedom existed for anyone who might question slavery. The mobbings of their pastor, and the subsequent long record of terrorism, which Butler carefully catalogued, only toughened determination to prevent slavery from again enslaving them. They knew the lie of "abolitionist!" when it was applied to them, and the taunts and threats and acts against them "touched their Southern blood" so that they warmly welcomed the dignity Free-State resistance gave back to them.[19]

Proslavery forces, angered by the Free-State strategy of resistance and their own slipping support, took heart from the replacement of Reeder with the new governor, Wilson Shannon, and moved from threats and humiliations to deadlier acts. Yet they now faced organized opposition, so every killing triggered some resistance and complications. An Irish renegade from the Free-State Kansas Legion mob-killed one of its members but became the first proslavery casualty when the victim's sons badly injured him and another man during the attack. Then a Proslavery man killed a young Free-Stater in a dispute made to look like a claims controversy but in fact meant to frighten away Free-Staters. Proslavery sheriff Sam Jones had the well-known killer turn himself over to Governor Shannon, who freed him according to plan and had a friend of the victim arrested. Free-Staters rescued the accused, and Shannon prepared to use this act as proof of a secret organization thwarting the laws to repress Free-Statism. However, when the Free-Staters prepared to resist, Shannon abandoned this ruse of "insurrection" and worked out the first of several "peace treaties," this one to end the "Wakarusa War," which happily never began. The victory Free-Staters gained by preparations for violence, however, was a lesson they never forgot.

A few days before the treaty was agreed upon, proslavery forces killed another man: a Democratic colonel and an Indian agent fired at the passing suspect while a Democratic general and two Democratic judges watched approvingly. A month or so later, a riot occurred at an election in Leavenworth when Free-Staters tried to vote; several were hurt in the two-hour brawl, and a proslavery man was killed. The proslavery Kickapoo Rangers arrested seven Free Staters for the riot; unable to control his men, the Rangers' captain contrived to let most of the captives escape, but one was not so lucky. Proslavery people hacked Reese Brown brutally, and when they found that he clung to life, they kicked him, jumped on him, and spit tobacco juice on him until death finally provided intermission.[20]

Time, as had been feared, was working against any easy proslavery victory, and Democratic leaders in Washington and Kansas began to prepare for a more coordinated campaign of repressing the opposition. When Free-State leaders begged President Pierce to keep the peace, he issued a proclamation against both internal resistance to the law and external aggression, urging dependence on the control of federal troops and local militia. As was intended, this may have sounded even-handed in Camden and Canton but did not in Kansas, where the "local militia" were mostly deputized Southerners come to ensure slavery's triumph. Stephen Douglas headed a Senate committee that labeled the Kansas Legion an insurrectionary institution. Jefferson Buford led in his Southern "settlers," whom Sheriff Jones immediately deputized. U.S. marshals hired some of those new federal troops Pierce mentioned, and they knew their intended job. On May 17, young South Carolinian Andrew Hartlee wrote his mother that he was now "putting down" Free-Soilers in Kansas, having been hired at $1.50 a day, plus a 150-acre bonus if he stayed fifteen days. Action was expected to be brief.[21]

Shannon's ruse this time was more elaborate. Sheriff Jones, wounded while in Lawrence, became a victim of insurrectionists. Some Free-State leaders were arrested, including Robinson, while Democratic judge Samuel LeCompte got the Douglas County grand jury to condemn the *Lawrence Herald of Freedom* and the *Kansas Free Journal* as—that old legalistic mob standby—"public nuisances" and its Free State Hotel as a fort endangering public safety. These writs were never served, but a federal officer used them to declare Lawrence in a "state of revolt." When Buford's posse began to plunder on the outskirts of town, Shannon declared their action legal. On May 19 and 20 the posse killed one young Free-Stater each day in token terrorism; on May 21, a federal official arrested two men in Lawrence and dismissed the posse, probably to be able to claim personal and federal noninvolvement in the destruction. Sheriff Jones and the posse entered Lawrence: they sacked the two newspapers and threw their type in the river and attacked the Free State Hotel, consuming its liquor before burning it down. They partly burned the home of "Governor" Robinson and plundered stores and houses. They killed no one, in part because the Free-Staters decided not to fight; one rioter was killed by falling bricks as he worked to destroy the hotel. The next day one happy rioter, with plunder in his arms, told an Englishman they were going "to fight the nigger-worshipping crew to the last drop of blood."[22] Such was the dilemma of the Democratic leaders in Kansas: their hope lay in terror sufficient to intimidate resistance under a veneer of legalism, but this veneer, thin to begin with, peeled away at the words and acts of those intended to supply the supplemental terror.

Robinson's nondefense of Lawrence constituted a calculation that gross destruction of an undefending people's homes, businesses, meeting places and ideas would appear to the world indefensible and would be well worth the losses. He was right; of all the mayhem that marked these years of struggle in Kansas, the "sack" of Lawrence burned brightest in the distant memory. And it served to justify the perspective of those Free-Staters now set on retaliatory violence. Atchison spoke truly, if in ways he didn't understand, when he assured his troops outside Lawrence that the cowardly Free-Staters, who had not fired a shot, "tonight . . . will learn a Southern lesson they will remember."[23]

John Brown had led a group to aid Lawrence but arrived too late, seeing its flames in the distance. He and some followers soon gave terror for terror, with some interest, hacking to death five proslavery men, no more active in the movement than had been most Free-State victims, and leaving their bodies to announce to terrorists that their methods were a two-edged broadsword. In a small battle Brown's men also soundly beat a proslavery band. Other Free-Staters led an assault on the town of Franklin, killing one proslavery man and driving others away. At this point, the U.S. Army intervened to keep the peace. They convinced Brown's group to surrender, tacitly on the grounds that became more formal later: no prosecution. They also disbanded the proslavery Whitefield group, though the bulk of its members simply transferred to the Missouri band of Henry Reid, under whom they killed one Free-Stater and terrorized the women and children in a community. Buford killed a final Free-State man in this bloody June, but the federal troops now wanted peace, and neither side saw any immediate advantage in disrupting it.[24]

The scenario that Governor Shannon and other Democratic officials introduced had always suffered from an uncertain finale, but this ending made a bloody farce of their wishes, a bumpkin Pyramus and Thisbe tragedy of their high-laid, or at least high-sanctioned, plot. The only saving aspect of the whole performance was that the Missourians had been so long loudly mouthing their terrorist lines that the Lawrence debacle was seen to be the act of that now famous troupe of border ruffians. Such must have been in Democrats' minds as they pondered the only kind of play-doctoring historically possible: adding another act in the hope that it would end more to their liking. And David Atchison had long suggested the resolution to be tried in August: "If the General Government would only leave Kansas to the nurture of the 'Border Ruffians,' we would soon have peace in that quarter."[25]

On August 11, Governor Shannon ordered the militia to break up the Free-State legislature at Topeka as insurrectionary, and on the same day men of Buford's band riddled from ambush a Free-Stater. The next day Free-State men again invaded Franklin, where the murderers had gone; in the fighting two men were killed and ten wounded, divided equally between the two sides. The militia captain who had set up the first murder victim fled with his gang, and Free-Staters captured the fort of Colonel Titus, the man most associated with the sack of Lawrence, killing one of his men and badly wounding him. Proslavery people in Lecompton were not attacked, but they signed a "peace treaty" promising to respect Free-Staters' rights.

Missourians sent to Kansas militia members who began to force out settlers around Osawatamie, after a brief resistance and successful retreat of about thirty defenders under John Brown. Missourian Henry Reid, with a force of over 1,000, including 400 led in by Atchison, took charge and proceeded to devastate Osawatamie and its neighborhood: his men burnt down twenty or thirty homes in the town, sacked and plundered its post office and businesses, and burned seven farms in the area. Many people were killed; a federal officer later claimed to have counted thirteen mutilated bodies of victims. About 150 Free-State families were driven out. Just before this most effective attack on Free-Staters, Democratic officials in Kansas began writing Washington that Missourians, who were coming "to protect their friends and relatives," couldn't be controlled. They also expressed shock that James Lane was organizing people into agreeing to protect the polls, somehow related to "terror." When Governor Shannon left at the end of August, proslavery efforts seemed close to success. For the first time Missouri terror had done what its leaders had promised for two years: killed and expelled large numbers of Free-State opponents.[26]

Yet James Lane had 700 men clearly poised to attack Lecompton's proslavery settlement. The Missourians outnumbered them but had no stomach for such a serious fight. Federal troops refused the acting governor's orders, in their words, "to make war on Topeka." New governor John Geary entered the state determined to repress Lane's "insurrection," and random attacks on Free-Staters continued as he pursued Lane. Thomas Wentworth Higginson, bringing in some twenty-eight wagons of settlers, met nineteen going out with Free-Staters who told him, "The Missourians could not conquer us, but Governor Geary has." The temporary federal troops were primed to take proslavery action. Young Andrew Hartlee, his promised fifteen-day enlistment having stretched to fifteen weeks, wrote his mother on September 7 that a talk by the wounded Titus caused his troop to be "worked up for *revenge*" and that several political leaders, including Atchison and Doniphan, had sketched plans to burn Lawrence "to the ground, every house in it, take Lane and hang him, and drive his following from the Ter." Hartlee liked these ideas, as well as the $5,000 he'd heard was offered "for Lane's scalp." This was an old idea; Southern humor in late 1835 had flourished on rewards for abolitionist scalps, heads, and bodies. But Atchison's men had given mob-scalping a new currency on August 18 when one of them, on a bet, shot a passing Free-Stater, scalped him, and carried the bloody trophy to Leavenworth on a pole—and there killed another who expressed shock at the deed. When the victim's widow and some twenty neighbors came to claim the body, Atchison's merry men "captured," humiliated, and robbed them, killing two in the process.[27]

Hartlee and his fellow federal troops failed of their promised sport. Lane refused to disband and temporized, as Geary learned more about the true state of things. The Missourians went home in large numbers, the federal professional troops were not willing to act in a situation where Lane had offered so little excuse, and Free-State determination was clearly unbroken. Hartlee's final letter from Kansas, dated September 20, made clear what had happened. Governor Geary had been to his camp, given orders for Lane's arrest, and made it clear that he'd do anything "to be rid of the traitors, in a cheap way, and have Law and Order on his side."

Geary had come to Kansas, in fact, to save the national election for his Democratic Party, whose defeat throughout the North seemed possible if the Kansas conflict continued to manufacture Republican voters at the summer's pace. Geary himself explained he was "carrying a presidential candidate on his shoulders" and within a month decided that any semblance of "Law and Order" in fact depended on his accepting the de facto majority authority of Hartlee's Free-State traitors. Lane's terms were accepted in mid-October; he'd give in if Geary promised nonprosecution. Geary reported to Washington his arrest of Lane and 240 men and the confiscation of arms in mid-October, then he released them. The Geary–Free-State peace lasted through 1857, and all tenable expectation of using violence to promote a proslavery answer ended.[28]

Perhaps Geary's pacification of Kansas might have translated into Buchanan's pacification of Republicanism had the new president not shifted course again. Buchanan's initial reaction was in line with his manipulative instincts but not out of line with a policy of accepting Kansas realities. He decided to recall Geary, by this time hated by the South, and to replace him with Southerner Robert Walker. Walker went under presidential agreement to allow majoritorianism, and he arrived announcing that "the law of the thermometer"—not Free-Staters, of course—had decided the fate of Kansas. To have a Southerner preside over the acceptance of Free-State Kansas while announcing that the laws of nature, rather than human choice, had so decreed was the best way to package defeat.[29] Yet Buchanan shifted course, leaving his Kansas governor furious, his party bereft of any figleaf of principle, and his country stumbling on toward civil war.

Southerners hated to let go any slave hope, and they firmly held sway over Buchanan, if not over Kansas. Buchanan's pragmatism probably also played him false. While he was largely right that his party's central moral commitment had long been to defending the union by acquiescing in proslavery policies, he failed to recognize, unlike Douglas and, more dimly, Pierce, that the party needed some principle to offer the North if the drift away from the Democrats, clear from 1854 on, was to be stopped. Still, Buchanan might have followed where good politics and policy led had the Supreme Court not offered him renewed hope that slavery might yet triumph in Kansas.

The last of the core coterie of Andrew Jackson's supporters in public life provided the straw that Buchanan grasped at. Chief Justice Roger Taney decided to end conflict in the territories by judicial fiat. Though the Court had agreed on February 14, 1857, to decide the *Dred Scott* case on narrow noncontroversial grounds, within the week that resolution changed. Taney probably always wished a broad proslavery ruling; possibly Alexander Stephens influenced his fellow Georgian, Justice James Wayne, to push for this; certainly President-elect Buchanan cajoled a fellow Pennsylvanian, Justice Robert Grier, into going along with the broader decision to mask a bit the sectional nature of what was to be ruled.

Despite the jumble of concurrent opinions, there was no doubt that the Court majority in *Dred Scott vs. Sanford* asserted that all territories had to be open to slavery and denied both popular sovereignty and every historical precedent. And the chief justice said he spoke for the Court when he presented a large chunk of intellectual contradiction and historical disinformation to elaborate a position he had developed as Andrew Jackson's attorney general a quarter century earlier: blacks in the United

States were essentially property and, even if free, could never be deemed citizens or humans having legal rights. Disregarding majoritarianism, states' rights, and common practice, the Democratic Party's senior public figure and its newest president joined in announcing that the spread of slavery and the dehumanization of blacks were their nation's central sacred commitments. To advertise the solidarity of court and executive on these issues, Buchanan briefly chatted with Taney before announcing in his inaugural that the Supreme Court was to "speedily and finally" settle the slavery controversy, a verdict to which he would "cheerfully submit."[30] Speedy that verdict was, if far from final: two days later the *Dred Scott* decision was announced.

The ties between the Court's ruling and Kansas, in fact and in Buchanan's mind, are unclear. Certainly it had nothing to do with a Kansas that was ready to become a state and now had a solid Free-State majority. Even Taney was not about to announce that states could not ban slavery, though critics of this major decision were right in arguing it suggested that possibility. In Kansas political manipulation remained the only way to create another slave state, as proslavery Kansans well knew. Acting quickly because a Free-State legislature was about to end their formal power, the legislators by late fall had written their Lecompton Constitution, with a proviso that the vote on it would be with or without a clause prohibiting further slave importation but in no case interfering with the slaves already there. The Lecompton Constitution's argument for slavery depended on the absolute rights of property that the South had developed and that had made Adam Smith long the patron of the Democratic Party: "The right of property is before and higher than any constitutional sanction" and hence "property in slaves" was "inviolable."[31]

For awhile Buchanan supported Governor Walker in Kansas, whose promise of fair elections enticed Free-Staters to vote in the fall of 1857. Free-Staters won when Walker tossed out thousands of illegal votes cast where handfuls of people lived. Having failed like his predecessors to gain a slavery victory under some veneer of fairness, Walker was removed. Two things encouraged Buchanan to push for acceptance of Lecompton. In 1857, as in 1835, Southerners quickly demanded "works" to accompany the "words," this time of Roger Taney, that defined the nation's commitment to slavery. "Idle words," fumed the *Charleston Mercury* of the *Dred Scott* ruling, claiming that it was another "victory more fatal, perhaps, than defeat." The *Dred Scott* decision in fact whetted rather than satisfied Southern territorial appetites, and Kansas was still the only meal at hand. Pressure from Stephen Douglas also influenced Buchanan; Douglas continued to blame Free-Staters for the Kansas troubles, and in fact the man everyone knew to be Douglas's political representative in Kansas, U.S. Land Surveyor John Calhoun (from Massachusetts), became the leader of proslavery forces in politics, brag, and intimidation. It was Douglas's protégé Calhoun who presided over the writing of the Lecompton Constitution, with its careful provisions that he and his proslavery forces would supervise and count the vote.[32]

When Lecompton was ready for its vote in Washington, there had already been two Kansas elections on the document. The proslavery election overwhelmingly adopted Lecompton with slave importation to be continued; around 7,000 votes were cast, a bit over half of them probably legal. Before Buchanan had a chance to fire him, Walker's interim successor suggested that the Kansas legislature, now in

Free-State hands, call a clear up-or-down election on Lecompton. This election gave a majority of over 10,000 against the document. At this point Buchanan became a supporter of Lecompton, and Douglas an opponent.

Buchanan argued that Lecompton was the quickest settlement possible for the Kansas trouble, pointing out that once it was a state, the majority of voters could decide the slave issue. He chose not to notice that Lecompton's devisers had prohibited all amendment of it for seven years.[33] Douglas's opposition owed something to his clearer understanding of what was at stake in Kansas. Since the failure of the mob to fix slavery there, that issue had clearly wrapped one more fundamental to the country's future: to what degree would the Democratic Party modulate its proslavery stance with continued emphasis on majoritarianism? Faced with a fast-approaching rendezvous with Abraham Lincoln and the voters of Illinois, Douglas was made sharply aware of how hard it would be to run on Buchanan's platform of democracy rejected, or rather indefinitely deferred, to soothe proslavery caprice. Douglas brought his four-year courtship of the South to an end.

Back in Kansas, violence again briefly became the proslavery tack. Buchanan's new governor tolerated a new Southern militia, this one under wealthy Georgia planter Charles Hamilton. In March 1858 Hamilton captured ten or eleven Free-Soilers and had them all shot in cold blood, his defenders arguing that lack of prisons necessitated the military action against the helpless. Half of those shot lived by feigning death.[34] Hamilton was no better as soldier than as executioner. James Montgomery, leader of a Free-State "self-protective" group, defeated him without loss but reluctantly let him escape to Missouri on orders from federal troops. Another peace treaty followed; it lasted until the fall of that year, when Montgomery escaped assassination, killing one of his several attackers. In November and December he drove out many proslavery settlers in Linn County and then Bourbon County. By this time Kansas's federal administrators were unable to act against even such flagrant Free-State illegality. Still another governor fumed (this time with legitimate reason), begged for more arms and troops, and, like his predecessors, settled for a show of authority and peace on Free-State terms of amnesty and new fair elections. This time peace lasted, as Kansas became a state and Charles Robinson its first governor.

For half a decade, in fact, Robinson had guided a popular shadow government to steady victory and increasing popularity, despite the determined opposition of both the federal government and the Southern system of terror. And all this time, the Democrats, so happy to announce "revolution" in support of the "will of the people" in partisan farces in Maryland and Pennsylvania, never noticed, much less supported, the triumph of that principle in Kansas. In Rhode Island, the Democrats' central commitment to proslavery made all prominent support of Thomas Dorr, south of New York City, a "confidential" matter until his quick defeat rendered support for the principle he represented safely inconsequential. In Kansas, every leading Democrat advertised his unconcern for popular sovereignty if it questioned slavery.

Kansas was at peace. The nation's peace was another matter, made more difficult and less likely by both the events and resolution of the Kansas question and mobbings. Nathaniel Lyon was in Kansas with federal troops between March 1855 and August 1856, the full period of the earliest and worst of the Kansas troubles. He was sent to California in time to witness the conclusion of San Francisco's cleverer and much more successful proto-Republican use of the mob, carefully dressed in decorous vigilance committee garb. He returned to Kansas in 1859 in time to catch the conclusion of its riot years. His was one person's view and story—that, of course, of a sharply intelligent and irritable man close to the events. Yet his version of things honed and paralleled the always much vaguer central strand of "public sentiment" in the North.

Shortly after his arrival, just before the March elections of 1855, Lyon was sure that fraud and violence would again be used to carry out the voting's ordained purpose, to "give some appearance of proslavery strength in Kansas." Yet personal observation convinced him "that not in a single district are a majority of citizens in favor of slavery." Lyon expected that "the aggressions of proslavery men will not be checked, till a lesson has been taught them in letters of fire and of blood." After this election, with hordes of Missouri militia active, Lyon bitterly remarked on this mockery "of national greatness" and "our Glorious Union." Certainly the military had proved it could successfully "domineer over the people here," and effectively expand democracy, too, so that hundreds of voters appeared in districts where two dozen people lived.

By December 1855, before the major group clashes, Lyon predicted many of the results, locally and nationally, to come from "the over bearing domination of the proslavery people in Kansas towards the free-state men," who would eventually "have either to fight in self-defense or submit ignobly to the demands of the aggressors." Superficial observers might find some fault with "the Lawrence people," but they acted "through the unavoidable necessities of self-defense against unwavering and malignant prosecution which seeks to drive by violence and outrage the free citizens from the country." Missourians and the slave South had "been able to impose legislation and officers upon the people of Kansas, but find them rather unruly subjects." Hence, proslavery people clearly expected the federal government to "enforce their mandates," something that might be too reckless for "even President Pierce." Should the president act to aid proslavery, "it will only bring on the sectional strife more promptly," something which Lyon was "quite willing" to see happen and which he felt "the continued arrogance of the proslavery power will render inevitable": "I despair of living peaceably with our southern brethren without constantly making disgraceful concessions. But rest assured this will not always be."[35]

Lyon often expressed anger at Free-State passivity. Although the mass of armed Missourians at the March election made "effective resistance impossible," Lyon was amazed that "it was not resolutely attempted." In his next passage on the conflict, at the end of summer of 1856 and of the worst violence, after Lawrence's sacking and Brown's killings and Reid's murders and expulsions, Lyon was much harsher on "the wanton cowardice" and "the craven fear of Northern men in abandoning their homes and helpless families to the merciless outrages of the inexorable savages." Lyon's able and admiring biographer argued that such denunciations were unfair because Northerners found it hard to accept "a new code" of "a blow for a word, and a stab for a blow"; "braggartism and bullying, the pistol and the dirk, were instrumentalities better suited to the genius" of the South. Neither the biographer nor Lyon mentioned what quick learners the Free-Staters had proved in the new code. If they never gave quite tit for tat in the violence game, they'd used it often, at least once brutally, and well enough to win every round.

Lyon knew that the army in Kansas sometimes offered protection to Free-State people but also that its general role had been one of "subserviency to the proslavery schemes of the heartless villain," Secretary of War Jefferson Davis. When he claimed that "a proper manhood on the part of friends of freedom" would have stopped many barbarities, he wrote more truly of himself than of the Free-Staters. To follow orders from Washington was to abet violence against democracy, human freedom, and largely innocent citizens. Like much of his nation, Lyon obeyed, betrayed his own ideals and observations, and fumed at others, more than ready for the deeper break that would cost his life but that would let him act in step with his "proper manhood."[36]

Lyon came back to Kansas in September 1859 and was sent to the locus of trouble in December, as James Montgomery was driving out proslavery settlers for, Lyon wrote, "old grievances or vague suspicions." Lyon met Montgomery on Christmas Day and described their discussion in detail and with observational shrewdness. He immediately recognized how Montgomery was "conscientiously and absorbingly devoted to what he feels to be . . . his duty to society." Yet the "he feels" reflected clear reservations about this honest "disciple of the higher law," who was "more fanatical than reasonable." Montgomery spoke slowly at first, not out of evasiveness, Lyon felt, but out of hesitancy "to repeat the oft told story" of his and his community's griefs to someone who was probably unsympathetic. Involvement for both men grew as Montgomery spoke on and Lyon wrote on:

> He soon became earnest and warm. A red glow tinged his cheeks as he went through a long and minute detail of petty annoyances and brutal outrages to which the free people of Kansas had been subject, showing as a corollary the consequent necessity of the measures which he and his friends had adopted.

It must have been eerie for Lyon to listen to this "oft told story," once told by himself in his earlier letters, and to know that his chief responsibility was to repress this man who had acted on generous principles, with proper manhood, to protect the political and humane values that Lyon held—and had helped to attack out of his considerably more reasonable notions of "the requirements of the law."

On his 1859 arrival back in Kansas, Lyon rejoiced at the general peace he found, "and that, too with the ascendancy of free state principles." "Proslavery arrogance" had suffered "a handsome rebuke," although "at painful sacrifice of valuable life in martyrdom to the cause." Very recent events interacted with Lyon's memories of the core of the Kansas violence in the summer of 1856, some of whose influences

> are seen in the later fanaticism of poor old Osawatamie Brown in his attempt at Harper's Ferry. . . . The simpleton deserved his fate, though sympathy is natural for so earnest, sincere and brave a character. The people of the South make fools of themselves about this matter, as they always do on the subject of slavery. The affair will probably assume other shapes in the course of time.[37]

Those other shapes had been forming for a long time, as the South from 1835 on demanded that Northerners sacrifice their basic rights so that slaveholders might be assured more comfortable enjoyment of their property. Lyon's uncomfortable recognition that "fanatics" like Montgomery and "simpletons" like Brown represented "a proper manhood on the part of friends of freedom" not visible in his own conduct was a dangerous version of the truth that in the North had long been shaping, sharpening, and marching on.

Lyon was to put his various Kansas lessons to effective use in the spring of 1861, when he combined clever tactics and fatal force to quell a St. Louis mob, once again the coalition work of proslavery state officials and the city's Irish population. Lyon's efforts were so effective, in fact, that those groups suddenly decided they favored law and order and opposed federal intervention in earnest. A year later the Civil War, which Lyon welcomed though he guessed it might take his life, did just that.[38]

Kansas was no arena of saints and villains. The people who moved there represented pretty much the good or bad average American poor enough to consider moving on and well-off enough to do so. A small percentage came because they saw the territory as a testing ground between slavery and freedom, but these citizens were probably morally little different from their neighbors. A New England Congregationalist minister who took it upon himself to lead a small group of Maine lumberman to Kansas told Thomas Wentworth Higginson that it would have been theologically valuable for Higginson to have led the group because the time spent with those "emissaries" would have convinced even that cheerfulest of Unitarians of the truth of "innate depravity." The border ruffians always called their opponents, in accord with long Southern tradition, "abolitionists," but Lyons pointed out that that simply meant they were people who didn't want to do precisely what proslavery forces favored.[39] The great majority were no more centrally concerned about the slave than was Lyon. They were mostly good Americans, and thus reasonably good racists, who didn't care for slavery but who liked much less being pushed around. And with these motives, and some courage and good luck and leadership, they managed to defeat the determined actions of proslavery forces, both the Southern system of terror and the highest officials of their country.

Average Americans in Kansas, like those in Pardee Butler's congregation, cared about their liberty and about American democracy, which system they'd always been told and believed was the best in the world. And this holy of American holies was the first thing Southerners tried to kill in Kansas. Atchison's various organizations early on huffed personal threat but obviously hoped, as did federal officials, that a bit of voting violence would do the needed work. Atchison's associate Stringfellow told the Blue Lodges of Missouri that they should "exterminate" anyone "tainted with free soilism and abolitionism" but made it clear that their first duty was to go to Kansas "and vote at the point of the bowie-knife and revolver."[40] So they did in 1854, before they'd injured anyone; so they did in early 1855, when they'd "exterminated" but one, though by this time they had chalked up two personal humiliations to match their two polling saturnalias over the mocked authority of King Ballot Box.

That most Kansans kept asking for fair elections was what most infuriated proslavery and Democratic leaders, who feared the loss they knew they would suffer. So the Democratic Party affirmed its unconcern about majoritarianism when it irritated the South, its primary principle, over which it had been happy to urge revolution in Maryland and Pennsylvania and Rhode Island. Douglas himself often made clear that he'd be happiest if "popular sovereignty" flourished as theory by dying as a reality in Kansas. But the Americans there, ordinary enough, didn't let that happen. They fought politically better than they knew, so that "government of the people, by the people, and for the people shall not perish from the earth," and their "governor" understood (if they but vaguely) that they struggled in the very long run for the proposition that "all men are created equal."[41]

A great many people knew the danger to the union when its only national party so obviously and grossly jettisoned its only principle to promote slavery's cause; none saw this danger more clearly than Democratic judge and philosopher Frederick Grimké, who left his native South Carolina for a successful career in Ohio. Grimké shared with his sisters, Sarah and Angelina, great sharpness of intellect, in his case untainted with any worry that American democracy suffered from its exclusions of blacks and women. He saw clearly that Buchanan's refusal to submit the Lecompton Constitution to a clear vote concluded "a revolution in the character of parties most disastrous to the country." The worst event imaginable, "which hitherto has been skillfully warded off, appears now to be almost unavoidable, the conversion of national into geographic parties." Although Grimké believed real differences between the North and South were superficial variances due to slavery, he recognized that what he called Buchanan's "mere faux pas" left "no way out of the labyrinth."[42]

Free-State Kansans helped create this labyrinth because they had had some schooling in the nation's rough politics that Henry Miller learned about decades earlier in Missouri. That experience stood them in good stead in their meaner and more endangered frontier home. They also knew that they ought finally to be able to vote and that the votes ought to be counted close to fairly. They knew, as party leaders learned in the first political riots of the second party system, that the rules of this American sport and duty were flexibly vague but that it could not be a system where anything goes. Some clever jockeying and cutting of corners were parts of the game, but racing wouldn't survive the right to shoot the other fellow's horse. Nor could democracy survive a victory clearly carved by border ruffian bowie knives or shot from invading Missourian muzzles so that fifty votes were counted where one man lived.

After the war was over—indeed, soon after it began—Southerners were to say secession had nothing to do with slavery but with Southern rights, state or some other. There was little talk of this in the years leading to the Civil War, where "Southern rights" were a constant theme but one Southerners always tied to the right to enslave, to enjoy their property undisturbed, and to take it where they pleased. John C. Calhoun didn't mention slavery in his *Disquisition*, but no one, North or South, ever doubted that the only minority Calhoun wished safeguarded was proslavery's interests. One can imagine the fury of its author if some trenchant troublemaker, say John Quincy Adams had he lived to read it, had proposed the adoption of Calhoun's theory for a truly unprotected minority, like the nation's free blacks. On a more commonplace level, Lawrence Keitt might mention the injustice of the tariff in his litany of grievances, but this had not been a major issue since 1833 because there wasn't that much of a tariff.

That law and that judicial decision the South most praised in the 1850s both mocked states' rights to aid slavery. Roger Taney for the Supreme Court said that blacks could not be citizens, despite what many states wished to do and had long done. And the South's best-loved law, that against fugitive slaves, was the one that asserted federal authority over traditional state powers and prerogatives most completely. State courts, state law, state officials, and the will of the state's citizens were to be sacrificed to federal power to regain a few head of runaway chattel, whose dark skin overrode any state's right to determine its own citizenship. The answer that the South pushed to further its slavery interests in the decade leading to Civil War was that of active federal responsibility to serve them—in Kansas, in Cuba and other foreign areas, and in the Northern states. And for Northerners, the acquiescing in such demands created not only irritation but the "shame-faced feeling" of Pardee Butler's Kansas neighbors and the self-loathing that Lyon indicated.

In 1842 Unitarian minister Henry Furness had finally spoke his long-held antislavery opinions, though he knew that endangered his job and congregation, because he felt "the Curse of slavery had even left its own boundaries and enslaved the North." Bad as it was, slavery could be tolerated as "a local institution," but not if Northerners were forbidden "to wash their hands from its contamination." A decade of insistence by the South, and acceptance by their Northern Democratic allies, that the nation give up human rights, states' rights, and democracy if they interfered with slavery's protection and expansion convinced the majority in Kansas and in the North, most of them little sensitive to injustices to blacks, that some substantial resistance and risk were preferable to continued "disgraceful concessions" to an institution that had indeed "left its own boundaries" to demand their acquiescence, their rights, and their dignity.[43]

And at each demand, each coarse incident and argument, more Northerners found their self-respect salvageable only by turning against the South and the Democratic Party, which increasingly stood for nothing but slavery and snarling racism. Different things moved and maddened different people, and everyone clung as long as they felt they could to positions they hoped to be moderate enough to fend off catastrophe, but the movement in the North, under the infuriate Southern spur, was always in the direction of danger.

As early as 1835, with near-unanimity the South had declared its hostility to freedom of speech, of press, of assemblage, of petition, and of association, if those things were used to question slavery. In Kansas, no less clear and united, they proclaimed their scorn for self-determination and fair elections—again, if those contradicted slave interests. All these rights Southerners practiced and cherished, too, but not when they challenged the more fundamental right to enslave. Then, as in Kansas, when push came to shove came to shoot came to scalp, the South subordinated to its special institution all rights and decencies.

It was Preston Brooks's cane, speaking because a senator spoke vigorously about the crime against Kansas, that beat George Templeton Strong, racist enough so that he didn't think slavery a bad idea, into the Republican ranks. He'd long accepted that Southerners were somehow a little better than people in "the busy, money-making democracy" up north, but now he felt that "they are, in fact, a race of lazy, ignorant, coarse, sensual, swaggering, sordid beggarly barbarians, bullying white men and breeding little niggers for sale"—the extremity of this caricature owing much to Strong's long support of its chivalric opposite.

And it was his long Kansas experience that sharpened Nathaniel Lyon's conclusions on the brink of the Civil War. "Brags and threats," pouring "in torrents from the mouths of Southern orators," had swayed "the peace-loving North" to make steady concessions, which were then "produced as the most conclusive proofs that the craven, mercenary people of the North were unworthy to be associated under the same government with the bolder and more chivalric sons of the south." The time had long passed for "senseless wrangling," and Lyon rejoiced at the coming conflict that would free from bondage not slaves but "my principles, though this triumph may involve an issue in which I certainly expect to expose and very likely lose my life."[44]

For their part, antebellum Southerners, to protect the primacy of their right to enslave, erected a second right, to riot and use violence—again, especially in cases involving slavery. Or perhaps Alexander Stephens gave it a better name. In response to Preston Brooks's caning of Sumner, he drily commented that he didn't mind all kinds of rights being proclaimed in the North so long as the South retained "the right of the cudgel" to control them. And that right was used less effectively against Northerners and Kansans than it was against Southerners' own doubts and discussions about the institution around which they developed their economy, society, and loyalty. Such suppressed doubts also motivated the South's ex post facto insistence, by no one expressed more learnedly and lengthily than Stephens, that slavery and the cudgel had nothing to do with it.[45]

Epilogue

Vintage Violence

Man decides and Allah decides, and Allah decides more powerfully.
—Koran

Someone asked: "Then what are they fighting for?" "For Southern rights, whatever that is!"
—Mary Boykin Chesnut, *Civil War Diary*

Bystander: I think you are fanatical.
John Brown: And I think you are fanatical. "Whom the gods would destroy they first make mad," and you are mad.
—Interview after the raid at Harpers Ferry,
New York Herald, October 21, 1859

Oh God! Again
The pain of the spikes where I had sight,
The flooding pain
Of memory, never to be gouged out.
—Sophocles, *Oedipus Rex*

In 1848 a United States senator from New Hampshire, to distract attention from a failed slave rescue, introduced a bill to control riot in the District of Columbia, triggering the most vital and spontaneous debate on slavery in the nation's history. Over a decade later, an aging man, at the end of a shambling, commonplace farmer-merchant career, riveted the union's attention on another failed scheme to rescue slaves, dying in a way that caused people to wonder if self-sacrifice for others' liberty was madness or divinest sense. On the day of this man's execution, a handsome young actor deserted the Richmond theater to watch the rugged character make his final appearance in a way that mesmerized the memory of the actor and the nation. And a bit more than half a decade and some 620,000 lives later, that actor took the stage for the last time in the role that alone kept his memory alive. A few days later he was killed, carrying in his pocket a picture of the daughter of the just-retired senator from New Hampshire, a woman to whom he'd been close—probably engaged—possibly in order to be close to the man he'd long plotted to capture or kill.

These personal linkages between John Hale, John Brown, and John Wilkes Booth were among history's always intriguing coincidences, but the roles of all three were tellingly linked to evolving patterns of sectionally tinged violence. People were to

266

call all three men "mad," a claim still often found comforting about Brown and Booth, but any madness was wholly integrated to patterns of violence as sane as social sanction could make them.

In 1848 John Hale was the first American to be elected to the senate because of his antislavery position. He was already designated as the presidential candidate of the Free Soil Party, that midway point between Birney's principled gestures in the Liberty Party and Frémont and Lincoln's effective Republican modifications of them.[1] Known and liked more for his good humor than for any great abilities, Hale was a good stump speaker who had his full share of Yankee shrewdness. This allowed him to turn an incident mildly embarrassing to Northern political antislavery into a significant boost for it, by causing Southern opponents to talk like raging fools.[2] No one had done this so well since John Quincy Adams had encouraged and punctured Southern balloons of bluster in the House in the wake of Theodore Dwight Weld's congressional work.

In this case, the ill wind that blew Hale his problem and his opportunity came up the Potomac River, tragically for some seventy-two slaves attempting to escape in the ship *The Pearl*. Adverse winds and tides held back their ship until slave-catchers ended their dreams of freedom.[3] Nothing infuriated Southerners so much as when their always "kindly treated" but "ungrateful" chattel both emptied their pockets and belied their platitudes by trying to flee. The *Pearl* group of ingrates, owned by forty-one masters, were mostly "particularly valuable" and "pampered" house servants, and no one doubted that some abolitionist had financed Captain Daniel Drayton's attempt to help free them.[4] On the night of the slaves' capture, proslavery mobs roamed Washington threatening to take Drayton from jail for quick mob-justice and to destroy Gamaliel Bailey's antislavery *National Era*, the capital's best and largest newspaper.[5] People expected that Southerners would see that these mobs acted more effectively the next night.

Hale's personal response to the event was sympathy for the great price being paid by the *Pearl* blacks, now deposited in the slave pens and jails that conveniently dotted Washington for sale southward.[6] Hale's public action was wholly pragmatic. He finessed the oratory Southern senators had been preparing about the crimes of abolitionists by introducing a wholly innocuous bill against rioting in the District of Columbia, exactly modeled on the one in force in the neighboring slave state of Maryland.[7] The strength of Hale's strategy was that his bill was per se unobjectionable and, in the circumstances, a red flag to proslavery enthusiasts. They charged.

There was an element of comedy in the debate, Hale arguing with mock innocence that his legislation was a legal commonplace, and his opponents claiming that Hale's bill threatened the very union by questioning the South's right to riot against antislavery. Some congressional argument was powerful theater, but well rehearsed, with each actor carefully playing his chosen role. Hale's ploy created honesty by catching everyone off-guard. The passion of the proslavery response, as angry at moderates as at opponents, made clear not only how deeply the house was divided but also what a tract of political quicksand the middle ground was.

The South's elder statesman and leading intellectual first responded to Hale's proposal. John C. Calhoun claimed that at issue here was the "one question that can destroy this Union and our institutions," slavery, and that Hale's bill was clearly intended "to repress the just indignation of our people from wreaking their vengeance upon the atrocious perpetrators of these crimes, or those who contribute to them." In essense, Calhoun argued that all violence against slavery's opponents should be sanctioned as "just indignation." The proper Southern response, Calhoun asserted, was to prohibit "any of your sea-going vessels entering our ports," Southern or "our" ports including those of the nation's capital.

What Calhoun said harshly, Henry Foote of Mississippi expressed with blustering fury, whetted perhaps on remembering that the day before he had described the recent revolution in France as ending an "age of tyranny and slavery" and inaugurating one of "universal emancipation." Foote charged Hale with complicity in the slave theft and with "attempting to get up a sort of civil war." Were Hale not a coward, he would "unsheath his sword" and shed "his blood in the holy cause." Foote closed his diatribe by urging Hale to forsake the safety of the senate to voice his ideas in Mississippi, where he would "grace one of the tallest trees in the forest, with a rope around his neck," with all "high-spirited citizens" cheering and Foote himself actively assisting.[8]

Hale retained his cool amid this heat. He denied any knowledge of the *Pearl* rescue and made Foote admit that his charge here was baseless. He also invited the man soon to be famous as "Hangman Foote" to what Foote had called "the dark corners of New Hampshire," not to be hanged but to be debated. He also told Calhoun that it was good for the whole nation to know the South's conviction that slavery was not only "incompatible with the right of free speech," as had long been clear, but "that even the sacred rights of life and property must bow down before it." Hale spoke briefly. He well knew it was not what he said, but what Southerners were sure to say, that made his case.

Along with their avowal that mobbing in the service of slavery was no sin, Southerners asserted that any questioning of slavery threatened slave insurrection. Arthur Bagby of Alabama claimed that Hale's mentioning of national rejoicing at the wave of freedom sweeping Europe inferred "that the slaves of this country are to be permitted to cut the throats of their masters," while Foote said Hale was trying "to involve the South in bloodshed, violence, and desolation." Who would not respond as he did, Foote asked, who had seen "insurrection exhibiting its fiery front" in Mississippi? Foote well knew that the Mississippi insurrection with which he had close connection was a hysterical hoax, but only when a Northern senator insisted that Southerners' fear of insurrection was understandable did Southerners remember that their slaves were wholly happy. The other Mississippi senator, Jefferson Davis, who had earlier said that if Hale intended to raise any questions about slavery in the District of Columbia, he wished the union to end, "the sooner the better," now mocked all insurrectionary terror because the South had "no more fear of our slaves than . . . of our cattle."

Certainly Southerners had no fear of personal abusiveness. Calhoun sputtered in irritation that he "would just as soon argue with a maniac from bedlam" as with Hale, and Foote repeatedly said that Hale was "a maniac, or, if sane, you are a knave." He also, in one of the rhetorical transfers that Southerners made in discussions of slavery, claimed that Hale was "a gusty declaimer—a windy speaker— a—." Here he was cut off, as Calhoun had been, by those who still thought gross abusiveness improper in Senate debate. Hale knew how to draw the moral that would touch the North most deeply. He asked Calhoun if he imagined "that we of the North, with our faces bowed down to the earth, and our backs to the sun, had received the lash so long we dared not look up?" As in 1835, Southerners made it clear that Northerners, like slaves, had no right to question their will or words.

Those who tried to quiet the angriest Southerners also drew attack. For example, Calhoun derided North Carolinian Willie Magnum as urging a quiet that would soon "sign the doom of the whole." When Stephen Douglas of Illinois argued that the extremism of Southern response was "the best means to manufacture abolitionism" in the North, Foote charged that Douglas sought to win "golden opinions from all sorts of people" for political advantage. Calhoun sternly lectured that this attack on Southerners for "merely defending our rights" made Douglas's position "at least as offensive" as that of Hale.[9] South Carolina's Andrew Butler (who provided ex post facto pretext several years later for Preston Brooks's cane) concludingly lamented the 1848 debate's indication of "the approaching storm," with his section of the country "destined to be in a minority—a doomed minority."

After 1848, politics flowed toward Hale as the nation moved toward civil war. His run for the presidency in 1852 was ineffective, swamped by the country's fearsome hope for peace after 1850's compromises, but the North increasingly resented the Southern integration of violence, verbal and physical, to its slavery dedication.[10] As Weld had predicted, and as Stephen Douglas understood so sharply in the debate as throughout his career, the Democracy could no longer soothe every Southern outburst and demand without driving away crucial support in the North, mostly of people who neither much cared nor cared to think about slavery. Such, precisely, was the course of American politics after the death of Zachary Taylor, as the proslavery demands of the South and the efforts of feeble Northern presidents to appease them swallowed the work of moderates."[11]

Hale was to be largely forgotten as other leaders brought to harvest the politics he'd helped grow, but the nation was to remember sharply the two men who provided the dramatic finale to the era's sectional use of extralegal violence. The political acts of John Brown and John Wilkes Booth stand like vivid personal parentheses around the endless sentence of bodies consumed in the Civil War, their private fame or infamy emphasizing the connection of antebellum America's riotous street theater to the much more efficient killing in that sanctified tragedy. In a limited sense, Brown and Booth were similar heroes: melodramatic in their tendency to divide the world into the spotless virtue of their position and the intolerable vice of those they opposed, and heroes in that they gave their lives bravely, gladly, even grandiloquently for what they believed they believed. Still, the differences were great. Brown had a depth and dignity, grown of his hard life and long journey in Protestantism, that were lacking in Booth, conditioned by his quickly successful forays into theatrical and sectional melodramatics. Brown acted at crucial moments to counter the South's use of violence and to shift Northern response to it, while Booth killed in pathetic parody of Southern traditions of using violence to assert mastery.

"Mad" has been a favorite judgment on both men, in part because of the comfort of attributing to personal craziness the unthinkable destructiveness that nations and sections sanctify with reasons enough.[12] "Mad," too, often serves as soothing label for personal historic acts so unexpected they appear inexplicable: "stranger than fiction," since few would suspend disbelief had the event not actually occurred. Both men's madness could be and has been footnoted with familial references, but such methods allow "proof" that most in the nation were crazy. There is no evidence that the mind of either man was aberrational beyond the long-accepted patterns of social violence within which they acted.

If historians have sometimes escaped the puzzle of the two men by arguing insanity, contemporaries found similar comfort in conspiracy theory. The evidence for conspiracy is stronger. Brown's small, well-integrated band at the Kennedy farm near Harpers Ferry obviously conspired in some way to free slaves, for which purpose a small group of white abolitionists funded them.[13] The prevalent evidence is strong, though more ambiguous, that Booth was an agent of the Confederate government during most of his several months' stay in Washington, while he and a group of fellow conspirators plotted to kidnap President Lincoln.[14] Yet without the two men's personal visions, it is difficult to imagine the events associated with their names happening.

John Brown headed a large family of children and in-laws who accepted his convictions and followed his dictates (except about religion) with some resentment but also with a dedication as deep as his own. Yet it was the sons who led the father into the arena of sectional violence, going to Kansas in 1855 to help themselves to new land while helping the Free-State cause there. Their father stayed behind struggling with one of the several disappointments that punctuated his life, this one tied to Gerrit Smith's philanthropic effort to aid black Americans by providing farms for some of them in an isolated area of northern New York. Given the long reach of American racism, isolation was desirable, but this area of the Adirondacks, with its short season for growing and long one for wintering in livestock was too removed, too rocky, too mountainous, too cold to make the attempted community viable. Brown could remove the manipulative surveyor who first cheated the black settlers, but not the natural burdens of the area for farmers.[15]

When things didn't work out, Americans often moved on, frequently following family members who had decided a bit more quickly to try to make things work in the West. Brown went to Kansas certainly to visit his sons, possibly to consider settling, and clearly to make a political gesture in support of his long-held antislavery convictions. All Americans knew by late 1855 that Kansas was the locus of the battle, practical and political, between those who wanted to extend slavery and those who wanted to constrict it. Brown brought arms to Kansas in October 1855, either accompanied by or soon joined with plans to oppose slavery with militance. His first activities were the domestic ones of most settlers, but when proslavery violence erupted in the spring of 1856, Brown was ready to reply in spades.

Though Brown disliked slavery most of his life, his antislavery actions before Kansas were minimal. Neither speaker, writer, nor joiner, he responded to active abolition in 1834 by considering wheedling or buying a black child to raise as a member of his family. He also dreamed of getting "a school a-going here for blacks" because he believed that educated blacks "would operate on slavery like firing powder confined in rock."[16] Brown took no action, other than gaining his children's enthusiasm for welcoming the projected black sibling. Serious financial problems hit the Brown family about that time, never wholly to disappear. Brown aided fugitive slaves on occasion and at times strongly fought racial segregation in churches he attended. He was almost fifty in 1849, when he made his first sustained effort to help blacks by going to aid those in Gerrit Smith's Adirondack tract, a move effectively seconded by Brown's second major business failure. Long after his death, people reported that Brown had dedicated his life to antislavery after the murder of Lovejoy in 1837 and had long planned to use Virginia's mountains as a guerilla base for liberating slaves. Probably these people remembered backward, or perhaps they reported vague dreams, like those of adopting or schooling blacks in 1834.[17]

Fifty-five years old, Brown brought with him to Kansas a life of dedication to Calvinist religion; to praising and quoting Aesop, Jonathan Edwards, and Poor Richard; to morally educating his huge family; to rigid ideas of work and austerity; to generous communal paternalism; and to social and personal justice in accord with the demands of a benevolent, implacable, and inscrutable God, on whose character Brown did his best to model his conduct. Those who judged him harshly were partly right: from some angles, he was "very selfish and very intolerant with great self-esteem," a man whose "immense egotism coupled with love of approbation and his god idea" led him to believe "he was God's chosen instrument."[18]

Yet most Americans found it hard to brush off Brown's "god idea" when they found it embodied in someone so unswervedly brave and straightforward, so unaffectedly honest and self-sacrificing in aiding the oppressed—and with such confidence that he acted as God wished. People who fell within his orbit—his family, his workers, his townsmen, Northern intellectuals, Southern politicians, John Hale and John Wilkes Booth and Virginia governor Henry Wise—all admired the compelling strength of his character and his convictions.

Partly this influence on people grew from deep and practical tenderness blended with his severity. He liked to cook food for people; as much as possible, he took on himself the patient and messy business of nursing people during long illnesses; he'd go without sleep for days while trying to get newborn lambs on their feet; every night he personally tucked the blankets around his aged father when the latter went to bed; he loved to sing his children to sleep—though the lullaby they best remembered was "Blow Ye, the Trumpet, Blow."[19] Almost everyone noticed, too, the depth of his concern for justice, which made him often perceptively self-critical—especially regarding the dangers of his "haughty, obstinate temper," which made him "too much disposed to speak in an imperious or dictating way." He also noted social ills. For example, like several other American businessmen of the era, he believed that the nation's workaday religion, "the deification of pure selfishness," aided "material interests," often by debasing human ones.[20]

In a world of petty conning and compromise and calculation, of often grossly self-serving self-righteousness and sentimentality, Brown's absolute conviction, combined with tender love and capacity for cheerful self-criticism and self-sacrifice for others, made him something of a saint. Of course, saints are hard to live with. Frederick Douglass remembered how deeply impressed he was with the plain efficiency, cooperation, and devotion in Brown's spartan home, "where he was indeed the master of it, and indeed likely to become mine too, if I staid long in it."[21] Not about to be reenslaved, Douglass left in the morning. Brown's sons, as boys and men, felt much the same way. While no sons ever demonstrated greater filial devotion than they, Brown taught them to be honest, and they repaid him by telling him and anyone else who would listen the relief they felt at his absences.[22] It was tough love all around.

Brown's central "god idea" was the traditional Christian notion of blood atonement. When his oldest son, a boy of less than ten, had run up a considerable "debt" of punishment, mostly for sloughing off work, Brown laid on one-third of the strokes "masterly" with a blue-beech bough, and then took off his own shirt and ordered the lad to lay the final two-thirds payment on his skin, demanding that the boy hit harder until he drew small drops of blood from his father's back. Such effective blood punishment (drawn, its victim, John Jr., firmly believed, from the sermons of Jonathan Edwards) was central in Brown's antislavery career.[23] This theology, much like Nat Turner's, also conditioned Brown's quick grasp of the nature of Southern terroristic violence, surpassed only by that of Cassius Clay, who alone clearly saw slavery, mob law, and personal violence as one system. The stern Calvinist and the indulgent Deist shared not only a clear vision of the purport of Southern violence but some profound stubbornness of character, where all threat and danger only hardened their determination. Opponents might well kill them, but these opponets were dead wrong if they ever expected to win by mere intimidation. In 1855 a Missourian, on being told the group was traveling from New York to Kansas, told Brown, "You'll never live to get thar." Brown answered, very quietly, "We are prepared not to die alone," and the man from Missouri "slouched off."[24]

Missourians had done substantial slouching off from Kansas before John Brown arrived. They'd entered boisterously enough, expecting to cast the votes and intimidate the opposition to make Kansas a slave state. But the electoral fraud was too gross and the terroristic violence too slight. Brown, who, with his men, had been allowed to cross a bridge guarded by proslavery men when they simply displayed their well-loaded weapons, concluded that "*even* Missourians are amused with trinkets, or with those who wear them." He thought that unless the Free-State forces faltered, "*Kansas is free*."[25]

Because proslavery violence was far from over, Brown's career of blood was to begin. When Free-Staters were driven out of the proslavery center of Leavenworth in February, Brown realized that the time to "Buckle on our Armor" was approaching, though he perceptively concluded that it wouldn't come "until warmer weather." On May 21–22, a United States marshal led rioters into Lawrence under slight legal camouflage and "abated the nuisance" of free press and assemblage by ruining the antislavery newspapers and hotel. The killings of at least three young Free-State men in the preceding days also announced the dangers of resistance. A Free-State militia under John Brown Jr., with a small group of family members under his father, rode to protect Lawrence but arrived to see it in smoke in the distance. A messenger arrived with one Kansas-fresh piece of news that "much excited" the Free-Staters. He told of Preston Brooks's beating Charles Sumner senseless in the senate chamber for attacking "The Crime Against Kansas." When the smoke from Lawrence joined in John Brown's mind with the blows in Washington, he sensed the truth that the two events were linked in a Southern system of violent intimidation in service of slavery.[26]

The Free-State militia quarreled over its leader's freeing some slaves as they returned; the majority did not want to mix their cause "with 'niggers' or abolitionists." John Brown asked for volunteers for a special mission on Pottawatomie Creek, where at Dutch Henry's Crossing Judge Sterling G. Cato from Alabama, supported by "troops" from his native state under Jefferson Buford, had recently issued arrest warrants for the Browns and members of the Free-State militia and legislature. Four Brown sons and a son-in-law, plus an Austrian Jewish settler and James Townsley, who lived on the creek, volunteered. Brown pocketed a list of proslavery men on the Pottawatamie, the volunteers sharpened swords and sabers, and, to the cheers of those they left behind, they bumped off in Townsley's lumber wagon. They did nothing that first night because Townsley balked, claiming later that he'd had no inkling of the plan. Probably he'd learned reluctantly—as he drove into that dark night—of what John Brown had in mind when he talked about getting "away with some . . . vile emissaries before they get away with us."[27]

The following night Brown acted. His group went to the Doyles' place, took the father and two sons some distance from their home, and butchered them with sword and saber. Two similar "executions" followed quickly, and all five badly slashed corpses were left by edge of creek and road. Followers directly committed the sword killings, but old man Brown put a bullet through the head of old man Doyle, Brown's son claimed, about half an hour after Doyle was killed. In his only known gross deception, Brown always insisted in the East that he killed no one on the Pottawatomie, understanding how this grisly pile of corpses would suffocate some of the support he needed in future projects. Probably he personally killed no one so he could always deny doing so with technical honesty, while he put a bullet through the head of Doyle's corpse to affirm his responsibility and to sound to proslavery people the loud message that the silent corpses were to convey.[28]

Certainly everyone in the Kansas community knew full well who had planned and supervised the executions. Initially there was a general sense of horror at the mutilated corpses. Brown's own sons were sickened. Owen, "conscience-smitten," carried on "at an agonizing rate" for the killing he'd personally done, and two not involved were deeply shocked. John Jr. suffered a period of mental collapse, and quiet Jason told his father, "You have committed a very wicked crime." Brown, as true believer and as father, simply answered, "God is my judge."[29] However God viewed these mangled bodies, Kansas Free-Staters, once the shock was digested, judged the results of the Brown murders favorably. It was easy to list the crimes and killings on the other side as justification, and Brown's upping the ante of terror told proslavery people, despite some immediate retaliation, that the stakes of the terror game were high. Certainly some left or stayed away or decided to rely wholly on federal troops when they learned, as John Brown's settler brother-in-law, the Rev. Samuel Adair, put it, that "that gun which they have been firing is beginning to kick." Victims William Sherman and Allen Wilkinson had been proslavery toughs but were not involved with any known egregious act, and the Doyles were guilty of only the common Irish favoritism of proslavery. They were as innocent of any known crime as the hundreds of nonabolitionists and noninsurrectionists Southerners had killed or punished without qualm and with quelling effect. Adair pointed out the advantage of Brown's act: it made clear that Free-Staters would not demand conspicuous proslavery crime to act but would "not be particular" as they meted out murder "dollar for dollar and compound interest in some cases."[30]

Brown continued to fight briefly in Kansas, defeating a proslavery militia under Henry Clay Pate, before surrendering to Col. E. V. Sumner of the U.S. Army. A bit later, a proslavery minister murdered young Frederick Brown, the first of what were to be four family sacrifices to antislavery. When Brown left Kansas in October 1856, a year after he'd entered it, the Kansas violence was not over, but the state's path to nonslavery and the North's to nonextension was evident.

Such political realities didn't ensure Brown's success as a fund-raiser, but his next action was the most unambiguously successful one in his antislavery, or, for that matter, his economic, career. When he returned to Kansas a year later, there was "no discouraging news," so he had nothing to do and left. His 1858 return was more striking. A Missouri slave, Jim, crossed the river to ask for help for himself and his family, about to be sold away, and Brown took a small group to Missouri and rescued Jim, four fellow slaves, five others on a neighboring plantation, and another elsewhere, in the latter case killing planter David Cruise. With Missouri, Kansas, and federal officials all determined to get Brown and the stolen goods, human and otherwise, Brown evaded them for almost three months in the dead of winter to get all the former slaves safe to Canada. The notoriety of this act—Brown himself worked to publicize it on the trip and after—may have caused him to remove the projected base of his final plan to Virginia from Missouri.[31]

The slave rescue, apparently improvised on the spot in response to Jim's plea, occurred after Brown had adopted his "Provisional Constitution" for his republic of slave-freers and gained substantial support for his "Rail Road business on a somewhat extended scale." In the summer of 1859 he moved with twenty-three supporters to the Kennedy Farm near Harpers Ferry, his band again made up heavily of family members but now integrated, with young white and black co-conspirators. The one slave and four free blacks who were part of the group, one of them wrote, had their first experience of a society devoid of "hateful prejudice" or "a ghost of distinction" related to race.[32] To fend off suspicion, most of the men, after Brown led them in morning prayer, spent their days in the log loft, at times drilling from a military manual Brown admired, while teenage daughter and daughter-in-law, Ann and Martha Brown, provided the neighbors a front of familial ordinariness and the men fresh fruits and flowers.

The women had returned to New York and three men were left to guard the house when, on October 16, Brown and eighteen supporters swept down on and quickly controlled the town and arsenal of Harpers Ferry. Instead of leaving with the arms and some hostages for western Virginia's mountains when help failed to pour in, Brown dawdled. That night he stopped a train and then, as if to advertise his activity, let it pass through. By noon of the next day, Brown was effectively surrounded by local people and militia, and on the morning of October 18, Robert E. Lee directed U.S. Marines into the Engine House, where Brown and a few followers and hostages had retreated. A marine and four people of Harpers Ferry—a free black, an Irishman, a planter, and the town's mayor—had been killed, as had ten of Brown's men. Seven, including a severely wounded John Brown, were captured and lived to be legally hanged. Five male participants and the two women escaped.[33] Brown never made clear why he so purposelessly squandered these lives by being "too tardy" in leaving after he'd gained all that might have aided him. He claimed that he'd been misled by a "desire to spare the feelings of my prisoners, their families, and the community at large," though even such sentimentality would have been best served by the practical course: to get arms and get out.

After capture, Brown always admitted, perfectly accurately, that "it was my own fault as a leader that caused our disaster," for which young men whom he loved gave their lives and on which some older white ones had staked funds and potentially their freedom, without helping any black, and with near-maximum sacrifice of life.[34] In fact, Brown betrayed his promises to all these people and their confidence in him, but Brown—and, more strangely, they, so far as we know—never doubted that "Christ put a sword in my hand, and there continued it so long as he saw best, and then kindly took it from me." Brown wrote that he was at first disappointed in himself "in not keeping to *my own plans*" but had come to conclude that "God's plan, was infinitely better, *no doubt*; or I should have kept to my own." Perhaps Brown dallied out of some subconscious recognition that his death would do more to end American slavery than any number of guerilla rescues could.

He wrote a teacher of his youth that he'd always been confident that "in the *worst event*," his effort at Harpers Ferry "would certainly pay." In his terms and those of other Americans who deeply hated slavery, pay it did, largely because Brown conducted the business so flawlessly in the month and a half between his capture and his hanging.[35] In both interviews and letters from Harpers Ferry, Brown offered the nation as seamless a blend of the homely—advice to his wife about feeding "the old spotted Cow" and to his children about needing to learn the music of the broom or the scythe before that of the piano—and the holy and the heroic, understated American style, as the United States would ever find. In everything was apparent Brown's simple faith and dignity and family feeling and intelligence and courage, without a touch of whine or bluster or meanness of spirit. Such rare virtues made many in the North consider the value of both violence and self-sacrifice related to those people whom, actively or indifferently, they'd deprived of all liberty, justice, and protected dignity.[36] No one really noticed the one thing conspicuously missing in Brown's talk: any concern or thought about those who had died or would die with him. God worked through John Brown, and the others who gave their lives were rather insignificant adjuncts of this joint venture.

When Brown was hanged, few would have disputed the judgment of the old antislavery warrior Joshua Giddings, like Brown in mind and character, his metaphor as naturally commercial as Brown's verb "pay": "Brown and his friends have sold their lives well. Nothing has ever so aroused the North, or struck such terror in the South as the Harpers Ferry raid." Now few could evade "the great question, whether we are to protect and uphold slavery or not."[37] This owed much to the clarity with which Brown posed the basic issue. Had he acted against the enslavement of anyone powerful and respected, Brown argued, "it would have been all right" and then some, in everyone's eyes. He could be condemned comfortably only by those who denied any divine agency or who believed that God was "a respecter of persons"— comfortable white persons—and a despiser of black ones. Brown put in compellingly theological and personal terms what Henry David Thoreau put more literarily. How could anyone question the success of Brown's action, which "has liberated many thousands of slaves, both North and South," people who had long ceased to consider that principles mattered, could be acted on, and were worth living and dying for?[38]

Theodore Dwight Weld's "Events" had long been leading Americans toward Brown's final conclusion that "the crimes of this guilty land: will never be purged away; but with Blood," in quantity hard to imagine by those upset by the drops he'd caused to be shed. Yet Brown's grim self-righteousness in taking life and cheerful self-righteousness in giving his own and those of people he loved became spur to the long-feared national "tramping out the vintage." Passionate preacher, reformer, and conspirator Theodore Parker, dying of consumption in Italy, wrote in praise of Brown, when he learned the old man was to die from his consuming passion, in words that precisely duplicated Brown's final thought a week before he uttered it. Parker had once hoped that American democracy might blot out slavery in some "less costly ink," but now he knew there would have to be a deadly "pilgrimage . . . through a Red Sea."

This red sea closed only when Brown's captor, Robert E. Lee, another simply devout American whose convictions seldom encouraged him to question deeply his conduct, surrendered the sword he, like Brown, believed Christ had given him, used to redden the land, and then taken away. Yet the conflict's most famous bit of bloodshed was still to come, horrifying because it was personal and just outside the numbing mass slaughter both sides continued to glory in. On the same page where Parker predicted the red sea, he noted the irony of Virginia's state shield; a man—who should have been black, Parker suggested—standing on a tyrant and chopping off his head, accompanied by the phrase "Sic semper tyrannis."[39] And such, of course, were the words of John Wilkes Booth as he leaped in front of history's footlights, having shot President Abraham Lincoln in the back of the head.

John Brown's "truth" may have marched on with this bullet as well. Booth lied when he told his sister and the public that he'd rushed from the Richmond stage to Harpers Ferry bravely to aid in Brown's capture; he merely went to watch him hanged. But he probably spoke truly when he expressed his hero-worship of Brown, "a man inspired, the grandest character of this century."[40] Brown would not have been surprised about his possible influence on this final bullet. His god was just but expunged sin through the blood of lambs and good shepherds as well as wolves.

John Wilkes Booth's reasons for killing Lincoln were perhaps as muddled to him as they are to us. As with the tradition of Southern violence out of which the act grew, specific circumstances may have mattered less than its gross symbolism of rightness proved by power. Booth was a Marylander, raised in the northern part of the state, where for some time free blacks had outnumbered slaves. His English-born father, Junius Brutus Booth, who owned slaves but disliked slavery, was arguably America's greatest Shakespearean actor and unarguably its most prominent alcoholic eccentric. Booth's mother was devoted to her children, especially the handsome John, and to their impossible but equally devoted father. The "marriage" was extralegal until 1851, a decade after the birth of their youngest child, because Booth's long-deserted legal wife only then learned of her husband's second family and gained a divorce. The youngest of the sons who were to follow their father onto the stage and who shared some fear of following him into mental weirdness, Booth was a child when his father's bouts of oddity or insanity ended with his death in 1852.[41] Dashingly handsome and with much of his father's ability to convey bursts of overwhelming passion, especially as a snarling villain, the young Booth served a reasonably brief apprenticeship in minor and secondary roles in Philadelphia and Richmond before becoming a well-paid and perhaps too-praised "star" in places like Montgomery, Alabama; Rochester, New York; and Boston.[42]

The vagueness of Booth's politics has contributed, reasonably enough, to the tendency to attribute his killing to insanity, or twisted ambition causing him to seek fame in some dramatic public role. The latter explanation perhaps contains some truth, though Booth's acting career was a solid monetary success and a substantial aesthetic one. Yet he, like others, recognized limitations in his skill, or at least in its development. Actor, manager, and friend John Ellsler claimed that had Booth lived, he would have "stood, head and shoulders, above all the artists of the time," but Ellsler added in the same sentence that Booth was "not a finished actor, far from it"—"a blooded colt, full of action, full of fire, necessitating a master hand to . . . keep him down to good work." Ellsler described him in 1863, at a time when Booth had been on stage seven years and a star for five, perhaps a bit late for a master hand or mind to take the reins. Booth told his closest confidant of child- and adulthood, his sister Asia Booth Clarke, that he regretted his early success in the South, where "even his errors were extolled," and told her, "If I shine, it must be in the rough."[43] This Booth most admired old tragedian Edwin Forrest, whose powerful acting style was increasingly called rant approaching self-satire.

The better model closer to home, himself named after Edwin Forrest, may have been part of the problem. Brother Edwin, well established on the New York stage, was probably brighter and was certainly more literary and harder working than his younger brother. Edwin was in the process of becoming what he was to remain for decades, the nation's great serious actor, at a time when "high" culture appreciated and theater allowed more closely controlled and thoughtful overall effect to replace the earlier Romantic emphasis on the surprising moment of transporting passion. The Booth family was close, something that often walks hand and hand with high competition, and brothers with much greater intellectual and moral resources than John Wilkes might have felt rankled that his most successful performance in New York City came when Edwin arranged for all three acting brothers to star in *Julius Caesar*. Edwin's *Hamlet* was becoming the longest running and most praised Shakespearean production in American theatrical history during the time John Wilkes prepared his Ford's Theatre drama.[44] Asia reported that Edwin, a strong Unionist, and John Wilkes had "stormy words" in these years, presumably over politics but heated on some professional jealousy and their different personalities. This personal conflict reverberated in Booth's political argument that duty to country might be paramount to obligation to justice, except "in a struggle *such as ours* (where the brother tries to pierce the brother's heart)."

The political reason that Booth gave for hating Lincoln was that the president planned to make himself emperor or king, a political fantasy largely personal to Booth. His other "ideas" were standard Southern political truisms: much verbiage about "rights" and "honor" and "justice," all loved in the South, and all the hated target of Republicanism. In 1860 Booth still tied the good terms to unionism. "This union is my mother," he said, doubtless with some subthought of the woman who had provided the practical and emotional center in the chaotic Booth household. The threat to the union came only from the North.[45]

The South asked but its "just rights," especially the right to enslave without any-one raising treasonous doubts about this sacred institution, a "happiness" for blacks and "a social and political blessing for us." Given Lincoln's election and Northern willingness to let people who disliked slavery "spread their damned opinions throughout the land," Southern secession was wholly justified and would prove dis-astrous to the North. Booth's solution was the one that the South had demanded in 1835 and exulted over as beginning to happen in 1856 in the Senate and in Kansas: terroristic violence exported northward to stop antislavery people from speaking, writing, gathering, or voting. Such "rights" were acts of aggression which forced slaveholders to fear for their rights of property and which somehow induced "my very servant to poison me in my sleep." To question slavery was to attack trea-sonously the union; hence John Brown's execution was the proper model for han-dling all abolitionists. States' rights were sacred—except every basic human right of Northern states or citizens. If the North was unwilling to control its citizens with le-gal acts and executions that ended all discussion of slavery, extralegal violence was needed. "When treason weighs heavy in the scale," Booth boomed, "it is time for us to throw off all gentler feelings of our natures and summon resolution, pride, justice, ay, and revenge."

Booth reiterated the Southern argument of 1835 with coarse simplicity of mind. All who raised any questions about slavery were, in Booth's mind and spelling, "tradors" to the union and the Constitution. Thus the North, if it cared about "justice to the South" and calculated its own interests, would enact laws expunging basic lib-erties and/or take action to mob-kill and -cower anyone who showed a treasonous lack of enthusiasm for slavery. Booth's fustian was the bargain-basement version of what Hale's riot bill had triggered and what had been driving the North Republican-ward for years. "If the South would spare us its brag and bad rhetoric," wrote a Northerner in 1860 who shared some of Booth's racial and ethnic prejudice, "it would paralyze any Northern free soil party in three weeks."[46]

Booth's 1864 statement involved the same argument in more coherent and de-spairing form. Slavery remained "*one of the greatest blessings* (both for themselves and us)." The United States was "a favored nation . . . formed for the white, not the black man," despite the latter's lucky "elevation" by being owned by Southern-ers, who never showed as much harshness to their chattel as Northern fathers used on their sons. "Heaven knows," Booth assured the world, "no one would be willing to do more for the negro race than I," despite blacks' terrible tendency to "ingrati-tude." But what could highly theoretical philanthropists like Booth do when blacks were so inevitably incompetent that slavery was the only possible alternative to "an-nihilation"? The "very nomination of Abraham Lincoln" demanded that the South go to war, because whites would retain not "a single right" and would face "either extermination or slavery for *themselves* (worse than death)." The abolitionist Re-publicans "were the only traitors in the land," not because they wanted to end slav-ery but "on account of the means they have ever endeavored to use." Hadn't they shown "fiendish glee" when "enticed away" slaves had killed Booth's kindly neighbor, Edward Gorsuch, trying merely to collect his "property" in Pennsylvania? While all abolitionists should have been hanged with John Brown, Booth's admiration for Brown's courage led him to conclude, weirdly enough, that Brown would never have endangered the union over the slavery issue. Yet Booth, whose sense of "duty" and "justice" had by now led him to aid "in the capture and execution" of Brown, was "proud of my little share in the transaction." Despite the wondrous beauty of slavery to blacks, whites, and God, Booth, like most Southerners by this time, insisted that slavery had absolutely no relation to the war—which he also insisted would have not happened had the North not treasonously raised concerns about slavery.

Such intellectual argument was grounded in racial, class, and ethnic snobbery, grown partly of Booth's insecurities as a chivalric Southerner. Asia, who as a youngster had been "lonely together" with John Wilkes, loved her younger brother intensely, shared to some degree his pro-Southern, antiblack, and anti-other impulses, and remembered him in perceptive detail. She recalled the patience required to help her slow-learning brother memorize a dramatic part, one that a young black girl picked up quickly just by casually listening to them. "Hark to that thick-skulled darkey," said the boy. "She has sharper wits than I." Probably she had, so the inferiority of the "little black ape" or "monkey" must be innately racial, the product of that thick skull, because attention to evidence threatened comforting presumption. The kind of racial kindness Booth had in mind when he claimed that he more than any person would help the blacks, were that a possible task, is suggested in his childhood charities: he brought candy back from Baltimore, gathered black youngsters round, and threw it on the ground with the cry, "After it, nigs! Don't let the dogs get it!"[47]

He despised white workingmen and Irish immigrants, who were less accustomed than the "nigs" to grub in the dirt for candy he chose to throw. When very young, Booth offered his "first evidence of undemocratic feeling" by refusing to share a table with white workers. As a teenager Booth was an active Know-Nothing, despising these "pressing hordes of ignorant foreigners." During the Civil War, Asia reported, "nothing grated this fierce Southern partisan so sorely as beholding the easy enlistment of Irishmen who were wild to free the nagur." His hatred of Lincoln showed the same snarling snobbery: "This man's appearance, his pedigree, his coarse low jokes and anecdotes, are a disgrace to the seat he holds. Other brains rule the country."[48] Such invective was, again, Southern commonplace, but it took on an odd quality of transference in the mouth of this illegitimate son of a talented alcoholic who himself spent most of his free time in bars and bordellos.

Booth was clearly Lincoln's superior in appearance and had much charm and sweetness as well. Edwin, like others, remembered him as "of gentle, loving disposition, very boyish and full of fun." Asia's love of him lay in the same qualities, as probably did that of Lucy Hale, though her family destroyed and suppressed all records of this attachment. One wonders how Booth felt toward her. Booth told Asia he "undesignedly fell in love with a Senator's daughter," the very use of the adverb creating some doubt about the impression it was intended to give. Junius Brutus Jr. wrote Asia that John Wilkes was up all night in early February 1865 composing a valentine and poor letter to Miss Hale. Ellsler described Booth as "merry, jovial and liberal to a fault," fond of children's company, and always "manly" and "honest"— though Booth wholly deceived him, as he did a prostitute friend, with "remarkable enthusiastic outbursts, in the interest of the Union Forces." Apparently Booth never really left off acting, even with close business- and bedfellows.[49]

Asia's account of his early Confederate career, sketchy and based on what Booth told her as it is, is helpful. By mid-1863 Booth gave his time to the South where he could do "most good," not in the army but as a spy and a supplier of mind (his intelligence worth that of "twenty men," he claimed), money, and needed goods. His profession permitted him to move across enemy lines without much suspicion. He traveled to Kansas and to Canada to meet with proslavery agents, and in 1864 he came to Washington, probably at the Confederacy's behest, as the central figure in a plot to kidnap Lincoln, to be held for a large ransom: Confederate independence. When events on the battlefield outran this conspiracy, Booth and a few others decided to kill the "tools" they hated, Lincoln and William Seward;[50] the latter had been the South's second favorite Southern target since Preston Brooks felled Charles Sumner. What manly person, South Carolinian John Lyde Wilson had asked in his popular tract on dueling, would accept humiliating defeat when some gentlemanly violence could show where all blame lay?

Injured in his dramatic leap from box to stage in Ford's Theatre, Booth escaped with a companion to northern Virginia, where he hoped to be acclaimed and protected as a hero. Thomas Jones discovered the two men near his home, Booth in much pain and consumed with two ideas: escape and what the world said of his deed, "what mankind thought about it, what different classes thought about it." Jones told him that the act "was gratifying news to most men of Southern sympathies" but that he could expect little help. Jones brought Booth what he most craved, newspapers, and the assassin "lay there . . . reading what the world had to say about his case. He seemed never tired of information on that one subject." He must have felt sore-hearted at what he read. Whatever journalists' secret sympathies, Booth was given none of the verbal glorification showered on Preston Brooks for an act far less brave. The war had changed some things. When Booth was discovered and shot dead, his purported near-last words sounded like something from one of his melodramas; "Tell Mother I died for my country."[51] By this time, even he must have known that the country he killed and died for, that of slavery fenced round with violence, was dead.

Booth once gave his sister Asia a pike John Brown had planned to use to rescue slaves, a gift to Booth from Brown's most distinguished brief captive, Lewis Washington, of the "father of the country" family. He also told Asia that he'd acknowledged Brown as a hero on the scaffold when "he beheld the old eyes straining their anxious sight for the multitude he had vainly thought would rise to rescue him. . . . His heart must have broken when he felt himself deserted." Such was Booth's false projection into Brown's eyes, and the reflective prediction of his own final grief. His last words were, "Useless, useless."[52] Such words were a fitting epitaph over the long practice of using violence to quell questioning of slavery, that social hope for which his deed was a pathetic—and tragic—last act.

John Hale had calculated on the South's ready resort to verbal excess and commitment to riotous violence when rankled, John Brown calmly awaited his god's use of his death for the benefit of slaves, and John Wilkes Booth desperately sought his vindication as slavery's latest violent savior in the next newspaper. These sanctifying agents, secular and divine, had long told both North and South largely what they wanted to hear about the nation's one deeply divisive moral issue. The sectional attitudes of most Americans toward slavery hadn't changed a lot in the century, the South determined to keep it, the North wishing it somehow would go away, and both considering the union more important than any concern over the situation of African Americans. After the 1830s, when a few voices on both sides accurately pointed out that the national choice was between accepting or rejecting slavery as a central part of its economic, political, and ideological system, the settlement of silence crumbled stone by stone. Sectional commitments less changed than came into clearer focus, hardened by differing systems of and responses to social violence, ones in which Hale, Brooks, Brown, and Booth all worked. And the two systems of sectional violence, whetted on slavery, slowly whittled away the uneasy undiscussed consensus—until blood aplenty and numbers and money and maybe John Brown's terrifying, just god purged the land of slavery.

Useless?

Notes

AAS	American Antiquarian Society, Worcester, Massachusetts
AlaDAH	Alabama Department of Archives and History, Montgomery, Alabama
AusPL	Austin Public Library, Austin, Texas
BPL	Boston Public Library, Boston, Massachusetts
ChiHS	Chicago Historical Society, Chicago, Illinois
CinHS	Cincinnati Historical Society, Cincinnati, Ohio
CLUM	Clements Library, University of Michigan, Ann Arbor, Michigan
ColU	Books and Manuscripts, Columbia University Library, New York, New York
ConnHS	Connecticut Historical Society, Hartford Connecticut
CorU	Department of Manuscripts, Cornell University, Ithaca, New York
DU	Manuscript Department, Perkins Library, Duke University, Durham, North Carolina
EU	Special Collections, Woodruff Library, Emory University, Atlanta, Georgia
FC	Manuscript Department, The Filson Club, Louisville, Kentucky
HSMo	Historical Society of Missouri, St. Louis, Missouri
HSPa	Historical Society of Pennsylvania, Philadelphia, Pennsylvania
IllHS	Illinois Historical Society, Springfield, Illinois
JHL	John Hay Library, Brown University, Providence, Rhode Island
KanHS	Kansas State Historical Society, Topeka, Kansas
KyHS	Kentucky Historical Society, Frankfort, Kentucky
LC	Manuscript Division, Library of Congress, Washington, D.C.
LDSA	Latter-Day Saints Archives, Salt Lake City, Utah
LSU	Department of Archives and Manuscripts, Louisiana State University, Baton Rouge, Louisiana

MaHS	Massachusetts Historical Society, Boston, Massachusetts
MdHS	Maryland Historical Society, Baltimore, Maryland
MeHS	Maine Historical Society, Portland, Maine
MinnHS	Minnesota Historical Society, St. Paul, Minnesota
MissDAH	Mississippi Department of Archives and History, Jackson, Mississippi
NCDAH	North Carolina Department of Archives and History, Raleigh, North Carolina
NF	Manuscript Collection, Nook Farm, Hartford, Connecticut
NHHS	New Hampshire Historical Society, Concord, New Hampshire
NYCMA	New York City Municipal Archives, New York, New York
NYHS	New York Historical Society, New York, New York
OhHS	Ohio Historical Society, Columbus, Ohio
RIHS	Rhode Island Historical Society, Providence, Rhode Island
SCDAH	South Carolina Department of Archives and History, Columbia, South Carolina
SCHS	South Carolina Historical Society, Charleston, South Carolina
SHC	Southern Historical Collection, University of North Carolina, Chapel Hill, North Carolina
SHSMo	State Historical Society of Missouri, Columbia, Missouri
SHSWi	State Historical Society of Wisconsin, Madison, Wisconsin
SyU	Manuscripts Division, Arents Library, Syrcuse University, Syrcuse, New York
TenHS	Tennessee Historical Society, Nashville, Tennessee
TexSA	Archives, Texas State Library, Austin, Texas
UAla	Special Collections, University of Albama, University, Alabama
USC	Manuscript Division, South Caroliniana Library, University of South Carolina, Columbia, South Carolina
UTex	E. C. Barker Texas History Center, University of Texas, Austin, Texas
UVa	Manuscripts Department, University of Virginia Library, Charlottesville, Virginia
WRHS	Western Reserve Historical Society, Cleveland, Ohio
YU	Historical Manuscripts Collection, Sterling Library, Yale University

Periodicals

AlaHQ	*Alabama Historical Quarterly*
AmHAAR	*American Historical Association Annual Reports*
DR	*Democratic Review*
EssIHP	*Essex Institute Historical Publications*
HEdQ	*History of Education Quarterly*
IaJHP	*Iowa Journal of History and Politics*
IrAmHSJ	*Irish American Historical Society Journal*
JAH	*Journal of American History*
JLHS	*Journal of the Lancaster Historical Society*
JMissH	*Journal of Mississippi History*
JNH	*Journal of Negro History*
JSH	*Journal of Southern History*
JSocH	*Journal of Social History*
LaHQ	*Louisiana Historical Quarterly*
MoHR	*Missouri Historical Review*
MVHR	*Mississippi Valley Historical Review*
NAR	*North American Review*

NEQ	New England Quarterly
NR	Niles' Register
NYH	New York History
OhAHP	Ohio Archeological and Historical Publications
PaMHB	Pennsylvania Magazine of History and Biography
SA	Slavery and Abolition
SCGHM	South Carolina Genealogical and Historical Magazine
SCtHSY	Supreme Court Historical Society Yearbook
SWHQ	Southwestern Historical Quarterly
TenHM	Tennessee Historical Magazine
TKanHS	Transactions of the Kansas Historical Society
WisHSP	Wisconsin Historical Society Proceedings

Chapter One

1. Columbia, S.C. *Southern Times*, August 28, 1835; *Richmond Whig* in *Globe*, August 22, 1835; Philadelphia *National Gazette* in *National Intelligencer*, August 14, 1835, and in *NR* 48 (August 22, 1835): 434, 439. On September 5, 1835, Niles reported that he had found over 500 articles on different violent incidents in the past two weeks, clear proof that *"society seems everywhere unhinged"* (*NR* 49:1).

2. *New York Evening Post*, September 2, 1835. The Baltimore riots of 1812 were of major importance, and several cities, especially Boston, had eruptions in the mid-1820s. Two historians of New York City riots have argued that mobs were a constant of the pre-1830s and present rich evidence if one follows largely a "legal disturbance" definition of riot. They both, however, see 1834 as ushering in much more major conflict and, less convincingly, argue that the end of the eras they cover—in one case about 1840 and in the other the early 1830s—marked a shift from communal to class rioting. Paul O. Weinbaum, *Mobs and Demagogues: The New York Response to Collective Violence in the Early Nineteenth Century* (Ann Arbor, Mich., 1979); Paul A. Gilje, *The Road to Mobocracy: Popular Disorder in New York City, 1763–1834* (Chapel Hill, N.C., 1987).

3. Joseph Story to Mrs. Story, March 7, 1829, in William W. Story, *Life and Letters of Joseph Story* (Boston, 1851), 1:563; William Anders Smith, "Anglo-Colonial Society and the Mob, 1740–1775" (Ph.D. diss., Claremont Graduate School, 1965), 19–20. Sydney George Fisher, August 6, 1834, commented on the shift in usage from "mob" to "the people" to suggest the lower classes. *A Philadelphia Perspective: The Diary of Sydney George Fisher, Covering the Years 1834–37* (Philadelphia, 1967), 5, 13.

4. *Baltimore Republican*, August 20, 22, 1835; *Richmond Whig* in *Globe*, August 20, 1835. "Contagion" as cause was argued in the Columbia, S.C., *Southern Times*, August 28, 1835, and the *Delaware State Journal*, in *National Intelligencer*, August 14, 1835.

5. John William Ward, *Andrew Jackson, Symbol of an Age* (New York, 1962), 46–78; Mary W. M. Hargreaves, *The Presidency of John Quincy Adams* (Lawrence, Kans., 1985), 281–303.

6. James Parton, *Life of Andrew Jackson* (Boston, 1860), 1:439–88; Robert Remini, *Andrew Jackson and the Course of American Empire, 1767–1821* (New York, 1977), 116–43, 178–86.

7. *Journal of Commerce* in *Globe*, October 19, 1835. The *Globe* claimed that the *Journal*'s opinion was the real disgrace and that Americans would mob the editor were they not so "good-natured" and "law-abiding." Samuel Flagg Bemis offers a good account of the West Indies affair: *John Quincy Adams and American Foreign Policy* (New York, 1949), 457–68.

8. Samuel Gwin, one of Jackson's friends and political advisers, and Robert Walker, whom Jackson strongly supported for the Senate against a much more democratic candidate, were in the center of a nest of Jacksonian speculators in Indian lands. The papers of the New York and Mississippi Land Company, in the WiHS, make clear the political ties of one group of land speculators, who were delighted that much of the process of land sale went ahead under Jackson's friend, William Carroll, "to give tone and protection to the operation's going on." David Hubbard to John Bolton, November 1835; R. N. Bolton to Lewis Curtis, February 16, 1837.

9. The closest and least self-serving account of Jackson's convictions about removal is that of his close friend in the White House, William B. Lewis, printed in Parton, *Life of Jackson*, 3:501–8.

10. Andrew Shiner, "Diary," February 22, 1833, f.52, LC; *American Annual Register* 7 (1831–32): 114–120; Kenneth S. Greenberg, *Honor and Slavery* (Princeton, 1996), 20–22; Parton, *Life of Jackson*, 3:385–93; David Crockett, *A Narrative of the Life of David Crockett* (Philadelphia, 1834), 13. The book was ghostwritten by Thomas Chilton, seemingly from Crockett's oral account and under his close supervision, as James Shackford in *The Life of David Crockett* (Chapel Hill, N.C., 1955) makes clear.

11. *National Gazette*, March 15, 1834; John Munn, "Diaries," March 4, 1837, 12:49, ChiHS; *Baltimore Patriot* in *Portland Advertiser*, September 4, 1835. On the emptiness of the "will of the people" see Louis Hartz, *Economic Policy and Democratic Thought: Pennsylvania, 1776–1860* (Cambridge, Mass., 1948), 309–20, and Woodrow Wilson, *Division and Reunion, 1829–1889* (New York, 1898), 115.

12. Joseph Sill, "Diary," December 12, 1832, January 28, 1833, HSPa, suggests the puzzled response to Jackson's contradictory pronouncements. Richard Ellis argues that Jackson had a clear-cut ideology of states' rights tied to democracy rather than slavery. *The Union at Risk: Jacksonian Democracy, States' Rights and the Nullification Controversy* (New York, 1987), esp. 13–40, 187–98. Yet the politics of slavery was deeply involved, especially after the Jefferson-Jackson national successes undercut the old eighteenth-century idea of democratic localism and encouraged thinkers in both movements to unite democracy with Adam Smith's economic "natural law," that great sanctifier of all status quo private power, including slavery.

13. Abraham Lincoln, "Address before the Young Men's Lyceum," *Collected Work*, ed. Roy P. Basler (New Brunswick, N.J., 1953), 1:108–15; *Cincinnati Courier and Enquirer*, August 28, 1841; John Ashworth, *"Agrarians" and "Aristocrats": Party Political Ideology in the United States, 1837–46* (London, 1983), 131. Thomas R. Hietola argues the racist roots of Democtaric foreign policy in *Manifest Design: Anxious Aggrandizement in Late Jacksonian America* (Ithaca, N.Y., 1985).

14. Parton, *Life of Jackson*, 1:254–64; *History of Tennessee with a Sketch of Moore County* (Nashville, 1886), 806–7; Detroit, July 15–16, 1833; near Williamsport, Maryland, January 15–16, 1834; Baltimore, August 9–11, 1835.

15. Richard Maxwell Brown, *Strain of Violence: Historical Studies of American Violence and Vigilantism* (New York, 1975), 23; Eliphalet Price, "The Trial and Execution of Patrick O'Connor," *Palimpsest*, 1 (1920): 86–97; James Sterling, *Letters from the Slave States* (London, 1857), 282–83.

16. Andrew Jackson to Amos Kendall, August 9, 1835, Jackson Papers, LC. Jackson wrote in positive reply to Kendall's request for approval of his policy of letting postmasters intercept abolition mail.

17. *Globe*, August 20, October 5, December 21, 1835; *Baltimore Republican*, August 22, 1835.

18. *Baltimore Republican*, August 21, 1835; *Philadelphia Herald*, January 1, March 10,

1834; *Richmond Compiler*, February 16, 1834. The last writer, in good Southern fashion, insisted that, "though a cool and considerate man," he was "ready to whet my knife."

19. *Richmond Whig*, March 28, 1834; *Baltimore Republican*, April 18, 1834.

20. Deborah Logan, "Diary," February 16, 1834, HSPa. Parton offers a rich survey of these delegations and Jackson's often very hostile responses (*Life of Jackson*, 3:548–57).

21. Samuel F. B. Morse, *Imminent Dangers to the Free Institutions of the United States through Foreign Immigration* (New York, 1835), 3.

22. On the fraud see David Grimsted, "Robbing the Poor to Aid the Rich: The Baltimore Bank Swindle," *SCtHSY* (1987): 44–47. Ellicott's special deposits plan, requested by Taney in late 1832 and probably drafted then and shown to the president after his reelection, exists— misdated in pencil as "1837"—in the Taney Papers, LC. Taney and Jackson followed it except for the features of currency-banking control that Ellicott suggested.

23. Charles Sellers, *The Market Revolution: Jacksonian America, 1815–1846* (New York, 1991), follows the contours of Arthur Schlesinger's classic argument in *The Age of Jackson* (Boston, 1945), as well as broadens it, to contend that opposition to the rise of capitalism was central to Jacksonianism. Marvin Meyers, *The Jacksonian Persuasion: Politics and Belief* (Stanford, Calif., 1957), 76–107; Daniel Walker Howe, *The Political Culture of the American Whigs* (Chicago, 1979), 23–42, 96–122.

24. Barrington Moore, *Social Origins of Dictatorship and Democracy: Lord and Peasant in the Making of the Modern World* (Boston, 1966).

25. John C. Munroe, *Louis McLane* (New Brunswick, N.J., 1973), 415–24, chronicles the second-term struggle between Taney and McLane for Jackson's favor and appointment to the Supreme Court.

26. Andrew Jackson to A. J. Donaldson, April 23, 1835, Jackson Papers, LC.

27. William Lloyd Garrison, *Thoughts on African Colonization* (Boston, 1832); Lydia Maria Child, *An Appeal in Favor of Americans Called Africans* (Boston, 1833), 123–47; William Jay, *Inquiry into the Character and Tendency of the African Colonization and American Anti-Slavery Societies* (New York, 1835), 11–124; P. J. Staudenraus, *The African Colonization Movement, 1816–1865* (New York, 1961).

28. Bertram Wyatt-Brown, *Lewis Tappan and the Evangelical War against Slavery* (Cleveland, 1969), 68–86; Frank Luther Mott, *American Journalism* (New York, 1962), 200–228; Leonard Richards, *"Gentlemen of Standing and Property": Anti-Abolition Mobs in Jacksonian America* (New York, 1970), 20–27, 71–73.

29. Roberts Vaux to Frederick Tuckett, April 26, 1835, Vaux Papers, HSPa.

30. James L. Penick, *The Great Western Land Pirate: John Murrell in Legend and History* (Columbus, Mo., 1981), 94–105, 158–67.

31. W. Sherman Savage, *The Controversy over the Distribution of Abolition Literature, 1830–1860* (Washington, D.C., 1938), 8–26.

32. Glover Moore, *The Missouri Controversy, 1819–1821* (Lexington, Ky., 1952), 10–22; Charles B. Going, *David Wilmot, Free-Soiler* (New York, 1924), 94–155; Chaplain W. Morrison, *Democratic Politics and Sectionalism: The Wilmot Proviso Controversy* (Chapel Hill, N.C., 1967), 52–74, 180–81.

33. *Natchez Courier* in *Baltimore Republican*, December 19, 1835, January 8, 1836; Henry A. Foote, *Casket of Reminiscences* (Washington, D.C., 1874), 257; James E. Cutler, *Lynch-Law: An Investigation into the History of Lynching in the United States* (New York, 1905), 114–15. The Mississippi *Advocate of Liberty* suggested that the crime of the man killed in jail was that he revealed the emptiness of the evidence against one man brutally murdered in the summer's insurrection scare. Printed in Thomas Brothers, *The United States of North America as They Are* (London, 1840), 510.

34. Small fines were levied in Portland, Maine, and Montpelier and Newbury, Vermont.

35. *New Orleans Commercial Bulletin* in *Kennebec* (Me.) *Journal,* August 8, 1835.
36. Patrick Sharkey and James B. Kilbourn to Gov. Hiram Runnels, July 7, 1835, MissSDAH; *Lexington* (Ky.) *Intelligencer* in Brothers, *United States,* 509.
37. Helen Catterall, ed., *Judicial Cases Concerning American Slavery and the Negro* (Washington, D.C., 1926–37), 3:201, 225–26, 301–2, offers typical examples from Alabama and Mississippi, the latter written by William Sharkey, who showed rare human understanding of the law's need to acknowledge the powerlessness of slaves.
38. Foote, *Casket of Reminiscences,* 259–61.
39. Philadelphia, mid-July 1835; Colerain, Massachusetts, and New York City, November 1835; Orville, New York, February 1835.
40. "Humanity" letter, July 24, 1835, *Vicksburg Register,* August 13, 1835; letter from a Ohio Methodist describing scene he witnessed in Yazoo County, Mississippi, July 1835, Marius Robinson Clipping Book, WRHS.
41. Richards, *"Gentlemen of Standing,"* 52–54. The *Globe,* September 16, 1835, offered a résumé of Southern insistence that illustrations in abolition journals were intended to excite slaves "to revolt and massacre." Jackson's 1835 message claimed that the pictures were "addressed to the passions of the slaves." Quoted in Jean Fagan Yellin, *Women and Sisters: Antislavery Feminists in American Culture* (New Haven, 1984), 4. Yellin deals closely with abolitionist imagery, 3–26. The fullest survey of the controversy's iconography is Phillip Lapansky, "Graphic Discord: Abolitionist and Anti-Abolitionist Images," in Jean Fagan Yellin and John C. Van Horne, eds., *The Abolitionist Sisterhood: Women's Political Culture in Ante-Bellum America* (Ithaca, 1994), 201–30.
42. *Richmond Enquirer,* July 28, August 14, 1835; John Tyler, "Speech at Gloucester, Virginia, 1835," in Lyon Gardiner Tyler, *Letters and Times of the Tylers* (Richmond, 1884–94), 1:572–81; Richards, *"Gentlemen of Standing,"* 52–71.
43. *Washington* (D.C.) *Mirror,* August 8, 1835.
44. William Jay to Roberts Vaux, November 16, 1835, Vaux Papers, HSPa.
45. *Richmond Enquirer,* July 21, August 14, 25, 1835. The last quote was in a letter by "H," a Virginian, first published in the Philadelphia *National Gazette,* August 21, 1835. William Freehling argues, quite wrongly, that few arguments for slavery as a positive good or demands that the North curb basic liberties came from outside South Carolina until the 1850s. *The Road to Disunion: Secessionists at Bay* (New York, 1990), 290–95.
46. *NR* 48 (August 29, 1835): 461–67, reprinted a host of these resolves. Typical of the immediate Southern response to them was the reaction of the *Clinton* (Miss.) *Gazette,* September 19, 1835, which greeted them as "a matter of exultation to the South," insuring that "ere long, the abolitionists will be intimidated and silenced."
47. John Quincy Adams, *Memoirs of John Quincy Adams, Comprising Portions of his Diary, 1795 to 1848,* ed. Charles Francis Adams (Philadelphia, 1874–77), 9 (August 20, 1835): 260; *Richmond Enquirer,* June 9, July 28 (reporting New York City resolves of July 22), August 14, 1835; *Petersburg* (Va.) *Constellation,* August 16, 1835; Petersburg, Virginia, resolves of August 10, 1835, in *Baltimore Gazette,* August 12, 1835.
48. *Charleston Patriot,* September 9, 1835; Boston Meeting of August 21, 1835, in *Boston Centinal,* August 22, 1835.
49. Woodville, Mississippi, meeting, July 25, 1835, in *Woodville Republican,* August 1, 1835; *New Orleans Commercial Bulletin,* January 23, 1836; *Richmond Whig* in *Vicksburg Register,* August 27, 1835; *Alexandria Gazette,* September 3, 1835; *Richmond Enquirer,* August 14, 18, 1835.
50. *Kennebec* (Me.) *Journal,* August 26, 1835. One finds similar images of bloodbath or explosion in most of the Southern gubernational messages of late 1835 or early 1836, such as those of Governor White of Louisiana and Governor McDuffie of South

Carolina, both printed in the *New Orleans Commercial Bulletin*, December 8, 1835, January 5, 1836.

51. "Calm Observer" in Columbia, S.C., *Southern Times*, October 2, 1835; John Quitman, *Message of the Governor to the State of Mississippi and to Both Houses of the Legislature* (Jackson, 1836), 5–6.

52. Letter from New York, September 12, 1835, in Augusta (Ga.) *Chronicle*, reprinted in *NR* 49 (October 3, 1835): 77.

53. Columbia, S.C., *Southern Times*, October 16, 1835; *Richmond Enquirer*, August 25, 1835.

54. *New York Journal of Commerce* and *New York American*, August 27, 1835; *New York Evening Post*, August 14, 27, 1835.

55. Richmond resolves, August 4, 1835, in *Enquirer*, August 7, 1835; *Charleston Courier* in *New York Evening Post*, October 14, 1835. *New York Courier and Enquirer* and *Boston Mercantile Journal*, quoted in James M. W. Yerrington, ed., *Proceedings of the Anti-Slavery Society . . . on The Twentieth Anniversary of the Mob of October 21* (Boston, 1855), 14–15; *New York Times*, August 19, 1835; *Baltimore Gazette*, August 21, 1835; *New Bedford* (Mass.) *Mercury*, October 3, 1835; Columbia, S.C. *Southern Times*, July 10, 1835; George McDuffie, *Annual Message,* in *New Orleans Commercial Bulletin*, December 8, 1835.

56. October editorials in the *Boston Mercantile Journal* and *Commercial Gazette, Cincinnati Evening Post,* and *Boston Chronicle* quoted in Yerrington, *Twentieth Anniversary,* 15–17; James Henry Hammond to Mordecai M. Noah, August 19, 1835, Hammond Papers, LC.

57. Amos Kendall to Andrew Jackson, August 7, 1835, and Jackson to Kendall, August 9, 1835, Jackson Papers, LC.

58. Kendall to Alfred Huger, August 9, 1835, in *National Intelligencer*, August 11, 1835; Philip Hone, *Diary of Philip Hone,* ed. Allan Nevins (New York, 1927), August 13, 1835, 155.

59. Amos Kendall to J. D. Townes, August 20, 1835, and to Samuel Gouvernor, August 22, 1835, in *NR* 40 (September 5, 1835): 7–9; Samuel Gwin to Martin Van Buren, August 15, 1835, Van Buren Papers, MissDAH. The Van Buren Papers, LC, contain several letters from the South telling the candidate that his election was dependent on appeasing Southern fears of abolition.

60. *Globe*, September 2, 1835; *New York Times*, August 19, 1835; *Kennebec* (Me.) *Journal,* August 19, 1835, and, quoting the *New York American*, September 16, 1835.

61. *New York Commercial Advertiser*, August 21, 1835; *Lexington Observer* in *Vicksburg Register*, October 1, 1835; *U.S. Telegraph* in *Globe*, October 3, 1835; *Boston Advocate* in *New York Evening Post*, October 2, 1835.

62. *New York Evening Post*, August 26, 27, 28, September 1, 2, 4, 8, 10, 1835.

63. *New York Evening Post*, September 21, 28, 1835; *Report of the Postmaster General,* 24th Cong., 1st sess., Senate, December 1, 398–993; Richard John, *Spreading the News: The American Postal System from Franklin to Morse* (Cambridge, Mass., 1995) 257–83.

64. Albany Resolves in *Globe*, September 9, 10, 1835; *New York Evening Post*, September 10, 1835; *Richmond Enquirer* in *NR* 49 (October 3, 1835): 75; Martin Van Buren to William Schley, September 10, 1835, in *Augusta* (Ga.) *Courier,* reprinted in *Globe*, October 6, 1835.

65. *Richmond Whig* in *NR* 49 (October 3, 1835): 75. The *Baton Rouge Gazette*, October 17, 1835, said the Albany resolves, trumpeted as Van Buren's "confession of faith," showed the South "the writing on the wall" because they evaded advocating "that legislation which is indispensible to the existence of the Republic."

66. *NR* 49 (October 3, 1835): 65, 80. On August 28 the *Post* first attacked the *Argus* for its pro-mob stance and on October 1 claimed that it, unlike the *New York Times,* would never grind out "whatever music they are bid." The *Globe* waited until September 9 to point out the

Post's "errors and eccentricities," a few days after the usual silencer of dissent, loss of federal patronage, proved ineffective. On September 18, the *Globe* wrote the *Post* out of the party entirely for its "eutopian temper" in defense of abolitionists' right to speak and publish.

67. *New York Evening Post*, October 3, 10, 12, 15, and 30, 1835. The "radicals" were the object of attack of Jackson, Van Buren, Kendall, and every other administration leader, in stark contrast to the alignment suggested by Arthur Schlesinger and others (*Age of Jackson*, 19–92).

68. *New York Evening Post*, September 4, 7, 15, 17 (quoting the *Charleston Courier*), 19, 1835.

69. New Haven resolves of September 9, chaired by Jacksonian governor Henry W. Edwards. The resolutions of Chautauqua, New York, endorsed Kendall's positions, denied Congress's authority over slavery in the District of Columbia, and hinted that abolitionists should be extradited to the South, while an Oneida grand jury, after indicting leading abolitionists, urged the public to destroy their communications networks. *Globe*, October 8, 22; 1835; *New York Evening Post*, October 12, 15, 29, 1835.

70. *Globe*, September 27, 1835. There is a fuller account of these riots in the next chapter.

71. North Carolina legislative resolves, in the *New Orleans Commercial Bulletin*, December 11, 1835. This paper reported the annual messages of Southern governors, most of whom demanded that the North act to prevent what Clement Clay of Alabama called "a demonic spirit of hostility in our own households."

72. *Baltimore Republican*, January 22, 1836; *Globe*, October 29, 30, 1835; *New York American*, January 21, 1836, printed Marcy's address, which Van Buren sent immediately to Southern leaders; William Rives to Martin Van Buren, January 29, 1836, Van Buren Papers, LC; W. Sherman Savage, *Abolition Literature*, 51–52, and John Niven, *Martin Van Buren: The Romantic Age in American Politics* (New York, 1983), 399–400; Elizur Wright to Theodore Weld, March 24, May 19, 1836, in Gilbert Barnes and Dwight Dumond, eds., *Letters of Theodore Dwight Weld, Angelina Grimké and Sarah Grimké* (New York, 1934), 1:280–81, 304; *Account of the Interviews between the Anti-Slavery Society and the Committee of the Legislature of Massachusetts* (Boston, 1836).

73. Andrew Jackson, "Seventh Annual Message," in J. D. Richardson, ed., *Messages and Papers of the Presidents* (Washington, 1896), 4:1394; Clyde N. Wilson, ed., *The Papers of John C. Calhoun* (Columbia, S.C., 1980), 13:53–67, 144–69; W. Sherman Savage, *Abolition Literature*, 61–81. Donna Lee Dickerson, *The Course of Tolerance: Freedom of the Press in Nineteenth-Century America* (New York, 1990), 81–113, explores these issues.

74. Duff Green, "Prospectus," September 15, 1835, in *Woodville* (Miss.) *Republican*, October 31, 1835; *Augusta* (Ga.) *Chronicle*, August 26, 1835.

75. *Globe*, August 22, September 16, 1835; *Richmond Enquirer*, August 4, 1835; *Baltimore Republican*, February 3, 1836.

76. *Richmond Whig* in *New York Evening Post*, September 4, 1835; *Natchez Free Trader* in *Mississippian*, October 16, 1835.

77. *Mississippian*, August 21, 1835; *New Orleans Courier*, August 27, 1835, March 4, 1836; *Vicksburg Register*, November 19, 1835; *NR* 49 (February 6, 1836): 387.

78. *Alexandria Gazette* in *Baltimore American*, September 19, 1835; *NR* 49 (September 19, October 3, 1835): 33, 65–66; *Georgetown* (D.C.) *Metropolitan* in *New York Evening Post*, September 11, 1835; *Globe*, October 7, 1835. The *Globe* began to claim, wholly inaccurately, that it was only nullifiers who abused the North.

79. *Lowell Times*, September 25, 1835, and *Richmond Compiler* in *NR* 49 (October 3, 1835): 74–75; Richmond, Virginia, meeting September 24, 1835, in *Globe*, October 2, 1835; Governor Vroom's message in the *New York Evening Post*, November 11, 12, 1835.

80. *NR* 49 (October 3, 1835): 65, and quoting the *Boston Courier*. William Lee Miller

covers the most lasting of the civil liberties controversies in Congress, the gag rule, and John Quincy Adams's ability to turn Southern fury to antislavery advantage in *Arguing about Slavery: The Great Battle in the United States Congress* (New York, 1996).

81. *New Hampshire Patriot* in *Baltimore Republican*, August 24, 1835; *Globe*, August 24, 1835. Antiblack riots occurred in Philadelphia, July 13, 1835, and in Pittsburgh and Burlington in August.

82. Letter in the *Rochester Democrat* in the *U.S. Telegraph*, August 10, 1835; *NR*, 48 (August 1, 1835): 380-81; Wendell Phillips, *Speeches, Lectures, and Letters* (Boston, 1891), 2:11, 25–26.

83. *Globe*, October 3, 1835.

84. "Veto" in *New York Evening Post*, October 1, 1835.

85. "Plebian" in *New York Evening Post*, August 26, 1835. On October 16, 1835, Plebian sent in a letter from "Draco Slick of Mobville, Lynchiana Territory" attacking the "cold and calculating" town resolutions of the North which failed to express "a manly determination to hang, draw and quarter all who dared to open their lips on the subject of slavery" as "the Southern Chivalry" wished. Slick lamented the attitudes of the "vulgar multitude" in the North, except for "that part of the mercantile community which has been enlightened by their pecuniary intercourse with the high-minded South."

Chapter Two

1. James A. Thome and John W. Alvord to Theodore Weld, February 9, 1836, in Gilbert Barnes and Dwight Dummond, eds., *Letters of Theodore Dwight Weld, Angelina Grimké, and Sarah Grimké* (New York, 1934), 1:256–62.

2. *Marion* (Ohio) *Visitor* in *NR* 57 (October 14, 1839): 41; James H. Anderson, *The Life and Letters of Thomas Anderson and His Wife . . .* (Columbus, Ohio, 1904), 52–113. Bill had lived in Marion for a year and was "very industrious, lively, good-natured, and withal so competent" as a laborer, butcher, barber, and fiddler that all liked him. Marshall, a Methodist, led the riot of Quakers who crowded into the room where the Virginians retreated, while Marshall let Bill out the back. One Quaker tripped and wrestled with slavecatcher Robert McLanahan so Bill could get away. Anderson's account of this riot is the best for any fugitive slave rescue: straightforward, detailed, and with a wealth of newspapers quoted: the *Visitor* justifying the mob as proving "a band of armed assailants are not able to trample on our laws with impunity" and claiming that many anti-abolitionists took part; McLanahan's version of events from the *Richmond Whig*, October 26, 1839, and state newspaper reaction, with the Democratic papers stressing their racist argument that this showed how far Whigs/abolitionists "intend to go to place the black man on an equal footing with the white" (*Ohio Statesman*, February 17, 1840).

3. Wendell P. and Francis J. Garrison, *William Lloyd Garrison: The Story of His Life*, 4 vols. (New York, 1885–89); Parker Pillsbury, *Acts of the Anti-Slavery Apostles* (Concord, N.H., 1883); George W. Julian, *The Life of Joshua Giddings* (Chicago, 1892); Louis Filler, *The Crusade against Slavery, 1830–1860* (New York, 1960); Ralph Korngold, *Two Friends of Man* (Boston, 1950); Walter M. Merrill, *Against Wind and Tide* (Cambridge, Mass., 1963); Merton L. Dillon, *Benjamin Lundy and the Struggle for Negro Freedom* (Urbana, Ill., 1966); Dorothy Sterling, *Ahead of Her Time: Abby Kelley and the Politics of Anti-Slavery* (New York, 1991); Carolyn Karcher, *The First Woman in the Republic: A Cultural Biography of Lydia Maria Child* (Durham, N.C., 1994).

4. David Donald, *Lincoln Reconsidered* (New York, 1956), 19–36, and *Charles Sumner and the Coming of the Civil War* (New York, 1961); John L. Thomas, *The Liberator: William*

Lloyd Garrison (Boston, 1963); David Brion Davis, *The Slave Power Conspiracy and the Paranoid Style* (Baton Rouge, 1969); Stanley Elkins, *Slavery: A Problem in American Institutional and Intellectual Life* (Chicago, 1958), 140–206.

5. Gilbert H. Barnes, *The Anti-Slavery Impulse, 1830–44* (New York, 1933); Dwight L. Dumond, *Anti-Slavery* (Ann Arbor, Mich., 1961); William and Jane Pease, *Bound with Them in Chains: A Biographical History of the Anti-Slavery Movement* (Westport, Conn., 1972); Martin Duberman, ed., *The Anti-Slavery Vanguard: New Essays on the Abolitionists* (Princeton, 1965) and *James Russell Lowell* (Boston, 1966); Howard Zinn, *The Politics of History* (Boston, 1970), 137–66; Aileen Kraditer, *Means and Ends in American Abolition: Garrison and His Critics on Strategy and Tactics, 1834–50* (New York, 1969).

6. Bertram Wyatt-Brown, *Lewis Tappan and the Evangelical War against Slavery* (Cleveland, 1969); Lewis Perry, *Radical Abolitionism, Anarchy, and the Government of God in Antislavery Thought* (Cornell, 1973); Peter Walker, *Moral Choices: Memory, Desire, and Imagination in Nineteenth-Century American Abolition* (Baton Rouge, 1978); Robert Abzug, *Cosmos Crumbling: American Reform and the Religious Imagination* (New York, 1994); David Brion Davis, *The Problem of Slavery in the Age of Revolution, 1770–1823* (Cornell, 1975); Louis S. Gerteis, *Morality and Utility in American Antislavery Reform* (Chapel Hill, N.C., 1987); John Ashworth, *Slavery, Capitalism, and Politics in the Antebellum Republic* (Cambridge, Eng., 1995), 125–91; Lawrence J. Friedman, *Gregarious Saints: Self and Community in American Abolitionism, 1830–1870* (Cambridge, Eng., 1982), 2–5. Friedman states most strongly the idea that abolitionists "must be studied neither as figures of influence nor as radicals who failed. They were evangelical missionaries who contributed quite inadvertently and secondarily to sectional tensions and the Civil War." Such a conclusion I think wholly wrong; certainly the "must" is indefensible.

7. Ronald G. Walters stresses the ordinariness of abolitionist values in *The Antislavery Appeal: American Abolitionism after 1830* (Baltimore, 1976); and Robert Fogel gives some attention to abolition actions in relation to political context in *Without Consent or Contract: The Rise and Fall of American Slavery* (New York, 1989), 281–387.

8. Merton I. Dillon, *Elijah Lovejoy, Abolitionist Editor* (Urbana, Ill., 1961); Edward Beecher, *Narrative of Riots at Alton in Connection with the Death of Rev. Elijah P. Lovejoy* (Alton, Ill., 1838).

9. In the urban riots which combined anti-abolition and antiblack elements, official and press anger against abolitionists was prevalent, but the level of destructiveness of the mob almost always accelerated when blacks became the victims.

10. A student in Lane Seminary to Lyman Beecher, May 17, 18, 1838, in Barbara Cross, ed., *Autobiography of Lyman Beecher* (Cambridge, 1961), 2:431. Philadelphians especially stressed amalgamation as cause and excuse: Sydney George Fisher, *A Philadelphia Perspective: The Diary of Sydney George Fisher, Covering the Years 1834–37* (Philadelphia, 1967), May 19, 1838, 50. Augustus Pleasanton, "Diary," May 17, 18, 1838, HSPa; John S. Warner, *Report of the Committee on the Police* (Philadelphia, 1838), 12. Foreigners who described abolition riots tended to emphasize strongly racist fears of amalgamation as cause: Gustav de Beaumont, *Marie; or, Slavery in the United States*, trans. Barbara Chapman (Stanford, 1958), 117–31, 243–52; Edward Abdy, *Journal of a Residence and a Tour of the United States . . .* (London, 1835), 1:354–68; 3:316–45; Thomas Brothers, *The United States of America as They Are* (London, 1840), 197–98.

11. *New York Commercial Advertiser*, June 13, 21, 1834; *Courier and Enquirer*, June 23–26, and July 7, 1834; Linda Kerber, "Abolitionists and Amalgamators: The New York City Race Riots of 1834," *NYH* 48 (January 1967): 28–39; Paul O. Weinbaum, *Mobs and Demagogues: The New York Response to Collective Violence in the Early Nineteenth Century* (Ann Arbor, Mich., 1979), 21–33.

12. The anger against foreigners, like that over amalgamation, was certainly an emotional additive to the attack on abolition, as in a much lesser way was the occasional huffing about abolition's incorporation of women and children. Certainly British and Irish temperance supporters bothered no one seriously, nor did that movement's much more extensive integration of women and children into its public campaigns ever earn much denunciation.

13. Thompson mobs: Portland, Maine, in August and four in Massachusetts: Lynn and New Bedford in August, Abington in September, and Salem in October. May mobs: Haverhill, Massachusetts, in August, Montpelier and Rutland, Vermont, in October. Weld mobs in Ohio: Circleville, February; Putnam, March; Granville, May; Chardon and Painesville, October.

14. Leonard Richards, *"Gentlemen of Standing and Property": Anti-Abolition Mobs in Jacksonian America* (New York, 1970), 74–81, stresses the tie between organizational effort and mobs correctly but in overstated terms. In only three cases did a mob attack an attempt to organize a society divorced from a primary effort to lecture (or to set up a press). Richards's graph for Illinois suggests the problem: in that state mobs may have increased as antislavery societies formed, but all or almost all of the riots were in Alton, attacking not organization effort but Elijah Lovejoy's newspaper. Commonly the correlation was in fact the reverse of the Richards's pattern: attacks on speakers or the press precipitated local organizations.

15. Weld was hurt in Circleville, Ohio, in February, the lecture notes were destroyed in Worcester, Massachusetts, in August, and the signboard in Boston in October, all 1835.

16. That most anti-abolition riots in the second half of 1835 were calculated gestures to appease the South explains much of the difference in Boston's communal response to its convent and its abolition riot that Theodore M. Hammett explores in "Two Mobs of Jacksonian Boston: Ideology and Interest," *JAH* 62 (1976): 845–68.

17. Quoted in *NR* 49 (October 3, 1835): 72; *The Mob at Troy* (Troy, 1836). On the Jacksonian's proslavery stance, see Richard H. Brown, "The Missouri Crisis, Slavery, and the Politics of Jacksonianism," *South Atlantic Quarterly* 65 (1966): 55–72; Thomas B. Alexander, *Sectional Stress and Party Strength* (Nashville, 1967).

18. William S. Lincoln, comp., *Alton Trials* (New York, 1838).

19. Flamen Ball to Salmon P. Chase, September 4, 1841, Chase Papers, HSPa; Henry W. Wilson, *History of the Rise and Fall of the Slave Power Conspiracy in America* (Boston, 1872–77), 1:556–57.

20. Nantucket Island, Massachusetts, August 1842; Portland, Maine, September 1842; Hancock, New Hampshire October 1842; Harwich, Massachusetts, September 1848. The first three riots suggest "contagion," the action of one community strengthening the option of riot in another.

21. This batch of riots concentrated in Boston, Philadelphia, upstate New York, and Ohio, all antislavery centers where anti-abolition riot occurred in 1835–36.

22. Weld to Arthur Tappan, Joshua Leavitt, and Elizur Wright Jr., November 22, 1833, in Barnes and Dumond, *Weld-Grimké Letters*, 1:120. For a fuller outline of Weld and his followers' intellectual positions and tactics, see Weld to J. F. Robinson, May 11, 1836, in ibid., 1:295–98.

23. Cassius M. Clay, *Life of Cassius Marcellus Clay: Memoirs, Writings and Speeches . . .* (Cincinnati, 1886), 55-56.

24. John Quincy Adams, *Memoirs of John Quincy Adams Containing Portions of his Diary From 1745 to 1848,* ed. Charles Francis Adams (Philadelphia, 1874–77), August 10, 1835, 9:251; letter to the citizens of Bangor, Maine, July 4, 1843, in the *British and Foreign Anti-Slavery Reporter*, September 20, 1843, 169–70; Thomas H. Gallaudet to Leonard Bacon, May 14, 1838, Bacon Papers, YU.

25. Elizur Wright to Leonard Bacon, April 27, 1837, Bacon Papers, YU.

26. *Liberator* 1 (May 28, 1831): 22.

27. 1861 Syracuse Anti-Slavery Society Statement and Resolves, reprinted in Samuel May, *Recollections of Our Anti Slavery Conflict* (Boston, 1869), 393–96.

28. Barnes, *Anti-Slavery Impulse*, most thoroughly deals with this term borrowed from the English movement, esp. 48–49, 66.

29. Child, *Appeal*, 95–97; American Anti-Slavery Society to Weld, February 20, 1834, and Weld to J. F. Robinson, May 1, 1836, in Barnes and Dumond, *Weld-Grimké Letters*, 1:125–26, 295–98.

30. Elkins, *Slavery*, 193–200.

31. May, *Recollections*, 174–77. Southern moderates on slavery like Henry Clay denounced Channing's "arrogance and presumptiousness" as much as that of other abolitionists. To John Pendleton Kennedy, May 16, 1839, Kennedy Papers, Peabody Institute, Baltimore.

32. William Ellery Channing, *Slavery* (Boston, 1835), 130–48, 164–65. The *Baltimore Gazette*, October 5, 1835, reported Charles Leete Stone's original story and Thompson's reply in the *Boston Atlas*. Stone claimed a student said that Thompson had told him "every slave should cut his master's throat," but he couldn't remember where or with whom this private interview occurred.

33. Channing, *Slavery*, 54–62; John L. Thomas, *Liberator*, 211–15.

34. Adams, *Memoirs*, January 8, 1836, 9:268.

35. Bacon's life is covered eulogistically in Theodore Davenport Bacon, *Leonard Bacon, A Statesman of the Church* (New Haven, 1931).

36. Beecher left Lane Seminary when the trustees moved to repress the students' discussing abolition and stayed away until the policy was promulgated, thinking he could remain in the "rebels'" good graces by calling them "a set of glorious good fellows," and especially anxious that wealthy Lewis Tappan not think he opposed them. Cross, *Autobiography of Lyman Beecher*, 2:327–9; Beecher to Weld, October 8, 1834, and Huntington Lyman to James Thome, October 4, 1834, in Barnes and Dumond, *Weld-Grimké Letters*, 1:170–73. A letter from Henry Ward Beecher to Chauncy Howard, November 1834, Beecher Papers, NF, repeated the family line: the students were self-indulgent, Beecher was a reasonable abolitionist, Lane Seminary was flourishing despite the "Locomotive" students, and free discussion was never threatened, "if they will not carry it out of all proportion." Lawrence T. Lesick, *The Lane Rebels: Evangelicalism and Antislavery in Antebellum America* (New Jersey, 1980) covers the conflict carefully.

37. Catharine Beecher, *An Essay on Slavery and Abolition with a Reference to the Duty of American Females* (Philadelphia, 1837), 38, 7, 27–31. Kathryn Kish Sklar argues that Beecher may have defended her father particularly strongly, in part because she felt drawn toward acts of "symbolic paracide." *Catharine Beecher: A Study of American Domesticity* (New York, 1973), 46–47, 134–37.

38. Leonard Bacon's letters richly chronicle the hatred of moderate antislavery people for abolitionists largely because of how clearly they illumined the emptiness of any uncontroversial answer. Walter Laurie offered Bacon a large salary to head the Colonization Society in New England, July 25, 1834, and a series of letters from late January 1835 show the pressure and arguments used to induce Bacon to lead the moderate American Union against the abolitionists. E. A. Andrews reported everyone's "depression of spirits" about its success when Bacon refused. Andrews to Bacon, March 22, 1835. Bacon Papers, YU.

39. Leonard Bacon to Joel Hawes, March 22, 1836, Bacon Papers, YU. Over a year later, Bacon was being congratulated for his anti-abolition sermons.

40. Leonard Bacon, *Review of Pamphlets on Slavery and Colonization* (New Haven, 1833). On pages 6–7, Bacon offers a good example of his care in exposing Garrison's care-

lessness. He shows how Garrison shoved together as one statement three sentences taken from different writers in a pamphlet. Yet, despite Bacon's strong and valid criticisms, he also carefully ducked the larger issues Garrison raised.

41. Birney memorandum, December 22, 1838, in Dwight L. Dumond, ed., *The Letters of James Gillespie Birney* (New York, 1938), 1:478–81.

42. Wright to Bacon, February 24, 1837, and several partial drafts of a Bacon reply, the fullest fragment dated May 1, 1837, Bacon Papers, YU.

43. The first time Bacon in his letters suggested more opposition to those who insisted that blacks be removed from the country than to abolitionists was in a letter to C. S. Henry, May 14, 1838, Bacon Papers, YU; Leonard Bacon, *Slavery, Discussed in Occasional Essays, from 1833 to 1846* (New York, 1846); Theodore Davenport Bacon, *Bacon*, 233–34. Part of Bacon's conservatism related to his insistence that blacks would probably not survive in the United States except in the hottest climates, an idea that may have appealed to Lincoln, too.

44. May, *Recollections*, 37–38; Ralph Ellison, *Invisible Man* (New York, 1947), 13–14, 438.

45. May, *Recollections*, 37; John L. Thomas, *Liberator*, 224–34, 452–59; Anthony Benezet, *A Short Account of the Part of Africa Inhabited by Negroes . . .* (Philadelphia, 1762), 43. The strongest attack on charges of "abolitionist extremism" was Wendell Phillips, "Philosophy of the Abolitionist Movement" in *Speeches, Letters, and Lectures* (Boston, 1884), 98–153. It is also the best example of "vituperation" against Northern nonabolitionists.

46. Cassius M. Clay, *Writings of Cassius Marcellus Clay*, ed. Horace Greely (New York, 1848), 271. Historians commonly quote, in proof of Garrison's vileness of pen, less what he said about slavery than his justification of the use of biblically strong language, i.e., Elkins, *Slavery*, 193.

47. Stanley Harrold, *Gamaliel Bailey and Antislavery Union* (Kent, Ohio, 1986), 81–108, 184–196. Next to Greeley's *Tribune*, the *National Era* had the widest nationwide circulation, steadily growing from 11,000 to 25,000 between 1847 and 1853, and exchanging with sixty papers in slave states, largely because, in the words of an Illinois farmer, "It is a candid paper and hard to beat" for its political or literary content. Lewis Tappan to John Scoble, November 14, 1847, January 8, 1853, in Annie H. Able and Frank J. Klingberg, eds., *A Side Light on Anglo-American Relations, Furnished by the Correspondence of Lewis Tappan and Others* (Washington, 1927), 228–310; Lucius Reynolds to Asa Talcott, December 1, 1850, Talcott Family Papers, NF.

48. *Liberator*, January 1, 1831. James Lakey of Cincinnati reported one Garrison speech replete with careless errors, such as statements that Essex County, Massachusetts, produced more than South Carolina and that Thomas Jefferson wrote the Constitution. "Diary," April 19, 20, 1853, CinHS.

49. Donald, *Lincoln Reconsidered*, 19–36; Richards, "*Gentlemen of Standing*," 131–55.

50. Richards, "*Gentlemen of Standing*," 150–52; Paul A. Gilje, *The Road to Mobocracy: Popular Disorder in New York City, 1763–1834* (Chapel Hill, N.C., 1987), 164–66; Isaac Stearns, *Right and Wrong in Mansfield, Massachusetts* (Pawtucket, Mass., 1837).

51. The information on this riot and its participants comes from three local histories: Charles H. S. Davis, *A History of Wallingford, Connecticut* (Meriden, Conn., 1870), 231, 417, 430–31, 503–5, 549–51, 581–82, 591; Robert E. Mitchell, *A History of New Haven County, Connecticut* (New Haven, 1893), 420–21; Franklin Curtis, *Meriden, Connecticut's Early History* (Hartford, 1923), 1:225, 253, 357–62; 2:107, 113, 121, 361–62, 400–409, 555. Rev. Arthur Granger was in an immediate sense a victim of the riot. Despite a majority of twenty-eight to fifteen congregant petitioners in his favor and the support of a Congregational consociation in 1838, which argued that the church was the proper place to consider slavery like "all subjects that pertain to the relationships men sustain to each other and to God," Granger

was dismissed from his Meriden pastorate in the summer of 1838. Nine months later he became minister of a larger church in Middletown, Connecticut, and from there was called to Providence, Rhode Island's High Street Church (Charles H. S. Davis, *Wallingford*, 231, 505). Granger's letters suggest the way the riot moved him toward abolition and out of favor with the state's Congregational leadership: Granger to Leonard Bacon, December 1, 10, 1837, Bacon Papers, YU.

52. May, *Recollections*, 153–55; "Anti-Slavery 'Riot' at Montpelier in 1835," *Green Mountain Free Man* (July 11, 1877), VerHS; David M. Ludlum, *Social Ferment in Vermont, 1791–1850* (New York, 1939), 149–151.

53. In addition to the Meriden and Montpelier mobs, this was true in Utica, October 21, 1835; Troy, New York, June 1836; Cincinnati, July 30, 1836; Alton, Illinois, November 7, 1837.

54. Edward Magdol, *The Anti-Slavery Rank and File: A Social Profile of the Abolitionists' Constituency* (New York, 1986), especially the tables on pp. 47, 68–71, 87; John Jentz, "The Antislavery Constituency in Jacksonian New York City," *Civil War History* 27 (June 1981): 101–22; James E. Mooney, "Anti-Slavery in Worcester County: A Case Study" (Ph.D. Diss., Clark University, 1971); Judith Wellman, "The Burned Over District Revisited: Benevolent Reform in Mexico, Paris, and Ithaca, New York, 1825–1842" (Ph.D. diss., University of Virginia, 1974); Alan M. Krout, "Forgotten Reformers: A Profile of Third Party Abolitionists in Antebellum New York," in Lewis Perry and Michael Fellman, eds., *Antislavery Reconsidered: New Perspectives on the Abolitionists* (Baton Rouge, 1979), 119–45.

55. Magdol suggests that rank-and-file abolitionists more closely represented the general breakdown of Protestant denominations, with Methodists, Baptists, Quakers, Presbyterians, and Congregationalists numerous and only Episcopalians underrepresented. Donald Mathews, *Slavery and Methodism: A Chapter in American Morality, 1780–1845* (Princeton, 1965), is an able account of the issue in the nation's largest denomination. John R. McGivigan, *The War against Proslavery Religion: Abolition and the Northern Churches, 1830–1865* (Ithaca, N.Y., 1984), explores the church tensions abolition generated. Richard Carwardine suggests the general attitude toward slavery in evangelical faiths tended to follow closely that of the general public in *Evangelicals and Politics in Ante-Bellum America* (New Haven, 1993) 133–74.

56. John White Chadwick, ed., *A Life for Liberty: Anti-Slavery and Other Letters of Sallie Holley* (New York, 1899).

57. Sarah Grimké to Jane Smith, September 30, 1837, Grimké Papers, TexHS; William H. Brisbane, *Speech of William H. Brisbane . . . Containing an Account of the Change in His Views on the Subject of Slavery* (Hartford, 1840), 9–10; James G. Birney to Ralph R. Gurley, July 12, 1832, in Dumond, *Letters of Birney*, 1:8–10; Weld to Lewis Tappan, March 9, 1836, and Angelina Grimké to Weld, August 12, 1837, in Barnes and Dumond, *Weld-Grimké Letters*, I: 273, 417; John Brown to Henry L. Stearns, July 15, 1857, in Louis Ruchames, ed., *John Brown: The Making of a Revolutionary* (New York, 1969), 46; Thomas I. Mumford, *Memoir of Samuel Joseph May* (Boston, 1873), 18–19.

58. Henry Stanton, *Random Recollections* (New York, 1886), 69–70. Abby Folsom may have had bouts of insanity, but she had sharp wit, too. Being hauled out of a church meeting by Stephen Foster and another, she informed the congregation: "I'm honored more than my Savior was. He went into Jerusalem riding an ass. I go out of this room riding upon two" (Chadwick, *Life for Liberty*, 116).

59. Edmund Fuller, *Prudence Crandall: An Incident of Racism in Nineteenth-Century Connecticut* (Middletown, Conn., 1971). Letters from Phileo's daughter, Elizabeth Goodwin, to her brother between February and July 1847 suggest Phileo's eccentricities, his "abuses" of his wife "beyond conception," and Ralph Waldo Emerson's patience with his "extremely

malapropos" views on poetry: Calvin W. Phileo Papers, ConnHS. Fuller reprints a description of George Thayer's interview with a lively eighty-four-year-old Crandall in Elk Falls, Kansas, suggesting a happy personal ending for her.

60. Kelley-Foster Papers, AAS; Donald Kennon, "A Knit of Identity: Marriage and Reform in Mid-Victorian America" (Ph.D. diss., University of Maryland, 1981) deals richly with the Kelley-Foster relationship (127–37, 197–212, 305–29). Blanche G. Hersh, *The Slavery of Sex: Feminist Abolitionists in America* (Urbana, Ill., 1978), 218–51, discusses, in a more generalized way, abolition-feminist marriages.

61. Robert H. Abzug, *Passionate Liberator: Theodore Dwight Weld and the Dilemma of Reform* (New York, 1980); Milton C. Sennett, *Abolition's Axe: Beriah Green, Oneida Institute, and the Black Freedom Struggle* (Syracuse, 1986); John D'Entremont, *Southern Emancipator: Moncure Conway, The American Years, 1832–1866* (New York, 1987).

62. Stanton, *Random Recollections*, 71; letter of May 10, 1852, reprinted in C. B. Galbreath, "Anti-Slavery in Columbiana County, Ohio," *OhAHP* 30 (October 1921): 390. The writer claimed that the speech contained sophistry obvious to him if not to others, but he followed the usual anti-abolitionist habit of offering no examples.

63. Weld to Angelina Grimké, March 12, 1838, in Barnes and Dumond, *Weld-Grimké Letters*, 2:592–603. On March 1, Weld had written a letter outlining his moral faults (575–85).

64. Hazel Wolf, *On Freedom's Altar: The Martyr Complex in American Abolition* (Madison, 1952), 50.

65. See Chapter 3 for many examples, or the Epilogue for a discussion of the debate in the United States Senate of April 20, 1848, where Senator Henry Foote, with the full support of John C. Calhoun, Jefferson Davis, et al., invited colleague John Hale to Mississippi to be mob-hanged for the crime of introducing a bill against rioting in the District of Columbia. *Congressional Globe*, 30th Cong., lst sess., Appendix, 500–508.

66. George Thompson to William Lloyd Garrison, September 15, 1835, and Samuel May to Garrison, September 9, 1835, Antislavery Letters, BPL; *Salem Register* in the *Baltimore Gazette*, November 3, 1835; George Thompson, October 15, 16, 1835, and A. Rand to Thompson, December 3, 1835, in George Thompson, *Letters and Addresses of George Thompson, during His Mission in the United States* (Boston, 1837), 13–14, 32–33; *The Mob at Troy* 6–18; Kerber, "Abolitionists and Amalgamators," 28–39; William Thomas, *The Enemies of the Constitution Discovered . . .* (Utica, 1835), 26-29; James G. Birney to Charles Hammond, November 14, 1835, in Dumond, *Letters of Birney*, 1:264–65; Joseph and Owen Lovejoy, *Memoirs of the Rev. Elijah P. Lovejoy* (New York, 1838); Ellen D. Lerned, *History of Windham County, Conn.* (Worcester, 1880), 2:492–94; Weld to Lewis Tappan, March 9, 1836, in Barnes and Dumond, *Weld-Grimké Letters*, 1:270–75. The last document is a full statement of the abolition position on race.

67. Canterbury, Connecticut, September 9, 1833; Canaan, New Hampshire, August 10, 1835; James G. Birney to Lewis Tappan, July 15, 1836, in Dumond, *Letters of Birney*, 1:342–44; Weld to Ray Potter, June 11, 1836, in Barnes and Dumond *Weld-Grimké Letters*, 1:309–l0; May, *Recollections*, 39–71; Lewis Tappan to Weld, July 10, 1834, in Barnes and Dumond, *Weld-Grimké Letters*, 1:155.

68. May, *Recollections*, 39–71; Lewis Tappan to Weld, July 10, 1834, in Barnes and Dumond, *Weld-Grimké Letters*, 1:155.

69. William S. Osborne, *Lydia Maria Child* (Boston, 1980); Karcher, *First Woman*, 181–94; Phillip G. Wright and Elizabeth F. Wright, *Elizur Wright, The Father of Life Insurance* (Chicago, 1937); *The Works of Charles Follen, With a Memoir of His Life* (Boston, 1842), 1:330–85.

70. Hawes, popular pastor of Hartford's First Congregational Church, had been convinced of the abolitionist position since 1834, a stance his congregants knew about. Yet he remained

silent on the issue, even when Leonard Bacon moved against his more forthright brother, Rev. George Hawes, until after Lovejoy's killing in 1837 and several long discussions with Weld. Even then, he nearly lost his pulpit for a single antislavery sermon. Joel Hawes to Amos A. Phelps, June 30, 1834, "Anti-Slavery Letters," BPL; Julia Grew to Laura Kingsbury, March 18, 1835, Kingsbury Papers, NF; Leonard Bacon to George Hawes, March 22, 1836, and G. Hawes to Bacon, June 20, 1836, Bacon Papers, YU; Weld to Lewis Tappan, June 8, 1837, in Barnes and Dumond, *Weld-Grimké Letters*, 1:398; Joel Hawes to James G. Birney, December 7, 1837 in *Emancipator*, June 6, 1837.

71. May, *Recollections*, 146; Julia Ward Howe to sisters, November 29, 1856, in Laura E. Richards and Maria Howe Elliott, *Julia Ward Howe, 1819–1910* (Boston, 1915), 168; J. W. Nevin to Weld, June 2, 1835, in Barnes and Dumond, *Weld-Grimké Letters*, 1:222–23.

72. Joseph Sill chronicled the course of Furness's pulpit support of abolition from 1841 to 1854, and all quotes are from his manuscript diary in the HSPa; Elizabeth Geffen, "William Henry Furness, Philadelphia Anti-Slavery Preacher," *Pennsylvania Magazine of History and Biography* 72 (July 1958): 259–91, handles Furness's career well, though she dates his open abolition from 1839, while offering no evidence to refute Sills's chronology. Furness's close friend Lucretia Mott wrote James Miller McKim as early as May 8, 1834, that she expected Furness to speak out against slavery soon. Anna Davis Hallowell, *The Life and Letters of James and Lucretia Mott* (Boston, 1884), 119.

73. The opposition to Furness's abolition came primarily from the church's wealthiest congregants, both Sill and Furness suggest, such as Tevis, James Taylor, Evans Rogers, Isaac Elliott, Samson Toms, and artist Thomas Sully.

74. Charles Burleigh to H. C. Benson, December 26, 1835, Anti-Slavery Letters, BPL; Thome to Weld, March 31, 1836, in Barnes and Dumond, *Weld-Grimké Letters*, 2:285.

75. Thome and Alvord to Weld, February 9, 1836, in Barnes and Dumond *Weld-Grimké Letters*, 1:256–62.

76. Sarah Grimké to Weld, June 11, 1837, in ibid., 1:403; Chadwick, *Life for Liberty*, 74.

77. The quotations are from Chadwick, *Life for Liberty*, 74, 82, 107. Holley's warmly witty letters offer a wonderful "social" history of abolition.

78. The resolves in Danville, Kentucky, where Birney first tried to published an abolition newspaper, were like those in Cincinnati, though leaders of the meeting more strongly condemned riot. Birney left when his opponents bought out his intended printer. The fullest primary record containing the documents of threat, support, and "solution" is contained in Dumond, *Letters of Birney*, 1:185–251.

79. *Cincinnati Republican*, January 18, 25, 1836; Ohio Anti-Slavery Society, *Narrative of the Late Riotous Proceedings against the Liberty of the Press in Cincinnati* (Cincinnati, 1836), 9–11; Robert Lytle speech, Lytle Papers, Box 44, CinHS. The only person at the meeting openly urging a mob was local Democratic official Charles Hale, who repeated the amalgamationist/insurrectionist charges and who proved Birney's vileness by saying he'd seen the abolitionist ignore whites "to talk with one of the biggest and most blackest niggers he'd seen." Quoted in Patrick A. Folk, "The Queen City of Mobs: Riots and Community Reactions in Cincinnati, 1788–1848" (Ph.D. diss., University of Akron, 1978), 77. Folk covers press response in these controversies quite thoroughly, and Stephen Ellingson, "Understanding the Dialectic of Discourse and Public Action: Public Debate and Rioting in Antebellum Cincinnati," *American Journal of Sociology* 101 (1995): 100–144 deals with how Cincinnati's 1836 debates shifted in response to threats and mobbings. Richards labels Hale, mistakenly I think, as "a prominent Whig from Pennsylvania."

80. Christian Donaldson to William Greene, February 3, 1836, in W. Greene Papers, CinHS; *Philanthropist*, January 29, 1836; Birney to Lewis Tappan, March 17, April 29, 1836, in Dumond, *Letters of Birney*, 1:310–12, 318–19.

81. The April mob began after a black youth won a personal fight with a white; Cincinnati's press uniformly condemned this mob: *Republican*, April 14, *Whig* and *Post*, April 15, 1836, and, vigorously, *Gazette*, April 12. Phebe Mathews to T. D. Weld, May 6, 1936, in Barnes and Dumond, *Weld-Grimké Letters*, 1:220. Standard histories of the city say several blacks were killed in this riot, but there is no mention of deaths in the press. Charles T. Greve, *Centennial History of Cincinnati* (Chicago, 1904), 597; S. B. Nelson, *History of Cincinnati and Hamilton County* (Cincinnati, 1894), 365.

82. Ohio Anti-Slavery Society, *Narrative of Late Riotous Proceedings*, 12–14; Folk, "Queen City of Mobs," 92–94. Of the Cincinnatians known to have acted in this mob and the one later in the month, Graham was a manufacturer, three were skilled mechanics, two had small businesses, and three were sons of prominent merchants or political appointees.

83. Notice of July 13 reproduced in Dumond, *Letters of Birney*, along with a threatening letter from Kentucky, 1:342–43; Kentucky handbill and *Cincinnati Journal or Western Luminary* quoted in Folk, "Queen City of Mobs," 100, 127; *Republican*, *Whig*, and *Post*, July 26, 1936; *Philanthropist*, July 22, 1836, attacked both the "mobocracy" of the three papers and the "wholly mercenary" motives of the anti-abolitionist business leaders.

84. The antimob *Gazette* proposed the meeting, but it was taken over by anti-abolitionists under Jacksonian appointees William Burke (president) and Morgan Neville (vice president), with Timothy Walker as secretary: *Pennsylvanian*, quoted in Brothers, *United States*, 369, a Jacksonian journal that emphasized the party credentials of the leading anti-abolitionists. *Narrative of Late Riots*, 23–25.

85. Charles Stowe, *The Life of Harriet Beecher Stowe, Compiled from Her Letters and Journals* (Boston, 1891), 84–85; letters from Timothy Walker and William Greene in *Whig*, July 27, 28, 1836; Folk, "Queen City of Mobs," 132–33.

86. *Republican*, July 23, 26, 1836; *Post*, July 24, 1836; *Whig*, July 19, 22, 23, 26, 27, 1836; Folk, "Queen City of Mobs," 134–40.

87. Anti-Slavery Society of Ohio address, reprinted in Ohio Anti-Slavery Society, *Narrative of Late Riotous Proceedings*, 17–18, and their reply to the committee in Folk, "Queen City of Mobs," 139. The *Philanthropist*, July 29, 1836, contained hostile stories from around the country about the city's "Corps Mobocratique," which suggested that Cincinnati's elite showed equal "alacrity in fulfilling an order form slaveholders for the destruction of a press" as it did in handling those for pork.

88. *Whig* and *Gazette*, August 1, 1836, gave the fullest accounts of the rioting, with the *Gazette* reporting the mayor's speech to the mob.

89. *Gazette*, August 3, 4, September 2, 1836; Folk, "Queen City of Mobs," 151–59; Greve, *Centennial History*, 601–2; Clarissa Gest to Erasmus Gest, August 2, 1836, Gest Papers, OhHS; Harriet Beecher Stowe to Calvin Stowe, printed in Charles Stowe, *Life of Harriet Beecher Stowe*, 82–84. There was less description of the damage to black homes, but a letter tells of a "colored woman" who supported herself and six children by weaving and sewing. She had her house sacked, her furniture burned in the streets, and her thirty silver dollars of savings stolen, along with about $50 worth of clothing she was making—only because she was known to be industrious—"while the police of our Cossack city looked tamely on." James to Thomas Lakey, January 12, 1837, James Lakey Papers, CinHS. This woman never received compensation for her losses, but Salmon Chase won damages of $1,650 in civil suits against seven rioters.

90. *NR* 57 (October 5, 1839): 83, and 61 (September 11, 1841): 32; Nicholas Longworth letter quoted in Folk, "Queen City of Mobs," 215; the weekly *Cincinnati Chronicle*, September 11, 1841, gave a very close, hour-by-hour account of these fights, suggesting that whites and blacks were probably killed, and mentioning both rape and theft against the African Americans.

91. The *Courier and Enquirer* ran a barrage of antiblack stories and opinion in August before the riot; the quotes are from September 6, 9, 11, 15, 21, 23.

92. *Observer* and *Telegraph* quoted in Folk, "Queen City of Mobs," 260–62, also 280–81; Charles R. Morris, *American Catholic: The Saints and Sinners Who Built America's Most Powerful Church* (New York, 1997), 79; John Werner, *Reaping the Bloody Harvest: Race Riots in the United States during the Age of Jackson, 1824–1849* (New York, 1986), 126–32. Werner says two of those convicted received slightly larger fines and two-month sentences.

93. Birney to *The Signal of Liberty*, September 29, 1841. A letter to Birney from Joseph Sullivan, September 11, 1841, described the riot, "headed by persons from Ky" (Dumond, *Letters of Birney*, 2:632–36).

94. *Philanthropist*, September 11, 25, 1841. The issues less changed between 1836 and 1841 than came to be defined as struggle not between abolitionists and Northern elites but between abolitionists and the Democratic Party, which honed its racism to new levels and was left alone as the defender of proslavery mobs.

95. James Thome to Weld, July 16, 1836, in Barnes and Dumond, *Weld-Grimké Letters* 1:314. The argument of abolitionist racism appears in Leon Litwack, *North of Slavery: The Negro in the Free States, 1790–1860* (Chicago, 1961), 214–46; Walker, *Moral Choices*, 245–57; Friedman, *Gregarious Saints*, 95; Philip Foner, *Frederick Douglass: A Biography* (New York, 1964), 75–83, 136–56. All argue prejudice centered on Douglass, using essentially the material developed balancedly by Benjamin Quarles: "The Breach between Douglass and Garrison," *Journal of Negro History* 23 (April 1938): 144–54.

96. William Birney to James Birney, August 7, 1843, Dumond, *Letters of Birney*, 2:750–53; account and papers from Folk, "Queen City of Mobs," 330–51.

97. Child, *Appeal*, 195, 207. Karcher, *First Woman*, describes richly Child's earlier and later antislavery views (157–68, 267–94).

98. Theodore Dwight Weld, *American Slavery as It Is: Testimony of a Thousand Witnesses* (New York, 1939). The shift toward Weld's emphasis suggests the relation of the 1835 riots to it: *The Evils of Slavery and the Cure of Slavery* (Newburyport, 1836).

99. Jane Grey Swisshelm, *Half a Century* (Chicago, 1880), 91. Lysander Spooner, *The Constitutionality of Slavery* (Boston, 1847), and Henry I. Bowditch, *Slavery and the Constitution* (Boston, 1849), represent the two sides of the issue, well covered in William Wiecek, *The Sources of Anti-Slavery Constitutionalism in America, 1790–1848* (Ithaca, 1977), and more briefly in Gerteis, *Morality and Utility*, 43–61.

100. *DR*, 16 (January 1845): 6. This was one of the more reasonable discussions of abolition by this intellectual organ of the Democratic Party, which specialized in name-calling against all those who claimed that slavery was more than "a minor evil in a national point of view." Abolitionists were "a corps of as blood-thirsty and merciless janissaries as ever disgraced and terrified the dominions of Mahmount . . . , these mulatto saints of Oberlin and Peterborough" or "those babbling miscreants . . . who were willing to betray their country and the cause of humanity, deny their Redeemer, blaspheme their God, and devote their children to slavery, for the sake of personal notoriety." *DR*, 23 (August 1848): 93; 28 (June 1851): 501; 27 (December 1850): 519.

101. Charles G. Finney to Weld, July 21, 1836; William T. Allan, Sereno W. Streeter, John W. Alvord, James Thome to Weld, August 9, 1836; and Thome to Weld, September 9, 1836, in Barnes and Dumond, *Weld-Grimké Letters*, 1:318–19, 323–29; 339–41.

102. Garrison and Garrison, *William Lloyd Garrison*, 2:333–65. Jean Yellin Fagan and John C. Van Horne, eds., *The Abolitionist Sisterhood: Women's Political Culture in Ante-Bellum America* (Ithaca, 1994), gives a rich sense of the variety of antislavery and feminist perspectives among abolitionist women.

103. John G. Whittier to Angelina and Sarah Grimké, August 14, 1837 and Weld to A. and

S. Grimké, August 15, October 10, 1837, in Barnes and Dumond, *Weld-Grimké Letters,* 1:423–7, 452–9. Friedman argues that the "woman issue receded as abolitionists of all stripes came to see female work as essential to their widening circle" (*Gregarious Saints,* 129–59).

104. Perry, *Radical Abolitionism.* The approach toward anarchism in theories of extreme negative government can be equally seen in much Jeffersonian-Jacksonian thought, as well as in such diverse thinkers as John C. Calhoun and Henry David Thoreau.

105. *Liberator,* August 12, 1842; Abby Kelley Foster letter in *Liberator,* May 22, 1846; Edmund Quincy to Richard D. Webb, September 22, 1844, Quincy Papers, MassHS; Jacob Heath quoted in Galbreath, "Anti-Slavery in Columbiana County, Ohio," 392.

106. Fanny Garrison Villard, ed., *William Lloyd Garrison on Non-Resistance* (New York, 1924), 25–26. Lewis Perry deals with the issue in *Childhood, Marriage, and Reform: Henry Clarke Wright, 1797–1870* (Chicago, 1980).

107. Nathaniel Peabody Rogers to William Garrison, February 1, 1846, *Liberator,* February 21, 1845; *National Anti-Slavery Standard,* December 12, 1844. Carlton Mabee describes the nonresistants sympathetically in *Black Freedom: The Nonviolent Abolitionists from 1830 through the Civil War* (New York, 1970). Adin Ballou, *Christian Non-Resistance in All Its Important Bearings, Illustrated and Defended* (Philadelphia, 1846), developed these ideas most systematically.

108. Much of the nation's press for the first time printed Anti-Slavery Society resolves when disunionism underlined the fanaticism long charged. See *NR* 66 (May 18, 1844): 192. Yet Garrison's hope of avoiding Civil War is clear here: "The only exodus of the slave to freedom, unless it be one of blood, must be over the ruins of the present American church, and the grave of the present union."

109. Abby Kelley Foster to William Lloyd Garrison, September 6, 1843, Garrison Papers, BPL.

110. *Liberator,* May 31, 1844; John Weiss, "Diary," January 23, 1861, Belcher-Jennison-Weiss Papers, MassHS.

111. Garrison and Garrison, *William Lloyd Garrison,* 40–41. Garrison introduced his joke with Benedick's quip from *As You Like It* that, when he'd announced he'd die a bachelor, he hadn't thought he would live to marry.

112. The temperance movement followed the same pattern: Joseph R. Gusfield, *Symbolic Crusade: Status Politics and the Temperance Crusade* (Urbana, 1963); Barbara Epstein, *The Politics of Domesticity: Women, Evangelism, and Temperance in Nineteenth-Century America* (New York, 1981); and Ian R. Tyrell, *Sobering Up: From Temperance to Prohibition in Ante-Bellum America, 1800–1860* (Westport, Conn., 1979).

113. Weld to James G. Birney, January 22, 1842, in Dumond, *Letters of Birney,* 2:663; Richard H. Sewell, *Ballots for Freedom: Anti-Slavery Politics in the United States, 1837–1860* (New York, 1976), 80–106.

114. Alvan Stewart to Samuel Webb, November 13, 1841, and to Myron Holley, December 16, 1839, in Alvan Stewart Papers, NYHS; Clay to Chase, September 1843, Salmon P. Chase Papers, HSPa; Birney to Joshua Leavitt *et al.* January 10, 1842, in Dumond, *Letters of Birney* 2:645–657.

115. Betty Fladeland, *Men and Brothers: Anglo-American Anti-Slavery Cooperation* (Urbana, 1972), 221–301; Augustus Wattles *et al. The Condition of People of Color in the State of Ohio, with Interesting Anecdotes* (Boston, 1839); John G. Fee, *Autobiography* (Cincinnati, 1880); William H. Pease and Jane H. Pease, *Black Utopias: Negro Communal Experiments in America* (Madison, 1963): Stanley Harrold, *The Abolitionists and the South, 1831–1861* (Lexington, Ky., 1995), 87–106.

116. Smith offered to give forty acres of land to 3,000 blacks in 1846 and to 500 whites in 1850, but how much was finally given and how many in fact benefited is uncertain. May, *Rec-*

ollections, 321–29; Ralph V. Harlow, *Gerrit Smith: Philanthropist and Reformer* (New York, 1939), 242–85. Harlow handles well the dubious aspects of Smith's benefactions, as well as the problematic quality of Smith's ties to politics, Kansas, and Harpers Ferry (312–422).

117. Abzug, *Passionate Liberator,* 152–55; Weld to Ray Potter, June 11, 1836, in Barnes and Dumond, *Weld-Grimké Letters,* 1:309–10; Weld to James G. Birney, January 22, 1842, in Dumond, *Letters of Birney,* 2:663. Weld's position suggests elements of truth in Eric Foner's and Louis Gerteis's class analysis, though it joins the South, accurately I think, to a kind of capitalism tied peculiarly to long-term credit and the market economy. Eric Foner, *Free Soil, Free Labor, Free Men: The Ideology of the Republican Party Before the Civil War* (New York, 1970), and *Politics and Ideology in the American Civil War* (New York, 1980); Gerteis, *Morality and Utility.*

118. Weld to Sarah and Angelina Grimké, January 5, 1838, in Barnes and Dumond, *Weld-Grimké Letters* 2:514–15. While publicly Weld held in check his detestation of slave owners, his private invective made Garrison sound gentle, or at least an amateur in abuse. Slave owners were "the thieves, the man stealers, the whore mongers," guilty of "adulteries, bloody baptisms, human burnt offerings and . . . hellish tramplings on God's image," making the church itself "ring with blasphemies and reek with lust and smoke with the blood of its damnable abominations." To Lewis Tappan, November 17, 1835, in ibid., 1:244. Weld's historical reputation suggests how historians devised an alternative to strawman Garrison, both anti-abolitionists like Avery Craven who wished to make clear that they were not proslavery, and abolition enthusiasts like Gilbert Barnes and Dwight Dumond who wanted to show that their heroes were not unreasonable fanatics.

119. Weld to Angelina Grimké Weld, January 2, December 27, 1842, in ibid., 2:885, 947–49; Joshua Giddings to his son Addison, August 15, 1842, Giddings-Julian Papers, LC.

120. John Greenleaf Whittier, *Anti-Slavery Poems: Songs of Labor and Reform* (Cambridge, Mass. 1888). The story of Webster and the more tragic one of Calvin Fairbanks are well told in Randolph P. Runyon, *Delia Webster and the Underground Railroad* (Lexington, Ky., 1996).

121. John Demos, "The Anti-Slavery Movement and the Problem of Violent Means," *New England Quarterly* 37 (December 1964): 501–26; C. Vann Woodward, *The Burden of Southern History* (Baton Rouge, 1960), 47–61; Perry, *Radical Abolitionism,* 231–67; Friedman, *Gregarious Saints,* 196–222.

122. Gerrit Smith, *Abstract of the Argument on the Fugitive Slave Law . . . on the Trial of Henry W. Allen . . .* (Syracuse, 1852), 9; Garrison in *Liberator*, December 16, 1859; Chadwick, *Life for Liberty,* 179.

123. Alvan Stewart to Samuel Webb, June 25, 1840, Stewart Papers, NYHS; Thomas Jefferson, *Notes on the State of Virginia* (1785) in *The Portable Thomas Jefferson* (New York, 1975), 215; Adams quoted in Frederick Grimké to William Greene, May 8, 1848, Greene Letters, CinHS. This brother of the Grimké sisters also came north, served ably as a judge in Ohio, and wrote a probing defense of conservative democracy and Democrats. He told Greene that "John Randolph and John Quincy Adams were the two most mischievous public men America had produced," seeing them as the most serious challengers to the happy union of democracy and slavery Jefferson and Jackson had sanctified.

124. William Elder to Salmon P. Chase, May 24, 1845, Chase Papers, HSPa; John P. Parker, *His Promised Land: The Autobiography of John P. Parker . . . ,* ed. Stuart Seely Sprague (New York, 1996), 90–151; John Rankin, Autobiography, Rankin-Parker Papers, DU; William R. Smith to Gerrit Smith, June 9, 1851, and Eliza Smith to G. Smith, June 10, 1851, Gerrit Smith Miller Papers, SYU; *The Case of William L. Chaplin: Being an Appeal to All Respecters of Law and Justice . . .* (Boston, 1851); Harrold, *Abolitionists and the South,* 64–83.

125. Detroit, July 1833; Brookville, Pennsylvania, late 1835; Boston, August 1836; Har-

risburg, 1842; Chicago, November 1846; Carlisle, Pennsylvania, May 1847; Christiana, Pennsylvania, September 1851. Several fugitives escaped during arguments or distractions or in crowds that protectors provided, probably about as many were aided by actual rioting.

126. *Albany Argus* in *Richmond Enquirer*, July 31, 1835; *Philadelphia Enquirer*, August 17, in *New Orleans Bulletin*, September 1, 1836. The New Jersey riot was triggered when the slave's owner, William Christian, tried to get him away before legal action was completed, fearing his escape. Christian told the crowd that Sam—the slave name of Severn Martin—had run off not because of slavery but to escape his slave wife's jealousy and that the white owner had no interest in the substantial house and property Martin had accumulated in seventeen years of hard-working freedom—unless Martin was childless, which Christian knew he was.

127. Three rioters in the Latimer case served some months of their one-year sentence; at Carlisle, eleven of thirty-six indicted were convicted, and served eight months of their three-year sentences, while Booth spent a month in jail. Of the few convicted in the Wellington, Ohio, rescue in 1858, none served as much as three months.

128. George R. Crooks, *Life and Letters of Rev. John McClintock* (New York, 1876), 143–81; Earl E. Sperry, *The Jerry Rescue* (Syracuse, 1924), 21–29; May, *Recollections*, 379–81.

129. U.S. District Court, Pittsburgh, in *New Orleans Courier*, August 2, 1836. The Virginia owner received $1,440 for the two slaves rescued in 1835, while $4,800 was assessed rescuers of three slaves in South Bend in 1850.

130. *New York Tribune*, March 17, 1854; Vroman Mason, "Fugitive Slave Law in Wisconsin," *WisHSP* (1895): 122–40; Frederick Merk, "Rescue of a Fugitive Slave in Wisconsin," typescript, SHSWi; Jane Corss to Fannie ———, January 18, 1855, Booth Papers, and Charles Sumner, August 8, 1854, May 12, 1859, and Wendell Phillips, March 31, 1855, to Byron Paine, Paine Termbook, SHSWi.

131. *New York Tribune*, August 26, 27, 1850.

132. *Philadelphia Public Ledger*, March 29, 31, June 25, 1838; Solomon Northup, *Twelve Years a Slave, A Narrative . . .* , (Auburn, N.Y. 1853); Carol Wilson, *Freedom at Risk: The Kidnapping of Free Blacks, 1780–1865* (Lexington, 1994).

133. Galbreath, "Anti-Slavery in Columbiana County, Ohio," 380–88. Galbreath reported that the black's foster mother described her character as much like Mrs. Stowe's mischievously unmanageable Topsy.

134. Charles E. Stevens, *Anthony Burns, a History* (Boston, 1936); Thomas Wentworth Higginson, *Cheerful Yesterdays* (Boston, 1898), 147–65; Theodore Parker, *A New Crime against Humanity* (Boston, 1854), 4. The diary of Daniel F. and Mary D. Child, in the MassHS, traces the intense passions of the case between late May and early July, with the Irish strongly supportive of the owner and large numbers of rural people, touched by Burns's plight, pouring into town to feel furious at the sight of their militia and their courts so determinedly denying Burns's freedom. The society also has a number of letters from Burns, both before and after his Massachusetts friends bought his freedom, and some broadsides used to attract rural people to town, as well as ones that help explain the indifference to Batchelder's death, such as this one duplicated in huge letters: MURDERS, THIEVES and BLACKLEGS EMPLOYED BY MARSHAL FREEMAN!!!

135. Clarence M. Burton, *History of Wayne County and the City of Detroit, Michigan* (Chicago, 1930), 2:1123–24; Silas Farmer, *History of Detroit and Wayne County and Early Michigan* (Detroit, 1890), 1:345–46; David M. Katzman, *Before the Ghetto: Black Detroit in the Nineteenth Century* (Urbana, 1973), 11–12.

136. William E. Farrison, *William Wells Brown: Author and Reformer* (Chicago, 1969), 248; James Oliver Horton and Lois Horton, *Black Bostonians: Family Life and Community Struggle in the Antebellum North* (New York, 1979), 81–128; May, *Recollections*, 285–92; Higginson, *Cheerful Yesterdays*, 155–59. Sperry, *Jerry Rescue*, 42, reprints Lucy Watson's

statement about the help black women gave to this escape. The fullest account of black actions in fugitive slave rescues is Jane H. Pease and William H. Pease, *They Would Be Free: Blacks' Search for Freedom, 1830–1861* (New York, 1974), 206–32. James Oliver Horton and Lois Horton add some material in *Black Bostonians* and *In Hope of Liberty: Culture, Community, and Protest among Northern Free Blacks* (New York, 1997).

137. Parker's account is reprinted along with other telling documents in Margaret Hope Bacon, *Rebellion at Christiana* (New York, 1975), 16–36, 45–60, 89–109. Parker's account is vigorous, moving and melodramatic. I accept it as largely accurate in the broad outlines but question many of its dramatic details (such as the killed slave-catchers at Gap Hill) and interpretations. See Roderick Nash, "William Parker and the Christiana Riot," *JNH* 96 (1961): 24–31. More solid is the account by a man familiar with the participants and era, William U. Hensel, *The Christiana Riot and the Treason Trials of 1851: An Historical Sketch* (Lancaster, Pa., 1911), very accurate and remarkably detailed. One can learn, for example, the average age of treason trial jurors (fifty-three) and their average weight (178 pounds), 74. The trial is recorded in *United States v. Hanway*, 3d Circuit Court, S. Wall Jr. 139, April 1852, and much detail is in *A Full and Correct Report of the Christiana Tragedy . . . Presented in Evidence Before Alderman Reggart . . .* (Lancaster, 1851). Jonathan Katz, *Resistance at Christiana, the Fugitive Slave Riot* (New York, 1974), 284–90, gives good material on the questions that have been raised about the authenticity of Parker's narrative, written with much help from Canadian blacks. Thomas P. Slaughter, *Bloody Dawn: The Christiana Riot and Racial Violence in the Ante-bellum North* (New York, 1991), is the most recent and broadest study.

138. William Still, *The Underground Railroad* (Philadelphia, 1872), 348–68; Hensel, *Christiana Riot*. Slaughter deals with the various stories about Parker's mother-in-law, Cassandra Harris, in *Bloody Dawn* (80–85).

139. Hensel, *Christiana Riot*, 67, 411. The complaints of prejudice against Hanway's conviction were less convincing than the evidence for national and local Democratic support for it: *The Report of Attorney General Robert J. Brent to His Excellency Govr. Lowe in Relation to the Christiana Treason Trial* (Annapolis, 1852). National reaction to the trial, and the quote from the Boston *Christian Register*, September 20, 1851, are in Roderick Nash, "The Christiana Riot: An Evaluation of Its National Significance," *JLHS* 65 (1961): 65–91.

140. These figures I take from Stanley W. Campbell's close study, *The Slave Catchers: Enforcement of the Fugitive Slave Law 1850–1860* (New York, 1968), 167–69, 184–89.

141. Joseph Osborne, "Diary," January 30, 1856, OhHS; Samuel May, *The Fugitive Slave Law and Its Victims* (New York, 1861), 50–60; Julius Yanuck, "The Garner Fugitive Slave Case," *MVHR* 40 (1953): 47–60.

142. Sill, "Diary," October 18, 1850; February 8, 9, March 10, 16, 1851, HSPa.

Chapter Three

1. William H. Hauser to Julia Conrad, September 15, 1841, Conrad Papers, CinHS.

2. Rollin G. Osterweis, *Romanticism and Nationalism in the Old South* (New Haven, 1949), represents the traditional vision of the graciously romantic South, and Robert Baldick, *The Duel: A History of Dueling* (New York, 1965), presents the high-flown vision of chivalric dueling.

3. Clement Eaton, *The Freedom-of-Thought Struggle in the Old South* (1940; reprint, New York, 1964), and "Mob Violence in the Old South," *MVHR* 29 (December 1942): 351–70; John Hope Franklin, *The Militant South, 1800–1861* (Cambridge, Mass., 1956). Eaton, more than any historian before or since, emphasized the negatively repressive character of group violence in the antebellum South, while Franklin's study remains the most inclusive and balanced survey.

4. Bertram Wyatt-Brown, *Southern Honor: Ethics and Behavior in the Old South* (New York, 1982); Grady McWhiney, *Cracker Culture: Celtic Ways in the Old South* (Tuscaloosa, 1988); Dickson D. Bruce Jr., *Violence and Culture in the Ante-Bellum South* (Austin, 1979). Kenneth S. Greenberg, *Honor and Slavery* (Princeton, 1996), ties the values closely to "mastering."

5. *Grand Gulf Advertiser*, June 27, 1835; *Augusta* (Me.) *Age*, May 24, 1837; *New Orleans Courier*, May 2, 1837: "Murder still continues rife among us," sighed the editor. Louisiana Attorney General, *Report on Crime in New Orleans*, 1857, quoted in James Stirling, *Letters from the Slave States* (London, 1857), 140–44. This Democratic legal document, intended to encourage vigilante action against New Orleans's Know-Nothing administration, urged "summary justice on the criminals whom the law is unable to reach, or who, possibly, represent the law."

6. William Winans, Centreville, Mississippi, to his sister, Amelia Thompson, June 17, 1836, Winans Papers, MissDAH; Joseph A. Graves, Kentucky, to Robert Lowery, December 8, 1847, Richard James Hooker Papers, SHC.

7. William H. Thomson, Spring Ridge, Mississippi, to Ruffin Thomson, December 4, 1859, Thomson Papers, SHC. Thomson said all the wounded seemed likely to recover, but in a letter of January 12, 1860, he reported that Dr. Reynolds had died.

8. Amelia Boswell to Cousin Elizabeth A. Boswell, August 13, 1847, Amelia Boswell Papers, UAla; Mary Hart, "Diary," March 10, 1847, USC; Petition from Orange County, April 1842, Gov. John Morehead Papers, NCDAH; R. R. Rose to Preston R. Rose, June 14, 1852, Preston R. Rose Papers, UTex. Whig governor Morehead was a rare politican who rejected such pleas, telling the petitioners he was unwilling to grant licenses to maim even "to a poor married father of four or five children," and the next day rejecting a similar communal request for a pardon for Thomas Strother that argued that both the convicted and all the witnesses were too drunk to remember what happened. Morehead, Letterbook, April 18, 19, 1842, Moorhead Papers, NCDAH.

9. James L. Stirling, Mississippi, to brother Lewis Stirling, October 29, 1837, Lewis Stirling Papers, LSU; *New Orleans Courier*, August 24, 1829, in *NR* 37 (September 26, 1829): 68–69.

10. James Norman Smith, "Autobiography," Wallace A. Jones Papers, UTex; Andrew Schirmer, "Journal," SCHS; William R. Hogan and Edwin A. Davis, eds., *William Johnson's Natchez: The Ante-Bellum Diary of a Free Negro* (Baton Rouge, 1951): the duels (November 21, 1836), 148; (November 14, 1837), 202; (September 11, 1841), 346–7; other quotes and incidents, 527, 354, 56–63. Smith was the rare Southerner who showed some pride and courage in preventing bloodshed, and Schirmer reported violence with the tart matter-of-factness—and regularity—most diarists reserved for the weather.

11. The South's most active duelist was Alexander McClung, once governor of Mississippi, who made a career of killing or beating opponents in duels and "rencontres" to compensate for legal, political, and economic incompetence and chicanery. McClung killed about a dozen people in a twenty-year period, before most honorably killing himself in 1855 (Franklin, *Militant South*, 39). The rules for one of his brutal duels are in *North Carolina Standard*, August 30, 1837.

12. *A Full Report of the Commonwealth of Virginia vs. Thomas Ritchie, Jr.* (Richmond, 1846); *Pennsylvanian*, March 7, 1846.

13. Quoted in McWhiney, *Cracker Culture*, 170. McWhiney accepts Perry's conclusions, though the book is chockful, and prideful, of personal abusiveness and violence on a staggering scale.

14. Nathan Warren to Gov. H. G. Runnels, February 24, 1835, MissDAH; John E. Campbell, Mt. Home, Texas, to his brother, August 25, 1860, Campbell Papers, UTex; "A Southron," *The Code of Honor: or, The Thirty-nine Articles* (Baltimore, 1847), 23. Fifty-four

citizens of Madison County supported Warren's request on the grounds that his violence was no reason "to rob said Warren's family and children of so large an amount" (October 7, 1834, MissDAH).

15. Harriet Martineau, *Society in America* (New York, 1837), 2:155; William L. Yancey to the *Alabama Baptist*, February 10, 1845, Yancey Papers, AlaDAH; *Philadelphia Public Ledger*, September 21, 1838; W. L. Yancey to Ben Yancey, September 8, 1838, Misc. Mss., SCHS.

16. Jack K. Williams's competent recent survey *Dueling in the Old South: Vignettes of Social History* (College Station, Tex., 1880) offers the shortest introduction to the chivalric school on this topic, as well as a good bibliography of earlier works, most of them with a similar heroic perspective. Williams also reprints the best-known of many dueling manners guides, that of ex–South Carolina governor John Lyde Wilson, published in 1838, *The Code of Honor, or Rules for the Government of Principals and Seconds in Dueling*, with its interesting discussion of how drunk a gentleman had to be to palliate his insults. Public testimony to the character of a challenger *and* to his being boozed beyond recollection of what he said was sufficient to assure high-toned settlement without resort to the field of honor, Wilson counseled. "A Southron" offered etiquette advice on proper gestures, comments, and epistolary style in *Code of Honor,* esp. 22–25.

17. *New Orleans Delta,* June 26, 1847; letter from St. Mary's, Georgia, printed in *NR* 48 (March 14, 1835): 18. The next week *NR* reported that the three Kings had been arrested (48 [March 21, 1835]:42.

18. *NR* 41 (December 26. 1831): 247; *American Annual Register* (Philadelphia, 1830–31), 213; *Baltimore Republican,* August 4, 1836; *Federal Union,* quoted in *New Orleans Commercial Bulletin,* September 11, 14, 1833; a postscript, "I had like to forgot, to tell you . . . " in a letter from Rachel O'Connor to brother David Weeks, March 7, 1828, David Weeks Papers, LSU; *Little Rock Gazette,* probably March 30, in *Pennsylvanian,* May 2, 1846.

19. *Augusta Chronicle,* quoted in *Philadelphia Public Ledger,* July 26, 1838; *Morgan* (Ala.) *Observer,* December 1838, quoted in Theodore Dwight Weld, *American Slavery, as It Is: Testimony of a Thousand Witnesses* (New York, 1839), 194; *Vicksburg Sentinel,* June 14, 1838; Jackson *Mississippian,* November 9, 1838; *New Orleans Courier,* August 13, 1840; *Hagerstown* (Md.) *Courier and Enquirer* in *Philadelphia Public Ledger,* April 30, 1838; *Virginia Advocate,* January 26, 1838, in Weld, *American Slavery,* 201.

20. *Danville* (Va.) *Reporter,* August 27, 1836, in *Philadelphia Public Ledger,* September 7, 1836; Frederic Hudson, *Journalism in America* (New York, 1873), 762–64. In a decade and a half, *Sentinel* editors and writers killed two and wounded two challengers, while suffering four fatalities and two injuries in public murders, in part because, in addition to its Whig politics, the paper vigorously reported the personal and political economic chicanery that characterized Mississippi in the hard times, 1837–1844.

21. Lewis Collins, *History of Kentucky* (Frankfort, 1966), 2:78; *Norfolk Beacon* in *Portland Argus,* July 8, 1835; William F. Gray, *From Virginia to Texas* (Houston, 1965), December 25–26, 1835, 57–58. Matthew Powell wrote a letter describing the Chuckatuck tragedy: William Cooper came to town to kill Samuel Whitfield Jr., but missed two shots at his enemy as the latter was entering a carriage. Out of bullets, Cooper took a sudden interest in a fair fight and yelled, "I'm unloaded," at which announcement Whitfield shot him, and the black by accident. Whitfield was beating Cooper with a gun when Josiah Parker shot him in the back and proceeded to beat him to death with a gun. In the *Richmond Enquirer,* July 14, 1835.

22. J. Orlando Harrison, Vicksburg, to Jilson P. Harrison, September 30, 1835, Harrison Family Papers, KenHS; *New Bedford Gazette* in *Portland Argus,* September 26, 1835; *Manchester* (Miss.) *Herald,* in Jackson *Mississippian,* July 31, 1835.

23. V. Bruce Adams, Jack Williams, and Greenberg emphasize class segregation in types of

violence, while McWhiney and Wyatt-Brown see violence in service to a code or tradition of honor that served to protect communal and familial norms. A second strand of Wyatt-Brown's rich interpretation, what he calls a Tocquevillian "tyranny of the community," a concern for reputation defined in large part by what one's neighbors thought and said, in a competitive, insecure, and frazzled society, seems more accurate (*Southern Honor*, esp. 34–71, 462–93).

24. An account of the Potter trial was printed in the *Raleigh Star*, September 22, 1831, Potter's version of events in the *Tarborough* (N.C.) *Free Press*, October 4, 1831, and an account of his murder in the *Caddo* (Tex.) *Gazette*, March 12, 1842. Potter's letter of resignation due to "an untoward event," November 12, 1831, is in the Governor Montford Stokes Letterbook, NCDAH, and details of the business, from someone who was in contact with both Mr. and Mrs. Potter, are in A. R. M. Sandoss to John D. Hawkins, August 30, 1831, Hawkins Papers, SHC.

25. Thomas B. Chaplin, "Journal," May 10, 13, 1845, SCHS. Toomer was a nephew of Chaplin's stepfather, with whom Chaplin struggled long for control of his mother's wealth. Chaplin's journal, edited by Susan W. Walker, has been printed in Theodore Rosengarten, *Tombee, Portrait of a Cotton Planter* (New York, 1986), 349, note 170.

26. Chaplin, "Journal," May 3, 1845, SCHS. Chaplin's grammar is telling here: he uses the generalizing "you" when laying out his misfortunes and reverts to the personal "I" form only when he talks of generosity and revenge. On October 29 the trouble with Toomer ended when he agreed to drop legal charges because Chaplin agreed to reveal who'd passed Toomer's remarks on to him.

27. Wilson's *Code of Honor*, in Jack K. Williams, *Dueling*, 88–89.

28. Augustus Baldwin Longstreet, *Georgia Scenes* (1835; reprint, New York, 1957), 1–3, 42–53.

29. Thomas Kirkman, "Major Jones' Fight," in William T. Porter, ed., *The Big Bear of Arkansas and Other Sketches Illustrative of Character and Incident in the South* (Philadelphia, 1843), 37–42, and "A Quarter Race in Kentucky" in Porter, ed., *A Quarter Race in Kentucky, and Other Sketches* . . . , (Philadelphia, 1847), 15–25. Johnson Jones Hooper, *Simon Suggs' Adventures and Travels* . . . (Philadelphia, 1848), 12, 118. In all this humor, the central themes include Southern economic chicanery, political demagogery, and violence that involved personal assertiveness to the destruction of communal standards and institutions. This emphasis, if strongest in George Washington Harris's *Sut Luvingood tales*, is omnipresent.

30. Ezekiel A. Powell in his memoirs recalled five murders of family members by relatives, most alcohol-related and none punished, in a small area of Alabama in a few years, as well as William Ferby's murder of his father and brother, for which he was hanged. "Fifty-five Years in West Alabama," *AlaHQ* 4 (1942): 501–6. *New Orleans Bee*, October 5, 1838, reported a brawl in which ninety-year-old Benjamin Alexander killed his grandson Thomas Hamilton with a dirk.

31. *Memphis Enquirer*, May 20, 1837; Sheilds McIllwaine, *Memphis down to Dixie* (New York, 1948), 102–3. Williams illustrates the common insistence on the duel's essential romantic-protective functions, using as his prime example Andrew Jackson's killing of Charles Dickinson, allegedly over Rachel's honor. Not only is there no shred of evidence for this interpretation, but the raft of documents in this case make clear how honor, as was so often the case, related primarily to calculatedly aggressive self-assertion. Jack K. Williams, *Dueling*, 18–19; "Southron," *Code of Honor*, 24. The full documentation of this duel as well as many other prominent political ones are included in the soberest and best work on American dueling, Don C. Seitz, *Famous American Duels: With Some Account of the Causes that Led Up to Them and the Men Engaged* (New York, 1929). Steven M. Stowe analyzes the rhetoric of some of the codes and formulaic political duels in *Intimacy and Power in the Old South: Ritual in the Lives of the Planters* (Baltimore, 1987), 5–49.

32. *Milledgeville* (Ga.) *Federal Union,* July 11, 1847; Matthew P. Blue, "History of Mont-gomery," mss., AlaDAH; Captain R. A. McLellan, *Early History of Limestone County, Alabama* (Limestone, Ala., 1927), 12–13; J. Stoddard Johnston, *Memorial History of Louisville from Its First Settlement to the year 1896* (Chicago, 1896), 1:91–92; *History of Ohio Falls Cities and their Counties,* (Cleveland, 1882), 312–13; *Little Rock Gazette,* March 2, 1842; Frances Anne Kemble, *Journal of a Residence on a Georgia Plantation in 1838 and 1839* (1863; reprint, New York, 1970), 292, 325–27.

33. Henry Whipple mentioned the fatal duel over hogs, and McLellan reported that one Jones brother murdered another in an affray over a chair. The murderer in this case fled Alabama because another brother had recently been legally hanged for a public murder of their brother-in-law. *Bishop Whipple's Southern Diary, 1843–44,* ed. Lester Shippee (New York, 1968), November 24, 1843, 30; McLellan, *Limestone County, Alabama,* 16–18.

34. The *Memphis Enquirer* concluded sarcastically that the Jackson-Gholson duel ended "most 'honorably' according to the rules of genteel murder" (May 20, 1837). Potter's purgation claim appeared in a public letter printed in the *Tarborough* (N.C.) *Free Press,* October 4, 1831.

35. Samuel and Mary Gregg to Mr. and Mrs. George W. Smythe, November 20, 1835, Smythe Papers, UTex; Thomas H. Maddox, "Reminiscences," Maddox Papers, SHC. Maddox described another duel, famous for the brawling fracas afterward—two dead and Jim Bowie and another hurt—in great detail without a word about why.

36. Abbeville Petition, 1838 Grand Jury Presentments, SCDHA. The large planter–dominated legislature paid no attention to these requests or dismissed them as "unnecessary," well-knowing weapons' contribution to class as well as personal intimidation. *NR* 53 (September 16, 1837): 35 reprinted an Alabama law typical of the attempts to prevent sale and wearing of such weapons, similar to those against dueling in both their frequency and ineffectiveness. Hugh McVay message, printed in *Mobile Register,* November 15, 1837.

37. Schirmer, "Journal," May 25, 1839, SCHS. A Mr. Fell had the foot and Mr. Herrot had the mouth. J. L. Petigru to R. F. W. Allston, July 2, 1857, Allston-Pringle Papers, SCHS; Mary P. Harrison, North Carolina, to brother Jilson P. Harrison, Harrison Family Papers, KenHS.

38. *New Orleans Courier,* February 15, April 22, 1836, quoting the *Washington Globe* and, at length, the *New York Sunday Morning News.*

39. *New Orleans Courier,* February 15, 1836. The *New Orleans Commercial Bulletin* agreed, adding that a hefty fine to be used by the state for widows or orphans would prevent duels in those few cases where a participant had neither family nor debts (March 1, 1836).

40. *DR,* 11 (October 1842): 422.

41. A. B. Burleson to Ed Burleson, November 19, 1860, Burleson Papers, UTex; Joel R. Poinsett to Benjamin F. Perry, December 16, 1850, Perry Papers, AlaDAH.

42. Historians continue to accept Brooks's attack in terms of Sumner's personal abuse of Butler, attacking the Massachusetts senator's "tasteless villification" or more creatively asserting that Sumner described Butler as a "harlot, pirate, falsifier, assassin and swindler." Sumner charged that Butler was always quick to defend "the harlot, slavery" and mentioned (accurately) Butler's "deviation from truth" and "proclivity to error" in his discussion of American history and the New England Emigrant Aid Society. Yet the essential analogy of Butler to Don Quixote was gentle, even affectionate, compared to that of Stephen Douglas as Sancho Panza *and* Danton, of David Atchison as "Cataline . . . reeking of conspiracy," or of John V. Mason of Virginia, described as having "the prejudices" of Butler "but without his generous impulses." The speech was harsh about slavery and the South—especially South Carolina and Virginia—but in verbal abusiveness, personal and sectional, it was neither notable nor comparable to commonplace Southern rhetoric in Congress, much less the brutal vulgarities that poured from Brooks, Lawrence Keitt and the Southern political and press es-

tablishment in exultation over the deed. Charles Sumner, *Recent Speeches and Addresses* (Boston, 1856), taken from the *Congressional Record*, 595–602, 610–11, 648, 687–90; Bertram Wyatt-Brown, *Yankee Saints and Southern Sinners*, (Baton Rouge, 1985), 198; Jack K. Williams, *Dueling*, 26.

43. Preston Brooks to J. H. Brooks, May 22, 1856, printed in *SCGHM* 52 (1951): 1–4. When Brooks felt the need two months later to refresh his reputation by dueling with Anson Burlingame "somewhere outside the District," Burlingame suggested Canada. Not getting the joke, Brooks replied through an intermediary that Canada was too far and that if Burlingame didn't choose another spot, he would "expose the matter." Burlingame's reply, through an intermediary, perhaps caused Brooks to forget this matter: "It will disgrace us forever if we have anything more to do with that vile set." Brooks to Burlingame, July 21, 1856; Burlingame to L. D. Campbell, August 1, 1856, Burlingame Papers, OhHS.

44. *Richmond Whig* and *Richmond Enquirer* quoted (along with other equally rabid editorial responses) in John S. C. Abbott, *South and North; or, Impressions Received during a Trip to Cuba and the South* (1860; reprint, New York, 1969), 257–73.

45. Petition to Governor for Mary DuBois, 1835, signed by forty-six citizens including Henry S. Foote and George Coulter, Governors' Petitions, MissDAH.

46. *Vicksburg Sentinel*, September 28, 1837. The editor reported that these three actions were just the grossest of recent numerous "minor outrages" by lynchers.

47. Henry A. Foote, *Casket of Reminiscences* (Washington, D.C., 1874), 262; Myra C. Glenn, *Campaigns against Corporal Punishment: Prisoners, Sailors, Women, and Children in Ante-Bellum America* (Albany, N.Y., 1984).

48. J. H. Green account, April 10, 1845, of the story of the one survivor who subsequently murdered and was hanged at Auburn (N.Y.) Prison, *Lexington True American*, June 3, 1845; Joseph Williams, *Old Times in West Tennessee: Reminiscences* (Memphis, 1873), 201–3.

49. *St. Louis Republican*, April 4, 1838, in *Philadelphia Public Ledger*, May 12, 1838; letter from Grand Gulf, August 15, 1836, to a brother in Pennyan, New York, in *New York Evening Post*, September 13, 1836; Alfred W. Arrington, *The Desperadoes of the Old Southwest* (New York, 1849), 16.

50. *Alton Telegraph* and the St. Louis correspondent of a New York paper, quoted in Parker Pillsbury, *Acts of the Anti-Slavery Apostles* (Concord, N.H., 1883), 64–65; anonymous, "St. Louis Diary," June 25, 1836, HSPa, remembering the event he'd witnessed two months earlier; Newel Knight, "Autobiography," 20, LDSA.

51. Bennet H. Barrow, *Plantation Life of Louisiana, 1836–1846, as Reflected in the Diary of Bennet H. Barrow,* ed. Edwin Adams Davis (New York, 1967), June 17, 1842, 262. On Luke Lawless, see *St. Louis Observer*, July 21, 1836; Robert Patterson, "Journal," July 3, 1835, HSPa; J. Thomas Scharf, *A History of St. Louis, City and County* (Philadelphia, 1883); Thomas H. Benton, May 11, 1844, and Luke Lawless, June 12, 1835, to Thomas Reynolds, Reynolds Papers, MoHS.

52. *New Orleans True American*, August 4, 1838, in *Philadelphia Public Ledger*, August 13, 1838; Jewell L. DeGrummond, "A Social History of St. Mary's Parish Louisiana from 1845–60" (M.A. thesis, Louisiana State University, 1948), 126; *Liberator*, December 4, 1857.

53. *Natchitoches Herald* in *NR* 61 (November 6, 1841): 149. The victim, named Boatwright, was killed for speaking out against "the barbarous cruelties" of both Regulators and Moderators in Shelby County, Texas. His fate suggests the wisdom of Southerners not noticing, or at least not noting, mob brutalities.

54. Letter from Natchez, January 4, 1835, printed in *NR* 47 (January 3, 1835): 373; *Natchez Courier*, quoted in *Vicksburg Register*, January 22, 1835; *Rodney* (Miss.) *Telegraph*, quoted in *Baltimore American*, February 14, 1835. Wyatt-Brown gives good background on Foster's financial-legal chicanery preceding the murder in the concluding section of *Southern*

Honor (462–93), while Terry Alford provides an account of the Foster family background in his rich study of one of their slaves, *Prince among Slaves* (New York, 1977).

55. Henry Clay Lewis, *Odd Leaves from the Life of a Louisiana "Swamp Doctor,"* ed. John Anderson (Baton Rouge, 1962), 68, 81, 133–37.

56. George Washington Harris, *Sut Lovingood's Yarns*, ed. M. Thomas Inge (New Haven, 1966), 174–75.

57. Elias Canetti, *Crowds and Power* (New York, 1963), 223.

58. Rachel O'Connor to David Weeks, July 11, 1829, in David Weeks Papers, LSU; *Galveston News*, July 15, 1856; Frederick Law Olmsted, *A Journey through Texas; or A Saddle-Trip on the Southwestern Frontier* (New York, 1857), 386–88; *Louisville Journal*, May 14, 1857.

59. Evan Thompson, *The Feud of Gerrard County, Kentucky* (Louisville, 1849). This feud was familial in structure but essentially the product of political intimidation and medical-financial rivalry. Lela R. Neill, "Episodes in the Early History of Shelby County" (M.S. thesis, Stephen F. Austin State College, 1950); Samuel Asbury Papers on Regulator-Moderator War, especially Thomas Ashcroft typescript, "Thrilling Incidents," TexSA.

60. *NR* 66 (August 24, 1844): 428, and, quoting *Van Buren* (Ark.) *Intelligencer*, 67 (September 14, 1844): 19. The Arkansas paper stated that Jones and White had also killed a man named Moss in Arkansas: the murderers had been hired by one Piercy, who paid them a racing mare.

61. Samuel Asbury Papers, UTex, has much material, original and copied, on the Rose-Potter battle and on Potter's life, including letters, addresses, and poems by Potter and the court records of Rose's case. The UTex's Preston R. Rose Papers testifies to the family's zest, violence, and constant economic scheming. Alfred W. Arrington's "faction," *The Rangers and Regulators of the Tanaha; or, Life among the Lawless* (New York, 1856), paints a harrowing picture of Rose, his pack of dogs trained to attack people, and his brutality, including cutting the heart out of a man who repeated Tom Paine's charge that Jesus was a bastard. Methodist leader John H. McLean defended his ancestor in a review of Arrington's narrative in the Asbury papers and in *Reminiscences of John H. McLean,* (Nashville, 1918), 4–22. Gray, *From Virginia to Texas*, discussed Potter's early role in Texas politics, where, despite mistrust of him, Potter's intelligence and legislative experience gave him in 1836 "an ascendancy over the rest of the body" (90–91, 129).

62. Alexandre Barde, *L'histoire des Comités de la Vigilance des Attakapas* (1861), trans./ed. Henrietta G. Rogers (M.A. thesis, Louisiana State University, 1936); Corydon Fuller, "Diary," October 16, November 15, 1857, CLUM; Arrington, *Desperadoes*.

63. The killers' justifying letter was sent to the *Grand Gulf Advertiser* and reprinted in the *New Orleans Commercial Bulletin*, August 24, 1841. Stories taken from New Orleans, Arkansas, and St. Louis papers were reprinted in *National* (D.C.) *Intelligencer*, August 31, September 4, 1841, and *NR* 61 (September 1, November 6, 1841): 3, 149–50.

64. *Quincy* (Ill.) *Whig* in *NR* 58 (August 15, 1840): 375. Northern Democratic officials were prominent in several abolition mobs—Utica, Montpelier, Cincinnati, Troy—but no Northern official could compare with Governor Lilburn Boggs of Missouri, who, while in office, organized or authorized mobs against Mormons, Osage Indians, and Iowans, the latter in a border dispute of the kind that often involved officials.

65. Thomas M. Allen, Columbia, Missouri, to John A. Gano, August 26, 1853, John A. Gano Papers, HSPa.

66. Ashcroft, "Thrilling Scenes," Asbury Papers, UTex., 18, 53–57. A petition from eighteen men and a letter of December 18, 1841, from one signer, N. B. Garner, to the Texas government asked for protection against wholly ruthless men "having no fixed principle tending to the good of the community." Garner himself had had some slaves stolen and, when he com-

plained of this "regulating," was driven with his family from his home (Samuel Asbury papers, UTex).

67. For a contrary argument, see Bertram Wyatt-Brown, "Community, Class, and Snopesian Crime: Local Justice in the Old South," in Orville Vernon Burton and Robert C. McMath Jr., eds., *Class, Conflict and Consensus: Antebellum Southern Community Structures* (Westport, Conn., 1982), 173–206. I find no evidence of the extralegal system offering "social control by the poor over the rich" (179). Both systems of justice were slanted sharply in favor of the "respected," with esteem and hence what one could get away with depending significantly, though far from wholly, on wealth.

68. Petition from Port Gibson, May 1, 1834, Governors Papers, MissDAH. McMurty served over nine months of his sentence before he escaped with the murderer. Sheriff Hamilton reported the escape on June 4, 1834: "The Scoundrels here who assisted Skinner in getting away has succeeded in indighting me for his Breaking of goal. The trial comes on today and if hard swearing will do it I have no doubt that I shall be fined."

69. Captain Slick Papers, UAla, offers a rich selection of newspaper and court records related to the Alabama movement, at one point 600 strong. Huff collected only $22.50 and Hale $100 plus $216 costs. Martin didn't sue, but his son "pumped 18 or 20 shot from a pistol" into one Slicker, for which he was fined $100, while all the Slickers involved, including the wounded victim, were fined $10. James W. Bragg, "Captain Slick, Arbiter of Early Alabama Morals," *Alabama Review* 11 (1958): 125–34, gives the movement competent sympathetic treatment.

70. James Petigru to Jane Petigru North, December 2, 1854, in *The Letters and Speeches of James Louis Petigru, the Union Man of South Carolina* (Washington, D.C., 1928), 350–51; James E. Cutler, *Lynch-Law: An Investigation into the History of Lynching in the United States* (New York, 1905), 114–15; *St. Louis New Era* in *NR* 58 (August 1, 1840): 347.

71. *Louisville Journal*, May 14, 1857. On the Texas case, on the Brassos in 1838, see Weld, *American Slavery as It Is*, 102.

72. *Wilmington Chronicle* in *Fayetteville Observer*, January 13, 1840; *Raleigh Register* in *Liberator*, January 22, 1841; William H. Battle to Lucy M. Battle, March 21, April 4, 1842, Battle Papers, SHC; Duplin County Court Records, Spring 1842, NCDAH, and in the same place, the petition of 300 citizens, along with letters from Joseph T. Rhodes and Jeremiah Pearsall, April 6, 1842, and in May, after the jailbreak, one with more than 150 signatures for the only remaining prisoner, John M. Morehead Papers. The Governor's Letterbook contains his first reply to the petitioners, April 28, 1842, and his pardon of Fountain on May 23.

Chapter Four

1. *New Orleans Bee*, September 19, 1835.

2. *National Intelligencer*, August 26, 1835; Gov. George McDuffie, *Annual Message*, 1835, quoted in Edwin L. Green, *George McDuffie* (Columbia, S.C., 1936), 153–54.

3. *Liberator* 1 (December 3, 1831): 194. The incident occurred on November 16. Reports circulated that James Thome was mobbed in 1834, but these were untrue. Thome reported his return to Augusta, Kentucky, in late 1837 to a warm welcome from the community, former slaves, and his family, now devoted teachers in the "colored department" of the local Presbyterian church, where blacks comprised a full third of the membership. In 1839 Thome helped a slave woman, about to be sold south by a guardian before her young masters came of age, to escape to Canada and mentioned the incident at an Oberlin meeting. A listener foolishly named Thome when he wrote up the story for a youth magazine. In fear of arrest, Thome briefly fled Ohio. Thome to Theodore Dwight Weld, December 25, 1837; August 27, Novem-

ber 22, 1839, in Gilbert Barnes and Dwight Dumond, eds., *Letters of Theodore Dwight Weld, Angelina Grimké, and Sarah Grimké* (New York, 1934), 1:501–4, 2:793–95, 814–17.

4. John G. Fee, *Reminiscences* (Chicago, 1891), 97–99, 113–52, recounts these mob attacks. Richard D. Sears, *Day of Small Things: Abolitionism in the Midst of Slavery, Berea, Kentucky, 1854–1864* (Lanham, Md., 1986), is rich in primary data. Sears quotes two Fee letters of 1858 that explore the personal ties and blame the mob attack on Clay's "standing aloof" (45).

5. Prof. Benjamin Hedrick was mob-driven from Chapel Hill in 1856; a Mr. Payne, who ran as a Republican for Congress, was forced out of Demosville, and J. R. Whittemore from Newport, both in Kentucky in 1859; and editor S. Harbaugh was mob-propelled from Lexington, Missouri, in July 1860, when his paper announced for Lincoln. The Virginia cases are discussed later.

6. *New York Daily Sentinel* in *Liberator* 1 (September 24, 1831): 155; *Richmond Whig* in *NR* 38 (August 22, 1835): 440; letter of David F. Robertson in *Richmond Enquirer*, August 11, 1835; *Norfolk Beacon* and *Richmond Compiler* in *Baltimore Republican*, August 15, 1835.

7. Robert Gage to James McKibben Gage, August 31, 1835, James McKibben Gage Papers, SHC; *Darien* (Ga.) *Telegraph* in *NR* 41 (December 24, 1836): 272.

8. Eugene Walter, *Terror and Resistance: A Study of Political Violence, with Case Studies of Some Primitive African Communities* (New York, 1969), is the classic exposition of the politics of terror, and the way in which extreme arbitrariness abets effectiveness.

9. *Richmond Enquirer*, August 9, 1835; letter to *Richmond Whig*, August 12, 1835; *National Intelligencer*, August 27, 1835. The latter indulged in common Southern logic, if unusual analogy: the fault was really that of "Northern fanatics" who drove Southerners "to a pitch of jealousy, compared with which Othello's feelings are those of assured confidence."

10. *New Orleans Advertiser* in *New York Evening Post*, September 2, 1835.

11. *Louisiana Courier* in *Vicksburg Register*, September 10, 1835; *Charleston Patriot* on an incident in Columbia on September 8 and on one in Orangeburg District a few days later where "Judge Hang presided," and *Aiken* (S.C.) *Telegraph*, September 11, 1835, in *New York Evening Post*, September 17, 1835, and *Portland Advertiser*, September 26, 1835. A similar case, grown of the same hysteria, I label "criminal" rather than "abolition" because the Charleston mob, led by ex-Governor John Lyde Wilson, accused the barber they beat, tar-and-cottoned, and tossed in jail of selling cotton stolen by slaves. Andrew Schirmer, "Journal," August 21, 1835, SCHC; *Charleston Patriot*, August 21, 1835.

12. *Portland Argus*, August 11, 1835; Otis's letters of description and explanation of September 3, 6, and 9 appeared in the *Portland Advertiser*, September 7–9, 1835. Otis had written abolitionist lecturer Amos A. Phelps asking him to speak in Portland on the "glorious cause" (March 7, 1834, A. A. Phelps Papers, BPL).

13. *Baltimore Republican*, June 25, 1835; *Augusta* (Me.) *Age*, June 29, 1835. William R. Hogan reports a happy ending (I guess) for this story. Kitchell was later admitted to the Texas bar, even though "sundry respectable citizens" of Georgia had driven him away as an abolitionist, because he'd turned respectable after that. Hogan, *The Republic of Texas* (Norman, Okla., 1946).

14. *Norfolk Herald*, in William Lloyd Garrison, ed., *The New "Reign of Terror" in the Slaveholding States* (Boston, 1860), 60–61; *New York Independent*, December 29, 1859; Julian A. Selby, *Memorabilia and Anecdotal Reminiscences of Columbia . . .* (Columbia, S.C., 1905), 131.

15. "Cosmo" letter of November 20, 1859, from Salisbury to *New Bern* (N.C.) *Progress* in Garrison, *New "Reign of Terror,"* 77–79.

16. *New York Herald*, January 18, 1860, and the Charleston incident in same month, Garrison, *New "Reign of Terror,"* 131, 112; New Orleans incident, November 1860, William Lloyd

Garrison, ed., *A Fresh Catalogue of Southern Outrages* (Boston, 1861), 69; *New York Independent* in Garrison, *New "Reign of Terror,"* 63; *Oxford* (Miss.) *Intelligencer,* September 12, November 14, 1860, in Donald Brooks Kelley's rich "Harper's Ferry: Prelude to Crisis in Mississippi," *JMissH* 67 (November 1965): 367–68.

17. *Richmond Dispatch* and letter of F. Snow, December 28, 1859, in Garrison *New "Reign of Terror,"* 75–76, 102; letter from Clio to *Charleston Mercury,* in Garrison, *Fresh Catalogue,* 19–21; letter from Chappel's Depot, February 6, 1860, in Garrison *New "Reign of Terror,"* 105, and the trick on the Italian organ grinders, 96.

18. *Augusta* (Ga.) *Evening Dispatch,* December 29, 1859, and *Charleston Mercury,* December 31, 1859, in *New York Tribune* in Garrison, *New "Reign of Terror,"* 35–41. In four cases, people mobbed claimed that the impetus for action against them came from people who owed them money; at least in four others mobbing activity was directly related to confiscating property.

19. *Belfast* (Me.) *Age,* in Garrison, *New "Reign of Terror,"* 84–85; report of Duncan L. Clinch and William T. Bird, in the *Savannah News,* in Garrison, *Fresh Catalogue,* 23–24.

20. *Indianapolis Journal,* December 24, 1859.

21. *Liberator* 1 (December 3, 1831): 194.

22. James Blair killed Dr. Shepherd in Columbus, Mississippi (Garrison, *New "Reign of Terror,"* 121); R. T. Sherman letter, in November or December 1860, in Garrison, *Fresh Catalogue,* 55.

23. Rev. W. J. Weiss to his mother, January 6, 1861, Belcher-Weiss-Jennison Papers, MaHS; letter from Memphis, November 6, 1860, in *Cleveland Plain Dealer,* and letter of Samuel J. Halle to *Memphis Argus,* December 11, 1860, in Garrison, *Fresh Catalogue,* 51, 64.

24. Milledgeville correspondent of *Savannah Republican,* November 22, 1860, in Garrison, *Fresh Catalogue,* 66. The mob had wanted to hang a Lincoln man but settled on a poor man from the North who had trouble explaining himself.

25. John Townsend, *The Doom of Slavery in the Union: Its Safety out of It* (Charleston, 1860), 3. Townsend claimed "every Douglas Democrat, and every Bell and Everett supporter" in fact favored Lincoln and had "abolitionist proclivities."

26. Anna P. Hannum, ed., *Quaker Forty-Niner: The Adventures of Charles E. Pancoast on the American Frontier* (Philadelphia, 1930), 111–15.

27. Charles Colcock Jones Jr. to his father and sometimes his mother, October 6, 11, 1859, October 9, 27, 1860, May 4, 1861; Rev. Charles C. Jones to his son, May 9, 1861, in Robert Manson Myers, ed., *The Children of Pride: A True Story of Georgia and the Civil War* (New Haven, 1972), 524–25, 613–14, 624, 672–76. The report of a victim, William T. Reynolds, son of a Savannah merchant, said that on November 18, 1860, Jones promised him protection, but the mob picked him up four days later (Garrison, *Fresh Catalogue,* 54–55).

28. *Richmond Enquirer,* September 25, 1835. On the Virginia debate, with strong sectional roots, see Joseph Clark Robert, *The Road from Monticello: A Study of the Virginia Slavery Debate of 1832* (Durham, N.C., 1941), and Alison G. Freehling, *Drift toward Dissolution: The Virginia Slavery Debate of 1831–32* (Baton Rouge, 1982).

29. Letter from Kanawha Salines, September 6, 1835, in *Lynchburg* (Va.) *Democrat,* September 14, 1835, in *NR* 49 (October 3, 1835): 76–77; *Richmond Enquirer,* August 4, 1835.

30. *Philadelphia Public Ledger,* May 28, 1838; *Kennebec* (Me.) *Journal,* January 29, 1839. In 1845, Virginians kidnapped three Ohioans, and legal maneuvers between the two states ended in stalemate. *NR* 69 (September 20, October 4, 1845): 41, 67; *NR* 70 (January 9, 1845): 296.

31. Robert McColley, *Slavery and Jeffersonian Virginia* (Urbana, Ill., 1964), 147–62; Donald Mathews, *Slavery and Methodism: A Chapter in American Morality, 1780–1845* (Princeton, 1965), 62–87, and *Religion in the Old South* (Chicago, 1977), 170–208; John L.

Eighmy, *Churches in Cultural Captivity: A History of Social Attitudes of Southern Baptists* (Knoxville, 1972), 25–30; Anne C. Loveland, *Southern Evangelicals and the Social Order, 1800–1860* (Baton Rouge, 1980), 208–56. The rich black-white religious ties in the South are movingly explored in Mechal Sobel, *Trabelin' On: The Slave Journey to an Afro-Baptist Faith* (Westport, Conn., 1979) and *The World They Made Together: Black and White Values in Eighteenth-Century Virginia* (Princeton, 1987), and illustrated in John Boles's bibliographic essay "The Discovery of Southern Religious History" in the book he edited with Evelyn Thomas Nolen, *Interpreting Southern History: Historiographical Essays in Honor of Sanford W. Higginbotham* (Baton Rouge, 1987), 510–48, and his other writings on Southern religion, especially his editing of an excellent collection, *Religion in the South: Essays* (Jackson, Miss., 1985).

32. *NR* 69 (October 11, 1845): 90; Clement Eaton, "Mob Violence in the Old South," *MVHR* 29 (December 1942): 363–64.

33. *Salem* (N.C.) *Peoples' Press*, October 4, 1851; *New York Tribune*, September 29, 1851. Such threats were effective against not only their victims but anyone else holding deviant opinions, but they did not end private hostility or even touches of public opposition to slavery by men and ministers who were respected, cautious, and lucky. Patricia Hickin chronicles one such career in "Gentle Agitation: Samuel M. Janney and the Anti-Slavery Movement in Virginia, 1842–1851," *JSH* 37 (May 1971): 159–90, and one sees a similar pattern in the personal reminiscences of a Methodist preacher from Maryland's Eastern Shore, John Dixon Long, *Pictures of Slavery in Church and State . . .* (Auburn, N.Y., 1859).

34. *Wheeling Intelligencer*, August 18, 1856; *New York Tribune*, September 12, 1856; *Kanawha Valley* (Va.) *Star*, February 3, 1857.

35. *Wytheville* (Va.) *Telegraph*, November 22, 1859, and *New York Herald*, January 1, 1860, in Larry Gara, *The Liberty Line: The Legend of the Underground Railroad* (Lexington, 1961), 87; *New Orleans Courier*, December 29, 1859; *Washington* (Pa.) *Tribune* and *New York Tribune*, in Garrison, *New "Reign of Terror,"* 67–68, 93, 101, 114–17; *Richmond Enquirer*, November 15, 1859; *Alexandria Gazette*, in Garrison, *Fresh Catalogue*, 48.

36. Cassius M. Clay, *Writings of Cassius M. Clay, including Speeches and Addresses,* ed. Horace Greeley (New York, 1848), 130–78. Clay's basic enlightenment convictions are sketched best in the same work (18–30). Many others contributed to the Kentucky antislavery movement, from bravely feisty editor William Shreve Bailey to dubiously proslavery editor George D. Prentice. The broad contours of the movement in Kentucky up to 1850 are handled well in Asa E. Martin, *The Anti-Slavery Movement in Kentucky prior to 1850* (Louisville, 1918), as are its religious aspects in John Boles, *Religion in Ante-Bellum Kentucky* (Lexington, 1976), 101–18. Will Frank Steely, "Anti-Slavery in Kentucky, 1850–1860" (Ph.D. diss., University of Rochester, 1956), is rich on this period, while Lowell H. Harrison, *The Anti-Slavery Movement in Kentucky* (Lexington, 1978), offers a concise overview. The standard biography is David L. Smiley, *Lion of White Hall* (Madison, 1962), especially good on the Faulknerian Gothic of Clay's later years, though less evocative of the man in his prime than Clay's honest, if often careless, autobiography, and the early writings Greeley edited.

37. Cassius M. Clay, *The Life of Cassius Marcellus Clay; Memoirs, Writings and Speeches* (Cincinnati, 1886), 80–81; Clay, *Writings*, 78. Though he hated intensely the Wickliffes, father and son, an early issue of the *True American*, June 17, 1845, praised Wickliffe, "giving the devil his due," for his legal defense of a black.

38. Clay, *Life*, 82–85; Clay to Salmon P. Chase, September 1843, Chase Papers, HSPa.

39. See Clay, *Writings*, 127–28, for an 1843 open letter to the people of Kentucky, and ibid., 220, on his more general dislike of mobs; on his racism *and* his dedication to the sociopolitical rights of blacks and his hostility to any plan of forced colonization, see ibid.,

292–95, 337–40. Marshall's angriest charge speaks well of Clay: "The negroes might well, as we have strong reason to believe they do, look to him as a deliverer." W. L. Barre, ed., *Speeches and Writings of the Hon. Thomas F. Marshall* (Cincinnati, 1858), 207. William Freehling offers a contrasting picture of Clay as primarily a racist who cared very little about slavery and much about "whitening" Kentucky and about "land speculation" in *Road to Disunion: Secessionists at Bay* (New York, 1990), 460–72. Clay admitted—and sometimes virulently expresed—racism and worked to make his position viable to Kentuckians, but he was the only Southern politician or spokesman to insist that blacks were entitled to basic human and civil rights and opportunities. Few Kentuckians or antislavery people, white or black, doubted his basic commitments. Stanley Harrold, "Cassius M. Clay on Slavery and Race: A Reinterpretation," *SA* 9 (1988): 42–53, and *The Abolitionists and the South, 1831–1861* (Lexington, Ky., 1995), 131–45.

40. Clay to Chase, September 1843, January 9, 1844, Chase Papers, HSPa; Clay, *Writings*, 31.

41. *True American*, June 3, 24, 1845, in Clay, *Writings*, 217, 224. Such gross personalisms shouldn't obscure Clay's intelligence when denouncing slavery itself, as in his letter of April 1844 (*Writings*, 141).

42. Clay to Chase, July 3, 1845, Chase Papers, HSPa, explains clearly the rationale for his brutally personal early remarks.

43. Clay, *Writings*, 302, 258, 316; Marshall, *Speeches*, 208–9, and, quoting the offensive editorial of August 12, 196–97.

44. Clay, *Writings*, 289–91, 303–4, and *Life*, 107. The circular he printed on August 15, 1845, Clay sent to Chase; it is in the latter's papers, HSPa.

45. Clay's *Appeal*, August 18, 1845, in *Writings*, 298–300; Clay, *Life*, 107–108. *NR* 69 (September 6, 1845): 14–15, printed some of the proceedings, and Marshall, *Speeches*, 199–209, reprinted his talk. Clay claimed that it was largely the Democratic Party, still led by ex-vice president (under Martin Van Buren) Richard Mentor Johnson, that organized the mobbing (*Writings*, 304–305; *Life*, 23). One reason for Marshall's anger was Clay's republication in the *True American* of an antislavery speech that Marshall had made years earlier (*Writings*, 208).

46. Clay, *Writings*, 305–8; Lewis Collins, *History of Kentucky* (Frankfort, 1966), 2:51; William E. Connelly and E. M. Coulter, *History of Kentucky* (Chicago, 1922), 2:812. On Vaughan's editorship, see Clay, *Writings*, 335–36 and *Life*, 175, as well as the letter from James to Thomas Lakey, August 24, 1847, Lakey Papers, CinHS, praising Vaughan's greater "effect" as an editor. The tie of others in Kentucky to Clay's fate is clear in the way mobs took advantage of the attack on him to sack the mildly antislavery *Georgetown Christian Intelligencer* and to tar and feather several free blacks in Lexington (*NR* 68 [August 30, 1845]: 408–9).

47. *Louisville Journal* in *NR* 69 (September 6, 1845): 15; Greeley, Introduction to Clay, *Writings*, vii. The *Lexington Observer*, August 23, 1845, offered a good example of Democratic mob praise, but Clay exulted in how general the riot condemnation was and how tentative the support for it (*True American*, October 28, 1845, in Clay, *Writings*, 327).

48. Clay, *Writings*, 470, and letter to the *New York Tribune*, December 10, 1846, 475–78; Clay to Chase, June 30, 1846, Chase Papers, HSPa; and Clay letter in *NR* 70 (July 11, 1846): 294.

49. Clay, *Life*, 185–86. Clay labeled Marshall, whom he despised, as the instigator (*Life*, 129–31, 494). Clay's emancipation plan followed the form earlier used in the North: a prohibition of slave sales out of the state, the freeing of slave women born after a certain date at the age of twenty-one, and some encouragement of voluntary emigration by blacks, but a ban on any forced exile of those freed.

50. Frederick Law Olmsted, *A Journey through Texas; or A Saddle-Trip on the Southwestern Frontier* (New York, 1857), 12–13.

51. Explanations of Clay's actions are in his letters to Salmon P. Chase in the HSPa: June 4, July 5, October 23, 1855, and in Clay, *Life*, 240–59. Fee covers his own fascinating career with straightforward simplicity in his *Autobiography* (Cincinnati, 1880), the best source about the warm if uneasy friendship between the two Kentuckians, so deeply opposite except in their antislavery. Clay gave land to Fee to settle his group in central Kentucky and circulated Fee's antislavery pamphlets, doubtless hoping to add a religious adjunct to his economic antislavery politics (esp. 89–93).

52. The public split between the two men began at a July 4, 1856, picnic, just when the Republicans were clearly the waxing power in the North. Here Clay chose strongly to denounce a comment Fee made about a "higher law," though Fee forced him to admit that he wouldn't obey the Fugitive Slave Law. Fee reported overhearing someone say then, "Fee is religiously right; Clay is politically right." Fee blamed Clay's "notion of expediency" for the trouble (*Autobiography*, 103–26). Sears, *Day of Small Things*, uses Fee's letters richly.

53. *Richmond Enquirer*, August 25, 1835.

Chapter Five

1. Occasionally people essentially "abolitionist" in the Southern definition were labeled "insurrectionist," but I include them in the other category. For example, William Smithyman was beaten until he confessed he was an "insurrectionist" and then was tar-and-feathered in Senatobia, Mississippi, in January 1861, without anyone suggesting a slave uprising. *St. Louis Democrat*, reprinted in William Lloyd Garrison, ed., *A Fresh Catalogue of Southern Outrages* (Boston, 1861), 63.

2. Solomon Northup, *Twelve Years a Slave, A Narrative . . .* (Auburn, N.Y., 1853), 188–90; *NR* 53 (October 28, 1837): 129; *New Orleans American* in *New York Evening Post*, October 27, 1837. Two companies of United States troops were sent there, and three free blacks and nine slaves were hanged, quickly but after (I think) a legal trial.

3. Historians have sometimes argued wrongly that the profit motive prevented antebellum mob killings of blacks: Hugh Davis Graham and Ted Robert Gurr, *The History of Violence in America* (New York, 1969), 791. For a view of slave insurrections very different from mine, see Herbert Aptheker's *American Negro Slave Revolts* (New York, 1934), richly researched though sometimes carelessly reported. Aptheker accepts everything whites said on these occasions without consideration of the gross improbabilities of the stories and evidence. More recently, Winthrop Jordan accepts as real a Civil War insurrection where my reading of his evidence is that it was a "whipped-out" white fantasy. *Tumult and Silence at Second Creek: An Inquiry into a Civil War Conspiracy* (Baton Rouge, 1993).

4. On these South Carolina developments the classic study is William Freehling's *Prelude to Civil War: The Nullification Controversy in South Carolina, 1816–36* (New York, 1966).

5. E. P. Guion to Thomas Ruffin, August 28, 1831, Thomas Ruffin Papers, and Elizabeth Watters to John Haske, August 16, 1831, C. W. Broadfoot Papers, SHC; *Liberator* 1 (September 3, 1831): 140–43, printed many of the first letters and reports, all of which estimated the number of insurrectionists at 300 to 800 and most of which provided white leaders to the blacks. The literature on Nat Turner's revolt is rich but pays little sustained attention to the militia and citizenry's torture and killing of innocent blacks after its repression. Henry Irving Tragle, ed., *The Southampton Slave Revolt of 1831* (Amherst, 1971), is the excellent standard collection of primary and secondary material; other works are by Eric Foner, Stephen Oates, and Herbert Aptheker. John W. Cromwell "The Aftermath of Nat Turner's Insurrection," *JNH* 5 (1920): 208–34, puts the innocent death toll, on the basis of local black memory, at 120.

6. Pleasants in the *Richmond Whig*, quoted in the *Columbia* (S.C.) *Centennial*, August 31, 1831, and *Roanoke* (N.C.) *Advocate*, September 15, 1831; minister's letter from the scene, quoted in Frank Shay, *Judge Lynch: His First 100 Years* (New York, 1938), 41–42. The *Roanoke Advocate* printed a letter from one of the Murfreesboro troops under Elisha H. Sharp who went to Southampton, detailing several of their black killings and the militia's pocketing, cooperatively with some Southampton whites, $23 and a gold watch taken from three victims (October 31, 1831).

7. Emma Mordecai to Ellen Mordecai, September 2, 1831, with a postscript signed "E." in another hand, Mordecai Papers, SHC.

8. Mary E. D. Manning, Woodlawn, Virginia, to Elizabeth Roberts, October 21, 1831, Jonathan Roberts Papers, HSPa. The *Tarboro* (N.C.) *Free Press*, October 18, 25, 1831, has fairly full reports on "rumors" in Delaware and Maryland as well as farther South.

9. V. I. Trist, Charlottesville, to Nicholas P. Trist, September 25, 1831, James I. Otey Papers, SHC.

10. Turner's religious motivation is clear in Thomas R. Gray's transcript of *The Confessions of Nat Turner* (reprint, Miami, 1969), the honesty of which created fury in the Southern press which preferred Nat as snarling savage. *Richmond Enquirer*, 12–14, 1831; *Elizabeth City* (N.C.) *Star*, December 31, 1831.

11. James F. McRae, August 7, 1830; L. D. Henry, September 3, 1830; and W. Burgwyn and John I. Paskur, November 15, 1830, to Gov. John Owens, Owens Papers; Tryam McFarland, September 3, 1831, to Gov. Montfort Stokes, Stokes Papers, NCDAH. Clement Eaton's "A Dangerous Pamphlet in the Old South," *JSH* 2 (1936): 323–33, and John Spencer Bassett, *Slavery in North Carolina* (Baltimore, 1899), 98–107, support this white conspiratorial use of Walker's pamphlet, while Charles Wiltse endorses Truman Nelson's "plausible speculation" that slaves actually widely knew Walker's work, smuggled south in old clothes that Walker sold to sailors: Wiltse's edition of Walker's *Appeal* (New York, 1965), viii–xii.

12. Governor Montfort Stokes's "Letterbook" for December 1830 shows much of this private fear and official response. A. M. Kirkland to Catherine Ruffin, January 10, 1831, Ruffin-Roulhac-Hamilton Papers and Thomas Ruffin to Annie Ruffin, December 30, 1831, Thomas Ruffin Papers, SHC.

13. Robert S. Parker to Rebecca Maney, August 29, 1831, John Kimberly Papers, SHC. Parker also gave a general description of the Murfreesboro troops' activity at Southampton, where the Virginia militia began the practice of poling heads.

14. Samuel Whitaker to Montfort Stokes, August 26, 1831, Stokes Papers, NCDAH. The Stokes Papers in late August and September are full of hysterical letters and reports from citizens chronicling in detail marches and massacres and burnings that never occurred, some of which Whitaker felt obliged to send on with a note: "None of this news do I believe." *Edenton Gazette* in Fayetteville *Carolina Observer*, October 26, 1831.

15. The fullest report of the plot discovery was in the Fayetteville *Carolina Observer*, September 14, 21, 1831; Jeremiah Pearsall, Kenansville, to Samuel Langdon, September 19, 1831, Langdon-Young-Means Papers, SHC. Maj. Gen. Nathan B. Whitfield reported the whole fantasy, plus some "rascally whites" involved in the plot, on September 12, but two days later he more cautiously referred to rumors growing out "of some discovery of intended insurrectionary movements," with those blacks mob-murdered "killed as examples." Letters to Gov. Montfort Stokes, Stokes Letterbook, NCDAH.

16. Pearsall to Langdon, September 19, 1831, SHC; *Newburn* (N.C.) *Sentinel*, September 15, in *Tarborough* (N.C.) *Free Press*, September 20, 1831. There were by this time decriers of the plot rumors, men like George Whitaker and George E. Badger, October 4, 1831, who warned Governor Stokes about "the cruel and undeserved" killing and torture of slaves (Stokes Letterbook, NCDAH); or young Lewis Tillinghast, who laughed as early as September 14 at all the "raw head and bloody bones stories," attacked the "brutal and savage man-

ner" of whites, and, as a militia member, hoped the insurrection would come quickly: "One might as well be killed as drilled to death" (letter to James Tillinghast, William N. Tillinghast Papers, DU). Less common were editors who dared suggest the brutal folly of whipped-out proofs (*Newburn Spectator and Literary Journal*, September 23, 1831) or the vicious fantasy of all the rumors (*Raleigh Register*, September 21, 1831):

> The flying rumors gather'd as they roll'd
> Scarce any tale was sooner heard than told,
> And all who told it added something new,
> And all who heard it, made enlargment, too.
> In every ear it spread, on every tongue it grew.

17. *Wilmington Recorder*, September 21, in *Raleigh Star*, September 29, 1831; R. Lazurus, Wilmington, to Ellen Mordecai, and ?, Petersburg, Virginia, to Mrs. Richard Lazurus, both October 9, 1831, and Mrs. Ann Davis to Magdelan de Rosset, September 13, 1831, Mordecai Papers, SHC, all suggest the depth of panic.

18. Duplin County Court Records, September 30, 1831; and letters of John R. Donnell, October 4, and James Wright Jr., December 5; James Wright Sr. affidavit, November 16, 1831, and counterpetitions signed by 163 citizens asserting no "rational doubt" could exist of the slave's guilt, Stokes Papers, and Stokes's respite, October 3, and pardon, December 5, Stokes Letterbook, all NCDAH. Old Wright's testimony was most telling: he urged each mob-attacked slave "to acknowledge any thing that he thought would please them, and tell the same tale they told" as the only way to lighten their sufferings.

19. William Gaston to Susan Donaldson, September 22, 1831, Gaston Papers, SHC; Isaiah H. Spencer, Hyde County, September 20, 1831; John Borland to Roscius Borland, August 31, 1831; Clinton citizens letter, September 13, 1831; Petition against the pardon of Jerry, November 11, 1831, Stokes Papers, NCDAH.

20. John Borland to Roscius Borland, August 31, 1831, Stokes Papers, NCDAH; Fayetteville *North Carolina Journal*, October 5, 1831. Donald Mathews argues this general case in *Religion in the Old South* (Chicago, 1977), and rich detail is given in Jane Cornelius, "Slave Marriages in a Georgia Congregation," in Orville Vernon Burton and Robert C. McMath Jr., *Class, Conflict, and Consensus: Antebellum Southern Community Structure* (Westport, Conn., 1982), 128–45, and in several good studies in the collection edited by John Boles, *Masters and Slaves in the House of the Lord: Race and Religion in the American South, 1740–1870* (Lexington, Ky., 1988).

21. Charlotte Hooper to son John De Bessiere Hooper, September 20, 1831, Hooper Family Papers; Moses A. Curtis, "Diary" September 23, 1831; Lewis Williams to William Gaston, December 21, 1831, Gaston Papers, all SHC. The Curtis diary between September 9 and October 5 is rich in reports and reflections, both intelligent and idiosyncratic, on the panic.

22. Richmond County Supreme Court Minutes, September 30, 1831, Court Records; Petition of forty-seven citizens of Duplin County, October 14, 1831, and letter of W. L. Menouson, October 15, 1831, Stokes Papers, and letter of Stokes to Gov. James Hamilton of South Carolina, November 18, 1831, and Address to the Assembly, November 22, 1831, in Stokes Letterbook, all NCDAH.

23. The first reference to the *Liberator* as cause of Southampton that I've discovered was in *Tarborough* (N.C.) *Free Press*, September 6, 1831, which reported that it was published in "Boston or Philadelphia." The *National Intelligencer*, by the time it reported the charge that most Southern papers copied, on September 18, 1831, had learned where Garrison published. Gov. John Floyd of Virginia solemnly assured that state in his annual message of December 31, 1831, that Turner's insurrection was "designed and matured by unrestrained fanatics in

some of the neighboring states." Quoted in Henry W. Wilson, *History of the Rise and Fall of Slave Power Conspiracy in America* (Boston, 1872–77), 1:192.

24. Lewis C. Gray, *History of Agriculture in the Southern United States to 1860* (Washington, D.C., 1933), 2:903; *Mississippian*, May 14, 1834; Thomas Shackleford, *Proceedings of the Citizens of Madison County, Mississippi, at Livingston in July, 1835, in Relation to the Trial and Punishment of Several Individuals Implicated in the Contemplated Insurrection in this State* (Jackson, Miss., 1835); *Baton Rouge Register* in *Woodville Republican*, May 23, 1835. Good August weather lessened the crop loss (*Mississippian*, October 16, 1835), but William Winans of Centreville, Mississippi, wrote his brother Obadiah that the early summer rains diminished the crop by from one-third to one-half, (November 14, 1835, Winans Paper, MissDAH). One of the best pictures of the region's economic and social realities is the diary of William Munn in ChiHS. On March 12, 1834, Munn wrote, "Suddenly all is changed— Confidence is gone and money is also—The merchants on whom our success depended have yielded to the storm." A Yankee in background and a Calhounite in political persuasion, Munn moved to the area in 1831 as a storekeeper but soon became a planter; like most others in the area, he invested heavily on credit in land and slaves and desperately hung on when the boom fizzled in the late 1830s. Munn was away at the time of the insurrection panic but returned to the area in late 1835 and became a member of the Committee of Thirteen in its dormancy in 1836. The best literary source for this time and area is Joseph G. Baldwin's *Flush Times in Mississippi and Alabama* (New York, 1853), which turns these years of men desperately plotting advantage and profit into solid comedy.

25. Shackleford, *Proceedings*, 6–8. Although a slave woman "revealed" the plot, there is no suggestion that she was ever "interrogated" or punished.

26. Shackleford, *Proceedings*, 8–11; Jesse Mabry letter of July 13, 1835, in *Grand Gulf Advertiser*, August 4, 1835. Anonymous, *The Life and Adventures of John Murrell* (Philadelphia, 1849), printed a letter with the best description, melodramatic but convincingly detailed, of the first beatings and hangings at Beattie's Bluff and of the crowd frenzy surrounding them very much in Vergil Stewart's style (112–20).

27. Two letters provide the most accurate record of the known events. A detailed chronology was made by a visitor to the area at the time, published in the *New York Evening Star*, and the official press release, probably written by Shackleford for the July 11 *Clinton Gazette*, was printed in *NR* 48 (August 8, 1835): 404. One other letter contains accurate description of part of what happened, this one from Tyger Bayou, Mississippi, taken from the *Charleston Courier* by the *New York Evening Post*, August 6, 1835. The Donovan letter to his wife of July 7 was communicated by Donovan's father, Thomas, "our respected fellow citizen," to the *Maysville* (Ky.) *Eagle* at the end of July and reprinted in *National Intelligencer*, August 7, 1835.

28. The Earle torture was described in a letter from "Humanity," July 24, 1835, in the *Natchez Courier*, August 7, 1835, while a Livingston reply of August 20 was printed in the *Vicksburg Register*, September 17, 1835. This didn't contest the description but mocked "the unnatural sympathy" for a monster like Earle. The ties to Boyd are suggested in a letter from Madison County, August 24, 1835, to the *Natchez Courier*, reprinted in *Baltimore Republican*, September 2, 1835; Shackleford, *Proceedings*, 16.

29. Letter of Patrick Sharkey and James B. Kilborn to Gov. Hiram Runnels, July 2, 1835, Governor's Papers, MissDAH; letter to *Lexington* (Ky.) *Intelligencer* in *U.S. Telegraph*, August 5, 1835. Sharkey and Kilborn pointed out the stupidity of denying legal process after the date of the alleged insurrection, when the plot was exposed and the leaders hanged, but the letter explained why mob killings went on: "I never saw a people so blind with excitement. The populace are . . . out for blood." George C. Osborn, "Plantation Life in Central Mississippi as Revealed in the Clay Sharkey Papers," *JMissH* 3 (October 1941): 277–88, offers an

interesting sketch of Patrick Sharkey, who came to the area poor from Tennessee in 1817 and became a wealthy planter, but one who believed slavery indefensible. A Whig, he allowed much independence to his slaves and advocated stiff laws against injuring slaves. His cousin, for eighteen years Mississippi's chief justice, had a poor education but was very "able and sagacious" in judgment, well illustrated in his protecting his relative by playing up the "super-eminent authority" of the vigilantes: John F. H. Claiborne, *Life and Correspondence of John A. Quitman* (New York, 1860), 1:474; Henry A. Foote, *Casket of Reminiscences* (Washington, D.C., 1874), 259–61. William Freehling sees the Sharkey episode as proof of county "local-ism," although the majority of the whites killed were not locals. He also says Sharkey later sued his tormentors and collected $10,000, a claim for which I've found no evidence. *The Road to Disunion: Secessionists at Bay* (New York, 1990). 110–13. A letter from Mississippi, September 20, 1835, in *Baltimore Gazette*, October 22, 1835, described Ned's attempts to buy his life by implicating others, but by this time the mob, its killing mood over, decided the rev-elations were "of revenge." The Clinton mulatto victim, Vincent, "obstinately refused" to co-operate (*Grand Gulf Advertiser*, July 28, 1835).

30. Shackleford, *Proceedings*, ii–iv; *Mississippian*, August 7, 1835.

31. Shackleford, *Proceedings*, iv–13; Foote, *Casket of Reminiscences*, 255. Foote also wrote movingly about how fear of mob anger kept him from aiding his friend Lee Smith when he saw a mob beating him with rods, from protecting Vincent from mob death, and from taking the case Vincent's former owner, a widow, wanted to press against the mulatto's murderers (255–59).

32. Edwin Miles, "Mississippi Slave Insurrection Scare of 1835," *JNH* 42 (1957): 48–60. Miles records the land and slave holdings of the committee members (50). Hudnold, with 2,700 acres and 118 slaves, was by far the wealthiest, but all except Dr. Mitchell were sub-stantial planters. The focus on steam doctors came at the end of a campaign by other doctors to ban these briefly popular practitioners. In the spring, Chief Justice William Sharkey over-turned as unconstitutional the conviction of a steam doctor under the new law (*Woodville* (Miss.) *Republican*, May 2, 1835).

33. Shackleford, *Proceedings*, 25. Three of those killed and most of those exiled were from Hinds County, where the *Jackson Banner* reported that no slaves had heard of the plot, quoted in *Grand Gulf Advertiser*, July 14, 1835. The Earles were from Warren County. Lau-rence Shore, "Making Mississippi Safe for Slavery: The Insurrectionary Panic of 1835," in Burton and McMath, *Class, Conflict and Consensus*, 96–127, argues that the incident shows Southern fears of white divisions about slavery.

34. Shackleford, *Proceedings*, 9–11, 26–34; Claiborne, *Life of Quitman*, 1:138. Southern papers were insistent on the authenticity of Stewart's pamphlet, though there was some Whig and nullifier doubting. An able account of the real Murrell is that of James L. Penick, *The Great Western Land Pirate: John Murrell in Legend and History* (Columbia, Mo., 1981), which sensibly bears out early local reports of Murrell as small-time criminal: Joseph Williams, *Old Times in West Tennessee: Reminiscences* (Memphis, 1873), 247–49; James Phalen, *A History of Tennessee . . . with a Sketch of Madison County* (Boston, 1888), 821; Park Marshall, "John Murrell and Daniel Crenshaw—Some Facts with Regard to these Crim-inals . . . ," *TenHM* 6 (1920): 3–9.

35. Stewart's fiction came out under two pseudonyms: Augustus Q. Walton, *A History of the Detection, Conviction, Life and Designs of John A. Murel, the Great Western Land Pirate* (Cincinnati, [1835]), and a revised and expanded version that also reprinted Shackleford's pamphlet, H. R. Howard, *The History of Virgil Stewart and His Adventures in Capturing and Exposing the Great "Western Land Pirate" . . .* (New York, 1836). Stewart gave some plausibility to his story by including some known crooks on his list, the most prominent of whom was Alonzo Phelps, long in jail in Mississippi under a death sentence. Phelps peti-

tioned the governor in March 1834 for a delay in his execution so he could write his memoirs, proving he had "always been a friend to the widow and orphan," to help financially some poor acquaintances, "if the sail of it shall equail my expectations." Phelps was still around in 1836, by which time he had learned he was a Murrellite and had written a fifty- to sixty-page manuscript in which he informed the governor that he had considered breaking jail to join the insurrection but refrained "from considerations of humanity." Alonzo Phelps to Hiram Runnels, March 3, 1834, Governor's Papers, MissDAH, and affidavit of Phelps's lawyer, Henry Foote, April 15, 1836, in Howard, *Stewart*, 261–62.

36. Walton, *Murel*, 33–35, 53–58, 65–78; Howard, *Stewart*, 7–8, 12–13, 127–150, 204–15, 169–75; Philadelphia *National Gazette*, August 27, 1834. Clanton, elected probate judge in Yallabusha County, had sixty-six fellow citizens testify to his character and thirty-seven of them swear that Stewart was a thief in a public letter Clanton wrote to the *Pittsburg* (Miss.) *Bulletin*, July 2, 1835. "Howard" claimed that the original pamphlet was printed in February and that Stewart sent it to judges and police officers as well as secretly circulated it; by May, Clanton had gotten his affidavit circulated and signed. Stewart's vigilantes beat a "confession" against Clanton out of Islam Medford, insisting it was "voluntary" since the beating stopped before Medford talked. Clanton and a Colonel Jarrot wrote a pamphlet against Stewart that I've not been able to find. Stewart's hopes are clear in his exaltation after the Livingston killings in a letter to Yallabusha opponent George N. Saunders: "It would be as much as a man's life is worth to interfere with me in anyway. . . . I said Clanton's feelings would bleed some day. . . . I have lived to see it." *Mississippian*, July 17, 1835; *Grand Gulf Advertiser*, August 4, 1835; Columbia, S.C., *Southern Times*, August 28, 1835.

37. Mabry letter in Shackleford, *Proceedings*, 8–11; Anon., *Murrell*, 119–21. Most detail on the real Mabry appears in Christopher Morris, "An Event in Community Organization: The Mississippi Slave Insurrection Scare of 1835," *JSocH* 22(1988): 42–53.

38. Eric Hobsbawm, *Primitive Rebels . . .* (New York, 1959), 1–26, 175–83. Leslie Fiedler's introduction to George Lippard's *The Quaker City; or The Monks of Monk Hall* (1846; reprint, New York, 1970), vii–xxxii, offers a good sketch of the genre as international phenomena; and I published an abridgment of a Northern example, *The Almighty Dollar!*, in *Notions of the Americans, 1820–1860* (New York, 1970), 245–59.

39. Foote, *Casket of Reminiscences*, 250–51; Howard, *Stewart*, 269–73; New Orleans City Council Chamber Report, mss., LSU; *Mississippian*, August 7, November 13, December 25, 1835; Columbia, S.C., *Southern Times*, September 11, 18, 25, 1835; *Moulton* (Ala.) *Whig*, August 26, 1835; *NR* 48 (August 8, 1835): 403–5; *Baltimore American*, August 10, 1835; Robert Coates, *The Outlaw Years: The History of the Land Pirates of the Natchez Chase* (New York, 1930), 169–302, and a host of other "popular" histories and novels; Eudora Welty, "A Still Moment," *in The Wide Net* (New York, 1943), 73–94; William Gilmore Simms, *Richard Hurdis; or, The Avenger of Blood* (New York, 1854), 10–11, and *Border Beagles, a Tale of Mississippi* (Chicago, 1885), first published in 1838 and 1840. Though the latter was set around Beattie's Bluff, Simms excluded all mention of the slave plot but reproduced in both books much of the communal and class distrust found in Stewart's tale plus, in *Hurdis* especially, much familial hatred. Simms also claimed that he had conferences with Stewart "prior to the publication" of the original Murrell story.

40. Anon., *Murrell*, 56; Walton, *Murel*, 13, 21, 42–44. Howard, *Stewart*, repeated and expanded most things in Walton, but cut a few things, like Murrell's trusting Stewart immediately, "for d——d if I could not see hell dance in your eyes," and some of the least believable details such as Murrell's quick trip to South America and conversion to Catholicism (33, 46–49). Perhaps some of these changes were concessions to Stewart's new, and much more reputable, publisher, the Methodist Harper Brothers.

41. Walton, *Murel*, 29–33; Howard, *Stewart*, 59–60. *Stewart* has Murrell give this lecture

322   *Notes to Pages 152–59*

only to "the most vicious and wicked disposed ones," and with some promise of liquor and white women along with a strange ritual indoctrination.

42. *Nashville Banner*, July 15, 1835; *Manchester* (Miss.) *Herald*, quoted in *Vicksburg Register*, July 30, 1835; *Clinton Gazette*, July 11, 1835, pasted in LC copy of *Murel*; Shackleford, *Proceedings*, 7–10; *Mississippian*, August 14, 1835; *Columbus* (Miss.) *Democratic Press* in *Baltimore American*, August 4, 1835.

43. George Wyche to Hiram Runnels, July 8, 1835, Governor's Papers, MissDAH; letter from Vicksburg, July 11, to *Lexington Intelligencer*, printed in *Kennebec* (Me.) *Journal*, August 12, 1835; William Thomson, Raymond, Mississippi, to Hannah Thomson, July 12, 1835, Thomson Papers, SHC.

44. *Mississippian*, July 17, 1835; Shackleford, *Proceedings*, 5. The letter from Brandon was dated June 25, 1835.

45. *Mississippian*, August 14, 1835; *NR* 48 (August 22, 1835): 440. A story, identical in both the *New Orleans American* and the *Louisiana Planter* of July 13, included the first mention of abolition in connection with the plot, of the loose kind that had followed Nat Turner's insurrection in the *New York Evening Post*, August 3, 1835.

46. M. Overman letter and Wilkinson County Meeting, in *Woodville Republican*, October 24, December 5, 1835. David Hubbard similarly tied abolition to Murrell in a private letter to John Bolton, August 23, 1835, New York and Mississippi Land Company Papers, SHSWi.

47. William Winans to Obadiah Winans, November 14, 1835, Winans Papers, MissDAH. Winans, like most Southerners of his education and generation, had called slavery an evil, which was enough to blast his brief foray into politics two decades later. William Cooper Jr., *The South and the Politics of Slavery, 1828–1856* (Baton Rouge, 1978), 1–4. Winans's image of the volcano as symbol of Southern society is so common in these months that Duff Green felt obliged to say, "It is *not* true that the South sleeps on a volcano." *U.S. Intelligencer* in *NR* 49 (October 3, 1835): 74.

48. Shackleford, *Proceedings*, 24, and 12, where he called all leaders "highway robbers, murderers and abolitionists"; Howard, *Stewart*, 58–59, 90. Anon., *Murrell*, 48, turned the added note into a letter from George Thompson.

49. *Mississippian*, August 14, 28 (letter of Rev. E. Battle), 1835.

50. John Quitman, *Message of the Governor to the State of Mississippi and to Both Houses of the Legislature* (Jackson, 1836), 5–6; *Columbus* (Miss.) *Democratic Press* in *Baltimore American*, August 4, 1835; Eugene Genovese, *The World the Slaveholders Made: Two Essays in Interpretation* (New York, 1969), 99.

51. *New Orleans Bee* in *New York Evening Post*, August 27, 1835; Quitman, *Message*; letter of Quitman to Colonel Burch, August 23, 1823, printed in Claiborne, *Life of Quitman*, 2:84; Joseph Ingraham, *The South-West* (New York, 1835), 2:123–28, 259–61; Norfolk *American Beacon* in *New York Evening Post*, August 21, 1835. Jefferson was a prime authority in the scientific racist tract Southerners praised most in the late 1830s, J. H. Guenebault, *Natural History of the Human Race* (Charleston, 1837).

52. The Battle letters were printed in the *Port Gibson Correspondent*, October 3, 1835, and the *Mississippian*, August 28, September 11, 1835; the Clinton report and resolves were in the *Clinton Gazette*, September 12, 1835.

53. Thomas R. Dew, *Review of the Debate in the Virginia Legislature of 1831 and 1832* (Richmond, 1832), 13, 20–21, 48–49. There is passing mention of Adam Smith (19), but Dew's argument parallels, indeed exceeds that of the Scotsman concerning the sanctity of property (47–69). Drew Gilpin Faust offers interesting socio-psychological interpretation of proslavery thought in *A Sacred Circle: The Dilemma of the Intellectual in the Old South, 1840–1860* (Baltimore, 1977), stressing George Fitzhugh's atypicality and the close parallels in Northern and Southern unease with aspects of untrammeled capitalist acquisitiveness (112–31).

54. Recent studies of Southern economics, immigration, urbanism, industry, religion, politics, and family reinforce similarities to the North, though patrons of paternalism and folk culture steadily press an abstract opposite case. There were some sectional differences, of course, but few that are not most clearly explained by the simple existence of slavery and the somewhat larger pockets of uneducated poverty among whites that slavery helped perpetuate. The various articles in John Boles and Evelyn Thomas Nolen, eds., *Interpreting Southern History: Historiographical Essays in Honor of Sanford W. Higginbotham* (Baton Rouge, 1987), offer solid summaries of recent studies. Stephanie McCurry suggests how slavery helped shape class interactions and especially family gender patterns in *Masters of Small Worlds: Yeoman Households, Gender Relations, and the Political Culture of the South Carolina Low Country* (New York, 1995).

55. Karl Marx, *Capital: A Critique of Political Economy*, ed. Frederick Engels and trans. Samuel Moore and Edward Aveling (New York, 1967), 1:236; Ezekiel A. Powell, "Fifty-Five Years in West Alabama," *AlaHQ 4 (1942): 507–11*; Col. James R. Creecy, *Scenes in the South and Other Miscellaneous Pieces* (Washington, D.C., 1860), 107; Ingraham, *Southwest*, 2:84–91; *Mississippian*, January 10, 1834; ad for a new paper to be published by V. N. Smith in Madisonville, in *Grand Gulf Adviser*, July 7, 1835. John Ashworth argues that the South was noncapitalist because there was little wage labor and because planters did not think only of profit maximization in *Slavery, Capitalism, and Politics in the Antebellum Republic* (Cambridge, Eng., 1995), 80–121. Yet Southern slavery involved a great deal of hiring out of wage labor with the owner collecting the wages, a practice retained to enhance the system's maximization of profit. And if one defines a bourgeois society (as many economists of all stripes do) as one where profit maximization always determines choice, no bourgeois society has ever existed.

56. George Fitzhugh, *Sociology for the South*, in *Ante-Bellum*, ed. Harvey Wish (New York, 1960), 49–54; William Harper, *Slavery in the Light of Social Ethics* (1836), 564–68, and James H. Hammond, *Slavery in the Light of Political Science* (1845), 647, both in E. N. Elliott, *Cotton Is King, and Pro-Slavery Arguments* (Augusta, Ga., 1860); Harper in *Morton vs. Thompson*, May 1854, in Helen Catterall, ed., *Judicial Cases Concerning American Slavery and the Negro* (Washington, D.C., 1926–37), 2:442; R. F. Charles, Mount Meigs, Ala., to Peter Bacot, November 13, 1836, Peter Bacot Papers, USC; J. W. Menzies to Alexander St. Clair Boys, June 5, 1842, Boys Papers, OhHS; B. F. W. Allston to his wife, December 7, 1836, Allston-Pringle Papers, SCHS; Rose to Thomas B. Huling, Huling Papers, UTex. The evidence supports James Oakes's conclusion that the planter ideal was "a model of efficiency. Its premise was black inferiority, its organizing principle was the absolute control of the master, its structure was bureaucratic" in a way that encouraged not close ties to the black workforce but a "conscious effort to create social distance between management and labor." *The Ruling Race: A History of American Slaveholders* (New York, 1982), 153–55, xi. Drew Gilpin Faust argues Hammond's profit concerns in *James Henry Hammond and the Old South: A Design for Mastery* (Baton Rouge, 1982), 105–34.

57. Mary Boykin Chesnut, *Diary from Dixie*, ed. Ben Ames Williams (Cambridge, Mass., 1980), September 21, 1861, 142; Francis Anne Kemble, *Journal of a Residence on a Georgia Plantation in 1838 and 1839* (1863; reprint, New York, 1970), 69–77, 287–89, and Robert Manson Myers, ed., *The Children of Pride: A True Story of Georgia and the Civil War* (New Haven, 1972), passim.

58. Carl Degler, *Neither Black nor White: Race Relations in Brazil and the United States* (New York, 1971); Peter Kolchin, *Unfree Labor: American Slavery and Russian Serfdom* (Cambridge, Mass., 1987). Frank Tannenbaum, *Slave and Citizen: The Negro in the Americas* (New York, 1967), and Stanley Elkins, *Slavery: A Problem in American Institutional and Intellectual Life* (Chicago, 1958), 52–80, argue the protectiveness of Latin American slavery.

59. Susan B. Eppes, *The Negro in the Old South* (Chicago, 1922), 83; Claiborne, *Life of Quitman*, 1:81; black woman quoted in Randolph Campbell, *Southern Community in Crisis: Harrison County, Texas, 1850–1880* (Austin, 1983), 142; John P. Parker, *His Promised Land: The Autobiography of John P. Parker,* ed. Stuart Seely Sprague (New York, 1996) 110–15; Rev. F. L. Cherry, "A History of Opelika, Alabama," *AlaHQ* 15 (1963): 255–59; Thomas Jefferson to Joel Yancey, January 17, 1819, in Edwin Morris Betts, ed., *Thomas Jefferson's Farm Book* (Princeton, 1953), 43.

60. *Jim, a slave v. the State*, 15 Ga. 535, July 1854; *Moran v. Davis*, 18 Ga. 722, August 1855; *Johnson v. Lovett*, 31 Ga. 187, August, 1860 in Catterall, *Judicial Cases*, 3:36, 45–46, 79.

61. *Jordan v. the State*, 22 Ga. 1855, June 1857; *Martin v. the State*, 2 Ga. 494, June 1858; *Moran v. Davis*, 18 Ga. 722, August 1855, in Catterall, *Judicial Cases*, 3:55–56, 63, 46.

62. Eugene Genovese argues that Southern law offered considerable human recognition and protection for slaves, but the evidence for this is highly ambiguous. Certainly he is wrong in his generalizations that "the courts moved to eliminate the excuses for killing blacks," that "a slave could kill a white man in self-defense and escape conviction," or that white punishment for killing and maiming slaves increased as "time went on." *Roll, Jordan, Roll: The World the Slaves Made* (New York, 1976), 34–38. Along with North Carolina courts, those in Kentucky, Alabama, Mississippi, and (most steadily) Tennessee tended to recognize slaves as about three-fifths human, the proportion James Madison claimed reasonable in the *Federalist Papers*, no. 54. A. E. Keir Nash, "Fairness and Formalism in the Trials of Blacks in the State Supreme Courts of the Old South," *Virginia Law Review* 56 (1970): 84–100; "A More Equitable Past?: Southern Supreme Courts and the Protection of the Ante-Bellum Negro," *North Carolina Law Review* 48 (1970): 197–241. Thomas D. Morris handles well the question of law and violence (183–248), in a study especially rich on the economic orientation of slavery: *Southern Slavery and the Law, 1619–1860* (Chapel Hill, 1996).

63. Southern fiction as well as history might well make more use of these cases, richer in Southern Gothic than anything but the best of Henry Clay Lewis, Faulkner, and Flannery Connor. In one Mississippi case, slaves George and Josephine were tried for the murder of a white one-year-old, the only person to die from arsenic put in the Jones's family tea one afternoon. Old retainer George, crippled, was angry about being made to do some fieldwork and newly bought Josephine was "vexed" at being beaten twice, once by Jones and once by an overseer, at Mrs. Jones's insistence. Jones testified, attempting to get George's conviction overturned and to get Josephine convicted, and under cross-examination implied that he had (1) briefly imprisoned Elsey, his longtime slave, when she'd said she had put the first Mrs. Jones in the grave and would do the same to the second; (2), turned Elsey into the fields when her (and apparently his) daughter Lethe by whom he now had an eighteen-month-old child; reached maturity (3), often had sex with Eliza, the chief slave witness against Josephine; and (4), had sex with Josephine on the steamboat when he returned from New Orleans with his new purchase a week before the poisoning. George had also slept with Josephine but testified that she was planning to run off with another slave, Charles. Justice Alexander Hardy provided hilarious patriarchal comic relief for this Southern family portrait by ruling that Jones's sexual testimony was appropriate evidence because, if Jones "was in the habit of sexual intercourse with her [Josephine], she was not discontented with her condition." It's hard to believe that the case could have happened anywhere outside of Yoknapatawpha County. *George (slave) v. State* and *Josephine (slave) v. State*, 39 Miss. 570 and 613, October 1860 and 1861, in Catterall, *Judicial Cases*, 3:372–76.

64. *Bryon v. Walton*, 14, 20, suppl. 33, Ga., August 1853, June 1856, March 1864, in Catterall, *Judicial Cases*, 3:35, 50–51, 88; see also 39, 43–46.

65. Chesnut, *Diary*, April 20, 1861, 44. I discuss this "genteel tradition" in *Melodrama*

Unveiled: American Theater and Society, 1800-1850 (Berkeley, 1987 [1968]), 220–48, and *Notions of the Americans,* 14–22. Harriet Martineau's discussion of honor stressed how, in both North and South, it was commonly camouflage for fearful conformity but that only in the South did violence, "the device of terrorism," secure complete non-notice of obvious realities. *Society in America* (New York, 1837), 2:129–36, 155–68.

66. Charles G. Sellers, "The Travail of Slavery," in *The Southerner as American* (Chapel Hill, 1964), 40–71, and William Freehling, *Prelude to Civil War,* 328–60, stress political sources of guilt, while Gaines M. Foster puts more emphasis on religion's contribution to elements of tension rather than guilt. "Guilt Over Slavery: A Historiographical Analysis," *JSH* 56 (November 1990): 665–94.

67. Ingraham, *South-West,* 192–201; Cassius M. Clay, *Writings of Cassius Marcellus Clay,* ed. Horace Greely (New York, 1848), 426; Brian Steel Wills, *A Battle from the Start: The Life of Nathan Bedford Forrest* (New York, 1992), 27–37; Robert Remini, *Andrew Jackson and the Course of American Empire, 1767–1821* (New York, 1977), 55–56, 132–33. Theodore Dwight Weld, *American Slavery as It Is: Testimony of a Thousand Witnesses* (New York, 1939), 174, listed several prominent Southerners who established much of their wealth as slave-traders, and Frederic Bancroft, *Slave-Trading in the Old South* (Baltimore, 1931), esp. 365–81, makes clear the respectability of prosperous traders. Michael Tadman amply documents the centrality of frequent slave buying and selling to the South's economy in *Speculators and Slaves: Masters, Traders, and Slaves in the Old South* (Madison, 1989).

68. *Southern Literary Journal:* 1 (November 1835): 189–93, and quoted in *Woodville (Miss.) Republican,* February 6, 1836, and several other papers. Cooper's article stressed the main threads of the proslavery argument of late 1835: because blacks were "an inferior variety of the animal, man," slavery was a protective kindness to them; slaves were made unhappy only by agitators and were much better off than the European lower classes; divine approval of the institution was proved by its profitability and made clear in the sacredness of property rights; and slavery freed the South of the "mobs and riots" that debased the North.

69. Chaplin, "Diary," May 4, 5, 1845, with penciled note added after Civil War, SCHS; Andrew Shiner, "Diary," fols. 52–54, LC; James Gordon, "Diary," July 20, 1835, MdHS.

70. Chesnut, *Diary,* July 24, August 5, November 11, 1861, 93, 104, 158; Northup, *Twelve Years,* esp. 194–201. Northup's picture of his fellow slaves Patsey and Uncle Abram offer rich testimony to both the full humanity of slaves and the distortingly tragic influences of slavery.

71. Mary B. Blackford, "Notes Illustrative of the Wrongs of Slavery," 2, 5, 17–20, 23, Blackford Family Papers, UVa. Blackford made notes between 1832 and 1866 in this journal, a good example of the evangelical humanity of Southerners mobbed to public silence. But neither mob nor law kept Blackford from steadily teaching a few blacks to read the Bible in Sunday school, though threats caused her to turn away most of those who wished to attend, out of her sense that communal tolerance would end if she taught more than a handful at a time, 15–16, 20–21.

72. Chesnut, *Diary,* April 20, August 5, 1861, 44, 104; Kemble, *Journal,* 176, 201, 238, 273–74; Rachel O'Connor to Mary C. Weeks, September 15, 1828, to David Weeks, June 22, 1829, January 19, 1833, and to A. F. Conrad, October 26, 1835, when she had apparently rehired Patrick because of his ability, despite "so many privadoes of the blackest color" (David Weeks Papers, LSU); Bennet H. Barrow, *Plantation Life of Louisiana, 1836–1846, as Reflected in the Diary of Bennet H. Barrow,* ed. Edwin Adams Davis (New York, 1967), August 3, 1840, 206-7; *Columbus* (Miss.) *Democratic Press* in *Mississippian,* July 31, 1835, and *Grand Gulf Advertiser,* August 14, 1835.

73. Petition of Elisha Blackman to the legislature of South Carolina, November 8, 1839, November 24, 1845, and Replies, Slavery Petitions, SCDAH; *Gordon v. Blackman,* December 1844, in Catterall, *Judicial Cases,* 2:393.

74. Petition for William Primm, January 11, 1848, to Texas legislature and Reply, quoted in Harold Schoen, "The Free Negro in the Republic of Texas," *SWHQ* 40 (1936): 112. Primm brought his five mulatto children with him from Louisiana to Texas; at least one of them married a white (ibid., 170).

75. Barrow, *Diary*, on others' brutality to slaves and hospitality to him, 148, 202, 211, 225, 227, 235; on his own cruelties, 104, 239, 242, 341, 376. Robert Fogel and Stanley Engerman, *Time on the Cross: The Economics of American Negro Slavery*, 144–48, claim whipping was a rarity by using only a list the editor compiled of whippings in 1840–41, neglecting those punishments not specifically marked as whippings, and paying no heed to the text for these years, which talks of things like whipping all the house servants at one time, and "all field hands" at another (181, 192–93).

76. Theodore Rosengarten, *Tombee, Portrait of a Cotton Planter* (New York, 1986), February 19, 1849, 456–58; William Johnson, *William Johnson's Natchez: The Ante-Bellum Diary of a Free Negro* (Baton Rouge, 1951), August 18–19, 1844, 500. In his diary Chaplin vented fury against Sandiford, "this demon in human shape," but he and his fellow jurors did what they'd been convened to do: pronounced the death of the crippled slave an accident. Wyatt-Brown discusses this case and much else in his able account of the South's general tolerance of violence to slaves, *Southern Honor: Ethics and Behavior in the Old South* (New York, 1982), 362–401.

77. *State v. Orr and Stovall*, 1848, UAla; Sumter District Docket, 1827–54, Court Records SCDAH; Governor John Morehead, Letterbook, October 23, 29, 1842, NCDAH; Catterall, *Judicial Cases*, 2:85–86, 193–94; 3:151–52. Michael Hindus mentions the Cheves incident in his valuable section on black justice in South Carolina, *Prison and Plantation: Crime, Justice and Authority in Massachusetts and South Carolina* (Chapel Hill, N.C., 1980), 39–61.

78. Petition in favor of pardon for Motley and Blacklege, and reply of Governor John Hall, January 1854, and later petitions, SCDAH; Catterall, *Judicial Cases*, 2:440.

79. Basil Manly Jr., Pittsboro, North Carolina, August 12, 1844, to his father, Basil Manly Papers, UAla; *New Orleans Courier*, September 12, 1840; George M. Wharton, Tuscumbia, Alabama, April 13, 1850, to William F. Cooper, Cooper Family Papers, TenHS.

80. W. E. B. Du Bois, *Souls of Black Folks*, in *Writings*, ed. Nathan Huggins (1903; reprint, New York, 1986), 491.

81. Alexandre Barde, *L'histoire deo Comités de la Vigilance des Attakapas* (1861), trans. and ed. Henrietta G. Rogers (M.A. thesis, Louisiana State University, 1936), 286–93; *New Orleans Bee*, April 11, 12, 1834, and *New Orleans Courier*, April 10, 1834. George Washington Cable, "The 'Haunted House' in Royal Street," in *Strange True Stories of Louisiana* (1889; reprint, Gretna, La., 1994), 200–219, is a richly researched and deeply felt sketch of the incident which makes clear how well-known the woman's cruelty was long before the incident, though this did nothing to lessen her social position. For knowledge of this source I'm indebted to Susan Perez Castillo, who used it to consider the ties between literature and history in an unpublished paper, Milan Conference on National Memory and Historical Meaning, June 1996.

82. *Southern Literary Journal* 1 (November 1835): 193; *Vicksburg Register*, August 20, 1835.

83. *New Orleans American* in *New York Evening Post*, October 27, 1837; *NR* 53 (October 28, 1837): 129; R. L. McGuire, "Diary," October 1837, LSU; Northup, *Twelve Years*, 188–90. Northup wrote that slaves often discussed insurrection but desisted because potential leaders recognized the pragmatic difficulties.

84. Letter from Opelousas, September 26, 1840, in *New Orleans Courier*, October 1, 1840; *New Orleans Picayune* in *Liberator* 10 (September 18, 1840): 151; *Courier*, September

12, 26, October 1, 3, 1840; *NR* 59 (October 10, November 14, 1840): 88, 176; Basil Manly Jr., Pittsboro, North Carolina, to father, August 12, 1844, Manly Papers, UAla.

85. *New Orleans Courier*, December 22, 1840, June 4, 1842; *NR* 59 (January 9, 1841): 296, and 63 (December 3, 1842): 212; *New Orleans Bulletin*, July 23, 28, 1841; *New Orleans Bee*, July 26, 1841; Barrow, *Diary*, July 17 to July 28, 1841, 236–37.

86. *New Orleans Delta*, February 2, 1846, in *Pennsylvanian*, February 28, 1846.

87. William P. Gould, "Diary," December 23 to December 26, 1856, AlaDAH; James B. Clark to Thomas W. Clark, December 1856, George B. Wright Papers, MinnHS. Gould made clear why data about these late insurrection panics is so piecemeal: "The *Montgomery Journal* thinks it's injudicious to publish details or the doings of excited Public meetings." Yet he wrote of reports of scares in twelve slave states, not including South Carolina, where panic also occurred: Mrs. R. F. W. Allston to son Ben, January 1, 1857, Allston-Pringle Papers, SCHS.

88. *Nashville Union*, December 10, and other Tennessee papers in *New York Tribune*, December 10–18, 1856; James Stirling, *Letters from the Slave States* (London, 1957), 299–301; Iris H. McClain, *A History of Stewart County, Tennessee* (Columbia, Tenn., 1965), 36–37; *History of Tennessee . . . with a . . . Sketch of . . . Stewart . . . Counties* (Nashville, 1886), 900–901; William F. Cooper to father, December 29, 1856, and Halladay, Chatham and Company to Matthew D. Cooper, December 16, 1856, in Cooper Family Papers, TenHS; John Killebrew, "Recollections," 166–67, TenHS; Catterall, *Judicial Cases*, 2:565–69.

89. Rudolph L. Biesele, *The History of the German Settlements in Texas, 1831–1861* (San Marcos, Tex., 1930), 202–3; Andrew F. Muir, "Free Negroes in Jefferson and Orange Counties, Texas," *JNH* 33 (April 1950): 199–203; Frank Smyrl, "Unionism, Abolitionism, and Vigilantism in Texas, 1856–1865" (M.A. thesis, University of Texas, 1961), 27–33. Muir found that the area's free black population fell from sixty-three to twenty-nine after the riots, suggesting that some thirty blacks were permanently driven out.

90. *Texas State Gazette*, March 11, 1859, quoted in Smyrl, "Unionism," 36–37; Wesley Norton, "Methodist Episcopal Church and the Civil Disturbances in North Texas," *SWHQ* 68 (January 1985): 324–29; *Dallas Herald*, June 20, 1860, in Smyrl, "Unionism," 48. See also Wendell G. Addington, "Slave Insurrections in Texas," *JNH* 35 (October 1950): 414–17.

91. *Houston Republican*, July 28, 1860, in *Anti-Slavery Standard*, August 18, 1860; Cincinnati *Christian Luminary*, January 12, 1860, in William Lloyd Garrison, ed., *The New "Reign of Terror" in the Slaveholding States* (Boston, 1860), 29–30; *Dallas Herald*, August 31, 1859, in Smyrl, "Unionism," 38.

92. Letters from Fort Worth and Marshall, Texas, both August 12, 1860, and from Judge John H. Reagan, August 18, 1860, in John Townsend, *The Doom of Slavery in the Union: Its Safety Out of It* (Charleston, 1860), 34–37; letter from Houston, August 23, 1860, in James E. Cutler, *Lynch-Law: An Investigation into the History of Lynching in the United States* (New York, 1905), 122; various Texas papers in *New York Tribune*, August 18–23, 1860, and *Anti-Slavery Standard*, August 18, 1860; John M. Snickerson, September 13, 1860; and M. W. Chapin, December 15, 1860, to Elisha M. Pease, Pease Papers, AusPL; Addington, "Slave Insurrections," 419–35. William H. White, "The Texas Slave Insurrection of 1860," *SWHQ* 52 (January 1949): 259–85, presents rich data while arguing that the plot was real.

93. Norton, "Methodist Episcopal Church," 321–40, tells Bewley's story and includes his dying letter and the conclusion of the *Texas Advocate* and of D. R. McAnally in the St. Louis *Advocate*. See also the account of Rev. H. W. South from Kansas in *New York Times*, and the *Canton* (Ill.) *Register*, October 23, 1860, both in Garrison, *Fresh Catalogue*, 25, 42, 47.

94. Frederick Anthon letter of September 18, 1860, to *Chicago Press and Tribune*, in Garrison, *Fresh Catalogue*, 7–10. For similar accounts of insurrection charges as a cloak for stealing property, see the story of a Bourbon County hotel owner in the same source (25–26)

and that of E. C. Palmer, wealthy land speculator of Cooke County, reported in the *Marshall* (Tex.) *Republican* between November 12 and December 17, 1859, in Smyrl, "Unionism," 40–44.

95. Smyrl, "Unionism," 4–9; James A. Baker, "Diary," October 18 to November 6, 1860, UTex. Baker's diary tells of a number of actions and "resolves" related to the year's lynching turmoil.

96. Letters from Marshall and from Fort Worth, Texas, both August 12, 1860, in Townsend, *Doom of Slavery*, 35–38. Jordan's *Tumult and Silence at Second Creek* illustrates how quickly, even during the war, sexual fantasies came to the fore under the prospect of slave freedom; here planters concentrated on whipping out the names of specific women that slaves had in mind as the particular object of their insurrectionary fervor.

97. Lucilla McCorkle, "Diary," August 26 to September 30, 1860, UAla.

Chapter Six

1. Henry Miller, "Diary," March 23, August 5, 1838, fols. 20–21, 90–97, HSMo.

2. Richard McCormick, *The Second American Party System: Party Formation in the Jacksonian Era* (Chapel Hill, N.C., 1966).

3. Some general questions about women's public participation are raised in Mary Ryan, *Women in Public: Between Banners and Ballots, 1825–1880* (Baltimore, 1990).

4. Nancy Rash, *The Paintings and Politics of George Caleb Bingham* (New Haven, 1991), deals with the politics of these paintings, which are tied to broad patterns of Whig humor (120–94). For slightly differing political interpretations of them see Jean H. Baker, *Affairs of Party: The Political Culture of Northern Democrats in the Mid–Nineteenth Century* (Ithaca, 1983), 277–79, and Elizabeth Johns, *American Genre Painting: The Politics of Everyday Life* (New Haven, 1991), 91–99.

5. This was the one highly destructive non-election political riot, though it has been commonly seen as tied more centrally to ethnic-religious hostilities.

6. The growth over time of fall election violence reflected the increasing importance of federal, and especially presidential, politics.

7. Ezekiel A. Powell, "Fifty-Five Years in West Alabama," *AlaHQ* 4 (1942): 563.

8. Henrietta Embree, "Diary," November 2, 1856, UTex.

9. Anson Buttles, "Diary," March 21, April 5, November 8, 1859, SHSWi; Lemuel Sawyer, *Blackbeard*, ed. Richard Walser (Raleigh, N.C., 1952), 12.

10. David Crockett, *A Narrative of the Life of David Crockett* (Philadelphia, 1834), 71–76, 107–13; John R. Kimball to Augustine P. Kimball, October 28, 1839, Kimball Papers, MoHS; Henry A. Foote, *Casket of Reminiscences* (Washington, D.C., 1874), 265–67; police reporter of *New Orleans Picayune*, November 18, 1840, in Mervin Coulter, ed., *The Other Half of Old New Orleans . . .* (Baton Rouge, 1939), 45. Arrested for riot for disturbing the peace, this Jacksonian argued his own case, stressing that he hadn't made as much noise as many mechanical gadgets that went unmuzzled: "Ain't I as much consequence as a steamboat or locomotive, in the eyes of the law? But I knew it would be so. I knew that once Harrison got elected our liberties would be swamped."

11. *Washington* (D.C.) *News*, May 30, 1857; Thomas H. Espy, November 20, 1840, and John Hamilton, December 12, 1840, to Thomas B. Huling, Thomas B. Huling Papers, TexHS; Frances Trollope, *The Domestic Manners of the Americans*, ed. Donald Smalley (New York, 1949), 102.

12. Ronald Formisano's argument that mass political meetings were an adaptation of revival practices to elections has some truth, but Charles Grandison Finney argued that revival

techniques were partly necessary to gain the religious attention of people used to the stirring excitement of political campaigns. Formisano, *The Transformation of Political Culture: Massachusetts Parties, 1790s to 1840s* (New York, 1983), 262–67; Finney, *Lectures on Revivals of Religion* (New York, 1835), 251–55.

13. Mary A. Trousdale to William Trousdale, November 15, 1856, Trousdale Family Papers, TenHS; James S. Buck, *Pioneer History of Milwaukee from the First Settlement . . .* (Milwaukee, 1890), 253–54.

14. Edmund Cooper to William F. Cooper, March 20, 1836, William F. Cooper Papers, TnHS.

15. Minerva Blow to Susie Blow, May 20, 1861, Blow Family Papers, MoHS. Joseph Sill, "Diary," February 22, 1844, HSPa, offers a good description of one political fund-raising ball. See also Robert Gunderson, *The Log-Cabin Campaign* (Lexington, 1957), 135, 190, 245.

16. *DR* 8 (September 1840): 198; two Jacksonian songs printed in *Baltimore Republican*, May 7, 1834. On political songs, see Vera B. Lawrence, *Music for Patriots, Politicians, and Presidents: Harmonies and Discords of the First 100 Years* (New York, 1975).

17. Seba Smith, *The Life and Writings of Major Jack Downing* (Boston, 1834). Jennifer Schwartz makes an excellent analysis of the importance of humor to the Lincoln-Douglas debates, contrasting the Democrat's abusiveness with the Republican's gentler and more inventive use of comedy to make his position palatable to his racist audience. "The Uses of Humor in the Lincoln-Douglas Debates" (honors thesis, University of Maryland, 1992).

18. *DR* 8 (September 1840): 200; James Russell Lowell, *The Biglow Papers* (London, 1859), 78–80.

19. Francis Lieber to his son, July 10, 1840, Lieber Papers, USC; Jesse B. Strawn, "Reminiscences," Folio a-b, WRHS. Gunderson, *Log-Cabin Campaign*, chronicles the 1840 Whig gimmicks richly but without much sense of their positive ties to democracy.

20. Cody Raquet, Philadelphia, to Henry Raquet, September 2, 1840, Raquet Family Papers, UTex; Joseph Osborne to Hickey Paulson, September 15, 1840, Osborne Papers, OhHS; M. V. (Buck) Harrison, Missouri, to Jilson Harrison, April 26, 1840, Harrison Papers, KyHS.

21. Pearce, quoted in almost all papers, including the *Vicksburg Register*, June 4, 1835; Calvin Goddard to John Cotton Smith, April 8, 1837, John Cotton Smith Papers, ConnHS; *DR* 1 (December 1837): 23; 17 (September 1845): 169. No year went by when the *DR* failed to lament how American politics had become "the game of public plunder" (30 [April 1852]: 372).

22. Earl F. Niehaus, *The Irish in New Orleans* (Baton Rouge, 1965), 228; Joseph M. Cord to Thomas Vaux, July 8, 1857, Vaux Papers, HSPa; Joshua Fletcher testimony, Pennsylvania General Assembly, House of Representatives, *Report of the Minority Committee to Enquire into the Causes of the Disturbances . . .* (Harrisburg, 1839), 83; Thomas Brothers, *The United States of North America as They Are* (London, 1840), 309.

23. James K. Polk, *Polk: The Diary of a President . . .* , ed. Allan Nevins (New York, 1952); Moore, July 14, 1853; DeCordova, August 5, 1853; Clark, July 3, 1853; Bell, June 17, 1853, to Elisha M. Pease, and Pease to Lucinda Pease, October 10, 1853, in Elisha M. Pease Papers, AusPL.

24. Glyndon G. Van Dusen, *Thurlow Weed, Wizard of the Lobby* (Boston, 1947); Fawn Brodie, *Thaddeus Stevens, Scourge of the South* (New York, 1959); George Templeton Strong, *Diary*, ed. Allan Nevins and Milton Halsey Thomas (New York, 1952), August 19, 1864 3:475.

25. J. L. Jenckes to William Greene, June 22, 1841, Greene Papers, CinHS; Strong, *Diary*, March 19, 1861 3:111; Hawthorne to Sophia Peabody, March 15, 1840, and to William Pike, June 9, 1853, in Randall Stewart, "Hawthorne and Politics: Unpublished Letters to William

Pike," *NEQ* 5 (1932): 240, 254. "Loaves and fishes" was a commonplace term in these years, perhaps influenced by John Randolph's tart observation that the nation swarmed with "politicians of seven principles, that is five loaves and two fishes." Quoted in *DR* 13 (August 1843): 132.

26. John C. Calhoun, "Senate Report," *NR* 48 (June 13, 1835): 265–72, and *A Disquisition on Government* (Charleston, 1851); Henry Winter Davis, *The Origin, Principles, and Purposes of the American Party* (n.p., 1855), 13; C. A. Packard to Charles F. Chandler, January 31, 1857, Chandler Papers, MeHS.

27. The *Globe* set the standard for partisanship in journalism, while the *Philadelphia Public Ledger* represented the vigor, honesty, and social conscience of the penny press at its best.

28. Houston, February 15, 1855, in *Congressional Globe* (1854–55), 1:724; *DR* 30 (April 1852): 366–78; Benjamin Gratz Brown to Orlando Brown, August 6, 1852, Brown Papers, NF. Domestic peace wouldn't last between the sections, Brown wrote, "unless some bone of contention from *abroad* is thrown to them" (August 4, 1849).

29. M. B. Williamson to Elisha M. Pease, April 9, 1846, Pease Papers, AusPL; David Grimsted, "Robbing the Poor to Aid the Rich: The Baltimore Bank Swindle," *SCtHSY* (1987): 46–47. William E. Dodd deals richly with Walker's land speculation in defrauding the U.S. government, with the complete cooperation before, during, and after of Jackson's friends and officials, and with other frauds where Walker and his fellow Mississippi Democrats cheated less profitably. *Robert J. Walker, Imperialist* (Chicago, 1914), 10–21. On the Houston affair and the successful enrichment of Jackson's friend through an arranged speculation in public land, see Marshall de Bruhl, *Sword of San Jacinto: A Life of Sam Houston* (New York, 1993), 113–22.

30. John Hynes to Eddy and Kirkpatrick, September 8, 1841, November 20, 1842; William Wilson to Henry Eddy, February 14, 1843, Massac Papers, IllHS.

31. Thomas B. Stevens to Orlando Brown, July 2, 1849, Brown Papers, KyHS; Samuel Fowler in *NAR* 77 (July 1853): 52; E. Peshine Smith to Henry C. Carey, October 17, 1856, Edward Gardiner Papers, HSPa. The plaint that politics was merely "a trade" and "mode of money-making" was unceasing (*Philadelphia Public Ledger*, September 15, 1836).

32. The police indictment was for an election riot in the Southwark area of Philadelphia: *Philadelphia Public Ledger*, October 3–6, 1838. The Cincinnati riot of Christmas Day, 1853, between Irish Catholic police and German liberal paraders is described later in this section.

33. Leon Cyprian Soulé, *The Know-Nothing Party in New Orleans: A Reappraisal* (Baton Rouge, 1961), 55–58; Philip Hone, *Diary of Philip Hone,* ed. Allan Nevins (New York, 1927), January 1, 1840, 451; James F. Richardson, "Fernando Wood and the New York Police Force, 1855–57," *NYHSQ* 50 (1966): 5–40; *Philadelphia Public Ledger*, September 28, 1838.

34. Strong, *Diary*, November 6, 1854, 2:196; Augustine E. Costello, *Our Police Protectors: History of the New York Police . . .* (New York, 1885), 143. De Francias Folsom, *Our Police* (Baltimore, 1888), 43–44, discussed one political tough arrested 147 times in a bit more than a year—and always released on bail. New York City's chief engineer, Alfred Carson, in 1850 attacked the political use of firemen by expelling 124 leading toughs and promising to publish the names of all culprits, police, aldermen and magistrates active in the system. The Democratic aldermen backed down from their vote to expel Carson but also tabled a resolution to condemn magistrates who freed arrestees before examination. New York City Board of Alderman, *Documents* (New York, 1955), 16–18: September 3, June 6, 1850, September 15, 1853.

35. Alco petition, January 4, 1834; Van Horn and Smith, May 20, 1835; Williams, October 28, 1834; Peebles, n.d. [1835] to Hiram Runnels, Governor's Papers, MissDAH; Clinton Terry to Elisha M. Pease, June 8, 1856, Rose Papers, AusPL.

36. *Albany Evening Journal* in *NR* 59 (September 26, 1840): 54, and *NR* 64 (March 11, 1843): 42. The statistics for Pennsylvania and New York are telling of the general pattern:

Pennsylvania	*Average number of Pardons per Year*
Thomas McKean (1799–1808)	258
Simon Snyder (1808–17)	110
William Findlay (1817–20)	144
Joseph Heister (1820–23)	101
John A. Schultze (1823–29)	121
George Wolf (1829–35)	71
Joseph Ritner (1835–38)	27
New York	
DeWitt Clinton (1817–22, 1824–28)	250
Robert Yates (1822–24)	140
Van Buren-Throop (1818–30)	112
William Marcy (1831–37)	133
William Seward (1838–41)	68

37. *Cincinnati Chronicle*, February 13, May 8, 1841; *NR* 63 (December 24, 1842): 258; 67 (February 1, 15, 1845): 352, 384, the last quoting *Pennsylvanian*; Salmon P. Chase to Rev. L. Warren, April 28, 1855, Salmon P. Chase Papers, OhHS.

38. Alexander Long, "Autobiography," Alexander Long Papers, CinHS; Philadelphia *Public Ledger*, October 13, 1838; *NR* 59 (October 3, 1840): 73–79, reprinted the documents on a similar dispute in New Jersey.

39. *New York Tribune*, November 7, 1856; D. Clark, Hartford, to Elisha M. Pease, Pease Papers, AusPL; E. Peshine Smith to Henry C. Carey, September 12, 1858, Edward Gardiner Papers, HSPa; Clay, *Writings*, 279. Erwin S. Bradley denies that Cameron made the comment often attributed to him: *Simon Cameron: Lincoln's Secretary of War* (Philadelphia, 1966), 420.

40. John S. Kendall, *History of New Orleans* (New York, 1922), 1:207–8; Foote, *Casket of Reminiscences,* 135; John B. Glentworth indictment, January 26, 1841, NYCMA; Anon., *The Election Frauds of 1838* (New York, 1838). Glentworth's "defense" admitted every foul act but waxed righteous that he was never properly paid with money or office and was deprived of fair legal opportunity to implicate more of his friends. "I only claimed rights under as binding a contract as was ever made by honorable men" (Anon., *Election Frauds*, 52). NYCMA has records of a number of cases of election cheating in these years—bipartisan, but mostly by Democrats: December 10, 1832; December 6, 1838; November 22, 23, 29, 1839; May 18, 1841; November 20, 1843.

41. James Richardson, *New York Police, Colonial Times to 1891* (New York, 1970), 84–92; William Marcy to D. S. Dickinson, October 25, 1847, Marcy Papers, NYHS.

42. James McCullough to R. W. Curran, October 22, 1844, William Preston Papers, MdHS; *Philadelphia Public Ledger*, October 6, 1838; Edward M. Shepard, *Martin Van Buren* (1888; reprint, Boston, 1909), 453; *NR* 66 (July 6, 1844): 304. In 1838, Maryland passed a law against political wagers, with the fines going to the school fund. Bernard Steiner, *Citizenship and Suffrage in Maryland* (Baltimore, 1896), 32.

43. John Glenn Jr. to William Wilkins Glenn, November 10, 1844, Glenn Papers, MdHS; "Extracts from the Journal of Gibbins Adams," October 17, 1840, *EssIHP* 82 (1946): 81; John Russell to Spencer Russell, November 5, 1848, Russell Papers, IllHS; State Committee Cir-

cular, October 8, 1856, in John Bruner Letters, FC. John Russell also mentioned two men killed "on the day of the election in an adjoining parish," suggesting how deadly "customary" political violence often was, perhaps especially in the South.

44. On Elliott's sales see *New Orleans Picayune*, April 17, 1844, and Niehaus, *Irish in New Orleans*, 79–80. New York papers printed in Philadelphia *National Gazette*, April 11, 1834; William Baughin, "The Development of Nativism in Cincinnati" (M.A. thesis, University of Cincinnati, 1963), 94–95, 116; *Missouri Republican*, April 4, 1848; *New Orleans Picayune*, November 11, 1853.

45. *Remarks on the Maryland Report on Secret Societies* (Baltimore, 1856), 11–14. Good examples of the shock and anger, entwined with prejudice, at mass-naturalization voting practices can be seen in Strong, *Diary*, November 6, 1838, 1: 94 and John Day Caldwell, "Diary," August 4, 1840, CinHS.

46. These fascinating documents are arranged chronologically by district as Grand Jury Presentments, SCDHA. Occasionally the many grand jury pleas for weapon limitations stressed the special need for controls around polling places. An Irish immigrant in Cuthbert, Georgia, reported violent "political strife" and "dishonesty of all hues" at its 1848 election. Annette McDonald Suarez, ed., *The Journal of Andrew Leary O'Brien . . .* (Athens, Ga., 1946), 43.

47. Sill, "Diary," September 11, 1832, HSPa; John Clancy to Roberts Vaux, October 5, 1860, Vaux Papers, HSPa; John F. Charles to Samuel Gordon, Gideon Alkire, and William Luzzader, [October 1844], Miss. Papers, IllHS.

48. *Baltimore Republican*, January 1, February 15, 1836; *Baltimore American* figures on the votes by ward for mayor and the registry law in *NR* 55 (October 6, 20, 1938): 81, 114; Riot indictment, May 20, 1840, NYCMA; R. R. Ward to William Greene, William Greene Papers, CinHS. Niles became a strong advocate of registry laws after the New York City political riots of 1834, and he reported approvingly Massachusetts's stiff fines for illegal voting: *NR*46 (May 24, 1834): 210; *NR*47 (December 27, 1834): 278. Truly effective registry laws came only when the Republicans defeated the Democrats in the North after 1858.

49. *Washington Globe*, October 23, 1837; Anson Buttles, "Diary," March 12, 1860, HSWi.

50. Thomas Ford, *The History of Illinois, from Its Commencement as a State in 1818 to 1847* (Chicago, 1854), 88; "Pulling Teeth in Mississippi," in William T. Porter, ed., *The Big Bear of Arkansas and Other Sketches Illustrative of Character and Incident in the South* (Philadelphia, 1843), 167; Schirmer, "Journal," September 6, 8, October 10, 1831; September 2, October 4, 11, 1832; April 1, 1833; October 14, 1834, SCHS.

51. John Black to John A. Quitman, November 14, 1835, Claiborne Papers, MissDAH; George Quinan to Elisha M. Pease, February 16, 1846, Pease Papers, Aus PL; Nimrod Porter, "Diary," March 13, 1840, SHC.

52. *New Orleans Bulletin*, October 12, 1842.

Chapter Seven

1. *NR* 47 (October 18, 1834): 97; Julia Grew, Philadelphia, to Laura Kingsbury, October 16, 1834, Kingsbury Papers, NF.

2. The best document suggesting the political ideology derived from the "Bank War" is Treasury Department official William Gouge's *A Short History of Paper-Money and Banking in the United States* (Philadelphia, 1833), with its unease over many economic developments and its faith that all would work fairly and profitably if the government didn't act.

3. Philip Hone, "Diary," March 19, 1834, and quoting Daniel Webster, April 2, 1834, NYHS; R. H. Wilde to Gulian Verplanck, April 1, 1834, and other letters, Verplanck Papers, NYHS. All Whig and neutral papers reported with shock the naturalizations made just before

the election, at least 800 of them, according to the responsible *New York American*, printed in Philadelphia *National Gazette*, April 15, 1834.

4. New York *Commercial Advertiser*, October 1, 1834; *New York Evening Post, New York Daily Advertiser*, and *New York Commercial Advertiser*, November 6–8, 1832, in Paul O. Weinbaum, *Mobs and Demagogues: The New York Response to Collective Violence in the Early Nineteenth Century* (Ann Arbor, Mich., 1979), 12–13. Weinbaum argues that this riot was not greatly different from earlier troubles, but in terms of gravely wounding police, it was the worst riot before the Civil War. Weinbaum and Paul Gilje say that one policeman was killed, but I think this is the victim, long unconscious and expected to die, who eventually recovered. Weinbaum, *Mobs and Demagogues*, 8; Paul A. Gilje, *The Road to Mobocracy: Popular Disorder in New York City, 1763–1834*, (Chapel Hill, N.C., 1987), 139.

5. Sill, "Diary," October 9, 1832, HSPa, offers a good description of the property destruction in this small riot.

6. *New York Courier and Enquirer, New York American*, and *New York Journal of Commerce*, April 8, 1834.

7. *New York Courier and Enquirer* and *New York Journal of Commerce*, April 9, 1834; *Baltimore Republican*, April 14, 1834.

8. *NR* 46 (April 12, 1834): 100–101; John Schneider, "Mob Violence and Public Order in the American City, 1830–65" (Ph.D. diss., University of Minnesota, 1971), 62–76; Joel Headley, *Great Riots of New York* (New York, 1873), 66–78.

9. The chronology of events is fairly clear, although Democratic and Whig accounts jibed only on the police injuries: *New York Standard* in *New Orleans Courier*, April 20, 1834, and *Daily Advertiser* in *Baltimore Gazette*, April 19, 1834. The worst injuries were to Capt. John Munson, who had many ribs and a collarbone broken and a head wound by a hatchet that penetrated the bone; and to watchman Ludowick Smith, initially said to be mortally wounded, who recovered from having "a side of his face completely crushed by a kick."

10. *New York Courier and Enquirer*, April 10, 1834, and *New York Sun*, April 11, 1834.

11. Davy Crockett, *An Account of Col. Crockett's Tour to the North and Down-East* (Philadelphia, 1835), 48–49; *NR* 46 (April 19, 1834): 115–16, 122–24; *New York Sun*, April 12, 1834. The Jacksonian *New York Standard*'s inventive explanations, including that the brutal police beatings happened "by mistake," are reprinted in Thomas Brothers, *The United States of North America as They Are* (London, 1840), 297–99; *New York Evening Post*, April 12, 1834. *NR*, 46 (July 26, 1834): 365 discussed the records of those convicted, one of them having spent seventeen of his thirty years in jail. The indictments of eight men for the riot are in NYCMA, May 16–17, 1834.

12. Philadelphia *American Sentinel*, October 8, 10, 13, the last date reporting on the Patterson-led meeting; *National Gazette*, October 6, 14, 1834; *Philadelphian*, with Mrs. Perry's comment, in *NR* 47 (November 1, 1834): 136; Inquest Report of October 13, in *Hazard's Pennsylvania Register* 14 (October 1834): 253.

13. The Philadelphia *National Gazette*, October 15, 1834, published the three somewhat conflicting eyewitness accounts of the event, and *NR* 47 (October 18, 1834): 104–5 reprinted various Philadelphia press versions.

14. Henry Arcularius, "Report of April 21, 1834," in Aaron Clark, *Communication on Election Peace* (New York, 1834), 132, 158–65.

15. Asher Taylor, *Recollections of the Early Days of the National Guard, Comprising the Prominent Events in the History of the Famous Seventh Regiment . . .* (New York, 1865), 131–38.

16. These writings began a Democratic practice of issuing reports on riots that tarred their opponents and camouflaged their own involvement that lasted through the 1850s. Their

propaganda had some success, inasmuch as political violence in this era is commonly treated as a peculiarly Nativist–Know-Nothing proclivity.

17. *New York Courier and Enquirer*, quoted along with a good sample of other New York press response in *Baltimore Gazette*, April 11, 1834.

18. *Baltimore Republican*, November 23, 1835. This theme was common between November and April 1836, in the *Republican*, but largely disappeared after the spring local elections, doubtless because Jacksonians knew the issue was sure to hurt them in the less-populated rural slave areas.

19. Bernard Steiner, "The Electoral College for the State of Maryland and the Nineteen Van Buren Electors," *AmHAAR* (1895): 129–70, covers the dispute and its background. Steiner pointed out that the Maryland setup drew praise from James Madison in *Federalist* no. 63.

20. Anonymous Whig pamphlet, rumored to have been written by Governor Thomas Veazey, *A Brief Outline of the Rise, Progress and Failure of the Revolutionary Scheme of the Nineteen Van Buren Electors . . .* (Baltimore, 1837), 5–6, which reprinted the Van Burenite electors' statement and the Whig reply (15–36).

21. Speech of John V. I. McMahon to Baltimore meeting of September 26, and proclamation of Governor Veazey of November 8, both in *NR* 51 (October 1, November 12, 1836): 71, 165–66. A. Clarke Hagensick, "Revolution on Reform in 1836: Maryland's Preface to the Dorr Rebellion," *MdHM* 57 (1962): 346–66, offers a careful account of the aftermath of Whig reform. The planter-dominated areas of Maryland were induced to accept this diminution of their power with one "reform" provision that touched their deepest commitments: slavery could be abolished in the state only by the unanimous vote of the legislature. The election figures are mentioned by Benjamin Latrobe Jr., "Diary," December 7, 1836, Latrobe Papers, MdHS. Latrobe hated this "most unprincipled party movement" that threatened "anarchy" or "at least the credit of state," which might disrupt the canal and railroad projects from which he earned his livelihood as an engineer.

22. Anon., *Brief Outline*, 4, and quoting "Resolves" of Frederick Whigs, 60; Van Buren electors' statement in Steiner, "Electoral College," 143–44, and on the convention (November 16–19), 160–61; *NR* 51 (November 26, 1836): 193.

23. Pennsylvania General Assembly, House of Representatives, *The Report of the Minority Committee Appointed to Enquire into the Causes of the Disturbances . . .* (Harrisburg, 1839), 3; *NR* 55 (December 8, 1838): 225.

24. William M. Meigs, *The Life of Charles Jared Ingersoll* (Philadelphia, 1897), 208–20. Meigs spends much time denying that his ancestor was really proslavery but quotes much that belies his argument (5, 229–46).

25. Burton A. Konkle, ed., *The Life and Speeches of Thomas Williams* (Philadelphia, 1905), 1:107–25, gives good background on the controversy as well as Williams's passionate Whig response.

26. *Harrisburg Keystone, Philadelphia Inquirer*, and *United States Gazette*, December 3, all in *NR* 55 (December 5, 1838): 237; *Spirit of the Times*, September 13, 1838; Williams speech, March 21, 1839, in Konkle, *Life and Speeches*, 1:122–23; Pennsylvania House of Representatives, *Report of the Minority Committee,* 14–15. The September statement of lynch enthusiasm in the coming election was whetted on Jacksonian pleasure at the mob burning of abolitionist Pennsylvania Hall. Ingersoll took the occasion to argue, regarding the coming election, that "fraud may be opposed by violence, even to the death of the wrong-doer," while his organ, *The Spirit of the Times*, not only seconded his endorsement of lynch-law but waxed wroth that the *Philadelphia Public Ledger* dared both to criticize the recent riot and to arm itself "to intimidate an insulted people, whose honorable and natural feelings upon the question of *amalgamation* they had wantonly and outrageously abused." Quoted in *Philadelphia Public Ledger*, September 24, 26, 1838.

27. *Harrisburg Telegraph*, December 6, and Philadelphia *American Sentinel* in *NR* 55 (December 8, 1838): 237; Williams to his wife, December 6, 1838, in Konkle, *Life and Speeches*, 1:112–13.

28. The official letters and replies between Harrisburg and Washington, including the elaborate attempts to fudge the federal official status of the mob leaders Ritner named in his letter of December 7, are in *House Executive Document*, 25th Cong., 3d sess., no. 28, and were printed in *NR* 55 (January 5, 1839): 294– 97. A Democratic legislator told of the plans to blow up the militia train: *National Intelligencer* in *NR* 57 (September 7, 1839): 28. Augustus Pleasanton, "Diary," December 5, 6, HSPa, describes the militia action well.

29. *Philadelphia Sentinel*, October 21, 1840, and *United States Gazette* in *NR* 59 (October 24, 31, 1840): 118, 132; *Kennebec* (Me.) *Journal*, January 2, 1839.

30. Robert Patterson, "Reminiscenses," December 8, 1838, HSPa; Ruell Williams, Philadelphia, to son Joseph, December 9, 1838, Ruell Williams Papers, MeHS; *Philadelphia Public Ledger*, December 7, 1838, in an editorial arguing that this political farce was a continuation of the "demonic delight" shown over the work of the year's earlier anti-abolition mob.

31. Richard Rush to T. W. Dorr, December 23, 1833, Dorr Papers, JHL. Dorr made the one-third estimate in a letter to John Quincy Adams, October 22, 1841, when requesting him to lecture for suffrage extension. Probably two-thirds was closer; the electorate expanded by about a quarter when voting rights were modernized.

32. A good account of the political context of the Dorr War is Francis Bowen's article, "The Recent Contest in Rhode Island," *NAR* 58 (April 1844): 371–435. Recent studies add valuable material but limit the complexities of the situation by seeing it largely as democracy/radicalism/republicanism versus aristocracy: Chilton Williamson, *American Suffrage, from Property to Democracy, 1760 to 1860* (Princeton, 1960); Marvin E. Gettleman, *The Dorr Rebellion: A Study of American Radicalism, 1833–49* (New York, 1973); George M. Dennison, *The Dorr War: Republicanism on Trial, 1831–1861* (Lexington, 1976). Better in paying attention to the complex local realities are Peter J. Coleman, *The Transformation of Rhode Island, 1790–1860* (Providence, 1963), 255–94, and the classic study of Arthur May Mowry, *The Dorr War; or The Constitutional Struggle in Rhode Island* (Providence, 1901).

33. A copy of the request to Van Buren, May 31, 1833, and his reply is in the Dorr Papers, JHL, as are Dorr's letters from jail to Catherine Williams telling of his work, and complaining during the winter of the cold and want of air, sunshine, and newspapers, December 13, 1844, January 18, March 7, 1845. *NR* reprinted many of the pleas for Dorr and flashed irritation that Dorr refused to take the oath of allegiance: 66 (July 27, 1844): 339; 67 (February 1, 8, 1845): 352, 361–63; 68 (March 22, 29, 1845): 37, 54.

34. Dorr's antislavery is clear in his letters to William M. Chase, July 25, 1837; James G. Birney, December 26, 1837; and Edmund Quincy, n.d., all in Dorr Papers, JHL. Dan King, *The Life and Times of Thomas Wilson Dorr, with the Outlines of the Political History of Rhode Island* (Boston, 1859), was the honest work of an active Dorrite, who saw Dorr as a martyr to the cause of democratic principle, fighting exclusion from the suffrage of men of all sorts, including many who were wealthy (23–24, 58). He also saw Dorr's weakness as a leader: "He thought too well of the world, and his standard of ethics were placed too high for practical purposes" (289). Two other accounts by Dorrites are Mrs. F. H. Green, *Might and Right: By a Rhode Islander* (Providence, 1843), and Jacob Frieze, *A Concise History of the Efforts to Obtain an Exchange of Suffrage in Rhode Island . . .* , 3d ed. (Providence, 1912), the latter by a man who turned against Dorr when he turned toward violence.

35. Whig Charles N. Tilley urged Dorr to withdraw on February 9, 1837, and by the spring he and other Whig reformers were adamant that the Constitutionalists should support the Whigs who were on record for Charter changes (Dorr Papers, JHL). Thomas Sprague Jr. to

John Bacon Francis, January 27, 1836, and J. B. F. to Colonel Thurston, March 23, 1837, John Bacon Francis Papers, RIHS.

36. Charles Randall to Dorr, January 20, 1836, March 16, 1837, Dorr Papers, JHL. Randall lamented that the party had no "*good fat offices*" to aid the ambiguous attractions of ideology.

37. John Bacon Francis to Henry D. Gilpin, February 20, 1837; Christopher Allen, June 5, 1836, and "W.G.G.," Charleston, S.C., March 31, 1836, to John Bacon Francis, Francis Papers, RIHS.

38. William Ennis to Dorr, March 16, 1840, Dorr Papers, JHL. Dorr's letters begging Francis to run or to let his name stay on the ballot, and the latter's refusals, are from January and early February 1840, the same time Dorr wrote Rantoul, Brownson, and Everett for lecture aid.

39. Alexander H. Everett to editor of the *New Age*, November 8, 1841, Dorr Papers, JHL.

40. *NR* reported the Dorr returns from the *New Age* and the later indications of fraud and the high court declaration of unconstitutionality: 61 (January 8, 15, 1842): 289, 320; 62 (March 12, 1842): 52; 63 (January 7, 1843): 290. On the Newport vote, see Twenty-Three Citizens of Providence, *Address to the People of the United States* (Providence, 1842), 9. Dorr's honesty and the more manipulative vision of the real politicians in the movement are clear in the letters between Dorr and Dutee J. Pearce, November 21, December 13, 1841, Dorr Papers, JHL.

41. John L. O'Sullivan to Dorr, August 9, 1841, Dorr Papers, JHL. O'Sullivan's friendship predated Dorr's 1839 union of convenience with the Democracy. When O'Sullivan began his journal, he asked Dorr for an article on Roger Williams and for years continued to nag Dorr to write for the journal. O'Sullivan urged Dorr to turn himself over to the authorities for trial after his last nonbattle, to prove his courage and to "beard Charterism in its den" (July 1, 2, 1842). In 1842–43 O'Sullivan printed Dorr's engraving and several supportive articles in *DR*.

42. Henry Dorr to Thomas, May 28, October 25, 1841, and his "Opinions on the Suffrage," January 1842, Dorr Papers, JHL. The letter of Dorr's personally faithful parents, begging him "to pause before you pass the Rubicon," is a touching document, as is a puzzling thank-you note to his mother for some clothes she had sent: "You are the only person related to me . . . who entertains toward me any feelings of kindness." Sullivan and Lydia Dorr to Thomas, April 8, 1842, and Thomas to Lydia, May 6, 1842, Dorr Papers, JHL.

43. Alexander Ming, May 13, 1842; William S. Balch, April 19, 1842; and Allen M. Sniffen, April 20, 1842, promised Dorr Tammany's military support (Dorr Papers, JHL). *NR* 62 (May 21, 1842): 179–80 chronicles the New York noise well, which people like William Cullen Bryant and Samuel Tilden also supported. The Dorr Papers, JHL, have a number of letters of belligerence to Dorr from Philadelphia and New England.

44. Orestes Brownson to Dorr, May 14, 1842, with Dorr's bitter note of Brownson's "action" added; John L. O'Sullivan to Dorr, May 14, 1842, on Connecticut governor Chauncy F. Cleaveland's position, and May 18, 1842, on his writing resolutions for the New York legislature. Silas Wright, April 16, 1842; Thomas Hart Benton, April 16, 1842; Levi Woodbury, April 15, 17, 1842; William Allen (Ohio), April 15, 1842; and Edmund Burke, May 17 1842; to Dorr, Dorr Papers, JHL. On May 19 Burke pointed out Southern opposition to support, and *NR* 63 (January 21, 1843): 323 printed sections of Wright's letter.

45. Dorr to Dutee J. Pearce, December 13, 1842; Dorr Speech, March 19, 1842; Dorr to Aaron White, April 4, 1842, Dorr Papers, JHL; Dorr speech of May 15, 1842, *NR* 62 (May 21, 1842): 180. There is an element of unaware self-satire in Dorr's "military" letters, such as the one to Bradford Allen, May 8, 1842, Dorr Papers, JHL.

46. John A. Brown to Dorr, May 5, 1842, Dorr Papers, JHL; Tyler letter, April 11, 1842, in *NR* 62 (April 23, 1842): 116.

47. Dorr in Woonsocket to Henry DeWolfe, May 19, 1842; and Suffragists Samuel H. Wales, Eli Brown, et al., to Dorr, May 18, 1842, Dorr Papers, JHL. Letters to Dorr from Rhode Island in May and June were mixed, but reports of sliding support predominated. The fullest are from Aaron White, who told Dorr he could expect little local support for a fight, personal or financial. The popular feeling against Dorr's appeal to force is clear in the letters of Providence defender W. M. Bailey, May 17, 19, 1842, and his sister Harriet Bailey, June 14, 1842, to their mother about what Harriet called "that door [Dorr] to misery" (Dorr Papers, JHL).

48. Henry B. Anthony, *The Dorriad*, reprinted in Mowry, *Dorr War*, 392, the best perhaps of the avalanche of satires, broadsides, and cartoons the Dorr nonbattles triggered. The only fatality was from Massachusetts—Alexander Kirby, a forty-year-old father of six, and a factory worker who was a great reader (King, *Life of Dorr*, 147–48). George Templeton Strong's *Diary*, ed. Allan Nevins and Milton Halsey Thomas (New York, 1952), suggests the laughter at the absquatalations (May 9, 23, June 29, 1842, 1:180–84).

49. Dorr speech, May 3, 1841, Dorr Papers, JHL; S. S. Rider, "Nine Lawyers' Opinion," in *Providence Express*, March 16, 1842, appended to *Bibliographical Memoirs of Three Rhode Island Authors* (Providence, 1880). In the only other stab locally at a theory of government, Joseph Cowell claimed that "the Sovereign People now fill the throne abdicated by the King" so they could "change the form of government whenever and in whatever manner soever they pleased." *Letter to Samuel Ward King of Rhode Island* (Providence, 1842), 23–25.

50. John Quincy Adams, *The Social Compact* (Providence, 1842), 18, 31; *DR* 10 (June, July 1842): 78–79, 602–7. The Southern reaction is well shown in a letter that mocked Dorr's position that "any majority without regard to color and condition" could "overturn the existing Government" (William A. Graham to Paul C. Cameron, May 20, 1842, Duncan Cameron Papers, SHC). John C. Calhoun, always quick to see slavery implications, had attacked "the authority of numbers" over law in the 1836 Jacksonian Maryland stab at "revolution."

51. Daniel Webster, *To the Supreme Court in the Case of Martin Luther . . .* (Boston, 1842), 25. Dennison argues that this was in fact the result of the conflict but puzzlingly claims that this *reversed* earlier national commitments to direct democracy and "traditional revolutionary ideology" in order to set up "the leviathan state" (*Dorr War*, 35, 63–65, 200–205).

Chapter Eight

1. The Liberty, Free Soil, and Republican Parties in the North rose without much serious violence, perhaps because of their experience in the political game prior to their truly contesting power. In the South, of course, the few individuals who supported the Republican Party drew mobs.

2. The conclusion locally and nationally about the May riots in Philadelphia was that response was not quick and harsh enough—that, in Strong's words, "irresolution and old grannyism in general" prevailed. George Templeton Strong, *Diary*, ed. Allan Nevins and Milton Halsey Thomas (New York, 1952), May 11, 1844, 1:233; *NR* 66 (May 18, 1844): 192; R. I. Ingersoll to George Cadwalader, May 20, 1844; Cadwalader to R. I. and Joseph S. Ingersoll, May 24, 1844; Cadwalader Papers, HSPa; Strong, *Diary*, April 9, 1845, 1:258.

3. The quotations from and about Scott are in William Baughin, "The Development of Nativism in Cincinnati" (M.A. thesis, University of Cincinnati, 1963), 151. Baughin's able study escapes the easy dichotomies used to simplify the cross-hatching of political, ethnic, religious, and class loyalties over issues such as slavery, temperance, and public schools.

4. Gustavus Myers, *History of Bigotry in the United States* (New York, 1943); Seymour Martin Lipset and Earl Raab, *The Politics of Unreason: Right Wing Extremism in America*

(New York, 1970); David Bennett, *The Party of Fear: From Nativist Movement to the New Right* (Chapel Hill, N.C., 1988). Richard Hofstadter offered the softer version of this interpretation, emphasizing the movement's "paranoid" aspects, rooted in social change and "rootlessness," in *The Paranoid Style in American Politics and Other Essays* (New York, 1965), as did David Brion Davis, "Some Themes of Counter Subversion: An Analysis of Anti-Masonic, Anti-Catholic and Anti-Mormon Literature," *MVHR* 47 (1960): 205–24, an argument Michael Holt supports in his work, most sharply in "The Politics of Impatience: The Origins of Know Nothingism," *JAH* 60 (1973): 309–31. The several older information-filled local studies by Catholic scholars are also informed by the bigotry/insecurity hypothesis.

5. Among the best local studies suggesting the complexity of American Party support and commitments are Jean H. Baker, *Ambivalent Americans: The Know-Nothing Party in Maryland* (Baltimore, 1977); Louis Dow Scisco, *Political Nativism in New York State* (1901; reprint, New York, 1968); Peyton Hurt, *The Rise and Fall of the "Know Nothings" in California* (San Francisco, 1930); Robert D. Parmet, "The Know Nothings in Connecticut" (Ph.D. diss., Columbia University 1966); and three studies of Massachusetts: William G. Bean, "Party Transformation in Massachusetts . . . ," (Ph.D. diss., Harvard University 1922); John R. Mulkern, *The Know-Nothing Party in Massachusetts: The Rise and Fall of a People's Movement* (Boston, 1990); and Virginia Campbell Purdy, *Portrait of a Know-Nothing Legislature: The Massachusetts General Court of 1855* (New York, 1989).

6. L. C. Porter, "Diary," [July?] 1855, FC. Know-Nothing pamphlets often complained of the repeal of the Missouri Compromise line, which had long helped prevent any federal focus on slavery. Thomas R. Whitney, *A Defense of the American Policy* (New York, 1856), 216–21, 275–77; Frederick R. Anspach, *The Sons of the Sires; A History of the Rise, Progress and Destiny of the American Party* (Philadelphia, 1855), 142–43.

7. Two able regional studies of Know-Nothingism best suggest this argument. W. Darrell Overdyke, *The Know Nothings in the South* (Baton Rouge, 1950), v–vi, makes clear how the importance of the American Party related to its unionism and its resistance to proslavery politics, though the book is marred by some claims as excessive as those of Overdyke's sources; Southern cities, he says at one point, became "filters to retain the weaker, the less capable and less desirable" immigrants, "the scum of European almshouses, prisons and asylums" (11). Tyler Anbinder, *Nativism and Slavery: The Northern Know Nothings and the Politics of 1850s* (New York, 1992), offers rich detail (especially about the makeup of the party) and argument but is mistaken that the Know-Nothings were "essentially a Northern party," while the movement in the South "bore little resemblance to its Northern counterpart." His evidence that Know-Nothings "opposed the extension of slavery" is also weak, based largely on the complicated maneuvering and coalitions bound to occur in a fluid politics (xii–xiii, 45, 145–57). Michael Holt argues the insignificance of slavery issues to Know-Nothingism's sudden success by insisting that slavery had been on the political menu for decades, while socioeconomic strain and disgust with politics were the real concerns. This argument neglects both the nation's growing difficulty in dodging the slavery bullet after 1845, and that social strain and disgust with politics we have always with us. Holt, *The Political Crisis of the 1850s* (New York, 1978), 3–4. Holt's *Forging a Majority: The Formation of the Republican Party in Pittsburgh, 1848-1860* (New Haven, 1969) suggests better the tangled web of issues in these years, as does William E. Gienapp, *The Origins of the Republican Party, 1852–56* (New York, 1987).

8. An account of a Beecher lecture in a letter from Esther ———, Hartford, Connecticut, to Jane Corss, January 2, 1855, Sherman Booth Papers, SHSWi. *NR* regularly reported instances of immigrant "dumping" by foreign jurisdictions from the early 1830s on, often in the form of municipal reports or complaints: 47 (October 11, 18, 1834): 89–90, New York City complaining especially of Austria, and Albany of Chatham, England; 55 (September 15,

1838): 43–47, United States of Jamaica and Baltimore of Germany and England; 71 (November 28, 1846): 193, the United States of Hamburg and Mecklenburg. These reports were often sympathetic to the people, regularly listing in the 1840s the appalling numbers of those who died or arrived ill from the voyage. For instance, the *Boston Traveller* reported that one ship arrived with one-sixth of its about 150 immigrant passengers dead and with another twenty needing to be taken to the almshouse deathly ill, with no one having "a copper." *NR* editor John Hughes commented, "Political economists may have their views, but Christians have their duties. . . . We may not pick and choose too scrupulously. . . . Man may not disown his brother man, and lock up his abundance without sin lying at his door" (72 [May 8, 1847]: 155).

9. Samuel C. Busey, *Immigration: Its Evils and Consequences* (New York, 1856), quoting statistics compiled by "Ex-Senator Clemens of New York City," 115. This was a Nativist tract with working-man sympathies, rich in such statistics and complaints, including that of New York mayor Fernando Wood, who wrote President Pierce, January 2, 1855, charging that "this port has been made a sort of penal colony for felons, and paupers, by local authorities of several of the continental powers" (70). Busey also attacked the "money power" and "the capitalists of this country," always "allies of Great Britain, . . . the great antagonist of American labor" (13, 24, 34-44, 81).

10. Joseph H. Allen, *NAR* 79 (October 1854): 418. The Irish editor of the *New Orleans Crescent* complained, "What fools, what fools" the Irish were, "the dupes and victims . . . of demagogic natives—who are the true criminals." September 11, 1852, March 29, 1854, quoted in Earl F. Niehaus, *The Irish in New Orleans* (Baton Rouge, 1965), 210–11, 216; Joseph Osborne to Governor Joseph Vance, December 23, 1844, copied in his "Diary," Osborne Papers, OhHS.

11. *NR* used these terms as well as other similar pairings: "the industrious and honest poor" versus the "putrescent masses," or "the industrious and down trodden masses" versus the "cast off population of aristocratic governments" (43 [September 29, 1832]: 68; 52 [June 10, 1837]: 226; 67 [January 18, 1845]: 309). American Party apologists often made such distinctions, as in Whitney, *Defense*, 167–68. The most able of the American Party pamphleteers, Frederick Saunders, not only praised immigrant contributions but hailed that "as a nation we are essentially eclectic in character, receiving constant accession to our numbers from all parts of the globe." *A Voice to America: The Progress and Prospects* (New York, 1856).

12. T. C. Grattan offered a survey of such views in developing his own: *NAR* 52 (January 1841): 198–206. See also, for examples, *Philadelphia Public Ledger*, September 19, October 2, 1838; Catherine Sedgwick's "The Little Mendicants," in *Pennsylvanian*, May 2, 1846; Martin Spalding, *Miscellanea, Comprising Reviews, Lectures, and Essays* (Louisville, Ky., 1855), lviii–lix.

13. Joseph Mannard, " 'Maternity of the Spirit': Women Religious in the Archdiocese of Baltimore, 1790–1860" (Ph.D diss., University of Maryland, 1986); Bennett, *Party of Fear*, 41–47. Two works, loosely based on real incidents, fueled Know-Nothing sentiment in Massachusetts and Maryland: Thomas F. Caldicott, *Hannah Corcoran: An Authentic Narrative of Her Conversion from Catholicism, Her Abduction from Charlestown, and the Treatment She Received in Her Absence* (Boston, 1853), and the much saltier Josephine M. Bunkley, *The Testimony of an Escaped Novice from the Sisterhood of St. Joseph, Emmetsburg, Md.* (New York, 1855). The stories share a common tone with the fetid "class" writings of George Lippard, *The Quaker City; or The Monks of Monk Hall* (Philadelphia, 1846). See David Reynolds, *Beneath the American Renaissance: The Subversive Imagination in the Age of Emerson and Melville* (New York, 1988).

14. Thomas T. Gantt to Lusinka Brown, August 20, 1855, Campbell-Brown-Ewell Papers, TenHS. Protestant writers often showed uneasiness about celibacy, perhaps because they as-

sociated sexuality with lower things, as when the Episcopal *Banner of the Cross*, generally Catholic-friendly, denounced Catholicism's "celibacy that severs every tie that binds man to his country" (July 27, 1844).

15. William L. Stone of the *New York Journal of Commerce* first promoted the account of Maria Monk and then, upon investigation, exposed its falsity. Reported in *Baltimore Republican*, May 30, 1836; *NR* 51 (October 15, 1836): 98, and 52 (August 12, 1837): 370. *NR* also reported the second nonvirgin birth: 55 (October 20, 1838): 117. Charles Hale lambasted the Know-Nothings in *The Convent Committee, Better Known as the Smelling Committee, in the Exercise of Their Onerous and Arduous Duties at the Ladies' Catholic Seminary, Roxbury* (Boston, 1855).

16. Charles R. Morris, *American Catholic: The Saints and Sinners Who Built America's Most Powerful Church* (New York, 1997), 69. This argument was central in most Know-Nothing writing, as well as in less polemical discussions, often bolstered by relatively official church teachings as well as the occasional comments of incautious American Catholics like Orestes Brownson: Samuel F. B. Morse, *Foreign Conspiracy Against the Liberties of the United States*, (New York, 1839), 20–22, 57–69; Whitney, *Defense*, 53–54, 89–97; Saunders, *Voice to America*, 141–48, 285–88; "Review of *Romanism in America*," NAR 89 (July 1859): 273–74.

17. This was a central theme in several *NAR* articles in the 1850s, such as those by C. C. Shackford (79 [October 1854]: 373–77), and Selma Hale (82 [January 1856]: 120–28), and in the most sophisticated of critiques of political Catholicism, "Civis," *Romanism Incompatible with Republicanism* (New York, 1854). It was a main point of contention in the most famous and perhaps the best of these debates, that between Archbishop John Purcell and Alexander Campbell in Cincinnati in 1837, reported well, with a good sample of reaction, in Baughin, "Nativism in Cincinnati," 41–43. There is a corrected stenographic transcript of the Purcell-Campbell debate, *A Debate on the Roman Catholic Religion* . . . (Cincinnati, 1837), showing that it was less nasty than its Hughes-Breckinridge predecessor.

18. Alexis de Tocqueville, *Democracy in America*, trans. Henry Reeve (London, 1835), 2:222–36. A significant part of Orestes Brownson's Catholic writings insisted that the absolute moral truths of the church alone checked the dangerous vagaries of democratic private judgement. His Catholic political essays are in volumes 15 to 18 of *Brownson's Works* (Detroit, 1882–87); volumes 4 to 8 concentrate on his anti-Protestant essays.

19. Portrayals of Protestants in "official" Catholic publications were as vacuously vicious as most of those on popes and Jesuits in anti-Catholic tracts. For example, Boston's *Catholic Sentinel* said anyone who aided societies to make available "heretical and fanatical Bibles" were "the adopted children of Belial—canting, faithless mock-moralists," and it singled Methodism out for attack as the faith where "hypocritical cobblers, tailors, and tinkers, without education, intelligence, or intellect abandon their honest calling and native element of happy ignorance, and mount the pulpit, like mad preachers, with the *unrighteous, sacrilegious*, heretical dogmas of the Don Quixote of fanaticism, John Wesley." Quoted in *NR* 48 (April 4, 1835): 78–79. Jay P. Dolan intelligently works to define a "Catholic ethos," including its strong anti-Protestant teachings, largely in terms of authority but in ways that in fact suggest great ties to other religions' ethos. *The American Catholic Experience: A History from Colonial Time to the Present* (Notre Dame, 1992), 221–40.

20. Ray Allen Billington, *The Protestant Crusade, 1800–1860: A Study of the Origins of American Nativism* (Chicago, 1938), is the standard account of anti-Catholicism in the era, a careful resumé of the extremest (and extremist) positions. At the same time, Billington neglects the reasonably equitable give-and-take between Catholic and Protestant sources, fails to place the extreme position in relation to the broad spectrum of Protestant views, and neglects the intellectual and theological complexity that underlay the broad argument. The "or-

dinary" Protestant position toward Catholicism was modulated not only by genially vague theology and ecumenical goodwill but also by the calculation of able church strategists like Presbyterian Leonard Bacon who deemed attacks on Catholicism as "eminently unwise" because he saw, as did Catholic leaders, that persecution could only strengthen that church's hold on its members. To W. C. Brownlee, July 28, 1837, in Bacon Papers, YU.

21. *The Controversy between Rev. Messrs. Hughes and Breckenridge on the Subject "Is the Protestant Religion the Religion of Christ?"* (Philadelphia, 1833). An 1835 oral debate between the two enthusiasts was little better except in being much shorter. Dolan deals ably with the changes within Catholicism in *American Catholic Experience,* 101–24, as does Morris in *American Catholic,* 3–80, the latter stressing its Irish orientation.

22. Philadelphian Joseph Sill suggested the element of intellectual curiosity in response to much Catholic-Protestant "discussion." He went to a Hughes-Breckinridge debate in 1835 and thought that Breckinridge had the best of several arguments but that his manner was "unpleasant," while Hughes was personally more genial; in 1844 he read pamphlets by Bishop Kenrick, Reverend Cotton, and Reverend Furness on church differences; in 1845 he attended lectures on toleration, especially toward Catholics, given "very effectively to a large audience" by a Reverend Giles; in 1853 he went to hear the "celebrated Anti-Papal Lecturer Gavazzi, speak in a manner very earnest and impassioned" ("Diary," March 25, 1835; March 23, 29, 1844; February 14, 17, 26, 1845; May 24, 1853, HSPa). Gavazzi, an ex-friar from Bologna who left the church because of its opposition to Garibaldi, was the most influential of the anti-Catholic speakers of the mid-1850s. Alessandro Gavazzi, *The Lectures Complete of Father Gavazzi* (New York, 1854).

23. Differing American/Catholic notions of lay influence underlay the age's many "trustee" controversies. The best-known of these controversies took place in Philadelphia in the 1820s, but there were major conflicts into the 1850s in such places as Baltimore, Norfolk, New Orleans, New York City, and Buffalo. The issues in these struggles are handled in Patrick J. Dignan, *A History of Legal Incorporation of Catholic Church Property in the United States, 1784–1932* (Washington, 1933), and Patrick W. Carey, *People, Priests and Prelates: Ecclesiastical Democracy and the Tensions of Trusteeism* (Notre Dame, 1987); the latter is more balanced.

24. James F. Connelly, *The Visit of Archbishop Gaetano Bedini to the United States of America* (Rome, 1960); Richard Shaw, *Dagger John: The Unquiet Life and Times of Archbishop John Hughes of New York* (New York, 1977), 278–87. The tour of Kossuth in the United States in 1852 also hardened the sense among some Americans of the Catholic Church's broad hostility to political liberalism.

25. Robert Hueston, *The Catholic Press and Nativism, 1840–1866* (New York, 1976). In private writings, the prevalent attitude of ordinary citizens toward Catholicism was one of curiosity more than hostility, though one finds an occasional attack, such as that of a young Massachusetts woman who reported approvingly a traditional jeremiad sermon where the minister suggested that national catastrophe was nigh because of "atheism, infidelity, Blasphemy, Sabbath-breaking, slavery, popery," letting the Irish vote, and especially lack of personal piety. Or a letter of an Illinois man, his religion stronger than his spelling: "my nabour hood is become much mixed with Europians and them almost eunaimously papists which is verry disagreable to us which makes me intent to lieve hear as soon as posibal." Frances Elizabeth Gray, "Diary," November 11, 1835, MaHS; William McCutchin Jr. to his father, March 24, 1840, McCutchin Family Papers, ChiHS.

26. Lovejoy's anti-Catholicism was a variant of that of Lyman Beecher's *Plea for the West* (Boston, 1835), essentially a sense of intense competition for people's souls in the "new" arena, but was sharpened by the attack of Catholic periodicals on him for his antislavery views and by the legal glorification, by an Irish-American Catholic judge, of the mob that de-

stroyed his press. On Father Mathew, see Colm Kerrigan, *Father Mathew and the Irish Temperance Movement, 1838-1849* (Cork, Ire., 1992), and John Francis Maguire, *Father Mathew: A Biography* (London, 1863), which details his American visit (460–519).

27. Charles H. Haswell, *Reminiscences of an Octogenarian in the City of New York* (New York, 1896), 375. On Hughes's and the Catholic Church's fight for parochial funding and against the public schools in New York, see Vincent P. Lannie's excellent *Public Money and Parochial Education: Bishop Hughes, Governor Seward, and the New York School Controversy* (Cleveland, 1968). John Francis Maguire in his good *The Irish in America* (London, 1868) developed what became the standard interpretation about the public school controversy in terms of reading the Protestant Bible, 431–35. Catholic periodicals continued to urge citizens "to break off from our neck the yoke of State despotism, put on them by Jacobinism in the shape of the school system." *Freeman's Journal*, quoted in Richard J. Purcell and John F. Poole, "Political Nativism in Brooklyn," *IrAmHSJ* 32 (1941): 38.

28. Hughes quoted in Lannie, *Public Money*: on Jews, 33, on Quakers, 68, and on Red Republicanism, 253. On the Hughes-Seward alliance, see Glyndon Van Deusen, *William Henry Seward* (New York, 1967), esp. 67–71. A New York Whig supporter lamented that Seward gained nothing for his work for Hughes except opposition from "a bigotry mainly Presbyterian." E. Peshine Smith to Henry C. Carey, June 14, 1854, Edward Gardiner Papers, HSPa.

29. James Lakey, "Diary," September 12, 1853, Lakey Papers, CinHS; Philip Hone, *Diary of Philip Hone,* ed. Bayard Tuckerman (New York, 1889), October 30, 1841, 2:96–97. Jane Grey Swisshelm wrote that her defense of the public schools in Pittsburgh in 1849 at the time when Bishop R. R. O'Connor was attacking them led to her paper's loss of both Catholic readers and Protestant advertisers, while all political papers avoided questioning the Catholic position. *Half a Century* (Chicago, 1880), 150–53.

30. A. P. Peabody in *NAR* 74 (April 1852): 456. The "Bible controversy" was most central in Philadelphia, but the development of different positions over time is clear in an excellent article by Vincent P. Lannie and Bernard C. Diethorn, "For the Honor and Glory of God: The Philadelphia Bible Riots of 1840," *HEdQ* 8 (1968): 44–106.

31. Purcell and Poole, "Political Nativism in Brooklyn," 25–26; John Hancock Lee, *Origin and Progress of the American Party in Politics* (Philadelphia, 1855), 20–25; Saunders, *Voice to America,* 245–60, 280–88. Some suggested that naturalized citizens should be barred from holding office, just as the Constitution barred them from becoming president. Under the Federalists in 1798 a fourteen-year naturalization period was briefly in effect. Massachusetts Know-Nothings took one vicious action against immigrants, sending about 1,300, most of them from charity institutions, back to Europe (Mulkern, *Know-Nothing Party,* 103).

32. In places this proscriptive theory wasn't practiced. In Louisiana, for example, the Know-Nothing candidate for governor was a Catholic, as were the wife and daughters of a Kentucky gubernatorial candidate (Overdyke, *Know Nothings,* 292).

33. Ralph Waldo Emerson, January 26, 1855, quoted in George H. Haynes, "A Know-Nothing Legislature," *AmHAAR* (1896): 187. The Know-Nothings' central emphasis on a political issue involved with electoral corruption strengthened its appeal to the always solid American majority professing dislike of "politics." With Civil War looming and no easy answers, it was comforting to blame corruption on unprincipled politicians, much as subsequent historians found relief in the "blundering politicians" theory.

34. Jean H. Baker, *Politics of Continuity: Maryland Political Parties from 1858 to 1879* (Baltimore, 1973), 21, 32-33; Haynes, "A Know-Nothing Legislature," 178–79; Holt, "Politics of Impatience," 329; Purdy, *Portrait of Legislature,* 116–45. Anbinder rejects this contention, largely by showing that Know-Nothing lodge membership broadly paralleled their community's occupational makeup, but this is precisely the point: the composition of Know-Nothing leaders (and active membership) was close to representative, which created

strong contrast to the much more elitist power structure of the older parties (*Nativism and Slavery*, 34–40).

35. Charles E. A. Gayerre, *Address to the People of Louisiana on the State of Parties* (New Orleans, 1855), 4, 6, 34–38.

36. Initially Know-Nothing lodges supported candidates by private effort rather than public endorsement. This "secrecy" became a central object of Democratic attack after it had ended.

37. Edward H. Savage, *Police Records and Recollections; or Boston by Daylight and Gaslight* . . . (Boston, 1873), 113–16. Anspach, *Sons of the Sires*, 119–20, discussed the way Catholic attempts to silence these preachers aided the movement.

38. Strong, *Diary*, December 15, 1853, 2:140.

39. *New York Tribune*, May 29, June 5, 6, 1854, described these riots.

40. Purcell and Poole, "Political Nativism in Brooklyn," 47–50; *New York Tribune*, November 8, 1854; *Brooklyn Eagle*, November 6, 1856.

41. *New York Tribune*, November 17, 18, 1854.

42. *Baltimore American*, November 3, 1857.

43. A. T. Andreas, *History of Chicago* (Chicago, 1884–85), 1:453, 615–16; *New York Tribune*, April 23–26, 1855.

44. Charles T. Greve, *Centennial History of Cincinnati* (Chicago, 1904), 2:729–30; S. B. Nelson, *History of Cincinnati and Hamilton County* (Cincinnati, 1894), 366–67; Sister M. Evangeline Thomas, *Nativism in the Old Northwest, 1850–1860* (Washington, D.C., 1936), 120–121; *Catholic Pilot*, May 21, 28, 1853; Baughin, "Nativism in Cincinnati," 122–27, 60–68. Anger at Kirkland's arrest for street-preaching was sharpened by the police's failure to act against Catholic mobs who broke up meetings of L. Gustiniani in 1852 and 1853 and who were blamed for burning a church where he spoke.

45. Timothy Walker's speech was printed in the *Cincinnati Gazette*, January 19, 1854.

46. Charles Cist, *Cincinnati in 1851* (Cincinnati, 1851), 45–47; Baughin, "Nativism in Cincinnati," 177, 191–92; Greve, *Cincinnati*, 2:732–33; *New York Tribune*, April 3, 5, 6, 7, 1855; Osborne, "Diary," April 5, 1855, Osborne Papers, OhHS. Rumors also appeared that visiting Kentuckians were central in destroying the ballot boxes to protect bets they had placed on the American Party to win.

47. William S. Merrell, "Diary," April 2–6, 1855, CinHS.

48. Gantt to Brown, August 20, 1855, Campbell-Brown-Ewell Papers, TenHS. While job competition was not a major reality, especially in the South, in these economically good years, the anti-establishment nature of Know-Nothing politics had some strong class reverberations in the hatred of "an aristocracy of wealth, which is the worst of all aristocracies," that resounded especially strongly in the slave South, whose planter leaders talked much of their superiority and of the degradation of white workers compared to their slaves (Whitney, *Defense*, 311).

49. Walsh has often been praised by pro-Democratic historians in search of a "radical" common man: Arthur Schlesinger Jr., *The Age of Jackson* (Boston, 1945), 409–10; Sean Wilentz, *Chants Democratic* (New York, 1984), 326–35. In terms of his writing, Judson was the most respectable and class-oriented of these figures, turning out coarsely vigorous popular fiction and never using his writings specifically to bribe and blackmail, as did Slamm and Walsh. Jay Monaghan's biography of Judson is fairly good, though its interpretation never goes beyond its title: *The Great Rascal: Life and Adventures of Ned Buntline* (Boston, 1952). Michael Denning deals with the class elements in Judson's fiction and the larger genre of which it was a part: *Mechanic Accents: Dime Novels and Working-Class Culture in America* (London, 1987), 102–3.

50. Testimony of George and Henry Clunk at trial for 1852 election riot, printed in the

Missouri Republican, December 27, 1872. These trial clippings are in a "St. Louis history" folder in the MoHS, as is a typescript titled "Mobs and Riots" that covers the 1850s disturbances.

51. J. Thomas Scharf, *A History of St. Louis, City and County* (Philadelphia, 1883), 2:1837; John Schneider, "Mob Violence and Public Order in the American City, 1830–65" (Ph.D. diss., University of Minnesota, 1971), 118; Buntline telegram, quoted in Monaghan, *Great Rascal*, 203.

52. Thomas Lynch, *The Volunteer Fire Department of St. Louis* (St. Louis, 1880), 91; Scharf, *St. Louis*, 2:1840–41.

53. *St. Louis Democrat* in *New York Tribune*, August 12, 1854; Scharf, *St. Louis*, 2:1838–40; *Missouri Republican*, August 10, 12, 1854; *Western Casket*, September 18, 1854; Schneider, "Mob Violence," 122–31, and "Riot and Recreation in St. Louis, 1854–56," *MoHR* 68 (1974): 175.

54. Thomas LaMotte to his wife Ellen, September 16, 1854, and Henry Hitchcock to Ellen Ervin, August 7, 8, 1854, Hitchcock Papers, both in MoHS.

55. Schneider, "Mob Violence," 134, and "Riot and Recreation," 179–82. Thomas Gantt, who was active in the 1854 patrol, wrote the state legislation the Democrats passed. John F. Darby, *Personal Recollections of Many Prominent People I Have Known* (St. Louis, 1880), 436–37.

56. E. A. Hannegan to David Atchison, July 1, 1853, Atchison Papers, SHSMo; Thomas Hart Benton, letter of March 21, 1851, and speech of 1852 and David Atchison on "tyrants," quoted in William Nisbet Chambers, *Old Bullion Benton: Senator from the West . . .* (New York, 1970), 381–408. The Atchison papers are rife with anger at Benton for being a "trimmer" on slavery. On O'Blennis's economic, political, and riotous activities in St. Louis before his conviction for an "honorable" murder, see Charles Van Ravenswaay, *St. Louis: An Informal History of the City and Its People, 1764–1865* (St. Louis, 1968), 311–12.

57. On the 1854 riot see Overdyke, *Know Nothings*, 105–6. On the 1855 riot see *Louisville Courier*, May 7, 1855. Neither of these riots involved the numbers, intensity, and communal concern of another in the Louisville spring of 1854. Young and wealthy "Matt" Ward was acquitted for the killing of a schoolmaster because "honor" was invoked and money was involved. The mob was angered by the case's illustration of how often the legal system provided less equal justice under law than justice for sale on a per capital basis. However, the riot also involved proslavery Democrats' attempt to discredit the Whig friends of the Wards, especially defense attorney (and the man who attempted the last compromise before civil war) John J. Crittendon, and character witness George Prentice. Wholly nonpolitical in its ostensible motive, the Ward riot was in fact the major predecessor of what, sixteen months later, became known as "Bloody Monday."

58. *Louisville Courier*, April 30, 1854, May 7, 1855; *Louisville Journal*, May 8, 1855. The *Times* distinguished between the just popular anger of the Ward riot, which it liked, and the "calculated" quality of the spring election riot (May 11, 1855).

59. *Louisville Times*, May 6, 1855; *Louisville Journal*, August 1, 1855. Prentice's religious tack probably owed something to the fact that, while Kentucky had a small immigrant population (4.1%), its Catholic population was even smaller (3%), with the Protestant and nonreligious Germans being much less certain Democratic allies.

60. John Cleland, "Memorandum Book," July 17, 1855, FC. In a later note, Cleland said, "The questions of the day are Catholicism and Slavery" (November 4, 1856).

61. *Louisville Times*, August 3–5, 1855; *Louisville Journal*, August 5, 1855. The *Louisville Times* steadily claimed that the Know-Nothings were disguised abolitionists determined to destroy the South's "undisturbed enjoyment of her peculiar institutions" (August 2, 1855).

62. *Louisville Courier, Louisville Journal*, and *Louisville Times*, August 7–8, 1855; Stod-

dard Johnston, *Memorial History of Louisville from Its First Settlement to the Year 1896* (Chicago, 1896), 1:100; Wallace B. Turner, "The Know Nothing Movement in Kentucky," *Filson Club Quarterly* 28 (1954): 278–79.

63. Stoddard Johnston, "Journal," in Scrapbook 3, Johnston Collection, and L. C. Porter, "Diary," August 25, 1855, both in FC.

64. The major fireboy clashes occurred on March 21, 1846 (a constable badly hurt); September 25, October 22 (one fireboy killed and many injuries and arrests), and November 28, 1847; October 10, 1848; April 14 and July 16, 1850; and June 2, 1851. Injuries and/or property destruction resulted from all. Jacob Frey, *Reminiscences of Baltimore* (Baltimore, 1893), 89; J. Albert Cassedy, *The Fireman's Record* . . . (Baltimore, 1891), 26–36.

65. Thomas Spaulding, *The Premier See: A History of the Archdiocese of Baltimore* (Baltimore, 1989). Carroll's first book, *The Great American Battle* (New York, 1856), centered in extreme anti-Catholicism, but subsequent pamphlets stressed sectional unity, a concern that led Carroll to add a theme more common among Democrats to her second major work, *The Star of the West* (Boston, 1856): expansionism as a substitute for internal argument. Janet Coryell has written a sensible biography and interpretation that traces Carroll's shift to Republicanism. *Neither Heroine nor Fool: Anna Ella Carroll* (Kent, Ohio, 1990).

66. Joseph Mannard, "The 1839 Baltimore Nunnery Riot: An Episode in Jacksonian Nativism and Social Violence," *Maryland Historian* 11 (1980): 13–27. The street-preacher incident occurred in July 1853.

67. Frey, *Reminiscences*, 90–92.

68. Frank Towers deals broadly with the Baltimore party struggles in these years, especially valuably in regard to the class tensions that crisscrossed the struggle: "Ruffians on the Urban Border: Labor, Politics, and Race in Baltimore, 1854–61" (Ph.D. diss., University of California, Irvine, 1993).

69. *Baltimore Sun* and *Baltimore American*, October 12, 13, 1854; *Baltimore Sun*, September 22, October 27, 30, 1855; *Baltimore Patriot*, October 19–23, 1855; *Baltimore American*, November 19, 1855; *New York Tribune*, September 13, 1856, quoting Baltimore papers. Baker, *Ambivalent Americans*, 128–34, offers good generalizations about the violence and suggests well the interest and ideological cleavages in the political struggle.

70. *Baltimore Sun* and *New York Tribune*, September 16, 19, 1856; *Baltimore Sun*, October 6, 1856; *Baltimore American*, October 9, 1856.

71. *Baltimore Patriot*, November 5, 1856; *New York Tribune*, November 6, 8, 11, 1856; J. Thomas Scharf, *Chronicles of Baltimore* . . . (Baltimore, 1874), 550–52.

72. Francis Ligon Report (1857), quoted in Scharf, *Chronicles of Baltimore*, 558–63. The *New York Tribune* followed the city's response to Ligon's report and planned action closely: October 15, 30–31, November 2, 6, 1857; *Baltimore American*, November 3, 1857; *Baltimore Sun*, November 5, 1857.

73. Mayor Thomas Swann, quoted in Overdyke, *Know Nothings,* 255. Swann, in his *Address on Municipal Affairs* (Baltimore, 1857), claimed he was always "the uncompromising advocate of law and order." More convincingly, he orchestrated comparative urban crime and fire statistics to show that Baltimore was better off than other cities (5–6, 11–15).

74. Scharf, *Chronicles of Baltimore*, 565, quoting from Matthew P. Andrews, *Tercentenary History of Maryland* (Baltimore, 1925), 785.

75. *Baltimore Sun* and *Baltimore American*, November 3, 1859. The Democratic state legislature, after refusing to seat Baltimore's elected Know-Nothings, issued a "fraud" report, featuring dramatic "cooping" tales of men who claimed they were forcibly drugged and made to vote repeatedly. It's possible that something like this may have happened as someone's idea of fun, but certainly Baltimore Know-Nothings had no lack of better and cheaper ways of cheating to assure victory. Maryland General Assembly, *Baltimore City Contested Election—*

Papers in the Contested Election Case, 1859 . . . (Annapolis, 1860); Scharf, *Chronicles of Baltimore*, 470–75, 583. In 1859 there were only minor injuries.

76. The fullest history of these events remains John S. Kendall, *History of New Orleans* (New York, 1922), 1:169–227. Leon Cyprian Soulé, in *The Know-Nothing Party in New Orleans: A Reappraisal* (Baton Rouge, 1961), argues that Creole-American tensions underlay the conflict, though this theme is stronger in the introduction and conclusion than in the body of the account. Earl F. Niehaus offers rich general information about older Catholics and the Irish in *Irish in New Orleans*.

77. *Louisiana Courier*, March 15, 1854; *New Orleans Bee*, March 15, 22, 1854. The Whigs held the mayoralty, 1846–54, but state Democrats put the police under the control of their party by removing the mayor's appointive power.

78. *New Orleans Picayune*, March 26, 1854; *Louisiana Courier*, March 28, 1854.

79. *New Orleans Bulletin*, September 12, 14, 16, 18, 1854; *Louisiana Courier*, September 15, 20, 1854; *New York Tribune*, September 16, 19, 1854; Helena Kirchoff to Fritz Kirchoff, September 14, 1854, Kirchoff Papers, SHC.

80. *New Orleans Bulletin*, November 1, 7, 8, 1855; *New Orleans Picayune* in *New York Tribune*, November 16, 1855; Overdyke, *Know Nothings*, 242–45.

81. *New Orleans Bulletin*, June 3, 11, 1856; *New Orleans Picayune*, June 3, 1856; *Louisiana Courier*, June 1, 4, 1856; Kendall, *New Orleans*, 197–98; Niehaus, *Irish in New Orleans*, 228.°

82. *New Orleans True Delta* in *The States* (D.C.), November 6, 1857; Louisiana Attorney General, *Report on Crime in New Orleans* (New Orleans, 1858); Kendall, *New Orleans*, 212. The attorney general's report was released to justify and abet the vigilantes.

83. Richard Maxwell Brown, *Strain of Violence: Historical Studies of American Violence and Vigilantism* (New York, 1975), 134–43; Robert Senkewicz, *The Vigilantes in Gold Rush San Francisco* (Stanford, 1985), 104–19, 170–88. Louisiana proslavery Democrats used vigilantism more politically effectively in the Attakapas area: see David Grimsted, "Né D'Hier: American Vigilantism, Communal Rebirth and Political Traditions," in *People and Power: Rights, Citizenship and Violence*, ed. Loretta Valtz Mannucci (Milan, 1992), 93–105.

84. *New Orleans Delta*, May 28, June 2, 6, 1858; *Louisiana Courier*, May 30, June 3, 1858; Kendall, *New Orleans*, 212–18.

85. Kendall, *New Orleans*, 218–24; *New Orleans Delta*, June 4–5; *New York Tribune*, June 7–8, 1858; James Norman Smith, "Autobiography," 123–24, Wallace A. Jones Papers, UTex.

86. *New York Tribune*, June 9, 10, 12, 1858; John M. Claiborne to Thomas Claiborne, June 9, 1858; Kendall, *New Orleans*, 1:224–27, and "The Municipal Election of 1858," *LaHQ* 7 (1924): 466–79. George Templeton Strong lamented that the New Orleans group, unlike the San Franciscans, failed of a "unanimous uprising of the conservative men and property-holders of the community, compelled in self-defense to put down rampant scoundrelism, even at the expense of violated formalities and legalities" (*Diary*, June 5, 1858, 2:403–404).

87. *The States*, June 8, 1857; R. M. Boyer, Georgetown, to Ann Eliza Hawley, June 9, 1857, Hawley Papers, MinnHS; Andrew Shiner, "Diary," June 1, 1857, LC.

88. Citizens of the District of Columbia, *The Military Execution of American Citizens by Order of the President: An Appeal to the People of the United States* (Washington, 1857). The three Democratic papers in the capital—*The States, Union*, and *News*—tried to deny the evidence, but with such clumsiness that its truth was clear. The final "defense" was the report of a grand jury, carefully stacked by the Democrats.

89. See, for example, the Maryland General Assembly, *Baltimore City Contested Election*. This pattern was followed later by post-Reconstruction Democratic legislatures who "investi-

gated" their predecessors to prove their purity and create the documents subsequent historians followed.

90. The Baltimore and St. Louis riots of 1861 were very much a continuation of the alliance of proslavery politicians and partly Irish mobs, as were the draft riots of 1863, though always with many complicating elements. The "politics" of this era in border areas are well explored in Baker, *Politics of Continuity*, 47–62, and Robert E. McDowell, *City of Conflict* (Louisville, 1962).

91. Lewis D. Campbell, *"Americanism": The Speech of the Hon. Lewis D. Campbell of Ohio* (Washington, D.C., 1856), 2; "An Old Clay Whig," *Reflections and Suggestions on the Present State of Politics* (Nashville, 1856), 6–7, 9–12, 27–28, 75. Here, as in many of these writings, Know-Nothing anti-Catholicism was attributed to what these writers saw as that church's proslavery position. For example, see Louisiana Democratic State Central Committee, *Extracts from the Speech of the Hon. Alexander Stephens* (New Orleans, 1855), 9.

92. William K. Sebastian, *Substance of the Speech of Hon. William K. Sebastian, Made for Democratic Mass Meeting of Helena* [Ark.] . . . (Washington, D.C., 1855), 15–17, 22.

93. Lawrence M. Keitt, *Speech of Lawrence M. Keitt in the House of Representatives* (Washington, D.C., 1855), 1–2, 7–8.

Chapter Nine

1. Nancy Rash, *The Painting and Politics of George Caleb Bingham* (New Haven, 1991), 151–54. Bingham described the election visits from Missouri as "infamous expeditions of organized rowdyism" and was amazed that slavery interests failed to see how such tactics were sure to "arouse a fierce opposition in the entire North."

2. George Fort Milton, *Stephen Douglas and the Needless War* (New York, 1934) argues that Douglas was always antislavery and offers vigorous attack on the "ambitious fanatics" who opposed him and used war to win power (149–66). Robert W. Johannsen, *Stephen A. Douglas* (New York, 1973), is a more reasonable interpretation, centering on Douglas as "a consummate politician" with "an almost obsessive devotion to 'the voice of the many'" (vii). Damon Wells Jr., *Man in Motion: The Last Years of Stephen Douglas, 1857–6,* 1968 typescript, LC, is a good analysis of Douglas's principles.

3. *Richmond Enquirer*, December 5, 1853. Most abolitionist opinion in the North agreed that slavery was foreordained for Kansas by the passage of the Kansas-Nebraska Act, as did the *New York Tribune*, May 24, 1854. Henry Ward Beecher to Mrs. Hale, n.d. [1854], Hale Family Papers, NF. Samuel A. Johnson, *The Battle Cry of Freedom: The New England Emigrant Aid Company in the Kansas Crusade* (Lawrence, Kans., 1954), is the standard account, and Richard Abbot, *Cotton and Conscience: Boston Businessmen and Antislavery Reform, 1854–1868* (Amherst, Mass., 1991), 28–49, a more recent one. Eli Thayer, *A History of the Kansas Crusade: Its Friends and Foes* (New York, 1889), deals richly with the hostility of New England abolitionists to the Kansas Free-State movement (74–164).

4. John H. Jewett, *Speech of John H. Jewett of Kentucky* . . . (Washington, D.C., 1856), 3. The twenty killings in 1857 by Iowa vigilantes are recorded in the rich and careful article by Paul Black, "Lynchings in Iowa," *IaJHP* 10 (1912): 189–99. My Kansas body count is probably low. Oswald Garrison Villard, using government reports, suggests that about 200 "lost their lives" in the conflicts. *John Brown, 1800–1859* (Boston, 1910), 264. The best personal account by a proslavery settler, for example, describes six deaths a bit too vaguely for me to include, four Free-Staters murdered and two proslavery men killed in a battle with Lane's men. R. W. Williams, *With the Border Ruffians: Memoirs of the Far West, 1852–1868* (1907; reprint, Lincoln, 1982), 82–86.

5. Roy F. Nichols, *Franklin Pierce: Young Hickory of the Granite Hills* (Philadelphia, 1958), argues the president's impartiality and blames trouble in Kansas on claim jumpers and northern fanatics, essentially the position also of Philip Klein, *President James Buchanan: A Biography* (University Park, Pa., 1962). Elbert B. Smith, *The Presidency of James Buchanan* (Lawrence, Kans., 1975), is more realistic about the administration's pro-southern slant.

6. William E. Cornell, *James Henry Lane: The "Grim Chieftain" of Kansas* (Topeka, 1899); Wendell H. Stephenson, *The Political Career of General James H. Lane* (Topeka, 1930); Don W. Wilson, *Governor Charles Robinson of Kansas* (Lawrence, Kans., 1975). The fullest handling of the later debates, by a man who despised all the Free-State leaders, is James C. Malin's two-volume *John Brown and the Legend of Fifty-Six* (Philadelphia, 1942). This work has been influential in distorting historical understanding of the Kansas conflict. While correct in insisting on John Brown's lesser role in Kansas and vigorous in pointing out others' errors, Malin so delights in every mote in others' eyes that he never notices the beam of evidence he determinedly neglects: the threats, intimidation, and violence from proslavery forces that engendered the broad resistance and anger.

7. The recent study by Homer E. Socolofsky, *Kansas Governors* (Lawrence, Kans., 1990), 33–78, is less detailed than William E. Connelley, *Kansas Territorial Governors* (Topeka, 1900).

8. William O. Lynch, *Population Movements in Relation to the Struggle for Kansas* (Bloomington, Ind., 1925), collects the demographic statistics, with Missourians comprising the largest state group, and people from the old Northwest the most significant regional group. Paul Gates, *Fifty Million Acres: Conflicts over Kansas Land Policy* (Ithaca, 1954), 1–105, details the land controversies, exacerbated by opening the territory before surveying was done, that reverberated in the conflicts.

9. D. W. Wilder, *The Annals of Kansas, 1541–1885* (Topeka, 1886), reprints the extreme proslavery laws of this legislature 72–75. Wilder's book contains the best chronology of the conflict with a rich presentation of basic documents (45–341). Also valuable for reprinting sources is A. T. Andreas, *History of the State of Kansas* (Chicago, 1883), 81–179. The best narrative of the events is still Leverett W. Spring's *Kansas: The Prelude to the War for the Union* (Boston, 1885), vigorous and relatively fair. The more recent interpretation is represented best, but badly, by Alice Nichols, *Bleeding Kansas* (New York, 1954). *The Report of the Special Committee Appointed to Investigate the Troubles in Kansas: With the Views of the Minority of Said Committee*, 34th Cong., 1st sess. (Washington, 1856), presents a wealth of data on the early conflict in a form making clear the political passions tied to the struggle.

10. D. F. Jamison to David Atchison, March 25, 1856; Atchison to A. R. Corbin, March 16, 1856; C. F. Jackson to Atchison, January 18, 1854. In a letter to Corbin, December 14, 1855, Atchison claimed he worked "not to excite but to control and keep within proper bounds the over-excited" (Atchison Papers, SHSMo).

11. The Westport resolves of July and October 1854 are in John H. Gihon, *Geary and Kansas: Governor Geary's Administration in Kansas* (Philadelphia, 1857), 29–31; *Squatter Sovereign*, quoted in Thomas H. Gladstone, *The Englishman in Kansas* (New York, 1857), 278. The Gihon-Gladstone volumes are the best of the "primary" accounts, both Free-State in orientation: the latter has an able introduction by Frederick Law Olmsted.

12. Missouri paper quoted in Gladstone, *Englishman,* 264; Roy V. Magers, "The Raid on the Parkville *Industrial Luminary,*" *MoHR* 30 (1935): 39–44. The Frederick Starr Papers, SHSMo, contain rich clippings and letters from a young minister in Weston, Missouri, of Northern birth, Yale education, and Free-Soil principles who managed to avoid the frequently threatened mobbing. His case shows how much latent communal resentment proslavery tactics aroused when anyone had the courage, skill, and good luck to question the label "abolitionist" as excuse for violence. A public meeting exonerated Starr when he was given a

chance to explain the circumstances surrounding the bill of charges against him, in this case all admitted: he had refused to sign a proslavery petition, helped organize Missourians interested in going to Kansas, taught slaves to read, privately urged a woman to free a talented slave, and once had ridden in carriage with a black.

13. Wilder, *Annals,* 64. A different William Phillips was a *New York Tribune* correspondent who wrote *The Conquest of Kansas, by Missouri and Her Allies* (Boston, 1856), the Free-State counterpart of G. Douglas Bretherton, a *New York Herald* reporter, who wrote *The War in Kansas: A Rough Trip to the Border . . .* (New York, 1856). Both books have a lot of data—and overheated rhetoric.

14. *Squatter Sovereign* account, quoted in Gihon, *Geary,* 48–49; Gladstone, *Englishman,* 283. Gladstone reprinted the bloody-bones rhetoric of threat from the proslavery *Kickapoo Pioneer* and other sources that put the South's message in verbal form (23–26), making clear the intent to frighten Free-Staters away by bluster and threat.

15. Wilder, *Annals,* 70–71, 118; Pardee Butler, *Personal Recollections of Pardee Butler* (Cincinnati, 1889), 63–80, 106–9.

16. Malin, *John Brown,* developed this idea to disparage Free-State "moralism." The most serious proponents of the racist explanation for opposition to slavery expansion remain Eugene H. Berwanger, *The Frontier against Slavery: Western Anti-Negro Prejudice and the Slavery Extension Controversy* (Urbana, Ill., 1967), and James A. Rawley, *Race and Politics: "Bleeding Kansas" and the Coming of the Civil War* (Philadelphia, 1969). Berwanger and Rawley did good service by calling attention to the deep racist strand in Republican or proto-Republican politics but paid little heed to the louder racism of the party opposed. See Eric Foner, *Free Soil, Free Labor, Free Men: The Ideology of the Republican Party before the Civil War* (New York, 1970), and David Potter, *The Impending Crisis, 1848–61* (New York, 1976), 199–224, 297–327. Potter's is a good handling of the Kansas issue, if not wholly free of Malin's malign influence.

17. Charles Robinson, *Kansas Conflict* (New York, 1892), 151. Robinson quotes much of this speech, remarkable for how fully it includes the later Lincoln position, with lesser elements of equivocation and of racism. Robinson stressed the Declaration of Independence as "the rule of faith and practice" of the nation which could "be cherished only by those who believe 'that all the nations who dwell upon the earth are made of one blood.'" He quoted copiously from Kansas and Southern editors and leaders who argued that laws and mobs ought to take life and freedom from all "abolitionists," and he pointed out what most Free-Staters by this time accepted: that "abolitionist" meant everyone who dared "to have an opinion upon the subject of the rights of man in any respect differing from theirs." To illustrate his point in local terms and symbols, with which everyone was familiar, Robinson quoted the remark "of one of the chivalry, whose name is suggestive of hemp factories [Stringfellow], 'had I the power I would hang every abolitionist in the country, and every man north of Mason and Dixon's line *is* an abolitionist.'" And such threats came from a group of men who deemed it perfectly honorable to teach that "the Declaration of Independence is a lie; . . . that marriage is a mockery; that the parent shall not have possession of his own child, nor the husband his wife; that education is a crime; that traffic in human beings is a virtue." Robinson concluded that Free-Staters could take heart from the fact that they fought for liberty not alone but with the eyes and hopes of history, the world, and the nation on them, both "the millions of freeman and the millions of bondsmen" (145–52).

18. Robinson, *Kansas Conflict,* 169–76. Robinson's account suggests well the general Free-State strategy and his personal confidence that the political compromises contributed to his broader goals. He later strongly supported Susan B. Anthony's 1867 attempt to give women the vote in Kansas.

19. Butler, *Personal Recollections,* 37–44, 50–52, 63, 108–10, 135–36.

20. Gihon, *Geary*, 45–73.

21. Wilder, *Annals*, 109–10; Andrew T. Hartlee to his mother, May 17, 1856, William Hartlee Papers, SHC.

22. Gladstone, *Englishman*, 45. Gladstone offers a vivid eyewitness account of the sacking (31–46).

23. Atchison quoted in Gladstone, *Englishman*, 34, and also in Wilder, *Annals*, 12. Parrish points out accurately that there were slightly varied reports of this speech, that the *Squatter Sovereign* later gave a highly legalistic version of it, and that Atchison much later denied it, claiming he only visited Lawrence to insure the peace. Still, at the time Atchison did not disown the common report. William Earl Parrish, *David Rice Atchison of Missouri, Border Politician* (Columbia, Mo., 1961), 201–2.

24. Oswald Garrison Villard offers the most intellectually nuanced and morally balanced view of Brown's acts at this time (*John Brown*, 79–266). Spring, *Kansas*, 137–94, gives a good account of the summer's Kansas events.

25. Free-Stater Samuel Anderson, who had fought under Brown and took over his troops, described these and subsequent events well: KanHS *Collections* 2 (1894): 290–91. Richard B. Foster's testimony also covers these events (2:227–28). David Atchison to A. R. Corbin, March 16, 1856, Atchison Papers, SHSMo.

26. Edwin V. Sumner to Colonel Cooper on his orders from Shannon, and Persifer Smith to Cooper, August 29, 1856, in *House Executive Documents*, 34th Cong., 3d sess., pt. 2:64, 77; Gihon, *Geary*, 92–101.

27. Daniel Woodson to P. St. George Cooke, September 1, 1856; Cooke to Woodson, September 2, 1856; Geary to Cooke, September 28, 1856, *House Executive Documents*, 34th Cong., 3d sess. pt. 2:90–91; 1st sess., pt. 1:151; Thomas Wentworth Higginson, *Cheerful Yesterdays* (Boston, 1898), 205; Andrew T. Hartlee to his mother, September 7, 1856, William Hartlee Papers, SHC; Gladstone, *Englishman*, 302–3. Gihon, who went to Kansas as Geary's assistant, pointed out that upon his arrival, information from both friends and Washington directed "all his proclivities" to the proslavery side, though evidence "at length forced [him], though unwillingly," to see that justice sided mostly with the Free-Staters (*Geary*, iv).

28. Andrew Hartlee to his father, September 20, 1856, William Hartlee Papers, SHC; Geary, quoted by Allan Nevins, *The Ordeal of the Union* (New York, 1947), 2:484; Geary to William Marcy, October 15, 1856, *House Executive Documents*, 34th Cong., 3d sess., pt. 1:169.

29. Walker's speech is printed in *TKanHS* (1889–96), 5:328–41. James P. Shenton, *Robert John Walker: A Politician from Jackson to Lincoln* (New York, 1961), 154–55.

30. Don E. Fehrenbacher, *The Dred Scott Case: Its Significance in American Law and Politics* (New York, 1978), 70, 308–14 and, on the substance of the decision, 335–88; Klein, *Buchanan*, 269–72. Kenneth Stampp deals with the national politics tied to Kansas in *America in 1857: A Nation on the Brink* (New York, 1990), 144–81, 266–331.

31. Wilder, *Annals*, prints the Lecompton Constitution (177–91), with the section of proslavery electoral control and prohibition of all amendment for seven years (189) and the clause extolling the absolute sanctity of slave property (183). He provides returns for the various elections in late fall of 1857 and January 1858 (192–94, 206–8).

32. *Charleston Mercury*, April 20, 21, 1857, quoted in Fehrenbacher, *Dred Scott*, 449–50, in an excellent chapter on the national reverberation of the Lecompton controversy (449–84). George D. Harmon, "President James Buchanan's Betrayal of Governor Robert J. Walker of Kansas," *PaMHB* 53 (1929): 51–91, covers the two men's relation closely.

33. Buchanan message to Congress, February 2, 1858, supporting Lecompton, discussed in Fehrenbacher, *Dred Scott*, 469–70.

34. J. P. Jones to James W. Denver, June 3, 1858, KanHSC *Collections* 5 (1896): 526.

35. Lyon letters of March, April, and December 1855 in Ashbel Woodward, *Life of General Nathaniel Lyon* (Hartford, 1862), 209–14.

36. Lyon letter of August 1856 and Woodward's comments, *Life of Lyons* 215–18. Perhaps Lyon had even more personal reasons for unease about his own stance. In a letter not used by his biographer, he wrote to Atchison complaining of one person's "outrageous and unprincipled conduct" toward some proslavery people (June 8, 1855, Atchison Papers, SHSMo).

37. Lyon letters of September, December 5, and later in December, 1859, in Woodward, *Life of Lyon*, 229–33.

38. Woodward, *Life of Lyon*, 243–54.

39. Higginson, *Cheerful Yesterdays*, 198–99; Lyon letter of August 1856 in Woodward, *Life of Lyon*, 215.

40. Benjamin F. Stringfellow, quoted in Gladstone, *Englishman*, 80. At another public meeting, Stringfellow, after urging the murder of all Northerners coming to Kansas, voiced his version of the patriarchal theory: in the North "every man who works for his living is a slave and every poor white working woman a whore. The North has no gentlemen and no intelligence. The country is carried forward by Southern intelligence and capital alone." Stringfellow denied making the remark, but when testimony about this poured in and one man proved quite happy to duel over who was the "liar," Stringfellow changed the subject to the more arcane matter of who reported his remark and with what propriety. Frederick Starr to his father, February 22, 26, 1855, Starr Papers, SHSMo.

41. Gary Wills's moving account of Lincoln's intellectual journey to a more inclusive national ideal reveals in fact a path much traveled, or stumbled along, in these years. *Lincoln at Gettysburg: The Words That Remade America* (New York, 1992).

42. Frederick Grimké to Alexander St. Clair Boys, January 1, 1858, Boys Papers, OhHS. Grimké's major work was *Considerations upon the Tendency of Free Institutions* (Cincinnati, 1848), perhaps the best attempt to create a "political philosophy" from Jacksonian party positions.

43. Furness sermon, quoted in Joseph Sill, "Diary," July 3, 1842, HSPa; Butler, *Personal Recollections*, 49–50.

44. Strong, *Diary*, May 29, 1856, 2:275. Lyon, Ft. Scott, Kansas, January 27, 1861, in Woodward, *Life of Lyon*, 235, 239.

45. Alexander Stephens to Thomas W. Thomas, May 25, 1856, Stephens Papers, EU; Stephens, *A Constitutional History of the Late War between the States . . .* (Philadelphia, 1868). Here Stephens espoused extreme racism while disingenuously insisting that both North and South, including such figures as Roger Taney, were in fact antislavery (2:28–34, 260–61).

Epilogue

1. Theodore C. Smith, *The Liberty and Free Soil Parties in the Northwest* (New York, 1897); Richard H. Sewell, *Ballots for Freedom: Anti-Slavery Politics in the United States, 1837–1860* (New York, 1976).

2. Richard H. Sewell, *John P. Hale and the Politics of Abolition* (Cambridge, Mass., 1965) is an able biography, conscious of Hale's weakness as well as appreciative of his abilities and contributions.

3. *Slavery at Washington* (London, 1848) gives some data about the slaves before and after the attempt, and Daniel Drayton, *The Personal Memoir of Daniel Drayton* (Boston, 1855), tells the story, with much documentation, from the view of the man who captained the rescue

ship and who was long jailed for the crime but was pardoned by Millard Fillmore just before the latter left the presidency.

4. *The Globe,* April 18, 20, 1848; *National Intelligencer,* April 18–22, 1848.

5. Stanley Harrold, *Gamaliel Bailey and Antislavery Union* (Kent, Ohio, 1986), 124–27. Drayton printed a transcript from the *New York Tribune* of how Mr. Radcliff and other Washington leaders tried to use the mob threat to get Bailey to leave (*Personal Memoir,* 49–53).

6. John Hale to his daughter Elizabeth, April 18, 19, 1848, Hale Papers, NHHS. The letters of praise that poured in suggest the anger at Southern arrogance and Northern proslavery kowtowing to it that girded later Republican success in the North.

7. The quotations from the debate are taken from my condensation of it in *Notions of the Americans, 1820–1860* (New York, 1970), 312–26. The full debate is in the *Congressional Globe,* 30th Cong., 1st sess., appendix (Washington, D.C., 1848), 500–510.

8. Henry A. Foote, *Casket of Reminiscences* (Washington, D.C., 1874), 74–77, made clear his moderate politics, his personal liking for Hale, and the embarrassment he felt about his "fumy" and "rabid" response on this occasion. Foote's French Revolution speech was used by Drayton's attorneys to argue that slaves were induced to run off by that day's congressional paeans to the glories of freedom, many of them by Southerners (Drayton, *Personal Memoir,* 27, 73).

9. The damage Hale did them shows in Northern Democrats' loud denunciations of Hale's attackers. The *Democratic Review* lashed out in its common vein against "the incendiary and basely selfish strivings" of abolition's "fools and fanatics," but it found Calhoun, always subject to "childish excesses of unbridled passion," impossible to respect when he responded in "words we could only expect in a maniac or common driveller." Of Calhoun's many "hot-brained and foul-mouthed followers," the worst was that "senseless demagogue" Foote, whose "disgusting rant" was beyond the pale "of the most abandoned leader of a street mob" and whose talents made him better suited for a hangman than a legislator. So disturbed was the editor that he made the *Review's* only suggestion that slavery, "the cursed legacy of English cruelty and avarice," would end—"eventually" (DR 22 [May 1848]: 471–72).

10. Van Buren gained just over 10 percent of the votes in 1848, while Hale garnered about 5 percent four years later, somewhat closer to the numbers Birney attracted in 1844 than to those of the ex-President as Free-Soiler.

11. Of the several attempts of historians to blame "blundering politicians" for the Civil War, the most cogent is that of Elbert B. Smith, who argues that Pierce and Buchanan's unwillingness to resist Southern demands ensured the North's turning away from the Democats. *The Presidency of James Buchanan* (Lawrence, Kans., 1975), 143–65, 196–98; *The Presidencies of Zachary Taylor and Millard Fillmore* (Lawrence, Kans., 1988), 91–122, 257–60.

12. The leading historian arguing Brown's insanity is C. Vann Woodward, mistaken about some of his evidence and connecting madness with intense religious commitment: "John Brown's Private War," in *America in Crisis,* ed. Daniel Aaron (New York, 1952), 109–30. A modified mental instability theme is found in the articles by Bertram Wyatt-Brown and Robert E. McGlone in Paul Finkelman, ed., *His Soul Goes Marching On: Responses to John Brown and the Harpers Ferry Raid* (Charlottesville, 1995), 10–38, 213–52. The attack on Brown from historians more proslavery and hostile to abolition has placed more emphasis on his business ambition and failures and his antislavery as part of another dishonest speculation. See James C. Malin, *John Brown and the Legend of Fifty-Six* (Philadelphia, 1942); Hill Peebles Wilson, *John Brown, Soldier of Fortune* (Boston, 1918), and Robert Penn Warren, *John Brown: The Making of a Martyr* (New York, 1929), who argued that the slave "never bothered his kinky head about the moral issue" (332). Booth's insanity is most stressed in two popularized family histories, Stanley Kimmel, *The Mad Booths of Maryland* (New York, 1969), and Gene Smith, *American Gothic* (New York, 1992).

13. Otto J. Scott, *The Secret Six: John Brown and the Abolitionist Movement* (New York, 1979), stresses the maladjusted fanaticism of Brown's financial supporters, and Jeffery Rossbach, *Ambivalent Conspirators: John Brown, The Secret Six, and a Theory of Slave Violence* (Philadelphia, 1982), argues shared religious emphasis, market values, social concerns, and racial theories.

14. William A. Tidwell, James O. Hall, and Winifred Gaddy, *Come Retribution: The Confederate Secret Service and the Assassination of Lincoln* (Jackson, Miss., 1988), is richly researched and makes clear Copperhead-Confederate enthusiasm for assassination and consideration of it at the highest level of Southern officials. Still, the case is argued in one direction and lacks any "smoking gun" in regard to the final murder. Clayton Gray, *Conspiracy in Canada* (Montreal, 1957), offered, in popularized form, much of the material that made clear Booth's long connection with and support from Confederate agents. William Hanchett, *The Lincoln Murder Conspiracies . . .* (Urbana, Ill., 1983), 58–89, argues that the final killing was personal, without denying Confederate support for Booth's plan to abduct Lincoln. See also Thomas Reed Turner, *Beware of People Weeping: Public Opinion and the Assassination of Abraham Lincoln* (Baton Rouge, 1982).

15. Oswald Garrison Villard, *John Brown, 1800–1859* (Boston, 1910), 73–111. Villard's richly researched biography codified and corrected the vision of early Brown supporters and biographers and provided the basic data used in subsequent studies. Thomas Wentworth Higginson wrote a strong description of the north Elba experience and of the family there after Brown's execution: James Redpath, *The Public Life of Capt. John Brown* (Boston, 1860, 60–72.

16. John Brown to his brother Frederick, November 21, 1834, in Franklin Sanborn, *The Life and Letters of John Brown, Liberator of Kansas and Martyr of Virginia* (Boston, 1891), 40–41.

17. Villard, *John Brown, 45–57,* covers the evidence related to the "origins" of the Harpers Ferry idea.

18. George Gill, a Brown supporter active in the slave raid to Missouri, to Richard J. Hinton, July 7, 1895, reprinted in an excellent collection of source material: Louis Ruchames, ed., *John Brown: The Making of a Revolutionary* (New York, 1969), 239–41.

19. The memories of the Brown home life of James Foreman, George B. Delamater, and children John Jr., Salmon, and Ruth Brown Thompson all suggest the same traits. In Ruchames, *John Brown,* 171–97.

20. John Brown to Henry L. Stearns, July 15, 1857, in Villard, *John Brown,* 6–7; reported by W. A. Phillips, a Kansas correspondent for the *New York Tribune,* in Ruchames, *John Brown,* 220. The Stearns letter, written to the young son of a friend who'd asked about his life, shows Brown's sweetness, humor, values, and shrewd self-honesty at their best. At about the same time he told his daughter, "If I had my life to live over again, I should do very differently with my children. I meant to do right, but I can see now that I failed" (Ruth Brown Thompson, quoted in Ruchames, *John Brown,* 187).

21. Frederick Douglass, *The Life and Times of Frederick Douglass* (Hartford, 1882), 309–10. His children's accounts all suggest intense love and admiration for their father but also a salty and realistic sense of his excess and folly at times, both in their upbringing and in their relations to his antislavery actions. Perhaps their limited rebellion from him was clearest in religion, in which none of Brown's sons had much interest. They often told him "he trusted a little too much to providence" in ways that threatened his, and their, lives (Salmon Brown in Ruchames, *John Brown,* 199).

22. Even after their father's execution, the young at North Elba told Higginson how much they loved and admired their father—and how relieved they had always felt when he left home (Redpath, *Public Life,* 70).

23. John Jr. account in Sanborn, *Life and Letters,* 91–93.

24. Salmon Brown in Ruchames, *John Brown,* 194–95. The work that best integrates Brown's actions into broader patterns of politics and violence is Richard O. Boyer, *The Legend of John Brown: A Biography and History* (New York, 1972).

25. John Brown to *Akron* (Ohio) *Summit Beacon,* December 20, 1855, in Ruchames, *John Brown,* 97–100.

26. John Brown to his family, February 1, 1856, in Sanborn, *Life and Letters,* 222; Salmon Brown account in Ruchames, *John Brown,* 199–200.

27. Salmon Brown account in Ruchames, *John Brown,* 200–202, which also reproduces the 1879 account of the murders by participant James Townsley (205–11).

28. James Malin covers fully the development of the proofs of John Brown's active involvement in the Pottawatomie murders in the face of his own and his earliest biographers' denials (*John Brown,* 393–404). Malin's description of Brown (and of anyone who liked him) involves imperceptive diatribe, but his full search of press accounts makes amply clear the element of mutualness in Kansas mayhem and of his central point: that Brown's Kansas career was much less important to the Free-State cause than that of several other steadier leaders.

29. Villard, in his account of the Pottawatomie killings—richly researched, morally sensitive, complexly damning of Brown—records the revulsion of the sons at their father's deed and the immediate shock and then greater justification of the act by the Free-State settlers (165–88).

30. Samuel Adair to Mr. and Mrs. Hand and other friends, May 30, 1856, copy in Villard Collection, ColU.

31. Villard, *John Brown,* 362–90; account of reporter William A. Phillips, in Ruchames, *John Brown,* 222–26.

32. Brown to Thomas Wentworth Higginson, February 12, 1858; Osborne P. Anderson, *A Voice from Harper's Ferry* (Boston, 1861), 23–24. The fullest account about Brown's associates, that of Richard J. Hinton, *John Brown and His Men: With Some Account of the Roads They Travelled to Reach Harper's Ferry* (New York, 1894), also gives a good account of the Missouri slave rescue (199–228). Benjamin Quarles, *Allies for Freedom: Blacks and John Brown* (New York, 1974), is the fullest treatment.

33. Villard, *John Brown,* 426–55. Possibly a slave or two, briefly armed after "liberation" by Brown's men, were also killed, but the evidence, as always about such chattel, is vague.

34. Transcript of public interrogation of Brown, October 19, 1859, and letter to Heman Humphrey, November 25, 1859, in Ruchames, *John Brown,* 126, 131, 157.

35. Brown to E. B. of Rhode Island, November 1, 1859, and to the Rev. H. L. Vaill, in Ruchames, *John Brown,* 137–38, 143–44.

36. Both Sanborn, *Life and Letters,* 578–615, and Ruchames, *John Brown,* 136–66, print Brown's ten letters to his family from jail.

37. Joshua Giddings to J. Miller McKim, October 29, 1859, Cornell Anti-Slavery Collection, CorU.

38. Brown's speech in court after the verdict, in Villard, *John Brown,* 498–99; Henry David Thoreau, "The Last Days of John Brown," in *Reform Papers,* ed. Wendell Glick (Princeton, 1973), 149.

39. Brown note given to a guard, December 2, 1859, in Ruchames, *John Brown,* 167; Theodore Parker to Francis Jackson, November 24, 1859, in James Redpath, *Echoes of Harper's Ferry* (Boston, 1860), 77. Parker partly misremembered Virginia's seal, where a woman, not a man, slays tyranny.

40. John Wilkes Booth, quoted in Asia Booth Clarke, *The Unlocked Book: A Memoir of John Wilkes Booth,* ed. Eleanor Farjeon (New York, 1938), 124. Clarke's book was written well after these events, so the Booth quotations were filtered through long memory.

41. The best account of the English-born father's stage career and personal life is Stephen Archer, *Junius Brutus Booth: Theatrical Prometheus* (Carbondale, Ill., 1992). John Wilkes's "insanity" has commonly been proved by the many weird actions, on and off stage, of his father. It is impossible to know if the elder Booth were insane or if his "mad" actions and letters were, as most theater people believed, Booth put-ons to excuse the many betrayals of audiences tied to the alcoholism that punctuated his long career as a star in the United States.

42. Gordon Samples, *Lust for Fame* (Jefferson, N.C., 1982), covers Booth's stage career. By far the most popular and praised role of both Junius Brutus and John Wilkes was Shakespeare's Richard III, in the melodramatic version of it that Colley Cibber crafted, but they also triumphed in non-Shakespearean plays featuring melodramatic vile heroes.

43. John A. Ellsler, ms. on John Wilkes Booth, Ellsler Papers, WRHS; Clarke, *Unlocked Book,* 108–12. Similar opinions are in Ellsler's published *The Stage Memories of John Wilkes Booth* (Cleveland, 1950), 120–29.

44. Charles Shattuck offers a rich evocation and study of Edwin's best role in *The Hamlet of Edwin Booth* (Urbana, Ill., 1969). In 1862 John Wilkes played three weeks in New York, his Hamlet scorned but his Richard III much praised, though not by his now best-known critic, Walt Whitman, who judged it imitative of the husk but not the heart of the elder Booth's interpretation (Samples, *Lust for Fame,* 76–85).

45. Clarke, *Unlocked Book,* 112, 124–25. Booth passed out copies of a letter, seemingly much like that of 1864 with an attached assassination squib, just before he killed Lincoln. Almost identical versions of the 1864 writing were published in the press, and it is reprinted in Francis Wilson, *John Wilkes Booth: The Fact and Fiction of Lincoln's Assassination* (Boston, 1929), 50–54. The longer and more chaotic speech exists in manuscript in the Hampden-Booth Theatre Library in New York and is probably a speech Booth prepared for an anti-Republican gathering in Philadelphia just prior to the Civil War. I quote from a typescript of the document that Professor Terry Alford kindly shared with me.

46. George Templeton Strong, *Diary,* ed. Allan Nevins and Milton Halsey Thomas (New York, 1952), February 10, 1860, 3: 8.

47. Clarke, *Unlocked Book,* 136, 82, 97, 107–8. Clarke claimed that John Wilkes's politics diverged from those of his father and brothers because of his identification with the South, "where masters were gods" (63).

48. Clarke, *Unlocked Book,* 63, 105–6, 114, 124–25.

49. Edwin Booth to Nahum Capen, July 28, 1881, and Junius Brutus Jr. to Asia Booth Clarke, February 1865, in Clarke, *Unlocked Book,* 202–3, 198–200, 120. Edwin's letter suggested John Wilkes's fear of Lincoln's monarchical aspirations and Edwin's sense of his younger brother's talent and limited intelligence: "a rattle-pated fellow, full of quixotic notions" (Ellsler, ms. on Booth, Ellsler Papers, WRHS).

50. Clarke, *Unlocked Book,* 115–22. Here is reprinted also a speech of co-conspirator John Surrat, made in late 1870, describing the kidnap plot but denying that assassination was ever discussed (159–65). Francis Wilson, *Booth,* offers the standard interpretation I largely follow here but should be read in conjunction with the much more richly researched conclusion of Tidwell, Hall, and Gaddy in *Come Retribution.*

51. Thomas A. Jones account of Booth in hiding in Maryland, Clarke, *Unlocked Book,* 171–82; Mrs. T. K. B. Holloway personal remembrance of Booth's death in Francis Wilson, *Booth,* 207–16.

52. Clarke, *Unlocked Book,* 113–14; George Alfred Townsend, *The Life, Crime, and Capture of John Wilkes Booth* (New York, 1865), 36–37.

Index

Types of mobs are indexed under subheadings within the general category "Riots," while specific mobs are indexed by place, year, and type under the name of the state where they occurred.